D1566819

BLACK WORKERS IN WHITE UNIONS

JOB DISCRIMINATION IN THE UNITED STATES

BLACK WORKERS IN WHITE UNIONS

JOB DISCRIMINATION IN THE UNITED STATES

WILLIAM B. GOULD

Cornell University Press   ITHACA AND LONDON

First published 1977 by Cornell University Press.
Published in the United Kingdom by Cornell University Press Ltd., 2–4 Brook Street, London W1Y 1AA.

International Standard Book Number 0-8014-1062-2
Library of Congress Catalog Card Number 76-50263
Printed in the United States of America by Vail-Ballou Press, Inc.
Librarians: Library of Congress cataloging information appears on the last page of the book.

To my mother and father

Contents

Preface

This book deals with the law and reality of employment discrimination, and places particular emphasis upon race and labor unions. I have drawn upon numerous interviews with union and employer representatives as well as some government officials in order to assess the impact of decrees, governmental efforts to eliminate discrimination, and the extent to which private behavior meets the standards of law as enunciated by the courts and the agencies. Moreover, my experience both as consultant to the Equal Employment Opportunity Commission and as plaintiffs' counsel in litigation in the federal courts (coupled with my previous representation of both unions and employers) provided me with many insights derived from firsthand observation.

In a sense, this book is more than a professional assessment, for I have seen racial discrimination ever since I was a small child. I know what it means to be black in America, and I am quite familiar with the thinking of many whites in this country as it relates to the race issue.

I became a lawyer because of the Supreme Court's desegregation decisions, and by the time I entered law school I had decided to specialize in labor law—a choice partially motivated by my belief that the law might be used to eliminate racial inequities in employment. My thinking about the issues under discussion in this book has evolved over a considerable period of time.

The landscape has been altered during that period. As farm mechanization has hastened the exodus from agriculture, industrial employers, disproportionally numerous in the North of the United States, have attracted southern black workers who are products of another society and environment. This kind of migration has accentuated the bitterness between the races throughout the world, although discord has been most pronounced in the United States—a country which bears the legacy of slavery, the black codes, Jim Crow, and "separate but equal." The migration has been essential to the advance of the Western economies. But the price of economic growth is racial conflict.

As a result, the ever-present tension between equality of opportunity and the nation's actual practices has become more severe. White insecurity about race which is predicated in substantial part upon sex, a retracting economy which makes the majority cling to their cherished economic advantages, and black violence and crime in the cities—all these factors have been significant as America has become a swirling political caldron where the dominant issue is race, even though carefully chosen code words obfuscate and sanitize the real issues.

This book could not have been written without assistance, including the cooperation of people who live with the problems under discussion. The Ford Foundation provided financial assistance in the form of a grant. I am grateful to Charles Joiner, former dean of Wayne State Law School and now judge in the Eastern District of Michigan, and Thomas Ehrlich, former dean of Stanford Law School and now president of the Legal Services Corporation, who were supportive and encouraging as I proceeded with my research. Both provided facilitative assistance, and Judge Joiner guided me in my search for research funds.

Among those who generously provided time and cooperation—many cannot be identified because they could not speak "on the record"—are the following: Douglas Fraser, vice-president of the United Automobile Workers, Detroit; Anthony Connole, formerly special assistant to Mr. Fraser; William Lucy, secretary-treasurer of the American Federation of State, County, and Municipal Workers (AFCME), Washington, D.C.; Jerry Wurf, president of AFCME; Alex Fuller, civil rights director of the United Steelworkers of America, Pittsburgh; Paul Spiegalman, attorney-at-law, Berkeley; Ed Wallace, Project Outreach, Los Angeles; Stuart Herman, attorney-at-law, Los Angeles; Walter Connelly, labor counsel to Firestone Tire and Rubber Company, Akron; Donald Pfeiffer, labor relations department, General Motors Corporation, Detroit; Sydney McKenna, Ford Motor Company, Dearborn; Harry Alston, civil rights director, Amalgamated Meat Cutters Workers, Chicago; William Raymond, Office of Federal Contract Compliance, New Orleans; Rayfield Mooty, Ad Hoc Steelworkers Committee, Chicago; Ernest Green, A. Philip Randolph Foundation, New York; Daniel George, Washington, D.C.; and John Wilks, former director, OFCC, Washington, D.C.

Nathaniel Pierson, formerly director of the Construction Project in the Office of Federal Contract Compliance, Department of Labor, and now director of Equal Employment Opportunity in the Veterans Administration, delivered talks to my Employment Discrimination Seminar at Stanford Law School, which were helpful in the course of writing this book. Tyree Scott of the United Construction Workers of Seattle provided much useful information about the Seattle Decree. Lou Ferrand and Sally Kenyon of the Justice Department were similarly helpful.

John de J. Pemberton of University of San Francisco Law School (formerly deputy general counsel of the Equal Employment Opportunity Commission [EEOC]), George Bodle, attorney-at-law, Los Angeles (formerly chairman of the American Bar Association, Labor Law Section), and William Brown, III, attorney-at-law, Philadelphia (formerly chairman of EEOC) all read the manuscript and provided useful comments and criticism. To them I am particularly grateful. The responsibility for any deficiencies that may be found in the book is mine alone.

Many students helped in the preparation of the manuscript. Foremost is Jeremiah Collins, Stanford Law School, 1976, for he shouldered the bulk of the work on the notes and, even more important, also provided editorial criticism which has resulted in textual alterations. Oscar Rosenbloom, Stanford Law School, 1975, did much research for me in the summer of 1973. Research was also done by Jose Renya, Stanford Law School, 1976; Robert Knox, Stanford Law School, 1976; Ralph Jones, University of Michigan Law School, 1972; Lynn Coe, Harvard Law School, 1972; Joaquin Avila, Harvard Law School, 1973; and Barry Moon, Wayne State Law School, 1972. P. Alan Zaragozza, Stanford Law School, 1978, checked the text and footnotes for inaccuracies, and prepared the Table of Cases and Index.

I am also grateful to Marsha Turner, Julia Connolly, and Sarah Coates, who typed the final drafts of the manuscript.

My wife, Hilda, and my three sons have put up with the long hours of work and the emotional ups and downs involved in a project of this dimension. Their tolerance has been essential to its completion.

A portion of Chapter 13 was originally published in the *Stanford Law Review* under the title "The Seattle Building Trades Order: The First Comprehensive Relief against Employment Discrimination in the Construction Industry," 26 *Stanford Law Review* 773 (1974). I wish to acknowledge permission to use portions of some of my other articles which were previously published: "Some Limitations upon Discipline under the National Labor Relations Act," 1970 *Duke Law Journal* 1067, copyright by *Duke Law Journal*; "Black Power in the Unions: The Impact upon Collective Bargaining Relationships," 79 *Yale Law Journal* 46 (1969), used with the permission of the *Journal* and Fred B. Rothman & Co.; "Negro Revolution and the Law of Collective Bargaining," 34 *Fordham Law Review* 207 (1965), © 1965 by Fordham University Press; "Labor Arbitration of Grievances Involving Racial Discrimination," 118 *University of Pennsylvania Law Review* 40 (1969), © 1969 by the *University of Pennsylvania Law Review* and used with the permission of the *Review* and of Fred B. Rothman & Co.; "Seniority and the Black Worker: Reflections on Quarles and Its Implications," 47 *Texas Law Review* 1039 (1969); "Employment Security, Seniority, and Race: The Role of Title VII of the Civil Rights Act of 1964," 13 *Howard Law Journal* 1 (1967).

My hope is that this book may make some contribution to the reduction of the misery and suffering of those to whom fate has arbitrarily and irrationally denied opportunity.

WILLIAM B. GOULD

Stanford, California

BLACK WORKERS IN
WHITE UNIONS

JOB DISCRIMINATION IN
THE UNITED STATES

Note: An asterisk following a note number in the text indicates that the corresponding note at the back of the book is substantive in nature. Numbers without asterisks indicate notes that are wholly citations.

Introduction

"Who among us would be content to have the color of his skin changed, and stand in his place? Who among us would then be content with the counsels of patience and delay?"[1] So spoke President John F. Kennedy thirteen years ago, goaded at that time into a search for legal remedies by the dangerous collision course created by civil rights demonstrations, hoses, police dogs, and "Bull" Connor's insistence that the South truly meant it when it said "Never" to integration of the races. Unkept promises and rising expectations produced not simply impatience but a wide spectrum of demands for equality in civil rights. But the form of protest shifted dramatically and abruptly in a short span of time. From the peaceful picket lines and marches of the early sixties, it changed to the riots in Watts in 1965, to more prolonged bouts of violence and arson in Detroit and Newark in 1967 and later to a large number of other urban centers, mostly in the northern part of the country. Despite the new era of "benign neglect" ushered in by the Nixon administration in January 1969, the fires that began to burn brightly more than a decade ago are not yet out; indeed they give every promise of breaking forth anew. Among the many challenges of the late seventies and the eighties is the resolution of racial problems in the courts and other forums which adjudicate disputes peaceably and rationally—and not in the streets.

The labor movement's response is ambivalent. While the unions purport to adopt a moral stance which is a notch above the country's, they have struggled against adhering to the requirements of new civil rights legislation. More than any other institutions, trade unions are the focal point of racial discord in our society. For the unions represent both the new immigrants and older groups who are pulling themselves up the ladder and who perceive their competitive status to be unstable and threatened. Paradoxically, the unions represent some of the most reactionary and insecure elements in American society as well as the "underclass," which is disproportionately black as well as Chicano and Puerto Rican. A principal obstacle to a more progressive labor movement in the United States is its unwarranted self-satisfaction and smugness about organizing new categories of workers. The effect is to disregard the interests of those who need protection most—the significant number of the poor who are members of racial minorities.

Thus, unions often constitute roadblocks to the achievement of nondiscriminatory employment practices. The urban migration has brought blacks face to face with a labor movement more firmly established than in the South. The confrontation is with the industrial unions born of a relatively egalitarian organizational philosophy in the 1930's, as well as with the racially exclusionary and conservative AFL unions. The principal issues involved in disputes between blacks and the unions are: (1) restrictions on admission to apprenticeship programs jointly administered with employers by both industrial and craft unions; (2) the denial of journeyman cards to qualified black nonunionists (3) refusal of admission to membership—even though no union today refers to a formal color bar in its constitutional rules; (4) the establishment of segregated or auxiliary locals for blacks; (5) the maintenance of separate lines of progression and seniority districts which prohibit or discourage transfers by blacks into relatively better paying and more desirable jobs held by whites; and (6) the absence of blacks and other minorities from policy-making elective and appointed positions inside the unions.

These factors were present at the time of President Kennedy's speech in 1963. They are present today—more than a decade after Title VII of the Civil Rights Act of 1964, the federal fair-employment practices statute, was enacted into law. The limited arsenal provided to minority-group plaintiffs by the 1964 statute and the hostility of the unions have made the problems seem more intractable today than they once appeared to be. Furthermore, governmental agencies charged with enforcing the act, hampered by both lack of appropriations from Congress and the absence of political will and competence, have failed to crack down effectively on offenders.

The unsympathetic attitude of the labor movement and business community has prevented the adoption of substantial remedies which might compensate blacks and consequently jostle the whites who might otherwise be the first to benefit from opportunities made available to the minority group. The difficulties are compounded by misunderstandings propagated deliberately by the labor movement—particularly its AFL wing, aided by its growing bank of scholarly allies.[2]*

Commenting on the labor movement's antedeluvian role in race relations is not union-bashing. The "choice" that AFL-CIO ally Bayard Rustin has recently posed to blacks—to "fight and strengthen the trade movement by wiping out the vestiges of segregation that remain in it or, . . . knowingly or unknowingly, [to] offer . . . themselves as pawns in the conservative's game of busting the unions"[3]—is hardly a real one. Rustin avoids discussion of the real institutional forces still at work against reform in the unions and obfuscates the options that are available.

To be sure, the patterns of segregation and exclusion constitute only one side of the ledger. One must repeat the litany of good deeds done if only to avoid being tarred by Rustin's brush as a stalking horse for management interests. Collective bargaining and the negotiation provided by grievance-arbitration machinery protects blacks as well as whites in a number of contexts. Blacks, because they congregate disproportionately in blue-collar jobs, are more apt than whites to be represented by unions, because the labor movement has been most successful in this area. (Estimates indicate that blacks make up 15 percent of the total union membership—a higher percentage than the percentage of blacks in the total population.)

As B. J. Widick has pointed out, the unions can be training grounds for minority-group leadership in the United States[4]—especially now that union staffs, like that of the American Federation of State, County and Municipal Employees, are active in the public sector and in hospitals, where blacks make up a large part of the work force.

Moreover, the unions, more than other important industrial institutions, are likely to be in the corner of social and economic reform and, to a considerable degree, of civil rights legislation as well: the AFL-CIO actively supports the elimination of racial discrimination in voting, housing, educational institutions, and most important, employment. Indeed, in a relatively rare act of self-abnegation, George Meany, representing the AFL-CIO, had proposed that employment-discrimination legislation be binding upon unions as well as employers before the Kennedy administration came forward with fair-employment-practices proposals. The problem has been that after the enactment of legislation that the AFL-CIO supported, it has not implemented the policies in a fashion that would make possible the erosion of union discrimination in this generation.

Even during the 1972 political campaign, the AFL-CIO Executive Council took the position that busing was a reasonable method of achieving desegregation in certain circumstances.[5] The AFL-CIO—as well as the UAW—refused to adopt a strategy or campaign of implementation. Yet the position itself was of some significance—especially in the context of the antiblack politics of 1972.

The positive aspect of the unions' relationship with minority groups is particularly evident in the public sector, because the public employee labor organizations are growing rapidly. A significant portion of union organizational effort is devoted to improving the position of minority-group employees. Nevertheless, though some unions are actively organizing the unorganized minority, this does not appear to be the principal interest of such executives as George Meany and Lane Kirkland, the president and the secretary-treasurer of the AFL-CIO. When asked by *Washington Post* reporters whether he had a "concern about organizing new workers," Meany replied, "To me it doesn't mean a thing. . . . I have no real concern about it, because the history of the trade union movement has shown that when organized workers were a very, very tiny percentage of the work force they still accomplished and did things that were important for the entire work force." Kirkland said, in the same interview, "I've never been concerned about what proportion of the working force is organized at any given time."[6]

This is the philosophy of those who are content with small preserves of organized aristocrats. The position of the CIO unions organized during the 1930's was that the labor movement represents all workers; its function is to organize the lowly, the disadvantaged, and the economically depressed. In contrast, the AFL, and the construction unions in particular, have traditionally organized only small sectors of an industry so that its membership could have benefits. Meany—a member of the Plumbers and Pipefitters Union—seems to follow in that tradition.

Before examining the post-1964 disputes between unions and blacks, it may be instructive to see what Meany and other trade union leaders were saying prior to the enactment of employment-discrimination legislation. How candid were they with outsiders about the labor movement's responsibility for racial discrimination?

When examined by the Congress about the building trades' role in employment discrimination affecting apprentices, Meany said: "We do not control that. The employer has absolute control even where an apprenticeship system is jointly administered and it is administered to see that the apprentice gets the proper training and that he gets the proper experience. . . . In practically every instance, the fellow who makes the choice as to who becomes the apprentice is the fellow who pays him his wages. That is the employer."[7]

That testimony was material for the gullible. In the construction and other industries, however, most apprenticeship programs are administered jointly by unions and employers. The construction unions, in a very substantial number of urban centers, establish the selection criteria for apprentices. The contractors are too weak and divided and, generally speaking, do not wield sufficient bargaining power to countermand union wishes regarding apprentices. Meany could confuse the issue because employers, subsequent to the selection of apprentices by apprenticeship committees, are not generally required to hire an apprentice they do not want. In the final analysis, employment is bestowed by the employer. Meany attempted to focus on this fact and draw attention from the major role played by craft unions in permitting access to the labor market even *prior* to the stage at which an employer may turn an apprentice away from a job. To be considered for a job, a worker—at least a minority-group worker—must gain entry to, and graduation from, an appenticeship. Here the building and construction trades have great power.

A few minutes later, Meany, during the same testimony, responding to questions about black membership, stated: "Well, in my own union there are Negroes. We have Negroes all over the country. . . . In a good many of the larger cities now we have considerable Negro membership where 20 years ago we didn't have any. So there is considerable improvement in that situation."[8] Meany did not say that minority membership in the Plumbers and Pipefitters Union was so small that even in the 1970's it hardly constitutes 1 percent of the total membership.

When questioned by Senator Quentin Burdick about the United Steelworkers' experience under state fair-employment practices statutes, former union president David McDonald said, "I must say that insofar as our personal experience is concerned, since we have no discrimination I have no experiences to report."[9] The United Steelworkers of America has been hit with thousands of charges filed with the Equal Employment Opportunity Commission alleging racial discrimination, as well as with a substantial number of lawsuits filed in federal district court. Though the black membership is approximately 30 percent, no black is in any elective policy-making position on the national level.

To some extent, such statements reflect not merely the attempt to mislead but also considerable naivete. During this period unions as well as employers—and indeed the public generally—thought that racial discrimination was limited to an isolated number of instances which represented an aberration from the general pattern and which had to be rectified case by case. The AFL-CIO thought of the statute as having prospective force only. The unions expressed disbelief when the Equal Employment Opportunity Commission (EEOC) and the courts began to deprive white union members of collectively negotiated seniority rights which they had possessed prior to the enactment of Title VII.

The pattern of debate since the enactment of Title VII makes evident the continuing fundamental resistance of a substantial portion of the labor movement to the elimination of discrimination in employment. No sooner was Title VII on the books than immediate attention was focused upon the issue of whether the statute had merely prospective force. Judge John Wisdom of the Fifth Circuit Court of Appeals asserted that "one of the most perplexing issues troubling the courts under Title VII" was "how to reconcile equal employment opportunity *today* with seniority expectations based on *yesterday's* built-in-racial discrimination."[10]

For years blacks have been locked into segregated departments and jobs where a no-transfer system barred the way to job advancement. Initially, of course, such practices developed, at least in the manufacturing industries, from the employers' discriminatory hiring practices. But the no-transfer system took the discriminatory hiring policy a step further and made it impossible for blacks to obtain better jobs.

Evident in all these practices were two factors. First, blacks generally had seniority districts carved around their jobs, and so did whites. Second, even though the effect was obviously discriminatory, similar systems existed in many portions of the country where a black face had never been seen. Accordingly, it could easily be established that the seniority system, in principle, was perfectly reasonable. As a result of internal union politics or management's concern with business efficiency, the parties could justifiably, without violating any law, in many instances arrive at a seniority arrangement which precluded the carrying over of seniority credit and in some instances entirely precluded transfer from one district to another. But these cases were exceptional; they resulted from past discrimination by the employer in hiring and also by the union insofar as the no-transfer system precluded upward mobility.

The AFL-CIO as well as its international and local union constituent members was not sympathetic to the plight of black employees caught up in the controversy over seniority rights. An inkling of this attitude was apparent in the testimony of AFL-CIO counsel Thomas Harris the year before Title VII became law. Speaking of the layoff of black employees who had been the most recently hired and the first to be laid off ("last to be hired, first to be fired"), and of the reason for such a discriminatory hiring policy, Harris said:

The AFL-CIO cannot . . . accept the premise that some sort of superseniority ought to be established for these Negro workers who generally were discriminated against for so long a period.
Even though discrimination ended 5 or 10 years ago, Negroes in the plant will necessarily not have seniority of any longer period of time than that, so when a layoff comes he is

the first to be victimized even though, as I say, the discrimination may have ended 5 or 10 years ago. . . . We don't think that can be taken care of by giving him superseniority. To do that would be unjust to the white workers who have been working there 15 or 20 years. We don't think that one form of injustice can be corrected or should be corrected by creating another.[11]

AFL-CIO sensitivity became even greater as the debate about Title VII wore on and as Senator Lester Hill of Alabama circulated a speech of his to southern trade union members stating that if the act was passed, white trade unions would lose accumulated seniority rights negotiated under collective-bargaining agreements. The AFL-CIO Civil Rights Department, in response, circulated a document, *Civil Rights: Fact vs. Fiction,* which gave the following assurance: "The law will probably put an end to discrimination—in employment—including discrimination in seniority systems. But it does not in any way interfere with existing job rights."

This document, written subsequent to the passage of Title VII, seemed to go further than Harris' assertions. When the Equal Employment Opportunity Commission held a meeting with union officials on May 5, 1966, to discuss guidelines for dealing with the past discrimination embodied in some seniority systems, the trade union reaction to changing the system was uniformly negative. William Schlitzer, at that time director of the Civil Rights Department of the AFL-CIO, said that he was "concerned" about newspaper reports and rumors concerning EEOC action with respect to seniority. Seniority, he said, was a complex problem, and the union seniority system, geared for ridding a plant of arbitrary inequities, was the fairest system in use.[12] The implication was that he thought EEOC and the courts ought not to tamper with it.

Emil Mazey, secretary-treasurer of the UAW, said that the commission's remedy for faulty seniority practices should be full employment. No simple solution of seniority problems was possible, he said, since custom and practice in each union were different. Erroneously citing the Landrum-Griffin Act as requiring ratification of any agreement affecting seniority, Mazey declared, "You cannot impose agreement upon the membership." To do so without ratification and without negotiation between the union and the employer would be in violation of the National Labor Relations Act. Donald Slaiman, later civil rights director of the AFL-CIO, said that the AFL-CIO had vigorously countered the notion that FEPC legislation would "undermine" seniority. If the EEOC was now to modify seniority arrangements, the unions which had said, "We told you that 'quotas' are not in the law," would be at a disadvantage in dealing with an unsympathetic membership. Segregationists would be able to say to the AFL-CIO leadership, "We told you so."

The AFL-CIO has never relented in its opposition to the reform of seniority systems that have discriminated against blacks in the past. This attitude, coupled with a pattern of opposition to other civil rights measures—including the Nixon administration's Philadelphia Plan—indicates that, contrary to the general impression, not merely the rank and file of local union leadership perpetuates discrimination in the country. The public's understanding is reflected in a statement of the

United States Civil Rights Commission in 1961: "Within the labor movement it-self civil rights goals are celebrated at the higher levels, but fundamental internal barriers tend to preserve discrimination at the workingman's level."[13] This state-ment should be regarded as incomplete, if not inaccurate. The AFL-CIO policy of not agreeing to implement Title VII serves to postpone the effectuation of the stat-ute's principles. Assertion of the leadership's innocence is simply the first in an arsenal of arguments that the AFL-CIO and its friends put forward to justify trade union misbehavior.

Much more pernicious is the view propounded by Derek Bok and John Dunlop: since a higher proportion of minorities are in jobs where unions represent the em-ployees in large numbers than in such nonunion occupations as office work and management, the unions have little or no impact upon any discrimination that may be practiced. According to Bok and Dunlop, "If [union] discrimination were truly a major factor in blocking Negroes from jobs, one would expect to find lower proportions of blacks working in heavily unionized occupations, such as crafts-men, foremen, operatives and laborers. But such is not the case."[14] The figures, however, hardly prove anything at all. The blue-collar jobs in which unions have representation rights are simply more easily obtainable by a large number of blacks who are recently arrived "immigrants" from southern agriculture and who may not have the credentials—whether job-related or not—for higher-echelon jobs. Moreover, the crucial inquiry in an investigation of work represented by unions should be whether minorities occupy the highest classifications within a union's jurisdiction.

Bok and Dunlop say that since "penetration of Negroes into higher skilled ca-tegories is even lower [in the automobile industry] than in skilled construction crafts," union discrimination does not play a role, because such unions as the UAW clearly have a positive position on race relations. In the first place, critics such as Bok and Dunlop fail to point out that the UAW, unlike the unions in the building trades, plays no role in the hiring process and that a substantial number of skilled tradesmen are hired by the employer from the street. Hence the unions in the building and construction trades are more responsible for hiring than is the au-tomobile union. Second, Bok and Dunlop assume that the UAW has clean hands in its dealing with race; although their arguments seem to fit neatly with those put forward by the construction trades to the effect that UAW rhetoric differs from UAW practices, which are even worse than those of the "maligned" construction unions. In fact, the devotion of the UAW to racial justice is by no means self-evident—particularly since the local unions and employers jointly administer ap-prenticeship programs in many auto plants in the country. Closer to the mark is the proposition that both the industrial and the construction unions have performed badly, with construction a poor second. Bok and Dunlop may know all this but may be attempting to highlight the fact that the late Walter Reuther's rhetoric did not comport with reality—a discrepancy which never ceases to delight the AFL unions.

The law, it is said, can be of relatively little assistance in ending discrimination;

primary reliance must be on programs negotiated between the parties themselves. In the construction industry, as this book endeavors to make clear, the plans negotiated between the parties themselves have had, for the most part, a very sorry history. Voluntary plans seem to be in disarray, in varying degrees, throughout the country—an especially unfortunate situation in view of the opportunities for knocking in closed union doors which have been established by federal court decisions. The voluntary agreements—which Bok and Dunlop praise—ignore the mandate for institutional reform issued by the courts and, when the goals of such agreements are not met, rely upon the very procedures left unchanged as an excuse for failure. The best that can be said for them is that the judiciary may in some instances make use of the plans in connection with the vast arsenal of judicial remedies. Moreover, the federal judges have become quite sophisticated in dealing with subtle employment discrimination as well as with "overt cases." Such critics as Rustin, Bok, and Dunlop seem to think that the courts can deal only with overt discrimination. The courts can also deal with practices that have a discriminatory effect and can fashion remedies for them.

Part I of the book traces the development of the law relating to racial discrimination, both generally and in the labor-management context, attempting to make clear the law's focus upon institutional behavior. In Part I, as well as in Part II—which deals with the accommodation between traditional labor-management relations and law—my views regarding the direction in which the law ought to move are developed. Some of my ideas have already won the day, but as a host of critics will point out, others have not—at least not just yet.

Part III, perhaps the book's most important section, dramatizes the importance of remedy and enforcement—after the standards for establishing liability have been promulgated. The numerous judicial decisions have undoubtedly contributed to a better moral climate.

The entire book demonstrates that the opportunity for employment is the key to the improvement of race relations in the United States. For a job changes the worker's aspirations for improving his own environment and for making available educational opportunities for his children. As the Fifth Circuit has noted, the right to work in an environment that is free of discrimination is an important and fundamental one, inasmuch as it "deals not with just an individual's sharing in the 'outer benefits' of being an American citizen, but rather the ability to provide decently for one's family in a job or profession for which he qualifies and chooses."[15] The impact upon the home and the well-being of the family is obvious.

Moreover, the benefits of employment radiate to affect the solution of other problems. If companies are required to hire fairly, without regard to race, and a similar obligation is imposed upon labor organizations selecting candidates for apprenticeship programs, the pressure grows to break down discriminatory housing barriers. The politically volatile issue of housing may decline in importance because of the development of more highly integrated neighborhoods; to achieve racial integration in previously white sections, the construction of low-cost housing may be necessary. Increased opportunities for employment are focal in a host of race relation issues. The elimination of discriminatory practices can have an impact on education and housing and probably ease the pain caused by imposed remedies.

PART I

THE DEVELOPMENT OF LAW
AND RACIAL DISCRIMINATION

1 | Overview of Constitutional Law
in Race Relations

In *Brown* v. *The Board of Education*[1] and its companion case, *Bolling* v. *Sharpe*,[2] the Supreme Court, on May 17, 1954, in an opinion authored on behalf of a unanimous bench by Chief Justice Earl Warren at the beginning of his judicial tenure, held that state-sponsored segregation in public education was unconstitutional under the Fourteenth Amendment and, where practiced by the federal government (as in the District of Columbia), the Fifth Amendment as well. *Brown,* one of the Court's great constitutional-law cases, has provoked much nationwide debate and controversy. The decision was significant not simply because it declared segregation in public education to be at odds with the Constitution but, equally important, because it was a moral declaration on race by the Court. It explicitly recognized what most Americans knew then, and know now, but would not then frankly state: that segregation as an institution was intended to stamp the badge of inferiority upon Negroes in the United States and to make them a separate caste of untouchables whose lot it was to receive what others did not want in all aspects of living. Segregation was and is a direct descendant of the heritage of slavery and discrimination which this country has imposed upon blacks. This fact is now so painfully apparent—thanks in large part to Chief Justice Warren's opinion in *Brown*—that it warrants Charles Black's simile (perhaps now outdated in light of contemporary sexual practices) to the effect that it is as obvious as the fact "that the imputation of unchastity is harmful to a woman."[3]

In charting the course for public understanding of the race problem in the United States, the Warren Court, in *Brown* and its immediate progeny, anticipated the work of both the President and Congress which began with voting legislation in 1957, 1960, 1964, and 1965, subsequently focused upon employment, public accommodations, and education in 1964, then shifted to housing in 1968 and back again to employment in 1972. The Court helped create the political climate for such matters by serving as a coordinate and equal branch of government, and thus made less necessary judicial activism that was independent of legislation. It seems quite clear that at the same time the Court's handiwork set in motion one of the most significant phenomena of the decade of the sixties: the rising expectations of the black community, which increasingly derided "the counsels of patience and delay" urged upon it by others.

Moreover, although President Eisenhower's view that law cannot change the hearts of men may have been accepted by many of his countrymen in the fifties, *Brown* demolished its validity. The law has made formerly respectable public expressions of racism by well-educated people completely untenable in America today. Though racist attitudes are still expressed in public in some quarters—and though such attitudes are deeply ingrained in many Americans—the Warren Court has changed the tone of American life as it relates to race relations.

Brown, though a positive force against racial barriers, postponed the devising of meaningful remedies for what was now admitted to be wrongful by putting over to the next term of the Court the formulation of a decree to implement the decision. In 1955, *Brown II* declared that the dismantling of segregated public school systems was to take place with "all deliberate speed."[4] The Court indicated that the parties to litigation would need time to take into account the complicated problems involved in adhering to *Brown I.* The Court also indicated that it wished to rely upon the expertise of the parties, which were themselves arms of government on the state and local level in a very delicately balanced federalist system, to formulate solutions for the problems posed by *Brown I.*

The basis for *Brown II* seems to have been a desire by the Court to give the deep South "breathing space" and time to adjust to the new rules of law declared by the Court on May 17, 1954. The country had become accustomed to the Hayes-Tilden Compromise of 1877—the reconciliation between North and South which was made at the expense of the Negro people—and the "separate but equal" proclamation of the Supreme Court in *Plessy* v. *Ferguson* in 1896.[5] But the deep South said "Never" to *Brown I* and *II* and utilized the time permitted by the phrase "all deliberate speed" to evade the Court's pronouncement. *Brown II* failed to realize that the defendants were not ready to comply in the absence of a very real prospect that they would be compelled to do so within a relatively short period of time. The body of law which the defendant school boards looked to was not *Brown I* and *II* but the legacy of *Dred Scott*[6] and *Plessy* v. *Ferguson,* which had declared the black person to be less than human and had specifically placed the state's *imprimatur* upon segregation. The South mobilized political support in the Congress, expressed in the "southern manifesto," which proclaimed hostility to the Court's decisions and revived the long discarded doctrines of interposition and nullification, once pet political theories of Senator John Calhoun—but surely no accurate guide to what was required by mandates of the Supreme Court ever since the Civil War. The Court had misgauged the temper and reactions of the country.

Too often evasion took the form of massive resistance. As Paul Brest has noted:

The District of Columbia and some school districts in the border states began to desegregate their schools almost immediately. The South responded to *Brown* with a barrage of measures designed to preserve and entrench segregation. State legislatures adopted resolutions of "nullification" and "interposition," which declared that the Court's decisions were without effect. They enacted statutes mandating school segregation; ordering state and local officials to take all measures within their authority to preserve segregation; terminating state funds for racially mixed schools; placing the public schools directly under the authority of the governor or state board of education with plenary power to close them; providing tuition grants to enable pupils to attend private schools; and repealing compulsory attendance laws.

Most of these schemes were struck down by lower federal courts. The Supreme Court's two major interventions were *Cooper v. Aaron,* 358 U.S. 1 (1958), which required Little Rock, Arkansas, to proceed with school desegregation in the face of state-inspired opposition, violence, and disorder; and *Griffin v. Prince Edward County School Board,* 377 U.S. 218 (1964), which ordered a county school system reopened after it had been closed for five years to avoid desegregation.[7]

Southern states adopted the tactic of utilizing pupil-placement statutes in the late 1950's and early 1960's. Brest has summarized the contents of one such statute:

The Alabama act, which served as the model for many southern states, directed districts to assign pupils to schools in accordance with a variety of nonracial factors, including the availability of school plants, staff, and transportation; the suitability of school curricula to the pupil's academic preparation and ability; his morals, conduct, health, personal standards and home environment; the psychological effect on the pupil; the effect of his admission on prevailing academic standards; and the possibility of friction, disorder and ill-will within the school and the community. Pupils were initially assigned as a matter of course to the school maintained for their race.[8]

The effect was to make mass integration impossible. And in the sixties, lower courts approved desegregation plans which permitted pupil assignment on the basis of residence, as well as so-called freedom of choice, even in the context of *de jure* or state-sponsored segregation.

The Court, of course, was itself to blame, because of the vagueness of the "with all deliberate speed" formula. Specifically, the Court left open the question of how and when its decree in *Brown II* was to be implemented. Whether *Brown I* required merely passive nondiscrimination or affirmative action by the government to eliminate segregation in the public school system was left unresolved. Eventually, the Court concluded that where there was *de jure* segregation, neighborhood attendance zones were unconstitutional if they, in fact, perpetuated segregation.[9] In 1968, the Court was to demolish freedom of choice and to say that *Brown* was to be implemented "now," without delay.[10]

The Court also left unanswered a troubling question which is still unresolved: Against whom is the decree to be enforced? The litigation in *Brown* arose in a *de jure* context: a southern state had supported segregation by means of laws and regulations. But what of the North, where *de facto* segregation exists—segregation which is not primarily or exclusively attributable to the state's alignment of school boundaries but to such factors as housing patterns and available social services. The state may not be said to be as responsible for the patterns that have developed (though that is a matter of considerable argument.)[11] Yet it seems that the psychological damage done to Negro children in a segregated setting, described in *Brown,* would have some applicability to the North, even though the state may not be as directly responsible. These problems, coupled with the facts that the human and financial burden of litigation rests on individual black plaintiffs and such organizations as the NAACP Legal Defense Fund, and that litigation is against individual school boards rather than the state government's educational department itself, delayed for fourteen years after *Brown* the integration mandated by the Court to eliminate *de jure* segregation.

The Court, operating under its "with all deliberate speed" formula, had denied certiorari (that is, review which is within its discretion) in a number of cases where lower court orders had proved to be harmful to the interests of black children: (1) cases upholding pupil-placement laws;[12] (2) cases requiring that the plaintiff exhaust administrative remedies before resorting to litigation;[13] and (3) cases holding that desegregation of one grade per year was all that *Brown* required[14] (even though, ironically, such a formula, if followed faithfully, would have desegregated all public school systems by the time of the 1968 "here and now" ruling).

Moreover, not until the sixties did the Department of Health, Education, and Welfare (HEW) become actively involved, as a result of the Civil Rights Act of 1964, in denying and threatening to deny all financial grants to school systems which did not desegregate. Only in 1971 did Chief Justice Warren Burger, speaking for a unanimous Court in *Swann* v. *Charlotte-Mecklenburg Board of Education,* [15] explicitly hold that the use of "ratios" as a "starting point" in desegregating southern *de jure* school systems is an appropriate judicially imposed remedy, specifically issuing a clarion call for careful scrutinization of one-race schools.

By 1964, Congress was fully aware of the difficulties involved in making *Brown I* a reality for black children in the United States and the fallacies of the "with all deliberate speed" formula contained in *Brown II*. This awareness partly explains the passage of provisions of the Civil Rights Act of 1964 which gave HEW the authority to cut off funds from school districts that continued to disobey the law. Yet the Congress, in enacting the most comprehensive fair-employment practices legislation ever put into effect by the federal government, committed many of the same mistakes that had already followed in the wake of *Brown I*. Proper enforcement tools were not provided until 1972. And at approximately the same time, the full panoply of judicial remedies available, as well as the law's applicability to *de facto* offenders, began to emerge.[16] Meanwhile, the Court adjudicated a heavy docket of race-relations cases.

Though some believe that the Nixon or Burger Court has exhibited caution and not significantly expanded upon the law previously staked out, most of the decided cases do not indicate that any substantial call for retreat has been sounded. But forebodings have been aroused by Chief Justice Burger's uneasiness about federal district-court interpretations of the Court's pronouncements on school desegregation[17]* and Justice Lewis Powell's insistence that one law be applied to both North and South (apparently without busing as a remedy for either area)[18] and by the Court's decision permitting racial segregation in clubs holding state liquor licenses.[19] Although the last decision erodes some of the dicta in the Court's previous "state action" holdings, it can nevertheless be regarded simply as a failure to apply desegregation principles to situations in which the Court is concerned (unjustifiably, in my view) with the competing considerations of privacy or private association.[20]

The Court has applied its decision in *Jones* v. *Alfred H. Mayer Co.,*[21] which held that the Civil Rights Act of 1866 prohibited racial discrimination in private housing, to swimming-pool membership associations,[22] as well as to nonstock corporations organized to operate community parks and playground facilities.[23] Racial discrimination and segregation engaged in by private parties is increasingly under attack—even by the Burger Court.

While the Court, in *Whitcomb* v. *Chavis,* evinced a reluctance to utilize the Fourteenth Amendment in cases in which black voters allege that redistricting dilutes a homogeneous black vote,[24] it has been exceedingly severe with political entities affected by the Voting Rights Act of 1965 that attempt to redraw voting boundaries where the effect is to dilute the black vote.[25] Moreover, in other Fourteenth Amendment cases, the Court has concluded that redistricting is unconstitutional where there is evidence of past discrimination.[26] Such conclusions may have definite applicability to employment-discrimination legislation. The Burger Court, though somewhat reluctant to be active in race-relations when the Constitution itself is at stake, may well interpret statutes enacted by Congress in an expansive fashion.

The Court, in *Keyes* v. *School District No. One, Denver, Colorado,*[27] concluded that where a portion of a school district is segregated, the remedy appropriately affects all of it. Justice William Brennan spoke for the majority:

Common sense dictates the conclusion that racially inspired school board actions have an impact beyond the particular schools that are the subject of those actions. This is not to say, of course, that there can never be a case in which the geographical structure of, or the natural boundaries within, a school district may have the effect of dividing the district into separate, identifiable and unrelated units. . . . In the absence of such a determination [however proof of state-imposed segregation in a substantial portion of the district will suffice to support a finding by the trial court of the existence of a dual system.[28]

In effect the Court indulged a ''presumption'' that segregated schooling in other portions of the district was not ''advantageous.'' ''Close examination'' of the connection between past segregation and the present system is required. The implications of *Keyes* for rectifying employment discrimination are enormous.

Subsequent to *Keyes,* the Court exhibited more caution in *Milliken* v. *Bradley,*[29]* where a 5 to 4 majority concluded that multidistrict busing to the white suburbs was not a justifiable remedy according to the facts of that case—in spite of a finding of intentional discrimination by both the city of Detroit and the state board of education. Chief Justice Burger, speaking for the majority, rebuked the district court for concluding that school district lines ''are no more than arbitrary lines on a map 'drawn for political convenience.' ''[30] Said the Court:

Boundary lines may be bridged where there has been a constitutional violation calling for inter-district relief, but the notion that school district lines may be casually ignored or treated as a mere administrative convenience is contrary to the history of public education in our country. No single tradition in public education is more deeply rooted than local control over the operation of schools; local autonomy has long been thought essential both to the maintenance of community concern and support for public schools and to quality of the educational process.[31]

The Court concluded in *Bradley* that the evidence must establish that there has been a "constitutional violation within one district that produces a significant segregative effect in another district."[32] Since, according to the Court, such evidence was lacking in *Bradley,* a constitutional violation could not be found. Justice Byron White, dissenting, noted that "the Court draws the remedial line at the Detroit School District boundary, even though the Fourteenth Amendment is addressed to the State and even though the *State* denies equal protection of the laws when its public agencies, acting in its behalf, invidiously discriminate."[33] Justice White's dissent stressed the "unwavering" posture of the Court and its view that a district court's remedial power does not "cease at the school district line."

Justice Thurgood Marshall, in a separate dissent, joined in by all four dissenters (Justices Brennan, White, and William Douglas), concluded that the Court was taking a "giant step backwards."[34] Justice Marshall declared, "Our Nation, I fear, will be ill-served by the Court's refusal to remedy separate and unequal education, for unless our children begin to learn together, there is little hope that our people will ever learn to live together."[35] Marshall expressed the fear that the Court's decision was "more a reflection of a perceived public mood that we have gone far enough in enforcing the Constitution's guarantee of equal justice than it is the product of neutral principles of law. In the short run, it may seem to be the easier course to allow our great metropolitan areas to be divided up each into two cities—one white, the other black—but it is a course, I predict, our people will ultimately regret."[36]*

Whether *Bradley* portends a shift backward in dealing with other racial issues as well remains to be seen. Notwithstanding expressions of concern and opposition by Chief Justice Burger and Justices Powell, William Rehnquist, and Harry Blackmun to the majority's somewhat expansive interpretations of Title VII,[37] similar caution has not been displayed in decisions on employment discrimination—although the Supreme Court has yet to confront major cases which require corporations and labor unions, because of their conduct toward black job seekers, to pay thousands or millions of dollars to private plaintiffs.

2 | Framework of Employment-Discrimination Law: An Introduction

The Presidential Executive Order

Ever since A. Philip Randolph's threatened march on Washington in 1941 resulted in an executive order by President Franklin D. Roosevelt prohibiting racial discrimination by those who contract with the federal government,[1] government contractors have, at least in theory, been prohibited from excluding blacks from their work forces. Under President John F. Kennedy's Executive Order 10,925,[2] issued March 6, 1961, contractors' and subcontractors' obligations were extended beyond the mere non-discrimination requirement to require them to undertake "affirmative action" to recruit and to promote minority-group workers—a duty which arises independent of any finding of discrimination. That is, a finding of discrimination is not necessary in order to find a violation of the affirmative-action provisions of the executive order. The operative words, however, are "in theory," because, until 1971, the federal government took no action to disbar or cancel the contract of any employer.[3]

Nevertheless, after President Roosevelt's action, all presidents—Truman, Eisenhower, Kennedy, Johnson, Nixon, and Ford—have supported the view that the government ought not to do business with those who discriminate on the basis of race.[4] The primary responsibility for enforcing contract-compliance obligations belongs to the contracting agencies themselves—the Department of Defense for defense contractors and the automobile industry; the Department of Health, Education, and Welfare for universities; and so forth. But since the Johnson administration, the Department of Labor, through its Office of Federal Contract Compliance (OFCC), has had supervisory authority. An equal-employment opportunity clause, however, is required only in contracts involving more than ten thousand dollars. In contracts for federally assisted construction projects, the total amount of the contract rather than the amount of federal assistance itself is determinative.

One difficulty with attacking labor-union discrimination through contract-compliance requirements is that the Labor Department is the agency created and designed to protect the interests of the unions. Whether proper or not, that at least has been the attitude of the unions and most administrations. Protection for black workers who are the victims of union discrimination is not a dominant concern of the department.

The executive order has never been applied to anyone besides a contractor. In my judgment, there is no reason why the unions should not be covered by its terms—just as subcontractors who do business with government contractors are under the affirmative-action obligation on the basis of their commercial contract with the contractor. Yet fundamentally political considerations have left the unions without cause for concern about meeting the order's requirements, even though a contractor is held to the responsibility to advise a union of his obligations. Moreover, a contractor is also committed to declare that the union with whom he bargains does not discriminate. But the executive orders have never forced any union to do anything at all—although a federal district-court decision in Ohio has implied that an executive order may require an employer to circumvent contractual hiring procedures which produce a lily-white work force.[5] The awesome sanctions at the government's disposal—cancellation of a contract and debarment of future contracts—are simply not used. The reasons are manifest. First, the contracting agencies that have the day-to-day responsibility for enforcement are not only understaffed (like all equal-employment agencies), but their primary interest is not equal employment opportunities. Rather, an agency, whether it deals with defense or transportation or any other concern of the government, is primarily interested in having its work done. Contract compliance, insofar as it involves equal-employment-opportunity obligations, interferes with the achievement of this important goal.

Furthermore, when OFCC does become involved, strong institutional concerns make it unsympathetic to the plight of black and other minority workers. These concerns were particularly significant during the term of Peter Brennan as Secretary of Labor. Brennan, in his capacity as president of the New York City Building Trades Council, was in open defiance of previous half-hearted measures to enforce laws against discrimination in employment. The fox was given the duty of guarding the chickens. OFCC has continued to stumble along with one reorganization after another and with staff positions unfilled; it has been unable to enforce programs in the construction industry because it does not even have any staff in such major cities as Detroit. For the most part, OFCC simply does not know which contracting agencies are actually requiring their contractors to maintain affirmative-action plans providing for the hiring of specific numbers of minorities within a specified time, and which agencies are ignoring their obligations under the executive orders.

It has been said that the executive orders have been ineffective because the government has been unwilling to spell out the precise nature of affirmative action. But the reaction in the construction industry when the OFCC adopted a tough stance in connection with the 1969 Philadelphia Plan, which formulated goals and timetables for minority hiring, belies that assertion. The objections were as plentiful—indeed, more so—as the government spelled out what was required with more exactitude. Furthermore (as Chapter 11 indicates), with the appointment of Secretary of Labor Brennan, the Nixon administration attempted to limit those state and local plans whose purpose has been more ambitious than the ones provided by the federal government.

The National Labor Relations Act and the Railway Labor Act[6]

In 1944, the Supreme Court held, in *Steele* v. *Louisville & Nashville Railroad*, that unions operating as exclusive bargaining agents for employees in an appropriate unit under the Railway Labor Act had an obligation to represent all such employees fairly, without discrimination.[7] The Court reasoned that if Congress had bestowed such broad bargaining authority upon unions and, in so doing, had sanctioned the practice of racial discrimination, grave constitutional questions would arise.[8] Accordingly, the Court found an implied statutory duty of fair representation and thus avoided constitutional issues. Noting that a strike was the minority's only recourse when an exclusive representative of the majority ignored the minority's interests, and that strikes contravened the statutory objective of achieving industrial peace, the Court said: "Requiring carriers to bargain with [a majority] representative . . . operates to exclude any other from representing a craft. . . . The minority members of a craft are thus deprived by the statute of the right, which they would otherwise possess, to choose a representative of their own, and its members cannot bargain individually on behalf of themselves as to matters which are properly the subject of collective bargaining."[9]

Yet the Court placed implied limitations upon its holding in *Steele,* and also indicated that the parameters of the case were blurred in some respects. In the first place, the Court explicitly stated that the statute did not deny a labor organization the right to determine membership eligibility. But the right of fair employment conditions and the corresponding freedom from the racial hostility of an exclusive representative are considerably more difficult to enforce without the right of membership in the union which is engaging in offensive conduct. If one cannot participate meaningfully in the decision-making process inside the union insofar as employment conditions are concerned, one's interests are more easily slighted or ignored. Black workers who are excluded from membership are not in a position to know the drift of union policy stances, let alone influence the decisions. Where racial exclusion is practiced, the minority's rights are abused with impunity and the practices complained of and enjoined in *Steele* can be continued with less difficulty than would otherwise be the case.

Until Title VII resolved the matter by designating as an "unlawful employment practice" the exclusion or segregation of members by unions because of race, the binding nature of the dicta in *Steele* was in dispute. In *Betts* v. *Easley*[10] the Kansas Supreme Court concluded that a union which excluded Negro workers from membership rights and thus from union participation in determining wages, hours, and working conditions was in violation of the Fifth Amendment by virtue of the governmental grant of exclusivity provided the union by federal labor law. The Supreme Court of California held that a union which excluded blacks from its membership could not enforce a closed-shop provision.[11] (The decision antedated the Taft-Hartley Act's prohibition of the closed shop.) The Sixth Circuit Court of Appeals, however, viewed unions as "private associations" whose membership policies are their own affair and, therefore, inappropriate for "interposition of judicial control."[12]

Another issue related to the applicability of *Steele* to the National Labor Relations Act (NLRA) involves the administrative process itself. For three years after *Steele* had been decided, the National Labor Relations Board (NLRB), which administers the NLRA, could not concern itself with union unfair labor practices inasmuch as the 1947 Taft-Hartley amendments establishing unfair labor practices for unions as well as employers were not yet law.[13] (Prohibitions against unfair labor practices by employers became law by virtue of the original National Labor Relations Act, or Wagner Act, in 1935.)[14]

But the board quickly recognized that the *Steele* holding made NLRB certification of a discriminatory union as an exclusive bargaining representative constitutionally suspect. Accordingly, it was held that rescission of certification was required when a union engaged in the conduct condemned by *Steele*. Yet the board, simultaneously heeding the dicta in *Steele* relating to membership eligibility, held that the establishment of auxiliary locals for Negro members—a favorite tactic for subordination practiced by many unions—could not be equated with the type of discrimination held unlawful by *Steele* and, therefore, was not an adequate ground for rescission of certification under the National Labor Relations Act.[15]

If this form of exclusion was to be tolerated, what kinds were not to be countenanced? The courts (which were confronted with an increasing number of unfair-representation cases after the Supreme Court ruled in 1953 that the *Steele* doctrine applied to the National Labor Relations Act as well as the Railway Labor Act)[16] did not always find the questions easy to answer. A union which prompted an employer to discriminate against blacks with regard to job classifications, discharges, layoffs, and washing and eating facilities was held not to be representing such workers fairly.[17] In *Conley* v. *Gibson,*[18] the Court held that a union must present grievances on behalf of black and white employees on the same basis. While the Fifth Circuit held that acquiescence to discriminatory conditions previously imposed by management constituted a fair-representation violation, the obligation was by no means clear.[19] How far was the union's protest to proceed before its duty was discharged? Should it attempt legal action? If so, of what kind—administrative-agency or judicial action? Must the union strike or use economic pressure? But suppose that the union was weak and striking employees were easily replaced by nonstrikers. Perhaps these concerns led the judiciary to be cautious about the forms of discrimination properly within the scope of *Steele*. In *Whitfield* v. *United Steelworkers,*[20] the Fifth Circuit, in dealing with a duty-of-fair-representation case involving segregated lines of progression, (or job ladders up which a worker was promoted) emphasized the "good faith" of the parties involved when they negotiated a seniority arrangement which fell far short of what the courts have required under Title VII. Judge Wisdom said:

The Union and the Company made a fresh start for the future. We might not agree with every provision, but they have a contract that *from now on* is free from any discrimination based on race. Angels could do no more.

. . . We cannot turn back the clock. Unfair treatment to their detriment in the past gives the plaintiffs no claim now to be paid back by unfair treatment in their favor. We have to decide this case on the contract before us and its fairness to all.[21]

Another difficulty thought to be inherent in *Steele* was that unfair-representation cases had to be brought in the federal courts. The National Labor Relations Board did not have jurisdiction over union unfair-labor practices until 1947. Moreover, it was not until seventeen years later that the board concluded, in *Hughes Tool Company*[22] that the failure to represent black workers fairly in a unit was an unfair labor practice within the meaning of Section 8 of Taft-Hartley. Until that decision, black workers confronted with discrimination at the hands of their union could only ask the board to refuse to certify the union as exclusive bargaining agent. This was a weak remedy. If the union had strength and power, the discriminatory conditions could continue without change; the refusal to grant certification might have no impact at all. A weak union might be hit harder by decertification, yet discrimination by management would continue unaffected. The federal courts could offer stronger remedies, but decisions such as *Whitfield* convinced many that they lacked the inclination. (In retrospect, this assessment appears to have been wide of the mark, for in the different and more turbulent era of the sixties and seventies, it was the federal judiciary that rejected the approach taken in *Whifield* and accordingly came to be regarded as a desirable forum in which to lodge cases.) Another reason for dissatisfaction with the judicial forum stemmed from the fact that court litigation was expensive and protracted; but by asking the NLRB for an administrative remedy, the charging party could obtain a board hearing without fees and costs and could be represented by NLRB counsel if the board decided to issue a complaint.[23]

The impact of *Hughes Tool Company* was therefore regarded as significant. The NLRB's power to issue cease-and-desist orders enjoining unfair labor practices (enforceable through the circuit court of appeals if not obeyed by the offending party) could now be leveled against a union which failed to represent black workers fairly. Such orders promised to be more potent remedies than decertification, and the NLRB was regarded as a more friendly, expeditious, and inexpensive forum than the courts.

Yet the duty of fair representation, under the rubric of both unfair-labor-practice cases and certification, has floundered for many reasons. First, the board, although it had taken the position in 1945 that it would not permit unions which had discriminated to use the act's representation procedures, undermined the effect of its own decision by holding that segregation could not be equated with discrimination *per se*.[24] Even though the board acts as the charging party's counsel and administrative procedures are generally more expeditious than those of the courts, the board has achieved relatively little under the duty-of-fair-representation provisions, and there appear to have been few charges filed before the NLRB. The board attempts to discourage litigation and to promote settlements—settlements which are not so class-action-oriented as those promoted by the EEOC. Moreover, investigation may not be symphathetic, since some board and regional-staff members assume that the NLRB is not a civil rights agency and therefore ought not to be involved in racial-discrimination questions. That attitude, if demonstrated clearly enough at the regional office, can quite easily discourage a potential charging party from filing anything at all.

This situation may be attributable to the fact that the board's constituency consists of labor and management and not the black and minority community. National Association for the Advancement of Colored People (NAACP), the Urban League (which is also actively concerned with employment issues), and black worker organizations generally have had virtually no involvement in the selection of NLRB members or general counsel—in sharp contrast to the AFL-CIO and the National Chamber of Commerce, both of which are significantly involved in such matters. Furthermore, the board's handling of other racial-discrimination disputes besides the duty-of-fair-representation cases does not give much reason for confidence in that agency.

For instance, when Judge Skelly Wright, speaking for the District of Columbia Circuit Court of Appeals in *United Packinghouse Workers* (*Farmers' Cooperative Compress*) v. *NLRB*,[25] concluded that invidious discrimination by an employer that did not involve a union might constitute an unfair labor practice within the meaning of the act, the board, on remand, avoided the issue by concluding that racial discrimination was not evidenced according to the record in that case—even though the same record might well have sustained a violation under Title VII.[26] In *Emporium Capwell*,[27] a majority of the board members held that when minority workers have attempted to protest alleged discrimination by forming a picket line, the existence of an exclusive bargaining agent, coupled with negotiated grievance-arbitration machinery, renders such conduct unprotected within the meaning of the act and thus exposes workers engaged in the activity to discipline and discharge. The board's decisions in both *United Packinghouse Workers* (*Farmers' Cooperative Compress*) and *Emporium Capwell* are questionable in my judgment. Both decisions have brought the board into conflict with the circuit courts of appeals, but in the latter case, the Supreme Court, by a vote of 8 to 1, sustained the board's judgment.

Title VII of the Civil Rights Act of 1964 and the 1972 Amendments: The Statutory Schemes

The proponents of fair-employment-practices legislation had always lobbied for cease-and-desist authority for Fair Employment Practices Commission (FEPC). Their model was the National Labor Relations Board. Ever since President Truman had infuriated the southern wing of his own party and triggered the breakaway of Strom Thurmond and other southern Democrats into the Dixiecrat Party during the 1948 campaign by his support of legislation providing for an FEPC with cease-and-desist authority, liberal supporters of civil rights legislation had rallied in favor of the idea. The essence of the scheme was that administrative procedures, while necessarily requiring enforcement in the courts when a responding party resisted the agency's cease-and-desist order, would be self-enforcing in many instances.

But cease-and-desist authority was not included in the legislative package which Congress passed when it enacted Title VII in 1964. The cease-and-desist provision was adopted by the House Judiciary Subcommittee Number 5, but the full Committee on the Judiciary rejected it, replacing it with a section authorizing what had now been named the Equal Employment Opportunity Commission to bring suits in federal court challenging employment discrimination.[28]* With this section, the bill passed the House,[29] but the Republican–southern Democrat filibuster threat, which had served to bury fair-employment-practice legislation ever since the 1948 campaign, made it impossible for even this weakened bill to prevail in the Senate. The result was some difficult negotiation between Senator Hubert Humphrey and the conservatives—and the emergence of the Dirksen-Mansfield amendments to the statute,[30]* which were the price for lifting the filibuster threat. Their purpose was to mollify legislators troubled by the prospect of effective change in racial relations. Mollification was to be accomplished in a number of ways; foremost were statutory provisions for deference to state fair-employment-practice agencies and the elimination of the EEOC's authority to bring suit in court.

State fair-employment-practice commissions have emphasized conciliation and have often approved "soft settlements" which did nothing affirmative for the complainant or the minority group involved.[31] Instead of investigating and building cases in which they could bargain from a vantage point of strength, the commissions have first attempted to negotiate settlements, frequently without a thorough investigation and factual support. This is not to denigrate the existence of such agencies altogether. Since the enactment, after World War II, of the New York law establishing a fair-employment commission, they have played an important role in changing American attitudes on race for the better. But in the 1960's, their posture was one of conservative weakness; because of this weakness—not because of federalist principles—the Dirksen-Mansfield amendments required that a complaining party take his charge to the state agency before going to the EEOC.[32]

More important was the impact of the amendments upon the EEOC itself. The agency was given no teeth. All it could do with a complaint was to investigate, find reasonable cause or no reasonable cause to believe that discrimination was taking place, and attempt to conciliate.[33] If the respondent union or company did not alter its behavior, the commission had no authority to do anything. It could not issue orders. It could not proceed to court. As a result of the Dirksen-Mansfield amendments, the EEOC was, in Michael Sovern's words, "a poor, enfeebled thing."[34] The second chairman of the commission, Stephen Schulman, was to say, in 1967, "We're out to kill an elephant with a fly gun."[35]

The individual could bring an action in federal district court if all administrative procedures available through Title VII availed nothing.[36] Moreover, the attorney general could bring an action in the event that there was a "pattern or practice" of discrimination.[37] In the main, however, the burden of bringing suit was to be placed upon individual workers and civil rights organizations such as the NAACP Legal Defense Fund.

Yet EEOC was not out of the fray. The authority to issue reasonable-cause findings carried with it the function of writing decisions and formulating the legal rationale for them. The commission was involved in the development of guidelines relating to such issues as seniority, testing, and—with reference to sex discrimination—maternity leave and state protective laws.[38] In sharp contrast was the state-commission practice of providing a one-sentence decision of "cause" or "no cause." In 1965 and 1966 the EEOC's decisions and guidelines were to establish a climate and framework for the federal court decisions that flowed from suits by individual workers.

Furthermore, the commission's willingness to hold public hearings dramatized the issue of discrimination. The bright light of publicity was not a substitute for judicial action—but many business and labor leaders were sensitive about airing their dirty linen before a critical public. Clifford Alexander, the commission's third chairman, criticized his successor, William H. Brown III, for not holding hearings.[39] In 1970, however, Chairman Brown held hearings in Houston, where black and Chicano workers had not shared in the benefits of the boom of the late sixties.[40] Brown characterized that metropolis—whose leaders claimed that the city had already achieved the statutory objectives—as a "sick city." Important hearings relating to the utility industry were held in November 1971.[41] All of this activity caused Chairman Brown to be castigated by Senator John McClellan,[42] just as Chairman Alexander had been criticized by Senator Everett Dirksen previously,[43] on the ground that the public hearings put undue pressure on business and labor. The commission was a catalyst. Moreover, its lawyers wrote *amicus* (friend of the Court) briefs in private law suits and provided other kinds of technical assistance as well.

But the EEOC's role was, nevertheless, diminished by its lack of enforcement authority. Despite the fact that a reasonable-cause finding was issued before conciliation took place, the commission entered into about as many "soft settlements" as had the state agencies. The Newport News Shipbuilding Agreement, was widely publicized—but it was ineffective because the commission played no policing role. Such circumstances, as well as the substantial backlog of cases which continue to plague the commission,[44] were attributable to inadequate budget and manpower and to general disorganization, rather than to the inability to go to court. They contributed substantially to the state of enfeeblement, and indirectly to the consensus that the commission should have more authority. The debate thus became not whether the statute should be changed—but *how* it should be changed. Thus developed the battle between the cease-and-desist adherents and those who believed that the EEOC should have the authority to go to court.

This controversy endangered the passage of the 1972 amendments to Title VII

(the Equal Employment Opportunity Act). The struggle pitted the Nixon administration and such friends as Senator Peter Dominick and Congressman John Erlenborn against the Senate liberals; the former favored EEOC court actions, and the
latter supported NLRB-type cease-and-desist orders which could subsequently be
enforced in appellate courts. Although many of the liberals who advocated cease-
and-desist authority for the EEOC characterized the debate as a liberal-versus-con-
servative dispute, the question of which of the two alternatives would be more effective was and is by no means susceptible to clear-cut resolution. The *New York
Times,* for instance, commented in an editorial of January 25, 1972.

> In the past, *The Times* has favored giving the commission this[cease-and-desist] power to
> enforce its own findings. We are still convinced that such an arrangement would represent a
> vast improvement over the present ineffectual method. But a strong case would be made for
> the idea that effective nonpartisan enforcement of the law may in the long run be more cer-
> tain through reliance upon the courts than upon a politically appointed commission whose
> members change with each Administration.
>
> Administrative agencies were given broad enforcement powers in the labor field because
> it used to be thought that the Federal judiciary had an antilabor bias. Whatever the truth of
> that estimate as applied to the courts in the 1930's, it is clearly untrue concerning their
> approach to racial discrimination today. Of the three branches of government, the judiciary
> has consistently been most vigilant in protecting minority rights in recent decades.
>
> Superficially, the cease-and-desist route holds out the promise of swifter action and more
> uniform administration of the law, but experience with N.L.R.B. hearing examiners
> suggests that they do not dispose of cases more rapidly than Federal district judges. As for
> the uniformity of interpretation, the harder issues will only be settled by appeal to the
> Supreme Court whether they originate in E.E.O.C. orders or in district court law suits.
>
> A closely divided Senate will decide today whether to substitute the court approach for
> the cease-and-desist order. If the final Senate vote is for cease-and-desist orders, the ques-
> tion will go to a House-Senate conference. There is satisfaction at least in the knowledge
> that either version of the bill would bring about an improvement over the existing feeble ar-
> rangement.[45]

The EEOC-court-action advocates argued that since the agency commissioners
were appointed by the President, the entire employment effort could be sabotaged
if an unsympathetic, politically motivated commission refused to issue cease-and-
desist orders. It was noted that the NLRB appointees operate in an arena where the
attitudes concerning policy had changed considerably, depending upon the administration that appointed the board members.[46] Yet this criticism was somewhat
off the mark, inasmuch as an unsympathetic EEOC could just as effectively scuttle
a court-action statute by refusing to file suits as it could a cease-and-desist statute
by refusing to issue orders. Moreover, a statute could more effectively resolve
both problems—as do the 1972 amendments—by providing what is in effect an
escape valve for individual plaintiffs—namely, the right of the individual to sue if
the commission takes no action or dismisses the charge.[47]

The cease-and-desist proponents said that the commission, as the agency
charged with the administration and interpretation of the statute, would have more
expertise than the courts, as well as a more sympathetic understanding of the
plight of victims of discrimination. Such characteristics could be brought into play

more directly and effectively through cease-and-desist authority than through a court-action scheme. Arguably, this has proved true under the National Labor Relations Act. Certainly, superior sensitivity to statutory objectives was evidenced by the board when the Wagner Act was first passed, at a time when federal courts were almost antedeluvian in their treatment of labor-management problems.

The same considerations, however, do not apply to Title VII litigation. The federal courts have paved the way and fashioned the law. The federal judges, in the main, have shown no lack of expertise or deftness in handling very complicated related problems. On the contrary, the judiciary, appointed with life tenure, may have accomplished more than the EEOC would have been able to if it had been faced with the primary or exclusive burden of responsibility under the statute. As the *New York Times* editorial notes, the courts have not demonstrated the deficiencies evident in the labor cases during the 1930's. Moreover, the proofs deduced in Title VII litigation make judicial procedure more suitable than its administrative counterpart. While an administrative agency operates in an informal setting which is, arguably, better suited to the industrial-relations situation, the problems connected with discovery in Title VII cases are much more complicated than those traditionally present in NLRB cases. In part, the complexity is attributable to the fact that Title VII litigations are often class actions involving large numbers of workers—and such actions involve examination of voluminous company files and documents. Perhaps a new atmosphere wil be created by the 1972 amendments and less resistance will obviate the need for much discovery of this kind. But there is no evidence on which to base such an assumption; indeed, the flood of procedural objections to EEOC litigation—mirroring the similar history involving private-plaintiff litigation in the 1960's—indicates that the opposite situation prevails.[48]

Another problem with NLRB-type powers is that they would have necessitated the hiring of a large number of trial examiners with some knowledge of Title VII law. Ideally, a good number of them should have been minority and women lawyers. Yet the effective civil service regulations on the federal and other levels may have the effect of disproportionately excluding minority lawyers as well as other types of minority personnel. Thus, the tooling-up for cease-and-desist orders could have presented many difficulties, because of the problems involved in trial-examiner selection.

On the question of whether the EEOC or NLRB route would have been more expeditious, the arguments are by no means one-sided. The proponents of cease-and-desist orders point to the NLRB experience: more than 90 percent of the charges are settled without a hearing.[49] Orders are generally issued by a trial examiner or administrative-law judge within eleven months after the issuance of a complaint by the general counsel.[50] The period of time compares favorably with the time it takes to litigate nonjury trials in the federal district courts, where most of the employment-discrimination cases are likely to arise. The cease-and-desist advocates, however, assume that the same percentage of defendants would be likely to settle under the provisions of Title VII as compromise their claims before the board under Taft-Hartley. But since no clear consensus is evident in American society concerning adherence to the dictates of Title VII and related civil rights legislation as currently interpreted by the courts, this would seem to be an unwarranted hypothesis upon which to operate. Title VII defendants do not seem particularly interested in settling their cases—and this will continue to be true until they are convinced that most judges will make discrimination an expensive proposition. Accordingly, one would assume that there is a greater likelihood that cases would be taken to the appellate courts. In sum, the question of which route would provide the most expeditious process is not completely answerable.

The amendments relating to court enforcement have another good feature. If the court itself has heard the evidence relating to the underlying claims of discrimination, it will probably be favorably disposed to issue relief which will effectively cure discrimination; it has a stake in the integrity and viability of its own order and decree. And the apparent reluctance of the courts to impose contempt sanctions in the public-education desegregation cases may be explained in part by the fact that the judiciary is extremely cautious in imposing sanctions of this kind upon a coordinate branch of government in the delicately balanced federal system. The contrast between the scheme provided by Title VII on the one hand and the operation of the National Labor Relations Act on the other bodes well for the former statute.

Under the National Labor Relations Act, the board, having issued its cease-and-desist order, must proceed to a circuit court of appeals to enforce it. But the circuit court of appeals has not heard the evidence and is not geared to deal with contempt problems. The trial courts are the institutions best able to handle contempt cases. Since they generally have heard the evidence upon which the decree is based, they are well prepared to deal with the disobedience which gives rise to contempt or, as is more often the case, the problems and new factors which where not anticipated at the time of the original order. Yet under the National Labor Relations Act, the district judges, who have often been called upon by the appellate court to determine which, if any, contempt sanction should apply, have not heard the evidence and, therefore, cannot address themselves to the issue with the same degree of expertise and vigilance that would be theirs if they had been the actual triers of fact.[51] Accordingly, the 1972 amendments appear to be superior to the National Labor Relations Act in some respects, since the federal district courts both hear the evidence and, if necessary, fashion contempt penalties.

Nevertheless, if a significant number of defendants are prone to negotiate settlements now that the threat of judicial involvement is more real, the cease-and-desist order might well be a preferable option, as long as the state agency takes a tough stance in enforcing the law and does not perform as have most state fair-employment-practice agencies.[52] The EEOC conciliation record, however, and its desire in many instances to obtain settlements rather than comprehensive relief do not indicate it will become tougher. For example, the EEOC's steel agreement of 1975 (discussed in the Conclusion), while providing for an extraordinary cash outlay by defendants in one settlement, nevertheless was very unsatisfactory: it stipulated an inadequate amount of relief on a per capita basis—particularly of the nonmonetary type—and the labor and management defendants dominated in administering and enforcing the decree. On the other hand, potentially more comprehensive relief has been negotiated in some EEOC conciliation agreements.[53]

Perhaps the best utilization of available remedies would have been to give the EEOC the option of issuing a cease-and-desist order or suing directly in federal district court, depending upon the particular circumstances of the case. But the proponents of court action for the EEOC were not willing to do so, since one of their reasons for disavowing cease-and-desist was their belief that the EEOC would be unable to perform a major judicial function by itself because, in its own way, the commission is committed to an attitude favoring the charging party or plaintiff and therefore to a generally expansive interpretation of the statute.

The poorly thought out "compromise" amendment between the EEOC and NLRB approaches advanced by Senators Jacob Javits of New York and Harrison Williams of New Jersey would have done little to provide the commission with suitable options. That amendment would have permitted the commission to have its findings filed with the federal court for the purpose of "certification," with substantial deference given by the court to the findings.[54] But the decision of the district court would be appealable to the circuit court of appeals and then to the United States Supreme Court. The Javits-Williams amendment had two significant defects: first, the absence of a cease-and-desist order which might prompt the parties to behave properly before going to court and, second, the requirement that the commission go not only to the circuit court of appeals, as under the NLRB scheme, but to the district court as well. The Javits-Williams amendment was the last-ditch effort supposedly intended to save cease-and-desist. To put the matter charitably, it was a misguided one, and if accepted it would have resulted in an enforcement mechanism much inferior to the two alternatives under discussion.

Although the 1972 amendments represent a great advance, the authorization of EEOC court involvement will mean little if that power is not effectively utilized. A critical question is whether EEOC will actively pursue judicial actions. William Brown, former chairman of the commission, had stated that the commission would be filing approximately 5 to 15 suits a month beginning in 1972, although he was first quoted as having taken an extremely pessimistic view of the time it would take to get EEOC "tooled up" for such action.[55] Unfortunately, during the first year the 1972 amendments were in effect only about 30 suits were filed. By the fall of 1973, however, the commission had filed about 140 suits[56]—approximately the same number filed by the Justice Department during its first nine years of pattern-and-practice authority. By the spring of 1975, the commission was involved in over 500 cases, and the general counsel's litigation staff had grown from twenty-two lawyers to three hundred.[57] Regional litigation centers have been established throughout the country. Yet, by 1976, the commission's impact was very slight indeed. Despite substantial budget increases, the backlog of cases had reached 120,000, and an intake of almost 60,000 complaints per annum was projected. One problem is that not enough EEOC lawyers have the trial experience that is a prerequisite for Title VII litigation. The commission's record compares unfavorably with that of the Justice Department, which commands a good deal of respect by virtue of its thoroughness in investigation and trial preparation.

An additional difficulty responsible for the commission's performance may stem from the EEOC chairmanship. The Nixon administration dropped William Brown III in 1973 and appointed John Powell in his place. This action was assumed to be retaliation for Brown's increasingly activist and outspoken stance. Yet Brown's appointment, after Clifford Alexander's removal as chairman by Nixon in 1969, was thought to be for a similar reason. To say that Brown was a surprise is to understate. Chairman Powell might have been, but that will always be a matter for speculation: his tenure was abruptly terminated early in 1975 by President Ford. Powell's replacement, Lowell Perry, resigned in April 1976 after less than a year in the post.

Another reason for the commission's relative ineffectiveness is that during the first four years litigation has been bogged down in procedural issues. The most prominent questions are whether conciliation must be undertaken by the commission prior to its instigation of litigation,[58]* and to what extent on EEOC suit is precluded by a pending private action, a previous judgment adverse to a private plaintiff, or a settlement of a related private suit.[59]* The difficulties of the commission resemble the plight of individual plaintiffs in the 1965 to 1968 period, when countless procedural issues were litigated by defendants—all for the purpose of delay; virtually all were eventually resolved in favor of plaintiffs.[60]*

Perhaps, however, the commission's difficulties are more fundamental than the procedural problems akin to those previously confronted by private plaintiffs. The commission was put together according to a cease-and-desist model. The five-member commission was patterned after the five-member NLRB, which performs a judicial function. Both before and after the passage of the 1972 amendments EEOC commissioners have not performed that function. The purpose of the commission is to investigate, conciliate, and bring law suits. These functions can, quite obviously, be better directed by one person than by a group, and the chairman is the principal policy maker. Four members have little to do, inasmuch as they do not participate in the administration of the commission and, unlike NLRB members, do not adjudicate disputes. Their role is often to criticize and backbite and make life difficult for the chairman.

Moreover, unlike his NLRB counterpart, the general counsel of the EEOC, who has authority to bring actions in federal district court,[61] does not influence an investigation and the consequent accumulation of facts. The board's general counsel investigates and tries the same case. The benefits of the latter scheme are obvious: the theory and scope of the case can be developed by conscientious selection of the evidence by those who actually try the case. The EEOC general counsel cannot select his evidence and cannot even determine the appropriate issue—for example, whether the case should involve both race and sex. The divorce between litigation and investigation also handicaps the general counsel in formulating an appropriate remedy. Indeed, many regional litigation centers that have been established as arms of the EEOC are not aware of pending cases—or, if they are aware, are unable to get such cases released by the investigative division of the commission for legal action.

Despite all these problems, at least the mechanism now exists through which to enforce the statute, and the sparks of litigation may begin to fly. Although few cases have been decided on their merits by a district judge in the years since the commission has acquired the authority to sue, ample groundwork for litigation has been laid by the substantive law that has been fashioned by the courts, primarily as the result of individual plaintiffs' actions under the 1964 act and secondarily by the Justice Department's pattern-and-practice litigation. Paradoxically, fundamental inequities in the employment relationship seem destined to survive the century even though the judiciary has created a body of law, based upon the Civil Rights Act of 1964 as well as other civil rights legislation, which has theoretically placed minority-group plaintiffs in a very favorable position. True, the decisions have not been uniformly beneficial for minority groups. But, on balance, they have achieved much more than was generally conceived possible by most sages[62]* at the time of the passage of Title VII in 1964. Interestingly, Congress, in the 1972 amendments, seems to have regarded these decisions favorably; it has given greater scope to the judiciary in devising remedies—particularly remedies involving the formulation of quotas, goals, and timetables to redress past discrimination under the statute.

Nevertheless, not all goals have been achieved. First, not all the basic issues have been resolved by the courts. Second, the courts may qualify some of the broad principles that have been enunciated. And, finally, the Supreme Court has not spoken on most of the major issues, although the ten opinions written by the Court—two by Justice Powell, three by Justice Potter Stewart and one each by Chief Justice Burger, Justice Brennan, Justice Blackmun, Justice Marshall, and Justice Rehnquist (plus an important decision by the Eighth Circuit while Judge Blackmun was sitting on the panel involved[63])—indicate a broad and sympathetic construction of Title VII.[64]*

The Court has denied certiorari in a number of instances where the lower courts have approved the position taken by plaintiffs—particularly in respect to quotas, goals, and timetable remedies.[65] Still, as the consequences of some of the decisions become apparent, what the reaction of President Nixon's appointees will be is uncertain. Uneasiness increases when the *entire* record of the Nixon-Burger court in connection with race relations is considered—although, as the preceding chapter indicates, the record has not been as bad and one-sided as it is generally made out to be by most civil rights proponents.

Other Aspects of the 1972 Amendments
Transfer of Pattern-and-Practice Authority

The attorney general has had authority to sue in pattern-and-practice cases ever since Title VII became effective on July 2, 1965. By the end of fiscal year 1973, however, only 107 actions had been brought—fewer than those instituted by the

EEOC in the first two years it had authority to sue under the 1972 amendments.[66] According to this measuring rod the record of the Justice Department is unimpressive. Ironically, liberal attorneys general such as Ramsey Clark and Nicholas Katzenbach—both of whom served in the Johnson administration—took very little action. A rash of actions were filed as the Johnson administration left office in 1968. This general record contrasts rather sharply with the more activist stance of the Nixon administration, an administration which was not very sympathetic to the plight of black people in general. Attorneys General John Mitchell and Richard Kleindienst filed most of the 107 actions. There seems to have been no major change in stance under the regimes of Attorneys General William Saxbe and Edward Levi. The Justice Department's involvement built to a crescendo in 1973 and 1974. Yet even in 1970, suit was filed in only two of the cases referred to Justice by EEOC for action. Justice utilized an only slightly larger number of EEOC referrals in 1971.

The poor record of the Johnson administration may be partly due to the emphasis given to voting-rights cases at that time. Also, the Justice Department took more than two years to make the determination that specialization according to subject matter was necessary. Only then did Justice create separate divisions to handle cases dealing with employment, voting, and so forth, departing from its previous practice of dividing all civil rights cases throughout the United States according to geographical region. The continuing conservatism of the department, which manifested itself in the Johnson as well as the Nixon and Ford administrations, is often described as "careful" or "lawyer-like." Such qualities are obviously beneficial in the processes of trial preparation and discovery. Furthermore, the resources of the Federal Bureau of Investigation, which are available to Justice but not, of course, to private plaintiffs or the EEOC, provide consequential assistance.

But the department lacks imagination and creativity in dealing with employment remedies. For instance, not until 1971 was the Employment Section convinced that the attorney general could successfully obtain back pay for the victims of discrimination. Moreover, in *Stamps* v. *Detroit Edison,* the department, while not explicitly *opposing* the private plaintiffs' request for punitive damages against the defendants, wrote memoranda to the court which suggested that the department would attempt to sever its portion of the case from the previously consolidated litigation if the court would hold—as it did—that punitive damages were authorized under the statute.[67] Despite the fact that its own Seattle building-trades decree, *United States* v. *Local 86 Ironworkers,*[68] demonstrated the importance of community-based organizations and their involvement in the implementation of court decrees, Justice opposed a similar involvement by the Association for the Betterment of Black Edison Employees in Detroit. The department's attitude was unsympathetic and shortsighted. Unable to enforce its own decree because its attorneys are based solely in Washington, D.C. (an experience from which the EEOC has profited by establishing litigation centers in major cities throughout the United States modeled on the regional offices of the National Labor Relations

Board), it was unwilling to support the private institutions which would perform that very task. Whether spitefulness, malice, or neglect was the motivation is almost beside the point. The point is that Justice had no interest in the enforcement mechanism in *Detroit Edison*—and such has generally been the case elsewhere.

Indeed, as we shall see, the lack of an enforcement or compliance effort has been one of Justice's principal shortcomings. It is attributable not only to geographical concentration in Washington but also to the fact that, unlike the National Labor Relations Board, Justice has no enforcement division whose job is to see that the great court victories that are chronicled in the department's press releases are translated into employment and income for black workers.

Finally, it must be noted that Justice has not lost a single case (many district court decisions have been reversed at the appellate level), although it has lost portions of some.[69] Yet its box-score mentality—its willingness to take only sure winners, in which abundant testimony supplements a strong statistical case—has contributed significantly to Justice's lack of courage in requesting strong remedies.

The 1972 amendments provided that Justice was to lose its authority to bring pattern or practice actions in the private sector. Arguably (although the statutory language is by no means clear),[70]* the authority is to be retained in the public sector, as it is also in connection with violations of the executive order. The arguments for and against Justice's continued involvement are carefully balanced. Superior investigative resources, expertise in particular industries, involvement in litigation already commenced, and the fact that the EEOC will not pick up all the slack in the territory vacated by Justice argue for its continued presence. Moreover, the EEOC is saddled with procedural requirements, such as the filing of a charge by the commissioner or an individual, the need for a reasonable-cause finding, and an attempt to conciliate, none of which impede Justice's statutory efforts. Hence Justice has never had to run the guantlet of procedural objections by defendants, which have plagued the EEOC. Although Justice has a tendency toward small-minded bureaucratic unimaginativeness, as well as an inability to follow through on its decrees, competition between the agencies is, on balance, a healthy phenomcnon—especially now that the EEOC seems prone to ape some of Justice's unattractive characteristics: arguing for limited class relief, refusing to support the punitive-damages remedy, and performing shoddily in enforcing and monitoring decrees that have been rendered. Accordingly, it appears that the phasing out of Justice by the 1972 amendments was not a good move by Congress.

Office of Federal Contract Compliance

Both management and organized labor have often charged that the existence of the Office of Federal Contract Compliance fosters unhealthy competition among federal agencies having overlapping jurisdiction affecting employment and results in a proliferation of differing and potentially inconsistent standards. Thus when, at the time of the debate concerning the 1972 amendments, the AFL-CIO argued for the transfer of contract-compliance functions from the OFCC to the EEOC, it phrased its objection to the OFCC as opposition to multiforum litigation. But the motivation was the Philadelphia Plan, with its application of goals and timetables for minority hiring to the building trades, as well as other governmentally imposed plans. Recognizing the motivation, the civil rights groups, in an effort to support Philadelphia-type plans, and also in the belief that competition between agencies would keep each one honest, opposed the labor organization.[71]

Based upon this reasoning, the attempt to transfer OFCC functions to the EEOC in the 1972 amendments failed.[72] Ironically, labor's failure has redounded to its own best interests. The appointment of Peter Brennan as Secretary of Labor in January 1973 placed an enemy of the Philadelphia Plan and similar plans in charge of the program he opposed. In New York City, Detroit, Boston, and San Francisco, there has been a concerted effort by the federal government to undercut and invalidate more ambitious state and local government plans in the construction industry—that is, plans that are more ambitious than those developed by the federal government.[73]

Even prior to the Brennan appointment, a reorganization in the Department of Labor had placed the OFCC and its area coordinators under the Employment Standards Administration of the department. This weakened OFCC's position in the department and has hampered its budgetary efforts. In fact, the OFCC has no real budget of its own by virtue of the reorganization. The problem, however, is not simply one of staff and money. When the EEOC threatened to institute legal action against General Motors and General Electric on a national basis in 1973, it was pointed out that the contracting agency, the Department of Defense, operating under the presumably more stringent affirmative-action standards of the executive order, had approved what the EEOC was attacking.[74] Moreover, the OFCC had placed its imprimatur upon the Defense Department's action.

The lesson seems to be that the equal-employment opportunity interests need Cabinet-level representation. The EEOC, the Employment Section in the Civil Rights Division of the Justice Department, and the OFCC are all too far down the line. The OFCC is effectively under the thumb of its enemies—and the contract-compliance divisions of the contracting agencies do not make EEOC obligations their first priority.

Civil Rights Act of 1866

In *Jones* v. *Alfred H. Mayer Co.*[75]—one of the last and most important decisions of the Warren Court—the Court held that the Civil Rights Act of 1866[76] applied to private acts of discrimination in connection with the disposal of real estate. The Court held that the plaintiff, alleging that a real estate company had refused to sell him a house because of his race, was entitled to relief under Section 1982 of the code which was part of the 1866 act. The Court's reasoning indicated that a similar result might be found with regard to that section's parallel provision, Section 1981, which provides blacks with the same rights as whites to make and enforce contracts of employment.[77]* Moreover, the Court cited examples of racial discrimination that had concerned the Reconstruction Congress. Justice Stewart, writing for a seven to two majority, said:

The same Congress that wanted to do away with the Black Codes *also* had before it an imposing body of evidence pointing to the mistreatment of Negroes by private individuals and unofficial groups, mistreatment unrelated to any hostile state legislation. . . . The congressional debates are replete with references to private injustices against Negroes—references to white employers who refused to pay their Negro workers, white planters who agreed among themselves not to hire freed slaves without the permission of their former masters, . . .[78]

Accordingly, the dominant intention of Congress was to remedy employment discrimination independent of any support that it might have from the state governments.

Following *Jones,* the Third, Fourth, Fifth, Sixth, Seventh, Eighth, and District of Columbia Courts of Appeals all rules that Section 1981 applies to private employment discrimination.[79] And the Supreme Court finally resolved all doubts, in the decision of *Johnson* v. *Railway Express Agency, Inc.,* by holding that "Congress clearly has retained § 1981 as a remedy against private employment discrimination separate from and independent of the more elaborate and time consuming procedures of Title VII."[80]

Waters v. *Wisconsin Steel Works,*[81] a case decided in the Seventh Circuit, was the first situation in which the issue of the applicability of Section 1981 was faced by the judiciary. In *Waters,* the plaintiff had filed Title VII charges against the employer but not the union, which was sued in federal court. The Seventh Circuit said:

We hold that a right to sue under section 1981 for "private" racial discrimination in employment existed prior to 1964. By enacting Title VII of the 1964 Civil Rights Act, Congress did not repeal this right to sue. However, in order to avoid irreconcilable conflicts between the provisions of sections 1981 and Title VII, a plaintiff must exhaust his administrative remedies before the EEOC unless he provides a reasonable excuse for his failure to do so. Since we find on the basis of the material before us that plaintiffs have sufficiently justified their failure to charge Local 21 before the EEOC, we hold that the district court erred in dismissing plaintiff's complaint against the union. Accordingly, we reverse for trial on the merits of the plaintiff's complaint against Local 21 under section 1981 and against Harvester [the employer] under Title VII.[82]

While the Seventh Circuit found an independent basis for jurisdiction in addition to Title VII, it held that resort must be made preliminarily to the EEOC. The majority of circuit courts holding that the Civil Rights Act of 1866 is applicable to private employment discrimination have not so limited their decisions. Rather, they have followed the lead of the Third Circuit in *Young* v. *International Telephone & Telegraph Co.*[83] The court there stated that "due regard to the conciliation jurisdiction of the EEOC can be afforded by the district courts short of the erection of a jurisdictional bar." The Third Circuit therefore held that employees may bypass the conciliation procedures of Title VII. It did not, however, wish to have the conciliation features of the statute "entirely disregarded" and held that the availability of conciliation by the EEOC was a factor to be considered by the courts while determining whether to grant equitable relief to plaintiffs. Specifically, the court stated that a district court should focus upon the commission's power to initiate conciliation upon the request of employers, employees, and the unions. The Third Circuit said: "This power apparently may be exercised by the EEOC at any time, even during the pendency of a law suit brought pursuant to § 1981. The district courts may well find it appropriate to suggest in certain cases such resort to the healing remedies of conference, conciliation, and of persuasion."[84]

Of course, the effect of this ruling is to hamstring those plaintiffs who have not resorted to the EEOC prior to litigation and to place, in some instances, the burden upon them of seeking out EEOC conciliation procedures. (Most important class actions cannot be resolved through conciliation.) But one significant aspect of *Young,* as well as of *Waters,* is that EEOC procedures need not be exhausted prior to the filing of a suit in federal district court. As a practical matter, the court, even though it will not have jurisdiction over the EEOC, will probably attempt— either indirectly through the parties or by other means—to involve the EEOC in an expedited investigation and conciliation process. Therefore, charging parties or plaintiffs who would not normally have access to the EEOC because of its heavy backlog may, as a result of *Young* and the prestige and authority of the federal district courts, have a substantial portion of their discovery and investigative work done for them expeditiously by the commission. But neither the courts nor the sorely pressed EEOC has seemed to take advantage of the conciliation opportunity provided by *Young.* And the EEOC is not equipped to perform the detailed discovery that is required in Title VII action.

Moreover, in *Johnson* v. *REA,* the Supreme Court, albeit in dicta, enunciated a view of the relationship between Section 1981 and "the more elaborate and time consuming procedures of Title VII" which may indicate that even *Young,* let alone *Waters,* overestimates the role conciliation must play in Section 1981 suits. Justice Blackmun, after citing both *Waters* and *Young* for the proposition that "the filing of a Title VII charge and resort to Title VII's administrative machinery are not prerequisites for the institution of a Section 1981 action," commented:

We are satisfied, also, that Congress did not expect that a § 1981 court action usually would be resorted to only upon completion of Title VII procedures and the Commission's efforts to obtain voluntary compliance. Conciliation and persuasion through the administrative process, to be sure, often constitutes a desirable approach to settlement of disputes based on sensitive and emotional charges of invidious employment discrimination. We recognize, too, that the filing of a lawsuit might tend to deter efforts at conciliation, that lack of success in the legal action could weaken the Commission's efforts to induce voluntary compliance, and that a suit is privately oriented and narrow, rather than broad in application, as successful conciliation tends to be. But these are the natural effects of the choice Congress has made available to the claimant by its conferring upon him administrative and judicial remedies. The choice is a valuable one. Under some circumstances, the administrative route may be highly preferred over the litigatory; under others, the reverse may be true. We are disinclined, in the face of congressional emphasis upon the existence and independence of the two remedies, to infer any positive preference for one over the other.[85]

What are the circumstances which determine whether Title VII or Section 1981 is the preferable route for a particular plaintiff? Under Title VII, even with the 1972 amendments, employers or labor organizations with fewer than fifteen members or employees are not covered, nor are employers or unions in industries not affecting interstate commerce. The 1866 statute does not include these limitations nor, as *Johnson* indicates, does it require deference to state agencies, a conciliation period, or the other Title VII obligations. But the 1866 act has other limitations; the chief one is that its primary purpose is to combat only racial discrimination.[86] Thus, while Section 1981 has been held to bar discrimination against noncitizens,[87] arguably its provisions do not apply to national-origin discrimination unless race is involved,[88] to sex discrimination,[89] or to religious discrimination. Another important point is, of course, that a Section 1981 plaintiff does not have the help of the EEOC in investigating and litigating his case.

The statute of limitations governing timeliness of suit appears to apply for a longer period under Section 1981 than under Title VII in most instances, since Section 1981 refers to the relevant state statute of limitations rather than to Title VII's short 180-day period for filing charges[90] (extended in the 1972 amendments from the 90-day period provided in the 1964 act). But the effect of the 180-day limitation has been softened considerably by the development of the doctrine of "continuing discrimination," which permits a plaintiff to file charges more than 180 days after the incident which is his prime concern, as long as he alleges that the defendant's violation is not confined to that incident but constitutes a continuing course of conduct which still affects the plaintiff or his class.[91]* Moreover, the 180-day filing limitation does not determine the period of time over which a defendant's back-pay liability accrues. The 1972 amendments fix that period as no longer than the two years preceding the filing of charges[92]—a length of time approximately equivalent to that provided by the state statutes of limitations which are often applied in suits under Section 1981. (Prior to the passage of the amendments, the courts had ruled that the time limits for filing did not apply to back-pay determinations, and had either used state statutes of limitations[93]—in which case Title VII and Section 1981 would yield the same back-pay result—or assumed that back pay could be awarded from July 2, 1965, the effective date of the act[94]—in which case Title VII would yield the recovery of more back pay than Section 1981 would.)

In the main, differences between the state statutes and Title VII are beneficial to plaintiffs suing under the 1866 statute, and the state statutes do not seem to warrant repeal, inasmuch as most Title VII limitations are attributable to the filibuster threat and nothing else. If Congress, during the 1963–1964 debates on Title VII, had recognized that the Civil Rights Act of 1866 could be applied to private-employment discrimination, the filibuster threat would have disappeared.[95] Any filibuster would have come from the liberal proponents of civil rights legislation in opposition to limitations upon the Civil Rights Act of 1866.

3 | The Substantive Law of Title VII: An Introduction

Title VII and the "Private Attorney General"
Class Representation

Title VII of the Civil Rights Act of 1964 is the most comprehensive law relating to employment discrimination; most of the law that has evolved in this field has developed under that statute. Under the 1964 act, the Fifth Circuit has evolved the concept that not *all* Negro workers alleging discrimination on the basis of race need file charges with the EEOC and pursue available administrative remedies, inasmuch as "racial discrimination is by definition class discrimination."[1]* As in the public-accommodation cases arising under Title II of the Civil Rights Act of 1964, the plaintiff is deemed to be acting "not for himself alone" but, rather, as a "private attorney general" who puts on the "mantle of the sovereign" in the public interest.[2] The court and the EEOC have consistently held that a complaint filed with the EEOC protesting an individual injustice acts as a linchpin for an EEOC investigation into all employer or union practices related to race.[3]

Said the Fifth Circuit in *Jenkins* v. *United Gas Corporation* "In dollars, Employee's claim for past due wages may be tiny. But before a Court as to which there is no jurisdictional minimum . . . it is enough on which to launch a full scale inquiry into the charged unlawful motivation in employment practices. It is even more so considering the prayer for injunction as a protection against repetition of such conduct in the future."[4] The court also specifically noted the great potential for divide-and-conquer or "resist-and-withdraw" techniques when dealing with individuals rather than a group. This potential is particularly important in race cases in which an excluded group has been systematically fenced out and a slight advantage provided to one worker may effectively undermine group solidarity.[5]

Moreover, the courts have been particularly concerned about the danger that defendant unions and employers may attempt to play off one member of a group against another once litigation is imminent or has commenced. In such circumstances "a last minute change of heart is suspect, to say the least."[6] As the Fifth Circuit has said, "What has been adopted can be repealed, and what has been appealed can be re-appealed."[7] The same court said in *Jenkins* that "in the face of litigation'' changes in employment practices affecting some individuals ''are equivocal in purpose, motive, and permanence.''[8]

Even if a class action has not commenced, relief for a group may be obtained.[9] The Ninth Circuit Court of Appeals, however, in *Gregory* v. *Litton Systems, Inc.,*[10] was somewhat cautious in the absence of a class action. In denying group relief the district court had allowed, Judge Alfred Goodwin stated:

> In this case, Gregory [the plaintiff] did not seek reinstatement with Litton. As the result of a stipulation, he was to receive a money judgment. The wide-ranging injunction requested in Gregory's name could only benefit persons not before the court. Because no injunction was necessary to Gregory's chosen remedy, and because Litton was not shown to have a history of discrimination, or an intent to discriminate, there was no pressing need to fashion a remedy solely for the benefit of persons who were not before the court.

The court stated that nonparties to the litigation could benefit from a decree in some circumstances, even where the parties were not before the court, but emphasized: ''In this case, however, Gregory was seeking no prospective relief for himself, and affirmatively disavowed it. Except for ideologically interested *amici,* no one else before the court was seeking the rather broad and detailed injunctive relief fashioned by the decree. The injunctive benefits for nonparties, therefore, were neither incidental nor necessary to the resolution of the pending litigation.''[11]

Rule 23 of the Federal Rules of Civil Procedure provides for class actions, and that provision has been utilized in employment-discrimination cases. Under what circumstances and for what purposes may it be utilized? Rule 23 states that there are four prerequisites to the maintenance of a class action: ''(1) the class is so numerous that joinder of all members is impracticable, (2) there are questions of law or fact common to the class, (3) the claims or defenses of the representative parties are typical of all claims or defenses of the class, and (4) the representative parties will fairly and adequately protect the interest of the class.''[12]

The fourth consideration has spawned some of the most important litigation. Raising issues which relate to the question of ''standing to sue,'' on behalf of others who are not named plaintiffs, defendants often urge that a particular plaintiff is not an adequate class representative and that the litigation therefore cannot be maintained as a class action. In *Huff* v. *N. D. Cass Company of Alabama*[13] the Fifth Circuit, reversing an earlier decision *en banc,* (or with a full court) staked out the basic guidelines for resolving the question of class representation. The district court, in *Huff,* had conducted a preliminary evidentiary hearing on the plaintiff's individual claim and had found it lacking. The court therefore concluded that the plaintiff was not an appropriate member of the class, and hence could not adequately represent it. The Fifth Circuit recognized that, while maintainability of a class action may be determined on the basis of the pleadings filed by plaintiffs, a court may, and often will, permit discovery and hold an evidentiary hearing to decide whether a class action is appropriate.[14]

Such a hearing might reveal at an early stage the fact that the plaintiff could not represent the class:

A plaintiff who seeks to represent all employees on a claim of discriminatory denial of promotion might, if the case goes to trial, lose on his individual claim because it turns out that he was never employed by the defendant. Retrospectively one might say he lost "on the merits." Yet there is no doubt that the court could lay bare at a preliminary stage this fact concerning the plaintiff, and, having done so, conclude plaintiff was not a proper representative because he lacked the nexus with the class and its interests and claims which is embraced in the various requirements of [Rule 23].[15]

The important point in the Fifth Circuit's analysis is that such a plaintiff would be an inadequate class representative *not* because he had a losing claim, but because he lacked the required "nexus" with the class. Accordingly, the court held that "a class plaintiff [representing a group of workers] who otherwise meets the demands of 23(a) and (b) [prerequisites 1 and 2, above] should not be found to be disqualified solely by an advance determination that his claim is predictably not a winning claim."[16] Although such a plaintiff will often lack the required "nexus," this will not always be the case; as the Sixth Circuit has said, the failure of plaintiff's individual claim "is not dispositive, without more, of standing to prosecute the class action."[17]

The court, in *Huff,* recognized that "racial discrimination, which is by definition class discrimination, is a particularly virulent form of employment discrimination, because it is generally both subtle and pervasive";[18] therefore "the court trying a Title VII suit bears a special responsibility in the public interest to resolve the employment dispute by determining the facts regardless of the individual plaintiff's position."[19] In keeping with this policy, the courts have generally not been persuaded by the rather ironic solicitousness with which defendants have urged that one group or another might not be adequately represented by a particular plaintiff and that the class action should therefore be dismissed. For example, rejected applicants or discharged employees can represent a class including incumbents,[20] although in *Detroit Edison* the Sixth Circuit concluded that incumbents were not allowed to represent rejected applicants and individuals who were deterred from applying because of the defendant's reputation for discrimination.[21] In addition, union members can represent nonmembers.[22]

Standing to Sue

Issues very similar to those raised in such cases as *Huff* by the consideration of the adequacy of class representation arise when the courts must decide whether an organization has standing to sue under Title VII. The standing cases are broader in their coverage of workers who are not named as plaintiffs than their class-action counterparts.

In *Sierra Club* v. *Morton,* the Supreme Court implied that pleadings which allege harm to members of an organization provide the organization with a sufficient personal stake to justify suing.[23] (The Court made the point in explicit terms in the case of *Warth* v. *Seldin.*[24*]) The *Sierra Club* progeny at all levels of the federal judiciary provide the holding with a generous construction. Indeed, the Supreme Court, in *United States* v. *SCRAP,* held that standing can be provided where the nexus is extremely remote.[25] The injury alleged in the pleadings need not be economic.[26] Standing may be found even if only one member is affected by the conduct which is the object of the litigation.[27]

Another significant case is *Trafficante* v. *Metropolitan Life Insurance Company,*[28] where the Court held that a white tenant could protest racial discrimination against blacks in housing. Are white workers potential private attorney generals? Perhaps analogous are cases in which labor unions have sued on behalf of their members under Title VII. The courts have viewed the nexus among the members as insufficient for class-action purposes where possible conflicts of interest might exist—as between male and female members[29]—but nevertheless have held that unions possess the necessary standing for both statutory and constitutional purposes.[30]* That is to say, a labor union unqualified for class-action purposes because of the potential abuse which can develop from a situation in which a class representative has a direct conflict of interest with some of the members whom it can bind by means of a decree is, nevertheless, a "person aggrieved" within the meaning of Title VII.[31] The rationale is twofold: (1) The union has a direct interest in eliminating discrimination by virtue of its responsibilities under Title VII itself as well as under the duty of fair representation;[32] (2) general notions of standing permit unions which can bargain exclusively about conditions of employment to sue regarding the same matter.

The difficulty of asserting the same rights for white workers is greater, and the district courts which have ruled on the question have held that white workers cannot sue on behalf of blacks. Nevertheless, every worker's condition of employment is affected as a result of discrimination, and for this reason EEOC has accepted the concept of white-worker standing.[33] The public interest—a common concern of the judiciary in Title VII litigation—is antagonistic to a work environment which is polluted. It is more than arguable that white workers suffer psychological harm from employment patterns which inculcate attitudes of racial superiority and from the lack of interracial association—a theme which is sounded in *Trafficante*—where departments or jobs are segregated or complete exclusion is practiced. Furthermore, as in *Trafficante,* a white worker employed by a discriminatory company may be stigmatized in certain quarters—particularly if he has contact with the minority community.

Another reason for white-worker standing is that discrimination may produce divisiveness between black and white workers, undermining solidarity and thus harming the economic interests of both groups. Discriminatory employers could drive down the wage scale by playing off one group against the other. Ultimately, as is the case with whites living in a housing area which is "block-busted," white workers often have a direct interest in an employer's having a wide variety of racially balanced job classifications and departments. If a job becomes known as a "black job," the economic and vested interest in it may be depreciated in the workers' eyes. In the garment industry wage scales have gone down as the racial composition of the work force has changed. Segregated employment patterns may breed segregated housing and produce a flight of whites from a labor-market area.

White workers will want protection against such a phenomenon. The British Race Relations Act recognizes this concern by affirmatively protecting benign discrimination for the purpose of retaining a racially balanced work force and the avoidance of stigmatization of jobs, departments, and plants.[34]* Furthermore, a massive flight of whites can result in the same deterioration in the work place as takes place in housing and can lead to resentment, sporadic violence, and a consequent loss in the productivity and morale of all workers.

Finally, the white worker has an important economic interest in suing his employer, because if his union does not do so and is held financially liable, the judgment may be paid out of his dues or new assessments.

Under *Trafficante,* the employer may have standing as well. Stigmatization of the business operation may harm the employer socially and impair his ability to make business contracts. Crown Zellerbach, for instance, was harmed in San Francisco by boycotts, picket lines, and publicity aimed at its discriminatory conduct in Louisiana.

Moreover, in the event that the threat of contract-compliance enforcement becomes credible, economic loss may result from the loss of government contracts. The same interest is present if there is a threat of a union strike or economic action against employer adherence to the civil rights requirements of either Title VII or the executive order. In all respects, the white workers' economic interest can be injured; therefore, the argument for standing to sue is valid.

Finally, there exists the question of whether minority-worker organizations also have standing. The combination of decisions in *Sierra Club, Warth, SCRAP,* and *Trafficante* seems to answer in the affirmative, and in a whole series of cases, the right of such organizations to sue has gone unchallenged.[35] Indeed, some cases have specifically held that minority-worker organizations do have the right to sue.[36] Although Rule 23 class actions make secrecy and confidentiality for workers who wish to protest but not to be identified more feasible (and thus arguably provides a limited distinction from *NAACP* v. *Alabama,*[37] in which nondisclosure was deemed necessary), there are obviously circumstances in which no workers dare step forward because of fear of retaliation or violence. The trucking industry and the International Brotherhood of Teamsters provide obvious examples. Moreover, that union's members usually can show harm, including substantial economic harm, which can flow from a challenge opposed by the union leadership.

The involvement of a group or organization is likely to provide the communication vehicle—a. kind of information-clearing house—necessary for litigation. Involved organizations (the United Construction Workers Association [UCWA] of Seattle and the Association for the Betterment of Black Edison Employees) played a critical role in both *Local 86, Ironworkers*[38] and *Detroit Edison.* In both cases, the organizations have been involved in the relief. They are necessary for the monitoring and enforcing of their respective decrees. For this reason, the UCWA is promoting the formation of similar organizations in the Southwest under grants provided by the EEOC and others. Equally important, such organizations can spur new litigation against other defendants because the community and the organization's members become more sophisticated about their rights, and emboldened by virtue of solidarity and strength in numbers and awareness. Accordingly, the private-attorney-general concept and the promotion of beneficial and wholesome litigation are in keeping with the view that such organizations have standing. Moreover, punitive damages as a remedy provide a financial base by means of which such organizations may sponsor both the monitoring of their own decrees and the commencement of actions against other defendants who engage in discriminatory conduct.

One argument which has a negative edge is that the 1972 amendments provide organizations with the right to file an administrative charge on behalf of others.[39] The fact that the "person aggrieved" language in the statute was not thoroughly amended may argue for a different approach to organizational standing before the judiciary than before the administrative agency. Nevertheless, the contrary argument is that the amendments articulate a statutory philosophy promoting organizational standing, that the "person aggrieved" language swallows up the arguments, and that precedents are in favor of such a position. Curiously, the *Detroit Edison* decision appears to be the only one in which organizations have been dismissed as party plaintiffs under Title VII.

Another opposing argument is that standing undermines the exclusivity doctrine contained in the National Labor Relations Act. Yet mere standing undermines exclusivity no more than does any suit which challenges employment conditions negotiated by a union. Even involvement in the decree poses no threat, as long as the union is not supplanted.[40]* Both *Local 86, Ironworkers* and *Detroit Edison* have summarily rejected this argument, including minority-worker organizations in the decree.

The potential impact of more generous provisions regarding standing is three-fold: (1) more plaintiffs are likely to be enticed into suing, with consequent greater change in employment conditions; (2) more court action will embolden minorities to assert their statutory rights; and (3) the theory that the work environment is affected by discrimination provides another peg for broad relief improving all aspects of the employment relationship.

Statistical Evidence and the Burden of Proof

Having sanctioned class action as a means to remedy employment discrimination, the courts have expansively developed employment-discrimination law. The circuit courts of appeals have unanimously held that a prima-facie case of racial discrimination can be based on statistics showing that the number of minority members employed in the work force is severely disproportionate to the number residing in the relevant market area. The Fifth Circuit, in one of the leading cases involving voting discrimination, said: "Statistics often tell much and Courts listen."[41] The courts have followed the same approach in employment cases. Indeed, the Eighth Circuit Court of Appeals has said that the statistics may constitute *proof* of racial discrimination. The Fifth Circuit has held that statistics combined with facially "neutral" practices which discriminate constitute conclusive proof of discrimination.[42] Generally, however, the courts assume that statistics shift the burden and provide the defendant with an obligation to explain.

In the absence of special educational qualifications, which the employer or union generally provides, the labor market's minority population is observed for the purpose of comparison with the minority work force of the employer or union. And the labor market's minority population properly consists of those residing in the area rather than those working—inasmuch as the vicious cycle of unemployment, welfare, and discrimination excludes a disproportionate number of blacks from the work rolls.

In a construction-industry case, the Ninth Circuit Court of Appeals, computing the relevant area for consideration, said that even though the unions' jurisdiction extended beyond the urban area where blacks were congregated, the city could be used to establish a prima-facie case on the basis of statistics because "the City has the single largest population within their jurisdiction and is that area from which they would most likely draw the vast majority of workers for apprenticeship, referral and membership purposes."[43]

Definition of the appropriate labor market—a problem that the Office of Federal Contract Compliance has grappled with under the executive order[44*]—is important, both in the use of statistics and in determining the kind of relief to be made available if that relief involves the fashioning of goals or quotas. Even though the bulk of the minority population may be located outside a union's geographical jurisdiction, or an electric-power company's service area, such a population may be conveniently situated to apply for and obtain the jobs in question. For instance, the black residents of East Palo Alto, California, though outside Santa Clara County, which is beyond the boundary line of many craft unions' jurisdictions, are in a better position to work on a good deal of construction in that county than are many of its own residents, who are more distant from many of the jobs. The blacks are in a better location for work on Stanford construction projects than are the residents of San Jose, who are more likely to live within the union's geographical jurisdiction, since jurisdictional lines often follow county lines, and San Jose and Stanford are in the same county.

Judge Damon Keith, in *Stamps* v. *Detroit Edison,* rejected an electric-power company's argument that its service area was the appropriate base for statistics relating to its employment practices. The court said:

Defendant Detroit Edison's only response to the statistics has been its argument that a disproportionately small number of blacks is not employed at Detroit Edison since the area that must be considered is the area to which Edison supplies electricity rather than the labor market area. Private plaintiffs correctly point out that under this inadequate theory, the computation of statistics for a General Motors plant in Detroit, for instance, would not be based upon the working population in the Detroit area but rather any portion of the United States to which General Motors products were shipped.[45]

One argument against the use of statistics as evidence to establish a prima-facie case of employment discrimination arises from examination of Section 703(j) of Title VII, which states: "Nothing contained in this Title shall be interpreted to

require any employer [or] labor organization . . . to grant preferential treatment
to any individual or group because of race, color, religion, sex, or national origin
of such individual or group on account of an imbalance which may exist with respect to the total number or percentage of persons of any race, [etc.], employed by
any employer . . . or labor organization . . . in comparison with the total
number or percentage of persons of such race, [etc.], in any community, State,
section, or other area, or in the available work force in any community,
[etc.]."[46]* This so-called antipreferential-treatment or antiquota provision of Title
VII is violated only if a court grants "preferential treatment" simply "on account
of an imbalance" in a defendant's work force. Fairly characterized, the use of statistics by the courts does not constitute "preferential treatment" at all, and, in any
event, such treatment is not granted simply "on account of an imbalance."

   The Sixth Circuit expressed the dominant view when it held, in *United States* v.
IBEW Local 38,[47] that Section 704(j) "cannot be construed as a ban on affirmative relief against continuation of effects of past discrimination resulting from
present practices (neutral on their face) which have the practical effect of continuing past injustices,"[48] despite the fact that it is the remedies for such facially neutral practices that most often involve the use of "preferential treatment." The
court reasoned that the overall statutory scheme clearly contemplates such remedies and concluded that Section 703(j) only prohibits relief fashioned "solely
because of an imbalance in racial employment."[49] That is, the courts are only restricted from proceeding as if racial imbalance were a statutory violation per se;
they are not prohibited from taking the view that statistics demonstrating imbalance are properly to be accorded substantial weight in proving violations.[50]* That
the courts have remained safely within the bounds of this interpretation of Section
703(j) is clear on two accounts. First, the courts have generally viewed statistics
as capable of providing only the basis of a prima-facie case, rather than as constituting conclusive proof of a violation. This indicates that the courts are properly
declining to view imbalance as a violation per se. Second, the mere showing of
racial imbalance will not be accepted as the basis of a prima-facie case, since the
courts have generally required proof of severe disproportion. Even where the percentage of blacks in an employer's work force is only half the proportion in the
general population, a court may hesitate to accept that statistic as proof of discrimination,[51] although most courts would probably be convinced by such an
imbalance.[52]

   A more fundamental argument against the proposition that the use of statistics
violates Section 703(j) is that in deciding that a statistical argument proves a statutory violation, a court simply does not engage in any "preferential treatment."
Preferential treatment occurs—if at all—only when the court proceeds to fashion a
remedy for the violations found.[53] Therefore, the use of statistics is not governed
by Section 703(j), which speaks about the forms of relief the courts can grant
rather than the kinds of evidence which may be considered as establishing a violation.

   The Supreme Court, in considering the remedial provisions of the National

Labor Relations Act, has disregarded this kind of argument involving an artificially rigid line between what the courts may consider as evidence and what may be fashioned as a remedy. For example, in collective-bargaining situations it is clear that the National Labor Relations Board and the courts may not rely upon either party's refusal to make a concession as in itself a basis for establishing that bad-faith bargaining has occurred. Accordingly, when the NLRB has ordered a union and an employer to adopt specific contract terms as a remedy for unlawful refusal to bargain—even though the finding of unlawful refusal to bargain had been made without consideration of the offending party's refusal to make a concession—the Court has held that such a remedy is inappropriate under the Taft-Hartley statutory scheme.[54] Freedom of contract, said the Court, is so integral to the statutory philosophy that the board could not fashion the contract provisions itself. Unions and employers are formidably protected by the statute with regard both to the finding of a violation and to the remedy to be fashioned.

The difference between the NLRA and the Title VII situations may be that the fashioning of quotas is more essentially related to the goal of the latter statute: the promotion of equal employment opportunity for minorities. Moreover, no rigid quota-type requirement is imposed in any event, since defendants may rebut the statistical evidence presented by plaintiffs. The burden of rebuttal is, of course, fairly substantial, inasmuch as the courts presumably will hold that a high percentage of acceptance of black applicants does not dispose of the issue (since a discriminatory employer may have a reputation which will discourage all but "superblacks" from applying), and, in addition, it has been established that the fact that no individual instances of discrimination are evidenced does not negate the reliance on statistics. Indeed, the Tenth Circuit, in *Jones* v. *Lee Way Motor Freight*,[55] has held that even where blacks form a minority of the employees in a job classification from which they cannot transfer, the statistical absence of blacks in the job area to which they seek access proves discrimination—once again in the absence of proof of any specific instance of discrimination against an individual employee or applicant. The early Title VII cases—which arose shortly after the statute was enacted and therefore presented statistics that had evolved in the pre-act period—can be read as justifying the relevance of this evidence on the ground that a reputation for discrimination resulted in the continuance of discrimination after July 2, 1965.

To be sure, there appear to be limits to the rules of law thus established. For instance, in *United States* v. *Jacksonville Terminal Company*, a case that arose in the railroad industry, statistics were in effect "explained away" in light of an employer's adherence to a policy of hiring the "best qualified" workers for unskilled jobs because there was a surplus of experienced and skilled labor. The court said:

All of the persons so hired were white. In a stable or expanding industry, this fact would be damning, especially in regard to unskilled or semiskilled positions. Nevertheless, in the railroad industry, there is a plausible racially neutral explanation for the post-Act predominance of white workers in these jobs. The continuing decline in total employment compels many white workers experienced in skilled jobs to take employment in related unskilled or semiskilled positions, or face unemployment. For instance, a Welder may find work as a Welder Helper while he hopes that employment will again increase and he can regain his old job. Naturally this rollback tendency handicaps applicants who do not possess the skilled worker's qualifications. Manifestly the applicants who suffer most in competition for these jobs are black. Having been excluded from any but the most menial tasks in pre-Act years, they remain outside in post-Act times. Job assignments previously based on racial considerations are now founded on legitimate qualifications but the result is the same.[56]

This holding seems questionable in light of other Title VII rulings, inasmuch as the accumulated experience utilized against black applicants derived from a discriminatory employment situation. Instances in which white workers can be deemed to be more qualified in such a situation are probably the rule and not the exception. Nonetheless, *Jacksonville Terminal* serves to emphasize the proposition that there are some circumstances in which plaintiffs will be required to rely on evidence in addition to statistics once rebuttal has been introduced into evidence.

Why should statistics constitute prima-facie evidence of discrimination in appropriate circumstances? The Tenth Circuit declared, "In racial discrimination cases, statistics often demonstrate more than the testimony of many witnesses, and they should be given proper effect by the courts."[57] Moreover, where the standards for review by decision makers on employment are subjective, vague and elusive, statistics may be the best proof available. The Fourth Circuit has said in *Brown* v. *Gaston County Dyeing Machine Co.:*

Elusive, purely subjective standards must give way to objectivity if statistical indicia of discrimination are to be refuted. . . . In the absence of objective criteria applied to all workers alike, the statistics indicate that race is the only identifiable factor explaining the disparity between the jobs held by white employees and those held by black employees. The proof discloses no objective standards based on education, experience, ability, length of service, reliability, or aptitude to account for the preferential employment of white workers. . . .

In sum, the lack of objective guidelines for hiring and promotion . . . are badges of discrimination that serve to corroborate, not to rebut, the racial bias pictured by the statistical pattern of the company's work force.[58]

A further justification for the use of statistics is that direct evidence is difficult to obtain: "Racial discrimination will seldom be admitted by any employer."[59] The difficulty with requiring direct proofs is that defendants usually control the evidence. Applications are filed, inquiries and requests may be turned away, and discouraging responses and outright misinformation about job opportunities may be provided. Yet only defendants normally have possession of the evidence. Plaintiffs are in an extremely difficult evidentiary position, particularly with regard to hiring, because it is difficult or impossible to find rejected applicants, since they usually have no contact with an organization. Rejection can often discourage protest or the filing of a complaint. Lawyers must therefore have unfettered freedom to communicate with members of the class in order to encourage them to come forward with information about application rejections that cannot be uncovered through discovery and investigation of defendants' records because the potential applicant may have been discouraged from filing even a piece of paper with the company or application forms may have been destroyed after a period of time.[60] Moreover, it is extremely important for lawyers to have access to EEOC investigative files before commencing litigation in those few instances where the EEOC is able to carry on an investigation. The Fifth Circuit, in *H. Kessler & Co.* v. *EEOC,* has held that the nondisclosure provisions of the act[61] do not preclude access by an attorney to the investigative files prior to instituting litigation. Judge Elbert Tuttle spoke for the court:

It is difficult to understand how a grievant could amass the statistical information alone that would be necessary in order for him to know whether he had anything more than a suspicion of discrimination without access to the kind of information referred to in [the statute] concerning his employer's practices with regard to promotions, terminations and the like. One must ask how such a party could persuade an attorney to handle his case without having available some of the information which, under the various statutes, would come into the Commission's investigatory files. The courts of this circuit have previously found that competent lawyers are not eager to enter the fray in behalf of a person who is seeking redress under Title VII.[62]

Accordingly, because statistics can be crucial[63] in Title VII litigation, the lawyer's need to obtain access to information through the use of EEOC files or by communication with class members is not diminished but, rather, becomes more important.

Finally, the use of statistics as a tool for inferring discrimination in the absence of an explanation by the defendants is made more valid by the fact that the passage of Title VII evidenced Congress' distrust of employment patterns generally. The statistical absence of blacks or a severe disproportion between the number of those employed and the number in the labor market deserves some explanation in light of such legislative assumptions. The courts have been particularly concerned on this score when (1) discrimination was engaged in at some point in the past; (2) supervisors, interviewers, and union or company leaders involved in employment decisions are all or nearly all white; and (3) subjective standards are used in a situation where the first two factors are present. With regard to the first point, the Eighth Circuit has noted that past discrimination permits the "use of evidence of statistical probability to infer the existence of a pattern or practice of discrimination."[64] On the second and third points, once again, the Fifth Circuit, in *Rowe* v. *General Motors,* has taken the lead:

Blacks may very well have been hindered in obtaining recommendations from their foreman since there is no familial or social association between these two groups. All we do today is recognize that promotion/transfer procedures which depend almost entirely upon the subjective evaluation and favorable recommendation of the immediate foreman are a ready mechanism for discrimination against Blacks much of which can be covertly concealed and, for that matter, not really known to management. We and others have expressed skepticism that Black persons dependent directly on decisive recommendations from Whites can expect non-discriminatory action.[65]

Judge Keith sounded the same theme in *Detroit Edison* in supporting the probative value of statistics when subjective criteria had been utilized by the all white decision makers: "The record in the instant case demonstrates that Detroit Edison has an all white management and a nearly all-white supervisory work force. The record further demonstrates that management is represented in its dealings with defendant unions only by whites and, with the exception of plaintiff Willie Stamps, the unions are represented only by whites."[66]

Classwide Discovery in Individual Actions

Since the courts recognize that even an individual Title VII action must necessarily involve elements of classwide applicability, they have taken the position that even without certification of a class action the individual, in his capacity as a private attorney general, may invoke broad discovery relating to the entire work force. The Fifth Circuit, in the important case *Burns* v. *Thiokol Chemical Corporation,* has noted the relevance of information obtained by discovery, even outside the class-action context. Chief Judge John Brown spoke for the court:

The importance of obtaining an overall statistical picture of an employer's practices with regard to both Black and White employees does not depend on the presence of an alleged "pattern or practice" or a valid charge of class discrimination or class action. We categorically rejected this notion in *Georgia Power* v. *EEOC.* . . . There the EEOC sought historical, statistical information regarding both Black and White employees of Georgia Power. The Company objected to EEOC's Demand for Access to this evidence contending that because EEOC was only investigating the charge of an individual party that he was refused employment solely because of his race that the only relevant evidence was that relating to the filling of that particular vacancy. . . . Even though a suit seeks only individual relief for an individual instance of discrimination, and is not a "pattern or practice" suit by the government or a class action, the past history of *both* Black *and* White employees is surely relevant information. . . . It is therefore discoverable.[67]

This reasoning is predicated upon a number of factors. First, the private-attorney-general concept (that is, the private individual as representative of the public interest) is appropriate in connection with an individual suit because the elimination of some forms or aspects of discrimination improves the work environment for *all* employees[68]—especially because minorities may maintain class actions for *other* minorities[69] and whites may protest discrimination against blacks. Even if this were not so, the environment is certainly improved for employees and applicants of the same race, national origin, or sex.

Second, the composition of the work force may have a bearing on the inferences that can be drawn about an individual case. This fact was noted specifically by the Court in *McDonnell Douglas Corp.* v. *Green,* albeit in relation to the manner in which a plaintiff can rebut a defendant's allegations of a bona fide reason for refusal to hire rather than the manner of establishing a prima-facie case.[70]

Third, wide-ranging discovery is essential if a plaintiff's lawyer is to communicate with other applicants and employees in order to buttress the individual's credibility with regard to his own case. Moreover, such discovery, which must include names, addresses, and telephone numbers of workers,[71] is essential to develop evidence relating to the propriety of a class action. Indeed, the Fifth Circuit has specifically given its approval to evidentiary discovery preceding the hearing on maintainability of the class action, as it did the *Huff* case. In part, this process

of discovery is assisted by the use of EEOC investigative files. But despite the access provided by *Kessler,* the EEOC does not usually undertake investigations because of lack of staff to cope with the ever increasing flood of charges, and when investigations are set in motion, they are often incomplete. Accordingly, *Kessler* is quite often a source of comfort to academicians rather than lawyers.

Furthermore, even when such investigations are conducted and are thorough, further communication between lawyers and minority organizations and between applicants and employees may be critical (1) for corroborating information and testimony where there is a conflict in such testimony and evidence; (2) as the best means of gathering evidence for the purpose of establishing the maintainability of a class action and of identifying potential subclasses with different interests;[72] and (3) for providing informal notice to such members of the class so that they will be alerted to the fact that the action may have an impact upon their interests. In this way, such workers can effectively express those interests at the judicial proceeding. The court is better advised as to both the appropriateness of a class action and the nature of eventual relief which might affect large groups of workers. The due-process rights of all interested parties are best protected thus.

In connection with due process, the Supreme Court, in *Eisen* v. *Carlisle and Jacquelin,*[73] has held that plaintiffs, at their own cost, must notify identifiable class members prior to the trial in a securities action. *Eisen,* however, involved Federal Rule 23(b)(3), which governs actions for damages. Employment-discrimination cases are appropriately filed under Rule 23(b)(2), which covers equitable claims and damages arising in connection therewith.[74]* The Court specifically noted that its holding in *Eisen* did not apply to Rule 23(b)(2) suits.

McDonnell Douglas Corp. v. *Green:* Burden of Proof for Individual Plaintiffs

In *McDonnell Douglas Corp.* v. *Green,*[75] Justice Powell, speaking for the unanimous Court, promulgated guidelines for individual actions. These rules, however, again emphasized the group nature of discrimination and the societal inequities with which Congress was concerned in 1964 and 1972. In this case, an activist in the civil rights movement protested "vigorously" that his discharge, as well as the hiring practices of defendant McDonnell Douglas Corporation in general, was racially motivated. The protest tactics involved the respondent's illegally stalling his car (a practice engaged in by other members of the Congress of Racial Equality) on main roads leading to the petitioner's plant for the purpose of blocking access at the time of the morning shift change. A "lock-in" by CORE members also took place: a chain and padlock were set up to prevent occupants from leaving. The respondent's involvement in this phase of the protest was unclear, and the Court found it unnecessary to resolve legal questions connected with the lock-in.

Three weeks afterward, the defendant company advertised for qualified mechanics. When the respondent, a mechanic by trade, applied, he was turned down because of his involvement in the stall-in and the lock-in. Charges were filed with the city, and a suit was instituted.

The alleged discrimination related to both color and civil-rights activities. The Court pointed out that a complainant would carry the initial burden of establishing the existence of discrimination. The Court referred to four factors that should be established: "(i) that he belongs to a racial minority; (ii) that he applied and was qualified for a job for which the employer was seeking applicants; (iii) that, despite his qualifications, he was rejected; and (ivz that, after his rejection, the position remained open and the employer continued to seek applicants from persons of complainant's qualifications."[76]

The Court held that once these factors were established, the burden shifted to the defendant to "articulate some legitimate, nondiscriminatory reason for the employee's rejection."[77] According to the facts of the case, the Court concluded that "deliberate, unlawful" behavior aimed at the employer provided a legitimate nondiscriminatory reason. The Court stated that in rebuttal the plaintiff could establish that the defendant's reasons for discharging him were pretexts. In this connection, the Court indicated that evidence of disparate treatment as well as the employer's "general policy" on discrimination could be introduced into evidence to show pretext. Justice Powell summed up: "In short, on the retrial respondent must be given a full and fair opportunity to demonstrate by competent evidence that the presumptively valid reasons for his rejection were in fact a coverup for a racially discriminatory decision."[78] The Court subsequently put it in *Franks* v. *Bowman Transportation Co.,*[79] that where plaintiffs have "carried their burden of demonstrating the existence of a discriminatory hiring pattern and practice by respondents . . . the burden will be upon respondents to prove that individuals who reapply were not in fact victims of previous hiring discrimination."[80]

The concept here is similar to that of the rules relating to statistics. The burden is shifted to the party that has access to the information. Although *Green* involved a situation in which the job in question remained unfilled, the thrust of the decision is fully applicable to situations in which the job is not still open but another employee has been selected.[81] The reasoning in the case implies that if the minority employee or applicant seeking employment is qualified, the burden shifts to the defendant to show that the white worker selected is as well or *better* qualified.[82]*

4 | Discrimination, Seniority, and the *Griggs* Progeny

Even prior to the court holdings relating to statistics, the judiciary had startled those commentators who thought the fact that Title VII required a showing of specific "intent" to discriminate and was intended to be "prospective" (that is, to apply from July 2, 1965, the effective date of the statute, onward) limited the impact of the law. Could pre-1965 conduct be considered? If so, what relationship, if any, was it to have with contemporary employment practices which might be considered nondiscriminatory if considered without reference to the past?

The first major appeals court decision to confront this problem was *Local 53 Heat and Frost Insulators* v. *Vogler*.[1] In *Vogler,* the Fifth Circuit held that a union's policy of nepotism, though concededly neutral and nondiscriminatory *in vacuo* (that is, when considered in the abstract), was unlawful if there was a showing of past discrimination leading to the exclusion of minorities. The union had contended that the district court had improperly eliminated the union policy of exclusion of workers not related by "blood or marriage," because the remedy, a quota system to correct racial imbalance, was in effect a "penalty" and was in violation of the antipreferential-treatment provisions of Title VII. The court responded to this argument:

The District Court did no more than prevent *future* discrimination when it prohibited a continuing exclusion of negroes through the application of an apparently neutral membership provision which was *originally* instituted at least in part because of racial discrimination and which served no significant trade-related purpose. While the nepotism requirement is applicable to black and white alike and is not on its face discriminatory, in a completely white union the present effect of its continued application is to forever deny to negroes and Mexican-Americans any real opportunity for membership.[2]

The court, while avoiding the issue of seniority systems and their lawfulness under Title VII, noted that they were "not analogous to the exclusion of negroes from an all white union by a system of nepotism. While the former might for a limited time operate to exclude negroes, the latter probably would do so interminably."[3] The *effect* of nepotism—even if actually economically justified—was to continue in the present system the former exclusion of racial minorities, since the incumbent employees were predominately white. This continuation *Vogler* held to be unlawful.

Seniority

In American industrial unions, the institution of seniority serves two distinct functions. "Benefit seniority" determines an employee's rights to pensions, vacation pay, sick leave, parking-lot privileges, and other fringe benefits. Benefit seniority is generally computed on a plant-wide or company-wide basis and, therefore, is rarely relinquished when a worker transfers from one department or job to another. For that and other reasons, benefit-seniority systems have not been a focus of race-discrimination litigation to any great extent.

Much more controversy surrounds "competitive-status seniority"; the time spent or work experience in a job classification, department plant, or company is computed for the purpose of determining an employee's standing vis-à-vis other employees with regard to promotion and transfer opportunities as well as protection from layoff. It may also determine recall rights subsequent to layoff.

America's trade unions have adopted the principle of competitive-status seniority, not only because it eliminates favoritism toward employees, but also because it prevents the union from being inevitably caught in political cross fire, as it would be if it had constantly to choose among individual workers' competing claims according to their merits. While seniority is not the only basis for choosing among employees competing for promotions—qualifications play a role as well— in some industries, such as steel, the junior employee cannot be promoted over a senior worker unless he is "head and shoulders" better.

In contrast to benefit-seniority systems, in which plant—or company-wide— computation is the rule, competitive-status seniority systems may employ a variety of schemes. Although, in theory, the industrial unions in particular have supported plant seniority and the greatest opportunity for the greatest number, local seniority practices often contradict this egalitarian principle. The practices are not necessarily related to race. For instance, if junior workers realize that more obsolescent parts of the plant employ workers with more seniority, the former group may gather support at union meetings for a form of department or job seniority. Those workers with less plant seniority will want to build fences around themselves in order to protect their interests against outsiders. All occupations and professions engage in this sort of activity to some extent, and nothing in such labor-management practices violates civil-rights laws per se. Indeed, much in the legislative history of Title VII indicates that Congress was wary of tampering with seniority provisions negotiated in collective agreements.

This wariness first emerged when Senator Lester Hill of Alabama campaigned against the proposed law in 1963 and 1964 among white trade unionists who were opposed to the advancement of Negro workers and who were sensitive about potential dilution of their vested "rights," including seniority.[4] In response the AFL-CIO Rights Department issued a pamphlet to its constituent unions and their members. *Civil Rights: Fact vs. Fiction,* sought to assure union members that the proposed legislation would not interfere in any way with seniority rights possessed by such workers—unless a negotiated seniority system was itself discriminatory. Whether a system was discriminatory and the circumstances under which a finding of discrimination could be made were the critical issues—crucial issues that the framers of the statute never seemed to face squarely.

Legislative History

The first element of both the legislative history and the statutory language of Title VII that unions and employers pounced upon was that "intent" to discriminate was required by Section 706(g), which triggered judicial remedies when a respondent had "intentionally engaged" in unlawful activity.[5] Labor and management pointed out that if discrimination did occur as the result of a seniority system, it could not be said to have resulted from the unlawful intent prohibited by the statute. The proof, said labor and management, was that the very same seniority clauses existed in parts of the country where there were no blacks or other minorities in the labor force and where, therefore, no claim of discrimination could be raised because blacks were not present to be discriminated against.

The difficulty with this line of argument is that outside the criminal law, in tort law for instance, intent is not a matter of evil or improper motivation. An individual is presumed to be aware of the foreseeable consequences of his conduct, and from his conduct intent will be presumed. Moreover, in Title VII, the definition of unlawful conduct is extremely broad by virtue of the statutory language. Specifically, Section 703 states that it is an unlawful employment practice for an employer or union "to limit, segregate, or classify his employees or applicants . . . in any way which would deprive or tend to deprive any individual of employment opportunities or otherwise adversely affect his status as an employee because of race, color, religion, sex, or national origin." In unions, practices which "limit . . . employment opportunities" are also proscribed.[6] The words "adversely affect," "limit," and "tend to deprive" in Section 703 seem to negate any implications of a limited statutory concern in Section 706. Indeed, the courts have subsequently held that the language of Section 706 is intended to exempt from the remedial provisions only conduct which is unintentional in the sense of being accidental.[7]

A more vexing question which permeates Title VII is the relationship between the past and present. Senator Joseph Clark placed in the record the following exchange, in which he answered questions by Senator Everett Dirksen:

Question. Normally, labor contracts call for "last hired, first fired." If the last hired are Negroes, is the employer discriminating if his contract requires they be first fired and the remaining employees are white?

Answer. Seniority rights are in no way affected by the bill. If under a "last hired, first fired" agreement, a Negro happens to be the "last hired," he can still be "first fired" as long as it is done because of his status as "last hired" and not because of his race.

Question. If an employer is directed to abolish his employment list because of discrimination what happens to seniority?

Answer. The bill is not retroactive, and it will not require an employer to change existing seniority lists.[8]

The memorandum floor managers Clark and Clifford Case put together in consultation with the Department of Justice said:

Title VII would have no effect on established seniority rights. Its effect is prospective and not retrospective. Thus, for example, if a business has been discriminating in the past and as a result has an all-white working force, when the title comes into effect the employer's obligation would be simply to fill future vacancies on a nondiscriminatory basis. He would not be obliged—or indeed, permitted—to fire whites in order to hire Negroes, or to prefer Negroes for future vacancies, or once Negroes are hired, to give them special seniority rights at the expense of the white workers hired earlier. (However, where waiting lines for employment or training are, prior to the effective date of the title, maintained on a discriminatory basis, the use of such lists after the title takes effect may be held as unlawful subterfuge to accomplish discrimination.)[9]

Senator Clark also introduced a similar statement prepared by the Justice Department itself in rebuttal to the arguments of Senator Hill. This statement contained the following pertinent language:

First, it has been asserted that Title VII would undermine vested rights of seniority. This is not correct. Title VII would have no effect on seniority rights existing at the time it takes effect. If, for example, a collective bargaining contract provides that in the event of layoffs, those who were hired last must be laid off first, such a provision would not be affected in the least by Title VII. This would be true even in the case where owing to discrimination prior to the effective date of the title, white workers had more seniority than Negroes. Title VII is directed at discrimination based on race, color, religion, sex, or national origin. It is perfectly clear that when a worker is laid off or denied a chance for promotion because under established seniority rules, he is "low man on the totem pole" he is not being discriminated against because of race. *Of course, if the seniority rule itself is discriminatory, it would be unlawful under Title VII*. If a rule were to state that all Negroes must be laid off before any white man, such a rule could not serve as the basis for a discharge subsequent to the effective date of the title. I do not know how anyone could quarrel with such a result. But, in the ordinary case, assuming that seniority rights were built up over a period of time during which Negroes were not hired, these rights would not be set aside by the taking effect of Title VII. Employers and labor organizations would simply be under a duty not to discriminate against Negroes because of race. Any difference in treatment based on established seniority rights would not be based on race and would not be forbidden by the title.[10]

Finally, because of concerns expressed by the framers of the statute, Congress enacted Section 703(h), which stated that "bona fide seniority" systems were not to be regarded as unlawful.[11] Again, the issue in dispute was not resolved. The question of what was bona fide or unlawful remained unanswered. The ambiguity of legislative history was made no more unambiguous by the proviso. The essential questions of what was discriminatory and what were to be the rules relating to departmental and job seniority systems were left hanging.

The first round of problems confronting both the EEOC and the courts in connection with seniority all involved the question of whether, how, and at what rate incumbent blacks were to progress from segregated jobs.

Such seniority-line disputes have arisen in a number of situations. Quite often, black employees worked as helpers to white employees, filled in for them during vacations and absences, and had most, if not all, the experience and skills prerequisite for the white workers' jobs. Black employees, however, were paid at a lower wage rate and were in a separate seniority district. They were not permitted to transfer from one district to another or, even if they could transfer, they could not take seniority credits with them for the purpose of moving upward in their unit and protecting themselves against layoffs.

A step removed was a situation in which blacks were in a different department from whites but performed work that required skills roughly similar to those needed for jobs in the white department. Whites who had gone into the all white department did not require special training but, rather, were exposed to on-the-job "learning by doing" procedures. A no-training policy seemed arbitrary under the circumstances: relatively unskilled and inexperienced whites were hired from the street for jobs that were denied to incumbent blacks. The nature of the work and the experience of the whites who were hired, coupled with the fact that blacks were disproportionately congregated in low-level or undesirable jobs or departments, made it clear that legitimate economic aspirations of blacks were being threatened. Most Title VII litigation involving transfers appears to be in this category of cases.

Another problem in seniority disputes arises in situations where there is a difference in the skills required for jobs and where an employee transferring from one department to another would require special training to remedy his lack of preparation. These are the most difficult kinds of cases because speculation is inevitable about whether blacks who are in the lower-level job or department would have advanced in the absence of a discriminatory hiring policy. Another element of these cases is the reasonableness of the no-transfer policy in light of the substantial differences in skill or background required for jobs—an extreme example would be the prohibition of transfer from the job of janitor to that of airline pilot.

The EEOC Position and the Early Litigation

In *Whitfield* v. *United Steelworkers,* Judge Wisdom, speaking for the court, said:

The Union and the Company made a fresh start for the future. We might not agree with every provision, but they have a contract that *from now* on is free from any discrimination based on race. Angels could do no more.

It is undeniable that negroes in Line Number 2, ambitious to advance themselves to skilled jobs, are at a disadvantage compared with white incumbents in Line Number 1. This is a product of the past. We cannot turn back the clock. Unfair treatment to their detriment in the past gives the plaintiffs no claim now to be paid back by unfair treatment in their favor. We have to decide this case on the contract before and its fairness to all.[12]

Thus the pre–Title VII law, though scant, was opposed to efforts of black workers to compete effectively with whites who had been placed above them as a result of past discrimination. When the Equal Employment Opportunity Commission came into existence after July 2, 1965, it was immediately faced with hundreds of charges involving allegations of such discrimination. Employers and unions generally refused to award black employees seniority credits, relying largely upon *Whit-*

field. Accordingly, the commission's efforts at the conciliation stage of a proceeding were consistently thwarted. Consequently, the commission, early in the spring of 1966, requested me to formulate a report on the seniority problem and to advise the commission what, if any, position it should take on this issue—both when engaged in conciliation and when appearing as *amicus* in litigation. The report, submitted in the fall of 1966, attempted to respond to some of the numerous arguments raised against revising seniority arrangements and permitting black employees to rely upon past seniority credits when bidding for future job vacancies.[13] The AFL-CIO, in rebuttal to Senator Hill's vigorous campaign against Title VII predicated upon the notion that union members would lose their seniority rights, had said that white workers' seniority rights would remain intact. Of course, whatever assurances the AFL-CIO had given had no bearing upon how the statute should be interpreted. Closely related to the argument based on AFL-CIO assurances was the notion that human relations would suffer and the morale of white workers would deteriorate because their reasonable expectations of future job opportunities might not materialize if the statute was given Senator Hill's interpretation. The answer had to be that expectations attributable to segregation could not be realized under a fair-employment-practices statute. Moreover, as the Supreme Court had already stated regarding school desegregation, in *Brown* v. *Board of Education II:* "It should go without saying that the vitality of these constitutional principles cannot be allowed to yield simply because of disagreement with them."[14]

The legislative history indicated opposition to interference with seniority arrangements but no awareness of the problem. The overriding concern of Congress—to the extent that it focused on the particular matter—was that Title VII should not be interpreted to permit *unemployed* black workers to oust incumbent white employees by coming from the streets to take their jobs.[15]* This hypothetical concern differed dramatically from that under discussion in a number of respects.

In the controversy that swirled around the EEOC in 1965 and 1966, the following factors were relevant to the debate: (1) past discrimination was evident; (2) black employees were employed in an enterprise or industry, and their locked-in position and proposed escape routes gave rise to the litigation; (3) it was not proposed that incumbent white employees be displaced from the jobs they held.

Although the assertion had not been made during the legislative debate, it was contended before the EEOC that the courts and administrative agencies were not competent to deal with seniority and contract-interpretation problems. The Supreme Court had specifically encouraged the use of arbitration in labor disputes as resolution of this problem in the landmark *Steelworkers* trilogy cases.[16] But the resolution was that if complexities made judicial understanding difficult, a master with industrial-relations or labor-law expertise could be available. (Interestingly, the 1972 amendments specifically provide for masters in Title VII litigation.)[17]

Accordingly, my report stated that most seniority arrangements locked blacks into segregated job departments and were therefore unlawful under the statute.

Even though discrimination in hiring was the initial factor in the unlawful conduct, an unlawful no-transfer policy had brought seniority principles into play. The unlawful seniority and no-transfer systems meant that even though blacks were permitted to transfer after the effective date of the statute, they were unable to rely upon seniority credits that might well have been theirs "but for"[18] discriminatory transfer practices in the past. Unless the transfer prohibition could be regarded as reasonable (as would, for example, be the prevention of a janitor's transferring to an airline classification because of the extraordinary financial expense necessary to provide the required education), it was unlawful, and seniority credits were due to the black worker previously discriminated against. Of course, if the no-transfer policy was reasonable, it would be difficult to establish a violation of the statute, let alone devise a remedy providing for seniority credits. If the transfer prohibition was not reasonable and could therefore be regarded as unlawful, I considered the following possible remedies in the context of *Whitfield,* in which the employer utilized a valid line of progression.[19]*

1. As vacancies occur in any position in the line of progression, black employees would be permitted to bid on them in accordance with *plant* length-of-service seniority and thus jump ahead of white employees who are already moving up the ladder, if the white employees have less seniority according to a plant-wide basis of computation. The immediate obvious problem is that the differences in the degree of skill necessary for the job previously performed by the discriminatee and that required by the vacancy on which he bids may be considerable. Although Title VII will apparently require training programs of varying scope and expenditure, depending upon the circumstances, the training necessary to place an unskilled employee high on the line of progression, when other workers have had to climb the ladder step by step, is extensive as well as costly. Possibly, also, the vagueness implicit in the theory that remedies for Title VII violations should attempt to raise the victims of discrimination to their "rightful places" may make the filling of vacancies near the top provide windfalls for blacks at the expense of whites and thus raise the specter of preferential treatment.[20] The line between an appropriate remedy and preferential treatment is somewhat arbitrary and difficult to draw.

2. A compromise on the windfall aspect of "leaping" into a line of progression might be a "leap-in, leap-out" practice. This would permit Negroes to move into a vacancy anywhere on the line; but it would also require them to "leap out" of the line during a reduction of force, instead of moving to a lower rung of the ladder. While this practice would somewhat limit windfall possibilities, it would aggravate the training difficulties involved. For not only would the employer and the union have to bear the heavy costs of preparing employees for new assignments, but the investment would be wasted as soon as employment diminished.

3. The remedy I advocated permits, in my opinion, the best available reconciliation between equity—for both black and white groups—and business efficiency. If the line of progression is proper, blacks, as whites have done, should begin with the bottom job, but not simply because the whites have done so. Unless their

present skills entitle them to move higher, blacks should begin at the bottom because it is the best method of learning the next job on the ladder. In certain industries, the court—or the master—could make a finding that Title VII requires training programs which will facilitate the movement of blacks into the bottom jobs in the formerly white line.

The report also advocated "red circling" (freezing of black employees' wage rates when it would otherwise become necessary for them to take a wage cut in order to get into the formerly all-white progression line or department). Red circling would encourage black employees who would otherwise not transfer because they would be forced to suffer an economic setback, as was required in *Whitfield.* Moreover, the report proposed both "bump back" rights for black employees, permitting them to return to their formerly all-black jobs in case of a reduction in the work force, and a "residency" formula for seniority often used in industrial relations, which would enable a black worker to exercise his seniority rights after he acquired residency in the new job or department; the residency would be deemed the equivalent of a large amount of experience.

After the issuance of the report, the commission began to support the view that black workers were entitled to seniority credits where discrimination had been practiced in the past. The first federal-district-court decision, *Quarles* v. *Philip Morris,*[21] also adhered to this view. In *Quarles,* the company operated cigarette and tobacco manufacturing facilities that were divided into four departments: geen-leaf stemmery, prefabrication, fabrication, and warehouse shipping and receiving. Prior to 1955, only blacks worked in the stemmery and prefabrication departments, only whites worked in fabrication, and a "few" blacks worked in the "predominantly" white warehouse shipping-and-receiving department.

The number of blacks in supervisory positions was always very small. Prior to the passage of Title VII, what the court justly characterized as "token hiring" of blacks took place in the fabrication department in response to a presidential executive order. In 1966 and 1967, on the other hand, the percentage of new hires of blacks jumped astronomically. Most important is the fact that for many years interdepartmental transfers were prohibited. As a result, black workers could not be promoted into better paying jobs and thus could not accumulate seniority credits in the fabrication and warehouse departments. In the event of a business decline, some black employees could bump back and return to their former departments with seniority unimpaired, but others did not have this right.

The district court in *Quarles,* like the Fifth Circuit in *Whitfield,* dealt with a departmental structure with "many legitimate management functions. It promotes efficiency, encourages junior employees to remain with the company because of the prospects of advancement, and limits the amount of retraining that would be necessary without departmental organization."[22] Thus "legitimate management functions" were at stake in *Quarles,* just as "efficient management" problems were presented in *Whitfield.* But unlike *Whitfield, Quarles* held that, at least according to the facts of the case, the present consequence of past discrimination—the lack of accumulated seniority credits in the white fabrication department for blacks who transferred and who would have advanced at an earlier date but for the discriminatory policy—could be remedied by Title VII. In arriving at this conclusion, the court noted that plaintiffs do "not seek to oust white employees with less employment seniority from their jobs, but they do seek to be trained and promoted to full vacancies on the same basis as white employees with equal ability and employment seniority."[23]

In dealing with the proviso to Section 703(h) which states that "bona fide" seniority systems are not unlawful, the court properly concluded that any exceptions to Title VII's general prohibition of racial discrimination must be explicitly spelled out in the statute. Speaking for the district court, Circuit Judge John Butzner (sitting by designation) said: "Obviously, one characteristic of a bona fide seniority system must be lack of discrimination. Nothing in § 703(h), or in its legislative history, suggests that a racially discriminatory seniority system established before the act is a *bona fide* seniority system under the act. . . . The court holds a departmental seniority system that has its genesis in racial discrimination is not a *bona fide* seniority system."[24] Judge Butzner found that *"Whitfield* . . . is not controlling."[25] Said the court: "Congress did not intend to freeze an entire generation of Negro employees into discriminatory patterns that existed before the act."[26]

Two immediate problems not resolved by *Quarles* were soon addressed by the judiciary. In *Quarles,* the court pointed out that discrimination in hiring had continued after the effective date of Title VII and had ceased only in 1966. Would the result be different if the discrimination had not continued after July 2, 1965, the effective date of the statute? The first response was provided by the Eighth Circuit in *United States* v. *Sheetmetal Workers Local 36,*[27] a Justice Department pattern-or-practice suit, in which the court awarded retroactive seniority credits to black craftsmen excluded from the unionized sector of the construction industry, even though no specific acts of discrimination had taken place subsequent to July 2, 1965. The basis for the remedy in *Local 36* was that the defendants' reputation for discrimination had continued after July 2, 1965, and that nothing had been done to correct that reputation. Accordingly, black craftsmen were deterred from applying for jobs after the statute's effective date. In a similar vein, the Fourth Circuit, again speaking through Judge Butzner, has stated:

Since the employment statistics demonstrated that pre-Act hiring racially segregated both the general yard and the Barney yard, the burden shifted to the [company] to come forward with evidence to show that it had never discriminated in hiring black brakemen.

. . . We conclude, therefore, that the [company's] pre-Act hiring practices discriminated against black brakemen. Standing alone, however, pre-Act discrimination is insufficient to maintain a cause of action under Title VII; to be actionable, the proof must show present effects of the past discrimination. The present mechanism of discrimination, the government asserts, is the company's practice, embedded in its collective bargaining agreements, of denying black Barney yard brakemen who were employed before the company reformed its hiring practices their company seniority should they seek employment in the general yard.[28]

Therefore, if the past has lingered on through July 2, 1965, and has a "present effect," no evidence of specific instances of violations after July 2, 1965, is required. The pattern which persisted through 1966 in the company sued in *Quarles* is not a prerequisite for the application of that case's doctrine.

The rationale for the seniority cases and their lack of concern with events after July 2, 1965, can be understood more easily when one examines the first major circuit court of appeals decision. The Fifth Circuit Court of Appeals, in *Local 189, United Papermakers* v. *United States*,[29] another seniority dispute involving past discrimination, concluded that departmental or job seniority systems which deny blacks seniority credits they might have earned had they had access to previously all-white jobs to which they were now permitted to transfer, constitute a violation of Title VII. Judge Wisdom, speaking for a unanimous court, thus posed the issue:

One of the most perplexing issues troubling the court under Title VII: how to reconcile equal employment opportunity *today* with seniority expectations based on *yesterday's* built-in racial discrimination. May an employer continue to award formerly "white jobs" on the basis of seniority attained in other formerly "white jobs" or must the employer consider the employee's experience in formerly "Negro jobs" an equivalent measure of seniority? . . . We hold that Crown Zellerbach's job seniority system in effect at its Bogalusa Paper Mill prior to February 1, 1968, was unlawful because by carrying forward the effects of former discriminatory practices, the system results in present and future discrimination. When a Negro applicant has the qualifications to handle a particular job, the Act requires that Negro seniority be equated with white seniority.[30]

The defendants in *Local 189* maintained that the merger of black and white lines of progression had produced a "racially neutral system of job seniority." The court outlined the defendants' arguments:

The fact that the system continues to prefer whites over previously hired Negroes in filling certain vacancies does not in and of itself show racial discrimination. That effect, the defendants argue, is merely an ineradicable consequence of extinct racial discrimination. They point to evidence that Congress meant Title VII to apply prospectively only. Competitive seniority has an honorable place in the history of labor, and portions of the legislative history of the Act seem to immunize accrued rights of seniority against remedial measures. Thus Title VII § 703(h), specifically protects "bona fide seniority systems" from the operation of the Act. The defendants also maintain that insistence upon mill seniority would effectively bestow preferential treatment upon one race, which the Act by its terms positively forbids.[31]

Noting that *Quarles* had persuasively disposed of most of the issues, Judge Wisdom asserted that the proposition that the statute was intended only to be prospective was quite clearly answered in that case. But *Quarles* was hardly the end of the matter. In *Local 189* the court said:

The defendants assert, paradoxically, that even though the system conditions future employment opportunities upon a previously determined racial status, the system is itself racially neutral and not in violation of Title VII. The translation of racial status to job-seniority status cannot obscure the hard, cold fact that Negroes at Crown's Mill will lose promotions which, *but for* their race, they would surely have won. Every time a Negro worker hired under the old segregated system bids against a white worker in his job slot, the old racial classification reasserts itself and the Negro suffers anew for his employer's previous bias.[32]

Having concluded that the past was inseparable from the present, the court focused upon what it characterized as the "crux of the problem"—one which continues to confront the courts today: "how far the employer must go to undo the effects of past discrimination."[33] Three basic options were developed by the court. The first, labeled a "freedom now" approach, calls for the discharge of junior white incumbents and their replacement by blacks. Continuation of whites in jobs which blacks might have possessed but for discrimination was unlawful; this illegality could be remedied only by the ouster of the white workers. The second option—the one favored by unions and employers—was the *status-quo* approach, based on the theory that "whatever unfortunate effects there might be in future bidding by Negroes luckless enough to have been hired before desegregation would be considered merely as an incident of now-existinguished discrimination."[34] This option was rejected as unsatisfactory, because it could leave intact the past discrimination which reasserted itself in the present system.

The third possibility, which was adopted by Judge Wisdom, was the "rightful place" approach—advocated in my 1966 report to the EEOC.[35]* The court stated that the only conceivable defense of a seniority system which had a discriminatory impact was one based on business necessity: "When an employer or union has discriminated in the past and when its present policies renew or exaggerate discriminatory effects, those policies must yield, unless there is an overriding legitimate, non-racial business purpose."[36]

Finally, Judge Wisdom, the author of *Whitfield* as well as *Local 189*, distinguished the latter from the former. *Whitfield* involved a plan to eliminate segregated lines of progression, whereas the *Local 189*, unlike *Whitfield*, was concerned with "the measure of promotion from one job to another."[37] As the court pointed out, *Quarles* itself had thus distinguished *Whitfield:*

Whitfield does not stand for the proposition that present discrimination can be justified simply because it was caused by conditions in the past. Present discrimination was allowed in *Whitfield* only because it was rooted in the Negro employees' lack of ability and training to take skilled jobs on the same basis as white employees. The fact that white employees received their skill and training in a discriminatory progression line denied to the Negroes did not outweigh the fact that the Negroes were unskilled and untrained. Business necessity, not racial discrimination, dictated the limited transfer privileges under the contract.[38]

The court, in *Local 189*, concluded that the lines of progression in *Whitfield* were not "as functionally related" as in *Quarles* and, therefore, the business necessity was stronger in the former, pre–Title VII case. Moreover, in *Local 189* and a Fourth Circuit ruling in *Robinson* v. *Lorillard Corporation*,[39] the courts concluded that employees who would have to take wage cuts as a result of their transfer to previously all-white lines should have their wages red-circled—frozen at existing rates so that they would not be deterred from making the transfer. This remedy, of course, was as critical to black employees (particularly those with families and the attendant financial obligations) as the carry-over of seniority itself.

Without either, the black worker would be significantly deterred from transferring to work offering better opportunities.

Franks v. *Bowman Transportation Co.:* **Seniority for Rejected Applicants**

In *Franks* v. *Bowman Transportation Co.,* without referring to *Quarles* and *Local 189,* the Supreme Court held that the award of seniority credits to applicants rejected on account of racial discrimination is appropriate relief according to the remedial provisions of Title VII.[40] In *Bowman,* the district court had denied such relief on the ground that it was precluded by Section 703(h) of the act. The court of appeals for the Fifth Circuit affirmed.[41]

Justice Brennan, speaking for the majority, concluded that Section 703(h) was not "intended to modify or restrict relief otherwise appropriate once an illegal discriminatory practice occurring after the effective date of the Act is proved—as in the instant case, a discriminatory refusal to hire." The Court stated again its view that the policy outlawing the discrimination prohibited by Title VII should have the "highest priority." In order to attain the objective of making discriminatees whole by providing complete compensation, Congress, the Court said, had vested "broad equitable discretion" in the federal district courts to "order such affirmative action as may be appropriate, which may include, but is not limited to, reinstatement or hiring of employees, with or without back pay . . . , or any other relief as the court deems appropriate." The Court also referred to the fact that Congress, in the 1972 amendments to the statute, was particularly concerned to strengthen judicial remedial authority. Justice Brennan declared: "This is emphatic confirmation that federal courts are empowered to fashion such relief as the particular circumstances of a case may require to effect restitution, making whole insofar as possible the victims of racial discrimination in hiring. Adequate relief may well be denied in the absence of a seniority remedy slotting the victim in that position in the seniority system that would have been his had he been hired at the time of his application. It can hardly be questioned that ordinarily such relief will be necessary to achieve the 'make-whole' purposes of the Act."[42]

Fundamental in the Court's rationale for awarding seniority credits to rejected applicants was the importance of the credits in the employment relationship; and the facts that the remedial provisions of the National Labor Relations Act[43] are the model for those of Title VII, and that the former statute has been construed to provide workers "discriminatorily refused employment . . . an award of seniority equivalent to that which they would have enjoyed but for the illegal conduct."[44]

Chief Justice Burger partly concurred and partly dissented. The Chief Justice parted company with the majority—as did dissenters Justices Powell and Rehnquist—on the ground that "competitive-type seniority relief at the expense of wholly innocent employees can rarely, if ever, be equitable if that term retains traditional meaning. . . . In this setting I cannot join in judicial approval of 'robbing Peter to pay Paul.' "[45]

Justice Powell, writing a separate opinion in which Justice Rehnquist joined, expressed more basic disagreement with the majority. Justice Powell took the view that the Court's holding could not be "reconciled" with the statute's remedial provisions "or with fundamental fairness." According to the dissenting opinion, "retroactive" seniority is inappropriate, because seniority does not "directly affect the employer at all" and, unlike a back-pay remedy, the seniority remedy "penalizes" innocent, white workers. Without suggesting that Congress had intended to bar this type of remedy, Justice Powell concluded that the award of seniority resulted from a "preference based on a fiction," inasmuch as the discriminatee had not actually worked on the job after his rejection. The dissent declared: "This also requires an assumption that nothing would have interrupted his employment, and that his performance would have justified a progression up the seniority ladder. The incumbents, who in fact were on the job during the interim and performing satisfactorily would be seriously disadvantaged. The Congressional bar to one type of preferential treatment in Section 703(j) should at least give the Court pause before it imposes upon district courts a duty to grant relief that creates another type of preference."[46]

Finally, Justice Powell's dissent rejected an analogy to the NLRA, on the grounds that "in the usual case no one speaks for the individual incumbents," and much discretion should be accorded the district court under Title VII just as is the case with the Labor Board under Taft-Hartley.[47] Curiously, at no point did any of the three dissenting justices point up a feature that distinguishes between most factual situations under the two statutes: that the period of time during which those NLRA incumbents whose seniority is affected by a grant of retroactive seniority to discriminatees have been employed is relatively short, because the discriminatees are specific individuals—not members of a large class—who must file charges with the board within a six-month period fixed by the statute of limitations.[48] Under Title VII, members of the class need not file administrative changes.

The Impact of *Bowman* upon the Departmental-Seniority Cases

Does the Court's decision in *Bowman* alter any of the principles established in the departmental-seniority line of cases? There are two potential sources of conflict between those cases and *Bowman:* first, the question whether post-act conduct includes more than the mere operation of the seniority system itself—for example, specific acts of discrimination such as the job denials by defendants in *Bowman;* second, the problem of the extent of seniority relief—whether seniority credits for the period prior to July 2, 1965, may be awarded. The Court's view on both these issues are dicta, inasmuch as only instances of job denials subsequent to the effective date of the statute were presented. Consequently, seniority could not date back before July 2, 1965.

With regard to the first question, the Court's opinion is hardly a model of clarity. Justice Brennan said:

Whatever the exact meaning and scope of § 703(h) in light of its unusual legislative history and the absence of the usual legislative materials . . . it is apparent that the thrust of the section is directed toward defining what is and what is not an illegal discriminatory practice in instances in which the post-Act operation of a seniority system is challenged as perpetuating the effects of discrimination occurring prior to the effective date of the Act. There is no indication in the legislative materials that § 703(h) was intended to modify or restrict relief otherwise appropriate once an illegal discriminatory practice occurring after the effective date of the Act is proved—as in the instant case, a discriminatory refusal to hire.[49]

Justice Powell interpreted this assertion to require the "insulation" of seniority systems in existence on the effective date of the act against claims that such systems perpetuate pre-act discrimination.[50] Although, arguably, such a reversal of unanimous circuit-court decisions (the departmental-seniority cases were not even cited) represents the Court's judgment that most adjudicated cases of this type cannot now, as a practical matter, be disturbed or reversed, the Court's references to the 1972 amendments and Congress' approval of the departmental cases seems to undermine this view.[51] The same reasoning seems to apply to the argument that the Court intended to deprive black incumbents of seniority dating back before July 2, 1965. Possibly, Justice Powell—and perhaps Justice Brennan as well—intended to eliminate pre-act seniority where discriminatees are nonemployees and thus are seeking "fictional" seniority. Similarly, the justices may have intended both to insulate liability and to eradicate pre-act seniority awards in all-white plants.[52] Justice Powell notwithstanding, the Court did not dispose of such matters in *Bowman*.

Unanswered Questions Relating to Seniority
Remedies in Multiunion and Multicontract Situations

Could the same seniority remedies, including red circling, that were adopted in *Local 189* be fashioned in situations where transfer might involve different collective-bargaining agreements? And did it make any difference if the agreements were negotiated by individual locals of the same international or the locals were under one master agreement negotiated by the international?

The first of a series of cases to answer these questions was *United States* v. *Jacksonville Terminal Company*,[53] involving the multiunion railroad industry. In *Jacksonville Terminal*, Judge David Dyer, speaking for the court, concluded that if, in the past, discriminatory hiring had occurred in an industry, an appropriate remedy could provide for seniority carry-over from one union's craft, seniority system, and collective-bargaining agreement to those of another. Judge Dyer said: "That hoary collective bargaining agreements now mandate perpetuation of past aberrations from the governmental policy [against racial discrimination in employment] does not affect the propriety of judicial action. . . . Such agreements do not, *per se*, carry the authoritative imprimatur and moral force of sacred scripture, or even of mundane legislation."[54]

Similarly, in cases involving the International Brotherhood of Teamsters,[55] the courts have repeatedly provided a seniority-carry-over remedy for minority dockmen and local drivers who had been excluded from over the road drivers classifications in the past—even though that classification is under a separate collective-bargaining agreement with its own seniority system and is often represented by a different local union from the one that represents city drivers and dockmen. Accordingly, in both the multiunion railroad industry and the trucking industry, which is balkanized into local unions, the seniority-carry-over remedy has been utilized. Logically, the remedy should also be applied in the construction industry, for instance, in which black laborers have acquired skills usable in the sheetmetal and plumbing trades. In such instances, the right to transfer to the trade, which would eventually offer a higher rate of pay, might not be particularly attractive if the employee had to begin initially as an apprentice (at a lower rate of pay) or face the prospect of "sitting on the bench," unemployed, while journeymen or senior workers were referred out of the union hall before the minority worker. A further difficulty is the necessity for a fringe-benefit carry-over as well as a seniority and red-circling remedy. If black employees who are members of a labor union must sacrifice fringe benefits such as pensions in order to move to the jurisdiction of a different union with a fringe-benefit scheme of its own, the deterrents will be as great as in situations involving wage cuts. Perhaps the courts will have to integrate the fringe-benefit schemes of the respective unions so that an effective transfer can be made. But both the benefit and competitive-status aspects of seniority in such circumstances were specifically left unresolved by the Court in *Bowman*.

Further Thoughts on "Freedom Now"

A more fundamental question raised by *Local 189* relates to some of its underlying assumptions. For the Court had rejected the "freedom now" approach because of the same problems that had induced Chief Justice Warren to accept the "with all deliberate speed" formula in *Brown II*. Implicit in both approaches was the notion that a significant and sudden frustration of white expectations would produce racial tensions, which, in turn, would prove counterproductive to the implementation of both constitutional and statutory rights. Yet, in light of Title VII, "freedom now" was good logic. The only defense for a system which jeopardizes the black worker's assuming his rightful place is business necessity. Quite clearly, the erosion of white seniority rights, while posing serious human-relations problems which might conceivably erupt into violence or sabotage, has never constituted a business necessity within the meaning of Title VII. Indeed, in the construction industry, the award of seniority-referral credits to previously excluded blacks appears to apply even though the number of work opportunities for incumbent whites in the union diminishes. The Court said in *Bowman*, "We find untenable the conclusion that this form of relief may be denied merely because the interests of other employees may thereby be affected."[56] Moreoever, the Court cited with approval the Second Circuit's cogent statement: "If relief under Title VII can be denied merely because the majority group of employees, who have not suffered discrimination, will be unhappy about it, there will be little hope of correcting the wrongs to which the Act is directed."[57]

Although *Bowman* contemplates the displacement of white workers by blacks, even that case implies that blacks will advance up the job ladder *in the future* and will not immediately occupy the positions they would have occupied had there been no earlier discrimination. Therefore, the difficulty for the black worker in both *Bowman* and *Local 189* fact situations is that he must wait for vacancies to appear; in some industries, such as trucking and construction, the delay may be lengthy. Accordingly, the minority worker is not compensated for wrongs suffered until the white worker moves up the ladder, retires, or is discharged. Although the victims of discrimination may obtain back pay under both Title VII and the Civil Rights Act of 1866, a black worker who is not compensated while awaiting a vacancy which provides the opportunity for his rightful promotion is in the position of a segregated pupil in a public school whose rights may be vindicated at an uncertain date in the future.

If a minority employee must work for a time in each of several jobs along a line of progression before reaching the position which is rightly his, the wait can be very long. Some of the language in *Local 189* seems to imply that the courts would be reluctant to order a restructuring of transfer and promotion practices for the purpose of speeding the advancement of minority workers. Said Judge Wisdom:

> The [district] court's decision put the emphasis where it belongs: absent a showing that the worker has the ability to handle a particular job, the entry job [on the line of progression to which the employee transfers] is the proper beginning for any worker. Under the court's decree, employees still must move up through the various lines of progression job-by-job. As a further restraint, if a certain minimum time is needed in one job to train an employee for the next, a residency requirement may be imposed that will slow the rise of Negro employees. Under the system that is in effect at the mill now, and that is unaffected by the decree, that residency period is six months.[58]

To the extent that this dictum[59]* seemed to indicate that the burden would be on each black worker to prove, for example, that he had the ability to enter the line of progression at an advanced level rather than on the employer to justify the requirement of entry at a low level, the force of the court's statement was quickly eroded. For the Fifth Circuit has states, "We know that any facially neutral employment practice, such as requiring position-by-position advance up a line of progression . . . , which perpetuates past bias, for example, by slowing a discriminatee's advancement unnecessarily, is considered presently discriminatory . . . [unless the employer] can demonstrate that the practice is justified by business necessity."[60]

The business-necessity standard as it has evolved in the departmental-seniority cases is stringent. The leading cases defining the business-necessity test, *Robinson* v. *Lorillard* and *United States* v. *Bethlehem Steel Corporation*[61] enunciate a criterion remarkably similar to that proclaimed in cases arising under the equal-protection clause of the Fourteenth Amendment. Judge Simon Sobeloff, spoke for the Fourth Circuit in *Lorillard:*

> The test is whether there exists an overriding legitimate business purpose such that the practice is necessary to the safe and efficient operation of the business. Thus, the business purpose must be sufficiently compelling to override any racial impacts; the challenged practice must effectively carry out the business purpose it is alleged to serve; and there must be available no acceptable alternative policies or practices which would better accomplish the business purpose advanced or accomplish it equally well with a lesser differential impact.[62]

Judge Feinberg spoke in a similar vein for the Second Circuit in *Bethlehem Steel:* "Necessity connotes an irresistible demand. To be preserved, the seniority and transfer system must not only directly foster safety and efficiency of a plant, but also be essential to those goals [*Local 189* cited]. If the legitimate ends of safety and efficiency can be served by a reasonably available alternative system with less discriminatory effects, then the present policies may not be continued."[63]

The difficulty of squaring the business-necessity rule with a requirement of step-by-step advancement along a line of progression was well expressed by the Fifth Circuit in *Pettway* v. *American Cast Iron Pipe Co.:*

In an industry involving sophisticated machining processes such as many of the operations of this company, training of employees for skilled positions is a necessary function for the continued economic life of the business. However, a *departmental* seniority system is effective and efficient as an instruction program only as to those positions in a line of progression where the jobs below them on the ladder serve as prerequisite training steps. Thus in a departmental line of progression where the positions do not require specific training or where on-the-job experience in *another* department qualifies an employee, a departmental seniority system is not efficient and it is certainly not the best training method. The company . . . has failed to demonstrate that every position at the plant is so complex or specialized as to require, without exception, step-by-step job progression within each department.[64]

Obviously the *Pettway* explanation of the reasons why a departmental-seniority system cannot usually be justified by business necessity also applies to the requirement of a step-by-step progression after departmental seniority is replaced by plant-wide seniority. Unless step-by-step advancement, and the residency periods required along the way, are indispensable for training and there is no alternative, the practice violates Title VII if minority employees are impeded in their movement to their rightful places.

Accordingly, in some departmental-seniority cases the courts have not merely enjoined the use of departmental seniority while leaving the other elements of the transfer and promotion system unchanged, but have scrutinized the entire system in the light of the business-necessity test and have restructured or even eliminated[65] lines of progression in appropriate cases. They have also ordered entry at an advanced level of the line of progression, "job skipping" along the line, and reductions in residency requirements if business necessity does not justify delays in the movement of minority workers to their proper positions.[66] Through such remedies the courts can shorten the waiting period minority workers must suffer. But to eliminate completely the requirement of step-by-step progression is seldom possible, and vacancies at each step may come slowly.

The void between the discriminatee's present status and rightful place was filled by Judge Keith in *Detroit Edison,* in which, for the first time, a federal district court ordered front pay for "locked-in" incumbent blacks.[67] Accordingly, the discriminatee is paid at the rate he would have received had there been no discrimination. Front pay, like back pay, should be required of the parties in proportion to their responsibility for discrimination. The party that pays has an incentive to

move the black employee up the ladder as quickly as possible. The incentive for a
worker to refuse upgrading because he would receive high wages for a relatively
undemanding job can be easily eliminated by terminating front-pay liability either
upon a manifestation of unwillingness on the worker's part to accept a vacancy or,
as Judge Keith's order provides, after the employer or the union has found the
worker unqualified after three opportunities to advance into a high-opportunity
job. One district court moved further than Judge Keith and held that blacks may
immediately bump and displace incumbent whites as long as the latter retain the
pay rate of the job from which they have been ousted,[68] but that decision has been
reversed by the Fourth Circuit in an opinion which follows the lead of *Detroit
Edison* in providing for front pay for blacks rather than immediate promotion.[69]*
Seemingly, some of the human-relations problems envisaged by Judge Wisdom
would result from the bumping permitted by the district court—although the front
pay for whites would ease the transition to equality. Of course, blacks would more
expeditiously acquire the dignity and self-sufficiency inherent in work from which
they had been excluded if bumping rather than front pay was the remedy.

Seniority Credits for Workers Deterred from Applying

The remedies fashioned by the courts in *Quarles, Local 189,* and *Detroit Edison,* cases in which a large number of blacks had been locked into jobs from which
they could not be promoted, has led critics to say that employers or unions that
completely exclude blacks are less likely than those that limit transfer and promotion to be subjected to protest and litigation and, if sued, are confronted with less
potential liability and other difficulties. The first element is the more valid. As
numbers swell, so also do solidarity, strength, courage, and all other requirements
for effective militancy.

Of course, exclusion can be partially remedied by requiring the employer to hire
the black applicants whom he has rejected because of discrimination and to provide them with back pay and—under *Bowman*—seniority credits. But if the employer's conduct is egregious, the likelihood that large numbers of blacks will
have made applications for employment is very small, owing to the obvious futility of applying. Unless such employers are to be rewarded for the severity of their
discrimination, the courts should order qualified individuals who were deterred
from applying to be hired, with back pay and seniority credits. This approach has
already been adopted in trucking-industry cases with respect to incumbent employees who were deterred from requesting a transfer to jobs as long-distance
drivers.[70] To reject the "Biblically recognized claims of the meek"[71] would be
unwise in cases where minority workers have been excluded altogether from the
employer's work force instead of being locked into low-level jobs.

The Eighth Circuit's decision, in *United States* v. *Sheetmetal Workers Local
36,*[72] has paved the way toward an attack on lily-white unions and employers, and
on unlawful exclusion as well as illegal assignment to jobs. For in that case, black
nonunion construction workers were awarded seniority accumulated outside the
unionized industry. In *Detroit Edison,* as in *Sheetmetal Workers,* the defendants

were found to have a reputation for discriminatory hiring practices. In the former case, black skilled craftsmen available in the labor market who had been deterred from applying because of contact with their black community in which the reputation was known were awarded both seniority and back pay by the district court.[73]* The thrust of *Detroit Edison* was to require management as well as union members (through their treasuries) to provide compensation. Another difference from *Sheetmetal Workers* was that the relevant skills were not utilized in only one industry, as was arguably the case in *Sheetmetal Workers.* This difference, however, has been minimized by the Fifth Circuit's pointed reference, in *Jacksonville Terminal,* to the fact that experience need not be derived from the industry that is the subject of the litigation.[74] Moreover, in *Detroit Edison,* Judge Keith's decree was clearly aimed at employees who have accumulated partial skills through other employment, vocational schools, or related courses of study in other educational institutions.

From both *Sheetmetal Workers* and *Detroit Edison* two important principles have emerged and combined with those already present in such cases as *Local 189* and *Quarles* involving incumbents: first, an application for employment is not a prerequisite to the use of seniority credits accumulated by workers in low-level jobs or departments; second, nonincumbents or outsiders may be the beneficiaries, as well as incumbents. In both *Sheetmetal Workers* and *Detroit Edison,* outsiders were involved; thus those cases were different from *Local 189* and *Quarles.* In both *Sheetmetal Workers* and *Detroit Edison* a discriminatory reputation which would deter applicants was evidenced; in *Detroit Edison,* unlike *Sheetmetal Workers,* where no specific instances of discrimination were shown after July 2, 1965, discrimination was found to have been repeatedly practiced up to the time of trial in February, 1973. In effect, both cases have begun to erode the dicta in *Local 189* which had condemned "fictional seniority," or seniority based upon something other than time actually worked for the defendant employer or union.

In *Local 189,* Judge Wisdom had emphasized the difference between a situation in which incumbent blacks were awarded seniority credits for time actually worked with the company rather than for so-called fictional seniority. In countering the argument that the award of seniority credits to incumbent blacks constituted a form of unlawful "preferential treatment,"[75] Judge Wisdom said:

It is one thing for legislation to require the creation of *fictional* seniority for newly hired Negroes, and quite another thing for it to require that time *actually worked* in Negro jobs be given equal status with time worked in white jobs. To begin with, requiring employers to correct their pre-Act discrimination by creating fictional seniority for new Negro employees would not necessarily aid the actual victims of the previous discrimination. There would be no guaranty that the new employees had actually suffered exclusion at the hands of the employer in the past, or, if they had, there would be no way of knowing whether, after being hired, they would have continued to work for the same employer. In other words, creating fictional employment time for newly-hired Negroes would comprise preferential rather than remedial treatment. The clear thrust of the Senate debate is directed against such preferential treatment. . . .

No stigma of preference attaches to recognition of time actually worked in Negro jobs as the equal of white time. The individual victims of prior discrimination in this case would necessarily be the ones—the only ones—to benefit by the institution of mill seniority, as modified in the decree. We conclude, in agreement with *Quarles,* that Congress exempted from the anti-discrimination requirements only those seniority rights that give white workers preference over junior Negroes.[76]

Bowman largely undercuts the Fifth Circuit's view of fictional seniority. In *Bowman* the Fifth Circuit, "guided by"[77] Judge Wisdom's statement, declined "to take a giant step beyond permitting job competition on the basis of company seniority" by "creat[ing] constructive seniority for applicants who have never worked for the company."[78] The Supreme Court required precisely that "giant step."

Moreover, the Court held that if a pattern or practice of discrimination is proved, each rejected minority applicant is presumed to be entitled to a job, with retroactive seniority, unless the employer can show that the individual would not have been hired even in the absence of discrimination.[79] This approach seems to reject implicitly the notion that if there is any doubt that an individual has been the victim of discrimination, a class-wide seniority remedy which benefits that individual is "preferential treatment" prohibited by the statute. Thus *Bowman* largely vitiates the rationale behind Judge Wisdom's proscription of fictional seniority.

Does *Bowman* imply that an employer can be ordered to hire individuals who have been deterred from applying for a job and to give them credit for seniority? *Bowman's* implicit rejection of the need for absolute certainty in identifying the victims of discrimination, together with *Sheetmetal Workers,* Judge Keith's decision in *Detroit Edison,* and the trucking-industry cases regarding transfers,[80] seems to call for that interpretation, which the Second Circuit has adopted.[81] If qualified blacks or other minorities have been deterred from applying, they are entitled to seniority that is predicated on related work experience with another company or industry and that is fictional in that it does not purport to constitute time actually worked for the enterprise or union immediately involved in the litigation. Actually, in such cases, the potential for preferential treatment is less troublesome than in those involving incumbents, because the qualifications and consequent entitlement are more clearly evident—as was apparent not only in *Sheetmetal Workers* and *Detroit Edison,* but also in the trucking industry, where black and Chicano casual laborers, owner-operators, and employees of owner-operators had skills which are usually utilized only in that industry but were deterred from applying because of the discriminatory practices of both the Teamsters Union and the truckers.

If blacks are locked in with one company and they claim that they would have been promoted but for the discriminatory policy, uncertainty is greater, because whether a given individual would have taken the responsibility involved in progressing cannot be determined. Accordingly, doubts and necessary speculation increase the possibility of preferential treatment and windfalls for undeserving individuals. These doubts however, are significantly alleviated by the fact that locked-in employees will actually possess and use seniority only if they are qualified and willing to work. Nevertheless, what they actually would have done in the past to obtain transfers is uncertain. Those who were deterred because they either are journeymen or possess skills relevant to the trade are more easily identifiable. Speculation regarding incumbent employees is considered unimportant, however, because of the feeling of futility engendered in most black workers as a consequence of being discouraged from applying.

Moreover, in the seniority cases past entitlement is not the dominant theme in determining equitable relief if a presumption exists that the individual would have been promoted but for the discriminatory policy. The principal objective of the courts in the departmental-seniority cases is to ward off contemporary discouragement to those who may have been harmed in the past, the discouragement being loss of income, exposure to layoff, denial of promotion, and so forth. *Bowman* straddles the issues, emphasizing the seniority credit the individual "presumptively would have earned" and his subordinate status in the absence of the seniority remedy, as well as the "make-whole" provisions of Title VII, which are obviously tied to an award of back pay—compensation to those who have been injured in the past. To some extent, the Court's double-barreled approach and its emphasis on compensation may reflect judicial uneasiness, which is not felt if those who obtain seniority are incumbent employees who have actually worked in the establishment. Here liability exists with regard to a potentially larger and less well-defined class of workers. Nevertheless, the Court's willingness to resolve doubts by ruling against defendants once a "discriminatory hiring pattern" has been evidenced makes the future paramount and presumptive entitlement just that—presumptive and not very precise.

The departmental-seniority remedy de-emphasizes Judge Wisdom's concern with precision about the individuals who have been harmed. The seniority-credit award only roughly approximates the rights that would have been accumulated had there been no discrimination in the first instance. *Bowman* itself speaks of the seniority credit as what would be "presumptively" earned. Similar reasoning underlies the rationale for quota relief in connection with hiring and promotion.

The "Last-Hired, First-Fired" Controversy

Important in relation to seniority is a reputation for discrimination and the resulting deterrent that affects incumbents, applicants, and potential applicants. If an employer has such a reputation, it is futile for the minority worker to apply. Since junior black workers are harmed as a consequence of prior discrimination which excluded them from the hiring office, and since the operation of the seniority system causes the disadvantage to continue, junior blacks can be unlawfully harmed by a layoff. Under such circumstances, the principle of "last hired, first fired" can carry on the effects of the exclusionary practices which caused black employees to have junior status. The legislative history, however, argues against the ouster of incumbent whites by unemployed blacks. Moreover, unless the excluded black worker had special qualifications for the job at an earlier date, when discrimination was being practiced, it is difficult to perceive how he would have moved higher if there was no prior discrimination; or at least the presumption is more tenuous than in the *Local 189* cases, where the worker is an incumbent. Furthermore, unskilled or semiskilled workers who deprive white incumbents of promotional opportunities may come perilously close to occasioning the concern that Congress demonstrated in 1963–1964 legislation.[82] Credits provided for work experience should, however, be scrutinized carefully to determine their relevance to the job that is to be performed so that they will not be used as a shield to slow the advance of previously excluded blacks. That appears to be the lesson of the Fourth Circuit's holding in *Lorillard*. The 1973–1974 energy crisis, coupled with the downswing in employment opportunities in the early seventies, has exaggerated the country's concern with layoffs and the practice of "last hired, first fired."

The first court to confront this issue was that of Judge Fred Cassibry in *Watkins* v. *United Steel Workers Local 2369.*[83] Past discrimination was in evidence, and layoffs affected black employees with seniority dating back to 1951. All black employees except two who had been hired during World War II were laid off, since all the other blacks had been hired after 1965. In assessing whether the obviously adverse impact could be regarded as unlawful under Title VII, the court looked to the cases discussed above as well as to the more recent Fifth Circuit decision, *Rowe* v. *General Motors Corporation.*[84] In *Rowe,* statistics indicated that blacks did not acquire the same opportunities as whites for promotions and transfers to nonhourly salaried jobs. General Motors relied upon considerations of "experience" as the basis for promotion and seniority layoffs, as well as hiring. Chief Judge John Brown said in *Rowe:*

Starting with 1962 plant segregation and the policy of lay-offs and rehirings on some sort of "seniority" basis, the disadvantage suffered by the Blacks hired after 1062 in lay-offs and rehiring is the direct result of the prior segregation policy. This is to make Blacks continue to suffer long after 1965, the effect of race discrimination long after Congress has forbidden it either in current application or in some sort of reincarnation of days gone by. Although GMAD [General Motors' Atlanta plant] could rightfully consider the position of Whites who had been laid off for these reasons it could not—without more at least—treat the recently hired and governmentally twice emancipated Blacks as persons who once again had to go to the foot of the line.

Akin to this is the contention that "experience" was essential and only the long-employed Whites—and conversely, not the recently hired Blacks—had the "experience." Without gainsaying [the proposition] that *qualifications* are an employer's prerogative, the standards cannot be automatically applied to freeze out newly freed Blacks because for the years of its segregated policy, GM hired no Blacks to afford them an opportunity to acquire experience. And on this GM—apart from its incantation of "experience" needs—made no effort to show that in these ebb and flow lay-offs and rehiring that none of the affected Blacks was job-disqualified.[85]

To be sure, the factual pattern of discrimination in *Rowe* was buttressed by reliance upon an all-white supervisory work force's subjective evaluations, which the court properly regarded as suspect. But *Rowe,* coupled with the lines of authority referred to in other cases, set the stage for *Watkins.*

In *Watkins,* the court stressed the fact that the orders in seniority and referral cases attempted to cure contemporary discrimination—even though all the orders were predicated upon past segregation and exclusion. In *Watkins,* the court held that last hired, first fired, in the context of a judicial finding of past discrimination, was unlawful. Said the court: ''In this case, the relief ordered by the Court will not be designed to compensate the blacks who were not hired by the Company between 1945 and 1965. It will be designed to ensure that, because a Company hired no blacks for twenty years, the plant will not operate without black employees for the next decade. The beneficiaries of the order will be the blacks who will not work at the Harvey plant, but who would otherwise have been excluded because of the structure built upon the prior discrimination.''[86] The fashioning of the appropriate remedy raises questions of appropriate form and, most important, of who should bear the inconveniences, cost, and burden. (These matters are considered in more detail in Chapter 6.)

But the dominant view[87] seems to be reflected in the Fifth Circuit's reversal of the district court's decision in *Watkins.*[88] Concerned that this significant reversal might be cited as a precedent which might ''narrow'' or broaden'' the actual holding of the case, Judge Paul Roney, writing for the panel, stated:

We hold that, regardless of an earlier history of employment discrimination, when present hiring practices are nondiscriminatory and have been for over ten years, an employer's use of a long-established seniority system for determining who will be laid-off, and who will be rehired, adopted without intent to discriminate, is not a violation of Title VII of § 1981, even though the use of the seniority system results in the discharge of more blacks than whites to the point of eliminating blacks from the workforce, where the individual employees who suffer layoff under the system have not themselves been the subject of prior employment discrimination. . . .

We specifically do not decide the rights of a laid-off employee who could show that, but for the discriminatory refusal to hire him at an earlier time than the date of his actual employment, or but for his failure to obtain earlier employment because of exclusion of minorities from the workforce, he would have sufficient seniority to insulate him against layoff.''[89]

The Fifth Circuit's decision in *Watkins* is a significant one. The holding, however, is strewn with careful qualifications. First, if the layoff procedure was either adopted about the time that Title VII was enacted into law (or passage was imminent) or was simultaneous with the advent of black hiring, it seems probable that liability could be established on the ground that there was an intention to discriminate. In the absence of a claim that the procedure was a consequence of business necessity, *Watkins* leaves the way open to infer discrimination under such circumstances.

Second, the court in *Watkins* appeared to have been influenced by the facts that contemporary practices were nondiscriminatory and that discrimination had not been evidenced in the recent past. Two related concerns make these elements important. Evidence of contemporary or recent discrimination is relevant because such evidence indicates the attitude and behavior that defendants are likely to adopt in the future—and, therefore, the potential for wrongdoing which may necessitate a quota-type remedy reinstating laid-off black workers. As in the quota cases, there is no adequate alternative method of discouraging future illegalities.

And, as in the quota cases, this finding is a key factor, because the rights of blacks are being balanced against those of whites (in the quota cases both groups are usually applicants), and the judiciary may need reassurance on the question of whether the circumstances require drastic medicine. The absence of such a showing would heighten an always present concern that the antipreferential-treatment provisions of the statute are being ignored.

A third limitation in the *Watkins* holding relates to its requirement that "individual employees" establish that they are victims of "prior employment discrimination." In this connection, the court seemed to focus upon two categories of individuals: (1) the rejected applicant who could show that lack of seniority was attributable to a "discriminatory refusal to hire him at an earlier time than the date of his actual employment"; and (2) the deterred worker whose seniority position mirrored the defendant's "exclusion of minorities from the workforce."[90]

There can be no doubt that *Watkins* indicates apprehension about a preferential windfall for the decree's beneficiaries. The court declared, while noting that no plaintiff alleged the filing of applications or rejections: "Age, not race, is the principal reason the plaintiffs in the case did not have sufficient seniority to withstand layoff. All but one were under the age of legal employment when the Company commenced equal hiring."[91]

But what of future cases in which the laid-off minorities would be old enough to be employed at the time of the discriminatory conduct? If the work was unskilled or semiskilled—as was the situation in *Watkins*—a prerequisite for liability would appear to be recent or contemporary egregious conduct. Otherwise, the difficulties in establishing individual harm would become paramount. Such concerns should subside to some extent when dealing with cases involving skilled tradesmen or long-distance drivers—workers with relatively unusual or identifiable skills. If such minority workers were available in the relevant labor market and were deterred by a defendant's discriminatory conduct or reputation, the case would fit more adequately the liability contours adumbrated by the Fifth Circuit. The fact that such workers were hired and performed satisfactorily would make it less likely that they would benefit undeservedly and at the expense of others.

An intermediate situation exists where layoffs are triggered on a departmental- or job-seniority basis and where blacks have been hired for low-level jobs. Where there are a substantial number of blacks locked into this pattern, an appropriate remedy might be to allow such workers to defend their positions on the basis of plant-wide seniority—the same criterion used for *promotion* in the departmental-seniority cases, such as *Local 189*.

Yet, in spite of the many exceptions to the *Watkins* holdings, the opinion demonstrates that the law has limits in dealing with these issues. For where discrimination is practiced with force, the number of individuals with the courage to apply are few; and where discrimination is industry-wide (as it is in trucking and construction), the skilled workers available are scarce. Although preferential treatment, not business necessity, is the cadence to which *Watkins* marches, the fundamental judicial concern is apparently business necessity—a euphemism for money. If the district court's view of *Watkins* had been upheld, the potential liability and disruption for defendants would be substantial. The courts are not willing to impose large costs on defendants when they are least able to afford them—during an economic recession. While the federal courts are loud and clear on the proposition that the burden of discrimination is not to be placed on the shoulders of its victims, the reality is that minorities must look to the political forum for meaningful relief from unemployment.

One important qualification must be placed on this analysis because of the Court's decision in *Bowman*. The opinions of both Justice Brennan and Chief Justice Burger contemplate a front-pay remedy which provides compensation until the discriminatee attains his rightful position.[92] The remedy is expensive whether awarded to rejected applicants in *Bowman*, locked-in incumbents in *Detroit Edison*, or laid-off workers in *Watkins*. It may be that the Court did not fully appreciate the implications of such a remedy in *Bowman*. In the past, Chief Justice Burger seems to have shifted his view as the financial implications of legal standards have become clearer.[93] But the Court's willingness to shift the burden of proof to defendants when there is a "discriminatory hiring pattern" is a sign that it has left the door ajar for assessing liability in last-hired, first-fired cases under some circumstances.

When Does Discrimination Cease?

One final question applicable to all seniority cases relates to a showing about when discrimination ceases. The seniority cases are different from *Griggs* v. *Duke Power Co.*[94] and its progeny, inasmuch as the unlawful system is not permanently discontinued in the former cases. That is, the beneficiaries are those workers who either were employed while the discriminatory system was in effect or would have been employed but for the discriminatory hiring policy. As *Quarles* noted, after hiring discrimination ceases, those who are hired cannot carry with them employment seniority into other parts of the plant.[95]

But when does hiring discrimination cease? Suppose—as is often the case in large companies where the personnel office exercises limited control over the hiring practices of particular departments—one blue-collar craft or department has changed its practice and another has not. Is hiring discrimination at an end, the affected class no longer cut off from jobs? A liberal construction of the statute, in accord with its fundamental purposes, would conclude that discrimination does not stop and that the affected class is not truncated until hiring discrimination has ended in all blue-collar jobs to which, presumably, members of the affected class, locked into menial jobs, could under some circumstances advance.

Some support for this view is contained in the Supreme Court's *Keyes* decision, relating to school desegregation in Denver.[96] Only portions of the school district in Denver were segregated. Nevertheless, the Court concluded that the entire system was tainted by the segregation in part of the municipality. Accordingly, the busing remedy for those districts where intentional discrimination had been found was approved by the Court. It seems that a similar approach would apply to dis-

crimination in employment. Since such discrimination continues and employees
are unlawfully assigned to low-level jobs, the mere fact that some parts of a plant
have adopted fair hiring policies ought not to eliminate the seniority carry-over
rights of those who have been unfairly assigned despite some of the departmental
changes. In effect, this position accords with the Court's view regarding school
desegregation; all sections of a plant are tainted by the discriminatory hiring
policies of one division.

Societal Discrimination

The Supreme Court's landmark decision in *Griggs* v. *Duke Power Co.*[97] indicates that the bite of employment-discrimination law cuts more deeply than the
earlier discrimination cases have indicated. This case has implications for the entire economy—for craft, industrial, and public-employee unions, as well as for
nonunion workers. In the *Griggs* opinion, which its author, Chief Justice Burger,
has described as the high tribunal's most important holding since he has been a
member,[98] the question before the Court related to the requirement of high school
education and the passing of a standardized general intelligence test as conditions
of employment or transfer to jobs when (1) neither the education nor the test was
shown to be "significantly related" to successful performance on the job; (2) both
qualifications screened out Negroes at a "substantially" higher rate than whites;
and (3) jobs which were fenced in by the standards had been filled only by whites
in accordance with an earlier discriminatory policy. The Court held that Title VII
required "the removal of artificial, arbitrary, and unnecessary barriers to employment when the barriers operate" so as to discriminate. Chief Justice Burger wrote
for a unanimous Court: "The Act proscribes not only overt discrimination but also
practices that are fair in form but discriminatory in operation. The touchstone is
business necessity. If an employment practice which operates to exclude Negroes
cannot be shown to be related to job performance, the practice is prohibited." The
Court's decision seems to be predicated on a finding of past discrimination, as in
the seniority and nepotism cases. But the opinion's reasoning and language are
much more elaborate and have implications extending beyond those cases. The
Court said:

The objective of Congress in the enactment of Title VII is plain from the language of the
statute. It was to achieve quality of employment opportunities and remove barriers that have
operated in the past that favor an identifiable group of white employees over other employees. Under the Act, practices, procedures, or tests neutral on their face, and even neutral in terms of intent, cannot be maintained if they operate to "freeze" the status quo of
prior discriminatory employment practices."[99]

A more ambitious view of *Griggs* is buttressed by Justice Stewart's opinion in
Albermarle Paper Company v. *Moody,* where, speaking for the Court, he referred
to the statutory scheme of Title VII as a "complex legislative design directed at an
historic evil of national proportions." The Court asserted: "Title VII deals with
legal injuries of an economic character occasioned by racial or other antiminority

discrimination. The terms 'complete justice' and 'necessary relief' have acquired a clear meaning in such circumstances.''[100]

In effect, three types of cases have branched out from *Griggs*. The first relates to past discrimination and is akin to the nepotism and seniority cases, which dealt with neutral and inherently nondiscriminatory practices but with situations in which earlier practices were mirrored in contemporary neutral conduct. The second branch relates to those practices which are "fair in form, but discriminatory in operation." In many respects, this category presents the greatest potential for an expansive reading of Title VII and accordingly would appear to promise the greatest amount of litigation. The third branch relates to those practices which are "neutral on their face [and] operate to freeze the status quo."[101] A disproportionate exclusion of minorities by virtue of the practice appears not to be required (we shall put aside the question of the meaning of a disproportionate exclusion), although past discrimination which is not necessary to make out a statuatory violation in the second branch is a prerequisite of the third branch.

Characteristic of the second branch of cases is the Court's reliance on *Gaston County* v. *United States*[102] and the fact that the Court's opinion in *Griggs* cited none of the seniority or other earlier employment-discrimination cases. In *Gaston County* the defendant sought to escape the triggering mechanisms of the Voting Rights Act of 1965[103] by claiming that the small number of registered voters was not attributable to discrimination, the evil which the 1965 statute sought to eliminate, but was, rather, the result of the illiteracy of a large number of blacks. The Court noted that Negroes in North Carolina had received a segregated and inferior education and that a defense based upon illiteracy in such circumstances would simply carry on the discrimination engaged in earlier by the state school system— even though the past discrimination had been practiced by an entity separate and distinct from the voter registrars involved in the Voting Rights Act litigation. The *Griggs* Court declared: "Congress directed the thrust of the Act to the consequences of employment practices, not simply the motivation."[104] This interpretation has prompted the Court to say, in *Albermarle,* that unlawful employment practices may be engaged in, in good faith, and still incur monetary (back pay) liability for defendants as well as injunctive relief for workers. "To condition the awarding of back pay on a showing of 'bad faith' would be to open an enormous chasm between injunctive and backpay relief under Title VII. There is nothing on the face of the statute or in its legislative history that justifies the creation of drastic and categorical distinctions between these two remedies."[105]

Accordingly, this branch of *Griggs* seems to go far beyond most of the employment cases which have preceded it. It rests upon the proposition that certain practices carry with them the indicia of discrimination attributable to society in general and not—at least initially—to the particular employer or union involved in the litigation. This concept is of utmost significance, since this type of case imposes liability upon defendants for *de facto* societal as well as employment discrimination. It is also qualitatively different from the group of cases which rely upon statistics to infer discrimination.[106] For in the latter category, statistics are the means of determining how the defendant is behaving when more direct proof is difficult to obtain. *Griggs* looks outward to determine the impact of conduct which has been ascertained and inquires into the extent to which such conduct reflects societal inequities.

Griggs, insofar as it borrows *Gaston County* principles, goes far beyond the school desegregation cases, which have insisted upon a finding of *de jure,* or "intentional," discrimination by the defendant school district or state authority. In testing cases involving both public and private employers, the courts have begun to impose liability in *de facto* or "unintentional" contexts.[107]

Obviously, there are a number of fairly significant distinctions between *Gaston County* and *Griggs;* Chief Justice Burger, however, chose not to focus on any of them in his opinion. First, two areas of state government (voting and education) were involved in *Gaston County,* whereas the traditionally less closely regulated private sector (albeit a public utility) was the subject of *Griggs.* Moreover, private employers such as the defendant in *Griggs* did not have as great a legitimate opportunity as did the voting arm of the state to pressure educational institutions in the past, since discrimination in employment was not unlawful prior to 1965. (The fact that the Civil Rights Act of 1866 prohibited racial discrimination in employment before 1965 is of little consequence, since no one had the slightest inkling that this was so until 1968.)[108] By virtue of the Fifteenth Amendment, voting discrimination by a state has been unlawful for more than a hundred years. The Court in *Gaston County* did not, however, emphasize the unlawfulness of past discrimination. With regard to education, the Court specifically noted that its decision was not altered because of the fact that segregation in public education was lawful between 1896 and 1954.[109] Furthermore, the Court relied upon inequities in per capita expenditures for black and white schools—although the Court has never said that such inequities are *per se* unconstitutional and, indeed, in the later *Rodriguez* decision apparently held to the contrary.[110]

The second major difference between *Gaston County* and *Griggs* is that voting does not involve a business necessity comparable to that involved in employment. This difference is the "touchstone" in *Griggs.* Congress, in passing the Voting Rights Act of 1965, assumed that literacy tests were not a prerequisite or at least a significant prerequisite for voting; that is, voters can perform their duties because they are reasonably well informed through media other than written words and, thus, need not be literate. The same assumption cannot be made with regard to some unemployment positions and job classifications. Indeed, Congress was very careful, in enacting the 1964 employment statute, specifically to accord to employers and unions the right to use "professionally developed" tests.[111]

Third, although extending the right to vote to more blacks has the effect of diluting the voting rights of those whites (and blacks) who already have access to the franchise—an effect resembling that of the limitation of employment opportunities resulting from revision of seniority procedures—voting is less competitive than employment: there are a limited number of jobs available but a limitless number of votes to be cast. While the revision of a seniority system, for instance, may cause the postponing of the day on which a worker obtains a certain job, a given hiring or promotion system includes one worker or group of workers and excludes another worker or group. A depressed economy or a failing industry or company can exaggerate this problem of scarcity or a limited number of spaces available, particularly in situations involving layoffs. This is not so with voting. Accordingly, the tensions created by race-conscious remedies are more troublesome in the employment context. In any event, the Court in *Griggs* did not focus upon such distinctions, and references to them have not appeared in any of the cases decided under the authority of *Griggs*.

Indeed, the cases have moved far beyond the issue of testing itself. For instance, in *Gregory* v. *Litton Systems, Inc.*,[112] the Ninth Circuit held that an employer's reliance upon arrest records to determine the suitability of job applicants violates Title VII, because a black is more likely to have an arrest record than a white, and therefore such a procedure will screen out blacks disproportionately. This holding recognizes the fact that an arrest record is not always significant—particularly in light of the practice of police in many major cities of arresting for investigation. Furthermore, the Eighth Circuit Court of Appeals has extended this holding to convictions and stated that employer reliance upon convictions must generally be job-related.[113]

Perhaps the decisions in arrest-record cases such as *Litton Systems* are wrong, inasmuch as the Warren Court decisions regarding criminal procedure have the effect of making the arrest record potentially more significant, since conviction becomes more difficult. It may be desirable to move away from the notion that arrest records per se are to be excluded from consideration and toward a more commonsense approach analogous to that employed with regard to records of conviction.

This approach might include a consideration of several questions: (1) Is the arrest relevant to the work? An employer or apprenticeship committee would be permitted to make inquiries only about arrests that had some relevance. An employer that wanted to hire a guard or a night watchman for a woman's dormitory might be interested in the fact that an applicant had been arrested for rape. The fire department would want to know about an arrest for arson or for pushing people out of high buildings. If there was no demonstrable relationship between the crime for which arrest information was being sought and the nature of the work, the inquiry would not be permissible.

(2) If, preliminarily, the employer or apprenticeship committee was able to show a demonstrable relationship, the second question would be, Is the arrest itself likely to be significant? Presumably, for instance, an arrest for rape might be much more significant than, say, an arrest for murder, because rape convictions are notoriously difficult to obtain, even when the defendant is almost certainly guilty. Arrest for rape without conviction may be meaningful, especially because the embarrassment and other problems connected with a rape complaint may deter a woman from going to the police unless her case is a strong one[114]* (although,

no doubt, a certain percentage of rape complaints are groundless and are motivated by jealousy or other factors). On the other hand, an arrest but not a conviction for murder may be much less significant, inasmuch as witnesses are more likely to have a self-interest in testifying and there is no evident reason for reluctance on their part to do so.

(3) How recently has the arrest been entered on the employee's record? In the conviction cases themselves, the courts permit an employer to consider a conviction entered only within the past five years. In effect, despite the common belief that an employee is likely to be a recidivist, a time period limits the propriety of reliance on such a belief. (It may be well to limit the applicability of belief in recidivism in general, since if, for instance, one has been convicted of the murder of one's own spouse, one probably poses no danger whatsoever to the work force because of the peculiar passions that may arise in the marital relationship. The same kind of conclusion might apply to a murder that resulted from a lover's quarrel where there was no marital relationship.)

(4) What are the circumstances relating to the arrest? For instance, an employer, inquiring about an arrest, might find that it was relevant and likely to be significant within a permissible time period during which an employee might be presumed to be prone to recidivism; the employer would like to know, because of the fact that the employee made restitution, whether the arrest had not resulted in a conviction. Under such circumstances, it seems that the significance of the lack of a conviction and the presumption of innocence have little meaning indeed.

The *Griggs* progeny have not stopped with arrest records. The Eighth Circuit, in *Wallace* v. *Debron Corporation*,[115] declared unlawful an employer's rule requiring the discharge of employees who have wage garnishments. Here again, the basis for the court's holding is that socioeconomic inequities make blacks as a group more likely than whites to have their wages garnished.

Furthermore, the *Griggs* progeny may possibly have an impact on corporate relocations from the inner city to suburban areas, where a transfer affects minority-group workers more adversely than white employees. It is clear that the effect of such relocations is to exclude blacks. One distinction between this situation and other cases is that there is, arguably, a greater business necessity for the move to the suburbs—although the extent of the necessity depends upon the facts of each case. A second distinction is that a selection device is not directly at issue but, rather, a decision traditionally regarded as a management prerogative. As the cases decided under the National Labor Relations Act indicate, however,[116*] where such decisions have an impact upon employment opportunities, responsibility under protective labor statutes may be imposed, although admittedly those cases generally involve the duty to bargain and not employment discrimination as such. Moreover, the ultimate impact—and this is what gives rise to disputes—is upon employment opportunities and not upon the cause of the loss of such opportunities. A black employee is just as effectively deprived of work on a disproportionate basis as he was in the NLRB cases.

One criticism of the garnishment case is that there was no evidence that the dismissal of employees because of wage garnishments had a disproportionate impact upon blacks in the *employer's enterprise itself*. Proof of such an adverse impact presumably is significant because a fair-employment-practices statute purports to impose liability—even in the *Griggs* societal discrimination cases—upon an employer that engages in a practice that discriminates in some fashion. Thus a prerequisite is disproportionate exclusion not simply in society at large but in a particular establishment.

The requirement of proof may, however, be at odds with other requirements of the statute. In *Litton* the district court referred to the fact that the county of Los Angeles, where the employer's plant was located, had refused to rely upon arrest information in applications for employment and also to the fact that "Negroes nationally comprise some 11% of the population and account for 27% of reported arrests and 45% of arrests reported as 'suspicion arrests.' "[117] There was no reference to a disproportionate impact at the hiring gate of the particular plant. For instance, it may be impossible to show disproportionate exclusion in connection with wage garnishments or arrest records because an employer may recruit "superblacks" whose socioeconomic status may be on a par with, or superior to, that of the whites employed in the plant. If the recruitment policy of the employer, for some reason, brings in only blacks who are not representative of the labor-market population—a recruitment policy which may be unlawful because of its reliance upon word-of-mouth referrals by friends and relatives and which excludes qualified blacks—the labor market is too narrow to provide valid data for the determination of any discriminatory impact. In other words, in such situations it would be inappropriate to require a disproportionate impact on the plant, company, or union as a basis for a violation, rather than a general societal impact. Therefore, not merely a discriminatory impact is important in this connection, but also the matter of job-relatedness. After all, the selection devices, whether testing, arrest records, or whatever, must be fair and valid for both races in the appropriate labor market. If plaintiffs' cases are found to be inadequate because of a failure to prove an adverse impact on an atypical group of minority employees, potential applicants may be discriminated against because the selection device screens *them out* even though they can perform the work.

Accordingly, the recruitment policy must be fair enough to permit employees of both races who are likely to be successful workers yet have necessarily different backgrounds to have access to employment. Of course, problems arise not only because of the varying skills and educational backgrounds of workers from the same geographical area, but even more intensely if recent patterns of population migration come into play. To some extent, this issue overlaps that of the appropriate geographical area to be used as a base for determining whether the percentage of minority workers employed in a plant is really disproportionate to the number in the population as a whole.

To pose the problem in a dramatic and practical form one might ask whether *Griggs* applies to a northern plant which is recruiting employees who come directly from southern states which provide segregated, inferior educational opportunities or who reside in a community in the geographical vicinity of the plant but whose background is derived from another part of the country. One immediately recoils from the notion that the Court intended, through *Griggs,* to establish one law for the North and one for the South—even though this is exactly what has happened in regulations affecting education.[118*]

The difficulty is that the second group of cases that are offshoots of *Griggs*— cases which are not dependent upon earlier discrimination by an employer or labor union—have the effect of changing employment practices permanently. Unlike the cases dealing with past discrimination, there is not an affected class that has been harmed in a specific and identifiable way, that can reap the benefits of a transitional remedy (for example, the provision of seniority credits for transferees) after which the employer can return to the previous practice. *Griggs* itself involves inherently discriminatory practices: the use of examination and edicational requirements which, because of the plight of blacks in the country, would in a large number of instances mirror societal inequities. The lawfulness of a practice changes at the time society changes.

It is this assumption which argues for expanding the labor market net into the widest geographical area. *Griggs* is a national case. Yet the case is troubling, because of the assumption that the employer is ultimately permitted to return to the original practice if the underlying inequity can be eliminated. Since fair-employment-practice legislation is in some way related to the employers' behavior, presumably the defendant may be able to pressure or lobby for institutional changes which contribute to the inequities. The further an educational institution—to take an example— is from a plant, presumably the more difficult it would be for the institution to feel the wrath of an employer or labor union. This then is one of the strains inherent in legislation aimed at controlling the conduct of private parties and at fashioning appropriate remedies—yet which is focused upon the nation's socioeconomic ailments, simultaneously attempting a cure for them as well. We return to the subject in discussing remedies—particularly goals and timetables or quotas.

5 | Remedies (I): Quotas, Ratios, Goals, and Timetables

The basis for affirmative action is to be found in the remedial provisions of Title VII of the Civil Rights Act of 1964. Once a violation is found by the court under that statute, in addition to enjoining the conduct involved, the court "may . . . order such affirmative action as may be appropriate."[1] Under the 1972 amendment to the statute, more than an affirmative action obligation is thrust upon defendants who are liable—i.e., the court may order "any other equitable relief as the court deems appropriate."[2] It is interesting that Congress, when debating the 1972 amendments to Title VII, specifically rejected amendments which would have nullified pre-1972 judicial decrees requiring quotas.[3] Accordingly, whatever the debate about the authority of the district courts before 1972, Congress seems to have cleared up the matter by ratifying such decisions—a fact to which the Sixth Circuit Court of Appeals has specifically alluded.[4]*

Before examining the rationale for, and problems with existing judicial authority, it is important to note that in the President's executive order, there is an affirmative-action provision as well.[5] Ever since the Kennedy administration's revision of the executive order in 1961, this obligation has been imposed upon contractors regardless of whether discrimination had been engaged in by a particular defendant. The failure of a contractor to undertake affirmative action is itself a violation of the executive order.

Furthermore, even where neither the statute nor the executive order applies, the courts have the authority, in dealing with employment (as in other civil rights litigation) to exercise equitable discretion in fashioning relief by providing a remedy enjoining unconstitutional behavior. Indeed, the Court, in its landmark decision in *Louisiana* v. *United States,* has said: "We bear in mind that the court has not merely the power but the duty to render a decree which will so far as possible eliminate the discriminatory effects of the past as well as bar like discrimination in the future.[6]

Remedies fashioned by the courts are concerned with both past and future behavior, and the debate about quotas or goals and timetables as appropriate affirmative-action relief is inevitably linked to both. Without evidence of behavior which has either unlawfully excluded blacks or other minorities in the past or a practice which continues an exclusionary bias against minorities insofar as recruitment or advancement in the future is concerned, there is no basis for any relief in terms of quotas or goals.

If an employer or union engages in a practice which makes it unlikely or impossible for minorities to obtain employment in the future, the effects of past discrimination will probably be carried beyond the date of a decree which merely parrots the prohibition contained in a statute and permits the defendants to engage in their normal conduct without more than a "slap on the wrist." For instance, if a labor union has excluded blacks in the past, the retention of a requirement that sons of members receive preference for union admission may be enjoined.[7] The same holds true where the rule involved simply states that no new members can be admitted—although some courts may require proof that the practice, in fact, excluded blacks before issuing an injunction. The attempt of the judiciary here is to create a method similar or identical to the recruitment process that might have been in effect if the system was not discriminatory. The goal is to eliminate the artificial barriers which skew the employment process in favor of whites and against minorities.[8]*

To ensure that discrimination against minority workers does not persist, a more effective means of achieving the goal of nondiscrimination may be to fashion affirmative relief which, in addition to requiring advertising and notice of job opportunities to the minority community, contains an order establishing numbers, ratios, or goals. This may be the only way the statute can be made a reality for blacks and other minorities throughout the country. There are three principal reasons for this assumption. The first is that publicity coupled with the examination of previous barriers does not appear to have integrated the nation's work force.[9]* One of the major reasons for this is obvious. Where defendants engaged in significant discrimination before the decree, blacks may be deterred from applying because of the discriminatory reputation of the union or employer in the black community.[10] In addition to potential applicants who are discouraged as a result of their own experience or the experience of others in the community, or who are unable to apply for other reasons, many workers may not be aware of existing opportunities. The most pervasive campaign of publicity may not overcome any of these problems.

The second reason empirically demonstrates the first. The early prequota Title VII decrees have not been nearly as successful in promoting minority employment as those which contained quotas. Some of the most complicated and lengthy trials have culminated in decrees which have not produced minority referrals, employment, or union membership. The classic example is the St. Louis building trades litigation.[11] All the evidence indicates that the best results have been obtained where quotas or goals have been part of the relief. This explains the fact that since 1971 the Justice Department, and now EEOC under its new authority provided by the 1972 amendments, have requested quotas with increasing frequency.

Third, the experience with practices and litigation following *Brown* v. *Board of Education*[12] is instructive because the lack of specificity in the decree invited evasion. Like the uncertainty which early Title VII remedies demonstrated, there was much confusion on the part of the federal district courts regarding what

Brown required and, indeed, what its ultimate objective was. It was understood that, as a minimum, *Brown,* like Title VII, required passive nondiscriminatory practices instead of government-sanctioned segregation. About what else was required debate ensued, and defendants in both instances construed their obligations narrowly. Encouraged by the "with all deliberate speed" formula, defendant school boards took advantage of delay either to do nothing in the hope that litigation would not be commenced or, where the threat of resort to the judiciary was present, to engage in evasionary tactics such as pupil-placement laws. The result was the same as in the early Title VII litigation: the doors which had excluded blacks were formally opened. Yet nothing actually happened to promote the integration of education, just as very little happened in the early days of Title VII. Tokenism, at best, became the order of the day.

The pattern, therefore, became one of formal compliance with nondiscrimination regulations yet of the continuation of tenacious resistance by those who had discriminated in the past. Eventually the Court became impatient with this reality in dealing with the post-*Brown* desegregation cases; the first expression of this reaction was in Justice Arthur Goldberg's opinion in *Watson* v. *City of Memphis,* [13] involving the desegregation of a public park. Said Justice Goldberg:

Since the city has completely failed to demonstrate any compelling or convincing reason requiring further delay in implementing the constitutional proscription of segregation of publicly owned or operated recreational facilities, there is no cause whatsoever to depart from the generally operative and here clearly controlling principle that constitutional rights are to be promptly vindicated. The continued denial to petitioners of the use of city facilities solely because of their race is without warrant. Under the facts in this case, the District Court's undoubted discretion in the fashioning and timing of equitable relief was not called into play; rather, affirmative judicial action was required to vindicate plain and present constitutional rights. Today, no less than fifty years ago, the solution to the problems growing out of race relations "cannot be promoted by depriving citizens of their constitutional rights and privileges." [14]

This assertion was translated into the formula articulated by the Court in 1968, in *Green* v. *New Kent County School Board,* that segregation be "eliminated root and branch" and that it be achieved *"now."* [15] The Court, in *Swann* v. *Charlotte-Mecklenburg Board of Education,* [16] concluded that racial ratios were to be sanctioned in connection with the desegregation of public school systems. Chief Justice Burger said, in *Swann,* that while racial ratios were not mandated in all school-desegregation litigation, they could be regarded as an appropriate remedy in certain circumstances. [17]

With the lesson of *Brown* in mind, the federal courts began to move toward a more precise definition of the affirmative-action provisions of Title VII in a much shorter period of time. Moreover, during the summer of 1969, Assistant Secretary of Labor Arthur Fletcher enunciated the Philadelphia Plan, which, for the first time, provided for goals and timetables in connection with minority recruitment in the Philadelphia building trades under the executive order. [18] This pronouncement was challenged, and the challenge rejected, in *Contractors Association* v. *Schultz.* [19] The court upheld the plan as a valid exercise of executive power to impose conditions incident to contract, noting that it was "simply a refined approach" to the affirmative-action mandate of the executive order.[20]

On the issue of whether the goals and timetables set forth in the Philadelphia Plan constituted "racial quotas" prohibited by the equal-protection provisions of the Fifth Amendment, Judge John Gibbons, writing for a unanimous bench, simply stated without further rationale that the plan was a "valid Executive action designed to remedy the perceived evil that minority tradesmen have not been included in the labor pool available for the performance of construction projects in which the federal government has a cost and performance interest. The Fifth Amendment does not prohibit such action."[21]

Noting that the executive order did not require a finding of past discrimination and that, indeed, no such judicial finding had been made in the present case, the court, nevertheless, stated that the President, under the executive order, could remedy the "underrepresentation" of minorities in the construction trades in Philadelphia. Notwithstanding the absence of a need for such a finding, the court did cite the findings of the Department of Labor which characterized the problems as involving "obvious underrepresentation . . . due to the exclusionary practices of the unions representing the six trades."[22] In response to the argument that Title VII pre-empted the field of employment discrimination, the court held that the statute was not a limitation upon remedies which existed under the executive order.[23]

Plaintiffs had also argued that the plan required them to violate Section 703(a) of Title VII itself, which prohibits discriminatory hiring. The court responded:

To read §703(a) in the manner suggested by the plaintiffs we would have to attribute to Congress the intention to freeze the status quo and to foreclose remedial action under other authority designed to overcome existing evils. We discern no such intention either from the language of the statute or from its legislative history. Clearly the Philadelphia Plan is color-conscious. Indeed, the only meaning which can be attributed to the "affirmative action" language which since March of 1961 has been included in successive Executive Orders is that Government contractors must be color-conscious. . . . In other contexts, color-consciousness has been deemed to be an appropriate remedial posture.[24]

Shortly thereafter, the first and most prominent of a number of Title VII cases was filed: *Carter* v. *Gallagher*,[25] which resulted in a series of decisions by the Eighth Circuit Court of Appeals. Actually, *Carter* involved the equal-protection clause of the Fourteenth Amendment and the Civil Rights Act of 1866 rather than Title VII, inasmuch as it was decided prior to the 1972 amendments which made that statute applicable to state and local governments. However, as did all the courts confronted with the problem before the Supreme Court decision in *Washington* v. *Davis* (426 U.S. 229 [1976]), the Eighth Circuit assumed the applicability of EEOC guidelines under Title VII in determining that the tests were unlawful. Undoubtedly, considerations applicable under the Fourteenth Amendment apply with equal vigor to the antipreferential-treatment provisions of Title VII as well as to its broad prohibitions against discrimination on account of race.

In *Carter,* the federal district court found that the Minneapolis Fire Department had unlawfully excluded racial minorities on account of their race. The evidence indicated that of 535 employees in the fire department, none were black, Indian, or Mexican-American. Only two blacks had served in the fire department in the recent past. Blacks constituted 6.44 percent of the Minneapolis population in 1970. The court, relying in part on the prima facie evidence of the statistics, found that the hiring procedures of the department excluded applicants on the basis of race. Accordingly, the court ordered that an "eligibility list" of blacks, American Indians, and Spanish-surnamed applicants be established. The most important portion of the court's order provided for the "absolute preference" hiring of twenty minority members who would qualify on the basis of a validated civil service examination. In its first decision, *Carter I,* the Eighth Circuit rejected this part of the order. The court noted that the city charter and civil service provisions provide for preference for the fire-fighter applicant having the "highest rating." Judge Martin Van Oosterhaut, speaking for a unanimous bench said that this provision was inappropriate:

Under the [district] court's minority preference provision, a White person who, in a subsequently conducted examination fairly conducted and free of racial discrimination, obtains a higher rating than a minority person is denied employment solely because he is a White man. The fact that some unnamed and unknown White person in the distant past may, by reason of past racial discrimination in which the present applicant in no way participated, have received preference over some unidentified minority person with higher qualifications is no justification for discriminating against the present better qualified applicant upon the basis of race.[26]

The court distinguished *Carter* from the Fifth Circuit's *Vogler* decision, which two years earlier had approved an order requiring that one minority member be referred by the union for every white person, stating that the relief there had been granted to "specific persons who are wrongly denied membership."[27] Hedging against an attack on this distinction, however, the court noted that the issue of "reverse discrimination" had not been raised or considered by the Fifth Circuit. In *Carter,* there was no contention that the plaintiffs constituted an identifiable class who had made prior applications and been denied the job because of race. This reversal of the district court was itself altered as the result of the decision by the court *en banc.*

In *Carter II,* the court, this time with Judge Floyd Gibson speaking for the majority, concluded that some preferential relief was appropriate. Yet, at the beginning of the opinion, the court stated that "the absolute preference of 20 minority persons who qualify has gone further than any of the reported appellate cases in granting preference to overcome the effects of past discriminatory practices and does appear to violate the constitutional right of Equal Protection of the Law to white persons who are superiorly qualified."[28] The court reiterated the panel's reference in *Carter I* to the fact that there was no claim or showing that plaintiffs were "identifiable members of the class" who had made prior applications and were discriminated against because of race. Noting that the district courts have great power as courts of equity to fashion relief in enforcing both statutory and

constitutional guarantees of racial equality, the court cited preferences granted by
both the Ninth Circuit and the Fifth Circuit and a district court of North Carolina.[29] The court was troubled in *Carter,* however, by the "absolute" nature of
the preference. Something less than this absolute preference, phrased in terms of
numbers, was appropriate, in the court's view. The court pointedly referred to the
fact that none of the cases providing for numbers had established "absolute" preferences:

The absolute preference ordered by the trial court would operate as a present infringement
on those non-minority group persons who are equally or superiorly qualified for the fire
fighter's positions; and we hesitate to advocate implementation of one constitutional guarantee by the outright denial of another. Yet we acknowledge the legitimacy of erasing the effects of past racially discriminatory practices. . . . To accommodate these conflicting considerations, we think some reasonable ratio for hiring minority persons who can quality
under the revised qualification standards is in order for a limited period of time, or until
there is a fair approximation of minority representation consistent with the population mix
in the area. Such a procedure does not constitute a "quota" system because as soon as the
trial court's order is fully implemented, all hirings will be on a racially nondiscriminatory
basis, and it could well be that many more minority persons or less, as compared to the
population at large, over a long period of time would apply and qualify for the positions.
However, as a method of presently eliminating the effects of past racial discriminatory
practices and in making meaningful in the immediate future the constitutional guarantees
against racial discrimination, more than a token representation should be afforded. For
these reasons, we believe the trial court is possessed of the authority to order the hiring of
20 qualified minority persons, but this should be done without denying the constitutional
rights of others by granting an absolute preference.
   Ideas and views on ratios and procedures may vary widely but this issue should be
resolved as soon as possible. In considering the equities of the decree and the difficulties
that may be encountered in procuring qualified applicants from any of the racial groups, we
feel that it would be in order for the district court to mandate that one out of every three
persons hired by the Fire Department would be a minority individual who qualified until at
least 20 minority persons have been so hired.[30]

Judge Van Oosterhaut, the author of *Carter I,* dissented from the modification
of that decision. His dissenting opinion emphasized that the discrimination against
qualified white applicants had been in no way remedied by a 1 to 3 ratio rather
than an absolute preference for twenty individuals. The opinion also attacked the
majority's reliance upon the Court's *Swann* decision as authority for the use of
mathematical ratios, by noting that the constitutional rights of others were not
being limited or interfered with in the school-desegregation litigation.[31]

A month later, Judge Frank Johnson of Alabama in an important decision,
NAACP v. *Allen,*[32] ordered a ratio quota in litigation against the Alabama Department of Public Safety both for troopers and supporting personnel. The court noted
that there had never been a black trooper and that blacks were employed only in
the capacity of nonmerit system laborers. Said Judge Johnson, "This unexplained
and unexplainable discriminatory conduct by state officials is unquestionably a
violation of the Fourteenth Amendment."[33]

Because the job analysis and validation of state-trooper jobs would have taken
four or five years, since there were no black troopers who could provide a basis

for separate racial validation, and in light of the estimate of the cost of the validation, which was at least forty thousand dollars, the court concluded that a study of
this kind would be an "undue" burden. Judge Johnson ordered, however, that one
Negro be hired for each white until approximately 25 percent of both troopers and
supporting personnel was black. Interestingly, the court characterized the defendant's racial discrimination as a "blatant and continuous pattern and practice of
discrimination in hiring."

On appeal, the Fifth Circuit affirmed.[34] In so doing, the court undertook a constitutional analysis of the quota issue. In the first place, the court said, white employees could not constitutionally challenge a denial of public employment if the
selection procedures were unvalidated and if blacks were disqualified by them at a
higher rate than whites. In the absence of proper validation, the court concluded,
it would be illogical to argue that hiring on the basis of quotas produces unconstitutional "reverse" discrimination, a lowering of employment standards, or the appointment of less qualified or unqualified persons.[35] Emphasizing the propriety of
temporary relief which is color-conscious, the court held that racial classifications
for the purpose of establishing quotas were not per se unconstitutional but, rather,
an appropriate remedy for past discrimination:

> In the absence of an invidious purpose, a determination of unconstitutionality here would be
> clearly unwarranted. Even assuming for the purposes of argument, that action of a state of-
> ficial taken pursuant to a compulsory federal judicial order constitutes state action, the affir-
> mative hiring relief instituted *sub judice* fails to transgress either the letter or the spirit of
> the Fourteenth Amendment. Presuming further, that the federal chancellor's discretion
> should be subjected to the stringent compelling governmental interest test, the decree passes
> constitutional muster. No one is denied any right conferred by the Constitution. It is the
> collective interest, governmental as well as social, in effectively ending unconstitutional
> racial discrimination that justifies temporary, carefully circumscribed resort to racial cri-
> teria, whenever the chancellor determines that it represents the only rational nonarbitrary
> means of eradicating past evils.[36]

In *Morrow I,*[37] a majority of the Fifth Circuit approved a district-court order
based on a record quite similar to *Allen* but involving the Mississippi Highway Patrol (which, like the Alabama patrol, had never employed a black trooper). The
district court had simply enjoined racial discrimination as well as the use of a standardized intelligence test, precluded the practice of imposing requirements more
stringent than those that had been applied in the past five years, prohibited preference to applicants who had relatives employed in a department, and required an
affirmative recruiting program oriented toward the black population. The district
court, however, had specifically denied the individual plaintiff requested relief
relating to hiring, training, back pay, and more important, a minority-preference
or racial-quota system which would increase the percentage of black officers
employed by the state. On appeal, the state of Mississippi argued that "quota-
based relief would exceed the needs made out by the statistics in this case and
would constitute an unconstitutional preference."[38] But the Fifth Circuit side-
stepped the issue, finding no evidence that the recruiting measures ordered by the
court would not be sufficient to ensure the hiring of qualified minority employees

and no evidence to indicate that present qualifications needed to be changed in order to attain the same objective and, consequently, found that the district court's discretion had not been abused. The majority said:

Time may prove that the District Court was wrong, i.e., that the relief ordered was not sufficient to achieve a nondiscriminatory system and eliminate the effects of past discrimination. But until the affirmative relief the District Court has ordered has been given a chance to work, we cannot tell. There is no way that this Court can determine that the relief the Court ordered will not achieve the remedy to which the plaintiffs are entitled.

. . . The Court has retained jurisdiction to make the decree work. If it has ordered too much, it may modify the decree when it appears necessary. If it has not ordered enough, it may change the decree to require such additional relief as it determines to be necessary to remedy the wrong. There are no experts in the solution of problems created by racial prejudice.[39]

Judge Irving Goldberg, in his concurring and dissenting opinion, vigorously protested this portion of the majority opinion. The dissent noted that as a result of affirmative-hiring relief blacks would not be "forever . . . favored" over white applicants.[40] What was involved was temporary transitional relief. Referring to *Carter,* Judge Goldberg stated: "it is instructive to note that . . . the Blacks constituted a considerably smaller percentage of the general population (approximately 4%) and that the stigma of discrimination that emanated from the Minneapolis Fire Department did not approach the level of all-white legacy of the Mississippi Highway Patrol. Nonetheless, a majority of that Circuit recognized the appropriateness of ordering affirmative hiring relief."[41]

Characterizing the majority's affirmance of the denial of affirmative relief as an "unfortunate step backward in the fight for racial equality," Judge Goldberg referred to the "blatant statistical evidence and the long undeviating policy of discrimination" which, combined with the "public character" of the Highway Patrol, created a greater need for significant affirmative action than had been apparent in some of the earlier cases. In rebutting the majority's reliance on the Supreme Court decisions stating that the matter of relief was within the court's equitable discretion, Judge Goldberg noted that the district courts in those decisions had ordered "broad affirmative relief."[42] He also asserted that experience in racial-discrimination cases indicates that "the nature of the remedy is often the only relevant substantive issue at stake, and to permit broad notions of 'discretion' to supplant our duty to insure effective relief is an unfortunate abdication."[43] The dissenting opinion commented that no specific obligation was being imposed upon defendants. None of the traditional choices were presented: temporary one-to-one hiring, the introduction of priority-hiring pools, or a freeze on white hiring until the work force was effectively integrated.

In *Morrow II,*[44] the Fifth Circuit, persuaded by Judge Goldberg's dissent, reversed itself *en banc.* Pointing out the "limited role" of an appellate court in fashioning decrees, the court nevertheless remanded, with instructions to the district court to devise a decree which would have the "certain result of increasing the number of blacks on the Highway Patrol."[45] Left available to the district court were a number of options: "*temporary* one-to-one or one-to-two hiring, the creation of hiring pools, or a freeze on white hiring, or any other form of affirmative hiring relief until the Patrol is effectively integrated.''[46]

Fundamental to an understanding of the unusual step taken by the Fifth Circuit in *Morrow II* is an analysis of the rationale for the quota remedy and its relationship to the remedial philosophy of employment-discrimination legislation. Two principal themes run through the court decisions—and they are tied to Title VII law as enunciated by the courts. The first is that a quota is an attempt to compensate for the past and to remedy the wrongs done to blacks who were the actual victims of discrimination. In this regard, the remedy is an admission that many such workers cannot be found or encouraged to come forward to press their claims. Since the discriminatees are unidentifiable, the remedy must be based on race. Practically, it may be the sons of the fathers harmed by the practice occasioning the remedy who will benefit.

Inasmuch as the past provides an unsatisfactory rationale for devising a remedy, because it raises the specter of a preferential windfall for undeserving blacks at the expense of whites who were not responsible for discrimination, one must realize that the quota remedy looks to the future as well. Thus, a second theme is evident in the court decisions. The judicial remedy achieves three goals—although none of them can be completely separated from the past. First, the quota makes it less likely that defendants will discriminate in the future. Although many of the public-employment cases do not contain this ingredient, judicial inquiry will focus on the question of whether a defendant's conduct has been egregious. This was a factor in the Fifth Circuit's reasoning in both *Morrow II*[47] and *NAACP* v. *Allen.*[48] Quite often the court will be persuaded by the fact that a defendant has engaged in numerous or serious violations of the statute. As the Second Circuit noted in *Rios* v. *Enterprise Ass'n. Steamfitters Local 638,* "A pattern of long-continued and egregious racial discrimination which permeated" the industry justifies the quota remedy.[49]* Overt or deliberate discrimination is preferred—as is the case in judicial determinations of whether a punitive-damage remedy is appropriate under certain extreme circumstances. Here exasperation and distrust are the judicial responses to a defendant's conduct. The concept is that the remedy is necessary to deal with a civil law recidivist.

A second factor straddles both the past and the future. In *Morrow,* Judge Walter Gewin noted that the defendant's discriminatory reputation was "entrenched in the minds of blacks" and that it could not be "purged" without affirmative-hiring relief.[50] To the extent that this relief reaches out to young minority individuals who were not themselves victimized in the past, the concern is with the future. To the extent that it benefits those who were available for work in the past, the remedy applies to that time. Judge Keith's decree in *Detroit Edison*—because it attempted to compensate for past injustice with provisions for back pay and seniority as well as the hiring for a job of those blacks who had been deterred—was designed to benefit those who were actually available in the labor market during the relevant period of time, the time the defendant was discriminating.[51] In order to fashion such a remedy, one must be precise about identifying the employee, and the employer must have a monopoly or quasi monopoly on the utilization of the skills involved. In addition to those affected by the *Detroit Edison* and construction-industry cases, individuals who can be identified with precision as past victims are incumbent promotable employees with employment seniority. In other situations, the quota remedy assists those who may have been deterred but could not have been hurt and thus addresses the future alone. In both types of situation, however, a refusal to impose a race-conscious remedy because of uncertainty about whether an individual was a victim of discriminatory practices or of an employer's reputation benefits the wrongdoer who is responsible for the fact that the injury and identity of the individual cannot be determined with precision. As Judge Mansfield noted in *Rios* v. *Enterprise Ass'n. Steamfitters Local 638:* ''Any attempt to reconstruct what would have happened in the absence of discrimination is fraught with considerable difficulty. But the court is called upon to do the best it can with the data available to it.''[52]

The court may therefore regard the matching-up process as both futile and irrelevant—particularly if semiskilled and unskilled workers are involved. The problem comes into focus more clearly in seniority cases such as *Watkins* v. *Steel Workers Local 2369,* in which the ''last-hired, first-fired'' practice utilizing seniority in the context of past discrimination and a prior discriminatory reputation was held by the district court to be unlawful. The Fifth Circuit reversed, but Judge Cassibry's statements at the trial level remain instructive—even if not regarding the peculiar facts of *Watkins* itself:

> Here, blacks were simply not hired, and as a result, the victims of the original discrimination cannot be identified. On the basis of this distinction, the defendants argue that the segregated plant cases (Local 189, Quarles, etc.) do not provide authority sought by Movants here.
>
> But Title VII orders are not entered to right past wrongs or to compensate victims of pre-Act discrimination for their pre-Act injury. The orders in all of the cases involving seniority or referral rules are intended to prevent *present* discrimination. For example, in the segregated plant cases, relief was not entered to make whole the blacks who had been segregated before the passage of Title VII. Rather, it was designed to insure that, because there had been job segregation before the Act, blacks would not, for the next generation, continue to work in lower paying jobs than later-hired whites. Similarly, in this case, the relief ordered by the Court will not be designed to compensate the blacks who were not hired by the Company between 1945 and 1965. It will be designed to insure that, because the Company hired no blacks for twenty years, the plant will not operate without black employees for the next decade. The beneficiaries of the order will be the blacks who will now work at the Harvey plant, but who would have otherwise been excluded because of the structure built upon the prior discrimination.[53]

In *Watkins,* the remedy suggested involves racially proportioned layoffs with recall rights apportioned between separate racial pools, and thus some interference with existing incumbent white employees. Its reversal might have been anticipated by those familiar with the Fifth Circuit's ruling in *Bing* v. *Roadway Express, Inc.*[54] Judge Homer Thornberry, speaking for the court in a case in which incumbent employees sought seniority rights in over-the-road driving jobs from which they had been previously excluded, permitted such employees to figure seniority in competing with white drivers only from the "qualification date"—the time when they could have qualified for the jobs under the company's work-experience requirements subsequent to the date of employment.[55] That is, if the company required two years' work experience and the minority employee did not have it when he was hired, seniority could not be dated back to the time of hiring but, rather, to a date two years later. *Bing* is distinguished as a case in which peculiar skills are a prerequisite for employment in a relatively high-level job: the long-distance driver needs to possess a Class 1 license and may need some type of work experience. Yet it appears that *Bing* was wrongly decided under the authority of both *Watkins* and *Local 189*. The decision seems justified only when one recognizes the qualification date as a means of providing very rough and arbitrary estimate of time lost, and thus a formula which submerges emphasis upon the past.

While the district court in *Watkins* expressed solicitude about the granting of quotas in connection with entry-level jobs and, simultaneously, a concern about the unfulfilled expectations of white incumbents who compete for high-level jobs,[56] in fact, under *Local 189,* aside from the possibility of actually displacing a white worker, human-relations considerations do not constitute business necessity. Furthermore, the focus upon skills and the possible adverse effect on company profit, as well as safety considerations, relate to skills workers currently possess. As *Local 189* and its progeny candidly admit, there is much uncertainty about whether the minority employee would have actually progressed in the past. That uncertainty is resolved when one determines what his qualifications are today. The primary focus is upon the present effects of past discrimination. If the minority long-distance driver in *Bing* is able to perform today, it would seem that the reasoning of the district court in *Watkins* (which contemplates the actual displacement of white incumbents in a layoff and thus frankly acknowledges that avoiding such a result does not constitute business necessity) justifies employment seniority for those who have been discriminated against previously.

Moreover, while it is true that entry-level jobs are not involved in *Bing,* and that *Watkins* deals with unskilled and thus unidentifiable employees, actually the quantum of the jump from unskilled to skilled in *Bing* is not very great. In such cases, the courts should keep their eyes very carefully trained on circumstances under which whites come into a trade or job. That is why the Fifth Circuit, in *Franks* v. *Bowman Transportation Co.,*[57] was able to distinguish bidding and to provide company seniority for blacks who had been excluded from over-the-road jobs, because the evidence showed that the company had applied no rigid one-year experience requirement in the past. In part, this explains the willingness of the courts to fashion quota remedies in the construction industry for unidentifiable workers who have been excluded in the past and who are guaranteed dispatch according to quotas and referral from the union hall under the authority of the Fifth and Ninth Circuits' decisions in *Vogler* and *Local 86.*[58] The theme of the district court in *Watkins* and of the construction-industry cases is that quotas had to be fashioned even for situations in which white workers' employment opportunities are diminished—and they are diminished more substantially than when limitations are placed upon bidding for future job opportunities in industrial-union cases such as *Local 189* and *Quarles*. All the cases, both those involving industrial- and craft-union allocation of employment opportunities in connection with entry- and higher-level jobs and those relating to new hires of blacks and whites, are concerned about the delicate balance that must be struck between black and white employment interests. Even in *Carter,* where the interests of no incumbent white employees were involved and both races were outsiders, the court was careful to revise the district court's order so that white employees were not excluded *in toto* for a substantial period of time, thus providing the potential for the hiring of unqualified blacks. In the Fifth Circuit's *Jacksonville Terminal* decision[59] and the Seventh Circuit's *Waters II* holding[60] (which concludes that the last-hired, first-fired practice cannot be characterized as discriminatory per se[61]) more experienced whites extinguished the claims of newly arrived blacks to any seniority right whatsoever. The gist of both Judge Cassibry's opinion in *Watkins* and the construction cases makes the refusal to recognize black fictional seniority in *Jacksonville Terminal* and *Waters II* even more indefensible than in *Bing*—at least to the extent that the failure to recognize seniority is tantamount to continued unemployment for the previously excluded group and the gap between the inexperienced or unskilled new applicants and the incumbents is not wide.

In cases such as *Bing* which insist on qualification-date rather than employment-date seniority, as well as cases which reject quotas for jobs above the entry level, the same argument emerges *sub silentio* that courts discarded in the early job-seniority cases: that white employees will not stand for preferential treatment for blacks, and that human relations will, therefore, suffer. John Kaplan, makes this point: "It is clear that any attempt to secure preferential treatment for Negroes in the employment area will be extremely divisive. In addition to [other minority groups], whose economic well-being is not perceptibly better than the Negro's, those most affected by any job preference for the Negro would be the second generation Americans and the poor whites who have most bitterly resented his march toward equality."[62]

The prophecy is surely an accurate one, and it may argue for a form of a remedy which, at least where the employer is the primary offending party, places the burden upon management rather than on the white worker. President Nixon was able to win a resounding victory in 1972 by rallying those who were a rung above the black worker and by appealing to their belief that blacks were attempting to get something for nothing and to destroy the individual work ethic. Affirmative action makes many white workers angry. Blacks, of course, have been angry for years. It is not their feelings, however, with which Kaplan is concerned in his writings. Chief Justice Warren rejected the same kinds of arguments in *Brown II*. Judge Wilfred Feinberg specifically noted in *United States* v. *Bethlehem Steel Corporation* that the dissatisfaction of white workers was not a basis for a different result, and the Supreme Court has stated the same proposition in *Franks* v. *Bowman Transportation Co.*[63] As Judge Feinberg has stated, "If relief under Title VII can be denied merely because the majority group of employees, who have not suffered discrimination, will be unhappy about it, there will be little hope of correcting the wrongs to which the act is directed."[64] Kaplan's view has proved attractive to the courts in above-entry-level quota cases, however. Judge William Mulligan spoke for the Second Circuit in *Bridgeport Guardians, Inc.* v. *Bridgeport Civil Service Commission* while approving a district court's granting of quotas for applicants to the police department:

We are constrained however to find that the imposition of quotas above the rank of patrolman constitutes an abuse of discretion and is clearly erroneous. Initially, we observed that there has been no finding that the promotion examination is not jobdrelated. While past exclusionary hiring examinations do justify the quota remedy on entrance, there is no justification in our view for extending the remedy to higher ranks. We are discussing some 117 positions with time-in-grade requirements mandating three years' service as patrolman, sergeant, and lieutenant postponing promotion to captain for a minimum of nine years. While this factor will delay those of the minority groups who will become patrolmen, the imposition of quotas will obviously discriminate against those Whites who have embarked upon a police career with the expectation of advancement only to be now thwarted because of their color alone. The impact of a quota upon these men would be harsh and can only exacerbate rather than diminish racial attitudes.[65]

Similarly, Judge Edward Weinfeld, in *Vulcan Society* v. *Civil Service Commission*,[66] citing Kaplan as his authority, rejected long-term quotas because of white dissatisfaction with them: "Adjustments based upon racial classification, however well-intentioned, contain within themselves the seed of further divisiveness, regardless of their benevolent purpose. Attempts to make fair adjustments may be counterproductive and tend to generate resentments which serve to exacerbate rather than to diminish racial attitudes."[67]

Another factor involved in quota remedies, and one that is particularly relevant to public-employment litigation, relates to unvalidated selection procedures. Where discrimination has been engaged in the past—again, the same distrust is evident—quotas may be a temporary substitute for procedures which have been struck down. In some situations, courts such as the district court in *NAACP* v. *Allen* may even be unwilling to require validation because of the great expense involved.[68]

The dilemma is that both objective and subjective criteria for employment are suspect—especially once discrimination is evidenced in the record. Subjective criteria are likely to provide the best opportunity for employers or unions to allow their prejudices to influence the selection process—particularly where there was discrimination in the past and an all white or predominantly white reviewing board. This is the lesson of the Fifth Circuit's ruling in *Rowe* v. *General Motors Corporation*.[69] The court condemned unexplained racial statistics which indicated an exclusionary pattern and which were the product of subjective considerations. Closely tied to considerations underlying *Rowe* are both the lack of personal and social association between races in this country and the substantial difficulties involved in choosing between two or more applicants for positions in a variety of jobs, from janitor to university professor. Proponents of the "merit" system do not understand how difficult it is to ascertain merit where selection procedures are not validated. Kaplan, for instance, contends that employment applicants are rarely, if ever, relatively equal and that, therefore, a color-conscious choice by the selector will often result in the selection of an unqualified or an underqualified minority candidate. Kaplan phrases his contention thus:

In theory, less rigid than the quota would be the simple requirement that the fact that a job applicant is a Negro should be weighed somehow in his favor. This view can mean merely that where two applicants, white and Negro, are equal in terms of ability to perform the job, the Negro should be selected. Unfortunately, however, such a formulation has many disadvantages. Especially if the suitability for later promotion may be considered, the number of relevant qualities in which men may differ is so large that, in real life employment situations, equality of job applicants is relatively rare. Moreover, preference for the Negro, if it is to be more than marginally effective, must be considerably greater than this.[70]

Actually, the exact opposite is true. That is, most employee-selection situations present choices between candidates who are relatively equal in qualifications. Even Kaplan would have to concede that this is the lesson of unionized industries, most of which have adopted objective criteria, contained in seniority clauses, in their collective bargaining agreements in order to avoid this dilemma. These provisions demonstrate recognition by both labor and management that many promotion decisions involve facts about which reasonable men can disagree—and very often a dispute goes to an impartial arbitrator who must resolve the differences between the parties. All of this is also present in connection with problems related to racial and national-origin discrimination. The heart of the matter is that unions and employers have protected themselves against a continuous round of disputes through such provisions—and thus have proceeded on an assumption which completely contradicts Kaplan's thesis.

Even where seniority clauses are included in collective bargaining agreements, qualifications are a factor and disputes arise about whether an employee is qualified on a regular basis. The problem is that where subjective criteria are utilized, too often the applicant is found ''acceptable'' through consideration of personality and background which may mirror those of the interviewer or management officials who have the authority to make the decision. The lack of a definite criterion for deciding increases the scope and opportunity for racial prejudice. The other side of the coin is that many objective employment criteria are likely to be discriminatory as well. In the analysis of both *Local 189* and *Watkins,* one can see that seniority provisions may be discriminatory whether minorities have been locked into segregated jobs or excluded from the enterprise altogether. In *Local 86, Ironworkers,*[71] the refusal to improve the special program for jobs by ensuring that minorities receive all the classroom and on-the-job-training preparation that is provided to whites made it virtually impossible for black graduates to perform as journeymen and, moreover, unlikely that blacks would compete on the same level as white apprentices. It would, therefore, seem that under the authority of the *Griggs* progeny, a unitary, or integrated, and abbreviated program could appropriately be established for both races. Though in a testing situation a uniform standard might work to the detriment of blacks, because it would prevent the elimination of a competitive disadvantage for them, in a training situation the advantages of uniformity outweigh the disadvantages. (Establishment of an abbreviated unitary program, of course, has nothing to do with the standards to be applied in connection with admission to the program; dual admission standards for the races may be appropriate, inasmuch as standards may be differentially predictive for each race.)

Another argument indicating the compatibility of *Griggs* and its progeny with the unitary approach is that one is never certain about the scope of the class that should benefit from a decree. That is to say, it is always doubtful whether an individual black who will benefit from the decree would have been harmed had there been no discrimination in the first instance. This is especially true of craft-union cases where unidentifiable workers come forward to reap the benefits. Indeed, although the age limit for the special apprenticeship program in *Local 86, Ironworkers* was pushed up to compensate those who had been wrongfully excluded and were over the normal apprenticeship age, the special apprenticeship program appears to be dominated by young participants. Since imprecision about the affected class raises the specter of preferential rather than remedial treatment, it seems entirely appropriate to provide the same benefits to whites, even though they are not proportionately excluded by virtue of the arbitrarily long apprenticeship program—though it must be emphasized that the need for uniformity arises because of the peculiar disadvantages involved in a separate training prod gram. Although *Griggs* appears to present no legal obstacle to a unitary program, and although such a program lessens the danger of an arguably improper preference for the individual black who may not have suffered all the disadvantages of a culturally isolated, lower-income white, one must keep in mind that the dominant goal of both the quota decisions and the seniority cases—especially *Watkins*—is to assist minority workers who make future applications and bids for jobs.

A problem with reversing exclusionary practices for both races in the *Griggs* and training contexts is that the remedy fashioned by the court is aimed at correcting societal inequities imposed upon blacks. If one reverses the practice for whites as well, the imbalance or disadvantage which is supposedly harming the black worker's competitive status partially reappears. The very disability which was the object of judicial concern is resurrected, because previous discrimination has put blacks at a disadvantage. This problem, however, is not particularly troublesome, because in the types of situations considered in *Griggs* and its progeny one is less concerned with past discrimination by any particular party and, therefore, more likely to be balancing an unfounded advantage for whites against an unfounded advantage for blacks: a windfall to black beneficiaries who are not harmed in any sense by the defendant's previous unlawful practices.

The cases that give greater pause are the seniority cases and, particularly, litigation about the trucking industry, in which whites numerically dominate in jobs into which blacks (as well as those whites who have been unlucky enough to have been assigned with them to the city-driver classifications) are "locked."[72] One can imagine the political pressure on unions such as the International Brotherhood of Teamsters (as well as unions such as the United Steelworkers) to negotiate seniority and transfer rights for *both* races—even though only one had been held back because of race. In at least one case, the Justice Department itself acceded to this pressure and negotiated a consent decree providing for such transfer rights.[73] And Judge Joseph Sneed, writing for the Ninth Circuit in *United States* v. *Navajo Freight Lines,*[74] remanded a trucking case to the district court with instructions to consider seniority compensation for white local drivers—compensation which might assist them in their competition with nonincumbent employee blacks and whites. But there are two differences between this situation and the unitary apprenticeship program in *Local 86:* (1) the fact that the defendants discriminated against particular blacks through exclusion or locking in—even though this, admittedly, is a secondary consideration and; (2) the competitive-status consequences for blacks in the seniority system can be much more severe in the *Navajo Freight* fact situation. For in the seniority cases, blacks may be directly deprived of work. This is a much more remote possibility in the *Local 86* unitary apprenticeship program, where the deprivation for Negro apprentices and applicants may result from a greater influx of qualified whites who are attracted by the smaller sacrifice entailed by an abbreviated program which would boost them to journeymen level in a shorter period of time than the normal apprentice program.

The dilemma is twofold: (1) the difficulties of using objective and subjective criteria themselves (Kaplan notwithstanding); and (2) the fact that the formulation of remedies in the objective cases—those dealing with seniority, examinations, educational qualifications, and so forth—inevitably involves the courts in the same problems of race consciousness involved in the use of quotas. Quota remedies may simply be a more straightforward and simple means of balancing black and white economic interests without a good deal of the discord and potential for the undermining of black interests inherent in cases such as *Griggs, Local 86,* and the seniority cases. The greater the required precision in identifying the individual who was harmed in the past, and the greater the insistence on a purist remedy which is applicable only to one race, the greater the problems may grow.

In the absence of validated procedures, it becomes difficult or impossible to select the most qualified applicant. This is why the Fifth Circuit rejected the proposition that a white applicant could be constitutionally harmed by a racial quota where unvalidated procedures had been previously utilized. The court said in *Allen:* "The color-conscious relief which we affirm does require that the defendants temporarily institute race as the final determinative factor in their appointment of applicants to fill new openings on the patrol and its supporting staff. It is clearly contemplated, moreover, that the affirmative hiring procedure required could compel the defendants to employ a less qualified white ahead of a more qualified black applicant if the last person hired by the patrol was black and vice versa."[75]

Some courts have concluded that because of unvalidated procedures, as well as the difficulties always involved in employee selection, a minority employee may be selected as long as he or she is "qualified" in the sense that he or she meets minimum standards. The Fifth Circuit, however, is the first court to state definitely that the more qualified applicants of either race may be turned away when it is the turn of a member of the other race to be hired under the court-ordered quota. Were it not for the factors affecting the appropriateness of a quota remedy, such an employment practice would be clearly unlawful under Title VII itself.

One other theme, which crops up most often in public-employment cases where there is frequently no egregious, overt, or deliberate discrimination, is the need for the community to be served by all races. This is particularly important in police-hiring cases and other situations where the employee will have intimate contact with the public. In itself, this factor may serve as a partial justification for the quota remedy.

Constitutional Considerations

Two themes dominate the Fifth Circuit's approach to quotas in both *Allen* and *Morrow*. The first—emphasized in Judge Goldberg's dissent in *Morrow I*— is that where past discrimination is egregious, it is unlikely that anything short of a "certain result," that is, the actual hiring of blacks, will achieve the objective of integration. The second is that the relief is temporary. As the court said in *Allen:* "It is a temporary remedy that seeks to spend itself as promptly as it can by creating a climate in which objective neutral employment criteria can successfully operate to select public employees solely on the basis of job-related merit. For once an environment where merit can prevail exists, equality of access satisfies the demand of the Constitution."[76]

The emphasis on the temporary nature of the relief is woven through the Title VII cases as well.[77] If the quota relief is temporary, the shoals of unconstitutional racial classification are more easily skirted—even if the compelling-state-interest test applies to this kind of benign racial classification. In *Allen,* the court relied on both the absence of validation procedures and its view that the "collective interest, governmental as well as social, in effectively ending unconstitutional racial discrimination" was of paramount concern. Another point which the court did not make explicit is that while the Fourteenth Amendment's hostility to racial classifications is not solely or exclusively for the benefit of blacks or other racial minorities, in fact the backdrop for constitutional litigation is a concern with the protection of racial minorities and not of others.

The concept propounded by Judge Goldberg in *Morrow I* indicates some of this concern, as does also the Court's decision in *Brown*. After all, in our society the rationale for a suspect classification approach must to some extent provide the analytical foundation for quota remedies. Subsequent to *Brown,* the Court noted in the miscegenation cases such as *Loving* v. *Virginia*[78]* that the rationale for making racial classifications suspect is that "discrete and insular minorities" are often politically impotent and in need of judicial protection. Furthermore, as four members of the Court have said with regard to sex discrimination, in *Fontierro* v. *Richardson,* the rationale for suspect classifications is dependent upon a number of factors, the first of which is historical and political disenfranchisement.[79] In the case of blacks, much more than disenfranchisement was involved: slavery as well as the Black Codes and the "Jim Crow" separate-but-equal segregation which was itself encouraged by the Supreme Court's decision in *Dred Scott* and *Plessy* v. *Ferguson*.

Another important factor is the high visibility of the group involved. For most blacks, identification is relatively easy because of skin color and other facial and hair characteristics. Moreover, of course, these characteristics are immutable—and they bear no relationship to ability to perform work.[80] Finally, the Court in *Fontierro* noted another factor: that Congress had addressed itself to the problem and recognized that abuses were being engaged in against a particular group—in this case, women. Congressional recognition of abusive treatment of blacks has surely been even more noteworthy, resulting in the Civil Rights Act of 1964 as well as a host of other comprehensive statutes.[81]

A factor applicable to blacks that was not explicitly referred to in *Fontierro* is that racial classifications are perceived by society and especially blacks and other racial minorities as stigmatic, that the separation of the races denotes a status of inferiority for blacks. The community, both black and white, recognizes what the Court refused to recognize—that the stigma is inherent in racial discrimination.

Furthermore, as Paul Brest has pointed out,[82] racial classifications in the United States tend to reinforce the characteristics which the minority group is presumed to possess. That is, if blacks are not hired for, or promoted to, upper-level positions because they are deemed to be prone to undesirable conduct, such as high absenteeism, it may be that the group being treated poorly will respond with poor work habits. This, of course, will reinforce the perceived correlation between race and behavior and, accordingly, will reinforce the stereotype that whites have of blacks. As the Fifth Circuit said in *Allen* with regard to quota remedy: "By mandating the hiring of these who have been the object of discrimination, quota relief promptly operates to change the outward and visible signs of yesterday's racial distinctions and thus, to provide an impetus to the process of dismantling the barriers, psychological or otherwise, erected by past practices."[83]

The Supreme Court's ruling in *Griggs* seems to provide another basis for racial quotas. For in *Griggs* the Court, when striking down artificial requirements which screen out applicants and are not job-related, took into account the special position of blacks and presumably other racial minorities such as Chicanos that suffer educational inequities. If the position of the group qua group can be taken into account for the purpose of establishing a violation where a "neutral practice" reflects societal inequities, why cannot a remedy be fashioned on the same basis once a violation has been found? The principal concern in *Griggs* is that the practice complained of has a statistically significant exclusionary impact upon blacks because of the situation in which most blacks find themselves. In order to be certain that this is the case, such a statistical pattern must be presented in the course of the litigation. Without such a showing, there is not usually a basis for the *Griggs* remedy. In the quota-remedy cases, there must be a showing of (1) a long history of intentional racial discrimination; (2) a paucity if not a total absence of any positive efforts to recruit minorities at all levels of the work force; or (3) utilization of unvalidated selection procedures and other discriminatory practices. When such evidence is presented, it would presumably combine with the Court's assumption in *Griggs* and the rationale behind the suspect-classification cases such as *Brown* and *Fontierro* to argue conclusively for the quota remedy.

Yet there are lingering doubts which we must address. A major idea of Kaplan is that such remedies undermine the government's role as an educative force in society. The argument is that race-consciousness or racial classification are at odds with the government's abiding objective of pointing out the irrelevance of race to both qualifications and job performance. But the argument cuts two ways. If blacks and whites have the opportunity to work together at the same place of employment as the result of an effective remedy, it would seem that the same point is made. Surely, this is the best means of achieving any kind of understanding between the races. Kaplan, however, states:

The damage that such governmental action [erosion of a color-blindness principle through race-conscious remedies] can do is sometimes quite difficult to predict in advance. An argument can be made that the assimilation of the Puerto Ricans in New York was proceeding better before they were officially classified as Negroes for the purpose of perfectly well-intentioned programs. The effect of the law has been to stamp them more clearly as a group apart, a designation to which both they and the rest of the society could not help but react.[84]

The difficulty with this argument is that there is no evidence or factual basis in Kaplan's article to support this position. Similarly, he plays on another deeply emotive theme when he says:

One may, of course, question whether the society which we hope to build in the future should actually be completely color-blind. The presence of disparate groups in our culture contributes to its interest and its productivity, and one may well feel that we lose something when our Chinese restaurants are staffed by Negroes, Puerto Ricans, and Italians. *Nevertheless, the history of the Negro in America is such that for many generations to come, classification of the Negro as a distinct group can only evoke bitter memories.* At least with respect to the Negro, the type of society we probably should envision is one where color is completely irrelevant, not only to all governmental, but to all societal purposes. *It may be that the only possible way that this can be achieved is through intermarriage so complete that the Negro no longer exists as a Negro.*[85]

At no point does Kaplan contemplate the possibility of racial pride and its role as blacks begin both to participate in an integrated society and, simultaneously, to concern themselves with their heritage and history. One does not have to be a separatist or a black nationalist or to condemn interracial marriage to accept the view that pride and consciousness of a people's historical role is important to the race's achievement and success in society. Kaplan views the role of race consciousness as insignificant, inasmuch as blacks have apparently little in their tradition which would inspire pride and which does not involve bitterness and oppression. Curiously, this history of oppression is never mentioned in Kaplan's discussion of any justification for special treatment and remedies. No reference is made to the legacy of slavery, the Black Codes, and so on.

The final and most significant argument raised by Kaplan is that the claims of black workers cannot be distinguished from those of what Gunnar Myrdal calls the "underclass."[86] According to Kaplan, the competing claims of poor whites and other racial minorities generally are more "distinctive" than those of Negroes in the United States. This argument is quite similar to one put forth by Bayard Rustin in the reparation debate: "As a purely racial demand, [the] effect [of reparations] must be to isolate blacks from the white poor with whom they have common economic interests."[87] Kaplan says:

Though certainly the underclass contains a higher percentage of the nation's Negoes than of any other group (with the possible exception of the American Indian) at least two-thirds of its members are not Negroes and well over half of the Negro population of the U.S. does not belong to this underclass. In other words, the underclass forms just as distinctive a group in our society as does the Negro—and indeed membership in this group is a considerably better guide to the need for societal assistance or preference than is membership in the Negro "race." And though, with respect to the Negro members of this underclass, it is relatively easy to isolate specific types of deprivation at the hands of society and thereby explain their present status, the chances are that if we examine all the other members, we find that each of them, in one way or another, has somehow been injured by our society. At the very least, we can say that the great majority of the underclass have been without personal fault in their condition. Is it so very important, then, that one very specific type of deprivation was visited upon the Negro members of the underclass? One can, of course, argue that the Negro member has special psychological problems which are not shared by the rest of the underclass. Assuming this is true, its relevance on the issue of job preference is hardly clear. Moreover, we know very little about the other members of the underclass and it is well within the realm of possibility that many of them have psychological problems equal to those of the Negro. Certainly, they have had to confront their own obvious failure without the ready excuse available to the Negro.[88]

Is membership in the underclass a "considerably better guide to the need for societal assistance"—or, in the case of judicial remedies, those which create a preference? All Kaplan can perceive as peculiar to the Negroes are the "psychological" problems and not the myriad of historical circumstances, as well as those enumerated by the four members of the Court in dealing with suspect classifications in *Loving* and *Fontierro*. The notion that blacks are no more "distinctive" than the poor seems untenable in light of both *Griggs* and the suspect-classification doctrine.

More plausible, however, is the argument that a large number of groups may be themselves the victims of discrimination. In fairness to both Kaplan and Rustin, it must be said that they might well advocate relief for all claimants—although the tone of the Kaplan article is extremely negative with regard to all, as is the practical impact of his theme and proposals. In fair-employment litigation, this kind of argument was persuasive with Judge Charles Wyzanski, in *Castro* v. *Beecher,* and prompted the court to refuse to certify a class of blacks and Puerto Ricans and accordingly to fashion a remedy for those groups. The court said:

This court concludes that . . . examinations were discriminatory against minorities which did not share the prevailing white culture: that is, against groups such as blacks, yellows, browns, American Indians, persons reared in lands where the preferred language is not English, and even whites from backwood areas. . . . This court declines to follow plaintiffs' proposals for preferential hiring of these plaintiffs or other black and Spanish-surnamed persons. Quite apart from such constitutional problems as would be presented, . . . this court sees no reason to put blacks, for example, ahead of Indians, or Chinese, or whites who are in a comparable plight.[89]

The First Circuit reversed Judge Wyzanski on this point with a rationale which refutes the Kaplan-Rustin position quite persuasively. Judge Frank Coffin, speaking for the First Circuit, pointed out that the fact that discrimination might be practiced against other groups, including low-income families generally, did not undermine an action based on a complaint which was "less comprehensive in nature." Accordingly, the court rejected Judge Wyzanski's opinion as in effect presenting plaintiffs with a Hobson's choice: either to take on the burdens of other people or to "forego the vindication of their own rights."[90] Inasmuch as Judge Wyzanski's refusal to certify blacks and Puerto Ricans as a class was based on the same considerations as his refusal to award preferential treatment to that class, this refusal was similarly reversed. The court suggested that the district court might create two pools of eligible applicants: (1) black and Spanish-surnamed applicants who had failed any of the 1968 to 1970 examinations but who passed a new examination; and (2) applicants on present eligibility lists, who would be eligible as long as those lists remained valid under Massachusetts law, followed by applicants who had passed the new examination and who were otherwise qualified but not placed in the priority pool. The court suggested that a ratio of hires from the two pools be established. The ratio would depend on the number of those in the priority pool. This suggestion was followed by the district court in the spring of 1973.[91]

There are differences between the claims of Negro workers and other racial minorities; and there are differences between poor whites and other minority groups in that low-income whites do not form as identifiable a group which is likely to be discriminated against by supervisors, interviewers, and management and union officials because of the animosity of such individuals toward the group. The posture of the group may be the same, their educational plight resembles that of the black plaintiffs in *Griggs*. But they do not face the same resistance when unfreezing an existing pattern of exclusion is attempted. Moreover, as Boris Bittker has noted, "more than any other form of official misconduct, racial discrimination against blacks was systematic, unrelenting, authorized at the highest governmental levels, and practiced by large segments of the population."[92]

Furthermore, it is unlikely that other justifications advanced for preferences have applicability to poor white workers. Although whites below the poverty-income level possibly have the same unemployment ratio as blacks, the rapport with, and confidence in, police, firemen, and teachers from their own communities felt by blacks and Mexican-Americans do not appear to have a counterpart in attitudes of poor whites toward poor white functionaries. Poor whites seem to have as much confidence in a white policeman or fireman from a different income bracket as in one from their own. This is not to minimize the hostility that may yet exist because of income inequities and the distribution of wealth in this country. Yet, while the proposition cannot always be stated in the absolute terms, the relative lack of a cohesive homogeneous feeling would appear to make the preference less valid for low-income whites.

Similarly, a preference for minority skilled tradesmen may be extremely significant in terms of establishing "models" for ghetto youngsters—just as a black or Chicano lawyer might serve as models in the community in addition to providing needed services and expertise in connection with the community's causes. Once the poor white obtains better employment, there is less of a link or identification which ties him to his "group." Granted that blacks do not always want to identify with those whom they have left behind, they are more likely, nevertheless, to be models to aspiring or lower-income blacks.

It may perhaps be argued that if the preference is not underinclusive in scope (improperly leaving out those who are entitled to benefits), it is nevertheless overinclusive. This I interpret as the second part of Kaplan's argument, in which he states that Negroes are not as "distinctive" a group as low-income whites. The contention is that the black physician's son who has been sent to the best private school since age five is less deserving than the Polish auto worker's son who has been reared and educated in Hamtramck, Michigan. It should be pointed out, however, that the former will probably not be in the same labor market—and the one in which he will find himself will probably have no quota at all or a minimal one (assuming that he has taken advantage of the benefits with which fate has provided him). Morevoer, even though the black physician's son has been given societal advantages, the same hostility—particularly if he squanders his inheritance and competes in the automobile factory—if it exists, will be aimed at blacks in all economic strata. The member of a joint union-employer apprenticeship committee who dislikes blacks is unlikely to apply his hostility selectively, according to the economic level of the applicant he is considering.

The attempt by both Kaplan and Judge Wyzanski to point out that Mexican-Americans and American Indians are in some instances the objects of more grievous discrimination than blacks should not be a basis for disregarding the claims of either. The advances of one group should not be at the expense of another; the preference must be demanded by both. What is particularly important is that Professor Kaplan's arguments should serve as a basis for granting a preference to all—although, sadly enough, it appears that he is against a preference for any of the racial minorities.

This, of course, is not to argue against programs which are a benefit to the poor of all races. A coalition of racial minorities and progressive whites—in which the trade union movement participates—must undertake this kind of project. But such programs should not be confused with, or serve as a basis for, an attack upon racial minorities.

Finally, it is apparently the serious contention of Kaplan—and to some extent Bittker, in his important work *The Case for Black Reparations* indulges him on this—[93] that the problem of definition of race and consequently of impostors is a significant one. Kaplan states, "Granting that race is merely a cultural construct . . . one [cannot] simply say that one is a Negro if the culture treats him as Negro." I would think that one certainly can say that one is a Negro if one is treated as a Negro. He is a Jew who the Gentiles say is a Jew. Kaplan conjures up the horrors involved in testimony which would have to be given by expert witnesses relating to the "degree of kinkiness of hair, of skin color, of pinkness of palms, and many other factors which go into our definitions of a Negro."[94] It is interesting that neither Kaplan nor Bittker is able to cite any example of a white posing as a black in order to obtain the benefits of a preference. Although being an American Indian or Mexican-American does not appear to be as stigmatic as being a black, the fact is that there are no individuals who appear to volunteer to come forward and identify themselves as black. There could indeed be much confusion about this issue in light of the fact that many Negroes have "passed" as whites. Such individuals, however, would probably not wish to identify themselves as blacks because of the pain it would cause both family and friends. It is, of course, conceivable that dark-skinned swarthy individuals—some Jews or Italians—could be easily confused with Negroes. But since most people who have lived in the United States understand the way in which blacks are truly regarded in this country—and presumably Kaplan does also—it is hardly likely that people about whom there could be some confusion will volunteer to create it.

Training Remedies

It is generally assumed that unions and employers may devise special training programs on their own initiative in order to increase opportunities for blacks and other racial minorities. A large number of private parties have instituted "special hiring of the disadvantaged" programs, sometimes under the auspices of the National Association of Businessmen. In dicta the courts have indicated that the antipreferential-treatment provisions of Title VII do not prohibit special programs for black workers. Said Judge Wisdom in *Local 189:*

We conclude, in agreement with *Quarles,* that Congress exempted from the anti-discrimination requirements only those seniority rights that gave white workers preference over union Negroes. This is not to say that *Whitfield* and *Quarles* and Title VII prohibited an employer from giving compensatory training and help to the Negro workers who have been discriminated against. Title VII's imposition of an affirmative duty on employers to undo past discrimination *permits* compensatory action for those who have suffered from prior discrimination.[95]

The question of the lawfulness of training programs for one group in the absence of a finding of discrimination is a subject for another debate—presented by programs like those of the National Association of Businessmen.

In *United States* v. *Jacksonville Terminal,* the Fifth Circuit indicated that under some circumstances a black need not be the "best qualified" applicant where a finding of discrimination has been issued in his favor,[96] and the Eighth Circuit appears to have come to the same conclusion.[97] The landmark *American Telephone & Telegraph* consent decree provides for the hiring and promotion of minorities who meet minimum qualifications.[98]

The Court, in *McDonnell Douglas Corp.* v. *Green,* avoided a head-on confrontation with this issue, albeit holding that a defendant has the burden of showing the qualifications of the white worker who obtains the job for which a minority worker was passed over.[99] A rule of law protecting excluded minorities who are not necessarily the best qualified may be appropriate particularly in blue-collar jobs where the differences between workers is necessarily marginal and where little inquiry need be made regarding a worker's prior background and work experience.

Even among blue-collar workers, there are situations in which the worker is not presently qualified in the sense of possessing immediately marketable skills yet discrimination may be found and a remedy fashioned in connection with a denial of hire or transfer. One situation may be that of the "showcase" Negro. A black with marginal or submarginal qualifications may be hired and difficulties arise when satisfactory performance on the job is required. In *Long* v. *Ford Motor Company,* Judge John Feikens held that special training in such circumstances was mandated. The court said:

What must be understood in an analysis of this case is that a black man should not be hired just because he is black. A black person who is hired solely for appearance sake and is inexperienced and not given thorough job training is likely to fail. If that occurs and he is then fired, one may conclude that just as he was hired because he was black, so he was fired because he was black.

. . . It must be recognized that an inadequate job performance alone cannot justify what is otherwise a discriminatory termination. . . . Once hired, black people and other traditionally disadvantaged minorities *must* be given the job training necessary to enable them to perform their jobs.[100]

Judge Feikens' holding, however, was reversed by the Sixth Circuit and remanded for trial in light of the standards established by the Supreme Court in *McDonnell Douglas Corp.* v. *Green.* The court held that it was an error to hold the defendant company liable for failure to train the minority employee adequately "absent a showing that this failure constituted either dissimilar treatment from the training whites receive or treatment similar on its face but dissimilar in its effects upon racial minorities and unfounded on business necessity."[101]

In *Marquez* v. *Omaha District Sales Office*[102] the plaintiff was unlawfully locked into a Class 6 position with the company. His nonpromotional status and consequent inability to advance to intermediate job classifications which were prerequisite to the Class 9 managerial position he requested did not preclude a finding of a violation and the devising of an appropriate remedy. While rejecting advancement to Class 9 and conceding that the individual might never have reached that step of the ladder, the court suggested that the district court might consider promotion to Class 7 or 8, with back pay to compensate for the failure to promote earlier. *Marquez,* then, finds a violation and provides some relief for the minority workers who does not have the necessary qualifications to meet company standards at the time of the discrimination.

Similarly, the court, in *United States* v. *Local 86, Ironworkers,* [103] having found discrimination against black craftsmen, devised a special apprenticeship for blacks which was of shorter duration than that provided for a regular apprenticeship.[104] The 1974 consent decree negotiated between the Justice Department and the major trucking companies provides for the adoption of training programs or for cooperation with existing ones if the companies are not able to find a sufficient number of qualified black or Spanish-surnamed over-the-road drivers.[105]*

In all these cases the remedy seems to be predicated upon a number of factors. One is that the discriminatory policy of the defendant has discouraged the acquisition of sufficient skills, and those minority workers with an adequate background, if they are still in the vicinity, may no longer have the incentive or interest to apply. To some extent also the district court's *Detroit Edison* seniority remedy for those who had not applied fills the void—just as it does with regard to the quota remedy's inability to find the victims of past discrimination. Yet the general principle is not altered. For the aspirations of members of the minority communities are dampened in part because their fathers were not hired by the defendant, so that, unlike the white community, they have no model to encourage advancement. Accordingly, a group remedy providing training for blacks and Chicanos may be appropriate under certain circumstances. While the preferential-treatment problem is less severe because opportunities and not jobs are involved, the institution of a training program exclusively for minorities may present a greater problem. Yet the purpose of the remedy is to bring into being a fair employment pattern, a sharing of work opportunities by the races. A major concern in the quota cases is the possibility of a total or significant exclusion of white applicants, but if the training remedy does not produce that result, and if the remedy is predicated upon past exclusion or segregation, the preferential-treatment problem will not arise. This conclusion would seem to square with the Sixth Circuit's approach in *Long.*

In part, however, the training remedy, insofar as it attempts to revive dampened aspirations, can be seen as a device to acquaint the worker with a skill and make it less likely that he will be tempted by the culturally felt need for instant economic gratification to take advantage of other employment opportunities that may not provide as much long-term compensation. One of the most important problems in this context and throughout Title VII is that of business necessity, the "touchstone," as Chief Justice Burger refers to it in *Griggs.* The ability of the judiciary to establish Title VII violations is significantly dependent on the practicality of the remedy to be fashioned. A court may not presume that a no-transfer policy prohibiting a janitor from advancing to the classification of airline pilot is an unreasonable and unlawful policy—even where all janitors are black and all pilots are white. In view of the substantial gap in skills and education between the two groups, it is unlikely that many black janitors would have taken advantage of a transfer opportunity if it had existed in the first place. Furthermore, obviously such transfers could be expensive, inasmuch as the employer or union would have the burden of providing training on the order of a secondary school or university education. Although employers often pay for all or part of some form of education for an employee—sometimes as a matter of unilateral policy and sometimes in accordance with a collective-bargaining agreement—there are many limits on the kind of obligation private employers and labor unions can be expected to assume in lieu of the public-education system. To the extent that the skill difference is substantial, the defendant's responsibility for and implication in the employee's acquisition of skills is less plausible. After all, in our society this is the function of the public-school system—although the public schools have only recently abdicated vocational training to the unions. Even though the fundamental reasoning behind the approach to Title VII that I have advanced—and that the Supreme Court has confirmed in *Griggs*—is that an employer cannot take the job applicant as he finds him, because the entire society (public-school system, public and private housing agencies, and employers and unions) is involved in discrimination, the employer cannot bear the entire burden or an unduly significant part of the burden that ought to have been initially assumed by some other segment of society.

The issue, therefore, would appear to be the amount of training and education costs to be provided by the employer and the reasonableness of a particular remedy in light of the business-necessity standard. The central principle is that business necessity ought to be used as a criterion only to exclude the unqualifiable. Appropriate remedies should be devised for those who are qualified in the sense that they possess ability but not immediately marketable skills.

Although the Tenth Circuit, in *Jones* v. *Lee Way Motor Freight, Inc.*, seems to have concluded that additional costs are an appropriate element of the transfer remedy for previously excluded black drivers, in dealing with a no-transfer policy relating to city and over-the-road drivers the court said the training costs that defendant claimed would be involved in eliminating such a policy would be "somewhat illusory": "The training of a new city driver to replace the transferee will entail some costs, but we believe that these would not be substantial enough to outweigh the detriment to the plaintiffs of permanently locking them in city drivers' jobs."[106]

I am of the view that the courts should provide the same remedy where seniority credits are at issue. Some of the dicta in *Local 189,* as well as the views expressed by Judge Butzner in *Quarles,* seem to be against this proposition (despite the adherence of those cases to the business-necessity approach), in that they appear to assume that blacks must possess immediately marketable skills and be qualified for the jobs they seek at the time of litigation. Judge Butzner specifically distinguished *Whitfield* as a case in which seniority credits were not appropriate because of the wide divergence among skills required for previously all black and all white jobs. Although not as explicit as Judge Butzner in *Quarles,* Judge Wisdom seemed to regard *Whitfield* as a substantially different kind of case, partly for the reasons expressed in *Quarles*—although possibly Judge Wisdom may have been unduly concerned with distinguishing *Whitfield* inasmuch as he was the author of that decision. Judge Wisdom, in *Local 189,* stressed the fact that only qualified blacks could take advantage of the promotions coupled with seniority: "Both the court's decree and the existing collective bargaining agreement give Crown Zellerbach the right to deny promotions to employees who lack the ability or qualification to do the job properly."[107] And the court stated at the outset of its opinion, "When a Negro applicant has the qualifications to handle a particular job, the Act requires that Negro seniority be equated with white seniority."[108]

Finally, a narrow view of an employer's and union's obligation toward an employee lacking readily available skills is expressed by the court in the following statement:

Not all "but for" consequences of pre-Act racial classification warrant relief under Title VII. For example, unquestionably, Negroes, as a class, educated at all-Negro schools in certain communities have been denied skills available to their white contemporaries. That fact would not, however, prevent employers from requiring that applicants for secretarial positions know how to type, even though this requirement might prevent Negroes from becoming secretaries.[109]

This view seems relatively simplistic—especially in light of the implications of *Griggs*. If an employer or union has locked poorly trained and educated black workers into nonpromotable jobs, that employer or union should bear a portion of the responsibility. After all, in none of the seniority cases can an inability to translate skills into a promotion be blamed exclusively on any one party. The employer and labor organization in these circumstances form simply one link in the entire chain. They are responsible in that their hiring and no-transfer policies may have effectively cut blacks off from any opportunity or discouraged them from the on-the-job learning process because they had no hope of promotion, owing to the discriminatory policy. The same rationale advocated for an appropriate qualification date in *Bing* and *Bowman* applies here. Workers were deterred from acquiring qualifications—although they could have done so, since others acquired such skills in a short period of time, sometimes through on-the-job training. Unnecessarily, an arbitrary assumption is made about the past. Here more precision about the past is possible than in the ordinary quota cases, since the actual victim of discrimination is under consideration. If *Long* v. *Ford Motor Co.* is good law, the lack of such precision about the past will be fatal. Doubts about capabilities will be resolved quickly—as they are in the seniority cases, after the trial period often provided by collective agreement elapses.

The critical question in all Title VII litigation ought to be whether, where there was discrimination, the no-transfer policy was reasonable. To be sure, there are obvious examples of reasonable no-transfer policies, such as the above-mentioned refusal of an airline to establish a policy permitting promotion from janitorial or other unskilled jobs to the position of pilot. (The refusal to permit transfers from such unskilled jobs to jobs as stewardesses might be more questionable.) Where blacks do not have the requisite skills for promotion because they were in the past deprived of the opportunity to obtain the requisite experience, the remedy awarded must be a training program instituted by the employer and union (if the union is involved in such matters, as in the construction and printing industries), even if no such training program had been established for whites previously. The limitations of such remedies seem to me to be substantially synonymous with the reasonableness of the transfer policy. If the effect of permitting transfers—and seniority simply compounds the matter—is to require employers in effect to finance the entire secondary education of the job applicant, then it would seem the burden imposed is too great. The significance of *Jones* with respect to the training remedy may be regarded as limited, inasmuch as the court indicated the training costs were somewhat "illusory" and the jump between the two jobs involved—those of city and over-the-road drivers—does not appear to be great.

The Eighth Circuit Court of Appeals' decision in *United States* v. *St. Louis–San Francisco Railway Co.*[110] seems to carry more weight in support of this proposition. In that case the government sought to obtain relief which would reclassify black employees who were formerly train porters as brakemen by a merger of these two crafts and would, after the reclassification, allow the black employees to claim seniority accumulated as train porters. The court refused to accept the government's view that the train porter and brakeman classifications were in effect interchangeable. It was noted that the railroad porters performed many braking functions while working as porters, but the court said that some braking functions were not performed by the porters.

Accordingly, although the court ordered the company to make available brakeman positions to the black workers because of the discrimination involved in a no-transfer policy, only 50 percent of the train-porter seniority credit could be utilized by black employees in the brakeman job classification. On the other hand, the court ordered that a training program be made available to black employees who were not ready to advance at the time of the promotion opportunity. The court specifically stated that the possession of qualifications meant the capacity to perform rather than the possession of "immediately marketable skills."[111] *Frisco,* while disappointing on the seniority as well as the back-pay issue, is the first decision to recognize specifically the need for a training program as a remedy where blacks were by the nature of their previous work unready to bring to new categories all the experience necessary for the formerly all white jobs. Presumably, the court's holding in *Frisco* should be applicable to other fact situations where black employees have even a smaller percentage of the relevant experience. The bite of Title VII would obviously cost employers and unions a great amount of money in many instances.

The Segregation and Merger of Local Unions

A large number of American labor unions established segregated locals for blacks and whites. The AFL-CIO Civil Rights Department reports that most of them have been eliminated:[112] most of the mergers took place subsequent to July 1, 1965, the effective date of Title VII.

The most prominent offenders were the United Papermakers, Tobacco Workers

Union, Brotherhood of Railway Clerks, International Association of Machinists, International Longshoremen's Association (not to be confused with the West Coat ILWU) and American Federation of Musicians. Of the musicians' union James Petrillo, its former president and later director of its Civil Rights Department, has stated, "We had by far, more segregated locals than any international or local union. . . . The spotlight was on us."

The preliminary question—to which most of the unions which merged locals after Title VII became law anticipated the correct answer—was whether segregated locals would be countenanced because of the prohibitions in Title VII against segregation or classifications which "tend to deprive any individual of employment opportunities, or would limit such employment opportunities or otherwise adversely affect his status as an employee."[113] Assuming that Title VII does not explicitly address itself to this question, what characteristics of segregated locals might be regarded as at odds with the statute or its policy?

The analogy was drawn (and specifically formulated by Judge Irving Goldberg of the Fifth Circuit)[114] to the Court's decision in *Brown* v. *Board of Education*[115] and to Chief Justice Warren's reliance on sociological data indicating that separation of the races was psychologically harmful to black children. Although the attitudes of adult black workers have been shaped in many respects by the time they arrive at the work place—in a good number of instances because of the school segregation condemned in *Brown*—one might properly assume that there is a stigmatization for blacks in a separation of the races, at least one that has been imposed. The inferior jobs and working conditions that were assigned to the jurisdiction of black locals would tend to confirm this view (realities regarding race relations first commented on by the first Justice John Harlan in his ringing dissent to the majority opinion in *Plessy* v. *Ferguson*).[116]

Another unfortunate aspect of segregated locals was that whites who were in positions of power by virtue of their control of the better and more prestigious jobs and their relationship with employers who were almost always of the same race would not fully represent the interests of blacks who were not in the same local. Theoretically, it was arguable that this was not necessarily the case. In the Court's decision in *Brotherhood of Railroad Trainmen* v. *Howard*[117] the proposition was established that a union owed a duty of fair representation to Negro employees outside its unit who were members of another union. The actual limits of the *Howard* doctrine have, however, never been clear. Although the view presented is excessively narrow, in my judgment, Archibald Cox has taken the position that *Howard* was intended to apply only to black employees whose segregated unit and union were the result of an arbitrary racial exclusion that was made manifest by the similarity of work performed by black and white workers.[118] Moreover, as a practical matter, blacks were not represented by whites, and a duty, if it existed by virtue of *Howard*, was not enforced on behalf of the minority race. In any event, the question has been answered in the context of Title VII in *United States* v. *International Longshoremen's Association*,[119] a unanimous decision of the Fourth Circuit. In that case, Judge Butzner confronted the issue of whether the segregation of locals tends to deprive blacks of employment opportunities within the meaning of the statute and stated:

We agree with the district judge that the maintenance of racially segregated locals inevitably breeds discrimination that violates the Act. Racial segregation limits both black and white employees to advancement only within the confines of their races. The position that would rightfully be an employee's, but for his race, may be filled by a person of lower seniority or inferior capability because the job traditionally has been reserved for either a white person from one local or a black person from the other. Even though union officials strive in good faith to administer their duties impartially, they cannot avoid this inherent inequality, and its consequent violation of the Act. Indeed, so obvious is the discrimination that arises from segregated unions, that in every case, save one, courts have ordered or approved mergers.[120]

Yet the integration of such locals has raised many, if not more, problems than it appeared to resolve. Prior to the enactment of Title VII, the Sixth Circuit, in *Oliphant* v. *Brotherhood of Firemen*,[121] in rejecting a constitutionally based demand for admission to a labor union by excluded Negro workers, had asserted that acceptance of an application for membership would accomplish nothing, since the hostile white majority would always be in a position to outvote black union members. Despite the short shrift the court gave to potential black influence in the union's political process, the fact is that the court made a valid point. The admission of an oppressed minority would not necessarily solve any problem. It signified the submergence in many instances of black workers and their leadership. And it often meant the loss of property and assets for Negroes. (In Pittsburgh, blacks lost their own club, which outstanding jazz musicians looked forward to visiting when they were in the area.) In such circumstances, integration was at best a mixed blessing.

With the school-integration litigation in mind, the federal judiciary was not sympathetic to the demands for black separatism once Title VII was on the books. The outstanding example is *Musicians Protective Union Local 274* v. *American Federation of Musicians*,[122] in which Judge Edward Becker held that a Philadelphia Negro local refusing to integrate with its white counterpart in that city was lawfully expelled from the international for its defiant conduct. The court, noting the developing authority for the opinion that segregated locals are per se unlawful, found that the loss of "prestige, reputation and goodwill in the community" was irrelevant and that the thrust of the school-desegregation cases made the black local's position unlawful. The court said:

Applying the terminology for Swann [providing for unitary systems of education in which racial discrimination and segregation are to be eliminated "root and branch"] to the present situation, we find here the vestiges of what once was open segregation, now frozen into an inertial pattern of dual unionism based upon race. These vestiges of segregation are rooted in the history and identity of the separate locals. Thus, it only begins our inquiry here to say that the doors of both locals are now open to blacks and whites. The question is not mooted or ended by this fact, for the truth of the matter is that, in view of the no-raiding rule [under which neither the black nor the white local would raid one another], the continued existence of both locals will guarantee the continued existence of segregation in the Philadelphia unions. Against the background of decisions like

Swann, it becomes patently obvious that the IEB [the international] acted properly in determining that such a condition cannot be permitted, and that the IEB, like the school boards,
acted properly in coming forward with a plan to eliminate dual unionism based upon
race.[123]

While the *Musicians Protective Union* represents an approach from which there
will probably be no significant departure, the courts have nevertheless moved
some distance toward affording protection for the black minority confronted with
mergers. The courts have ordered that such mergers be conditioned upon transis-
tional agreements under which members of each local receive an allocation of executive-board seats and convention-delegate positions.[124] The duration of such
agreements varies and appears to be based on no precise logic—although it is generally keyed to the term a union officer would serve under the constitutional
bylaws of the organization in question. The time period has lasted as long as five
years.[125] It is clear in these cases as well as in those establishing race quotas that
the race-conscious remedy cannot be permanent.[126] The objective is to return as
soon as possible to a system which does not consider color.

Although the courts have not formulated a detailed rationale for the transitional
agreement, the remedy seems to be determined by a number of considerations.
First, it has been assumed that there is a significant nexus between union leadership and the employment conditions which are the essential concern of Title VII's
statutory scheme. That is, if segregation can be equated with discrimination for
the purposes of Title VII, it can be assumed that there was discrimination in the
employment relationship and that the union either actively participated or pas-
sively acquiesced. Moreover, in all the cases discrimination was engaged in while
unions were being desegregated. Thus, the potential roadblock to such remedies
which is established by the Court's decision in *Whitcomb* v. *Chavis,*[127] a reapportionment case in which it was held that blacks do not have a constitutional right
per se to a single-member voting district in areas where their cohesiveness would
be more politically potent, appears to be no roadblock at all. For the Court's
reasoning in *Whitcomb* was that a racial minority had not been submerged, in
violation of the Fourteenth Amendment, inasmuch as the district court in that case
had not found that blacks had obtained worse results in the political process than
they would have if there had been black representation through some other method
than the multimember-district procedure.[128] Discrimination in employment is
practiced by the lily-white leadership in most Title VII cases, in contrast perhaps
to the *Whitcomb* situation, in which segregation very definitely submerges the
excluded minority and harms its interests. In any event cases more analogous to
Title VII segregated local litigation are those involving the Voting Rights Act of
1965 in which the courts are dealing with defendants who are presumed, in contrast to those in the *Whitcomb*-type cases, to have engaged in discrimination in the
past. The Supreme Court has held that if the judiciary is confronted with voting
changes resulting from enacted legislation such as the Voting Rights Act of 1965,
the standard for unlawfulness is whether the change has a "potential"[129] for diluting the Negro vote.[130]

In Title VII cases, one method of fashioning the remedy is to find a nexus between the power to make decisions in the union's councils and employment patterns. The black minority is not likely to be voted into office, even in the absence of hostility, by whites who deem themselves the beneficiaries of discrimination. Although blacks have achieved some measure of representation as a result of the Chicago merger of the musicians' locals, it was after the imposition of a transitional agreement by the international. Moreover, in Washington and Pittsburgh blacks have been excluded from leadership positions even after the expiration of the transition agreement.

Various collective-bargaining decisions have a disproportionate impact on Negroes as opposed to whites. For instance, in Washington, two-thirds of the black members of the musicians' merged locals have left the union because the wage scale adopted by the all-white executive board is unrealistically high for black employers who have relatively marginal enterprises in the ghetto—enterprises which provide most of the jobs available to black musicians. As the wage scale is geared more to jobs from which blacks are excluded, black employers and their employees flee the unions' jurisdiction and, accordingly, weaken the black musicians' political base inside the merged institution even more. This is what has happened in Washington. This factor, coupled with the wide discretion afforded unions under the duty-of-fair-representation doctrine in connection with a host of collective-bargaining decisions,[131] makes black representation at the policy level vital.

In *Long* v. *Georgia Kraft Company*[132] the Fifth Circuit seemed to assume that transitional protective measures were remedies for the present effects of past discrimination without regard to employment opportunities in the present. The court characterized the issue thus: "The appellants point out that because of the long history of segregation in the unions and in the company, blacks have been unable to make the personal contacts and gain the prestige and respect necessary to win election to union offices. These 'present effects of past discrimination' will, they argue, prevent the black members of the merged union from assuming, even to a small extent, the leadership role they employed in the segregated Local 805."[133] Accordingly, *Georgia Kraft* seems to make employment patterns irrelevant to the establishment of the remedy (but in my judgment they must be taken into account in tailoring the remedy to a particular defendant).

Regardless of whether discriminatory employment patterns are a prerequisite for transitional relief, Judge Wisdom, speaking for the Fifth Circuit in *Georgia Kraft*, expounded the view that past segregation alone does not require court-ordered sharing of executive board seats by blacks and whites. Referring to the cases in which transitional agreements have been ordered, the court said, "In this appeal we recognize the right of members of an all-black local union to protective transitional arrangements when their local is merged with a formally all-white local."[134] The court also stated:

Because we recognize that transitional protective measures are a useful tool in the employment area we felt that it was necessary to discuss the subject although we hold that such measures are inappropriate in the instant case. First, almost a year has passed since the merger of the segregated locals. During that time, the transition from two segregated locals to a fully integrated local has taken place. We are informed that Local 804 has held its election of officers. At that election, a black, former member of Local 805 was elected to one of seven union offices. In addition, the nine-member Negotiating Committee charged with negotiating the collective bargaining agreement with the employer on behalf of employees represented by Local 804, has three black members. Also, of the seventeen shop stewards appoined by the President of the Local, seven are black, former members of Local 805. In short, blacks have now attained the leadership role which over a year ago, they sought through court-ordered transitional measures. The use of protective measures is addressed to the sound discretion of a court of equity. Before requiring the district court to order such relief, we must be convinced that the need for equitable relief still exists. In the case at bar, the transition has taken place. The need which once existed for transitional measures has dissipated.

Second, it must be remembered that this merger was not a court-ordered merger. The locals merged, admittedly because of the requirements of federal law, as a result of action by the International. It was, in fact, the refusal of Local 805 to ratify the terms of merger agreed upon by the negotiating teams which forced the International to intervene. This voluntary merger, rather than violating Title VII as the appellants appear to contend, brought the union into compliance with federal law. Protective transitional measures have been utilized only in the context of a court-ordered merger. This is not to say that their use is confined to such situations nor that segregated locals can escape the imposition of protective measures by effectuating a "voluntary" merger just prior to a court order. We feel, rather, that the voluntary nature of the merger in this case is an important factor to consider along with the time lapse in determining the need for protective transitional measures.[135]

Georgia Kraft, therefore, indicates that there are circumstances in which voluntarily negotiated mergers would require further equitable relief, such as the allocation of seats to black and white members of previously segregated locals. One of the factors to be considered by the court under the *Georgia Kraft* doctrine is the presence or absence of black representation that has developed without court-ordered allocation. This sensible consideration presumably applies to situations in which the voluntarily negotiated merger itself provides for an allocation of seats but the plan has expired and the blacks have been voted out. In other words, the mere establishment of a short transitional period which itself voluntarily provides for the allocation between the races does not preclude this kind of judicial relief at a later point. The Equal Employment Opportunity Commission has so held.[136]

In another and more recent decison of the Fifth Circuit, *Pettway* v. *American Cast Iron Pipe Co.,*[137] the court rejected a similar prayer for equitable relief. But in *Pettway,* as in *Georgia Kraft,* the court was careful to qualify its holding in a number of respects. Here a board of operatives was elected by employees, and in the past candidates had been segregated into two boards. With the dismantling of the segregated system, the court recognized that "input" by black employees would be invaluable, inasmuch as the board handled employee complaints. In rejecting the plaintiffs' request for cumulative voting (a form of voting which normally protects minority interests), the court pointed to several special factors which were present.

First, the plaintiffs did not contend that the defendants had engaged in "racial gerrymandering."[138] Second, black political power was increasing, since blacks made up approximately 50 percent of the company's work force—a substantial increase—and constituted a majority in three of the electoral districts and a large percentage in two others. Inasmuch as the jurisdiction of the board was already defined according to geographical and functional lines, the plaintiffs' request for cumulative voting would result in a multimember-district at-large vote which had been "frowned upon" in the reapportionment cases by the Supreme Court.[139]

The court opted for a special committee, including blacks, which would assist in the implementation of Title VII. At-large elections on a cumulative-voting basis would increase racial polarization, said the court, and thus counteract a fundamental objective Title VII.

Both *Georgia Kraft* and *Pettway,* while denying the claims put forward by the plaintiffs in those cases, adhere to the view that a transitional arrangement—even after a voluntarily negotiated plan has expired—is appropriate. Yet a host of troublesome questions arises about such remedies. The first relates to the presumed nexus between elective positions and employment. If continued employment discrimination is at the heart of the problems and is one of the principal justifications for the use of an allocation remedy even after the expiration of a merger plan providing for black representation, why not simply deal with the employment problem directly through quota hiring or a similar drastic remedy? Closely tied to this question is the commonsense argument that it is futile to reinstate a plan providing for representation when that plan has apparently failed to deal satisfactorily with employment discrimination and when the failure itself prompts demands for a *new* merger plan.

Moreover, all race-conscious remedies promulgated by the courts have been palatable because they were transitional. Permanently established racial classifications still seem to be condemned by the Fourteenth Amendment; indeed, the Third and Fourth Circuits have uncovered this fatal flaw in a merger case and have therefore declared that union bylaws which allocate seats on the basis of race impose unreasonable qualifications on the right to run for office.[140]

The Third Circuit has held that apportioning union offices between the "colored" and "white" races was unreasonable under the circumstances, because (1) there was no objective relationship between eligibility qualifications and the duties of the office involved; (2) the rules were to be in for an indefinite duration; (3) the argument that the union would "slip into a segregated status with a possible development of dual segregated local unions" was regarded as too "speculative"; and (4) other racial groups might be excluded.[141]

But suppose that segregation is not "speculative" and that blacks have been denied elective office by a predominantly white membership. Suppose also that other groups among the nonblack membership can run for office. If a specific time period is not sufficient in some Title VII cases, what period of time is satisfactory? Suppose that after whatever period of time is deemed appropriate employment discrimination continues. What should a court do under such circumstances?

Let us deal with the last of this series of problems first. It is apparent that no specific period of time is appropriate. The transitional agreement may leave discrimination untouched. Yet, if deficiencies in existing agreements allow the state of affairs to continue, they are probably attributable primarily to the fact that the duration of the agreement is too specifically defined. That is to say, because the defendant union recognizes that it can stop adhering to a decree within a specific period of time, it has no definite incentive to eliminate the underlying inequities which led to the imposition of the remedy. If, on the other hand, there is an element of uncertainty, or if there is certainty about the elimination of employment discrimination, the defendant may have a greater interest in demonstrating that a change in existing employment practices has taken place. If the court opts for a transitional agreement for an indefinite period tied to the elimination of employment discrimination, the remedy is more likely to be both legally and practically defensible because it goes closer to the heart of the problem of employment discrimination and the certainty that the remedy will expire when discrimination itself is terminated diminishes the specter of an unconstitutional, permanent racial classification.

Yet a transitional agreement of indefinite duration does not dispose of the first two issues. Why not simply deal with discrimination without reference to the union-leadership issue at all? First, the difficulty with ignoring union leadership is that *Georgia Kraft* appears to predicate transitional relief on the inability of blacks to obtain leadership positions owing to past discrimination elsewhere than in employment. Thus, the racially unrepresentative composition of union executive boards cannot be obliterated by a concern with employment patterns; *Georgia Kraft* indicates that it may have other causes. Moreover, such concern fails to take into account the frailties of the judicial process and the difficulties involved in enforcing the most comprehensive court orders relating to employment.

In the context of past discrimination, black representation may be a useful tool in implementing a decree relating to employment—particularly where the union has some involvement in referral to jobs. Black representation may be equally useful where the union purports simply to provide employers with a list of qualified employees, a practice sometimes engaged in by the musicians' locals. The opportunity and the temptation to suggest which employees are likely to be "more qualified" are too great. Subjective judgments will be made, especially if there is an immediate demand for musicians and no other sources can be utilized by the party making the request. The impact on blacks is likely to be adverse, because, as the Fifth Circuit has noted in *Rowe* v. *General Motors Corporation*,[142] where there has been discrimination in the past the chances are that there has been no association between the races and that whites in a position to make judgments are not apt to be familiar with the skills and capabilities of blacks. This potential for evasion of anti-discrimination requirements is limited when blacks are aware of employment opportunities because of the elective positions they hold. They can both check possible abuses by the white leadership and suggest blacks as qualified applicants.

The argument that reinstatement of a merger is futile seems to be fallacious because of the same considerations that apply to the duration of a decree. Though plans, whether court-ordered or voluntarily negotiated, may have failed because of knowledge that they would terminate without reference to the present con- tumacious behavior of the defendants, once the transitional decree is specifically linked to employment this situation may begin to change.

There are other objections to transitional decrees that have no termination date. If *Georgia Kraft* takes the position that the actual election of blacks is a basis for not ordering the allocation of seats, this is arguably but a step away from a state- ment that the *potential* for election of blacks similarly nullifies the necessity for relief. This is, in fact, the conclusion arrived at in *Pettway*. For instance, a case for such nullification could be made with clarity if it was obvious that black divisiveness prevented a victory which was mathematically possible—for ex- ample, if the combined votes for two black candidates equaled the average or the highest number of votes accumulated by successful white candidates. The ap- proach in dealing with such a situation might be similar to that employed by the Supreme Court in *Whitcomb* v. *Chavis,* where it was held that a multimember dis- trict in which it was more difficult for an identifiable Negro community to elect representatives was not violative of the equal protection clause if, in the Court's view, the showing indicated a lack of political success for blacks. Moreover, the Fifth Circuit has declined to order a racial ratio for a YMCA board of directors (previously segregated) in which the black minority was large enough to be regarded as potentially politically successful.[143] Of course, the smaller the minor- ity, the greater the possibility that black representation will be *dictated* by the white leadership, with results that will certainly be disastrous to all the parties in- volved.

Another objection is reflected in a perennial concern of the courts confronted with racial classifications: the prospect of further racial antagonism and divisive- ness. This is a theme of the *Pettway* opinion—although, ironically, there the Fifth Circuit saw the greatest potential for racial bitterness in at-large elections, in which blacks usually fail because they are outnumbered. This very phenomenon of discord gives rise to the need for the remedy. If, in fact, the classification is be- nign and is not designed to *thwart* black political ambitions, it cannot add to exist- ing problems and, furthermore, does not imply the harmful stigmatization of blacks which has been condemned by the courts ever since *Brown*. Where political power is involved, there is less chance of stigmatization than in employment-quota situations, where the minority applicant or worker may feel that he does not deserve the job because he was selected on account of his race (but such a feeling is unlikely, because the alternative of welfare or unemployment is far more de- grading).

Another problem arises because the voting blacks are not exclusively former members of the black locals which had been segregated. New members of the union of both races have now joined the merged locals. The problem, which always makes the court uneasy, is similar to the identifiable-class problem in employment: blacks may be the beneficiaries of relief even though they cannot show that they were harmed as individuals by the practices under attack. In the case of segregated locals which are merged, the fact that employment discrimination continues, as well as the forward-looking nature of the remedy, indicates, in the absence of evidence to the contrary, that all blacks, old and new members, are harmed and that, therefore, the relief is warranted.

6 | Remedies (II): Back Pay, Punitive Damages, Attorneys' Fees, and Test Validation

Title VII, in addition to providing for injunctive relief and affirmative action as remedies for statutory violations, empowers the courts to issue relief "with or without back pay."[1] The statutory language and policy are derived from the National Labor Relations Act, which empowers the National Labor Relations Board to fashion relief with or without back pay. The Title VII back-pay provisions are patterned on the Taft-Hartley model. Under the Taft-Hartley Act, more than compensation is involved in the award of back pay. The purpose is to implement the public-policy objectives contained in the statute.

The Circumstances under Which Back Pay Is Awarded

The leading decision on back pay is *Albermarle Paper Company* v. *Moody,* in which the Court, while noting that the back-pay award is not "automatic or mandatory," stated that the statutory scheme was aimed at "an historic evil of national proportions." The Court limited severely the power of the trial court to deny such a monetary remedy. Justice Stewart said, "Important national goals would be frustrated by a regime of discretion that "produce[d] different results for breaches of duty in situations that cannot be differentiated in policy.' ''[2]

The Court, in *Albermarle,* noted that the relevant statutory provisions in Title VII have dual origins. In the first place, the Court stated, the backdrop for antidiscrimination legislation is that the judiciary has a constitutional duty to eliminate the discriminatory effects of the past as well as the future. "Necessary relief" and "complete justice" acquire a "special meaning" under such circumstances. Second, the Court remarked that the "make whole" purpose of Title VII's remedial provisions was tailored according to that of the National Labor Relations Act. The Court stated, "We may assume that Congress was aware that the Board, since its inception, has awarded back pay as a matter of course—not randomly or in the exercise of a standardless discretion."[3] The presumption that back pay is to be awarded has been established with clarity.

Moreover, Justice Stewart also asserted that in class actions the victims of discrimination who are unnamed parties to the litigation need not file charges with the EEOC. This assertion is in keeping with the general theme of *Albermarle:* "Given a finding of unlawful discrimination, back pay should be denied only for reasons which, if applied generally, would not frustrate the central statutory purposes of eradicating discrimination throughout the economy and making persons whole for injuries suffered through past discrimination.''[4]

But under what burden of proof must such individuals establish their entitlement? It is interesting to recall (from Chapter 4) that courts have awarded seniority credits to black workers subsequent to the finding of discrimination in hiring, promotion, and transfers unless an individual can be immediately upgraded, and the courts have been relatively unconcerned with the question of whether a particular individual was harmed in the past and therefore deserves the credits as a form of compensation. An abiding theme which runs through the courts' opinions in cases dealing with these matters is that the relief is prospective, and doubts about whether the worker is qualified or qualifiable can be resolved at the time he has an opportunity to bid or work on the job in question. The inquiry with regard to back pay is more careful. Yet the difference is a matter of degree.

For as the Court has said in *Albermarle,* the applicable Title VII provisions have "twin statutory objectives." The "primary objective," which is "prophylactic" in nature, is stated in *Griggs:* "to achieve equality of employment opportunities and remove barriers that have operated in the past to favor an identifiable group of white employees over other employees." Back pay has an "obvious connection" with the purpose of the statute as set forth in *Griggs*. The Court said in *Albermarle,* "If employers faced only the prospect of an injunctive order, they would have little incentive to shun practices of dubious legality."[5] The Court specifically adopted the reasoning of the Eighth Circuit in *United States* v. *National Lead Industries, Inc.:*

Back pay awards play a crucial role in the remedial process. . . . They provide the spur or catalyst which causes employers and unions to self-examine and to self-evaluate their employment practices and to endeavor to eliminate, so far as possible, the last vestiges of an unfortunate and ignominious page in this country's history. If back pay is consistently awarded, companies and unions will certainly find it in their best interest to remedy their employment procedures without court intervention whether that intervention is initiated by the Government or by individual employees.[6]

The second purpose of the statute is to compensate workers who have been discriminated against—to make them whole by compensating them for losses incurred as a result of discrimination.

In light of these dual purposes, the approach of the courts to the question of who is entitled to recover monies in classwide actions becomes more intelligible. For the courts do not want to provide a windfall to plaintiffs and to "punish" the employer by imposing back-pay judgments on defendants when money is not properly owed. While the statutory purpose of back pay involves more than mere compensation, the fact is that there is no safeguard afforded the employer, as in the seniority and quota cases, where an award of seniority credits does not mean an automatic promotion; the employee must generally work his way up the line of progression and must often acquire "residency"—that is, a period of experience on the job—at his stops along the way, and above all, the employee will not be retained in an upgraded position if the employer or union defendant can show that he is unable to do the work. These elements of the seniority decrees, which prevent windfalls from accruing to undeserving employees and protect defendants from such consequences, are not immediately applicable to back-pay awards.

But this is as it should be. In fashioning a back-pay remedy, there is more concern with the past; even if the employee cannot perform properly now, perhaps he could have done so in the past. Age or physical disability may have changed his capability. Even if the employee could have qualified in the past, there may be no way of ascertaining his qualifications now, because jobs may not be available. To condition the award of back pay upon completion of employment would defeat the compensatory purpose of the back-pay rationale and would not be justified by the considerations which argue for limiting seniority remedies, such as the undesirability of promoting individuals who cannot perform a job. Accordingly, in the back-pay cases, the focus is on the question of whether there was, in fact, discrimination in the past. Nevertheless, setting the standards for determining individual entitlement in cases of classwide discrimination poses serious difficulties.

Albermarle, with its presumption that back pay is to be awarded and its concern that "complete justice" be provided by the judiciary as a matter of constitutional duty, points toward a liberal rule. In one of the first and most important cases to grapple with the problem, *Johnson* v. *Goodyear Tire & Rubber Company,* the Fifth Circuit referred to its previously expressed policy that the remedial provisions of the statute be given "wide scope . . . in order to remedy, as much as possible, the plight of persons who have suffered from discrimination in employment opportunities."[7*] Closely tied to this policy is the principle that the plaintiff and his or her attorney perform the functions of a "private attorney general" who seeks relief for the class in the public interest. The court said in *Johnson:*

The individual discriminatee has been locked into his undercompensated position precisely because he is a member of an unfavored class. . . .

Our holding does not necessarily mean that every member of the class is entitled to back pay. Individual circumstances vary and not all members of the class are automatically entitled to recovery. There should be a separate determination on an individual basis as to who is entitled to recovery and the amount of such recovery. . . .

In sum, it is our considered judgment that classwide back pay is available upon proper factual proof of an individual's claim when the aggrieved class has demonstrated cognizable deprivations based on racial discrimination by the employer in the employment relationship.[8]

In arriving at this conclusion, the Fifth Circuit confirmed what the courts have unanimously held—that individual class members are entitled to a remedy for classwide discrimination even though they have not filed administrative charges with the Equal Employment Opportunity Commission and are not party plaintiffs.[9]

Shortly after deciding *Johnson,* the Fifth Circuit, in *Pettway* v. *American Cast Iron Pipe Co.,* expressed the view that "once a prima facie case of discrimination against the class alleged is made out, a presumption for back pay arises in favor of class members."[10] Judge Tuttle stated that this presumption is "tempered by an initial burden on the individual employee to bring himself within the class and to describe the harmful effect of the discrimination on his individual employment position."[11] The court declared that an employee is not automatically entitled to back pay without a showing of qualification:

The *maximum* burden that could be placed on the individual claimant in this case is to require a statement of his current position and pay rate, the jobs he was denied because of discrimination and their pay rates, a record of his employment history with the company and other evidence that qualified or would have qualified him for the denied positions, and an estimation of the amount of requested back pay. The employer's records, as well as the employer's aid, would be made available to the plaintiffs for this purpose. The burden then shifts to the company to challnge particular class members' entitlement to back pay.[12]

In *Baxter* v. *Savannah Sugar Refining Corporation,*[13] decided shortly after *Pettway* and cited approvingly by the Supreme Court in *Bowman,*[14] the Fifth Circuit stated that where the employer had no objective criteria for employee selection, the job-related qualifications possessed by white workers who had advanced into the all white jobs should be considered in determining a standard by which to judge whether an individual black worker was actually qualified for promotion under a true merit system. The court held that once an individual meets the initial requirement of establishing that he "was available for promotion and possessed the general characteristics and qualifications . . . possessed by the higher paid white employees," the burden shifts to the employer, who is required to "demonstrate by clear and convincing evidence that any particular employee would have never been advanced." Significantly, the court concluded: "The court on remand will have to deal with probabilities. Any substantial doubts created by this task must be resolved in favor of the discriminatee who has produced evidence to establish a prima facie case. The discriminatee is the innocent party in these circumstances."[15]* As both *Albermarle* and the Fifth Circuit trilogy make clear, back pay is not merely a *permissible* remedy.

Under Title VII and section 1981 the injured workers must be restored to the economic position in which they would have been but for the discrimination—their "rightful place." Because of the compensatory nature of a back pay award and because of the "rightful place" theory, adopted by the courts, and of the strong congressional policy, embodied in Title VII, for remedying employment discrimination, the scope of a court's discretion to deny back pay is narrow. . . . . Once a court has determined that a plaintiff or complaining class has sustained economic loss from a discriminatory employment practice, back pay should normally be awarded unless special circumstances are present.[16]

Are there any conceivable "special circumstances" or exceptions to the presumption expressed in *Albermarle* which might make back pay inappropriate in some cases? The claim most often made is that an employer who in "good faith" believed that his practices were not unlawful should not be subjected to back-pay liability. Employers frequently point to the fast changing state of the law to substantiate their claim to good faith.

Such arguments are not limited to the problem of employment discrimination. For example, Boris Bittker, in discussing the question of reparations for blacks who have suffered from being consigned to segregated schools, has referred to the traditional judicial requirement that a defendant, to be subject to liability, must have engaged in acts which may reasonably have been considered unlawful at the time they were committed. But Bittker concludes that, whatever the merit of that kind of argument as a defense in cases of discrimination, it does not relieve public officials of liability for acts preceding *Brown* v. *Board of Education,*[17] since the NAACP litigation which began in the late 1930's and culminated in *Sweatt* v. *Painter*[18] and *McLaurin* v. *Oklahoma State Regents*[19] gave adequate notice of the holding which was admittedly first stated in *Brown*. Bittker comments that notice which might not suffice to establish criminal liability may nonetheless establish "civil liability, which routinely rests on such indefinite standards as 'reasonable care' and 'ordinary prudence.' "[20]

In *Albermarle,* the Court eliminated good faith as a defense in racial-discrimination cases arising under Title VII and related legislation. As Justice Stewart said, "A worker's injury is no less real simply because his employer did not inflict it in 'bad faith.' "[21] The Court took account of the fact that good or bad intent is irrelevant under *Griggs* and that to ignore this fact would be to invite the growth of an "enormous chasm" between the remedies of back pay and injunctions. The Court also declared that there was "no occasion" to determine the correctness of decisions in sex-discrimination cases where employers have relied on state protective laws which have been held to be inconsistent with, and therefore unlawful under, Title VII's ban on discrimination against women. The Fifth and Sixth Circuits have concluded that no damage recovery can be imposed where defendants were acting in good faith according to such protective legislation.[22]

The Ninth Circuit, however, in *Schaeffer* v. *San Diego Yellow Cabs, Inc.,* has taken a slightly different approach. In that case, a majority of the court, with Judge William Byrne dissenting, concluded that good-faith reliance on state protective legislation was not an adequate defense in all circumstances. The court eschewed "any hard and fast rule" and stated that the "merits of the plaintiff's claim and the public policy behind it must be balanced against the hardship on a good faith employer."[23] Therefore, in *Schaeffer* the court stated that after the district court for the Central District of California issued, in November 1968, its opinion in *Rosenfeld* v. *Southern Pacific Company*[24] holding that state laws relating to overtime could not serve as a shield against the prohibitions against discrimination on the basis of sex contained in Title VII, and the EEOC found in January 1969 that probable cause existed to believe that the employer had violated the act, reliance on the state requirements could no longer be viewed as evidence of good faith and could no longer serve as a defense against the damages claimed. The Ninth Circuit said:

We conclude, therefore, that Schaeffer is entitled to receive back pay for the extra hour per day from the day the Company had knowledge of both the *Rosenfeld* case *and* the Commission's decision in favor of Schaeffer (i.e., on some undetermined date subsequent to 1/22/69, to and including 10/7/69, the date the company allowed 9-hour daily employment for women).

We reject the argument that an employer should not be held for claims of back pay until a "final" court decision, such as our decision in *Rosenfeld* in June of 1971. It is unfair to force an innocent employee to forego his rights under law while litigation drags through the courts (which in, the *Rosenfeld* case, took nearly three years).

We do not understand that our earlier statements in *Rosenfelds's* penultimate paragraph (concerning perspective application of that decision) to bar the result we reach in this case. . . . We are not applying the *Rosenfeld* decision retroactively. The Company was in violation of federal law for a certain time prior to the date this suit was filed. *Rosenfeld* did not intend to automatically forgive all violations of Federal law that occurred prior to that decision. Plaintiff in this case had filed her suit in the district court well before the decision in *Rosenfeld* by this court. We stated in *Rosenfeld* that our decision would not necessarily affect actions pending prior to our decision.[25]

Does *Albermarle* allow for a good-faith defense for conduct engaged in prior to July 2, 1965, the effective date of Title VII? The argument is that the defendants had not been notified that racial discrimination was against the law. The Civil Rights Act of 1866,[26] however, as well as the Supreme Court's decision in *Steele*,[27] was in existence prior to that date. Racial discrimination in employment was unlawful prior to the effective date of Title VII; for instance, Judge Wisdom of the Fifth Circuit, in *Local 189*,[28] specifically noted that fact in connection with the award of seniority credits for the period before the enactment of Title VII. One factor which distinguishes the race cases from sex cases such as *Schaeffer* is that under no conceivable set of circumstances could defendants in the former be said to be relying on governmental requirements that did not accord with Title VII either before or at the time the statute was passed. Not only was the 1866 statute as well as the *Steele* decision in effect, but perhaps even more important insofar as employers are concerned, the President's executive order prohibiting racial discrimination by government contractors had been in existence for a long time. And ever since 1961 affirmative-obligation requirements have been imposed, as well as a no-discrimination pledge.

Unfortunately, one difficulty with awarding back pay to compensate for discrimination practiced prior to the effective date of Title VII in class-action seniority cases is presented by the existence of the Fifth Circuit's decision in *Whitfield* v. *United Steelworkers*,[29] in which the court refused to find the *Steele* doctrine a ban against the present effects of past discrimination. Therefore, most employers and labor organizations probably did not realize that Title VII law would develop according to the pattern of *Griggs*[30] and *Local 189*. With regard to conduct subsequent to the enactment of Title VII, however, certainly labor and management expectations about the meaning of the statute, which adhered to *Whitfield*, seem more to reflect wishful or optimistic thinking than to be grounded in fact. No specific legislation existed from which they could derive the kind of courage they displayed. Though some employers and unions may be regarded as "innocent" wrongdoers, the balance should be weighed in favor of those who were harmed by the perpetuation of discrimination in the teeth of Title VII.

In *Brown* v. *Gaston County Dyeing Machine Company*, a majority of the Fourth Circuit panel concluded that back pay could be awarded under the Civil Rights

Act of 1866 for the years 1960 and 1961. Judge Butzner, writing for the majority, simply stated: "The district judge's findings establish that the company violated 42 U.S.C. § 1981 by denying Brown [the defendant] a welding job because of his race from the time he applied in 1960 until he was employed as a welder-trainee in 1961. Brown, therefore, is entitled to back pay measured by the difference between the wages he would have earned had he been initially employed as a welder-trainee and his actual wages."[31] The difficulty with the Fourth Circuit's award of back pay in the circumstances is twofold: as Judge Franklin Dupree's dissent notes, the employer did take steps to improve the plaintiff's situation before even the effective date of Title VII; and the fact that racial discrimination by private employers was unlawful under the Civil Rights Act of 1866 was not known at the time the conduct was engaged in, because *Jones* v. *Mayer*[32] had not been decided as of that date. Nevertheless, the second point is to some extent countered by the fact that the executive order and *Steele* were in existence— although in *Brown* v. *Gaston County Dyeing Machine,* the employer's liability was independent of union action and therefore, presumably, *Steele* could not be said to be applicable. And the affirmative-action provisions of the executive order had just been promulgated at the time of the conduct which served as the basis for back-pay liability.

Of course, Judge Dupree's dissent relies on a factor which runs counter to the strong policy of a frequent and generous use of back pay expressed in *Albermarle* and by the Eighth Circuit in *National Lead.* Judge Dupree stated in his dissent:

In the few short years the Civil Rights Act of 1964 has been in effect much progress has been made in achieving its laudatory objectives. Some of this is the result of coercive court orders. . . . . The voluntary action of employers acting in good faith to eradicate the longstanding evils which existed prior to the statute have played a tremendous part in this progress. . . . [The majority's decision] may . . . encourage voluntary action and a softening of the racial prejudices responsible for pre-existing inequities in employment. With all deference, I suggest the contrary as being more accordant with reality. The concept of conciliation which pervades Title VII should also be engrafted on Section 1981. . . . Courts should be slow to employ harshly coercive remedies in cases where, as here, there has been an honest effort on the part of an employer to eliminate discriminatory employment practices and no current violation of any law has been found.[33]

Judge Dupree's dissent is not only inconsistent with the "make-whole" purpose of back pay, but it also ignores the second of the two bases for back pay, which both the Supreme Court in *Albermarle* and the Eighth Circuit in *National Lead* regard as the "more important" factor; the use of back-pay awards as a deterrent against discrimination. The fact is that, although substantial progress has been made since the effective date of the statute, most employers and unions have taken action which borders on tokenism instead of eliminating the last vestiges of discrimination as required by the courts. Accordingly, one of the principal justifications for back pay seems to remain substantially intact in the context of *Brown* v. *Gaston County Dyeing Machine.* Together with the quota or goals and timetables remedy, back pay is integral to the essential remedial portions of the statute.

Curiously, the Eighth Circuit in *National Lead*—in the same opinion that focused on the importance of back pay as a deterrent—took a more restrictive view than did the courts in other cases. In *National Lead* the court, dealing with seniority problems and unintentional discrimination, concluded that an employer could in good faith rely on a system which perpetuated the effects of past discrimination until the law of the circuit court explicitly countermanded such a policy. While the court thought that "the courts have at this point sufficiently delineated what constitutes acceptable and non-acceptable employment practices in the areas of seniority and hiring so that neither the employer or union can in good faith claim that they are unaware of what standards are expected of them under Title VII of the Act,"[34] it nevertheless refused to order back pay in the circumstances of the particular case. The court declared:

Despite what we have said as to the appropriateness of back pay, we do not make such an award here. In this Circuit, the law in regard to back pay has not been adequately defined to provide employers and unions with notice that they would be liable for a discriminatee's economic losses due to continuation of past or present discriminatory policies. However, where an employer and union have had ample opportunity to remedy an unlawful employment practice, they should be put on notice that they will be held responsible for the economic losses accruing to the parties injured by such unlawful employment practices.[35]

Albermarle seems to doom this approach. And even prior to the Supreme Court's decision, most courts had found "that an employer's alleged reliance on the unsettled character of employment discrimination law as a defense of back pay is unpersuasive."[36]* Even less had the courts been impressed by another argument often raised under the rubric of a "good-faith defense": that a defendant's efforts to nullify the effects of his past discrimination preclude the entering of a back-pay judgment against him. As the Fifth Circuit has properly stated, this use of the concept of good faith amounts to an attempt to resurrect a requirement of unlawful intent, in the teeth of *Griggs* and its progeny,[37] and is "totally irrelevant as a defense to a claim for back pay."[38] Any doubts are resolved by *Albermarle*.

The Statute of Limitations for Back Pay

Congress, when it was drafting the 1972 amendments to Title VII, was concerned that the act passed in 1964 seemingly provided no statute of limitations for back pay and that back pay could, therefore, be held to accrue from July 2, 1965, no matter how late a legal action might be brought.[39] Although the courts had not spoken on the issue, the Equal Employment Opportunity Commission had adopted the view that back-pay liability should extend to that date, and Congress was very much aware of the EEOC's judgment. Accordingly, the statute was amended to provide that "back pay liability shall not accrue from a date more than two years prior to the filing of a charge with the Commission."[40] Presumably this limitation does not apply to charges filed before the effective date of the amendments, March 24, 1972.

What is the appropriate statute of limitations for such charges? The leading case is *United States* v. *Georgia Power Company*,[41] in which the Fifth Circuit specifically considered the statute of limitations issue. The employer, taking a position that was accepted by the federal district court, contended that the 90 days (extended to 180 under the 1972 amendments) during which one must file a timely charge subsequent to the event complained of is the appropriate period for computing back pay. Judge Tuttle spoke for the court:

Though private complaints must be filed before the EEOC within 90 days, we cannot agree with the company that this period is the proper measure. The deadline is designed primarily to enhance the possibility of informal, out-of-court resolution of employment discrimination complaints through prompt administrative action. It is in no sense a limitation on the period for which one may receive backpay relief. Employment discrimination may as readily be a continuing course of conduct as a single event. Then too, an affected individual may not be aware of the discriminatory impact of certain employment practices until a pattern emerges as a result of the cumulation of numerous events over a substantial period of time. The remedial purpose of the Act would be frustrated were financial redress to be always limited to the 90-day period preceding the filing of a complaint.[42]

The court also asserted that such a statute of limitations for back-pay relief in pattern-and-practice suits brought by the attorney general under Title VII would be inconsistent with the approach taken under the Civil Rights Act of 1866, in which the courts look to state statutes of limitation to determine the appropriate cutoff period. Under Section 1981 the courts have applied a variety of state statutes of limitations: general statutes (which often run for a ten-year period),[43] contract statutes (often for a six-year period),[44]* tort statutes (generally for less than three years),[45] and statutes governing claims for unpaid wages (also generally for less than three years).[46] The court chose the unpaid-wages statute as most appropriate and analogous in *Georgia Power*. The court said:

Where federal laws create rights to back pay as part of general remedial relief courts have generally applied the appropriate state statute of limitations governing actions for unpaid wages.
    . . . The right of individual discriminatees to recover lost wages and like damages either in private class actions or the Attorney General's action is subject to Georgia's 2 year limitations period.[47]

The court rejected the contention that the contract statute of limitations should apply, inasmuch as the failure to contract was the heart of the complaint in this action.

Another approach is that employed by the Supreme Court in dealing with sit-in convictions of 1964.[48] The Court, looking to Title II of the Civil Rights Act of 1964 which made racial discrimination in public accommodations unlawful, set aside sit-in convictions imposed prior to the enactment of statute (thus avoiding an extremely troublesome constitutional question) on the basis of the retroactivity of Title II—even though Title II was not explicitly retroactive. The difference between the sit-in and the back-pay cases is that the civil rights legislation was being used to broaden and enhance the plaintiff's position in a fashion which arguably was consistent with an expansive and generous interpretation of the statute. In back-pay cases, the exact opposite is true, inasmuch as the back-pay recovery will be limited, since most arguments rely on theories or state statutes of limitations which run for a longer period of time and which would therefore compensate plaintiffs to a greater degree.

An approach which adopts the *Georgia Power* back-wages state statute of limitations (or another statute of limitations where the provision is approximately the same time) or a sit-in conviction analogy would preclude a recovery which goes back to July 2, 1965, and would seem to undermine to some extent the policy considerations outlined by the Eighth Circuit in *National Lead* and by the Supreme Court in *Albermarle*.

What if the applicable statute of limitations, whether chosen by looking to the analogous state statute or by some other method, allowed a recovery extending back before July 2, 1965? In *Pettway,* the Fifth Circuit held that in such a situation liability will not have accrued before July 2, 1965, even if claims are brought under Section 1981 rather than under Title VII. The court said:

The specific prohibitions of Title VII were adequate notice to employers post July 2, 1965. . . . Here, the company was put on sufficient guard by the enactment of Title VII to be found liable for back pay under section 1981 as of July 2, 1965. However, following the reasoning of this Court's decision in *Johnson* . . . we conclude that back pay awards under section 1981 should not cover any period of employment prior to the effective date of Title VII because of insufficient notice.[49]

In *Johnson* v. *Goodyear Tire & Rubber Company,* the same court had held that a "balancing of equities"[50] favored July 2, 1965, as the earliest date for back-pay liability. The court had said:

In an analytical void, free of the harsh history of employment discrimination which impelled Congress to enact Title VII, a court might conclude that a back pay award under § 1981 should extend back to the period permitted by the applicable state statute of limitations [prior to July 2, 1965]. It is an unfortunate legacy that private racial discrimination in the employment relationship was long tolerated. Therefore, in addressing ourselves to the problem of private employment discrimination, we think that notice of the proscribed conduct is an essential ingredient for the imposition of back pay. To impose remedial relief after the fact would indeed run against the grain of fundamental fairness which should hopefully be the outcome of any equitable decree.[51]

The Method of Computation

Once entitlement is established, the question of what constitutes the measure (or basis for computation) and amount of damages still remains. According to the thrust of *Albermarle,* the method of determination must not undermine the statutory scheme for making discriminatees whole. In *Pettway,* the court surveyed a number of formulas which have been utilized by the judiciary confronted with this problem. The court stated that it "should be emphasized that this is not a choice between one approach more precise than another. Any method is simply a process of conjectures."[52] Where lines of progression and seniority problems are involved, Judge Tuttle, in *Pettway,* noted that "exact reconstruction of each individual claimant's work history, as if discrimination had not occurred, is not only imprecise but impractical."[53]

The court first looked to Judge Keith's approach in *Stamps,* in which the court

146Black Workers in White Unions

averaged the rates of pay for several high-opportunity jobs in the skilled trades and
awarded each claimant back pay based on the average computed for pay-rate
progression purposes according to the number of years the worker had been employed, deducting interim earnings. Another example of the averaging method is
in *Sabala* v. *Western Gillette, Inc.,*[54] in which the court found from the testimony
of an expert witness that the average over-the-road driver earned 1.56 times as
much as the average city driver, and held that each city driver who had been discriminatorily denied transfer to an over-the-road job should recover back pay
1.56 times the amount of his actual earnings, minus those earnings. Also to be
subtracted was 10 percent of the estimated over-the-road earnings, since the
court determined that the average over-the-road driver spent that percentage in
employment-related expenses.

Another method, as *Pettway* noted, involves a comparability formula, or "representative employee earnings formula." An attempt is made to trace the progress
of white employees whose ability and length of employment are comparable to
those of the excluded minority workers and to compare the earnings of the two
groups. For example, in *United States* v. *Lathers Local 46,* Judge Marvin Frankel,
devising a compensatory back-pay formula for contempt of court related to the
exclusion of black and Puerto Rican workers from a hiring hall, stated that "a
claimant must prove as a first step a sufficient investment of time and effort to
show that he was ready, willing, and available to take work on referrals from the
Local."[55] To establish that he met this standard a claimant would have to show
that during a given month he either shaped (reported to) the hiring hall for five or
more days or shaped the hall or worked on a job or jobs for a total of eight or
more days. These requirements were referred to by the court as "objective criteria." If the claimant could show that he had complied with the objective criteria
within a given month, he might establish in back-pay proceedings that he had developed a "well-founded conviction" that future efforts would be futile. Evidence
the court would take into account in making this determination would include the
claimant's observations of what he has seen in the hiring hall, reports from other
excluded minority-group individuals, and statements by union representatives. If
the claimant established that he stopped shaping the hall owing to a "well-founded
cinviction," he could recover back pay for additional months beyond those in
which he met the objective criteria. The amount of back pay was set by a comparability formula: "For any month of eligibility a claimant is to receive the difference, if any, between average earnings of white union members performing
outside work (excluding foremen and deputy foremen for any month of service as
such) and permit holders, on the one hand, and the lesser amount the claimant
earned or should have earned. . . . Average earnings of white union members
and permit holders will be based in each period upon the total earnings of all such
individuals (divided, naturally, by their number) who either (i) shaped the hall for
at least five days, or (ii) shaped the hall and/or worked for at least eight days."[56]

Some of the workers could not be located and did not appear at the hearings.
But, under the National Labor Relations Act, it has been held that if the workers

meet the objective criteria, the back pay should be put in escrow pending location of the employees—on the theory that the employer or labor organization of which they are members is in the best position to find them and that any questions about their entitlement can be resolved in a hearing when such workers are located.[57] Moreover, the testimony in the back-pay hearings from April to November of 1972 indicated that a large number of workers had become "disgusted" with the blatant discrimination found by Judge Frankel.[58] The fact that white workers were called by name while blacks waited in the hall to shape for work and comments by other members of the affected group were offered as evidence in the back-pay testimony.

Several other methods of computation have been employed by the courts,[59]* but whatever method is followed, two principles expressed in *Pettway* should be the guide: "(1) unrealistic exactitude is not required, (2) uncertainties in determining what an employee would have earned but for the discrimination, should be resolved against the discriminating employer."[60]

Front Pay[61]

The back-pay cases include the assumption that monetary compensation ceases when nondiscriminatory hiring and transfer policies are instituted. It is to be recalled, however, that the "rightful place" approach to seniority disputes permits a black worker to achieve equality—to progress to the step on the job ladder that the individual would have occupied but for the discriminatory conduct of the defendant—only when vacancies permit the black worker to do so. The "freedom now" approach, which would have allowed the bumping of white incumbents by blacks so that they could achieve their rightful places immediately, was rejected by Judge Wisdom. The rationale for the rejection was not stated, but it surely could have not been that of business necessity. The reason is obvious: white workers would not stand for their own displacement, and, indeed, in relation to good human-relations policy, this kind of result would appear to be undesirable. But what of the black worker who has not achieved his rightful place at the time the new policies are adopted? Actually, the prior exclusion continues—and if turnover is slow, the wait for equality can be lengthy indeed. The resolution of the dilemma appears to lie in the concept of "front pay," which was first judicially stated by Judge Keith in *Detroit Edison,*[62] and which has been adopted by the Fourth Circuit.[63] Front pay provides compensation at the rate that would be paid for the job which constitutes the black worker's rightful place in the interim during which the worker waits for vacancies to develop. Such compensation should be paid by the party responsible for the discriminatory hiring that results in restrictions that thwart upward mobility.

The problem is more difficult in connection with layoffs. Here, the question is whether the seniority system will prevent discriminatees from holding any particular kind of position on the job ladder because of hiring discrimination. In *Watkins v. United Steelworkers Local 2369,*[64] Judge Cassibry determined the number of laid-off black workers to be reinstated by using the percentage that the present work force constituted in relation to the work force that existed at the time of the last new hires. This percentage was to be multiplied by the number of black workers on the payroll at that time. Accordingly, a percentage of the black workers was to be reinstated, and incumbent whites were not to be bumped. If the result was the employment of more than the required number of workers, nonetheless "the entire work force [should] receive wages based on a normal 40 hour work week, even if the number of hours actually worked [was] less than 40." Available work, according to the decree, was to be allocated "among the entire work force including the persons reinstated, until normal attrition or expansion of production [brought] the size of the work force to its most efficient level."[65] Back pay was to be awarded to those recalled.

Judge Cassibry's decree provides a form of front pay. Black workers receive what they would have been paid if there had not been discrimination in the past and if the consequences of such discrimination had not been carried forward into the present system. As in the first front-pay situation described above, *Detroit Edison,* the normal course of events would leave black workers uncompensated for discrimination previously practiced. The rights of white workers are not diluted—except to the extent that the union may be held responsible for hiring, and thus exposing white union members' dues payments to liability, a situation not present in *Watkins* but one which may arise in connection with union hiring halls operated by the construction unions and the International Brotherhood of Teamsters locals. In regard to recall rights, separate seniority pools were created for blacks and whites and a one-to-one ratio established. The expectations of white workers were interfered with, but the interference (even if it resulted in depriving the white worker of employment status altogether) appears to have a stronger foundation in the legislative history of Title VII. The Clark-Case memorandum, which dealt with the lawfulness of seniority under Title VII, condemns the use of "waiting lists" which are discriminatory and thereby postpone equality for black workers.[66] The percentage of workers immediately recalled enjoys both back and front pay, inasmuch as that percentage would have been employed despite the reduction in the work force if there had been no discrimination in the first instance.

Some industrial unions, such as the United Auto Workers, contended that rejected applicants unlawfully excluded from employment should be granted the remedy of front pay (as well as of back pay) rather than reinstatement with the seniority they would have had but for the discrimination. Title VII's remedial provisions are based on those of the National Labor Relations Act, and as the Court noted in *Bowman,* under that statute workers who have been dismissed or demoted because of unfair labor practices may displace incumbent workers who have less seniority or who were hired subsequent to the discrimination. The worker who is ousted as a result of application of the NLRA remedy is just as innocent of wrongdoing as is the white worker who suffers under Title VII. Indeed, the remedy of reinstatement is more appropriate under Title VII, in which a central objective is employment for minorities and the dignity, status, and security that are inextricably bound up with work in our society.

But there are circumstances in which monetary relief may be appropriate. The dissenters in *Bowman* noted that the question of which employee possessed seniority credits was of no concern to the employer (although in some situations, of which the Court was not aware, there may be a relationship between seniority and skill and therefore the employer *does* have a definite interest in the matter). Chief Justice Burger suggested that providing front pay would be more equitable than depriving whites of seniority when they had nothing to do with the discrimination. And Justice Brennan stated that the issue of fashioning other relief than seniority by placing the burden on a wrongdoer was not before the Court. The Court said: "Further remedial action by the district courts, having the effect of shifting to the employer the burden of past discrimination in respect to competitive status benefits, raises such issues as the possibility of an injunctive 'hold harmless' remedy respecting all affected employees in a layoff situation, . . . the possibility of an award of monetary damages (sometimes designated 'front pay') in favor of each employee and discriminatee otherwise bearing some of the past discrimination . . . and the propriety of such further remedial action in instances wherein the union has been adjudged a participant in the illegal conduct."[67]

Accordingly, the Court anticipates the awarding of front pay in the form of both ongoing payments as provided by Judge Cassibry—but for "all affected employees"—and lump-sum payments based on an assessment of future earnings. Presumably, the latter would be especially appropriate if either the likelihood of recall is not great or the potential for evasion in meeting future obligations for ongoing payments is great—for example, if work is contracted out. In connection with the former, for the first time the Court acknowledged that white employees may be compensated by means of a "hold harmless" remedy which would compensate whites for salary which they lost as a result of a remedy for blacks—and which was first propounded in the seniority context by Judge Sneed.[68] In *Bowman* and in last-hired, first-fired cases, it may take the form of "inverse seniority," which the United Auto Workers has proposed to the Big Three automobile companies for a number of years—providing senior whites with compensated layoffs while junior blacks continue to be employed.

If unions are involved in hiring or have a responsibility for fair hiring practices through the negotiation of a no-discrimination clause or if they are party to discriminatory seniority arrangements, they are liable for front-pay remedies. The labor movement will assume the burdens as well as reap the benefits of the remedies.

Punitive Damages

Punitive damages serve the same purpose as back pay. The Court's primary rationale for the rule in *Albermarle* is the same as the Eighth Circuit's in *National Lead:* back pay is a deterrent. Similarly, the punitive-damage remedy is a deterrent which attempts to make the defendants "an example" for the community. Well-reasoned cases have upheld the propriety of a punitive-damage award.[69] And the Supreme Court, without expressing a view about making punitive damages available under Title VII, has said in dicta that such relief is appropriate in actions proceeding under Section 1981.[70]

The availability of punitive damages under employment-discrimination legislation is particularly essential to the statutory scheme inasmuch as demonstrations, marches, the potential for violence as well as violence itself in the black community gave rise to the passage of the statute. Congress was concerned about the "unrest in the country today."[71] It is particularly important that plaintiffs in the black community be deterred from engaging in any form of self-help—and punitive damages are often seen as a substitute for self-help.

A second reason for the punitive-damage remedy, a reason which is part of the remedial statutory scheme of Title VII, relates to the fact that right to employment is extremely important and fundamental. The right to work in an environment free of discrimination affects not "just an individual's sharing in the 'outer benefits' of being an American citizen, but rather the ability to provide decently for one's family in a job or profession for which he qualifies and chooses."[72] Third, blacks who have been discriminated against by defendants can never be fully compensated by back pay or any of the other Title VII remedies. In addition to the pain and emotional suffering caused by employment discrimination, a black who has been deprived of his rightful place in the work force has been harmed in many other ways—for example, by being prevented from acquiring and enjoying the type of home or other possessions which would have been available had his income been higher or by suffering physical illness from being forced to work at a more dangerous or strenuous job than he would have had but for discrimination. These and countless other forms of harm, economic and otherwise, are not remedied by back pay. It is not clear whether compensatory damages besides back pay are available under the statute—and in any event, there is significant doubt that such damages can ever "remedy the future"—that is, encourage workers to apply for and take advantage of opportunities when they have been discouraged in the past.

An equally important point is that punitive damages are appropriate because they prompt the "private attorney general" and his client to stand up and protest discrimination. The award provides "an increased incentive for aggrieved individuals to bring suit"[73] and thus creates a greater deterrent to defendants' harmful conduct generally.

Finally, such money can often be used for the purpose of regulating union and employer conduct. For instance, the Association for the Betterment of Black Edison Employees, in *Stamps* v. *Detroit Edison Company,* prayed for punitive damages with a view toward obtaining money that could be utilized for monitoring adherence to the decree and bringing litigation against defendants who might emulate Edison and engage in similar conduct. The language of Title VII itself, in addition to judicial authority under Section 1981 and its parallel provisions, argues persuasively for punitive damages as well. Title VII was amended in 1972 to place in the judicial arsenal not only "affirmative action" but also any other appropriate equitable relief. Accordingly, although many courts have rendered punitive damages awards even though the statute is silent on the matter, under Title VII, the statute, through its explicit provisions relating to appropriate equitable relief, appears to support such relief.

Preliminary Injunctions

The Fifth Circuit Court of Appeals has held that a preliminary injunction may be obtained under Title VII without the threat of irreparable harm which is ordinarily required if preliminary relief is to be granted.[74] The court has stated that where a pattern or practice of discrimination is involved and the case has been filed by either the attorney general[75] or private plaintiffs,[76] such irreparable harm can be presumed. The court declared in a private-plaintiff suit, "Irreparable injury should be presumed from the very fact that the statute has been violated."[77] Among other considerations a court takes into account in determining whether a preliminary injunction should be issued is, first, whether there is a significant likelihood that the plaintiffs will prevail on the merits of the case at a full trial. In the context of Title VII litigation, this generally means that plaintiffs must present a prima-facie case on the basis of statistics. Second, the court must take into account the public interest involved. As with irreparable harm, the presumption is that the public interest supports an injunction against racial discrimination. Finally, there is the traditional consideration of whether harm to defendants would outweigh the need for preliminary relief. For instance, where back pay is requested as part of the injunctive relief, the practical problems involved in recouping such moneys if defendants prevail on their merits at the trial might in many cases argue against including back pay in the preliminary relief.

The EEOC has the authority, under the 1972 amendments, to sue against defendants in federal district court and to obtain preliminary injunctive relief. May an individual sue before the commission does, and—if the answer is in the affirmative—may the individual sue before the 180-day waiting period has elapsed? The Fifth Circuit, in *Drew* v. *Liberty Mutual Insurance Company*[78] noted that prior to the passage of the 1972 amendments plaintiffs could have filed suit for preliminary injunctive before the EEOC investigation and conciliation of unlawful-employment-practice charges. The court also took account of the fact that Congress was aware of the large EEOC backlog and therefore had provided for individual suits as well as those filed by the commission. Accordingly, the court, in *Drew,* held that preliminary injunctive relief could be sought by the individual without EEOC involvement and prior to the expiration of the 180-day period. Judge Tuttle spoke for the unanimous bench: "We conclude that in the limited class of cases, such as the present, in which irreparable injury is shown and likelihood of ultimate success has been established, (here this has been determined by the trial court), the individual employee may bring her own suit to maintain the status quo pending the action of the Commission on the basic charge of discrimination."[79]*

The significance, of course, is great, particularly if, as in *Drew*, retaliatory action by the defendant, in violation of the statute, is alleged. Few plaintiffs and lawyers will be willing to bring cases in federal district court if access to the courts is barred for at least six months and, as a practical matter, the EEOC (although it assigns priority to retaliation cases) can do very little or nothing because of its backlog.[80] (*Drew* has more significance for white female workers than for blacks, inasmuch as black workers could have brought suits for preliminary injunctive relief under Section 1981, without reference to Title VII.)

Attorneys' Fees

In *Newman* v. *Piggie Park Enterprises, Inc.*, the Supreme Court held that the award of attorneys' fees is an integral part of the statutory scheme of Title II—the public-accommodations provisions—of the Civil Rights Act of 1964. Rejecting the court of appeals' view that attorneys' fees should be awarded "only to the extent that the respondents' defense had been advanced 'for purposes of delay and not in good faith,' " the court took the broader view that "one who succeeds in obtaining an injunction under [Title II] should ordinarily recover an attorney's fee unless special circumstances would render such an award unjust."[81] The Court's rationale is highly relevant to Title VII cases, a point which was noted in *Albermarle*.[82] The Court said in *Newman:*

When the Civil Rights Act of 1964 was passed, it was evident that enforcement would prove difficult and that the Nation would have to rely in part upon private litigation as a means of securing broad compliance with the law. A Title II suit is thus private in form only. When a plaintiff brings an action under that Title, he cannot recover damages. If he obtains an injunction, he does so not for himself alone, but also as a "private attorney general," vindicating a policy that Congress considered of the highest priority. If successful plaintiffs were routinely forced to bear their own attorneys' fees, few aggrieved parties would be in a position to advance the public interest by invoking the injunctive powers of the federal court. Congress therefore enacted the provision for counsel fees—not simply to penalize litigants who deliberately advance arguments they know to be untenable but, more broadly, to encourage individuals injured by racial discrimination to seek judicial relief under Title II.[83]

At an early stage in the development of Title VII law, the courts held that the same presumption in favor of the award of attorneys' fees to prevailing parties should apply in Title VII litigation. Judge Alvin Rubin in the Eastern District of Louisiana said in an opinion affirmed by the Fifth Circuit: "Litigants under Title VII can obtain damages, and they are in this respect different from those who invoke Title II. But where Title VII suitors act on behalf of a class and successfully seek and obtain injunctive relief, they are acting as agents of the national policy that seeks to eliminate racial and other unlawful discrimination in employment."[84]

The appropriate standard in Title VII cases is the same as the one stated in

Newman—that a prevailing plaintiff should "ordinarily" recover an attorney's fee unless "special circumstances would render such an award unjust." The critical question is the size of the award. Two opinions are particularly instructive: Judge Robert Peckham's in *United States* v. *Local 3, Operating Engineers*[85] and the more detailed opinion of the Fifth Circuit in *Johnson* v. *Georgia Highway Express, Inc.*[86] In *Operating Engineers,* Judge Peckham asserted that the award of fees is "critical to the enforcement of the civil rights act" and that the "size of the award depends to some significant degree upon the underlying policy of encouraging litigation under the Act."[87]

The first factor emphasized both by the Ninth Circuit[88] and Judge Peckham is that the size of the award of attorneys' fees should be proportionate to the extent to which the plaintiff prevails in the suit. Other factors detailed in the Fifth Circuit's *Georgia Highway Express* opinion are: (1) the time and labor required; (2) the novelty and difficulty of the questions involved (the court noted that although the research and investment by counsel may be used by him in later cases, the plaintiffs' lawyer should not be "penalized for undertaking a case which may 'make new law.' Instead, he should be appropriately compensated for accepting the challenge");[89] (3) the skill requisite for performing the legal service properly (the trial judge is instructed to "closely observe the attorney's work product, his preparation, and general ability");[90] (4) the preclusion of other employment for the attorney owing to acceptance of the case (this factor appeared to relate to time conflicts created by complex litigation); (5) the customary fee for similar work (but in no event should the fee be below the minimum twenty dollars per hour prescribed by the Criminal Justice Act); (6) whether the fee is fixed or contingent on the amount of the award (the court concluded that the fee should not be greater than the amount the litigant is contractually bound to pay); (7) time limitations imposed by the client, particularly when new counsel is called in at a late stage of the proceeding; (8) the amount involved (the court stated that the amount of damages or back pay should be considered but that such considerations should not "obviate court scrutiny of the decision's effect on the law. If the decision corrects across-the-board discrimination affecting a large number of an employer's employees, the attorney's fee award should reflect the relief granted");[91] (9) the experience, reputation, and ability of the attorneys; (10) the undesirability of the litigation and the economic impact that taking unpopular cases can have on a lawyer's practice; (11) the nature and length of the professional relationship with the client, in view of the fact that a "lawyer in private practice may vary his fee for similar work in light of the professional relationship of the client with his office;[92] and (12) the reasonableness of the award in relation to other awards for similar cases.

Georgia Highway Express reflects a complex and somewhat conservative approach to determining the size of the attorney's fee. Although the standards must necessarily be hammered out on an ad hoc basis and the utilization of the standards by different judges will vary from case to case, the following passage is somewhat instructive about the court's general attitude:

To put these guidelines into perspective, and as a caveat to their application, courts must remember that they do not have a mandate under Section 706(k) to make the prevailing counsel rich. Concomitantly the Section should not be implemented in a manner to make the private attorney general's position so lucrative as to ridicule the public attorney general. The statute was not passed for the benefit of attorneys but to enable litigants to obtain competent counsel worthy of a contest with the caliber of counsel available to their opposition and to fairly place the economical burden of Title VII litigation. Adequate compensation is necessary, however, to enable an attorney to serve his client effectively and to preserve the integrity and independence of the profession. The guidelines contained herein are merely an attempt to assist in this balancing process.[93]

Some of the unease expressed by the courts in connection with commercial litigation involving class actions also seems evident in the *Operating Engineers, Georgia Highway Express,* and other attorneys' fees cases. Although the courts have held that public-interest and civil-rights-organization lawyers who are paid salaries are to be awarded attorneys' fees, the admonition that lawyers are not to become "rich" through these cases reflects the same kind of concern. (Many lawyers of defendants, of course, do become rich as a result of defending clients in this kind of litigation.) In many respects the concerns that have been voiced regarding large fees for plaintiffs' counsel in antitrust or securities-fraud class actions have little or no applicability to Title VII cases. It would seem that the proper concern of the judiciary is to guard against settlements which make plaintiffs' lawyers rich at the expense of members of the class who do not benefit from them and to protect those members if appropriate representations are not made on their behalf in class-action litigation.

Even if adequate attorneys' fees are awarded, the fact that Title VII class-action litigation is protected makes it likely that plaintiffs' attorneys must wait a long time before the fees are recovered—and meanwhile the costs of such litigation (also recoverable at the end of the contest) will pile up. Some lawyers of defendants are deliberately intransigent in order to exaggerate such problems. These realities make it impossible for most attorneys to take cases unless they are paid a large retainer; consequently, impecunious blacks and other minorities whom the law is supposed to protect go without counsel. Lawyers who could sustain the financial burdens are employed by large firms which generally represent defendants. The resolution of this problem is twofold: (1) foundation assistance for costs and, if possible, for attorneys' fees for plaintiffs' lawyers; and (2) a rule, similar to that applied to preliminary injunctions and front pay, providing an award of attorneys' fees and costs—both incurred and estimated for the immediate future—if plaintiffs have presented a prima-facie case that is not rebutted by the defendant's testimony and explanations. This rule would accomplish the purposes of the statute more than any other that could be devised under the statute. It would facilitate effective enforcement of the law by the private attorney general at a time when the government shows disinterest.

Testing

The most important Title VII case, *Griggs* v. *Duke Power Co.*,[94] concerned itself with the consequences of employment practices which, though neutral on their face, have discriminatory effects; this case established the job-relatedness criterion and placed the Court's imprimatur on the EEOC testing guidelines.[95] Moreover, in *Albermarle,* the Court, once again bestowing its approval on the guidelines, stated that even if job relatedness is evidenced, "it remains open to the complaining party to show that other tests or selection devices, without a similarly undesirable racial effect, would also serve the employer's legitimate interest in 'efficient and trustworthy workmanship.' . . . Such a showing would be evidence that the employer was using its tests merely as a 'pretext' for discrimination."[96]

The guidelines define discrimination as "the use of any test which adversely affects hiring, promotion, transfer or any other employment or membership opportunity of classes protected by Title VII . . . unless: (a) the test has been validated and evidences a high degree of utility . . . and (b) the person giving or acting upon the results of the particular test can demonstrate that alternative suitable hiring, transfer, or promotion procedures are unavailable for his use."[97] Persons using tests for selection purposes are required to have such examinations available for inspection for "indications of possible discrimination, such as instances of higher rejection rates for minority candidates than nonminority candidates." Moreover, the guidelines require separate racial validation where "technically feasible."[98] Are the guidelines to be applied by the federal courts? The Supreme Court specifically placed its imprimatur on the guidelines and encouraged the courts to defer to administrative-agency expertise. Moreover, some of the federal courts dealing with constitutional litigation brought against state and local governments prior to March 24, 1972, when Title VII became applicable to such entities by virtue of the amendments, looked to the guidelines for the purpose of establishing a framework to deal with the very difficult technical problems involved in testing.[99] In dealing with the private sector, the Fourth Circuit has, in the *Lorillard* cases,[100] specifically approved the guidelines. The Fifth Circuit, operating somewhat more cautiously, has taken the view that deference should be accorded the guidelines but that they need not be followed in every respect. Judge Tuttle spoke for the court in *United States* v. *Georgia Power Company:*

We view the reference by the *Griggs* court to EEOC guidelines as an adjunct to the ultimate conclusion that such tests must be demonstrated to be job related. We do not read *Griggs* as requiring compliance by every employer with each technical form of validation procedure set out in 29 C.F.R., Part 1607. Nevertheless, these guidelines undeniably provide a valid framework for determining whether a validation study manifests that a particular test predicts reasonable job suitability. Their guidance value is such that we hold they should be followed absent a showing that some cogent reason exists for noncompliance.[101]

The first step in establishing a testing violation of Title VII is normally[102] a finding that the test operates to exclude minorities in a statistically significant fashion. It must be established that the races differ in their rates of success on the test.

Although the courts have never determined—and probably could not determine—whether there is a precise figure that has general applicability, it would seem as though a mere marginal difference in the success rates would be inadequate. Other devices for discrimination may exclude besides the test; in such cases the test cannot be suspended. On the other hand, the Fifth Circuit has specifically stated that hiring through the utilization of other methods in spite of the use of the test does not remove the discriminatory taint of the test itself.[103]

Once a statistically significant adverse impact has been evidenced, validation or a showing of job-relatedness must be made by the employer or labor union. Validation can be "content validation"—determining whether a test measures directly the tasks that are to be performed on the job.[104] One of the best examples of such a test is one requiring that a typist type a certain number of words per minute. In some cases, a test can be "construct-validated" by showing that it accurately measures a specific trait, provided the trait is shown to be job-related.[105] But most tests cannot be validated for content or constructs and must instead be validated for "criteria relatedness." There are two ways of validating an examination for criteria relatedness: concurrently and predictively. Through the concurrent method employees who have already been hired are examined to determine whether there is a correlation between performance on the examination and performance on the job. In predictive validation, applicants as well as workers already on the job are scrutinized. In the predictive procedure no cutoff score screens out low-scoring workers who may do well on the job. Accordingly, the sample is more representative and the validity of the examination is not assumed prior to the validation inquiry. On the other hand, when the concurrent method is utilized, those who have not met the cutoff score are not at work and therefore their job performance cannot be examined. Consequently, the concurrent method is less desirable, since a broad spectrum of employees is excluded and the possibility of revising the cutoff score is more unlikely. Furthermore, the possibility of having minority employees examined as well as whites may often be technically unfeasible, inasmuch as minority members may have been screened out by the examination before they obtained employment status. Both methods suffer from a fundamental defect: they are necessarily dependent on subjective criteria of supervisors and thus may be troublesome where the supervisory work force is all white.

In undertaking criteria validation, first a job analysis must be prepared which sets forth the tasks involved in the job classification. Criteria for job success are established. The relationship between success on the examination and success on the job constitutes a validity coefficient. Such coefficients range from 0.00 to 1.00, and the coefficient 1.00 is representative of absolute validity. To qualify as nondiscriminatory, a test need not attain any particular validity coefficient. The guidelines merely state that the validation process must disclose that the test "evidences a high degree of utility."[106] "Utility" is not precisely defined. Three basic guidelines are, however, set forth. A low coefficient is acceptable when only a few applicants are to be hired from a large pool, or when few applicants not selected by means of the test become satisfactory employees, or when a job entails great human or economic risks. If none of these three conditions is present, a higher coefficient is called for.[107]

In addition to evidencing utility, a validity coefficient must be shown to be "statistically significant." According to the guidelines, this means that the size of the sample and the nature of the other elements of the validation process ensure that there is no more than a one-in-twenty chance that the relationship between the test scores and one relevant criterion indicated by the validity coefficient is fortuitous.[108]

The Fifth Circuit, however, indicated in *Georgia Power* that the courts may not adhere rigidly to the EEOC's one-to-twenty formulation.

Were the only criticism of the validation procedures the fact that there was a significance factor of 1 out of 15 or even 1 out of 10 instead of 1 out of 20, the employer might have better standing to complain that the guideline is arbitrary. We agree with the lower court that this, as well as other guidelines, must not be interpreted or applied so rigidly as to cease functioning as a guide and become an absolute mandate or proscription. Thus, Section 1607.5(c) must be read as setting a desirable goal and not a prerequisite.[109]

The EEOC guidelines take the view that since validity coefficients may differ for different races or ethnic groups, the examination must be validated for all races. This means that separate racial validations must be conducted. There is a possibility that the examination may be predictive at different cutoff scores for each race. That is, a black applicant or employee may score lower on an examination than a white worker yet perform just as well. Accordingly, the cutoff scores would be differentially predictive. The courts have been receptive to the need for differential validation. The Fifth Circuit took the position in *Jacksonville Terminal Company* that it is a *"non sequitur"* to conclude that blacks scoring lower than whites on the same test cannot perform the work as well. The court stated that what was required "most often [was] positive empirical evidence, of the relationship between test scores and job performance [by blacks]."[110] Subsequently, in *Georgia Power,* the Fifth Circuit, reversing the district court, stated:

Perhaps the most absolute bar to the action of the court below in accepting the work done by Dr. Hite as a final validation, particularly in view of our holding in . . . *Jacksonville Terminal Co.* . . . is the absence of any attempt to show that the tests did not screen out blacks as blacks. This minimum is designed to safeguard the key guarantee which the guidelines and the Act intend to assure—that the benefit of employment is not denied to blacks by the apparent neutrality of a facially objective ability test. . . . Although the significance of the concept of differential validity, viewed scientifically, is the subject of a considerable amount of professional debate, the possible fair employment implications are so great as to require separate racial group validation of tests in a case such as we have here in which there exists an available minority race sample of adequate size to conduct such a study.[111]

The availability of a large minority-group population or work force makes differential validation "technically feasible" within the meaning of the guidelines.

Unfair selection procedures which may violate Title VII in other ways may mask a differential impact of the tests which also violates the statute. That is, if the employer is selecting a very narrow group of black workers who may do extraordinarily well on examinations and have a high degree of educational achievement, they may score well on the examination—and this may mask the bias against those blacks who do not do as well but can compete in the work force effectively. On the other hand, in some instances there may be a very large number of minority applicants who, because they outnumber whites to a considerable extent at the hiring gate, are employed in larger numbers. While a prima-facie statistical case based on minority participation in the work force would show no violation of the act, the test may nevertheless unfairly screen out blacks and not take into account the fact that a large number of blacks are being turned away unfairly because the cutoff score fixed by the employer is not predictive for them.

Albermarle requires job relatedness, and where job relatedness is established, plaintiffs may show that a less discriminatory procedure is available to replace the one which has the differential impact.[112] This then is a modification of the "compelling state interest" standard applied in some equal-protection-clause cases which would seem to place the burden on the defendant to show the lack of a less discriminatory alternative. Moreover, the outcome of some of the constitutional litigation against the government prior to the enactment of the 1972 amendments indicates that the judiciary is a bit wary of moving too quickly in dealing with such matters.

The attitude of the judiciary is best demonstrated in two of the early public-employment testing cases: *Castro* v. *Beecher*[113] and *Chance* v. *Board of Examiners*.[114] In *Castro,* Judge Coffin of the First Circuit stated that a compelling-interest test requiring a showing of a lack of alternative means for accomplishing the legitimate purpose of employee selection could not be applied in its "full rigor" to racial-impact cases such as these. Said the court:

In effect, rigorous application of an alternative means test would, irrespective of history or purpose to discriminate, make it a denial of equal protection for a public employer not to utilize a racial quota, and accordingly, a denial of equal protection for the employer not to establish compensatory programs to remedy disparities of preparation. Such a result would be to translate what is a discretionary power of courts in giving relief into a mandatory standing obligation for employers. No employment case cited to us even arguably goes this far.[115]

In effect, the court placed the preliminary burden on the plaintiff rather than the defendant by stating that if expert testimony indicated that more than one method of adequate screening was available and if one was discriminatory and the other was not, the obligation on the defendant would be to use the nondiscriminatory method. Since, however, expert testimony was required, the absence of such testimony would not penalize defendants, since they would have no obligation, according to the court, to show that there was *no other* means of selecting employees.

In *Chance* v. *Board of Examiners,* Judge Feinberg, the author of *Bethlehem Steel,* wrote for a unanimous bench which held that examinations administered by the New York City Board of Examiners for the purpose of licensing supervisory personnel in the city's school system were unconstitutional. The court noted that, as in most of the testing cases, the examinations could boast of a "splendidly motivated genesis"[116] in that they had been designed to remove employee selection from a system of subjective choice (here involving political patronage) to an objective merit system. Nevertheless, the Second Circuit affirmed the district court's finding that no "strong showing of job-relatedness" had been made in connection with the examinations. The Board of Examiners contended that the statistical differences found by the district court between black and white success on the examinations were "insufficient to meet the constitutional test of invidiousness and [therefore did] not amount to a *prima facie* case of *de facto* discrimination." This was so, said the defendants, because white candidates passed the examinations at only one and a half times the rate of black and Puerto Rican candidates. It was contended that this difference constituted "mere under-representation" rather than the "gross unexplained disparity" that is a prerequisite for a prima-facie case.[117] Judge Feinberg, however, stated that not only the overall pass rate for all positions but also the pass rate for assistant-principal examinations had been considered, that the latter had a "magnifying effect" on the obstacles involved in passing the examinations seriatim, and that New York City had a much smaller percentage of minority principals and assistant principals than other large metropolitan school systems. The court, on the basis of these factors, found that a prima-facie case was presented.

Once this prima-facie case was established, said the Second Circuit, the defendants had the "heavy burden of justifying" examinations by showing their job relatedness. The court, in *Chance,* noted, however, that the Supreme Court had never applied the severe compelling-interest standard in cases in which the unconstitutional action "unintentionally resulted in discriminatory effects."[118] The court stated that the issue was a "difficult one" and therefore could not be resolved by "facile reference" to the cases that involved racial classifications that had been intentionally created. In any event, Judge Feinberg found it unnecessary to deal with this question, since he believed the examinations could be struck down as unconstitutional under the "more lenient equal protection standard." Because the district court found that appropriate examinations could be prepared but the defendants had not constructed such tests, the board had failed to meet even the requirements of the "rational relationship standard."

Lurking beneath the discussion of constitutional standards in both *Castro* and *Chance* is the question of whether defendants in Title VII and constitutional litigation can prepare examinations which will probably be predictive and job-related with a high degree of accuracy. The fear expressed in *Castro* is that a substantial burden on the employer will leave nothing but court-ordered quotas as the available option. In *Chance* the assumption by the Second Circuit was that the district court, by concluding that the Board of Examiners could produce an acceptable examination, had found the existing system unconstitutional according to the old "rational classification" equal-protection-clause standard. In *Georgia Power* the court specifically reversed the district court's conclusion that compliance with the guidelines was nearly always impossible.

PART II

LAW AND LABOR-MANAGEMENT RELATIONS

7 | Some Aspects of Taft-Hartley and Racial Discrimination

Racial Discrimination by a Union as a Ground for Denying Taft-Hartley Certification

Ever since the National Labor Relations Board's decision in *Hughes Tool Company*[1] in 1964 that a union violates its duty of fair representation under both Sections 8 and 9 of the National Labor Relations Act when it refuses to represent employees fairly because of race, the board has taken the position that a petition filed to revoke an existing certification held by such a labor organization is an appropriate procedure under Section 9. The theory stated by the board in *Hughes Tool* is that for the board to grant certification rights to an exclusive bargaining agent which engages in racial discrimination would constitute governmental aid and assistance to private parties engaged in racial discrimination, a result condemned by both the equal-protection clause of the Fourteenth Amendment and the due-process clause of the Fifth Amendment; the latter constitutional provision applies to an instrumentality of the federal government. For similar reasons, the board has held that a collective-bargaining agreement negotiated between a union involved in discriminatory conduct and an employer cannot serve as a contract bar or protection against a Section 9 representation petition filed by a rival union which is attempting to raid the employees represented by the discriminating incumbent union.[2]

Two important questions have remained unanswered, perhaps, in part, because of the infrequent use of the board's processes in unfair-representation cases. The first relates to the time that the racial-discrimination issue is raised by the parties. If a petition to revoke a certification is an appropriate means of denying government assistance to private parties that engage in racial discrimination, presumably the matter may be brought up at the time the union first petitions for representation. The difference between that situation and the situation in which revocation of an already issued certification is sought is that when the petition is heard for the first time the union may contend that it has not had a chance to demonstrate its good faith. Nevertheless, evidence concerning the likelihood that discrimation will take place at the particular enterprise or company involved may be inferred from the local or international's behavior and its employment practices. This is the position taken by the Eighth Circuit in *NLRB* v. *Mansion House Center Management Corporation.*[3]

In *Mansion House,* the court held that the board cannot constitutionally recognize, for the purpose of collective bargaining, a union which excludes employees from membership on grounds of race. The court said, "We conclude that the claim of racial discrimination allegedly practiced by a union seeking recognition as a representative bargaining unit under the Act is a relevant area of inquiry for the Board when the defense is appropriately raised before the Board upon a company's refusal to bargain."[4]

A central question in *Mansion House* related to evidence: Should the board rely on membership statistics as a basis for presuming union-membership policy on accepting nonwhites as members? The board answered negatively and appraised the discrimination charge on the basis of whether nonwhites had actually been rejected since 1968. The court properly repudiated this approach as "unrealistic." Referring to Title VII decisions as providing the applicable law on this issue the court said:

Statistical evidence may well corroborate and establish that a union has been guilty of racial practices in the past. In face of such proof, passive attitudes of good faith are not sufficient to erase the continuing stigma which may pervade a union's segregated membership policies. The fact that no minority applicant has been rejected by the union is not the sole test. When evidence suggests discrimination or racial unbalance the Board should inquire whether the union has taken the initiative to affirmatively undo its discriminatory practices. The admission policies of the union, the methods employed processing applicants, and the means utilized to publicize integrated membership and equal opportunity are only a few of the factors which deserve full scrutiny. . . .

In substance we hold the remedial machinery of the National Labor Relations Act cannot be available to a union which is unwilling to correct past practices of racial discrimination. Federal complicity through recognition of a discriminating union serves not only to condone the discrimination, but in effect legitimizes and perpetuates such invidious practices. Certainly, such a degree of federal participation in the maintenance of racially discriminatory practices violates basic constitutional tenets.[5]

The question of whether such practices constitute unfair labor practices in and of themselves is more complicated. The court took the board to task in *Mansion House* for the failure to consider such practices in connection with the company's defense in response to a refusal-to-bargain charge filed by the union against the company. Of course, *Mansion House* invites the employer to help himself, by determining initially that the union's policy indicates that it will not represent the employees fairly in the future. The court left to the board the question of how pretextual assertions (those utilized for the purpose of denying collective bargaining and not offered in "good faith") can be sorted out from other claims.

In addition to the issue of timing later resolved by *Mansion House,* a second problem that arises under the board's *Hughes Tool* doctrine relates in part to the question of so-called benign racial classifications. The *Hughes Tool* doctrine calls for the withholding of Section 9 certification whenever a union discriminates on the basis of race. Yet the board in some circumstances might wish to certify a unit on the basis of race. For example, although the board might generally be wise to withhold certification if a union's petition contemplates segregation of the races according to job classification or department, there may be circumstances where such a petition should be granted. The granting of such a petition will often increase the likelihood of collective bargaining, inasmuch as a large white constituency will probably vote against the union rather than be lumped with blacks in the same bargaining unit. There may be other advantages as well in a certification on the basis of race, but careful judgment is called for in making such assessments in a particular case.

Suppose, for instance, that a union asks for a separate grouping of black and white workers where it can be demonstrated that the white workers will be hostile to the upgrading of blacks and that the union's record indicates a lack of responsiveness on the part of whites. Should it make any difference whether another union is petitioning for the all or predominantly black unit and whether that union has a good record? In determining whether a craft-severance or separate representation petition is appropriate for skilled workers who seek to opt out of an overall industrial unit, the board has addressed itself to the question of whether the skilled workers are likely to be fairly represented in an industrial union and has inquired whether the industrial union has established a separate skilled-trade unit and has recognized and considered the peculiar interests and needs of a minority occupational group.[6]* Assuming the validity of benign classifications, there appears to be no reason why the board cannot undertake the same analysis with regard to racial minorities as it has with occupational minorities.[7]

The critical difficulty involved in the classification process is determining under which of two procedures, integration or separation, minorities are more likely to progress toward economic well-being. One factor to be considered, of course, is the attitude of each union. Another consideration is whether collective bargaining has flourished in the past where minority groups have bargained outside the structure of the largest union or the union representing the more skilled employee unit in the particular company or the industry generally. Another factor might be whether or not the industry is technologically integrated. Normally, technological integration of an industry is a reason for a single appropriate unit. But if the single union's record indicates a lack of responsiveness, might not the fact that the industry is integrated argue for more than one unit, on the theory that the employer and other labor organizations are more likely to pay heed to the minority group if economic pressure or a work stoppage in one unit will raise havoc or shut down the entire operation? These are all difficult questions to resolve in specific situations. But the board must face them if it is to remain faithful to its obligation under the statute to provide full freedom for all workers, including those that have been discriminated against or *may be* discriminated against if a collective-bargaining relationship is set up in which the parties are apt to ignore the interests and needs of black employees.

An important element in the rationale of both the *Hughes Tool* and *Mansion House* decisions is constitutional: to provide assistance to discriminatory labor unions in the form of certifications and bargaining orders is unconstitutional governmental or "state action." Bernard Meltzer has taken issue with this view, and much of his thinking appears to be based on the assumption that Title VII provides a remedy for discriminatees. Accordingly, in the opinion of Meltzer, the government has discharged its obligatioń under Title VII. Meltzer has declared:

A holding that the Constitution bars this jurisdictional approach has wholly unacceptable implications. It implies that all official agencies must have overlapping responsibility to uncover and develop remedies for racial discrimination. It also implies that the Constitution would prevent Congress from eliminating duplicative remedies by providing that a single agency should have exclusive jurisdiction over claims of racial discrimination by employers and unions. Whatever the wisdom of such exclusivity, there is no convincing basis for rejecting it on constitutional grounds.[8]

The difficulty with Meltzer's analysis—as this book makes clear—is that Title VII does not in fact provide for effective enforcement machinery. This lack impedes the efforts both of the government and the private attorney general. Thus the distinction between this situation and other state-action situations may be more a matter of form than of substance. And the constitutionality of a different judgment by Congress would also turn on whether the relief made available is designed to cure the evil. Meltzer assumes a very heavy burden in contending that Congress would be on safe ground if it eliminated all remedies but Title VII.

Breach of the Duty of Fair Representation as an Unfair Labor Practice

Of course, there has always been a major difficulty with a remedy which only denies certification to offending unions in Section 9 proceedings: strong unions engaged in a pattern of racial discrimination do not need to come to the board for representation rights, and, even if a petition for ratification and certification is filed, the union may continue to thrive without the aid of the law. Only when a proceeding is brought under Taft-Hartley's unfair-labor-practice provision, which empowers the board to issue a cease-and-desist order that is enforceable in the circuit court of appeals, can the unlawful conduct itself be actually enjoined. Accordingly, the question of whether racial discrimination by unions or employers violated Taft-Hartley's unfair-labor-practice provision confronted the board.

Even in the board's consideration of whether discrimination violated Taft-Hartley, the problems of black workers are hardly addressed. For the Supreme Court, long before the days of Title VII, held that union practices such as the operation of hiring halls are not per se violative of Taft-Hartley, in that they do not necessarily encourage union membership.[9] This conclusion defies reality; the hiring hall is a *de facto* closed shop, since in practice there is a requirement of union membership before referral to a job. The closed shop is illegal under Taft-Hartley—but the unions continue to use it, particularly when they have the benefit of a hiring hall. Moreover, even where blacks can become members, they have both quantitative and qualitative problems in obtaining referral—that is, problems with both the amount and the kind of work involved. Thus, aside from the question of the desirability of dealing with racial discrimination through Section 8 unfair-labor-practice provisions rather than Section 9 representation proceedings, the Supreme Court placed severe limitations on the board's ability to attack institutional discrimination by means of its unfair-labor-practice procedures.[10]

Nevertheless, the board undertook to attack racial discrimination more directly in 1964—through what the Supreme Court later characterized as its "tardy assumption" of jurisdiction over unfair labor practices.[11] That year, in the landmark *Hughes Tool* decision, the board held that failure by the union to represent bargaining unit employees fairly on account of their race was an unfair labor practice under Sections 8(b)(1)(A), 8(b)(2), and 8(b)(3). From the beginning of this controversy,[12] I have been of the view that Section 8(b)(1)(A), which makes it an unfair labor practice for a labor union or its agents to "restrain" or "coerce" employees in the exercise of their Section 7 rights to engage in concerted activities for the purpose of unionization and to protest what they deem to be unfair working conditions, presented the best opportunity to have unfair representation accepted as an unfair labor practice. First, as the board had previously stated in its *Miranda Fuel* decision,[13] workers have the right to be free from invidious treatment by a union, inasmuch as their right to "bargain collectively through representatives of their own choosing"[14] is contained in Section 7; the right cannot be restrained or coerced by labor organizations, according to Section 8(b)(1)(A). A second point was initially propounded by Michael Sovern:[15] the fact that employees have the "right to refrain"[16] from bargaining collectively through representatives of their own choosing under Section 7, and this right is premised on the concept that employees are deprived of the right to refrain by Section 9's bestowal on the union of the privilege to bargain as exclusive representative. Without the presence of Section 9, the argument runs, the union would not have legal sanctions for its authority to bargain for everyone within the bargaining unit, and the employee would have the right to refrain from adherence to the rules and regulations contained in the collective agreement and to bargain for himself.

Another basis for providing protection against racial discrimination under Section 8(b)(1)(A) is not mentioned in any of the opinions of the board or by other commentators: the right to "engage in other concerted activities for the purpose of collective bargaining or other mutual aid or protection,"[17] which is also contained in Section 7. The Supreme Court, in *NLRB* v. *Washington Aluminum Co.,* [18] required that this portion of Section 7 be given a broad interpretation. Employees protesting working conditions by means of a walkout, whether the protest is meritorious or not, are engaging in protected activity under the act.[19]* Accordingly, the board held, in *Tanner Motor Livery, Ltd.,* protests by employees and job applicants, including picketing with civil rights organizations against an employer's alleged racially restricted policies, are protected under this portion of Section 7.[20] Because their activity is protected, employees are immunized from discharge, although they may be permanently replaced by the employer unless management engages in an unfair labor practice which either causes or prolongs the walkout.[21]* Therefore, since black workers may be protesting discriminatory working conditions which are the result of unfair representation, the unfair representation constitutes restraint or coercion of an employee's right to engage in concerted activities for "other mutual aid or protection." A difficulty with this theory, however, lies in the fact that there may be many union practices which restrain or coerce Section 7 rights but do not interfere with the improvement of employment conditions and thus do not offend Section 8 (b)(1)(A).[22]* Congress deliberately limited the scope of that section by indicating that it was essentially aimed at union practices which involved mass picketing and violence—and was thus coextensive with Section 8(b)(2)—and which involved interference with employment rights based on the presence or absence of union membership or on a rule by which the union was attempting to enforce loyalty without proper business justification for the rule.[23] The Court has sounded this theme, stressing the narrow scope of Section (b)(1)(A), in *NLRB* v. *Teamsters Local 639* (*"Curtis Bros."*), where it was held that minority union picketing did not violate Section 8(b)(1)(A) even though it interfered with the ability of the majority of the group to work, because the section's legislative history included a prohibition against union violence, duress, and reprisals.[24] In *Local 639,* however, the court took pains to protect the right to strike contained in Section 13 of the act—and it quite properly indicated that Section 13 protected the right of a minority of the employees to engage in picket-line activity.

A more recent decision of the Supreme Court, *ILGWU* v. *NLRB* (*Bernhard-Altmann*),[25] appears to be more hospitable to the finding of a violation of the duty of fair representation under Section 8(b)(1)(A). In *Bernhard-Altmann,* the Supreme Court held that the execution of a collective agreement with a minority union in which that union was recognized as exclusive bargaining representative restrained and coerced the majority of employees of the unit in connection with their right, guaranteed under Section 7, to refrain from union activity. *Bernhard-Altmann* involved the utilization of Section 8(b)(1)(A) in a case in which the rights of the majority were being restrained or coerced, whereas the racial duty-of-fair-representation cases involve a minority. Yet this factor—that is, the restraint of the majority and not the minority—did not seem in any way essential to the Court's holding in *Bernhard-Altmann.* Moreover, the decision has been employed subsequently on behalf of a minority of workers in a unit.[26]*

Section 8(b)(2) makes it an unfair labor practice for a labor organization or its agents to "cause or attempt to cause an employer to discriminate against an employee in violation of subsection (a)(3) of this Section [this subsection makes it unlawful for an employer to discriminate on the basis of union membership or the lack thereof] or to discriminate against an employee with respect to whom membership in such organization has been denied or terminated."[27] Where blacks are not members of the union it seems plausible that discrimination against them is discrimination that has the effect of encouraging membership in the union and is, therefore, unlawful under this provision of Taft-Hartley. Accordingly, in *Hughes Tool* the board held, on the basis of the trial examiner's reasoning, that the failure to process a grievance of a Negro member of a segregated local violated Section 8(b)(2). The trial examiner rationalized that benefits were withheld which would not have been withheld if the Negro grievant had been eligible for membership in the white local. This rationale was expanded in *Local 12, United Rubber Workers* v. *NLRB*, in which the board concluded that Section 8(b)(2) was violated by the union's failure to process the grievances of blacks even where both races were members of the same union.[28]

In *United Rubber Workers*, there were separate seniority rolls for white males, Negro males, and females until March 1962. Both the board and the Fifth Circuit judged that the union contract provided for plant-wide seniority without regard to race or sex—even though their view of the practices, customs, and interpretations varied from that of the contract. Furthermore, in accordance with custom, racially separate plant facilities such as lunchrooms, rest rooms, and showers were maintained; the contract did not deal with these matters.

In August or September 1960, eight black workers were laid off, and in October 1969, a Mr. Buckner, having been notified that he was to be laid off again, inquired why a white employee with less seniority remained on the employer's payroll. Buckner was advised that the posted job that the white employee held was a "white job." Subsequently, Buckner and other black workers who were also to be laid off, executed affidavits to the effect that during the period of layoff subsequent to August or September 1960, new workers had been hired in violation of plant seniority rules. These affidavits were forwarded to the president of Local 12, United Rubber Workers, the exclusive bargaining representative of employees in the unit. Local 12 was requested to investigate and to take appropriate action. The black workers then appeared before the Grievance Committee and presented a more detailed complaint which charged that the original layoff and recall had not been in accordance with the contract's seniority provisions, and the complainants therefore demanded reinstatement with back pay; upon recall, the complainants wanted all the transfer rights set forth in the collective agreement; the complainants demanded the elimination of all color bars to plant privileges. The Grievance Committee nevertheless concluded that there was no contract violation and that the union, therefore, had no ground for complaint to the company. After this meeting, appeals were taken to the executive board of the union and the full membership. In March 1962, the complainants appealed the action to the union's international president, George Burdon. Burdon concluded that the decision refusing to process the grievances should be reversed.

Meanwhile, after Local 12's refusal to process the grievance, the President's Committee on Equal Employment Opportunity (a predecessor of the Office of Federal Contract Compliance) induced the union and the employer to arrive at a verbal agreement which resulted in the discontinuance of the no-transfer and no-upgrading policy for blacks. The complainants were reinstated, and apparently, thereafter, racial discrimination with regard to job opportunities, transfer, promotion, layoff, and involvement in the company's training program was discontinued.

Local 12, however, refused to process grievances concerning back wages; complainants therefore filed unfair-labor-practice charges alleging a violation of the duty of fair representation. The board found a violation of Section 8(b)(2). Curiously, the opinion sets forth no rationale for the finding. One theory, which was circulated at one point by some board members prior to a decision in the case, was that the segregated seniority lists and plant facilities encouraged white workers to remain union members and discouraged Negro workers from continuing as members. But this would be nothing more than a fiction in the worst sense of the word. It is equally plausible that black workers would attempt to become more active in the union on the theory that the union is most effective in determining employment conditions—or alternatively, that one is less effective if one does not participate in the political process of the collective-bargaining agent regardless of union strength. Accordingly, it would appear that the board's conclusion that a Section 8(b)(2) unfair labor practice is engaged in if the obligation of fair representation is violated does not pass muster.

Moreover, a few technical considerations in Section 8(b) (2) made both *Hughes Tool* and *United Rubber Workers* somewhat troublesome. We must remember that Section 8(b)(2) enjoins unions from engaging in conduct which will "cause or attempt to cause an employer to discriminate against an employee in violation of subsection (a)(3)." In *Miranda Fuel,* it was clear that the union had actively demanded and, indeed, achieved the derogation of an employee's status by depriving him of his seniority. The trial examiner in *Hughes Tool* equated the "action" taken in *Miranda Fuel* with the "inaction" evident in *Hughes Tool:* the union's failure to process the grievance. Probably, this difference is not very important, yet it seems that the framers of Section 8(b)(2) contemplated a more active role for the union. The statutory language becomes more troublesome when one realizes that under Section 8(b)(2) the union is only prohibited from causing an *employer* to discriminate against an employee in violation of Section 8(a)(3). Is the employer discriminating against a worker under Section 8(a) (3) when it fails to take action in response to a grievance which is never processed, the subject matter of the protest being racial discrimination rather than anything relating directly to union membership or the lack thereof—which is the subject of Section 8(a)(3), as well as 8(b) (2)? It would appear, then, that Section 8(b) (2) does not provide as solid a foundation for viewing a breach of the duty of fair representation as an unfair labor practice as is provided by Section 8(b)(1)(A).

The board in both *Hughes Tool* and *United Rubber Workers* has taken the position that Section 8(b) (3), making it an unfair labor practice for a union "to refuse to bargain collectively with an employer," [29] is also violated if the duty of fair representation is not carried out. Section 8(d), however, further defines the duty to bargain as "the performance of the mutual obligation of the employer and the representative of the employees to meet at reasonable times and confer in good faith." [30] As the *Hughes Tool* dissent stated, Section 8(d) contemplates and refers to a contractual relationship or the establishment of a contractual relationship between two parties, union and employer, and the "good faith" may be owed from each party to the other, rather than from both to the employees.[31] Neither the majority not the dissenting opinion was able to cite any legislative history—with the exception of one isolated statement[32]*—which could possibly support a Section 8(b)(3) violation in the *Hughes Tool* context. Moreover, as Sovern has noted, Section 8(d) speaks of "comparable obligations" between union and employer, and "of course, an employer can have no obligation comparable to the duty of fair representation."[33]

From a policy viewpoint, as opposed to a perspective that emphasizes legal requirements, the concept of "good faith" is admirably suited to the responsibilities imposed on the unions by the *Steele* decision. But even Archibald Cox, whose writings seem to have had much impact on the *Hughes Tool* application of Section 8(b)(3) to the duty-of-fair-representation cases, refused to argue for the idea's acceptance, conceding that the "point is open."[34] It would not appear that Section 8(b)(3) forms a proper basis for holding that a violation of the duty of fair representation is an unfair labor practice under Taft-Hartley.

In the leading decision on that matter, *Local 12, United Rubber Workers* v. *NLRB*[35] (an appeal of the *United Rubber Workers* decision), the court found a violation of Section 8(b)(1)(A) without considering Section 8(b)(2) and (3) issues. The court, speaking through Judge Thornberry, held:

Local 12 in refusing to represent the complainants in a fair and impartial manner, thereby violated section 8(b)(1)(A) by restraining them in the exercise of their section 7 right to bargain collectively through their chosen representatives. The mere fact Local 12's conduct may not have directly resulted in encouraging or discouraging union membership does not persuade us to alter our determination, for the language of section 8(b)(1)(A), unlike certain other provisions of section 8, is not restricted to discrimination which encourages or discourages union membership.

It is upon this point that we must respectively decline to concur on the reasoning of Judge Medina in *NLRB* v. *Miranda Fuel Co* . . . that since section 8(b)(3) was intended merely as a counterpart of the employer's duty to bargain collectively under section 8(a)(5), and since section 8(b)(2) requires a showing of discrimination by the employer under section 8(a)(3) which serves to discourage or encourage union membership, Congress must have intended that the application of section 8(b)(1)(A) should also be limited to conduct affecting union membership. This argument that section 8(b)(1)(A) should thus be restricted because section 7 rights are limited by these other enforcement provisions of section 8 is, as has been pointed out by one commentator in this area, to allow "the remedial tail to wag the substantive dog." . . . As exclusive bargaining representative, Local 12 had the duty to represent fairly all employees, union members and non-members alike. To adopt a narrow interpretation of section 8 (b)(1)(A) which would only protect the comprehensive section 7 right of employees to bargain collectively in those cases involving union conduct which encourages or discourages union membership would to a large degree render such right meaningless in the area of union administration of the bargaining agreement.

Moreover, the Board's recent assertions that fair representation constitutes an essential element of section 7 employee rights are even more convincing in light of the similarity in language between section 7 and section 2 of the Railway Labor Act, from which the Supreme Court in *Steele* perceived Congressional intent to impose such duty of fair representation upon the bargaining representative.[36]

Finally Judge Thornberry focused on two additional factors. The first is the question of pre-emption and the Supreme Court's holding that the board has exclusive jurisdiction over a matter which involves the employment relationship, as opposed to internal union affairs.[37] If employees could not utilize the remedial provisions of the statute which relate to the board's jurisdiction over unfair labor practices, it would be necessary for a worker to go to the courts to obtain effective relief. In other words, since a worker who had been unfairly treated in the employment relationship would not obtain adequate relief as the result of the revocation of a union's certification in a Section 9 proceeding, action essentially inconsistent with the Supreme Court's pre-emption doctrine would be imposed on him—resort to the judiciary for complete relief.

The second factor mentioned by the court is that the financial or other burden of suing defendants in federal district court would be considerably greater than in a proceeding before the board. Said the court:

The adequacy of the existing judicial remedies afforded individual unfair representation claims has been seriously questioned. Under current practice, the aggrieved employee is not only compelled to bear the substantial expense of an individual law suit, but must also face the burden of overcoming the strong judicial presumption of legality of union action in this area. Thus confronted with jurisdictional, monetary, and procedural obstacles, the individual employee may well find his right to fair representation as enforced by the courts more theoretical than real.[38]

In concluding that the breach of the duty of fair representation constitutes an unfair labor practice under Taft-Hartley, the court also took note of Title VII. Alluding to the fact that the controversy involved in the instant case had arisen three years prior to the effective date of Title VII, the court, nevertheless, stated that even if the matter had arisen subsequent to July 2, 1965, the complainants could seek redress under either Title VII or Taft-Hartley, or both. The court stated that the problem of overlapping jurisdiction would exist in the absence of its holding, since the Supreme Court had already held that relief from violation of the duty of fair representation could be obtained in the federal courts. The court said:

We recognize that while Title VII represents an appreciable addition to the protection afforded employee rights in the specific areas of discrimination covered by the Civil Rights Act, there continues to exist a broad potential range of arbitrary union conduct not specifically covered by Title VII which may also violate the union's duty of fair representation. The comprehensive right of an employee to be represented fairly and in good faith by his exclusive bargaining agent clearly encompasses more than freedom from union discrimination based solely upon race, religion and sex. The mere fact, therefore, that Congress has seen fit to provide specific protection to employees from union and employer discrimination in the area of civil rights in no way detracts from the legal and practical bases of our determination that a breach of the union's duty of fair representation constitutes a violation of section 8(b)(1)(A).[39]

Yet the board has not provided a forum that is superior to either the EEOC or the federal courts, despite the obvious advantages to which the Fifth Circuit referred. Very few charges alleging breach of the duty of fair representation, and an even smaller number relating to race or sex,[40] have been filed with the board. An examination of the issues which come before the board and of its response provides some insights into the lack of confidence in the board.

Some Implications of the Duty-of-Fair-Representation Doctrine

As Sovern has stated, presumably a union which is improperly representing employees and violates the duty of fair representation would not only be liable to have its certification rescinded but also would be unable to resort to utilization of the board's processes—particularly those relating to the union's right to enlist the board in support of its representation of employees within a bargaining unit. That is, such a union presumably should be denied use of the unfair-labor-practice machinery which the statute makes available to a union confronted with an employer who unlawfully has refused to bargain with its lawful bargaining representative. Until coerced by the judiciary in *Mansion House,* the board has refused to take this relatively small step.

In *Mansion House,* the Eighth Circuit, noting that membership in a labor organization is often a prerequisite for obtaining employment in the skilled trades and that a union which discriminates against blacks therefore "effectively deprives such employees of employment opportunities,"[41] concluded that the bargaining order could not be obtained by a union that engaged in such practices. To permit the use of the board's processes by such an organization would violate the Fifth Amendment of the Constitution and its condemnation of discrimination. Taking the same approach as the board and the Fifth Circuit did in connection with the representation issues under Section 9 as well as the duty-of-fair-representation issue under Section 8, the court stated that "any recognition or enforcement of illegal racial policies by a federal agency is proscribed by the Due Process Clause of the Fifth Amendment."[42] Accordingly, the court declared that if a governmental agency has merely recognized such a union as a bargaining representative, the government has "significantly become a willing participant" in the discriminatory practices. The court rejected the union's argument that the proviso to Section 8(b)(1)(A) which precludes the board's interference in a matter involving "the acquisition and retention of membership" should be construed as denying the board the power to withhold from a union which discriminates against blacks utilization of the administrative processes for compelling an employer to bargain. The court noted that the question of whether a union could use the board to assist it in a recognition dispute had not been discussed or contemplated by Congress when it enacted the proviso.

Mansion House leaves two major problems unresolved. The first is that, as in Section 9 proceedings, the impact of the decision is negative and defensive. The board is not utilizing the unfair-labor-practice machinery to require parties to cease and desist. Since *Mansion House* involved an allegation that the union would not represent black workers fairly because it excluded them from membership, the issue presented went beyond that confronted in the unfair-labor-practice context in *Hughes Tool,* in which discrimination against black *members* was involved. *Steele* had assumed that unions could exclude blacks from membership. A proviso of Section 8(b)(1)(A) stated that the statute was not intended to limit or restrict union rules relating to the acquisition and retention of members—and the legislative history of Taft-Hartley demonstrates that influential congressmen were concerned that blacks might obtain the right of admission to a union.[43*] Framers of the statute, such as Senator Robert Taft, sought to allay such fears.[44*]

Nevertheless, it seems that the board's unfair-labor-practice machinery (as well as its representation procedures) should be used against unions which exclude blacks from membership. In the first place, reliance on the proviso as a defense of a violation in such circumstances would just as effectively involve the government in private discrimination as in situations in which blacks are admitted to membership but still discriminated against in the employment relationship. Indeed, the *Mansion House* constitutional reasoning applies with equal validity to cases in which exclusion from membership is declared to be an unfair labor practice.

Second, it must be realized that whenever there is exclusion from membership, there is denial of job opportunities. The two are necessarily intertwined; therefore, an effective remedy must address itself to both. Finally, since Title VII itself has negated the dicta in *Steele* relating to the right of unions to exclude blacks, it should similarly override the proviso, in the interest of a uniform labor policy. Accordingly, *Hughes Tool, Mansion House,* and Title VII argue persuasively that a union's exclusion of blacks is an unfair labor practice under Taft-Hartley.

In addition to the problem of how to prove discrimination, the board is confronted with another issue on remand. The court discussed it thus:

There is a question whether the company here raised the issue of racial discrimination in good faith. The record demonstrates that the company did not suggest discriminatory practices to the union as the reason for its refusal to bargain. Nevertheless, aside from the public policy and national interests involved, we think constitutional limitations on the Board's process require recognition of a charge of racial discrimination as an appropriate ground of inquiry where a union's representative capacity is questioned. On the other hand, it should be clear that a refusal to bargain based on a union's alleged racial discrimination must not rest on pretextual grounds. The law in this area needs to be more fully developed by the Board. Prophylactic procedures may be needed by the Board to deter pretextual refusal to bargain with an authorized unit on the alleged grounds that the union is practicing discrimination in its membership. We leave this for the Board to work out.[45]

In a footnote, the court considered the "suggestion" that a refusal to order an employer to bargain might lead to labor unrest instead of putting a stop to discrimination. The court, citing Sovern, apparently was of the view that the union which was risking its life in a recognition strike would stop discriminating. Sovern said in the passage quoted in the note: "In almost all cases, this will be the choice [during the cessation of discrimination] urged by international unions, for few internationals now espouse racial discrimination. In fact, where racism is operative, it is frequently the choice of a local acting in defiance of a contrary policy stated but not vigorously enforced by its international."[46] Of course, these words were written before the full meaning of Title VII emerged. We have already seen that internationals as well as locals attempt to thwart the strictures of Title VII as a matter of stated policy. How long and how tenaciously the unions will cling to such attitudes is uncertain. But the unanimous policy of the AFL-CIO aimed at blocking any revision of seniority rules that was brought before the Equal Employment Opportunity Commission in May 1966[47] indicates that wherever discrimination develops as a consequence of economic selfishness on the part of white workers, the unions, generally speaking, cannot be expected to lead and educate such workers.

Mansion House raises a number of procedural and substantive problems which have not been fully resolved by the board. In response to that decision the board began to draft new rules providing for motions to disqualify labor organizations for certification as exclusive bargaining representatives and to revoke previously granted certifications.[48*] Under the proposed rules the motion to disqualify would have to be filed within five days after the tally of election ballots. Motions for disqualification would have to be raised in the manner noted above. Such motions could not be litigated at the pre-election hearing. Moreover, they could not be raised subsequent to the representation proceeding.

The purpose and effect of these regulations regarding the motion to disqualify would appear to be twofold. First, apparently, the rules were an attempt to convince labor organizations to correct their wrongdoing during campaigns and before the ballot box is utilized. Only if a labor organization is successful in the election will the board expend its resources to make a determination on a racial-discrimination issue. Second, the rules attempt to provide an element of stability by refusing to entertain *Mansion House* defenses against Section 8(a)(5) charges in an unfair-labor-practice proceeding subsequent to a Section 9 hearing, on the theory that it is not timely to raise the matter in such a proceeding. On the other hand, if there has been no certification, an employer may litigate the same issue by means of the board's unfair-labor-practice machinery—a formal, time-consuming process. The board's proposed regulations completely avoid the issue of what constitutes discrimination and leave the board's future adherence to the law of racial discrimination, as it has been promulgated by the federal courts, unresolved.

These draft regulations have never been formally proposed by the board, much less adopted. And, at least for the time being, the board has opted, in *Bekins Moving & Storage Company of Florida, Inc.* for a case-by-case approach to *Mansion House* issues, saying:

> We have considered whether we ought to attempt to define through rulemaking both the procedural and substantive parameters of our future consideration of issues such as those sought to be raised in this proceeding [a representation hearing in which the employer claimed that the union was disqualified from seeking an election by virtue of its discriminatory practices]. After much deliberation, we have concluded that we are not yet sufficiently experienced in this newly developing area of the law to enable us to codify, at this time, our approach to such issues.[49]

Nevertheless, the board's decision in *Bekins* was in keeping with the tenor of its proposed regulations. The board took the position that it is constitutionally compelled to engage in "a precertification inquiry as to a labor organization's willingness and capacity to represent employees on a fair and equal basis."[50] But it rejected the employer's request for such an inquiry before the election. The board will concern itself with the matter only if challenges are raised after the union wins the election.

In addition to this procedural limitation, the decision in *Bekins* implies a substantive limitation on the definition of discrimination which makes it appear more than arguable that the board does not intend to follow the Eight Circuit's instructions regarding adherence to Title VII law. The board carefully noted that primary responsibility for the administration of the civil rights laws as they relate to employment discrimination is in the hands of other agencies.[51] More important, the board emphasized a cautious ad hoc inquiry into both the nature and amount of proof and stated that to decline to certify a union was a "drastic" step. The board declared:

It is not our intention to take such a step [to decline to certify] lightly or incautiously nor to regard every possible alleged violation of Title VII, for example, as a ground for refusing to issue a certificate. There will doubtless be cases in which we will conclude that correction of such statutory violations is best left to the expertise of other agencies or to remedial orders less draconian than the total witholding of representative status. To reconcile these views with a full awareness of our own constitutional responsibilities will, we recognize, not always be an easy task, but the difficulties involved do not entitle us to shrug off our oath to uphold and defend the Constitution of the United States.[52]

Accordingly, it appears that the board will only refuse to certify if there is a serious or major instance of racial discrimination. The board's conception, of course, is significantly different from the view taken by the courts in accordance with Title VII: that racial discrimination in employment cannot be tolerated in any form. Perhaps a refusal to certify if violations are isolated or relatively minor would permit pretextual objections by unscrupulous employers attempting to avoid their collective-bargaining responsibilities. Yet, in light of the public policy against racial discrimination, such cases should be kept to a minimum—should be a rare exception to the general rule against tolerance of discrimination in any form.

Since *Mansion House* and *Bekins,* the board's record has not been outstanding. The most disappointing theme in the cases decided by the board is that a union cannot be disqualified as an exclusive agent if it is not responsible for *hiring* and its seniority system cannot be considered discriminatory in the absence of misbehavior on the part of the employer.[53*] Particularly pernicious is the board's failure to deal with unions' failures to protest hiring discrimination as prima-facie discrimination and therefore to conduct hearings which might focus on (1) the union's refusal to accede to protests against discriminatory hiring; (2) the union's refusal to press affirmatively for the elimination of discrimination barriers; and (3) the extent to which union policies relating to upgrading create a discriminatory environment which impedes fair hiring. This failure, coupled with an Old-Worldish antipathy toward the use of statistics as a measuring rod for discrimination, has limited the impact of the *Mansion House* doctrine.[54*] The principal beneficiary has been the International Brotherhood of Teamsters and its locals which operate under the National Master Freight Agreement in trucking. Even though numerous courts—and even the conservative Justice Department—have found the Teamsters' involvement in promotion bids discriminatory under national seniority contractual provisions, that union has escaped the *Manion House* net on the grounds that the Teamsters' Union does not control hiring and the Justice Department findings of discrimination by the union have not been litigated in a nationwide suit.

Jurisdictional Disputes

Under Section 8(b)(4)(D) the board is required to hold hearings arising out of work-assignment disputes between labor organizations and to make an award of work in such disputes.[55] An obvious question is whether the board can properly award work to employees represented by a labor organization which engaged in racial discrimination. In *General Motors Corporation* the board, confronted with a dispute between the UAW and the Die Sinkers, seemed to adhere to the concept expressed in *Mansion House* in a brief footnote dealing with the racial issue near the beginning of the opinion. The Board said: "The UAW offered to prove that all of the employees represented by the Die Sinkers are white, whereas many employees represented by the UAW, including some who would perform the disputed work if it were awarded to the employees represented by the UAW, are black. As the UAW made no offer to prove that racial composition resulted from discrimination by the Die Sinkers, the Hearing Officer properly rejected the proffered evidence."[56]

Even though the UAW did not charge racial discrimination in the proceeding (and most unions are reluctant to make such charges about their fellow unions in public), the refusal to consider the discrimination issue seems to have been erroneous on two counts: (1) mere "racial imbalance" appears to be a basis for withholding board assistance, according to the Eighth Circuit under the authority of *Mansion House;* and (2) when statistics of the kind introduced in *General Motors Corporation* are in evidence, the burden ought properly to shift to the party responsible to explain, at least, the reason for such statistics. In any event, in the more recent decision in *Local 440, International Longshoreman's Association,*[57] the board noted the existence of segregated locals, a segregated referral system, and the fact that the attorney general had instituted a pattern-of-practice suit under Title VII. The court had not granted the attorney general's request for an order compelling the merger of locals, hiring halls, and work gangs, although it had declared a prevailing work rule dividing work equally between black and white locals to be in violation of Title VII because it deprived longshoremen of equal work opportunities if either the black or the white group constituted a majority in a port. In *Local 440* there was not only evidence of racial discrimination but also of the kind of discrimination that directly provided the basis for an award the board would make through the award of work itself. Since the award would be made to an organization which lay claim to work because of racially discriminatory work-assignment rules, the Board would be actively encouraging discrimination. Accordingly, the board granted exclusive jurisdiction over all work in dispute to one or two black locals involved. The board said, "This grant represents an effort to eliminate racial discrimination by affirmative action in a manner which will, moreover, assure to all qualified employees in the Port Arthur area, whatever their union affiliation, an equal opportunity to engage in the disputed work."[58]

Three points should be made regarding the board's approach. First, eight years before the *Local 440* case the board had ruled on the same issue involving the same union in the same geographical part of the country—and the board specifically referred to its prior ruling.[59] Second, the board noted that the attorney general had instituted an action and that the relief requested had not been granted. The Board may have been looking at factors such as the involvement of the government as a basis for concluding that racial discrimination exists and, on the other hand, at the inability of another representative of the government to obtain the requested relief as a basis for intervening. Third, it was quite clear that the board's own remedy had been ineffective. The same pattern of discrimination attacked by the board persisted despite the agency's previous order.

Employer Liability under Unfair-Labor-Practice Provisions

One of the difficulties with the duty-of-fair-representation doctrine formulated by the Supreme Court in *Steele,* as well as with the more recent unfair-labor-practice concept contained in *Hughes Tool* and *United Rubber Workers,* is that it is one-sided. True, an employer may be derivatively liable. That is, if a union through its efforts coerces an employer into engaging in racial discrimination, the employer also commits a violation of the statute and must share the burdens of relief—specifically, by providing back pay.[60] But what if a union exerts effort in good faith but cannot convince a recalcitrant employer to cease its racially discriminatory practices? After all, while both industrial and craft unions play a major role in racial discrimination, employers are often primarily responsible. Discrimination frequently antedates the union—and much of it is attributable to management's hiring practices. Although the union may commence legal proceedings under Title VII against an employer,[61] is any relief available under the unfair-labor-practices provisions of Taft-Hartley? Can a remedy be obtained by a union which wishes to fulfill its obligations to represent all the workers fairly? Suppose, for instance, that blacks or Chicanos are congregated in low-paying jobs and that the union presses the employer to upgrade its minority workers. May it file an unfair-labor-practice charge alleging a violation by the employer of Section 8(a)(1), which exempts an employer from being subject to the "restraint and coercion" of employees exercising their Section 7 rights? Or must the union resort to enforcing the contract if it has adequate provisions, to altering its terms if they are inadequate, or to striking in order to change the employer's position?

This issue arose in *United Packinghouse Workers* v. *NLRB,*[62] in which union allegations that the employer had violated Sections 8(a)(1) and 8(a)(5) raised the question of whether or not the company had bargained in good faith prior to a union strike. The board had found that the company violated Section 8(a)(5) by refusing to bargain "meaningfully and in depth concerning actual racial discrimination practices then going on.''[63] The evidence indicated that all jobs with guaranteed weekly salaries during the year were held by whites and that none were held by Negroes or Mexican-Americans. Furthermore, one Chicano worker was paid a wage lower than that stipulated for the job he performed; all the other employees, who were white, were paid the proper wage. There were instances of arbitrary denial of overtime work to both blacks and Chicanos. Moreover, the company had segregated recreation facilities. The court noted that the trial examiner had found the following facts: "First, respondent takes office personnel and Anglo employees and their wives on a fishing trip; next it takes Anglo employees who do not wish to take along their wives; next it takes Latin and Negro employees without their wives. In 1965 and 1966 the Anglo trips were to a point about 700 miles away and lasted the best part of a week; the Latin-Negro trips were to a point about 300 miles away and lasted no more than 3 or 4 days.''[64]

In addition to protesting these practices, the union attempted to establish a seniority system, to provide open bidding for high-paying jobs, and to eliminate the practice of using employees in high-paying work while maintaining them in low-paying classifications. On the basis of these facts the board found a refusal to bargain by the employer, because it gave no "meaningful reasons" for its refusal to alter the status quo. But the board declined to hold that the employer's discriminatory practices in themselves violated the act—specifically, Section 8(a)(1)—and indeed the general counsel had explicitly decided not to prosecute the case on such a theory.[65]

The circuit court of appeals for the District of Columbia, after affirming the board's finding of a Section 8(a)(5) violation, held that the board had erred in not considering the possibility that the employer's racially discriminatory practices might constitute a violation of Section 8(a)(1). The court said, speaking through Judge Wright: "It is apparent that the Board has not felt itself unable to examine charges of union racial discrimination to determine whether they are true and, if true, what the effect is on the discriminated employees. No reason appears why employer discrimination is exempted from Board scrutiny.''[66]

The matter is a bit more complicated, and there are considerations to which the court did not allude. It is quite clear that the same Congress which passed Taft-Hartley rejected a fair-employment-practice statute despite President Truman's urgings both before and after the 1948 election; and Senator Taft and other legislators expressed the view that racial discrimination on the part of unions could legally continue despite the rather broad-gauged language of some of the new unfair-labor-practice provisions that had been made applicable to labor organizations by the 1947 amendments.[67] Nevertheless, the view that Taft-Hartley cannot be invoked against racial discrimination has been rejected by the board and the courts in several cases: *Steele, Mansion House, Local 440, ILA,* and—most relevant to the question at hand—the *Hughes Tool–Rubber Workers* decisions which establish that the duty of fair representation may be enforced by virtue of one of the 1947 amendments, Section 8(b)(1)(A). Since the same Section 7 rights that are protected by Section 8(b)(1)(A) are protected by Section 8(a)(1)—it must be noted again that the board and the courts have taken the view that employees may engage in protests against what they deem to be discriminatory working conditions and are protected by the statute from employer retaliation for such protests[68]—it would seem that if union racial discrimination violates Section 8(b)(1)(A), then employer racial discrimination must violate Section 8(a)(1). This conclusion is supported by the fact that Section 8(a)(1) is deliberately broader than Section 8(b)(1)(A). The former provision prohibits employer "interference, restraint and coercion," whereas the latter deals only with union "restraint or coercion." This language was deliberately chosen by a Congress which did not want to prohibit a wide variety of union practices which might "interfere" with Section 7 rights.[69] Accordingly, this difference in language argues for a stronger regulatory scheme for employers than for labor organizations.

Knowing that the overall framework of the act and such decisions as *Rubber Workers* argue for the proposition that an employer's racial discrimination is not necessarily immune from Taft-Hartley's unfair-labor-practice provisions, we come to a more specific question: In what circumstances, if any, does an employer's practice of discrimination "interfere with, restrain or coerce" an employee's Section 7 rights? The *Packinghouse Workers* court adopted the following analysis:

In the context of employer racial discrimination, the question reduces to whether that discrimination inhibits its victims from asserting themselves against their employer to improve their lot.

We find that an employer's invidious discrimination on account of race or national origin has such an effect. This effect is twofold: (1) racial discrimination sets up an unjustified clash of interests between groups of workers which tends to reduce the likelihood and the effectiveness of their working in concert to achieve their legitimate goals under the Act; and (2) racial discrimination creates in its victims an apathy or docility which inhibits them from asserting their rights against the perpetrator of the discrimination. *We find that the confluence of these two factors sufficiently deters the exercise of Section 7 rights as to violate Section 8(a)(1).*[70]

This rationale is by no means free from difficulties. The second portion of the two-pronged analysis is particularly vulnerable. For it is predicated on psychological studies similar to those employed by the court in *Brown* v. *Board of Education*.[71] Without making any judgment about the merits of that particular controversy, it is sufficient to note that in dealing with employment, the court has relied on the proposition that blacks, when discriminated against, are often burdened with the feeling and the badge of inferiority and are stigmatized and that the inevitable results are apathy and docility.[72] Nevertheless, it has become quite clear that discrimination often produces the antithesis of docility. The appearance of organizations such as DRUM,[73] the walkouts of a number of black caucuses and black organizations, and the demands that have been formulated in a number of industries indicate that discrimination can produce entirely different consequences. Of course, some of the material cited by Judge Wright evolved from a different era in our history. Today, as doors have begun to open, expectations have begun to rise and many black employees are bold enough to speak back. Moreover, the attitude and confidence of a northern auto worker on an assembly line are entirely different from those of his counterpart in a southern textile mill—a difference that has been apparent in labor-management relations generally.[74]

On the other hand, the clash of interests between aspiring blacks and the whites who are threatened by their advancement cannot be denied. The first branch of Judge Wright's two-pronged analysis is more valid.

Subsequent to the circuit court's decision in *Packinghouse Workers,* the board held on remand that it need not concern itself with the legal issues posed by Judge Wright, since, in any event, there was no invidious discrimination.[75] Again, as in *Mansion House,* in which a racially discriminatory union membership policy was alleged, as well as in *General Motors* in relation to Section 8(b)(4)(d), the board specifically refused to acknowledge the existence of statistics which, at a minimum, would establish a prima-facie case of discrimination under Title VII.

In *Jubilee Manufacturing Company,*[76] a sex discrimination case, the board rejected the approach taken by the District of Columbia Circuit Court of Appeals in *Packinghouse Workers.* The complaint alleged that the employer had violated Sections 8(a)(1) and (3) of the act by discriminating against women in granting wage increases and paying wage rates to male employees based solely on sex. Furthermore, the complaint also alleged that the employer violated Section 8(a)(5) of the act by insisting, to the point of impasse during negotiations, on contractual provisions upon which to predicate its authority to continue the practice of unilaterally granting wage increases and paying wage rates to its workers on a sexually discriminatory basis. The administrative law judge had concluded that the record did not establish a practice of discrimination based on sex. "He therefore found it unnecessary to decide whether an employer's policy and practice of invidious discrimination against its employees on the basis of race, color, religion, sex, or national origin interferes with or restrains the discriminated employees in exercising their Section 7 rights in violation of Section 8(a)(1) and (3) of the Act."[77] Having found that there was no discrimination on the basis of sex by the respondent, the administrative law judge concluded that the wage-rate pattern was a mandatory subject of bargaining within Section 8(d) of the act, and could therefore be negotiated until impasse.[78] Moreover, the administrative law judge found that the union rather than the employer was responsible for the impasse that was reached, and therefore no unlawful conduct could be charged against the employer.

This time, avoiding the question of the administrative law judge's finding of no discrimination because it had "serious doubts about [its] validity"—a position contrasting with the one previously taken in the *Packinghouse Workers* remand— the board specifically held that discrimination based on race, color, religion, sex, or national origin "standing alone" is not inherently destructive of Section 7 rights and, therefore, not violative of Sections 8(a)(1) and (3) of the act. The board said, "There must be actual evidence, as opposed to speculation, of a nexus between the alleged discriminatory conduct and the interference with, or restraint of, employees in the exercise of those rights protected by the Act."[79]* Accordingly, the board specifically expressed its respectful disagreement with the rationale in *Packinghouse Workers.*

In this connection, the board claimed that an employer's discrimination might well have the effect of creating a clash between racial or sexual groups but that this result was "by no means inevitable."[80] The board, referring to the weaknesses in Judge Wright's reliance on the "docility" issue, stated:

A continued practice of discrimination may, in fact, cause minority groups to coalesce, and it is possible that this could lead to collective action with non-minority group union members. Furthermore, docility is only one of several possible consequences of an employer's discrimination. In light of the increased militancy of minority groups today, it seems apparent that minority groups in different areas of the country, in different situations and at different times, react dissimilarly to discriminatory practices.[81]

With regard to the 8(a)(3) allegation, the board concluded that a policy and practice of invidious discrimination in the face of a union's effective efforts to eliminate such discrimination do not have the "foreseeable consequence" of discouraging union membership within the meaning of the act. The Board said on this matter: "Ineffective efforts in other areas, as for example when a union seeks successfully to gain a wage increase, may well result in a union's losing face with the employees it represents. Yet, to say that an employer's refusal to give a wage increase violates Section 8(a)(3) or (1) because of this loss of face seems to us beyond the reasonable intent of this Statute."[82]

The weakness of *Jubilee,* and the strength of *United Packinghouse Workers,* are related to the first portion of the two-step analysis. It seems likely that a clash between groups will take place as a result of discrimination even though it is not certain how the minority group will react. The steady stream of litigation under Title VII before the federal courts and the unwillingness of a large number of employers and labor organizations to change patterns and practices of racial discrimination seem to bear out this assumption. Consequently, the proper approach ought to be to expect such a clash and to impose a burden on the respondent to prove that one has not taken place in a particular instance. Where the burden is met, it should then be required that the charging party or the general counsel have the responsibility of coming forward with evidence showing that blacks or other racial minorities have been the victims of discrimination to such an extent that their aspirations have been completely supressed. The rebuttal will be difficult—but overcoming the first presumption will probably be even more difficult.

Racial Discrimination and Duty to Bargain Under Sections 8(a)(5) and 8(b)(3)

Section 8(a)(5)[83*] of the act was at issue in both *Packinghouse Workers* and *Jubilee.* In both cases, a union filed charges against an employer, alleging that the latter had not met its bargaining obligations with respect to race and sex discrimination issues. Under Sections 8(a)(5) and 8(b)(3)[84*] both labor organizations and employers have an obligation to bargain with each other in good faith.[85*] This does not require concessions by either party, and the board will not impose them—although recalcitrance and obstinacy at the bargaining table often reflect a state of mind which is inconsistent with good faith.[86*]

In the Supreme Court's landmark decision of *NLRB* v. *Borg-Warner Corp.,*[87] handed down in 1958, certain categories of matters that are subjects for the collective-bargaining process were established. The Court held that if an item under discussion was a mandatory subject for bargaining involving a term or condition of employment within the meaning of the statute, both parties are required to bargain to the point of impasse. Once impasse is arrived at and the parties are deadlocked, there is no obligation to bargain further. A failure to bargain until impasse will violate the statute. The parties, while obligated to discuss certain nonmandatory subjects for bargaining, are not under any compulsion to bargain to the point of impasse. Their insistence on doing so violates the statute, just as refusal to discuss a subject on any basis will similarly violate the law. Finally, the parties may not bargain about subjects that are illegal. A union or employer representative that insists on bringing up such a subject will run afoul of either Section 8(a)(5) or Section 8(b)(3).

The subject of racial discrimination and proposals for its elimination relate to employment conditions within the meaning of Section 8(d) of the act.[88] Accordingly, proposals for a no-discrimination clause or efforts to eliminate discrimination through the collective-bargaining process constitute mandatory subjects, and the party that refuses to discuss the issue runs afoul of the act. Conversely, an employer or union that adheres to the discriminatory status quo or proposes discriminatory alterations in the relationship or contract violates Taft-Hartley by giving cause for raising such an issue.

As is often the case, the principle is relatively easy to state but considerably more difficult to apply to a particular set of facts. For instance, in *Southwestern Pipe, Inc.* v. *NLRB*,[89] the board and the Fifth Circuit were confronted with the following situation. At the outset of contract negotiations, the union proposed and the employer accepted a simple no-discrimination clause which obligated both parties not to "discriminate against any employee or applicant for employment because of race, color, creed, national origin or sex." The employer, however, refused to accede to demands for a provision in the contract basing advancement upon seniority rather than merit. The union representative claimed that the merit system showed "on the surface" discrimination against blacks. The union then requested that the previous clause be dropped and replaced with one which reads: "Company agrees that it will not discriminate in rates of pay, rate of promotion or reclassification or any other employment condition or benefit on the sole basis of race."

Subsequently, the company put forward a comprehensive no-discrimination proposal which, in the court's words, set forth the company's

historical commitment to the Plans for Progress and the basic principles of equal opportunity for minority groups, reciting negative commitments in the language of the Civil Rights Act and Plans for Progress regulations, prescribing a program of affirmative action following the employer's existing contractual commitment as a subscriber to the Plans for Progress, calling for joint employer and union review of all employment histories to obliterate any vestige of discrimination to the full satisfaction of the union and the employer before conclusion of the negotiations proposing periodic review of work histories and practices to assure absence of discrimination and continued implementation of the Affirmative Action

Program, with participation of an outside expert advisory consultant on equal opportunity, providing that enforcement be through the specialized consultant, with administrative agency and judicial review as a final resort instead of arbitration, and discouraging undue publicity of racial discrimination problems being processed thereunder.[90]

Initially the union responded favorably, but subsequently it criticized portions of the proposal. The provisions the union found particularly objectionable stated that a disparity in wage rates within the range of rates provided for an employee's classification was not to be considered evidence of discrimination. Another provision the union found troublesome stated that discrimination was not to be inferred from the fact that employees of different classifications and disparate rates of pay were assigned to the same work. The board, affirming its trial examiner, had found that these proposals would preclude a review of the disparate nature of rates during attempts to assess discrimination and that union abdication would represent a breach of its duty to represent all employees in the unit fairly. Moreover, the board noted that in the past blacks had been locked into low-level jobs.

The Fifth Circuit saw the matter differently and rejected the proposition that these contractual proposals were necessarily interwoven into an earlier discriminatory pattern. The court concluded that the employer had "removed all racial barriers and segregated practices with the first Executive Order under the Eisenhower Administration."[91] This decision, more than arguably erroneous in light of its failure to consider the issue of past discrimination to which the Fifth Circuit has admirably addressed itself in the Title VII context in cases such as *Local 189, United Papermakers,*[92] *Vogler,*[93] and numerous others,[94] is important not so much for the result reached but because it illustrates the thorny problems that arise at the collective bargaining table when proposals and counterproposals are made by two parties, both purportedly attempting to eliminate all vestiges of discrimination.

The consequences, of course, for both parties may be significant. For the union, if it can demonstrate that the employer has engaged in an unlawful refusal to bargain and that the refusal either caused or prolonged a strike, the result is that striking employees are entitled to both reinstatement and back pay. In the case of an economic strike, which is not caused by unlawful conduct, the workers, though exercising a Section 7 right, do not possess the same rights as unfair-labor-practice strikers.[95] Also, the employer, if it wishes to lock out workers in order to improve its bargaining stance, may have its ability to do so lawfully considerably enhanced by the position it takes in good faith at the bargaining table. Accordingly, if it has bargained at length with an obstreperous and unreconstructed trade union, the chances of convincing the board and the courts that it has bargained lawfully to the point of impasse about a mandatory subject are good. The position is strengthened even more if it can be shown that the union itself insisted on a discriminatory approach to the problem instead of simply proposing, in good faith, a different remedy.

Can an employer or union, once a collective-bargaining agreement has been entered into, propose a modification of the agreement in order to end a discriminatory practice, and if so, can either eventually alter the agreement unilaterally if necessary? Section 8(d)(4) states that where a contract is in effect, the duty to bargain collectively implies that no party shall terminate or modify the contract without sixty days' notice prior to the expiration date of the contract. This means that the party that insists on such a termination or modification prior to the sixty days would ordinarily violate Section 8(a)(5) or 8(b)(3). The difficulty is that an unlawful act involving racial discrimination is at issue. The union is commanded by both *Steele* and *United Rubber Workers,* as well as Title VII, to take affirmative action to eliminate racial discrimination in employment. The employer under *Packinghouse Workers,* if that is good law (a matter which only the Supreme Court can decide), is obligated to eliminate invidious discrimination on account of race, and Title VII should call for the same obligation. Moreover, the courts have said on numerous occasions that collective-bargaining agreements containing clauses which are discriminatory have no impact on the parties' contractual or statutory obligations beyond creating liability, of course, for those who have negotiated such terms. That has been made clear in the Title VII seniority cases. Judge Dyer, speaking for the Fifth Circuit, has stated in particularly graphic language: "That hoary collective bargaining agreements now mandate perpetuation of past aberrations from the governmental policy [against racial discrimination in employment] does not affect the propriety of judicial action. . . . Such agreements do not, *per se,* carry the authoritative imprimatur and moral force of sacred scripture, or even of mundane legislation."[96]

Accordingly, it seems quite proper for a union or employer to modify contract provisions which are at odds with the commands of Taft-Hartley itself, as well as with Title VII and other civil rights legislation—particularly in light of the Supreme Court's judgment that the board should look at the federal labor policy expressed in all labor statutes while arriving at appropriate interpretations of the NLRA. This doctrine is evident in the Court's decisions in both *Southern Steamship Co.* v. *NLRB*[97] and *Textile Workers Union* v. *Lincoln Mills.*[98] In *Lincoln Mills,* the Court stated that "judicial inventiveness" in labor-management disputes should take into account the policies contained in other labor statutes.[99] And in *Southern Steamship,* the Court said: "It is sufficient for this case to observe that the Board has not been commissioned to effectuate the polices of the Labor Relations Act so single-mindedly that it may wholly ignore other and equally important Congressional objectives. Frequently, the entire scope of Congressional purpose calls for careful accommodation of one statutory scheme to another and it is not too much to demand of an administrative body that it undertake this accommodation without excessive emphasis upon its immediate task."[100]

The board has not always been faithful to the Court's instructions in *Southern Steamship* to take into account other statutes, such as Title VII. Indeed, it has ignored the relevant law of Title VII and in some instances even refused to note its potential relevance. Subsequent to its civil rights decisions, however, the board, when considering the relationship between Taft-Hartley and the 1959 Landrum-Griffin amendments dealing with internal union democracy, stated, in *Graziano*

Construction Company, that it must consider "the full panoply of congressional labor policies in determining the legality of a union fine."[101] At no point did the board take note of the fact that its position in Graziano is in complete contradiction to its refusal to consider Title VII and other civil rights legislation and their relationship to Taft-Hartley. The board's insensitivity to Title VII developments has caused it to run afoul of the views of the circuit courts of appeals, not only in *Mansion House* and *Packinghouse Workers,* but also in *Emporium Capwell* v. *NLRB,* in which the District of Columbia Court of Appeals, citing *Southern Steamship,* rebuked the board for its failure to take Title VII policies into account.[102] The view that Title VII is relevant to the NLRA has been confirmed by the Supreme Court in *Emporium Capwell* as well.[103]

The General counsel, albeit operating under a somewhat different standard in determining whether a complaint should be issued, seems to have had a better understanding of the strictures of *Southern Steamship* and *Lincoln Mills* than the five-member judicial arm of the board has. For instance, in one case the general counsel had occasion to consider, an employer association and a union had a collective agreement under which the union was recognized as the exclusive bargaining representative for all employees. The contract provided for an apprenticeship program. During the term of the agreement, the U.S. Department of Transportation ordered that all federal funds for highway construction in the area be withheld from the state for an indefinite period because federal-highway-construction contractors were not meeting their equal-employment-opportunity obligations under the executive order (the Justice Department had also filed suit under Section 707 of the 1964 statute against a number of unions, including the union involved, but no violation by this union was found). In order to remedy the unlawful conduct and to obtain a release of government funds, representatives of the state and of six crafts involved in highway construction entered into negotiations regarding a program which would, in the general counsel's words, "reasonably facilitate equal employment opportunity for minority citizens in those crafts." Federal and state officials viewed a coordinated program in which all trades participated as essential and, with regard to the union in question, determined that a twelve-week orientation and training course would suffice. The union took the position that such a program was inappropriate and in violation of its agreement, since it was inconsistent with its apprenticeship program, which required four years to complete. Although the union made alternative proposals to the officials involved, an impasse was ultimately reached on this point. The employer association, on the other hand, not engaging in bargaining with the union that was *independent* of the bargaining with government officials, accepted the plan devised by the government.

Accordingly, the union alleged that the employers' actions constituted a modification of the collective-bargaining agreement and, as such, were in violation of the requirements of Section 8(a)(5) of the act. The general counsel, however, refused to issue a complaint, concluding that, although employer-union discussion would "generally be required before an employer would be free to enter into a 'hometown' equal employment opportunity plan which has an impact upon existing collective bargaining agreements, further discussions between the Employer and the Union would have served no purpose since the Employer could not change the governmental position which had already been rejected by the Union.'' Consequently, even though the collective agreement was modified by virtue of the arrangement entered into between the employer and governmental officials, the employer had not rejected the collective-bargaining concept and therefore had not violated the statute. The general counsel specifically stated that the plan was devised in accordance with both the antidiscrimination prohibitions of Title VII and the affirmative-action provisions of Executive Order 11246.

A number of principles can be derived from the statements of the general counsel. It is quite clear that despite the language of the agreement unilateral changes or negotiations which affect the discrimination issue can take place during the term of the contract. Taft-Hartley presents no insurmountable barriers to appropriate unilateral modifications by either party. As a practical matter, moreover, an employer or labor organization may be in a very comfortable legal (as well as psychological) position if such modifications are made in conjunction with discussions with governmental officials. Such discussions and involvement with the government, however, ought not to be a *sine qua non* to the conclusion that the modification is permissible. If they were, employers or labor organizations would have to wait for the government, which is often slow-moving and poorly motivated, or invite governmental involvement—which most parties are unwilling or unlikely to do. There is no reason why employers and labor unions cannot propose and, where necessary, act upon modifications. Employers, of course, are in a position to implement the modification, and unions, if they have the economic muscle, can engage in a work stoppage to obtain it. In effect the government's inquiry would be similar to that employed in the Section 8(a)(5) context of *Packinghouse Workers* and *Southwestern Pipe:* an examination of the respective attitudes of the parties in order to determine whether one party insists on taking an unlawful position or to assess one party's open-mindedness regarding proposals that are put forward either to eradicate the underutilization of minority-group workers or to implement the policies of Title VII. Since discrimination issues constitute terms and conditions of employment within the meaning of Section 8(d) of the act, the party that avoids its bargaining obligation violates the statute.

The general counsel's opinion indicates that discussions with the government can suffice as negotiations within the meaning of the act, at least if the union has been notified and its position indicates that further discussion will not be productive. In essence, the union's attitude in discussions with government officials by both parties can lead to an impasse. If the union is not directly involved in any discussions with the government itself, perhaps the requirements of the statute are that *someone* must extend an invitation to the union to become involved in some fashion. Nevertheless, even this kind of effort may not be considered necessary if extending the invitation would in effect be a futile act. If the union, because of its earlier behavior as well as responses it may have made to various proposals and requests in the past, has foreclosed any kind of meaningful discussion, an invitation would seem to be futile. Even though a compelling case cannot be made, it would seem that an invitation may not be necessary if the union is, in effect, notified about such discussions and can attempt to involve itself by a demand for bargaining. In short, the traditional collective-bargaining-process requirements of Taft-Hartley need not necessarily be applied to this new and complex situation. Modifications of collective-bargaining-agreements, discussions with the government outside the context of the normal two-party relationship, and in some instances even a failure to invite the labor organization to participate may be perfectly appropriate under the act. In my judgment, they are consonant with the policies implicit in Title VII.

Another very important problem that arises from the duty to bargain relates to the emergence of black caucuses, black worker organizations, and an increasing interest by civil rights organizations in the day-to-day administration of contracts and employment conditions as they affect the elimination of discrimination. In many situations, particularly in automobile plants where black worker organizations have flourished and where union default in dealing with allegations of discrimination is involved, as in the relationship between the Utility Workers Union and the Detroit Edison Company, employers may find it necessary and often of critical importance to talk directly with such organizations. Such groups may frequently engage in walkouts, stoppages, and picketing in defiance of no-strike clauses and without union authorization if problems relating to employment discrimination are not resolved. If labor organizations do not effectively discharge their obligation to employees within the unit, the employer must be in a position to go forward and initiate discussions and proposals unless it wants to invite havoc. Furthermore, such organizations may often have standing to sue concerning such matters. Discussions before and after the commencement of litigation may be a prerequisite to resolution of such problems. After all, Title VII, even subsequent to the March 24, 1972, amendments to the statute, encourages the conciliation of disputes without judicial involvement. The objective is the negotiation of a conciliation agreement to which a minority-worker group or civil rights organization is party. How can such efforts be undertaken if employers (as well as labor organizations) foreclose discussions?

The difficulty, of course, arises from the exclusive-bargaining-representative concept. The Court, usually in relation to attempts by individuals to bargain for their own contracts, has explicitly stated that the obligation means the duty to treat with no others than the exclusive representative. Yet the matter is not so simple as this definition implies. Section 9 of the act, which establishes the exclusive-bargaining-representative principle, contains two provisos. The first states that "any individual employee or a group of employees shall have the right at any time to present grievances to their employer and to have such grievances adjusted without the intervention of the bargaining representative, as long as the adjustment is not inconsistent with the terms of a collective-bargaining contract or agreement then in effect." The second proviso is that such action is appropriate if "the bargaining representative has been given opportunity to be present at such adjustment."[104]

The first point that must be made is that the provisos have been uniformly interpreted as imposing no obligation upon management. They are simply directed to the question of what conduct an employer may, if it wishes, engage in without offending the exclusive-bargaining-representative principles contained in the first portion of Section 9.[105] Although the Second Circuit has held that a rival labor organization is a "group of employees" within the meaning of the Section 9 proviso,[106] the weight of judicial authority, and the opinion of the board, appear to indicate that such a reading of the statute is contrary to its central policies.[107] If black caucuses, black worker organizations, and civil rights groups generally are to be excluded on the same basis, the inquiry inevitably must focus on the question of whether such a group is a "labor organization" within the meaning of the act. For this purpose examination must be made of Section 2(5) of the statute, which provides that "the term 'labor organization' means any organization of any kind, or any agency or employee representation committee or plan, in which employees participate and which exists for the purpose, in whole or in part, of dealing with employers concerning grievances, labor disputes, wages, rates of pay, hours of employment, or conditions of work."[108] The definition, appropriately, has been given a broad gloss by the board and the court. In *NLRB* v. *Cabot Carbon Co.*[109] the Supreme Court held that Congress intended the term to include those groups which merely "deal" with the employer as well as the more traditionally structured unions which bargain collectively as representatives of the majority. The question is important, not simply for determining employer liability under Sections 8(a)(5) and (9), but also for determining whether other groups than unions are labor organizations for the purposes of the Section 8(b) provisions of the act when they resort to industrial warfare.[110]

The general counsel has taken the position that black individuals who join together "for the purpose of securing equal employment opportunities" do not necessarily constitute a labor organization within the meaning of Section 2(5). A number of factors appear to be important in this connection. The first is whether a civil rights or black worker organization attempts to "deal with" an employer in the same fashion as a labor union or work group with bargaining responsibilities. A critical question appears to be whether an organization attempts either to displace an incumbent union already present or, alternatively, to establish itself as some kind of collective-bargaining representative. If the facts do not bear out such an intent, and if an organization "sought to work with such incumbent unions in order to provide job opportunities for black employees through the establishment of a collective bargaining relationship," the general counsel has refused to issue a complaint based upon a finding that the term "labor organization" is applicable to the group. Difficulties, of course, arise when displacement is not the aim of the organization but when friction may occur, as it often will, between the labor organization and the black workers' group.

Suppose, for instance, the black caucus so distrusts the collective-bargaining representative that it attempts to assume some of the functions previously performed by the union, such as the referral of workers to job sites and the operation of hiring halls. The construction unions, for example, are specifically protected by Section 8(f) of the act in the operation of both apprenticeship programs and hiring halls. Suppose a black workers' group, as the United Construction Workers Association (UCWA) of Seattle did,[111] attempts to take over some of these functions because of unions have utilized them to exclude blacks from employment opportunities. Suppose such an assumption of responsibilities by a black workers' organization is ordered by a court, as was eventually done in Seattle during the summer of 1972.[112] The difficulty is that labor organizations will claim, even when they rely on institutionalized procedures to discriminate, that the assignment of some responsibilities to another organization is an attempt to displace the established union and therefore makes the black workers' organization subject to the provisions of Section 9 regarding labor organizations.

In my judgment, this view is not the better one. In previous chapters we have seen that arrangements such as seniority procedures have been suspended with regard to black employees because of their intrinsic relationship to past discrimination. Moreover, in the cases in which quotas have been imposed as remedies, as well as in decisions such as *Rowe* v. *General Motors Corporation*[113] where reliance on an all-white reviewing committee's subjective judgments, which resulted in patterns of promotion that were discriminatory, was held to violate Title VII, the theme has been the same: the elimination or modification of institutional procedures which are integral to the union's functioning. It does not seem in the least bit inappropriate for organizations such as UCWA and the Association for the Betterment of Black Edison Employees in Detroit to involve themselves and sometimes take control of certain functions previously performed by labor organizations without themselves being designated as labor organizations within the meaning of the act. The policy of Title VII is to eliminate discrimination. If organizations which are not a direct threat to the continued existence of unions as exclusive representatives assist in accomplishing this purpose, surely federal labor policy supports employer discussions with such organizations as a means of attaining this end.[114] William Lucy, the secretary-treasurer of the American Federation of State, County and Municipal Employees Unions, specifically stated that the existence of such organizations has kept unions more honest than they would otherwise be and has served as an incentive for them to concern themselves with equal-employment-opportunity programs.[115] Accordingly, it would appear as though doubts should be resolved in favor of finding that a black employees group is not a labor organization, unless there is a concerted and demonstrable attempt by the group to oust the union as exclusive bargaining representative. It simply will not do to say that the aims of such organizations may disparage or interfere with the labor organization's solution of its problems. For, in most instances, the emergence of black worker groups is directly attributable to the moral vacuum that exists because of the failure of labor organizations to take responsibility for the conditions protested. To the extent that there is disparagement it exists by virtue of the trade union's conduct.

Even if the result permits the employer to engage in discussions with other employee organizations than unions—and many employers have done so "en masse" when the alternatives of friction and protest activities where less attractive—limitations safeguard the exclusive bargaining representative's position. First, the agreement between the employer and employee group may not be inconsistent with the collective-bargaining agreement. The only proviso to this principle which now exists by virtue of both Title VII and Taft-Hartley authority is that such an employee group agreement may modify the collective-bargaining provisions if the provisions are inconsistent with antidiscrimination law. Second, the labor organization must be present during any such adjustment. Accordingly, if there is a basis for disagreement about the collective agreement's incompatibility with a case, the basic objectives of Section 8(d) are to be complied with in the sense that there will be give and take among all three parties, representatives of the minority-group workers as well as of labor and management, before the matter is settled.

The Union's Affirmative Obligation to Bargain and Employer's Managerial Prerogatives

The construction unions are deeply involved in the hiring of employees through their participation and dominance in joint union-employer apprenticeship committees and in hiring halls (some of which provide for exclusive referral by the union), although management often reserves the right to refuse jobs to those who are deemed to be unqualified. To some extent, these institutional arrangements reflect union power in the construction industry. Yet this kind of union involvement suits both parties: the employer does not concern himself with the recruitment of workers, and the union arrogates to itself power as well as responsibility. For the industrial unions, the situation is quite different. Normally, except for the longshore unions, they have nothing to do with hiring at all except on a very informal basis. The employer has exclusive responsibility. A union such as the UAW is concerned with General Motors' right to hire only after the worker has been on the job for a period of thirty days—at which time the worker is required to assume membership obligations to the extent of paying periodic dues and an initiation fee.[116]*

Curiously, however, a large number of collective-bargaining agreements purport to obligate both parties not to discriminate. Sometimes such antidiscrimination clauses specifically address themselves to hiring disputes as well as to promotion and employment status once the worker is on the job. Quite often, unions that have negotiated such agreements disavow any responsibility, on the theory that their lack of participation in the hiring process eliminates them from discrimination disputes—their antidiscrimination contract provisions notwithstanding. Moreover, trade union representatives will often assert erroneously that the law precludes their concern with such matters. This is utter nonsense. Even before the

enactment of Section 8(f) in 1959, the hiring hall had been lawful and not in violation of the closed-shop prohibitions. The Supreme Court so held in *Local 357,
Teamsters* v. *NLRB.*[117] There is nothing in the statute which limits or precludes
trade union involvement in management's hiring—only tradition and lethargy on
the part of the unions.

Converse questions are intriguing as a matter of law: Is a union liable, under either a Title VII or a duty-of-fair-representation charge, if it fails to come to the assistance of a potential employee who claims discrimination? To state the issue
with more scope: Does a union violate the law if it fails to police the employer's
hiring procedures to determine whether they are unfair? Presumably, a small minority of employees who believe they have been dealt with unfairly will actually
complain to any agency, private or public. If an institution is involved in the ev-
eryday relationship and focuses on this problem, complaints may be more likely to
emerge.

Is an employer obligated to bargain about such matters or be in peril of violating Section 8(a)(5)? It would seem that the questions of union and employer
obligations must be answered in the same way. For if a union is liable to an
applicant for a failure to represent him fairly, the most obvious way of doing so is
through the collective-bargaining process and by pressing the issue to the point of
impasse. The union can do so as a matter of law if the subject matter is a mandatory subject for bargaining within the meaning of Section 8(d). Moreover, in the
Section 8(a)(5) cases, such as *Packinghouse Workers* and *Southwestern Pipe,* the
assumption appears to be that if a union has a duty of fair representation, it *pari
passu* has an affirmative obligation at the bargaining table, and that the employer
who resists may violate Section 8(a)(5). Even though such cases have been primarily concerned with employment conditions after the worker is hired, there
seems to be no good reason why hiring would not be regarded as a "condition of
employment" as well.

May an obligation be found that is independent of a duty of fair representation?
What are the legal grounds for imposing on management the obligation to bargain
about hiring procedures? The first may be found in the antidiscrimination clause itself. If a provision in the collective-bargaining agreement purports to be applicable
to all aspects of the employment relationship, the failure by management to permit
union involvement may amount to a unilateral modification of the contract and
thus violate Section 8(d). In the absence of such a contract provision that relates to
hiring as well as other aspects of the employment relationship, an approach similar
to that of Chief Justice Warren in *Fibreboard Paper Products* v. *NLRB*[118] might
be employed. In that case, the Court, in considering whether unilateral subcontracting of maintenance work by management which resulted in the displacement
of incumbent union employees who had previously performed such jobs was a
mandatory subject of bargaining, relied partially on the prevalence of subcontracting clauses in collective-bargaining agreements negotiated between labor and
management as a basis for holding that bargaining about such matters was
bargaining about conditions of employment within the meaning of the act. Simi-

larly, the fact that antidiscrimination clauses are customary and frequently negotiated and that they do not specifically *exclude* the hiring process,[119]* argues in
favor of the matter's being properly regarded as a condition of employment under
the act.

But this argument is double-edged. Most unions do not in fact do what their
contracts claim they will. Indeed, it is not surprising that they take no role, inasmuch as rejected applicants do not constitute an organized or cohesive constituency which might place pressure on union leadership to act properly. On the other
hand, if a white rank and file elects the leadership, it may be indifferent at best
and hostile at worst. Either way, there is little attraction in the hiring area for the
union leader.. A trade unionist will not regard as in his own interest the taking of
such problems to the bargaining table or to arbitration. Accordingly, to the extent
that the Court takes note of this reality, the *Fibreboard* rationale may be at least
partially undercut. There are other arguments more formidably persuasive than
this one.

The first relates to the Title VII obligations thrust upon labor organizations by
the statute itself. The most relevant portion of that law states: "It shall be an
unlawful employment practice for a labor organization . . . to classify or fail or
refuse to refer for employment any individual, in any way which would deprive or
tend to deprive any individual of employment opportunities or otherwise adversely
affect his status as an employee *or as an applicant* for employment, because of
such individual's race, color, religion, sex, or national origin."[120] Critical is the
obligation to avoid the unlawful employment practice of "fail[ing] or refus[ing] to
refer for employment." If in fact the quoted passage indicates that Congress contemplated a union's failure to respond to discrimination in the hiring process, it
appears quite clear that the rest of the provision, Section 703(c)(2), is broad
enough to deal with applicants; indeed it specifically speaks of applicants.[121]*
Moreover, an expansive reading is buttressed by a broad statutory reference to
employment opportunities and the obligation not to engage in practices which
"would deprive or tend to deprive individuals of employment opportunities."
What can be more important in relation to employment opportunity than the right
to a job itself? This right is certainly as important as promotion and pay, and, in
light of the black-white unemployment differential with which Congress seemed to
be concerned, an obligation for both parties to deal with the hiring process seems
not unreasonable and indeed more consonant with congressional objectives than a
contrary result which would not place such an obligation on them.

Second, the statutory scheme of the National Labor Relations Act registers a
concern over the plight of unfairly rejected applicants or, more specifically, applicants rejected for reasons prohibited by the statute. Whatever the merits of *Packinghouse Workers* regarding racial discrimination by the employer alone, it seems
clear that *Southern Steamship, Lincoln Mills, Emporium Capwell,* and *Graziano*
require the board, the commission, and the courts to consider Title VII and the
NLRA, as well as other related labor laws. The Court, in *Phelps Dodge Corp.* v.
NLRB,[122] five years after the passage of the Wagner Act, held that discrimination

against applicants because of union membership violated the statute—just as discrimination against workers already hired would. Justice Felix Frankfurter spoke
for the Court:

> Discrimination against union labor in the hiring of men is a dam to self-organization at the
> source of supply. The effect of such discrimination is not confined to the actual denial of
> employment; it inevitably operates against the whole idea of the legitimacy of organization.
> In a word, it undermines the principle which, as we have seen, is recognized as basic to the
> attainment of industrial peace.
> . . . We have seen the close link between a bar to employment because of union affilia-
> tion and the opportunities of labor organizations to exist and prosper. Such an embargo
> against employment of union labor was notoriously one of the chief obstructions to collec-
> tive bargaining through self-organization. Indisputably the removal of such obstructions
> was the driving force behind the enactment of the National Labor Relations Act. The
> prohibition against discrimination in regard to "hire" must be applied as a means towards
> the accomplishment of the main object of the legislation. We are asked to read "hire" as
> meaning the wages paid to an employee so as to make the statute merely forbid discrimi-
> nation in one of the terms of men who have secured employment. So to read the statute
> would do violence to a spontaneous textual reading of 8(3) in that "hire" would serve no
> function because, in the sense which is urged upon us, it is included in the prohibition
> against "discrimination in regard to . . . any term or condition of employment." Contem-
> poraneous legislative history, and, above all, the background of industrial experience, for-
> bid such textual mutilation.[123]

Accordingly, the concern with discriminatory hiring expressed in *Phelps
Dodge,* the language of Title VII indicating that union responsibility is geared to
the hiring process, and the responsibility thrust upon employers by *Packinghouse
Workers* not to engage in invidious discrimination on the basis of race under Section 8(a)(1) all argue for an affirmative answer to the questions asked at the outset
of this section. Moreover, the Supreme Court, in *Brotherhood of Railroad Trainmen* v. *Howard,*[124] has taken the position that, under the Railway Labor Act (and
presumably the National Labor Relations Act as well),[125] a union has a duty of
fair representation which applies not only to employees currently employed in the
bargaining unit. In *Howard,* the question of a duty to applicants of fair representation was not posed. At issue in that case was the attempt by a union representing
all white brakemen to discriminate against black porters—a job classification
which appears to have been created for blacks and which encompasses many of
the duties of brakemen. It is therefore arguable that *Howard* is a special case
applicable only to a peculiar situation where the duties of two groups of employees overlapped considerably, where it appeared as though the job classifications had been created on the basis of race, and where the white union was able to
use its power effectively in a way that harmed black employees even more than
might have been the case if they were in the bargaining unit.[126] After all, the
black workers who constituted part of the bargaining unit, even though they probably would have been excluded from membership in the union that was the exclusive bargaining representative (an exclusion that indeed the Court's decision in
Steele seemed to countenance at the time), would have at least been in a position

to cast ballots in an election conducted under governmental auspices. Indisputably, the black workers in *Howard* were politically impotent.

Arguably, the Supreme Court, in *Chemical Workers, Local 1* v. *Pittsburgh Plate Glass Company*, [127] confirmed this narrow interpretation of *Howard*. In that case, the Court rejected the contention that employers had a duty to bargain about benefits for retirees. The union contended that such employees, though beyond the clutches of the appropriate bargaining unit, nevertheless could be regarded as employees to whom the union had a duty of fair representation by virtue of *Howard*. Justice Brennan, speaking for the Court, said in rejecting this argument:

> Since retirees are not members of the bargaining unit, the bargaining agent is under no statutory duty to represent them in negotiations with the employer. Nothing in *Railroad Trainmen v. Howard* . . . is to the contrary. In *Howard* we held that a union may not use the powers accorded it under law for the purposes of racial discrimination even against workers who are not members of the bargaining unit represented by the union. The reach and rationale of *Howard* are a matter of some conjecture. . . . But whatever its theory, the case obviously does not require a union affirmatively to represent non-bargaining unit members or to take into account their interests in making bona fide economic decisions in behalf of those whom it does represent. [128]

Nevertheless, there are policy reasons for answering the question of the duty to bargain regarding fair hiring affirmatively regardless of the thrust of *Howard*. Moreover, even according to Justice Brennan's dicta, it is questionable whether the reference to bona fide economic decisions can be read to include racial issues of the kind under discussion. Time and time again, the courts have noted that employment discrimination issues are different in kind from most collective-bargaining problems, which are susceptible to resolution through the majoritarian process. The majority's attitude has generally triggered discrimination problems.

Furthermore, it seems clear not only from the language of Title VII itself that unions are more likely to represent minority workers fairly once they are on the job and to have fewer difficulties with the white membership in doing so if they press for fair hiring policies on the part of management. The reason is that the more time that elapses before blacks and other minorities are hired at all or before blacks are hired into *all* departments and not assigned disproportionately to low-level and poor-paying jobs, the more divisiveness there will be within the union on the seniority issue. The more divisiveness there is on seniority, the greater the likelihood of clashes between blacks and whites which will pose a threat to worker solidarity and thus to the strength of the union. This, of course, is the theme sounded by Judge Wright in *Packinghouse Workers* in relation to NLRA unfair labor practices by employers and their impact on concerted activities under Section 7. A union that has a large black constituency—especially one that has its share of high-paying jobs—will act in a more even-handed manner, or, at least, be in a position to do so. Only by means of fair hiring practices can blacks be distributed throughout an enterprise. Only when they are will employees be less likely to divide on explosive racial issues.

Regardless of the Title VII implications, which may vary, depending on whether there exists an incumbent black work force, the seniority principle presents a problem for labor unions generally, especially if race is involved.[129] More recently hired blacks and those who have been hired and locked into jobs from which they will not be promoted can be harmed by the operation of a seniority system if they attempt to compete with whites for employment opportunities. The union is more effective in its dealings with the employer and it receives more loyalty from workers of all races if it attempts to alter the hiring process which makes the seniority system discriminatory. Moreover, blacks will have more confidence and trust in an organization which will probably be controlled by whites until a large number of blacks have moved into the work force.

Another factor in favor of a duty of fair representation and a duty to bargain regarding the hiring process is the definition given to "labor dispute" by the Supreme Court and the board in the Norris-La Guardia and Taft-Hartley acts respectively. The Court, in *New Negro Alliance* v. *Sanitary Grocery Co.*,[130] was confronted with the question of whether picketing to protest racial discrimination in employment has the same immunity from Norris-La Guardia's anti-injunctive provisions as it normally has in traditional labor-management disputes. The Court, holding that picketing to force the employment of blacks constituted a "labor dispute" within the meaning of the Norris-La Guardia Act (and thus could not be enjoined in a federal court),[131]* stated:

The desire for fair and equitable conditions of employment on the part of persons of any race, color, or persuasion, and the removal of discriminations against them by reason of their race or religious beliefs is quite as important to those concerned as fairness and equity in terms and conditions of employment can be to trade or craft unions or any form of labor organization or association. Race discrimination by an employer may reasonably be deemed more unfair and less excusable than discrimination against workers on the ground of union affiliation. There is no justification in the apparent purposes of the express terms of the [Norris-La Guardia] Act for limiting its definition of labor disputes and cases arising therefrom by excluding those which arise with respect to discrimination in terms and conditions of employment based upon differences of race or color.[132]

The significance is twofold. In the first place, the Court characterized a dispute about hiring as a "labor dispute." Second, it regarded such a "labor dispute" as necessarily synonymous with a protest against "discrimination in terms and conditions of employment." It is interesting that this is the exact language used in Section 8(b) of the act, which specifies the matters about which bargaining may take place.

Also important is the board's more recent decision in *Tanner Motor Livery, Ltd.*,[133] in which it was again called upon to determine whether picketing to protest an employer's allegedly unfair racial hiring policy can be characterized as a labor dispute—this time within the meaning of Taft-Hartley rather than Norris-La Guardia. The board, in *Tanner,* relied on the Court's previous ruling under Norris-La Guardia in *New Negro Alliance.* It characterized the definition of the term "labor dispute" in Norris-La Guardia as "substantially the same" as the definition in the National Labor Relations Act. Significantly, the board, in conceding that "not every concerted activity in furtherance of a labor dispute is protected by Section 7" stated: "An employer's hiring policies and practices are of vital concern to employees inasmuch as such policies and practices inherently affect terms and conditions of employment. Thus, in our opinion, the concerted activities of employees in protest of what they consider unfair hiring policies and practices are clearly within their Section 7 right 'to engage in other concerted activities for the purpose of collective bargaining or other mutual aid or protection.' "[134]

Moreover, in its second decision subsequent to remand by the Ninth Circuit in *Tanner*,[135] the board, declaring that the employees' picketing was not in opposition to union policy, noted that there was no indication that the union would not represent Negroes fairly once they were hired. One reason hiring policy has an impact on employees presently employed in a union is that discrimination in hiring may develop an environment in which white workers expect that racial priorities will be established in all aspects of the employment relationship. Judge Irving Goldberg said in *Rogers* v. *Equal Employment Opportunity Commission:*

It is my belief that employees' psychological as well as economic fringes are statutorily entitled to protection from employer abuse, and that the phrase "terms, conditions, or privileges of employment" in Section 703 is an expansive concept which sweeps within its protective ambit the practice of creating a working environment heavily charged with ethnic or racial discrimination. I do not wish to be interpreted as holding that an employer's mere utterance of an ethnic or racial epithet which engenders offensive feelings in an employee falls within the proscription of Section 703. But by the same token I am simply not willing to hold that a discriminatory atmosphere could under no set of circumstances ever constitute an unlawful employment practice. One can readily envision working environments so heavily polluted with discrimination as to destroy completely the emotional and psychological stability of minority group workers, and I think Section 703 of Title VII was aimed at the eradication of such noxious practices.[136]

Resistance to fair promotion policies may be encouraged if workers who regard themselves as the beneficiaries of discrimination see racism practiced elsewhere— for example, at the hiring gate. The few blacks who are hired may be extremely timid about asserting their rights because they properly regard themselves as fortunate to be employed in the first instance. Alternatively, black workers may feel bitterness and alienation, and these feelings may lead to the separation of the races in the work place. Accordingly, racial cleavages would develop which would undermine the solidarity with which *Packinghouse Workers* was concerned, and perhaps even more important, operate to prevent the achievement of an integrated work force which is the goal of both statutory and public policy.

Despite the Court's pronouncements in *Pittsburgh Plate Glass* about the limited impact of *Howard*, it is interesting that the board and the Fifth Circuit have held that some matters may be mandatory subjects for bargaining within the meaning of the act, under the *Borg-Warner* doctrine, even if nonunit employees are the objects of bargaining. For instance, in *Houston Chapter, Associated General Contractors*,[137] the board, with subsequent Fifth Circuit affirmance, held that a union's insistence on a nondiscriminatory exclusive hiring hall is a mandatory subject for bargaining in a right-to-work state. If an exclusive hiring hall is treated so solicitously for the purposes of *Borg-Warner* and Section 8(d), there appears to be no significant obstacle to reaching the same decision with regard to fair hiring policies—especially since the latter are buttressed by public policy—including those implicit in Title VII.

Furthermore, the board has held that a clause providing for the continued accumulation of seniority credits by employees while they are in a supervisory status is a mandatory subject for bargaining within the meaning of the act—even though it may have a direct impact on the manner in which supervisors perform their work, inasmuch as in some instances they may be tempted to return to the bargaining unit when there is a reduction in the supervisory work force or if they no longer prefer to be supervisors.[138] This decision, therefore, has radiations which spread in two directions. First, it serves as additional support for the proposition that hiring disputes are mandatory subjects for bargaining within the meaning of the act. Second, it seems to provide a basis for union involvement that moves in another direction, since the decision can be interpreted to mandate bargaining concerning the promotion of employees in the bargaining unit to supervisory positions or the employment of supervisors generally. The obvious objection to this interpretation of Section 8(a)(5) is that the unit's employees are not involved and, perhaps more important, that such bargaining represents an incursion into managerial prerogatives to an even greater extent than would be the case with regard to hiring.

Nevertheless, there are good grounds for taking the position that a demand that management institute or implement an affirmative-action program aimed at altering the racial composition of the supervisory work force constitutes a mandatory subject for bargaining. An obvious argument in support of bringing such a matter to the bargaining table is that the identity of supervisors has a direct impact on the working conditions of employees, particularly in mass-production industries, where there is a good deal of contact with immediate supervisors. The claim has been made on many occasions by black workers that an all- or predominantly white supervisory work force is insensitive to racial issues and may be prone to the use of racial epithets—a practice which has in some instances resulted in wildcat stoppages and consequent interruption of industrial peace. Moreover, black workers have often alleged that working conditions deteriorate if production workers in automobile plants, for instance, are predominantly black and supervisors are predominantly white, simply because fair treatment is less likely in such a situation. Accordingly, speedups and safety disputes may be more likely to occur.

Moreover, the board and the courts have held that, under Section 7, employee walkouts to protest management's appointment or retention of supervisors are for "mutual aid or protection." If one recalls that the Court and the board, in *New Negro Alliance* and *Tanner* respectively, have tended to equate working conditions which are properly protested under Section 7 and employment conditions which are the subject of Section 8(d), one can see that Section 7 cases are a basis for providing trade unions with the right to bargain with management concerning such subjects.

Furthermore, the realities that exist at plant level argue in favor of union bargaining rights on the issue. While trade unions generally take the position that they are unable to respond to employee discontent—particularly the discontent of minority-group workers—by attempting to replace certain supervisors with others, the fact is that racial clashes in, for instance, a number of automobile plants in both California and Detroit have resulted in a *de facto* involvement in the selection of supervisors by unions such as the UAW. Inevitably, if a union intends to play a significant role as an agent of the workers, it must address itself to their principal concerns. In a large number of instances, the focus of protest has been the question of supervision. Accordingly, the unions have addressed themselves, albeit on a *de facto* or informal basis, to programs to remedy the friction that exists. It is quite clear that one of the principal responses to this friction is change in racial composition.

Under the *Fibreboard* rationale, this evolving pattern forms a basis, together, once again, with Title VII policies, for concluding that the matter may be pressed to the point of impasse by unions. Even if the subject is not within the scope of mandatory bargaining, the matter can still be lawfully discussed. Where there is a pattern or tradition of promoting a number of employees into supervisory ranks very often, the case for bargainability grows more substantial. Here, also, the impact on employees and their promotional opportunities is real and direct—perhaps even more than is the case with hiring problems.

There is one principal legal obstacle: Section 8(b)(1)(B) of the act. This provision makes it an unfair labor practice for unions to "restrain or coerce . . . an employer in the selection of his representatives for the purpose of collective bargaining or the adjustment of grievances."[139]

In *Florida Power & Light Co.* v. *IBEW*, Justice Stewart, speaking for a majority of the Court, concluded that an attempt by a union to fine supervisor members was not *per se* a violation of section 8(b)(1)(B). The Court said:

Nowhere in the legislative history is there to be found any implication that Congress sought to extend protection to the employer from union restraint or coercion when engaged in any activity other than the *selection* of its representatives for the purposes of collective bargaining and grievance adjustment. The conclusion is thus inescapable that a union's discipline of one of its members who is a supervisory employee can constitute a violation of § 8(b)(1)(B) only when that discipline may adversely affect the supervisor's conduct in performing the duties of, and acting in his capacity as, grievance adjustor or collective bargainer on behalf of the employer.[140]

In *Laborers, Local 478* v. *NLRB*,[141] however, the board, with subsequent affirmance by the court of appeals for the District of Columbia, held that a union which attempts to remove a supervisor or to reduce his influence through the assignment of a "buffer" between him and the work force on the grounds that the supervisor is racially biased, violates Section 8(b)(1)(B) if it strikes for this objective. The scope of the board's decision is not entirely clear. On the one hand, the board stated that although "employees were free under Sections 7 and 13 of the Act to invoke their statutory rights with respect to these alleged unreasonable or unfair conditions . . . this is not to say . . . that the right to strike or engage in concerted activity because of unfair conditions of employment includes the right to dictate to an employer the selection of a particular supervisor.''[142] On the other hand, the board specifically rejected the following statement by the administrative law judge: ''It is immaterial whether the employees' basic dissatisfaction with Wilson [the supervisor] stemmed from his purported discrimination on a racial basis, or a reverse discriminatory intent by the employees. Whatever the dissatisfaction may have been the Union is barred by Section 8(b)(1)(B) from coercing and restraining the Employer in its selection of Wilson as its representative.''[143]

The board did not make clear why it rejected this language while reaching a conclusion along the same lines. And uncertainty as to the ultimate implications of the *Laborers, Local 478* decision is not dispelled by the opinion of the District of Columbia Circuit, in which the court stated: ''At oral argument, the union counsel assailed the Board's approach by asserting that the Board would find a § 8(b)(1)(B) violation whenever a union protested discriminatory conduct and the employer responded by replacing the offending supervisor. This does not follow, at least if the employer's replacement of the supervisor represents an independent exercise of his judgment as to the person who would best carry out the employer's obligation to refrain from discriminatory treatment.''[144] It is of course not at all clear what forms of protest by the union could succeed in persuading the employer to replace the offending supervisor while not running afoul of whatever principle the board and the court have in mind. In dealing with this uncertainty, it would seem appropriate that Section 8(b)(1)(B) be narrowly construed, in light of the Supreme Court's approach in *Florida Power & Light Co.* Thus, for instance, a stoppage because of alleged racially discriminatory conduct by a supervisor should be protected under Section 7 and bargained about under Section (8)(a)(5) if the objective is to *remove* the prejudiced supervisor, establish a buffer between him and the work force, or establish goals and timetables for minority hiring among supervisors. If the union attempts to involve itself in the actual *selection* of supervisors who will replace incumbents or retirees, the tension between Section 8(b)(1)(B) and the public policy contained in Title VII (which should have applicability to Section 7) grows more severe. In such a situation, I would hold that the matter is bargainable and a stoppage is protected.

Union Coercion under Sections 8(b)(2) and 8(b)(1)(A)
Section 8(b)(2) and Union Discrimination to Promote the Interests of Minority-
  Group Workers

In *Bechtel Corporation*[145] the board was faced with the following facts. The Bechtel Corporation was engaged by Potomac Electric and Power Company to construct a power plant at Morgantown, Maryland. In fulfilling its contract, Bechtel employed members of Local 832 of the Laborers' Union, as well as two employees who were members of a sister local, Local 74. During the three years that the PEPCO job had been in progress, there was a tacit agreement between Bechtel and Local 832 that those members of the union who wished to observe Dr. Martin

Luther King's birthday as a holiday would be able to do so. This policy had been completely voluntary, although most of the union's members had refrained from working. On Dr. King's birthday, when most union members were not working, one of the members of Local 74 came to the job site to obtain a set of kneepads which he intended to use for a personal project. Upon arriving at the job site the individual was asked by the general superintendent whether he would work that day with carpenters who were there. The employee agreed and worked a full eight hours.

The next day, the shop steward learned that the individual had worked on Dr. King's birthday. The following Monday some of the foremen expressed resentment that he had worked during this time, and the employee was consequently laid off shortly thereafter. The trial examiner found that the worker was therefore discharged for engaging in union activity and that the union had violated Sections 8(b)(1)(A) and 8(b)(2) of the act.

The board affirmed. Chairman Edward Miller, however, dissented. Agreeing that the discharge had been imposed because of refusal to adhere to union policy, but declaring that the layoff was "harsh treatment for a man whose only offense was to have no personal feeling of compunction about working on the day in question," the chairman concluded that the discrimination engaged in by the union would not "encourage or discourage membership" in the union within the meaning of Sections 8(a)(3) and 8(b)(2) of the act. Chairman Miller said: "Because I am not prepared to find the Union's desire to honor the late Doctor King to be so arbitrary, invidious, or irrelevant as to indicate that it was used as a mask for the hidden objective of encouraging or discouraging union membership, I am not ready to rush to the unrationalized conclusion that a violation of our Act occurred here. If there is some other more satisfactory basis for finding the violation, it does not appear in the Trial Examiner's decision or in any colleagues' *pro forma* adoption of his conclusion."[146]

If the refusal to work on Martin Luther King's birthday can be regarded as protected activity in the sense that an employer cannot penalize a worker for doing so—and it appears this should be the case, since the tacit agreement between the parties was to follow this procedure—it seems anomalous for an interference with the employment relationship grounded on this very same protected activity to be regarded as unlawful under the statute. Accordingly, it is more than arguable that the result achieved in Chairman Miller's opinion may be the more sensible one, inasmuch as it involved activity that may have been protected in the first instance under a *Tanner–Emporium Capwell* approach.

Moreover, to some extent my analysis intersects with Title VII and the manner in which the Equal Employment Opportunity Commission has interpreted its statute. In a case in which an employer had discharged a Negro employee because she influenced fellow Negro employees not to work overtime on the Saturday following the assassination of Dr. King, there was cause for believing that the employer violated the statute.[147] White employees, however, were not similarly disciplined; therefore, the *Bechtel* decision does not deal with the question of whether Section

704, which protects the right to protest violation of Title VII, is offended if such reprisals are engaged in, independent of a finding of disparate treatment. In my judgment, the cases which take the view that walkouts and picket-line activity fall within the jurisdiction of Section 704 would similarly protect a refusal to work on Martin Luther King's holiday, unless[148] the comprehensive collective agreement already has holiday provisions in detail.

Internal Union Discipline

The Court, in *NLRB* v. *Allis-Chalmers Manufacturing Co.*[149] (which was decided by a 5-to-4 vote), found that union fines against striking employees did not violate Section 8(b)(1)(A), at least in the circumstances of that case. In *Allis-Chalmers,* unlike *Bechtel Corporation,* the union did not actually attempt to interfere with the employee's employment status. In the former case, an internal union rule was involved—albeit a rule that might have an impact as devastating as a union's request that the worker be dismissed from a job or have his seniority credits reduced. Clearly, if the union's action led to either of those two results because the worker had crossed the union's picket line, a violation of the statute would be evident.

In *Allis-Chalmers* the Court, speaking through Justice Brennan, said that it would be "highly unrealistic" to hold that the words "restrain or coerce" contained in Section 8(b)(1)(A) "precisely and unambiguously [cover] the union conduct involved in this case." The Court stated:

National labor policy has been built upon the premise that by pooling their economic strength and acting through a labor organization freely chosen by the majority, the employees of an appropriate unit have the most effective means of bargaining for improvements in wages, hours, and working conditions. The policy therefore extinguishes the individual employee's power to order his own relations with his employer and creates a power vested in the chosen representative to act in the interests of all employees. . . .

Integral to this federal labor policy has been the power of the chosen union to protect against erosion its status under that policy through reasonable discipline of members who violate rules and regulations governing membership. That power is particularly vital when the members engage in strikes. The economic strike against the employer is the ultimate weapon in labor's arsenal for achieving agreement upon its terms.[150]

Allis-Chalmers, then, finds that the power of a union to fine its members derives its validity from the statutory policy favoring the exclusive-bargaining-representative status. But if, in a particular case, the fine enforces a rule which does not comport with statutory policies but instead "invades or frustrates an overriding policy of the labor laws the rule may not be enforced, even by fine or expulsion, without violating § 8(b)(1)"—as the Court stated in *Scofield* v. *NLRB.* A fine is therefore valid only if it "reflects a legitimate union interest, impairs no policy Congress has imbedded in the labor laws, and is reasonably enforced against union members who are free to leave the union and escape the rule."[151] Under *Allis-Chalmers* and *Scofield,* it is clear that pronouncements in *Lincoln Mills* and *Southern Steamship* that the board and the courts must consider the full range of federal labor policies and statutes have particular applicability to union-discipline cases under Section 8(b)(1)(A). In *NLRB* v. *Marine and Shipbuilding Workers,*[152] for example, the Court assumed the applicability of Landrum-Griffin Act policies in determining that a union had violated Section 8(b)(1)(A) by expelling a worker for filing an unfair-labor-practice charge; the union claimed that for a member to file a charge was a violation of its internal constitution. The Board itself expressly pointed out the applicability of Landrum-Griffin policies to a union-fine case, *Graziano.*

Other considerations of public policy have been relied on by the board to take out a Section 8(b)(1)(A) violation. For instance, the board, noting that the Court, in *Allis-Chalmers,* stressed the fact that the union's strike was lawful, found a violation where the union-imposed fines were on workers who had crossed picket lines which themselves were in breach of contract and hence unprotected and indeed unlawful under Taft-Hartley.[153]*

Allis-Chalmers and its progeny suggest a question which is closely related to the difficulty of accommodating the right of minorities within a union to engage in self-help with the concept of exclusive representation by the union, which speaks for the majority. (Indeed, the *Tanner* and *Emporium* cases both cite and rely on *Allis-Chalmers.*) May a union impose fines for employee disobedience in strikes in which either the union or a group of workers is taking a position on racial issues? From a consideration of *Marine Workers* and *Graziano,* along with *Tanner, Emporium Capwell,* and of course *Lincoln Mills* and *Southern Steamship,* it is clear that Title VII policies must be consulted in resolving this question in a particular case. And it would seem that a fine, expulsion, or other disciplinary measure which is directed against an employee for protesting a practice which may violate Title VII runs afoul of the *Scofield* prohibition of union measures which "impair" a policy "imbedded in the labor laws," even (perhaps especially) when the protest involves disobedience to the union's dictates regarding a strike or other matters. To elaborate this opinion it is desirable to focus on one particular form of protest, the refusal to pay union dues.

In *McGraw Edison Company*[154] the union disciplined an individual employee, one Arnold Blaine, for committing an act indicating "dual loyalty" by filing a decertification petition with the board, aimed at the ouster of the unions. The discipline—not as severe as expulsion—included a recommendation that Blaine be suspended indefinitely from membership, denied the right to attend local meetings, and denied the right to hold office in the local during his suspension. When Blaine refused to pay dues while his membership rights were denied to him, the union attempted to secure his discharge. This discharge attempt by the union (not the earlier impairment of Blaine's membership rights) then triggered the filing of an unfair-labor-practice charge by Blaine. Since, under prior holdings of the board and the circuit courts,[155] and in light of earlier judicial recognition of the Taft-Hartley Act's hostility to "free riders" who gained the benefits of union contracts without assuming union-membership obligations,[156] the union could lawfully expel a member or suspend his membership for the filing of a decertification petition, the union regarded its position as sound. But insofar as enforcement of the union-security provision was concerned, the board was faced with the second branch of the proviso, the statutory provision in Taft-Hartley governing union security, Section 8(a)(3)(B).

This provision states that an employer cannot justify discrimination against an employee for nonmembership "if he has reasonable grounds for believing that membership was denied or terminated for reasons other than the failure of the employee to tender the periodic dues and initiation fees uniformly required as a condition of acquiring or retaining membership."[157] The trial examiner in *McGraw* interpreted Section 8(a)(3)(B) to mean that employer discrimination imposed on a worker whose membership is impaired for any reason other than nonpayment of dues is unlawful. Therefore, the trial examiner asserted, "It is patent that since the disciplinary action was imposed upon Blaine because of the decertification petition, the Respondent could not lawfully seek his discharge under the 8(a)(3) provisos because that would constitute a reason other than the failure to pay dues."[158]

The union countered that an employee who was expelled or suspended occupied the same position as an agency-shop member who, while he did not choose to join the union and was thus perhaps not entitled to full political participation, was nevertheless obligated to pay dues.[159] The trial examiner agreed with the union that "Section 8(b)(2) and the Section 8(a)(3) provisos were designed to protect . . . the union from free riders." But he asserted that instead of supporting the union's contention that Blaine should be treated as an agency-shop employee who has declined membership but is required to pay dues, the "anti-free rider" rationale for the Section 8(a)(3) provisos actually undercut the union's contention, since "Blaine was willing to pay for his ride if accorded the rights and privileges of membership"—unlike the "free rider" who desired neither to join nor to pay but was required by the statute to do the latter.[160]

The board's decision, more narrowly based, essentially held that the combination of union discipline with enforcement of the union's security clause was hardly necessary to preserve the union's existence as an institution—the kind of consideration to which Congress presumably was attuned in formulating the "anti-free rider" concept in Section 8(a)(3). At the same time, the board noted that the sanctions would obviously have the effect of discouraging union members from invoking the board's representation procedures. The board, however, was careful not to say, as the trial examiner had, that the threat of discharge was unlawful, because membership would be denied for reasons "other than" the failure to pay periodic dues and an initiation fee. Rather, the emphasis of the board's *McGraw* opinion is on the protected nature of the activity which gave rise to the employee's problem and the combined weight of two powers exercised by the union—suspension and enforcement of the union-security clause. But the board said, "As our decision in this case is based on the coercive steps taken as a result of filing of a decertification petition, we need not pass upon whether a labor organization violates Section 8(b)(1)(A) through enforcement of a union security clause against a member whose membership was impaired for reasons unrelated to seeking access to Board decertification processes."[161]

This statement seems to imply that the *McGraw* reasoning is not confined to cases in which the union seeks the discharge of a member who refuses to pay dues because of impairment of his membership rights as retaliation for his having filed a decertification petition. The reasoning of the board (and, to an even greater extent, of the trial examiner) seems to be applicable to any case in which a union member's political rights within the organization have been impaired for reasons which do not comport with statutory policies—whether the reason is that the member has filed a decertification petition or that he has incurred unwarranted disfavor in some other way.

Such unwarranted impairment of political rights would seem to occur, and to justify a refusal to pay dues, where the refusal is on the part of black workers protesting discriminatory employment practices such as the operation of an unfair or unlawful seniority system or the exclusion of blacks from policy-making positions inside the union. In both situations the full participation in the benefits which should flow from union membership are being denied. Are not political rights being impaired in a very significant manner in both situations?

The board's decision in *General Motors*[162] indicates that where the union is not an "open" one or violates the duty of representation in other respects, financial support cannot be compelled. Admittedly, the board in *General Motors* was addressing itself to the question of a closed union which excluded employees from membership on the basis of race as well as other factors. Since Title VII prohibits such exclusion on the basis of race and inasmuch as formal exclusion has gone the way of all flesh, the same issue referred to by the board in *General Motors* does not seem likely to arise—in a racial context at least. Accordingly, the two most important circumstances are the denial of employment rights and the inability or unwillingness of the union to do something about it, and the exclusion from elective office.

The mere statistical absence of blacks from leadership positions however, should not *per se,* establish a basis for nonpayment of dues, in light of the rather extraordinary remedy involving self-help. Rather, blacks must show a definite willingness to run for office and must involve themselves in slate-making and press for the appointment of blacks to other important positions inside the union. If, in fact, all these efforts have failed because of the obduracy of whites, or if the effort is futile in light of past practices, it would seem appropriate to permit a nonpayment remedy.

Both *Allis-Chalmers* and the Court's decision in *IAM* v. *Street,*[163] which held that dissenting union members may protest political expenditures from a union treasury, require that dissidents affirmatively establish an evidentiary basis for their interest in opting out of politics and identify the objective they seek to attain through litigation. In *Allis-Chalmers* and *Street,* workers sought *disengagement* from elements of the union's political process. In the situation dealing with black dissidents, of the majority group objective is to share responsibility with others. The failure of a union to establish a civil rights department as a minimum and to take affirmative action to improve other aspects of the position of its black members should buttress a statistical absence or exclusion from leadership and indicate an attitude inconsistent with an intent to represent all members fairly. The board uses the same kind of considerations in determining whether a skilled occupational group is adequately represented by an industrial union, but the difference is that the skilled workers can sever themselves from the bargaining unit and establish their own group. The circumstances under which black workers may do this, if they exist at all, are limited.[164]

All of this, of course, is a substantial extension of the impairmant-of-membership rights involved in *McGraw*. The language of Section 8(a)(3)(B) does not solve all the problems that may arise. *McGraw* itself involved an approach which did not accept the literal language of the statute. *McGraw*'s policy seems consistent with the approach advocated here. If more passive but equally pernicious impairment of membership is not to occur in situations where it may affect race relations and employment, the principles of *McGraw* should be applied. Nothing will make the unions move more quickly than a threat to their treasuries. While black workers and their allies who wish to refuse to pay dues because of discrimination need only pay under protest, the essential danger for labor unions will remain. And that danger may make it easier for union leadership to explain to a hostile white membership why blacks are being promoted and endorsed on a slate for higher office. A more integrated leadership, moreover, can exert greater pressure on the employer to change discriminatory working conditions.

8 | Grievance Arbitration Machinery and Title VII

The Institutional Framework

Although unions and employers have negotiated arbitration provisions since the turn of the century, the arbitration process did not gain substantial impetus in this country until the advent of the War Labor Board and the conclusion of World War II.[1] The War Labor Board, which was established during the war in order to ensure uninterrupted production and a measure of equity for workers, attempted to encourage and in some instances to impose both no-strike and grievance procedures which culminated in arbitration—the selection of a neutral third party who would render a final and binding award resolving the differences between the parties. When World War II ended, the parties had begun to adapt themselves to the process, and it was natural that they should turn to many of the representatives of the War Labor Board, with whom they had become somewhat familiar and in whom they had sufficient confidence to request their assistance as third-party neutrals in negotiating collective-bargaining agreements. (Generally, in this country arbitration has not been used to resolve disputes over new contract terms as frequently as it is utilized in connection with disputes arising during the term of the contract and involving its interpretation. The former are called "interest" disputes and the latter "rights" issues.)

Accordingly, when the Taft-Hartley amendments were passed by Congress over President Truman's veto in 1947,[2]* the statute specifically encouraged the negotiation of the grievance-arbitration machinery and, in so doing, ratified a prior trend which had emerged before the War Labor Board became involved. Taft-Hartley attempted to encourage arbitration through two different statutory avenues: (1) Section 301, which made labor contracts enforceable through suits in federal district court—although, paradoxically, in the wake of that provision's passage, it was feared that the judiciary would usurp the arbitral role and make a mess of what the arbitrators had done;[3]* and (2) Section 203(d), which provides that "final adjustment by a method agreed upon by the parties is hereby declared to be the desirable method for settlement of grievance disputes arising out of the application or interpretation of an existing collective bargaining agreement."[4]

Yet the dominant inclination, apparent in the entire sweep of Taft-Hartley and its legislative history, as well as Section 301, was to discipline the unruly unions which had refused to adhere to their contractual responsibilities. A wave of strikes and what was deemed to be irresponsible trade union action at the end of World War II, triggered by the pent-up frustrations of workers who had operated under controls, provided the consensus necessary for the passage of what the unions then regarded as a "slave labor act." Moreover, the concern was that the judiciary, which had done an extremely poor job in dealing with labor disputes during the 1930's because of both its lack of expertise and its heavy-handed proemployer bias, would come back into the picture and eliminate the private process which had come to be accepted by both parties in many relationships. The concern became even greater when the Court resolved all doubts about the constitutionality of Section 301 in *Textile Workers Union* v. *Lincoln Mills*[5] and stated that federal substantive law was to apply to the interpretation of labor contracts. The first of many unanswered questions posed by *Lincoln Mills* related to both the source and the content of this new judicially created federal substantive law. On this subject, Justice Douglas, the author of the majority opinion, was disturbingly vague. The Court made mention of a few "shafts of light" which "illuminate our problem"; prominent among them were the congressional concerns discerned by the Court that there be uninterrupted production and that arbitration operate as the *quid pro quo* for the no-strike clause in the collective agreement.[6] But who would fashion this federal law—the courts or the arbitrators or others? One great difficulty associated with judicial intervention was the New York Court of Appeals' old *Cutler-Hammer* doctrine.[7] The judicial abuse created by *International Association of Machinists* v. *Cutler-Hammer, Inc.* was that the court, under the guise of determining whether a matter should go to arbitration in the first instance (the "arbitrability" issue), would inevitably become involved in the merits of the dispute and usurp prerogatives the parties had reserved for the arbitrator. The suspicion of potential wrongdoing was exaggerated by the fact that traditional common-law doctrine had declared arbitration agreements to be against the public policy. The reason for this suspicion was judicial apprehension about, and hostility to, the usurpation of functions normally performed by the courts.[8]*

Fears of a *Cutler-Hammer* approach were definitively put to rest by the Supreme Court *Steelworkers' Trilogy* decisions of 1960,[9] also authored by Justice Douglas. In the first two cases of the trilogy, *United Steelworkers* v. *American Mfg. Co.* and *United Steelworkers* v. *Warrior & Gulf Navigation Co.*,[10] the Court held that all doubts about arbitrability were to be resolved in favor of sending the matter to arbitration. The reason was that although the judiciary could not order the parties to submit to a process in which there was no promise to arbitrate,[11] the parties had bargained about the arbitrator's interpretation. The Court reiterated its view that the no-strike clause and arbitration provision were considered by both Congress and most parties which bargained about such matters as the *quid pro quo* for each other, and that public policy supported the negotiation of arbitration machinery *in lieu* of the strike weapon, which would interfere with production.[12] Accordingly, a policy favoring arbitration whenever possible was consistent with the general principle of some of the Taft-Hartley amendments indicating that final adjustment, particularly through arbitration, of disputes concerning the interpretation of collective-bargaining agreements was favored.

Moreover, the Court stressed the expertise of arbitrators—and stressed it to such an extent that probably most arbitrators would not recognize themselves in the *Steelworkers' Trilogy* opinion. The Court said:

The labor arbitrator's source of law is not confined to the express provisions of the contract, as the industrial common law—the practices of the industry and the shop—is equally a part of the collective bargaining agreement although not expressed in it. The labor arbitrator is usually chosen because of the parties' confidence in his knowledge of the common law of the shop and their trust in his personal judgment to bring to bear considerations which are not expressed in the contract as criteria for judgment. The parties expect that his judgment of a particular grievance will reflect not only what the contract says but, insofar as the collective bargaining agreement permits, such factors as the effect upon productivity of a particular result, its consequence to the morale of the shop, his judgment whether tensions will be heightened or diminished. For the parties' objective in using the arbitration process is primarily to further their common goal of uninterrupted production under the agreement to make the agreement serve their specialized needs. The ablest judge cannot be expected to bring the same experience and competence to bear upon the determination of a grievance, because he cannot be similarly informed.[13]

In the third of the three cases which came before the Court as part of the *Steelworkers' Trilogy, United Steelworkers* v. *Enterprise Wheel & Car Corp.,*[14] the Court held that inasmuch as it was the arbitrators' construction of the agreement for which the parties had bargained, the court had "no business" overruling an arbitrator because its interpretation of the agreement differed. Only when the arbitrator was unfaithful to the contract could the court properly reverse the award. A mere ambiguity in the opinion would not suffice for the purpose of reversal. The Court, however, stated that an award "based solely upon the arbitrator's view of the requirements of enacted legislation . . . would mean that he exceeded the scope of the submission."[15] Yet the Court said, "An arbitrator is confined to interpretation and application of the collective bargaining agreement; he does not sit to dispense his own brand of industrial justice. *He may, of course, look for guidance from many sources,* yet his award is legitimate only so long as it draws its essence from the collective bargaining agreements. When the arbitrator's words manifest an infidelity to this obligation, courts have no choice but to refuse enforcement of the award."[16]

Subsequently, the Court continued to encourage the arbitration process in a series of significant decisions. The Court held that an individual must exhaust arbitration machinery before pursuing the dispute in court.[17] Moreover, it held that failure by a union to process a grievance could only be attacked on the basis that the union had acted in bad faith.[18]

Furthermore, a 5-to-3 majority of the Court went so far as to say, in *Boys Markets, Inc.* v. *Retail Clerks Local 770,*[19] that, despite the broad prohibitions in the Norris-La Guardia Act against the issuing by federal courts of injunctions against work stoppages and picket lines, the *quid pro quo* policy and the encouragement of the arbitration process reflected in Taft-Hartley formed a basis for concluding that injunctions could be issued against strikes in breach of contract if the issue which gave rise to the strike was itself arbitrable. Accordingly, the Court, in a steady stream of decisions dealing with arbitration, has encouraged the process, and its decisions have permitted a proarbitration interpretation of Taft-Hartley to override other statutory concerns and policies, such as those contained in Norris-La Guardia. Meanwhile, the practices of the parties appear to reflect the same kind of positive attitude that is evident in the Supreme Court's opinions. Ninety-five percent of the collective-bargaining agreements negotiated between unions and employers contain arbitration clauses.[20]

In a large number of these contracts—an estimate is 83 percent[21]*—the parties have negotiated no-discrimination clauses, and disputes arising under such clauses may often proceed to arbitration. In a sense, the negotiation of such provisions and their coverage by arbitration might be regarded as indicative of good faith on the part of the parties. The assumption might be—and some of the courts appear to have made this assumption—that the public policy favoring arbitration ought to be applied with equal vigor in employment-discrimination situations. Yet there are certain basic differences between employment-discrimination disputes in the union-employer relationship and other kinds of problems which arise in the context of arbitration litigation previously before the Court. The Court, in *Glover* v. *Louis–San Francisco Railway*,[22] anticipated such differences by distinguishing exhaustion of contractual procedure requirements in duty-of-fair-representation cases involving race from those in which race is not an issue. The Court said in *Glover*:

In a line of cases beginning with *Steele* v. *Louisville & Nashville R. Co.* . . . , the Court has rejected the contention that employees alleging racial discrimination should be required to submit their controversy to "a group which is in large part chosen by the [defendants] against whom their real complaint is made." . . . And the reasons which prompted the Court to hold as it did about the inadequacy of a remedy before the Adjustment Board apply with equal force to any remedy administered by the union, by the company, or both, to pass on claims by the very employees whose rights have been charged with neglecting and betraying.[23]*

One reason for this kind of attitude is that in employment-discrimination cases—particularly those involving race—the basis for the confidence and trust in the parties' own machinery which the Court has expressed in other contexts does not exist. Congress, by passing Title VII of the Civil Rights Act of 1964, was in effect expressing the view that in a number of instances employment-discrimination matters were not being handled properly by labor and management. If the attitudes of the parties were sufficiently suspect to warrant the serious kind of legislative interference which Title VII represents, certainly a different kind of assumption should be applied in the arbitration of grievances involving racial discrimination from the kind applied in other situations. It would seem that the same basic distrust reflected by the legislation and by the Court in *dicta* in both *Steele* and *Glover* ought to apply to industrial self-government, which has admittedly pleased both unions and employers and has operated in accord with public policy in contexts where race is not involved.

The second important difference between the arbitration of disputes which involve discrimination problems and other kinds of labor disputes is that the courts were moved out of labor-management disputes by the National Labor Relations Act, and the encouragement of the arbitration process logically followed on the heels of the policy. But the statutory scheme of Title VII is entirely different. Here the courts, even subsequent to the 1972 amendments which gave the Equal Employment Opportunity Commission the authority to sue, have the major role in the effectuation of the rights guaranteed under the statute.[24]* Even though Title VII encourages the voluntary resolution of employment-discrimination claims without resort to litigation, the legislative history of arbitration and other private machinery is against judicial abdication.[25]* Accordingly, when the National Labor Relations Board has ruled against a Title VII plaintiff, the evidentiary record is not *res judicata* (that is, the parties are not bound by a prior factual determination) in federal district court, at least if the board did not consider racial-discrimination allegations.[26] The failure of the EEOC to find probable cause to believe that Title VII has been violated does not pretermit federal court action,[27] nor does any disposition made of the case by a state Fair Employment Practices Commission.[28] Indeed, in *Voutsis* v. *Union Carbide Corporation*[29] the Second Circuit said that an employee cannot be deemed to have elected to pursue state remedies exclusively if she entered into a settlement with the employer in the state proceeding. The Court said: "The Congressional policy here sought to be enforced is one of eliminating employment discrimination and the statutory enforcement scheme contemplates resort to the federal remedy if the state machinery has proved inadequate. The federal remedy is independent and cumulative . . . and it facilitates comprehensive relief.[30]

It is not clear whether the waiver of the right to sue as the result of an EEOC conciliation agreement would bar access to the federal court.[31]* The courts, however have gone so far as to say that a consent decree negotiated by the United States attorney general in a pattern-of-practice suit under Title VII does not bar a private right of action under the same statute.[32] Moreover, a suit by the attorney general which obtains relief short of that which private plaintiffs request in a subsequent action (for instance, the Justice Department has often detained relief *without* back pay) does not bar the consequent action.[33] *

In short, the entire thrust of Title VII is to make the federal courts the forums for all complaints and to establish a policy which is antithetical to any notion of limited access. This goal contrasts substantially with that of the National Labor Relations Act, which not only states that an administrative agency has exclusive jurisdiction over unfair labor practices, but which also specifically encourages arbitration itself—to such an extent that the board has devised procedures requiring the parties to initiate arbitration before seeking access to the board.[34]

Moreover, there are other features of the arbitration process as it relates to employment discrimination which may lead to hesitation in applying some of the underlying assumptions of the *Steelworkers' Trilogy* and other cases supportive of arbitration to antidiscrimination law. One troublesome feature is the paucity of minority-group arbitrators. It is interesting that the National Academy of Arbitrators, whose membership is involved in much important and prestigious arbitration (though by no means a significant percentage of all the hearings that take place in the country), claimed, as of April 1972, only four black and three women members in a membership of four hundred. The academy has no Chicano or American-Indian members. In 1974 and 1975 the status of blacks and women improved, but not perceptibly. These statistics compare very unfavorably with those of even the most discriminatory unions or employers—the parties that select the arbitrators.

On the other hand, the absence of minorities and women from the arbitral ranks does not by any means, in itself, constitute a persuasive argument against the appropriateness of arbitration. For the situation is similar in the federal judiciary, where the number of minority and female appointees is very small. Although statistics are relevant, the problem with arbitration involves more than the racial and sexual identity of the third-party neutrals.

The heart of the problem is institutional. The union controls the process from the employee's side, and there may not always be unanimity between union and worker. The union determines whether the case proceeds to arbitration and shapes its presentation.[35] The union may not urge the arbitrator to conclude that discrimination is the reason for discharge or discipline if a good relationship with an employer may be harmed or placed in jeopardy by an aggressive business agent. Charges involving discrimination or racism are serious matters, and some unions may be loath to press them against employers with whom they have stable relations. Moreover, a union is hardly likely to be enthusiastic about pressing charges which necessarily implicate itself—as is often the case with institutional practices which offend Title VII, such as the operation of seniority systems which lock minorities into low-level jobs.

Finally, one does not accuse arbitrators of venality when one points out that those appointed by labor and management must necessarily be responsive to their interests and not those of third parties who have no involvement in either the selection of, or "word of mouth" recommendations for, future cases. Arbitrators, like other people, are not often likely to bite the hand that feeds them, and therefore can be counted on to respond to the parties' conscious and subconscious expectations about standards to be applied in finding contract violations and the remedies to be fashioned therefor. These factors help explain the record that arbitrators have made for themselves in race-discrimination cases.

The treatment of such cases by arbitrators does not provide much basis for optimism about the arbitration forum and its ability to resolve discrimination disputes. In one of the earlier NLRB duty-of-fair-representation cases, *Local 12, United Rubber Workers,*[36] the board said that a union had failed to perform its duty of fair representation by refusing to process the grievance of a Negro worker.

The board, in fashioning a remedy for the violation, stated that the grievance should be processed through arbitration and expressed optimism about an arbitrator's resolution of the issue, since, the board said, the arbitrator could not act contrary to federal law. The Board declared: "When the Negro employees, in their efforts to utilize the grievance procedure of the 1962 contract to obtain backpay for the periods of layoffs, insisted upon a fair and valid interpretation of the contract, the Respondent refused to process the grievances relying upon the racially invalid interpretation which had been placed upon that and earlier contracts. . . . Obviously, an arbitrator would not have been bound by the racially invalid interpretation and might have awarded backpay."[37]

The arbitrator, however, who heard the case after the board did consider himself bound by the racially invalid interpretation and did not award back pay.[38] His decision, of course, contrasts with federal court decisions requiring back pay for wages due under similar circumstances if the parties have negotiated a discriminatory seniority system.[39]

Similarly, in *Hotel Employers' Association,*[40] an arbitrator relied on federal law in declaring invalid an agreement negotiated among civil rights organizations, employers, and civil rights agencies providing for statistical goals for the hiring and promotion of minorities. According to the arbitrator, the agreements were violations of both federal and state law. Not only do court decisions under Title VII and the executive order contradict this conclusion, but the courts themselves have devised such goals as a remedy for Title VII violations. Here once again the arbitral process produced a substantially different result, and one which was disadvantageous for the minority-group worker.

These cases are by no means unrepresentative. In the first place, arbitration cases involving allegations of racial discrimination are not likely to be successful at all. Of fifty-one reported cases involving such issues, thirty-four were dismissed.[41*] While these statistics are not out of line with arbitration win-lose ratios generally, they appear to contrast with the important victories obtained by plaintiffs in federal district court. More important, however, is the fact that arbitrators generally will not rely on public law in race cases—unlike the emerging trend in sex-discrimination cases, in which third-party neutrals look to both statutory and constitutional law with increasing frequency.[42] In the fifty-one race-discrimination cases, there are both references to public law and case citations in only five. In four cases, there is reference to law but no citation of cases. In an overwhelming number of cases, forty-two, there is no reference to public law and no citation of cases.

Particularly significant, when one considers both race and sex cases, is the strong correlation between victory or defeat for the grievant and the arbitrator's willingness or unwillingness to cite and apply public law. In the sex-discrimination cases, for instance, in nineteen reported decisions the grievance was dismissed, in twelve there was no reference to public law or any citation of cases, and in seven there was a reference to public law but no citation of cases. In none of the awards in which the grievance was dismissed was there both a reference to public law and citation of a case.[43] A similar pattern is evident in both the race and the sex cases.

To be sure, many arbitration awards uphold grievances predicated on racial discrimination—although many of the opinions have not contained a rationale which refers to discrimination as such.[44*] Most of the cases, however in which a grievance relating to discrimination is sustained involve discharge and discipline matters. There is more reluctance on the part of arbitrators to interfere in promotion disputes[45*]—although this deference to managerial prerogatives reflects arbitral attitudes toward promotion disputes in almost any context.[46*] Moreover, in the discharge cases, some sophistication is sometimes displayed. Typical is Arbitrator G. Allen Dash's reaction to racial tensions in a Pennsylvania post office dispute. Dash said:

This Arbitrator has not previously been involved in any arbitration case in which racial prejudice was so demonstrably present as was true in this instance. This is not to say that the management of the Williamsport Post Office was in any way racially motivated in discharging the grievant in violation of Article II of the National Agreement. But the underlying current that is evident throughout the background of this case, and the manner in which the grievant responded to the several situations with which he was faced on April 21, 1972, require the conclusion that racial prejudice contributed to the entire picture that culminated in his eventual discharge.

First, it is unfortunately necessary, on the basis of the record, to find that a number of the White Postal employees at the Williamsport Main Post Office and the Annex demonstrated obvious racial prejudice and bias in their reference to the grievant in names that deprecated his black race, belittled him as a person and caused him to feel that they did not consider him their equal. Constant exposure to such racial deprecation of a black employee's proper desire for personal worth and equal standing among his fellow employees can understandably result in reactions to on-the-job happenings that reflect themselves in failure to recognize the distinction between fellow employees and supervisors. In this situation, the Arbitrator is persuaded that top management of the Post Office did not give sufficient recognition to the grievants's [sic] repeated racial badgering by his fellow employees when it evaluated the Foremen's reports about the grievant's conduct on April 21, 1972, and decided to discharge him as a consequence thereof.

The fact that the grievant has a white wife has also exposed him to open racial prejudice and bias by some of his fellow employees who have expressed themselves in ways insulting to the grievant's wife, a participant in their interracial marriage. Questions raised by his fellow-employees in attempts to identify his wife, including questions as to the High School class of which she was a member go to the very heart of this situation. It is understandable that the black male member of an interracial marriage would strongly resent the taunts and aspersions of his fellow employees directed toward his white wife. It is evident to the Arbitrator that top management of this Post Office did not take sufficient cognizance of this matter when it decided to discharge the grievant for his actions . . . in that some of those actions arose out of a sense of frustration and a form of striking out against the racial prejudices his fellow employees had directed against his wife.[47]

Accordingly, the arbitrator rescinded the discharge that had been imposed because of the employee's "blowup" in response to the taunts. The arbitrator however, imposed a thirty-day suspension in lieu of discharge and reimbursed the employee with back pay only after to the thirty-day suspension period.

The dominant attitude in most awards, however, indicates understanding of the parties accused of discriminating, and hostility to, or misunderstanding of, the law. Sometimes these surface rather clearly in the form of attacks on the agencies charged with the administration of civil rights statutes. For instance, in *Hooker Chemical Company*, the arbitrator stated:

It is unfortunate for employers that Federal and State "Job Bias" rules can cause personnel activities to become somewhat "topsy turvy." Unions and executives in industry are being harassed, unfortunately, by actions of Federal or State "regulators." The new Federal Law giving the EEOC new powers to haul accused employers or unions into court, faced with a private law suit, or an order to dig out and disclose all sorts of data from personnel files can be somewhat burdensome. Employers and/or unions are faced with a big push on the part of bureaucratic officials (who do not have necessary expertise) to boost hiring, pay, and job status of women and minority groups. Recruiting, hiring, training, promoting, firing, and seniority provisions require careful handling.[48]

When an arbitrator is not hostile to public-law developments, he is likely to be simply unaware of them. Specifically, arbitrators often appear to be unaware of the fact that a finding of intent to discriminate is no longer significant in employ-ment cases by virtue of the Court's decisions in both *Griggs* and *McDonnell Douglas*.[49] In these cases and their progeny, the burden is often thrust upon the defendant union or employer to explain its action or conduct. We find the arbitra-tors striving for the Holy Grail of intent nevertheless. One example of such strained effort is the following statement by Edgar Jones in *Allison Steel Manufac-turing Company:*

The existence of discrimination for racial, religious, or other reasons is as hard to prove when suspected as it is to disprove when charged. An ancient judge once observed that "The devil himself knoweth not the mind of man," and the dilemma continues to frustrate trials of fact now as then. But because it is an ugly thing, as debasing to the doer as it is demeaning to the victim, justice requires the possibility of an unwarranted accusation be as seriously viewed as that of a true charge. Thus a proceeding in which alleged discrimination is the central issue of fact must, if anything, be more cautiously conducted and the evidence more carefully sifted than is routine in grievance arbitrations.[50]

Again, in *ITT Gilfillan, Inc.*, Arbitrator Howard Block said, "The Arbitrator is fully mindful of the difficulty of proving a charge of racial discrimination. He has carefully scrutinized the record with this consideration in mind. However, he can find no evidence of an intent to discriminate against the Grievants."[51]

Except in one reported decision,[52] the arbitrators seem to be unaware of a steady stream of decisions concluding that statistics can make out a prima-facie violation. And the same attitudes and lack of knowledge which prevail with regard to the standards under which discrimination is to be found apply to the remedies fashioned by arbitrators. No arbitrator has set goals and timetables or quotas for minority or female hiring or promotion, although Arbitrator Robert Howlett fash-ioned a strong affirmative-action award in *East Detroit Board of Education*.[53] In contrast to the courts, which have begun to award back pay under Title VII as a matter of course—and in contrast to the arbitral tendency to imply that arbitrators have the authority to award back pay even when an explicit command is lacking in the contract[54]*—the arbitrators seem reluctant to award back pay. This attitude is demonstrated not only in *United Rubber Workers*[55] but also in other cases in which arbitrators exercise discretion in specifying the remedy. For instance, in *G. C. Murphy Co.*,[56] decided by Arbitrator John Caraway, the company had maintained separate seniority lists for janitors and general warehousemen. Transfer from janitorial to warehouse jobs resulted in loss of seniority. The evidence showed that only one white was hired as a janitor in thirty-two years. In December 1971, a supplemental agreement was negotiated whereby the separate seniority lists were abolished and janitors were slotted into an integrated list on the basis of years of service with the company. The grievance was brought in behalf of four blacks whose classification had been changed to that of general warehousemen and who claimed back pay retroactively from the date of employment, or alternatively from the effective date of Title VII.

In denying their claim, the arbitrator made the following points: (1) the award of back pay under Title VII is discretionary; and (2) there was no contract language authorizing back pay. Neither point seems valid. As decisions such as the Supreme Court's decision in *Albermarle* and the *Johnson-Pettway-Baxter* triology make clear,[57] the courts now take the view that under Title VII back pay should be awarded unless special circumstances are present. And as to the second point, the absence of specific language authorizing a remedy of this kind has not troubled arbitrators in the past.

Finally, it goes without saying that none of the arbitrators or parties or—to be fair—grievants have seemed particularly interested in awards which include punitive damages. This has not always been the case in traditional labor-management controversies.[58]*

The failure of most arbitrators to consider the mandates of Title VII when fashioning their awards cannot be attributed simply to unfamiliarity with the law, nor is it merely the result of the arbitrators' reluctance to introduce the bugaboo of race into the cordial relationship which is presumed to exist between the parties (and between the parties and the arbitrator). Rather, arbitrators express a genuine concern that they might exceed their grant of power if they were to consult public law, despite the fact that the Court, in the *Steelworkers' Trilogy,* permitted arbitrators to look to "many sources."

The following comments are rather typical of the arbitral attitude toward the use of law: "Jurisdiction does not extend to interpreting the Civil Rights Act." "We are not the Equal Employment Opportunity Commission and should not put ourselves in its place in terms of our rights or ability to enforce the law which they administer." "It is not up to the arbitrator to interpret federal law." "My responsibility has only to do with determining if the Company has violated the Contract." "I . . . have no jurisdiction, as arbitrator to declare it [a clause bargaining away the arbitration of discrimination problems] to be illegal." "It is not for the Arbitrator . . . to speculate whether any State or Federal Agency or Court of Law, or the EEOC for that matter, will make a similar or contrary ruling. In the field of Industrial Arbitration, an impartial arbitrator is commissioned only to interpret the language the parties have negotiated—no more and no less.''

Such statements prompted some of the federal courts to conclude that the normal presumption in favor of ordering the parties to proceed with arbitration, dictated by the *Steelworkers Trilogy,* ought not to apply in discrimination cases—especially when there is a danger of conflict between implementation of the contract and of the law and especially when the law is in the form of either a consent decree providing for an affirmative-action program approved by a contract-compliance agency or an EEOC or state FEPC conciliation agreement. One important decision indicating the tensions between a quota remedy provided in a consent decree and the seniority provisions of a collective-bargaining agreement is *Stardust Hotel.*[59]

In this case, Edgar Jones was confronted with a consent decree negotiated between the Justice Department and the parties which called for a ratio of one black employee to every three employees placed on jobs as a result of "referral," upgrading, or otherwise in accordance with the collective-bargaining agreement, until blacks constituted 12½ percent of the designated work classifications. The decree provided that nothing was to be construed to require the discharge of any incumbent employee or the hiring of any unqualified worker. Moreover, the decree also stated that, in the event of a conflict between it and the collective bargaining agreement, "the provisions of this decree shall be controlling and deemed to supersede any conflicting provisions in said collective bargaining agreements.''[60]

Preliminarily, the arbitrator was confronted with the employer's argument that the matter was nonarbitrable under the authority of the federal court decisions which have undermined the presumption of arbitrability in employment-discrimination cases. One of the cases cited to the arbitrator was *Savannah Printing Union* v. *Union Camp Corporation,* in which the court stated:

If arbitration can result in obstructing or thwarting the eradication of racial discrimination in employment, an employer is not forced to go through with it. The new seniority provisions [dictated by OFCC seniority requirements] were entered into under the laws of the United States and pursuant to its public policy and cannot be diluted by private negotiations or arbitration. Union Camp cannot obey both the Government and an adverse arbitration award. . . . A contractual duty is excused in cases where intervening government regulations render performance impossible. . . . This does not mean that the arbitration section of the collective bargaining agreement is a nullity. It retains a vitality in all respects save those instances where resort to the arbitral process may prevent the employer from complying with Title VII and Executive Order 11246 and from implementation of the Affirmative Action Compliance Program.[61]

Jones, however, rejected the *Union Camp* reasoning as a "premature" conclusion that there would be conflict between the award and the requirements of law. Moreover, the opinion in *Stardust* noted that it was desirable to attempt to mesh the public policy contained in the Civil Rights Act with the collective-bargaining process.

On the merits—the question was whether the employer could advance a junior black worker in order to comply with the one-to-three ratio—the arbitrator found for the union. Stating that the consent decree was concerned with achieving equal employment opportunity with ''as little personal and institutional disruption as is consonant with the necessity for change,'' the arbitrator concluded that the seniority provisions should prevail under the circumstances. The reasoning set forth was that the quota provisions of the decree did not require a variation of the seniority clause. Jones said:

The district court, the government, and the affected parties to the consent decree quite evidently sought to be precise in their phrasing of the decree provisions. They might well have reached into the specific hotel areas in which employees working in a particular classification are to be found, requiring that each work assignment area ultimately reflect the same racial balance established as the goal for each of the classifications. . . . But it did not do so, and the reason is obvious enough. . . . There simply are not that many captains assigned to each of the rooms to allow for application of the remedial percentage of 12-½ percent. . . . Again, the decree might have empowered an employer to deviate from the seniority system in order to create additional job openings outside the contractual seniority track, but within a particular classification, to be filled by minority employees already occupying the classification. This is apparently what the Employer actually undertook to do unilaterally in this instance. This might well be a practical and less disruptive way to allow those Employers who wish to do so to respond more rapidly to attaining a nondiscriminatory racial balance. It would then have the effect of modifying the bargained seniority system by operation of law. Of course, the union might have consented to the creation of such fast track bypassing seniority, but it has not.[62]

A somewhat different theme was sounded by Arbitrator Adolph Koven in *Lockheed Missiles and Space Company.*[63] In this case, a Mrs. Portwood had filed a complaint with the EEOC because she was denied an opportunity for promotion in 1967. The commission found reasonable cause to believe that the statute had been violated. An agreement was ultimately reached, with the commission supervising the negotiations under which Mrs. Portwood was promoted and given back pay. The union then brought grievances on behalf of employees who were bypassed, in violation of the seniority agreement, by virtue of the settlement with the EEOC. An additional element was the fact that the company was a government contractor subject to Executive Order 11246.

Arbitrator Koven noted that Title VII had resulted in ''some disruption'' in seniority systems and that ''federal law is clearly paramount, and the EEOC and the courts are authorized by the law to fashion remedies . . . which supersede the collective bargaining agreement.'' Accordingly, inasmuch as the company had acted pursuant to ''EEOC compulsion,'' the arbitrator found that ''arbitral jurisdiction is absent to find that the Contract was violated when Mrs. [Portwood] was promoted. Moreover, to so find would be in clear violation of federal law.''[64]

Thus, on the one hand, in *Stardust* the arbitrator used the normal *Steelworkers' Trilogy* presumption of arbitrability and found no violations of the law or contract. In *Lockheed Missiles,* on the other hand, no presumption of arbitrability was employed. The arbitrator delved deeply into the ''requirements of enacted legislation.'' The arbitrator held that the contract, in effect, would violate the law, and thus arbitral jurisdiction was not present. Clearly, the arbitrator, confronted with a situation in which the collective-bargaining agreement would have compelled him to violate Title VII, reached the right result. And the reasoning, which obligates him in effect to stay his hand, seems as good as any. The arbitrator in *Stardust,* on the other hand, while faced with a situation slightly different from that in *Lockheed Missiles,* inasmuch as there was no agreement on the specific grievance in question, nevertheless resolved all doubts about the merits in favor of the agreement rather than the law. In so doing, he seemed to ignore the fact that hiring and promotion ratios or quotas will in many instances require the nullifying of seniority provisions in collective-bargaining agreements—even though the consent decree or the dictates of statutes do not specifically address themselves to the particular incident, before the arbitrator. *Stardust,* then, dramatizes the problems in reconciling contract and law and, perhaps more important, some of the reasons for the lack of confidence in arbitrators which are indicated in the court's decision in *Union Camp.*

The *Gardner-Denver* Decision

Many of the problems relating to the role of arbitration in Title VII cases were addressed by the Supreme Court in the decision of *Alexander* v. *Gardner-Denver Co.*[65] In this case, a black employee had been hired by the company to do maintenance work; two years after the date of hire he was awarded a trainee position as a drill operator. He remained on that job until his discharge a year later; the grounds for discharge provided by the company were that he was producing too many unusable parts that had to be scrapped. The employee filed a grievance under the collective-bargaining agreement between the company and the union, Local 3029, United Steelworkers of America. The grievance did not mention racial discrimination, but asserted that the employee felt that he had been "unjustly discharged" and requested reinstatement, back pay, and full seniority. The collective-bargaining agreement contained a no-discrimination clause and also a provision which stated that the employer could not discharge, suspend, or give a written warning notice to employees except for "just cause."

At the final prearbitration step of the grievance-arbitration procedure, the petitioner raised the question of racial discrimination. The grievance was rejected by the company, and proceeded to arbitration. Prior to arbitration, however, the grievant filed a charge of racial discrimination with the Colorado Civil Rights Commission, and this was eventually referred to the EEOC. At the arbitration hearing, the grievant stated that he had filed the charge with the Colorado commission because he "could not rely on the Union." But the union, at the hearing, introduced a letter written by the grievant in which he charged discriminatory treatment. The arbitrator held that the employee had therefore been discharged "for just cause," and, without reference to the claim of racial discrimination, upheld the company's position.

Mr. Justice Powell, speaking for a unanimous Court in *Gardner-Denver,* stressed at the outset the statutory preference for voluntary compliance and conciliation:

Cooperation and voluntary compliance were selected as the preferred means for achieving this goal [the elimination of discrimination in employment]. To this end, Congress created the Equal Employment Opportunity Commission and established a procedure whereby existing state and local equal employment opportunity agencies, as well as the Commission, would have an opportunity to settle disputes through conference, conciliation and persuasion before the aggrieved party was permitted to file a lawsuit.[66]

In response to the question posed in *Gardner-Denver*—whether the employee, by proceeding to arbitration, had selected his remedy and therefore barred the door to the federal courthouse—the Court stressed the essential role the federal judiciary has been provided by Title VII and the "plenary powers to secure compliance with Title VII" accorded the courts. The courts have held that an arbitrator's resolution of a contractual claim raising a discrimination issue was not dispositive and did not preclude judicial review. Said the Court: "In submitting his grievance to arbitration, an employee seeks to vindicate his contractual right under a collective-bargaining agreement. By contrast, in filing a lawsuit under Title VII, an employee asserts independent statutory rights accorded by Congress. The distinctly separate nature of these contractual and statutory rights is not vitiated merely because both were violated as a result of the same factual occurence." The Court also stated that the employee could not be deemed to have waived his rights under Title VII, even though a union might waive statutory rights through collective bargaining, such as the right to strike for the term of a contract. The Court compared the relinquishment of such rights through the collective-bargaining process with waivers under Title VII:

These [collectively bargained] rights are conferred on employees collectively to foster the processes of bargaining and properly may be exercised or relinquished by the union as collectively-bargaining agent to obtain economic benefits for unit members. Title VII, on the other hand, stands on plainly different ground; it concerns not majoritarian processes, but an individual's right to equal employment opportunities. Title VII's strictures are absolute and represent a congressional command that each employee be free from discriminatory practices. Of necessity, the rights conferred can form no part of the collective-bargaining process since waiver of these rights would defeat the paramount congressional purpose behind Title VII. In these circumstances, an employee's rights under Title VII are not susceptible to prospective waiver.[67]

A critical question not completely resolved by *Gardner-Denver* is the future role of arbitration in Title VII cases.[68*] Should there be a presumption against arbitrability by both the judiciary and the arbitrators? Is there any role for the arbitrators to play in such cases? On the one hand, the Court seemed to dismiss the role of arbitrators through its failure to accord any deference to these creatures of the collective-bargaining process in matters relating to public law. Furthermore, the Court indicated that providing a role for arbitration in such matters might undermine the arbitration process itself, inasmuch as one of its main benefits is informality and the "efficient, inexpensive and expeditious" processing of grievances which is a consequence. The Court contrasted this process to the detailed discovery and trial process in Title VII situations. The Court said: "A standard that adequately insured effectuation of Title VII rights in the arbitral forum would tend to make arbitration a procedurally complex, expensive and time-consuming process. And judicial enforcement of such a standard would almost require courts to make *de novo* determinations of the employees' claims. It is uncertain whether any minimal savings in judicial time and expense would justify the risk to vindication of Title VII rights.'' Accordingly, the Court concluded that a *de novo* hearing was warranted after the arbitral decision. The Court, however, indicated that the award could be "admitted as evidence and accorded such weight as the court deems appropriate."[69] At the end of this passage of the opinion—which appears at its conclusion—the Court added a significant footnote, number 21, which varies somewhat from the text of the opinion. Justice Powell said in footnote 21:

We adopt no standards as to the weight to be accorded an arbitral decision, since this must be determined in the court's discretion with regard to the facts and circumstances of each case. Relevant factors include the existence of provisions in the collective-bargaining agreement that conform substantially with Title VII, the degree of procedural fairness in the arbitral forum, adequacy of the record with respect to the issue of discrimination, and the special competence of particular arbitrators. Where an arbitral determination gives full consideration to an employee's Title VII rights, a court may properly accord it great weight. This is especially true where the issue is solely one of fact, specifically addressed by the parties and decided by the arbitrator on the basis of an adequate record.[70]

In order to assess properly the future role of arbitration in employment-discrimination claims it is important to review the judicial treatment of employment-discrimination arbitrations prior to *Gardner-Denver,* as well as the records of arbitrators.

The Election-of-Remedies Cases

The first case to be presented to a circuit court of appeals on the election-of-remedies issue was *Bowe* v. *Colgate-Palmolive Company,*[71] in which the Seventh Circuit reversed a district court holding that an election of remedies requiring a party to choose between the available forums was required *ab initio* (that is, at the initiation of the proceedings). The Seventh Circuit stated that the concurrent jurisdiction of arbitrators and the National Labor Relations Board was analogous to that of arbitrators and the federal courts charged with enforcing Title VII—and that the analogy was not merely "compelling" but, rather, "conclusive."[72] The court stated that a burden would be placed on the party that defended in each forum, but because of "crucial differences" between the processes and the remedy afforded in each forum, the election-of-remedies doctrine was inappropriate. The court stated that the arbitrator might consider himself to be precluded by a contract from providing the kind of remedy available in the courts under Title VII, and the court gave as an example the remedy of back pay. (This example would appear to miss the mark, inasmuch as arbitrators regularly fashion remedies of back pay.) Moreover, the court noted that in Title VII actions the court bears a special responsibility to resolve the dispute presented in the allegations regardless of the position of the individual plaintiff and the merits of his or her case. The class-action cases and those that expressed the notion that race discrimination is group discrimination have come to that conclusion.[73] The court said, "Accordingly, we hold that it was error not to permit the plaintiffs to utilize a parallel prosecution both in court and through arbitration so long as election of remedy was made after adjudication so as to preclude duplicate relief which would result in unjust enrichment or windfall to the plaintiffs."[74]

It is important at this point to explain what the Seventh Circuit left unexplained about the election-of-remedies doctrine, inasmuch as it has proved attractive to another appellate court—albeit for a temporary period which was cut short definitively by the Court's decision in *Gardner-Denver*. The traditional election-of-remedies doctrine was fashioned as a device to protect parties from being compelled to undergo repetitive and vexatious litigation. A party that has two alternative remedies and proceeds to pursue one of them will be precluded from seeking the other in certain circumstances. Those circumstances usually consist of a material change of position by the other party because of that party's reliance on the election. The doctrine applies most often when conflicting and inconsistent remedies are sought on the basis of conflicting and insistent rights. Thus, a party is protected from having a face in the future a different theoretical approach to the same set of facts (or an alternative set of facts supporting an identical approach to the one with which he is confronted in a given law suit). Although the doctrine of election-of-remedies and that of *res judicata* appear grounded in the same soil of equity, they are decidedly different. The election doctrine does not necessarily depend on the rendering of a judgment in the original action, while the existence of a prior final judgment is universally an element of the doctrine of *res judicata*. Because the former doctrine is a technical rule of procedure or judicial administration, grounded in considerations of equity, it is now considered largely obsolete, especially since the advent of *Federal Rules of Civil Procedure* for federal courts and their adoption by most states. It is now possible to plead totally irreconcilable fact patterns and seek irreconcilable remedies in the same action. Accordingly, the doctrine has long been in disrepute,[75] and it was thoroughly rejected by the Court in *Gardner-Denver*.[76]

The approaches subsequently undertaken by the Fifth Circuit Court of Appeals, in *Hutchings* v. *U.S. Industries*[77] and *Rios* v. *Reynolds Metal Company*,[78] and by the Ninth Circuit, in *Oubichon* v. *North American Rockwell Corporation*,[79] indicate reasoning that is more elaborate and satisfactory than that provided by any of the other courts prior to *Gardner-Denver*. The facts in *Hutchings* were as follows: The plaintiff, Hutchings, a black worker, had applied for the position of leadman, but the position was assigned to a white man who had less experience and seniority. Hutchings then filed a grievance complaining of the job assignment to an employee with less seniority, and the grievance was taken to the third step in the procedure, at which stage the grievance was decided against the plaintiff. Accordingly, the matter was not submitted to arbitration, and subsequently Hutchings filed a charge with the Equal Employment Opportunity Commission. Meanwhile, the leadman's position became open again, and after Hutchings applied for it, the company abolished the job. Again Hutchings filed a grievance, and this time the matter proceeded to arbitration. The arbitrator determined the company did not violate the agreement by refusing to hire a replacement for the job.

Here again, the court reversed a district court's granting of a company's motion for summary judgment based on the arbitration award. The Fifth Circuit noted that the federal courts "alone" were given the power by Congress to enforce compliance with the statute. The court, citing *Bowe,* stated that it had a special responsibility to determine the facts, regardless of the individual plaintiff's position. Considering the function of grievance-arbitration machinery against the backdrop, the court said, "An arbitration award, whether adverse of favorable to the employee, is not *per se* conclusive of the determination of the Title VII rights by the federal courts nor is an immediate grievance determination deemed 'settled' under the bargaining contract to be given this effect."[80]

The Fifth Circuit Court then declared that in arbitration proceedings, the arbitrator's role was to determine the contract right of the party as distinguished from the rights afforded by a statute such as Title VII. Moreover, Judge Robert Ainsworth, speaking for the court, said that the arbitrator might feel himself "constrained" not to provide the kind of remedies contained in Title VII. The court stated that a contrary decision would penalize the employee who had unsuccessfully pursued contractual remedies to conclusion and thus discourage reliance on voluntary compliance with the act, which, after all, is an objective of Title VII, as is stressed in *Gardner-Denver.*[81] In any event, the court concluded in *Hutchings* that the federal courts were the final arbiters under the statutory scheme.

The Ninth Circuit reached the same conclusion in *Oubichon,* a case which differs from *Hutchings* and most of the other election-of-remedies cases in that the plaintiff had not lost in the arbitral forum; rather, the company had settled his grievances by paying back wages for the time he had been docked and by removing a disciplinary warning from his file. The existence of the settlement gives *Oubichon* a dimension similar to that of the *Voutsis* case.[82] Judge Alfred Goodwin, speaking for the court of appeals, held that the settlement did not render the case moot, since the plaintiff alleged that the incident which was the subject of the settled grievances was "part of a chain of incidents indicative of a policy of racial discrimination," and proof of that claim would entitle him to a broader remedy than that afforded by the settlement of the particular grievances. Injunctive relief, for example, might be appropriate.[83]

Turning to the company's contention that by invoking the contractual-grievance mechanism the plaintiff had elected his remedy and was barred from suing under Title VII, Judge Goodwin first noted that the statute, which is quite specific about jurisdictional prerequisites, makes no mention of the effect of submission of a grievance to arbitration, and "thus the inference is strong that Congress did not intend to deny Title VII relief to employees who availed themselves of contractual remedies before coming to the courts."[84]

The court then proceeded to refute three arguments put forward by the employer. On each of these points the Supreme Court, in *Gardner-Denver,* subsequently approved Judge Goodwin's reasoning.[85]

First, he asserted that the "possibility of unjust enrichment by multiple recoveries . . . cannot justify a stringent election requirement [since] judicial relief can be tailored to avoid duplication and windfall gains."[86]

Second, he disposed of the argument that it would be "unfair" to provide the employee with a second forum (the federal courts) in which to pursue claims adjudicated in the arbitral forum, while the employer had no such "second string in his bow." The court noted that certain features of arbitration, such as the control of the process by the union rather than the grievant and the arbitrators' hesitance to provide the kinds of remedies mandated by Title VII, limit the protection arbitration affords to employees, while placing no corresponding limits on the protection afforded to employers. Thus to a large extent the fact that the federal courts are available to the employee but not to the employer is no more than an equalizing factor. "Moreover, to the degree that the procedure [of providing a second forum] is, on balance, less fair to the employer, the imbalance follows from the fact that the employer cannot, under Title VII, be the victim of discrimination, by an employee."[87] That is, only the employee is given the second forum of the federal courts, because only the employee can be the victim of the practices which Congress found it necessary to redress through Title VII, and which (as the very fact that Congress found Title VII to be necessary testifies) cannot be prohibited by arbitration alone. (In *Gardner-Denver* the Supreme Court, while citing *Oubichon* on this point, adopted a more precise analysis by recognizing that it is not really accurate to say that the employee has a "second string in his bow," because he is not really making a single claim in two forums; rather, he is urging a *contractual* claim before the arbitrator, and a *statutory* claim before the court.)[88]

Third, to the employer's assertion that providing a second forum would destroy the finality of arbitration, and hence its value to employers, the court responded that arbitration clauses are of such importance to employers (as the *quid pro quo* for no-strike clauses) that the lack of finality only in grievance procedures that raise Title VII claims would not lead employers to forsake the negotiating of arbitration clauses.[89] On the other hand, if resort to arbitration were to bar a Title VII suit, then employees would have every reason to avoid arbitration. Thus election-of-remedies rules would actually undermine arbitration, rather than fostering it.

Finally, the court refused to invoke the

principle of estoppel [which precludes a party from raising a claim by virtue of conduct which others may have depended upon to their detriment]. As a general proposition, parties who have freely agreed to submit their grievance to a fair and impartial tribunal having the power to decide should not seek another decision elsewhere on the same facts [citing *Newman* v. *Avco Corporation,* shortly to be discussed]. But Title VII cases do not lend themselves to solution by general propositions.

The purposes of Title VII and the federal labor policy of encouraging arbitration can both be served by a rule that an employee can seek more than one remedy but may not recover twice for the same injury.[90]

Accordingly, the court would hear the plaintiff's case despite the fact that he had invoked the grievance process, and despite the settlement, but would require him to prove that "what he received was not intended to be a complete settlement of his claim for money damages. If he can prove that the apparent settlement was not based on the full range of issues cognizable under Title VII, or that it was cognizable only as a partial settlement because the grievance arbitration machinery was limited in its available remedies, the plaintiff may press for additional money damages."[91]

In *Rios* v. *Reynolds Metal* the Fifth Circuit, speaking through Judge Griffin Bell, confronted the issue suggested by the last portion of *Oubichon*—whether the courts should defer to arbitration awards (or, in the *Oubichon* setting, to settlements) and, if so, what standards should be employed. The court, stating that the Title VII obligation was explicitly included in the collective-bargaining agreement in the form of a no-discrimination clause and that federal labor policy generally favored the settlement of labor disputes through arbitration, concluded that "the viability of arbitration depends upon the willingness of courts to enforce the arbitrator's award without reopening issues resolved by him."[92] On the other hand, the court referred to its previous holding in *Hutchings* that the federal courts have independent authority to remedy employment discrimination complaints pursuant to Title VII proceedings. Consequently, the court made an accommodation between the principle of *Hutchings* and the principle of deferral to a prior arbitration award "under limited circumstances." The court said:

We hold that the federal district court in the exercise of its power as the final arbiter under Title VII may follow a procedure of deferral under the following limitations. First, there may be no deference to the decision of the arbitrator unless the contractual right coincides with rights under Title VII. Second, it must be plain that the arbitrator's decision is in no way violative of the private rights guaranteed by Title VII, nor of the public policy which inheres in Title VII. In addition, before deferring, the district court must be satisfied that (1) the factual issues before it are identical to those decided by the arbitrator; (2) the arbitrator had power under the collective agreement to decide the ultimate issue of discrimination; (3) the evidence presented at the arbitral hearing dealt adequately with all factual issues; (4) the arbitrator actually decided the factual issues presented to the court; (5) the arbitration proceeding was fair and regular and free of procedural infirmities. The burden of proof in establishing these conditions of limitation will be upon the respondent as distinguished from the claimant.[93]

The Court in *Gardner-Denver,* however, rejected this "demanding deferral standard" because of its potential for making arbitration more legalistic and time-consuming and uncertainty "whether any minimal savings in judicial time and expense would justify the risk to vindication of Title VII rights."[94] Moreover, the Court in *Gardner-Denver* was concerned that employees who feared that the system might not protect their rights and that deference would be accorded to the award would bypass the process altogether. The Court said, "The possibility of voluntary compliance or settlement of Title VII claims would thus be reduced, and the result could well be more litigation, not less."[95]

If, however, a *Rios* v. *Reynolds Metal*-type deferral standard is rejected, an incentive to develop an effective arbitration procedure to eliminate discrimination is undermined. The Court's statement in *Gardner-Denver* about the tendency of workers to bypass procedures if deference is accorded misses the mark. The deficiencies in arbitration argue for tough standards of deferral—and the principal problem with *Rios* was that standards formulated in that decision were so ambiguous that both friends and foes of Title VII could praise them. I believe that, on balance, it is necessary to encourage the development of new arbitration procedures in Title VII cases. Although footnote 21 of *Gardner-Denver* may have a meaning somewhat akin to that of *Rios* v. *Reynolds Metal,* the Court's approach in the textual portion of the *Gardner-Denver* decision is a bit too severe.

The above-quoted portions of *Gardner-Denver* miss the mark in another respect as well. Justice Powell seems to assume that arbitration is much less formal than it really is. For several years the participants in, and commentators on, arbitration have railed against the expense, legalism, formalism, and delay involved in arbitration proceedings.[96] Justice Powell seems completely unaware of this phenomenon and the contemporary realities as he accurately states the reasons for the earlier increase in arbitration. Moreover, as footnote 21 implies, there are many cases of fact which do not raise contractual legal issues, and usually involve discharge or discipline, where an attempt to mirror Title VII fact-finding processes would not make arbitration proceedings more complex. On the other hand, those issues which present class-action-type problems of systematic discrimination are necessarily more complicated in any event. And even in the former group of cases, transcripts are often taken by a court reporter. Thus arbitration has already attained a degree of procedural complexity which Justice Powell seems to underestimate. Any additional complexities which might be necessary for an award to pass muster under a demanding deferral standard would therefore result in less change in the processes of arbitration than the Court seems to fear. Accordingly, the benefits lost through a *Rios* v. *Reynolds Metal*-type deferral standard are fewer than those contemplated by *Gardner-Denver*. Footnote 21, however, may make the differences between *Gardner-Denver* and *Rios* more academic than practical.

In contrast to the approach adopted by the Fifth and Ninth Circuits in *Hutchings, Oubichon,* and *Rios* was that of the Sixth Circuit in *Dewey* v. *Reynolds Metal Company*.[97] The plaintiff, Robert Dewey, claimed that he was wrongfully discharged because of his religious beliefs, and accordingly prayed for reinstatement with back pay. Simultaneously with bringing a grievance under the contract, Dewey filed a complaint with the Michigan Civil Rights Commission. The commission, as well as the arbitrator, dismissed the complaint. The EEOC, however, determined that there was reasonable cause to believe that an unlawful employment practice had been engaged in. The Sixth Circuit, in dealing with the effect of the arbitration award, noted that if an arbitrator had ruled in favor of Dewey, the award would have been final and binding on the employer, according to the *Steelworkers' Trilogy*.[98] Unlike the Ninth Circuit in *Oubichon,* and subsequently the Supreme Court in *Gardner-Denver,* the Sixth Circuit was persuaded by the apparent asymmetry of such a result. If the employer but not the employee was bound by the arbitration, the "efficacy" of arbitration would be "destroyed." Judge

Paul Weick wrote for the majority: "This result could sound the death knell to arbitration of labor disputes, which has been so usefully employed in their settlement. Employers would not be so inclined to agree to arbitration clauses in collective bargaining agreements if they provided only a one-way street, i.e., that the awards are binding on them but not on their employees."[99]

On rehearing, the same court stated that an employer would have no incentive to become party to arbitration procedures if employees could upset finality through suit in federal court. The Supreme Court affirmed the majority's denial of the plaintiff's claim by a 4-to-4 vote. It was never clear, however, whether the tie vote was on the religious-discrimination issue in *Dewey* or whether the justices had contemplated the arbitration aspects of the case.[100]*

Subsequently, the Sixth Circuit limited *Dewey,* even before the *Gardner-Denver* decision. In the first of two decisions prior to *Gardner-Denver, Spann* v. *Joanna Western Mills Company*[101] a discharge case in which the arbitrator granted reinstatement without back pay, a panel of the court declared its adherence to *Dewey* but emphasized the limited scope of the holding, and intimated "no opinion" on those issues beyond its reach. The court said, "We hold only that where all issues are presented to bona fide arbitration and no other refuge is sought until that arbitration is totally complete, *Dewey* precludes judicial cognizance of the complaint."[102]

In *Newman* v. *Avco Corporation,*[103] the Sixth Circuit explained further its characterization of the narrow holding in *Dewey.* In *Newman,* the plaintiff, a black worker, requested a transfer because of injuries sustained in an automobile accident. This request was denied, and, shortly after returning to the job from which transfer was sought, the plaintiff was discharged on the ground of inefficiency. Previously, the plaintiff had been suspended for inefficiency three days after assignment to the job and had not been given training which he claimed was due him according to the collective-bargaining agreement.

The plaintiff filed a timely grievance seeking reinstatement and amended it to include a charge of racial discrimination. The amendment was made because the union indicated that it would not allege racial discrimination in the arbitration proceeding. The plaintiff personally retained an attorney to argue the charge of racial discrimination at the arbitration hearing. A week after the hearing was held, charges were filed with the EEOC against both the company and the union alleging racial discrimination on the ground that the parties had failed to give blacks adequate training. Meanwhile, the arbitrator, after the filing of the charge with the EEOC, found against the plaintiff on all grounds and held that the discharge was for failure to perform the job adequately. As the Sixth Circuit's opinion notes, the arbitrator's opinion "seemed to ignore the plaintiff's underlying position that he could not perform other chores well because due to racial discrimination he had never been so trained."[104]

In *Newman,* the court distinguished between that case and *Dewey* because a motion for summary judgment had been granted by the district court and there was no

evidentiary record available as in the latter case. The Court also spoke of the
Dewey rationale as predicated upon the equitable doctrine which lawyers refer to
as estoppel. Judge John Peck said, speaking for the court:

Congress, intimately familiar with arbitration in labor-management contracts, employed no
language in Title VII which even intimates support for the election of remedies doctrine.
And several courts have squarely rejected it [citing *Hutchings* and *Bowe*]. We do not read
Dewey as based upon the adoption of election of remedies. The majority opinion of this
court in *Dewey* did not so characterize its reasoning. On the contrary, as has been indicated,
it seems apparent that the second ground relied on for the decision in *Dewey* was the doctrine of estoppel. This equitable doctrine holds that where the parties have agreed to resolve
the grievances before (1) a fair and impartial tribunal, (2) which had *power to decide them,*
a District Court should defer to the fact finding thus accomplished.[105]

The court reasoned that neither of these two factors was present in *Newman.*
Moreover, the court said that the employee really did not have the voluntary
choice of filing his grievance, since the collective agreement "required" prompt
filing. Judge Peck noted that it was claimed that a failure to file might have
confronted the plaintiff with a motion to dismiss for failure to exhaust contractual
remedies.[106] This, however, seems highly unlikely, inasmuch as an exhaustion of
contractual remedies has not been regarded as a prerequisite to the filing of Title
VII actions, and, moreover, the same rule seems to govern claims of racial discrimination arising under the National Labor Relations Act[107] as well as the
Railway Labor Act.[108] The court, in *Newman,* seemed to be on firmer ground
when it distinguished the situation in *Dewey* from that in *Newman,* where it was
alleged that there was a "long-standing conspiracy to maintain a system of race
discrimination participated in by both company and union [the contracting parties
which created the arbitration machinery and chose the arbitrator], an element totally lacking in *Dewey.*"[109] While the element may not have been totally lacking
in *Dewey,* the case was essentially concerned with idiosyncratic employee behavior, which, unlike racial discrimination, is not as likely to be the subject of a conspiracy.

Moreover, the court in *Newman* stressed that the union had declined to support
the claim that the discharge was caused by racial discrimination and this attitude
was noted by the arbitrator in deciding that there was no merit to the claim of
racial discrimination. In *Dewey,* the arbitrator, Mark Kahn, an able and respected
member of the National Academy of Arbitrators, specifically disclaimed consideration of statutory and constitutional claims. In the *Dewey* arbitration hearing, there
was no disagreement between the union and the employee in the presence of the
arbitrator, and the issues posed to the court were not even argued in the arbitration
forum.

The court in *Newman* emphasized a factor which the Supreme Court's decision
in *Gardner-Denver* seems to make irrelevant, except where the other factors of
footnote 21 are present: that the collective bargaining agreement did not contain a
provision prohibiting racial discrimination in hiring, promotion, or discharge. Ac-

cordingly, the court stated that substantial portions of the complaint either were not submitted to arbitration or were beyond the arbitrator's power of decision.

Distinguishing *Spann* from *Newman,* the court in the latter case stated that the plaintiff in *Spann* had been successful in obtaining reinstatement and thus was attempting to "accept the fruits of an award and then dispute its validity."[110] (*Oubichon,* however, as well as *Voutsis,* would seem to vitiate this distinction). The court noted, however, that some of the factors present in *Spann* were "arguably present" in *Newman.*[111]

Third-Party Intervention

The notion that the minority group's or individual's position will not be presented fully without the right of intervention for the grievant has special significance in the case of discrimination charges. The federal district court in *Dewey* noted that the plaintiff was not represented with his own counsel at the hearing.[112] If the discrimination charge involves the administration or negotiation of the collective-bargaining agreement (in which activity both the union and employer are involved), it is often possible that the union's viewpoint and interests are different from, or conflict directly with, those of the grievants. This potential is dramatized in *Spann,*[113] in which the union in fact brought the matter which led to the grievant's discharge to the employer's attention. As the Court noted in *Gardner-Denver* in refusing to require the court's deference to an arbitration award: "Harmony of interest between the union and the individual employee cannot always be presumed, especially where a claim of racial discrimination is made. . . . And a breach of the Union's duty of fair representation may prove difficult to establish. . . . In this respect, it is noteworthy that Congress thought it necessary to afford the protections of Title VII against unions as well as employers."[114] In the absence of distrust, it might have been unnecessary to pass the statute at all.

The question posed under the rubric of third-party intervention is whether the individual or minority group has the right to be notified of the arbitration hearing, and to participate in it with separate representation in the form of counsel or a civil rights organization in which he or she has confidence. The New York Court of Appeals has held that the individual has no third-party right of intervention, inasmuch as the union is the exclusive bargaining agent with authority to bind all employees within the union.[115] Notwithstanding the fact that the Railway Labor Act permits the individual to proceed in his own right by using that statute's adjudicative machinery (which is controlled by the union and the employer),[116] the NLRB has taken the position that it will honor an arbitration award even when the individual has no notice of the hearing. Therefore, it goes without saying that the individual under such circumstances has no right to representation.[117] The board's judgment is that even when the case involves an individual's discharge pursuant to a union-negotiated union-security clause, the discharged employee's absence does not destroy the hearing's validity so long as the *employer* takes a position at the hearing identical to that taken by the individual.[118]

In *Clark* v. *Hein-Werner Corp.*, a case involving a seniority dispute, the Wisconsin Supreme Court took a slightly different approach. In *Clark* the court held that a union was not performing its "fiduciary" duty of fair representation in a case involving conflicting employee claims. The court said: "Where the interests of two groups of employees are diametrically opposed to each other and the union espouses the cause of one in the arbitration, it follows as a matter of law that there has been no fair representation of a group. This is true even through, in choosing the cause of which group to espouse, the union acts completely objectively and with the best of motives. The old adage, that one cannot serve two masters, is particularly applicable to such a situation."[119] Concerning the argument that the employees' positions were considered by the arbitrator because the employer took the position of the plaintiff at the hearing, the court said, "Employees not fairly represented by the union should never be put in the position of having solely to depend upon the employer championing their rights under the collective bargaining contract."[120]

In *Humphrey* v. *Moore*[121] the Supreme Court considered an assertion that granting the right to employees to participate in a hearing was a necessary element in the duty of fair representation owed the workers. The Court found that, contrary to the dissident workers' allegations, they had in fact fully participated.[122] Nevertheless, one can conclude from the language of the opinion[123*] that the Court implicitly accepted the position that the right to intervene is part and parcel of the union's obligation to represent fairly, since the Court examined the issue factually rather than dismissing the question as a matter of law. We must keep in mind, however, that conflicting seniority claims of two different groups of employees were involved, and for the reasons enumerated in *Clark* by the Wisconsin Supreme Court, the United States Supreme Court may have been particularly sensitive to the third-party-intervention argument in such situations.

Somewhat supportive of this view is the Supreme Court's ruling in *Trbovich* v. *United Mine Workers*,[124] an election case arising under Title IV of the Landrum-Griffin Act, in which the Court held that union members have the right to intervene in such litigation even though only the Secretary of Labor has the authority to initiate actions charging election irregularities. The very same proposition holds true in the labor-arbitration context. The Supreme Court held, in *Vaca* v. *Sipes*,[125] that unless the contract states otherwise, the right to initiate a grievance and carry it through to arbitration rests exclusively with the bargaining representative of the workers. Just as Congress has designated the Secretary of Labor as the exclusive prosecutor for the litigation of election disputes, so Congress has supported the concept of an exclusive bargaining representative in connection with the administration as well as the negotiation of collective-bargaining agreements. But that does not mean that the exclusive bargaining representative must exclude all other groups from all discussions with employees at all times. This has already been made clear by the courts by reference to the provisos in Section 9(a) of Taft-

Hartley and the limited involvement that is permitted to both individuals and groups of workers in grievance adjustments.[126] Accordingly, it would seem as though some of the same considerations highlighted in *Trbovich* regarding the potential for relatively unenthusiastic processing of a protest in the absence of the interested party are applicable to the situation here.

Despite *Clark, Humphrey,* and *Trbovich,* the case law indicates no uniform trend toward a policy favoring third-party intervention. Arguably, the Supreme Court's rationale in *Alexander. v. Gardner-Denver Co.* and its reference to "the union's exclusive control over the manner and extent to which an individual grievance is presented"[127] constitute implied acceptance of the status quo. Yet the Court was hardly presented with a third-party-intervention issue in *Gardner-Denver.* Moreover, it did no more than make reference to Supreme Court decisions which involve the authority of the union to initiate a claim and not the right to intervene.

Nonetheless, hope for acceptance of a third-party-intervention approach in labor law received a setback in the Fifth Circuit's decision in *Acuff* v. *United Papermakers.*[128] In *Acuff* an arbitrator rejected the grievance of certain discharged employees and changed the discharge of others to disciplinary layoff, following a wildcat strike. The employees subsequently filed motions to intervene before the federal district court which had compelled the arbitration. In dismissing the employees' appeal from the district court's denial of their motions, the Fifth Circuit ignored the language previously used in *Humphrey* and relied heavily on *Vaca* for the proposition that third-party intervention would interfere with the union's right to control the grievance-arbitration process. After citing the rule in *Vaca* that the union, not the individual, has the right to compel arbitration of a grievance, the court stated, "It would be paradoxical in the extreme if the union, which is authorized to decide whether a grievance is to be pursued to the arbitration stage at all could be authorized to assume full responsibility for a grievance it did pursue, without the intervention of the individual union members immediately concerned."[129]*

Assuming the validity of the holding in *Clark,* the court stated that *Acuff* was distinguishable from that case inasmuch as "it [*Clark*] is a different case if the interests of different groups of employees are in irreconcilable conflict. Here the union could have and, as far as record reveals, did defend the rights of all employees with equal zeal."[130]

The *Acuff* opinion, however, is erroneous in distinguishing *Clark* from *Acuff.* Although the potential conflict of interests in exclusive union representation of wildcat strikers is not quite as direct and dramatic as it is in a seniority dispute, which was involved in *Clark,* nevertheless the difference between the two is not fundamental enough to provide a reason for deciding the cases differently. In an unauthorized work stoppage the union has a strong interest in guarding its treasury against strike liability. If the union can be shown to have instigated or aided the walkout, it may be liable for damages.[131]* At the same time, the union is obliged to argue for reinstatement or for scaling down penalties on behalf of the strikers.

A striker might testify that a union officer or committeeman told him to "down tools"—to say that the walkout was not initiated by workers independently of the union. Might not some unions therefore wish to keep such a grievant away from the hearing and without representation, even though the result would be discharge or suspension for the offending worker? The potential for the imposition of liability on the union may be the dominant concern of the union. These kinds of dilemmas for the union, as well as the fact that a perusal of the hearing transcript (if one is kept) can rarely inform a court about the enthusiasm with which the union presented the case, make the Fifth Circuit's search of the record for evidence of union zeal both irrelevant and futile.

The court's conclusion that it would be "paradoxical" to provide for third-party representation in light of the holding in *Vaca* is curious, especially because of the reasoning in *Trbovich*. If anything, the control *Vaca* affords the union in discharging its responsibilities would argue for a less limited right to intervene for those who might be out of favor with the exclusive bargaining representative. Under *Vaca,* unions will have little difficulty in refusing to take to arbitration those cases in which third-party intervention might cause them substantial discomfort. To say that because the union has the authority to interfere with the individual's right to compel arbitration, third-party intervention is to be denied once arbitration is under way defies common sense and sound logic.

When one considers the question of third-party intervention in the context of Title VII racial discrimination grievances, it is important to recall the Court's remarks in *Lincoln Mills* about the judicial role in Section 301(a) labor arbitration suits:

The substantive law to apply in suits under § 301(a) is federal law, which the courts must fashion from the policy of our national labor laws. . . . the Labor Management Relations Act expressly furnishes some substantive law. It points out what the parties may or may not do in certain situations. *Other problems will lie in the penumbra of express statutory mandate. Some will lack express statutory sanction but will be solved by looking at the policy of the legislation and fashioning a remedy that will effectuate that policy. The range of judicial inventiveness will be determined by the nature of the problem.*[132]

One must assume that Title VII is one of the statutes to which the courts are to pay heed in fashioning remedies that do not possess "express statutory sanction" but nevertheless lie in the "penumbra" of the statute's mandate. The Board's decision in *Graziano Construction Company*—let alone the Supreme Court's ruling in *Southern Steamship Company* v. *NLRB*[133]—requires that the board, under the National Labor Relations Act, must take into account the policies of other statutes, such as Landrum-Griffin[134] and the federal antimutiny laws.[135] In enacting Title VII, Congress recognized that black workers were underrepresented at the bargaining table, excluded unfairly and arbitrarily from leadership positions in unions (even when their numbers were large, inasmuch as generally whites would not vote for blacks in union elections),[136] and dealt with unjustly at the bargaining table by both unions and employers. Title VII was passed in order to remedy, among other things, the unique problems of racial minority groups in the United

States—problems to which most collective-bargaining representatives had failed to address themselves. Considering this failure, courts should seize the opportunity presented by *Lincoln Mills* and *Southern Steamship* and move toward either a form of trilateral arbitration (if a civil rights organization has entered into an agreement about hiring with an employer) or third-party intervention where appropriate. Objections may be raised to the entry of a third party on the ground that it would unduly disturb uniformity in the administration of plant grievances—a principle emphasized in both *Republic Steel Corp.* v. *Maddox*[137]* and *Vaca*. But the answer must be that "the rationality of the exhaustion doctrine (and other principles bound up in the notion of exclusivity) is dependent upon the fairness of the process to which the individual is remanded."[138]

In the *Hotel Employers' Association* award,[139] an arbitrator invalidated an employment agreement setting hiring goals in the absence of the organization which negotiated it. (The record did not show whether any invitation was actually extended to the organization.) It is certainly possible that notice to the organization and the opportunity to participate in the hearing would have exposed the arbitrator to the full clash of opposing viewpoints which should be an integral part of any hearing procedure. Perhaps the judiciary should either vacate the award or refuse to compel arbitration if such notice is not given in racial-discrimination cases[140] As the courts have already acknowledged in *Glover* and the other cases dealing with exhaustion of contractual grievance procedures, Title VII and racial discrimination stand on a special plateau which makes them different from most labor-management disputes.[141]

The most telling argument against third-party intervention is the one provided by both James Atleson and Bernard Meltzer:[142] that having one's own counsel or representative in a third-party-intervention procedure can work against the grievant's own interest, since the union may not be interested in assembling witnesses and information under such circumstances, and since the arbitrator may resolve doubts against the employee when it becomes clear that there are tensions between the union and the worker. The Court in *Gardner-Denver* specifically made reference to this lack of a "harmony of interest" in racial-discrimination cases.[143] The requirement of a *de novo* hearing in *Gardner-Denver,* coupled with the standards established in footnote 21 of the opinion, however, seems to make it more likely than ever that safeguards can be established to prevent such negative consequences of third-party intervention. (Of course, it should be noted that many minority workers may not want third-party intervention inasmuch as a large number of local unions will do an adequate job in protesting management discrimination on the basis of race.[144])

Another objection to third-party intervention relates to some of the practical problems that may be involved. One such problem would arise if a civil rights organization sought to intervene although there was no indication that Negro or other minority-group workers desired intervention. In such a case, the demand of what is, in effect, an interloper ought to be firmly denied. Only the minority-group workers' designee should be permitted to participate. If there is a dispute about the matter, means can be established to determine the employees' choice—just as they have been established in connection with the choosing of exclusive bargaining representatives.

A further objection is that many groups or individuals might desire to participate in the arbitration if a third-party-intervention rule or a similar one were promulgated. Obviously, a large number of interveners would pose practical problems of orderliness, and courts and arbitrators ought to require that a reasonably large number of workers request the involvement before intervention in the arbitration process is permitted.

Although third-party intervention may appear at first to be a radical proposal, in fact it should result in minimal disruption of the arbitration process. In many instances particularly if a grievance relates to a discharge, the union—primarily because of its omnipresent duty of fair representation—would process the grievance in a manner which would not make it necessary for the worker to involve a third party. Or a union which may not like a grievant or his case may invite participation by a third party in order to avoid a lawsuit. Moreover, some arbitrators already insist on hearing the testimony and requesting the attendance of individual employees when there is the slightest indication of a divergence of viewpoints between the union and the employees. Finally, the principle of exclusivity and the majority-representative rule are well protected by Supreme Court decisions such as *Vaca*—notwithstanding the Fifth Circuit's views expressed in *Acuff*. Indeed, the most telling argument against intervention is that unions will eventually become too selective in taking cases to arbitration. But, to a large extent, *Vaca* already encourages this selectivity. In any event, a third-party-intervention requirement such as that advocated here would seem to do little damage to the *Vaca* principle.

Some Proposals for Reforming the Arbitration Process in Title VII Cases
Patching the Leaky Ship

The most substantial argument against concerning oneself with the institutional deficiencies of the arbitration process and making proposals to cope with them is that it may really not be worth the effort. That is, the process is essentially private and involves contractual interpretation, whereas Title VII is statutory. In a sense, this distinction is the thrust of the analysis undertaken by the Court in *Gardner-Denver*. Yet footnote 21 indicates that arbitration has a role to play in Title VII cases—albeit a relatively minor one because, among other things, of the dim prospects for reform in the short run.

Nevertheless, I believe it is important that arbitration play a significant role in dealing with employment-discrimination complaints. Whether reform can be undertaken, especially along the lines prescribed in this chapter, may be questionable in light of the obstinate resistance of unions, employers, and arbitrators to any shift from the same old "business as usual" which has prevailed since World War II. It may be that what has evolved initially as an essentially voluntary and private forum cannot be altered to reflect the public policy considerations that are inherent in Title VII problems. After all, there are many aspects of the arbitration process which would necessarily be affected by reform. For instance, can arbitrators refuse to entertain class action or group discrimination claims filed by one worker whose own grievance may be without merit?[145]* What about the conventional arbitral wisdom concerning the propriety of an arbitrator's asking questions of the parties when the parties do not appear to be volunteering information? Certainly, traditional notions about leaving the parties to their own devices so as not to embarrass or disturb will at least need some re-evaluating in this context.

I believe there are a number of good reasons for choosing and encouraging reforms through the formulation of judicial doctrines. The major reason for using this method is that the Equal Employment Opportunity Commission is overwhelmed with charges: by early 1975 the EEOC already had a backlog of 120,000 complaints.[146] The expansion of Title VII coverage to federal, state, and local government employees makes the situation worse. Moreover, the 1972 amendments permit the appointment of masters in Title VII litigation if "the judge has not scheduled the case for trial within one hundred and twenty days after issue has been joined."[147] Accordingly, the statute specifically promotes the appointment of private parties, who are likely to be individuals with experience in labor-management relations. Since labor arbitrators may be appointed, it is important that the core of established arbitrators keep in step with the evolution of Title VII law.

Another major reason for pursuing reform is that failure to do so will lead to a lack of uniformity in Title VII adjudications and arbitration decisions. A highly undesirable consequence might be that substantially different results will be obtained in different forums. In most instances, the parties will be discouraged from utilizing arbitration—an outcome discouraged by the *Steelworkers' Trilogy* and its progeny, as well as *Gardner-Denver*.

Furthermore, public and private policy and law with regard to labor are to a considerable extent already intertwined, as is apparent from a further consideration of the Supreme Court's approach in *Vaca* v. *Sipes*.[148] In *Republic Steel Corp.* v. *Maddox*,[149] Justice John Harlan had concluded for a majority of the Court that the individual worker must exhaust grievance-arbitration machinery for the redress of contract grievances before proceeding into court. Justice Harlan stated that if workers could "side-step" the collective agreement and file suits in court, the uniformity and orderliness of an "exclusive method" would be undermined.[150] Then, in *Vaca* v. *Sipes,* the Supreme Court severely limited the role of the individual worker in cases challenging the union's decision not to process a grievance. Relying on the possibility that the parties might cease negotiating "detailed grievance and arbitration procedures" in accordance with national labor policy if the grievant could unilaterally proceed to arbitration, the Court said, "We conclude that a union does not breach its duty of fair representation, and thereby open up a suit by the employee . . . merely because it settled the grievance short of arbitration."[151] Thus the Court not only reaffirmed the *Maddox* exhaustion requirements, but also concluded that an individual does not have the right to proceed to arbitration on his own.

This vise was further tightened when the Court later, again in the *Vaca* opinion, addressed itself to an individual worker's right to sue in court after processing his grievance through the contractual machinery:

We think the wrongfully discharged employee may bring an action against his employer in the fact of a defense based upon the failure to exhaust contractual remedies, *provided the employee can prove that the union as bargaining agent breached its duty of fair representation in its handling of the employee's grievance.* . . .

It is obvious that the courts will be compelled to pass upon whether there has been a breach of the duty of fair representation in the context of many § 301 breach-of-Contract Actions. If a breach of duty by the union and a breach of contract by the employer are proven, the court must fashion an appropriate remedy.[152]

With a heavy and oppressive hand which has not been imposed on Title VII litigation or, for that matter, on the duty-of-fair-representation cases which involve racial discrimination,[153]* *Vaca* imposes on a worker the burden of proving that a union breached its duty of fair representation before a matter may be pursued in court. It is the logic employed in *Vaca* that is relevant to our theme. So intertwined are the public and private law considerations in labor grievances that *Vaca* will not permit a plaintiff to recover on a privately negotiated contract without first showing a violation of the statutory duty—the duty of fair representation. Any objection to the expansion of rights for minority-group workers premised on the theory that *Gardner-Denver* draws a sharp demarcation line between the public and private processes is necessarily compromised by the logic of *Vaca*. The demarcation line is becoming increasingly artificial in labor-management cases.

Another factor which argues for focusing on reform of the arbitration process is that most workers tend to think of the arbitration machinery as the court of first resort. There is an assumption that the worker should channel his grievance through this procedure. In a society which values and promotes integration of the work force and other sectors of public and private life, it seems highly undesirable to create two parallel procedures—one for discrimination complaints and one for those which do not raise discrimination issues. Dual processes would have the effect of divorcing minority-group complaints from the mainstream of employment-dispute procedures and encouraging unions and employers to believe that they are not to deal with discrimination complaints but to leave them to others, such as EEOC and the courts. This belief, of course, would be antithetical to one of the many principles of Title VII which encourages voluntary compliance—a principle stated in the Court's *Gardner-Denver* decision.

But, assuming that it is worthwhile to fashion arbitration procedures which meet the standards established in footnote 21 of *Gardner-Denver,* the question yet remains whether the *Gardner-Denver* approach rings the "death knell" for arbitration. The argument that lack of finality means the end of arbitration has always seemed false to me—and the Supreme Court reached the same conclusion in *Gardner-Denver*.[154]

A similar kind of reasoning was employed in a far more plausible context by

Justice Brennan in *Boys Markets, Inc.* v. *Retail Clerks Local 770*,[155] when, in order to justify the Court's reversal of a previous holding which viewed the Norris-La Guardia Act as a bar to the issuance of injunctions against breaches of no-strike clauses,[156] the Court stated that employers would have little incentive to enter into grievance-arbitration agreements if they were deprived of their most effective remedy, the injunction. But the fact is that employers had continued to enter into such agreements in more than 90 percent of the collective-bargaining contracts signed subsequent to the Court's 1962 decision which had previously *deprived* employers of the injunctive remedy.[157] The no-strike provision is one of the most important elements of the labor contract from the employer's point of view. But the attractions of arbitration were such that an inability (though not a complete inability)[158]* to secure effective relief for violations of the no-strike clause did not dissuade employers from continuing to agree to arbitration.

In *Gardner-Denver* the court responded with two basic points to the argument that arbitration would be undermined by a *de novo* hearing. In addressing itself to the question of whether employers were being dealt with unfairly because they, unlike the employee, did not have two "bites at the apple," the Court referred to Judge Goodwin's persuasive opinion in *Oubichon*[159] and stated: "The employee is not seeking review of the arbitrator's decision. Rather he is asserting a statutory right independent of the arbitration process. An employee does not have 'two strings to his bow' with respect to an arbitral decision for the simple reason that Title VII does not provide employers with a cause of action against employees. An employer cannot be the victim of discriminatory employment practices."[160]

With regard to the "death knell" argument which had been formulated by the Sixth Circuit in *Dewey*, Justice Powell stated:

It is not unreasonable to assume that most employers will regard the benefits derived from a no-strike pledge as outweighing whatever costs may result from according employees an arbitral remedy against discrimination in addition to their judicial remedy under Title VII. Indeed, the severe consequences of a strike may make an arbitration clause almost essential from both the employees' and the employer's perspective. Moreover, the grievance-arbitration machinery of the collective-bargaining agreement remains a relatively inexpensive and expeditious means for resolving a wide range of disputes, including claims of discriminatory employment practices. Where the collective-bargaining agreement contains a non-discrimination clause similar to Title VII, and where arbitral procedures are fair and regular, arbitration may well produce a settlement satisfactory to both employer and employee. An employer thus has an incentive to make available the conciliatory and therapeutic process of arbitration which may satisfy an employee's perceived need to resort to the judicial forum, thus saving the employer the expense and aggravation associated with a lawsuit. For similar reasons the employee also has a strong incentive to arbitrate grievances, and arbitration may often eliminate those misunderstandings or discriminatory practices that might otherwise precipitate resort to the judicial forum.[161]

The theme is two-pronged. A still relatively inexpensive and time-consuming forum remains available to both parties—and this is to the benefit of both parties. Accordingly, the Court's reasoning in *Gardner-Denver* with regard to the "death knell" argument provides an additional reason for encouraging the revision of arbitration procedures.

Furthermore, it is interesting that Judge Keith's ruling in *Stamps* v. *Detroit Edison* awarding punitive damages was in part predicated on the failure of the defendants to discuss and communicate with employees regarding protests registered about employment discrimination.[162] Even if a standard of judicial review more akin to that of the *Steelworkers' Trilogy* would more effectively accomplish the objective of creating an incentive for voluntary compliance, the fact is that the existence of a punitive-damage remedy may create a greater incentive than would any standard of judicial review. If the courts begin to assess punitive damages against defendants who have turned their backs on voluntary compliance and refused to negotiate voluntary procedures responsive to Title VII problems, a significant incentive in the form of potential multimillion-dollar liability will be present.

Nevertheless, it is quite possible that some parties will attempt to exclude discrimination grievances from arbitration in light of *Gardner-Denver* on the theory that the employee will go to court whether or not there is an arbitration clause. But in addition to a potential punitive-damage liability of the type fashioned by Judge Keith in *Detroit Edison,* it may be that the refusal to negotiate a no-discrimination clause itself constitutes a violation of both Taft-Hartley and Title VII. Furthermore, it would seem as though the party that resists inclusion of a no-discrimination clause in the contract may find itself in the position of resisting to the point of impasse on an unlawful position and therefore in bad-faith bargaining difficulties under the *Borg-Warner* doctrine.[163*] Such conduct would constitute a violation of either Section 8(a)(5) or Section (8)(b)(3) depending on whether the union or the employer was refusing to negotiate the clause.

Could an employer, however, refuse to arbitrate in response to a motion to compel arbitration under Section 301 of Taft-Hartley if the contract provides for finality and if the union and workers involved refuse specifically to waive their rights to institute a Title VII action? The Court in *Gardner-Denver* seems to have undermined an employer's position by stating that "prospective" waivers are invalid—at least according to the "circumstances" of *Gardner-Denver*.[164] (Moreover, even if employees themselves are involved in negotiating a waiver, the Court indicated that it must be "voluntary and knowing."[165] Accordingly, if, for example, an employee is alleged to have waived his rights under Title VII and other laws by having negotiated a promotion, it would appear that no waiver in such circumstances can be valid unless the employee was aware that he might be entitled to back pay and punitive damages and that he was waiving rights related to such matters.)

Even when the parties attempt to resist the arbitration of no-discrimination clauses by explicitly making finality the price of arbitration, it would seem that the courts, following the lead of the *Gardner-Denver* opinion, would still have to reach the same result and hold that an employee retains his right to sue under Title VII despite the contractual provisions. As the Court said, "The rights conferred [by Title VII] can form no part of the collective bargaining process since waiver of these rights would defeat the paramount congressional purpose behind Title

VII.''[166] Thus it seems clear that even express consent by the union to a clause purporting to grant absolute finality to arbitration of discrimination grievances would not eliminate the employees' right to sue under Title VII. Moreover, the union would not be fulfilling its duty of fair representation. Indeed, it would appear as though the union's duty extends beyond the mere use of grievance-arbitration machinery and obligates it to represent employees, if they so wish, in administrative proceedings.[167] A demonstrated willingness to perform either role, it seems to me, argues persuasively for the conclusion that a union has failed to meet its duty of fair representation.

Conclusion

Gardner-Denver seems to have sounded the right note in concluding that the arbitration process that is part and parcel of collective bargaining involves give and take and compromise which are foreign to Title VII. Arbitrators are the creatures of the collective-bargaining process and of the parties who are alleged to have discriminated.

The reticence of arbitrators in discrimination proceedings by no means reflects arbitral attitudes generally. It is true that arbitrators have not been as imaginative as they should be in fashioning remedies. Arbitrators have not, however, hesitated to fashion the remedy of injunctions and damages for violations of no-strike clauses or the remedy of back pay for a discharge without just cause, despite the absence of specific authority in the collective-barginaing agreement.[168] Of course, the difference between those cases and employment-discrimination cases is attributable to the fact that such awards are in accord with at least one party's conscious and subconscious expectations. In short, the parties ordinarily do not intend arbitrators to function as a miniature Equal Employment Opportunity Commission. In most instances, the parties do not view the no-discrimination clause as a grant of authority akin to the no-strike clause or the just-cause clause.

Typical of this point of view is the arbitrator's award in *Spann,*[169] where the arbitrator, albeit in accord with Supreme Court doctrine relating at least to situations not involving employment discrimination[170] relied on factors such as employee discontent to justify the denial of a remedy to a black worker who had been discharged for attempting to date a white co-worker. Quite obviously, plant morale and productivity are considerations, as the Supreme Court has declared in the *Steelworkers Trilogy*[171] which the arbitrator must take into account. But I doubt that the Sixth Circuit was on sound ground in *Spann* when it refused to entertain an employee's suit for back pay because, in essence, the biases of the white-worker community were offended. It seems unbelievable that such intent could be ascribed in the name of the *Steelworkers' Trilogy* to the Court, which, since *Brown* v. *Board of Education,*[172] has taken the lead in an unremitting attack upon racism in our society. The bruised feelings of white workers, even when they trigger morale and productivity problems, are not important enough to justify the limiting of Title VII rights.

In my judgment, the following proposals offer some solutions to the problems described above.

Selection of the Arbitrator

The arbitrator should be selected from a source that specifically promotes the use of arbitration for problems involving minority-group employees. For instance, the Center for Dispute Settlement of the American Arbitration Association has played a leading role in this respect, and parties that wish to have their awards accorded substantial weight should be required to obtain from such organizations a roster of arbitrators. (It would be a good idea for the EEOC and state agencies to maintain such lists themselves.) Though the arbitrator need not have the EEOC stamp of approval, it seems as though the parties should select a neutral third party from such a source or its equivalent. Footnote 21 of *Gardner-Denver* indicates that the arbitrator should have special competence to deal with the law of Title VII in rendering his award. Careful selection of such arbitrators seems to be part of the public policy which "inheres" in Title VII—to use the words of the Fifth Circuit's decision in *Rios* v. *Reynolds Metal*.[173]

Arbitration Procedures

If the claim of discrimination relates to a class of employees, the hearing should, if a no-discrimination clause is in the contract, delve into all the relevant information that relates to the class. If the union cannot obtain such information from the employer, it should file refusal-to-bargain charges requiring disclosure of that information with the National Labor Relations Board.[174]

Once arbitration is commenced, the employees, if they distrust union representatives, should be permitted to have their own counsel and representatives. This, it seems to me, is the central thrust of the provisos to Section (9) of Taft-Hartley referring to the accommodation between individual and group rights on the one hand and those of the exclusive representative contained in the provisos to Section 9(a) of Taft-Hartley on the other. The weight of authority seems to indicate that since arbitration cannot be initiated without the union's consent, the union can control the way in which the arbitration proceeds and not even permit the individual grievants to attend the hearing. This is a complete *non sequitur*. The right to intervene is completely independent of the right to initiate.

Arbitral Reliance on Public Law

Arbitrators are not considering the same complaint that comes before a federal district court unless they are reviewing the complaint in light of the requirements of Title VII. Although an arbitrator cannot exceed the contractual grant of authority provided him, there is no bar, particularly in discharge cases,[175]* to reliance on a statute such as Title VII in making arbitral determinations. In fact, the parties, when they negotiate no-discrimination clauses (which sometimes speak specifically of the law) and separability clauses, expressly purport to comply with the law by negotiating the contract. Indeed, the Court, in *Enterprise Wheel & Car,* specifically noted that the arbitrator may look to many sources.

There are three situations which perhaps dramatize the different approaches that arbitrators may take in relying on public law in arbitration hearings. In the first, for instance, a dismissal is at issue, and the question is whether the employee has been properly discharged under a contract provision which states that the employee may be dismissed only for "just cause." Here the arbitrator can easily apply Title VII considerations to the broad generalizations of the contract—just as many arbitrators for years have relied on essential notions of fairness and due process and "natural justice."

The second situation might be one in which a no-discrimination clause—sometimes negotiated with specific reference to Title VII and other civil rights laws[176]—coexists alongside a seniority provision, for instance, which has a discriminatory impact on the upward mobility of black workers. In this kind of situation the contract normally provides a separability clause as well—one which states that if one provision of the contract is declared to be unlawful, all other provisions are presumed to continue to exist as lawful clauses. The normal assumption is that the judiciary will make determinations under the separability clause. But if the no-discrimination provision is itself arbitrable, and especially if it makes reference to public law, the arbitrator would appear to have ample authority to use the combination of no-discrimination and separability clauses to strike down seniority provisions which run afoul of Title VII. If there is conflict between law and contract, the arbitrator must make a choice; while tradition argues for reposing such authority in the hands of the judiciary, there is no reason—assuming that arbitrators have or will be provided with the necessary expertise—why they should not perform such a function. Otherwise, the existence of the no-discrimination provision becomes rather meaningless.

A more difficult problem arises in the third situation—one in which the arbitrator has no authority derived from a no-discrimination provision. Although the arbitrator must presume that the parties intended to act lawfully—the separability clause generally supports that proposition—the arbitrator has no guidelines established by the parties. Here, the rather extraordinary remedy involved in disestablishing a discriminatory seniority system does not have the support it would have in the second situation. Nevertheless, in my judgment, if the arbitrator is unable to find authority to move forward affirmatively it would be at the same time irresponsible and inflammatory to impose affirmatively upon the parties an award which is clearly unlawful. Presumably the arbitrator would not issue an award he knew to be in violation of a Supreme Court decision such as *Brown* v. *Board of Education.* If the arbitrator blithely moves ahead and requires the parties to do what he knows is unlawful or has reasonable grounds to believe is unlawful, relying on the judiciary to rectify any mistakes at a later point, the arbitrator encourages the very antithesis of peaceful procedures: he encourages the minority-group workers to engage in self-help efforts in defiance of negotiated procedures. It would seem as though the obligation of the arbitrator under such circumstances is—where nothing else is possible—to stay his hand and to do nothing affirmatively which would result in illegality. When there is a clear conflict between contract and law, the arbitrator should refuse to come to the assistance of the parties who are discriminating. Therefore it seems to me that Arbitrator Koven's finding in *Lockheed Missiles* was an appropriate one—a finding of nonarbitrability when the contract ran afoul of the law.

Nevertheless, many cases will arise where the most competent arbitrator may be in doubt about the law because of a conflict of authorities or the lack of any authority. It seems to me that the parties, here again, should be very careful to choose arbitrators who are especially knowledgeable about Title VII. I would, however, subscribe to proposals for easing the arbitral burden. For example, Mark Kahn advocates that Title VII be amended to require the EEOC to issue an advisory opinion, when requested to do so by the union, employee, employer, or arbitrator, for use in a legal interpretation necessary for the rendering of the award.[177*] This requirement might also be helpful to arbitrators who wish to be less unpopular with the parties. A by-product would be the placing of blame for unwanted interpretations of the law on the hated agencies and courts.

The fact that special arbitration procedures have been negotiated to deal with employment-discrimination problems provides an element of optimism in an otherwise dreary landscape. The International Woodworkers of America and Weyerhaeuser Company entered into a settlement agreement on October 16, 1973, providing for such special procedures.[178*] Under a consent decree, Basic Vegetable Products, Inc., and the General Teamsters Warehousemen and Helpers Local 890 in California have done the same.[179] The approach of *Gardner-Denver,* while not reflecting an awareness of contemporary developments in arbitration and proposing a standard that may be too rigorous, if certain meanings are given to footnote 21, indicated recognition of the fact that reform requires a very long time. But not all cases can go to court, as the 120,000-case backlog at the EEOC demonstrates. That is why arbitration will remain important.

**Self-Help under the National Labor
Relations Act and Federal Labor Law**

[Industrial peace] would hardly be obtained if a substantial minority of the craft
were denied the right to have their interests considered at the conference table and
if the final results of the bargaining process were to be to the sacrifice of the
interests of the minority by the action of a representative chosen by the majority.
*The only recourse of the minority would be to strike, with the attendant
interruption of commerce, which the [Railway Labor] Act seeks to avoid.*[1]

Work Stoppages
The Status of Unauthorized Walkouts under the NLRA

Ever since *Lincoln Mills* and the *Steelworkers' Trilogy* promulgated the rule that
the no-strike clause and grievance-arbitration machinery are the *quid pro quo*s for
each other,[2] it has become increasingly clear that if the arbitration part of the
bargain is inadequate, the limitations imposed upon the strike weapon may well
become inoperative. The Supreme Court appeared to recognize this point in the
context of a safety dispute in *Gateway Coal Co.* v. *United Mine Workers*[3] where
Justice Powell concluded that a "work stoppage called solely to protect employees
from immediate danger . . . authorized by §502 [the safety provisions of Taft-
Hartley] cannot be the basis for either a damages award or . . . [an] injunction."[4] While, in my judgment, the ability of trade unions or employees to strike
in the face of a no-strike obligation contained in a collective-bargaining agreement
may not be *totally dependent* upon the adequacy or inadequacy of the arbitration
machinery insofar as employment discrimination disputes are concerned, the fact
is that the two things have a great deal to do with each other.

First, Sections 8(a)(1) and (3) of the National Labor Relations Act, as interpreted by the board and the courts, prohibit employer retaliation in the form of
discharge and discipline against workers who protest through a walkout or picketing what they regard to be poor working conditions.[5]* But when a union negoti-
ates a collective agreement which prohibits such practices through, for example, a
no-strike clause,[6]* the walkout becomes unprotected and the worker is exposed to
the above-noted penalties. The Supreme Court has limited the ability of employers
to discipline workers even when no-strike clauses exist. In *Mastro Plastics* v.
NLRB,[7] the Court held that a no-strike clause could not be read to prohibit a strike
that was called in response to unfair labor practices by the employer.[8]* The *Mastro Plastics* opinion noted that such unfair labor practices were destructive of the

"foundations" of the negotiated labor contract.[9] The language has convinced the board, over the strong objections of member John Fanning, that the *Mastro Plastics* exception to the unprotected nature of the no-strike violation was to be afforded only where the employer engaged in *"serious,* unfair labor practices."[10]

Second, under Section 502 of Taft-Hartley (the safety provisions), it is stated that "the quitting of labor by an employee or employees in good faith because of abnormally dangerous conditions for work at the place of employment of such employee or employees [shall not] be deemed a strike under this Act."[11] Accordingly, where it can be objectively ascertained that the requisite conditions exist and that the walkout took place in protest against them, the activity is protected and therefore employers may not discharge or discipline workers under such circumstances.[12]

Third, even without the presence of a labor contract or a no-strike clause, where a union is on the scene and is the exclusive representative, some strikes called without union authorization are unprotected within the meaning of the act. In *NLRB* v. *Draper Corporation,*[13] the Fourth Circuit set forth the proposition in its boldest terms. Emphasizing the concept of exclusivity and the disruption which unauthorized stoppages can cause in interstate commerce, the court stated:

> Even though the majority of the employees in an industry may have selected their bargaining agent and the agent may have been recognized by the employer, there can be no effective bargaining if small groups of employees are at liberty to ignore the bargaining agency thus set up, take particular matters into their own hands and deal independently with the employer. The whole purpose of the act is to give to the employees as a whole, through action of a majority, the right to bargain with the employer with respect to such matters as wages, hours and conditions of work. . . .
> The employees must act through the voice of the majority or the bargaining agent chosen by the majority. Minority groups must acquiesce in the action of the majority and the bargaining agent they have chosen; and, just as the minority has no right to enter into separate bargaining arrangements with the employer, so it has no right to take independent action to interfere with the course of bargaining which is being carried on by the duly authorized bargaining agent chosen by the majority. The proviso to section 9 . . . preserving to individuals or groups of individuals the right to present grievances to the employer, negatives by necessary inference the right on their part to call strikes for the purpose of influencing the bargaining being carried on by the chosen representatives of all the employees.[14]

The NLRB has proclaimed its fidelity to *Draper*[15] while at the same time holding that stoppages called without the union's authorization do not necessarily subvert majority rule where their objectives coincide with those held by the exclusive representative.[16]* The board accordingly has had an unrealistic and rarefied approach to wildcat strikes which assumes that if an identity can be inferred between the objectives of the union and the positions of the unauthorized strikers, the stoppage is not subversive of the collective-bargaining process and is consequently protected by the *Draper* rule. This has led the board to the completely erroneous conclusion that a mere disagreement about the timing of a strike, as distinguished from its substantive objectives, does not destroy the rapport between the union and the striking workers.[17] But the question of timing economic action, as the Court has noted in the context of lockouts in *American Ship Building Co.* v. *NLRB,*[18] is critical in the strategy of both the union and the company, specifically in connection with the union's decision to use or withhold the strike weapon. If the trade union leadership believe that September is the best time to shut down auto companies because economic pressure is greatest at the period of model changeover and therefore the likelihood that management will settle at the union's terms is increased, dissidents who choose to walk out in July are at odds with the union's objectives. Both the union and the employees want "more"—or at least they will say that they want "more" through their respective press releases. It should not matter what the substantive goals are or what each group says that it is pursuing by way of substantive goals. This is simply one example of the board's unwillingness to give the walkout protected status in defiance of the realities of industrial relations—that is, its reliance upon a unity of interest between the union and the worker as a test of defining what constitutes protected activity.[19]*

Moreover, while *Draper* seems to be predicated upon the notion that a walkout necessarily disparages the exclusive bargaining representative and the concepts surrounding it, no inquiries have been undertaken in the walkout cases to determine (1) whether individual action which leads to *any kind* of agreement is permissible—even a civil rights agreement outside the negotiated collective-bargaining agreement; or (2) whether in fact the walkout in a given situation is actually subversive of the exclusive bargaining representative concept. Just as the Court has taken the position that the board must be careful about inferring unlawful antiunionism from the use of legitimate economic weaponry by employers—that is, the lockout—and must look to the actual impact of such management efforts,[20]* so also it might be appropriate for the board to examine the actual impact of a strike called without authorization. One factor to be considered might be whether the walkout took place in an integrated industry where it was likely necessarily to involve workers other than a small group, and accordingly whether because of such power a small minority of employees was in a position to dictate to a majority regarding the employment conditions of all. Second, in considering the impact the board might determine whether employees and customers refused to cross the picket lines and assess the actual ability of the employer to function in the face of such a walkout. And third, it might consider the employer's actions in order to determine whether it was attempting to undercut the exclusive bargaining representative by dealing with the individuals in a manner forbidden by the statute—securing agreements without the presence of the union when the union was willing to proceed affirmatively. If this happened, and if the impact was serious, perhaps the *Draper* conclusion ought to apply. But it does not follow that in every situation activity which includes economic pressure necessarily disparages and undercuts exclusivity. Nor does it follow that this is the case where agreements are negotiated and implemented.

The Taft-Hartley Litigation on Racial Walkouts

The board had its first racial discrimination walkout case in *Tanner Motor Livery, Ltd.*,[21] where two white drivers employed by the company were active in civil rights organizations and demanded that a black driver be hired. Subsequent to the demand, one of the drivers was fired and filed a timely grievance under the labor contract. The union first decided against processing the grievance, and later a union-company panel proceeding ruled against the worker's reinstatement. Shortly after the first discharge, the second employee joined a picket line outside the establishment with a sign which bore the emblem "Jim Crow Shop." He was quickly fired.

The trial examiner found that both employees were discharged because of their protest against the alleged discriminatory hiring practices of the employer. He determined, however, that the firings did not constitute an unfair labor practice under the act. A unanimous board reversed his ruling, citing the Court's previous decision in *New Negro Alliance*,[22]* and holding that the workers involved in this protest were engaged in protected activity involving "conditions of employment" within the meaning of the act.

On appeal, however, the Ninth Circuit remanded the case to the board for consideration of the question whether employees who protested discriminatory hiring practices were required to act through their collective-bargaining representative where the representative had negotiated a contract with the employer. The court said that this question, "stated another way," was "to what extent does Section 9(a) [providing for exclusive bargaining authority] limit or remove the protection afforded by Section 7?" The court expressed the view that the purposes of the act, which in large part support the principle of collective bargaining, might be undermined if the employees could resort to picket-line activity in connection with "grievances" that should be settled in a "prescribed manner"—that is, by arbitration.[23]

The board on remand stated that the record did not indicate whether the employees in this case had attempted to act through their exclusive bargaining representative. Accordingly, the board found it unnecessary to decide whether the employees were filing a "grievance" under the Section 9(a) proviso or whether they were attempting to bargain individually with the employer. Holding that the employees were not "acting in derogation of their established bargaining agent by seeking to eliminate what they deemed to be a morally unconscionable, if not an unlawful, condition of employment," the board stated:

The Board cannot presume or conclude that, contrary to the course being urged by [the discharged employees], ... the Union knowingly would have taken the unlawful position that it would refuse to represent Negro drivers fairly if hired. Rather, we must assume that these employees were acting in accord with, and in furtherance of, the lawful position of their collective-bargaining agent. For the Board to find, therefore, that the employees' otherwise protected concerted activities herein were rendered unprotected by virtue of an existing collective-bargaining agreement between the Union and the Respondent would be offensive to public policy.

The board did not hold that the employer was in fact guilty of racial discrimination in hiring or that a violation of a civil rights law had occurred.[24] Consistent with its general refusal to examine the reasonableness of employee protest in the walkout context,[25] it found only that there was a reasonable basis for believing that the concern of the two workers was genuine, in the sense that it was not "grounded on contrived or flimsy evidence."[26] The evidence presented was the complete absence of black employees in the defendant's concern. Given a reasonable basis for belief, the activity was declared to be protected within the meaning of the act.

On the second appeal, the Ninth Circuit addressed the matter in the following fashion. The court noted that it had followed *Draper* in the past and that the board was citing cases where wildcat strikers' activity had been deemed protected because the strikers had supported the position of the union and therefore the employer did not have to choose between conflicting demands. Noting that the act itself did not provide an answer to the questions raised by *Draper* and the cases cited by the board, the Ninth Circuit took the position that the policies expressed in the act and Supreme Court decisions "applying these policies give us some guidance"[27] beyond the cases themselves. The case which the court found to be of primary significance, however, involved a very different issue.

This case was *NLRB* v. *Allis-Chalmers Manufacturing Co.,*[28] a decision involving Section 8(b)(1)(A) and the right of unions to impose fines upon their members, an issue decided by the Court in 1967. In *Allis-Chalmers* the union had called the strike against an employer in support of new contract demands, and union members who crossed the picket line during the strike were fined between $20 and $100. The Court held that such fines did not involve unlawful "restraint or coercion" within the meaning of Section 8(b)(1)(A) and therefore did not violate the statute. In arriving at this decision, the Court specifically took note of the fact that the doctrine of exclusivity and union responsibility was an important theme in federal labor law and that the use of disciplinary authority was an integral part of the union's role. The Court also noted that the authority given to the union was qualified by the duty-of-fair-representation doctrine first enunciated in *Steele*[29] and that it was not appropriate in the absence of specific instructions from Congress to limit union authority in this area. Similarly, the Court in a subsequent decision, *Scofield* v. *NLRB,*[30] held that union fines against employees who exceeded production quotas also did not violate the statute. The Court was, however, quite careful, despite the broad rationale employed, to qualify the opinion in a number of respects which the Ninth Circuit did not refer to in its second *Tanner* decision. Among the considerations which qualified the opinion were: (1) that the employees had the opportunity to vote on the strike prior to engaging in it; (2) that the fines were not excessive, but rather were relatively small; and (3) that the employees had assumed full membership obligations even though under the statute (probably unbeknownst to them) they were required only to pay dues and initiation fees.[31]* The court said in its second *Tanner* opinion:

In our view, *Allis-Chalmers* in particular recognizes a growing tendency to insure that an individual member's views are aired inside the union. Statutes and decisional law promote free speech and democratic decision-making processes within the union. Decisions like *Allis-Chalmers* and *Scofield* rely on these factors to give weight to a union majority's decision. In *Allis-Chalmers* and *Scofield*, the Court opted for concerted *union* activity, and upheld reasonable union sanctions against union members who sought to pursue a contrary course. If the union can expect a modicum of allegiance after a majority has made a decision, then the employer should be entitled to rely on that allegiance in negotiations with the union. The Court was upholding concepts of orderly bargaining which apply from either viewpoint.[32]

Accordingly, the Ninth Circuit viewed its adherence to *Draper* as representing the proper approach to this situation. At no point did the court address itself to any argument to the effect that the racial aspects of the case invited consideration of different public policy issues than had been present in *Draper* or any of the other cases discussed. Nor did the court consider the implications of Title VII of the Civil Rights Act of 1964 and the policies inherent therein. It simply noted that diverse interests were involved in the bargaining unit and that the union must take into account a variety of such interests in arriving at compromise solutions which would ultimately be approved by all employees within the unit.

The court took the position that the two employees who had engaged in the picketing in question had ''an obligation to go to the union with their desire for non-discriminatory hiring. The record does not demonstrate that they approached the union, nor does it indicate that the union gave its sanction to their actions. Thus, while the concerted activity does fall within section 7, the operation of section 9(a) deprives it of the protection to which it would otherwise be entitled.''[33]

Both the first and the second *Tanner* opinions of the Ninth Circuit concurred with the board's view that a protest against allegedly discriminatory activities here was concerted activity for mutual aid and protection within the meaning of Section 7. On this point the court as well as the board expressed no doubt. Subsequently, the board extended the scope of Section 7 in this area even further in *Washington State Service Employees State Council No. 18*,[34] where it affirmed a trial examiner's decision reinstating a white union organizer who was dismissed from the union because of her participation in picketing building trades contractors to promote job opportunities for the Seattle black community at the Seattle-Tacoma airport. (The background to these demonstrations is discussed in Chapter 13.) The charging party's employer objected to her participation in such picketing and contended that her involvement would make her ineffective as an organizer because the employees whom she was organizing would point to her as someone likely to be sent to jail. The charging party pointed out, however, that the employees she was organizing were approximately 50 percent black and that her outside activities would facilitate her organizational work. The trial examiner found that the activity was ''concerted'' within the meaning of Section 7 inasmuch as the charging party participated in her organizational efforts with employees of other employers and black trainees who were employees within the meaning of the act.[35] Moreover, the trial examiner stated, on the basis of both *Tanner* decisions and other decisions,[36] that the object of the picketing made it activity for mutual aid and protection within the meaning of Section 7. Accordingly, he found, and the board affirmed the decision, that the discharge of an employee for such activity was in violation of Section 8(a)(1) of the act.

The Ninth Circuit in its second *Tanner* opinion also addressed itself to the relevance of the presence or absence of an antidiscrimination provision in the collective-bargaining agreement. The court said that whether the charging parties in *Tanner* were seeking enforcement of a contract clause or seeking to instigate bargaining over such a clause, they nevertheless had an obligation to seek out the union before doing so—regardless of whether the contract contained an antidiscrimination clause. Just as the court neglected to address itself to the racial aspects of the case and the possibility of a different approach to the *Draper* authorized/unauthorized issues, so also did it deal in the same manner with the issue of the possible relevance of the presence or absence of an antidiscrimination clause in the collective-bargaining agreement. No attempt was made to determine whether grievance-arbitration machinery was available to test the question of whether the contract was being violated with regard to discrimination and, if it was available, whether the machinery was adequate to cope with the problem. In short, the kinds of issues raised by the Court, explicitly in *Alexander* v. *Gardner-Denver Co.*[37*] and implicitly in *Gateway Coal,* were not even considered, let alone discussed in any fashion by the Ninth Circuit in its second *Tanner* opinion.

In the next important decision, the board and the appellate courts switched roles completely. This time the board took a position hostile to the supporters of civil rights and the appellate court reversed the board. This case is *Emporium Capwell* v. *Western Addition Community Organization.*[38]

In *Emporium Capwell* the respondent, a San Francisco department store, had a collective-bargaining agreement with the Department Store Employees Union. The issue which triggered litigation involving Section 8(a)(1) before the board was a written warning to, and later the discharge of, two black employees subsequent to their picketing the store on their own time and calling upon minority races to boycott it on the ground that its management was "racist." The employer had a collective-bargaining agreement with the union which contained a no-strike, no-lockout clause, a no-discrimination clause, and a grievance machinery that provided for allegations of violations to be heard before an adjustment board (which was composed of the parties) and culminated in arbitration in the event that the union and management representatives appearing before the board reached an impasse.

In a series of meetings in early 1968 a group of employees, including the two blacks referred to above, submitted to union representatives a list of grievances involving alleged discrimination against racial minorities. The employees claimed that racial bias had prompted denials of promotion to minority employees and they specifically alleged that one employee, Russell Young, had been denied advancement because of race. The union, through its secretary-treasurer, Walter Johnson, designated a union committee to investigate the allegations, and shortly thereafter a detailed report was prepared. It referred to the "possibility" of racial discrimination. Johnson then presented the report to the Retailers' Council, and it was agreed that the grievances would be taken directly to the company.

A few weeks later, a group of ten employees requested an additional meeting with Johnson, and the problem of racial discrimination and the Young case were discussed again. It was agreed at this meeting that the parties would wait until September to meet again. The union in September took the position that the company had been acting discriminatorily and stated that it would demand an adjustment board proceeding, declaring that arbitration would produce a "long lasting effect" which would be of benefit to a large number of employees. Many of the minority group workers, however, took the position that such an approach was unsatisfactory and requested that the union picket the store. Johnson rejected this idea. He explained that the union was bound to seek a satisfactory resolution of the grievances under the procedures established by the collective-bargaining agreement. At the same time, he stated that the two black workers in question could do whatever they wanted "as individuals." Meanwhile, the matter was taken to the adjustment board but one of the black employees at this proceeding read a prepared statement objecting to the handling of the grievances on an individual rather than a group basis. He went on to state that the minority group employees wanted to talk to the president of the Emporium directly and to negotiate an agreement with him. Shortly thereafter, the minority employees walked out and did not attend subsequent meetings. Although they made an attempt to talk to the president of the company, he would not discuss the matter and referred them to the personnel director. Nothing further took place because the employees refused to follow this route, having previously advised the personnel director of the situation. In October the two black workers in question held a press conference at which they stated that the Emporium was engaging in racist conduct against minorities and that employees were planning to picket the store. On the following Saturday, the same two workers picketed and distributed handbills. The handbills charged racist conduct, referring to the Emporium as a "20th Century colonial plantation" and alleging that minority group workers were being treated the same way as blacks in the "slave mines of South Africa." The handbills also urged a boycott of the Emporium and indicated to shoppers that such a boycott had already been instituted.

A few days later the two workers were called in and given a written warning to the effect that if they did not refrain from picketing they could be fired. Despite the warning the picketing and distribution went on, and shortly thereafter the two workers were in fact fired.

The trial examiner held that while the two charging parties had engaged in "concerted activity" within the meaning of Section 7 of the act, they nevertheless lost their protected status by virtue of the collective-bargaining agreement. The trial examiner said:

The Union declined to submit their demands that grievances be prosecuted on a storewide rather than an individual basis, or to endorse their resort to the "dramatic" by way of picketing and the distribution of accusatory pamphlets. There is no basis in the evidence for a finding that the Union approved, endorsed, or in any way connived in the action taken by [these] employees. . . . It would be absurd to say that because they and the Union had a common ultimate objective, these four employees were somehow implementing or strengthening the Union in its position. They were acting outside the agreement and contrary to the Union's advice and urging. All the evidence indicates that the Union, their duly designated bargaining representative, was endeavoring in every way available to it under the agreement to adjust any and all cases of racial discrimination brought to its attention, and in at least one and apparently two cases had brought about the desired adjustment. It is also evident that it was prepared to resort to arbitration to enforce its position that racial discrimination in conditions of employment existed in Respondent's store, and it was handicapped in proceeding by the four employees' refusal to assist or to be represented by the Union in the matter.[39]

Accordingly, the trial examiner found the activity unprotected. But although he considered the question whether the picketing and leaflets demonstrated a disloyalty or inappropriate language which would render otherwise protected activity unprotected, no conclusions were made on this matter. The trial examiner, in this connection, articulated a theme which has become commonplace in the board's approach to employment-discrimination matters. He said: "Returning to the language of the pamphlets itself, the General Counsel correctly observes that such terms as 'racist pig' have become terms of common usage in the 'contemporary civil rights struggle.' (Parenthetically, it is noted that as adjudicators under the Act we do not belong in the contemporary civil rights struggle. Congress did not put us there.)"[40]

The board, without opinion, affirmed the trial examiner's opinion although stating in a footnote the following:

The sole issue presented for decision on this record is whether the conduct of the discharged employees was unprotected because in derogation of the duly designated exclusive bargaining representative. For the reasons stated by the Trial Examiner, we agree that the actions of the discharged employees in abandoning the contractual grievance procedure and seeking to initiate direct negotiations with Respondent by picketing and boycotting activities were not protected by the Act."[41]

The Court of Appeals for the District of Columbia unanimously reversed.[42] Unlike the Ninth Circuit, the court specifically took into account the fact that racial discrimination protests stand on a different plateau from protests over other working conditions insofar as they are limited by Section 9. The court, characterizing racial discrimination issues as "unique," stated: "we conclude that the Board's decision that these concerted activities were not protected by the Act is not supported by substantial evidence in the record and must be reversed. . . . We base this conclusion on the distinction between concerted activity involving racially discriminatory employment practices and other concerted activity involving other working conditions."[43]

The court noted that the right to be free from racially discriminatory employment practices is not dependent upon the existence of a no-discrimination clause in a collective-bargaining agreement. This point has been made dramatically in *Gardner-Denver* where a unanimous Court emphasized the "plenary" authority of the federal judiciary to remedy employment-discrimination complaints.[44] Judge George MacKinnon, speaking for the majority, noted that neither the board nor the trial examiner took account of the statutory bases of the rights asserted by the individuals who picketed and distributed handbills in this case—that is, Title VII and, more particularly, the protection afforded peaceful protest against allegedly discriminatory practices which is contained in Section 704(a) of that statute.[45]* These considerations, said the court, make protests against racial discrimination "quite distinct" from other kinds of concerted activity. In the case at hand, the court stated that the concerted activity involved factors other than the "major premise" which "underlies section 9(a)."[46] Echoing a theme contained in *Gardner-Denver,* the court said:

Subjection of the will of the individual to the will of the majority was the method Congress chose to preserve industrial peace and stability over matters in which individuals would most likely disagree. However, on the issue of whether to tolerate racial discrimination in employment the individuals in a union cannot legally disagree. The law does not give the union an option to tolerate *some* racial discrimination, but declares that *all* racial discrimination in employment is illegal. . . . Therefore, the underlying premise of Section 9(a) that the will of the individual must be subjected to the will of the majority does not authorize the approval of racially discriminatory employment practices, because the purposes of the minority group and the union in desiring to eradicate racial discrimination in employment cannot be at odds. . . .

While concerted activity over actual racial discrimination differs significantly from concerted activity over other working conditions and does not defeat the underlying premise of section 9(a), nonetheless we recognize that such activity as was engaged in here *does* interfere to a certain extent with the collective bargaining process. In abandoning the grievance procedures and seeking to bargain on their own, the picketers here rendered essentially ineffective the method of remedying grievances chosen by their collective bargaining representative and provided by the collective bargaining agreement.[47]

The court went on to say that it could not regard such "limited interference alone"[48] as a basis for removing the concerted activities from protective status under the act. In the first place, the court characterized the activity in *Emporium Capwell* as "less disruptive" to the collective-bargaining process than that involved in *Tanner*. In the latter case, the court noted, there had been no attempt to utilize the union representative or contract procedures before engaging in the concerted activity in question. Accordingly, the court focused completely upon the aspect of *Emporium Capwell* which had been left utterly unexplained by either the board or the trial examiner, namely the board's ability to find a violation in *Tanner* where no resort had been made to the union or contract procedures and its inability to find the same violation in *Emporium Capwell* where such an effort had been made.[49] The court also said the following, however:

We agree with *Tanner* that even when racial issues are at stake, one should be required to submit such disputes first to the union before one resorts to minority concerted activity. Without such a requirement, parties aggrieved by racially discriminatory employment practices would have little incentive to use the grievance procedures in the agreement, and certainly national labor policy favors the use of grievance-arbitration procedures to settle labor disputes . . . even when they involve racial discrimination. Though the exact role of grievance-arbitration procedures in enforcing rights created by Title VII is presently the subject of considerable dispute . . . we think grievance-arbitration procedures can play an important role in remedying racial discrimination in employment and should be encouraged.''[50]

Second, the court, in dealing with the *Draper* aspect of the issue, found that the union and the employees were in accord with one another and that therefore there was no disruption of orderly collective bargaining in the sense that the employees were demanding something different from the goals the union was pursuing. Third, although the court took note of the fact that the employees had insisted upon proceeding with their grievance on a group basis, and had therefore disrupted the proceeding before the adjustment board, it was of the view that this did not "wholly destroy" the Section 7 protection afforded, particularly in light of "the express protection mandated by Title VII and the limited interference with section 9(a)."[51] Curiously, the court then noted that while there was no evidence that the union's refusal to handle the discrimination problem on a group basis was indicative of bad faith, and the union could have properly regarded the way it chose to handle the matter as the "most efficacious method," nevertheless "it might be that these charges could have been better handled on a group or class basis."[52] Accordingly, the court said that even where there was no bad faith the possibility of a more efficacious or expeditious manner of resolving the issue as an option permitted the employees under the circumstances of this case to engage in self-help. The court said:

For example, the union might be vigorously processing individual grievances before an adjustment board, while it would be more efficient and thus preferable for it to be attempting to engage in collective bargaining negotiations with the employer for all minorities to eliminate all the discriminatory employment practices. In such a case, we do not think the method or means chosen by the union should preclude a minority group who has reasonable grounds for believing that the union is not proceeding against all discrimination from attempting to assert its claim of racial discrimination in a manner which it considers would be more successful. . . . We agree that the eradication of racial discrimination in employment cannot be subjected to such a restriction. Thus, the Labor Board, should inquire in cases such as this, whether the union was actually remedying the discrimination to the *fullest extent possible, by the most expedient and efficacious means.* Where the union's efforts fall short of this high standard, the minority group's concerted activities cannot lose its section 7 protection."[53]

Accordingly, the court took the view that the Section 9 exclusivity principle does not shield an employer under all circumstances from the burden of having to deal with two groups on the same subject. This, according to the court, was merely an "inconvenience" which was justifiable on the facts of this case. In its remand to the board, however, the court stated that the board might consider whether the language used made the picketing by the employees an act of disloyalty, which would render their status unprotected.[54]

Judge Wyzanski, in a separate opinion which is labeled a "dissenting opinion," also was of the view that the board should be reversed. He took note of the fact that the two employees wanted a change in management's hiring and promoting practices and that it could not be claimed that these individuals "were not acting in derogation of the union representative," but were rather attempting to "supplement, support, and make more explicit" the application of the collective agreement which had been negotiated.[55] Judge Wyzanski noted that the union was unwilling to make a "broad assault" on the employer and neither welcomed nor encouraged the steps taken by the two black workers in question. He went on:

It may be that the record does not show that the union interposed a firm veto. And we are not so unsophisticated as not to appreciate why this evidence is not and probably never would be available. We recognize that the union could have reasons which it might not choose to proclaim from the housetops why it did not want anything approaching what it might regard as a policy of employment based on affirmative measures to achieve racial balance.[56]

The Wyzanski opinion noted that national policy required affirmative actions as well as passive nondiscrimination. Most important, the opinion stated that the National Labor Relations Act as well as other statutes must reflect this basic policy, relying upon *Southern Steamship*.[57] A "more subtle reason" why such matters must be handled differently, said Judge Wyzanski, was that it was a "denial of justice to allow the white majority to have the power to preclude the non-whites from dealing directly with the employer on racial issues, whether or not this is in disparagement of the rights of the union representative."[58] He put it graphically in bold type:

TO LEAVE NON-WHITES AT THE MERCY OF WHITES IN THE PRESENTATION OF NON-WHITE CLAIMS WHICH ARE ADMITTEDLY ADVERSE TO THE WHITES WOULD BE A MOCKERY OF DEMOCRACY. SUPPRESSION, INTENTIONAL OR OTHERWISE, OF THE PRESENTATION OF NON-WHITE CLAIMS CANNOT BE TOLERATED IN OUR SOCIETY EVEN IF, WHICH IS PROBABLY AT LEAST THE SHORT-TERM CONSEQUENCE, THE RESULT IS THAT INDUSTRIAL PEACE IS TEMPORARILY ADVERSELY AFFECTED. IN PRESENTING NON-WHITE ISSUES NON-WHITES CANNOT, AGAINST THEIR WILL, BE RELEGATED TO WHITE SPOKESMEN, MIMICKING BLACK MEN. THE DAY OF THE MINSTREL SHOW IS OVER.[59]

The Supreme Court, over Justice Douglas' lone dissent, reversed.[60] Justice Marshall, writing for the majority, was careful to note that the trial examiner's finding that minority employees had attempted to "bargain" with the employer was undisturbed and that it was "important to have firmly in mind the character of the underlying conduct to which we apply [the central questions of labor policy raised by this case]."[61] Resolution of the question whether the dissidents "bargained" is a conclusion of law and not a finding of fact. It was disingenuous of the Court to say otherwise. The language and tone of the Court's opinion seems, however, to make Justice Marshall's note of caution relatively unimportant.

It is quite clear that the Court was extremely concerned about the problems which would arise if the grievance procedure was bypassed. In this connection, the Court referred to divisions among the workers which flow from competing claims, the inability of an employer to take "remedial steps satisfactory to all at once" and the ability of the grievance procedure to resolve group claims effectively—in contrast to self-help—because "one would hardly expect an employer to continue in effect an employment practice that routinely results in adverse arbitral decisions." Justice Marshall stated that self-help would exacerbate tensions, and that "the likelihood of making headway against discriminatory practices would be minimal." While stating that the board may have a role to play in connection with some race discrimination issues and noting that rights created under the NLRB might be "broadened to accommodate the policies of Title VII,"[62] the Court took the view that the inadequacy of Title VII relief was an issue for Congress to take into account and not the Court.

Reflections on *Tanner* and *Emporium Capwell*

The board's notion that the fair-employment activities and picket-line conduct of the two white workers in the *Tanner* case were "in accord with, and in furtherance of the lawful position of their collective bargaining agent"[63] requires an even greater act of faith than the board's general interpretation of the *Draper* rule which attempts to create accord between the union and workers when none exists.[64] It is quite clear that the union was unenthusiastic at best about the civil rights goals of the two workers. Although the board found that the first worker was dismissed on grounds that were a "pretext" for the employer's desire to rid itself of employees who took issue with its hiring policy, the union representatives twice refused to vote for the worker's reinstatement. The evidence adduced in *Tanner* indicates that the union sympathized with the employer's position. Contrarily, in *Emporium Capwell*, as Justice Marshall noted, the union attacked the company for racial discrimination and took the position that it would process the complaints (through arbitration if necessary), albeit it demonstrated less enthusiasm for this issue than the workers did. Moreover, the union was totally insensitive to the basic rule that race discrimination is group discrimination[65] and, therefore, refused to process the grievances on a group basis. Justice Marshall's view that an employer would not persist in following a pattern of discrimination and class actions and the potential for repeated misbehavior in an endless variety of circumstances. On the other hand, in both *Tanner* and *Emporium Capwell*, it may be argued that the union's hostility toward its civil rights–conscious members in no way establishes its hostility toward the goal of nondiscrimination. The union may take very severe measures against such independent actions as wildcat strikes yet be in total agreement with a policy that would remedy the irritations or injustices that gave rise to the stoppage. An initial problem with applying this view in *Tanner*, however, is the difficulty of translating an absence of hostility into the kind of accord between the parties required by the *Draper* rule. Unions as well as employers are responsible for much of the racial discrimination which exists in the country today. There is no evidence in *Tanner* that the international union would back the strikers' objectives, let alone any indication of sympathy on the part of the local. It does not seem possible that the board could have indulged in such an unjustified inference in light of the pattern of employment discrimination that has been evidenced in this country.

Again the situation in *Emporium Capwell* appears to be quite different. Not only did the union support the objectives of the black workers; it also protested their dismissals. This makes the board's finding of a violation in *Tanner* and no violation in *Emporium Capwell* completely implausible.

It is particularly interesting not only that the board's holding in *Tanner* sanctions a protected status for employees who did not proceed through their exclusive bargaining representative whereas the protected status has been denied workers who did so in *Emporium Capwell*, but also that in the former case the board declared "offensive to public policy" any collective-bargaining agreement negotiated by the parties which, through a no-strike clause or arbitration provision, would preclude dissident resort to self-help.[66] If one assumes, as the board did, that the union's position in *Tanner* was not being undermined by the workers' independent action, the procedures outlined in the collective-bargaining agreement would seem to be the appropriate means of resolving the dispute. The same holds true for *Emporium Capwell,* where the board (through its trial examiner), the court of appeals, and the Supreme Court all specifically noted the union's good faith as well as the fact that there was an arbitration remedy available which the union was willing to pursue. The Circuit Court of Appeals for the District of Columbia was not persuaded that this was enough, but the Supreme Court was.[67]

The contractual procedure in *Tanner* used a joint union-employer committee where both the employer charged with discrimination and an unsympathetic union voted against the reinstatement of the discharged worker. The board has taken the position that grievance procedures controlled by the union and employer are fair and deserve the same deference that is provided to negotiated procedures which culminate in impartial third-party arbitration.[68] Presumably, however, the procedural unfairness involved—the control of the machinery by the very parties who are alleged to be discriminating—would provide a sensible basis for the board's holding, in that the existence of this defect in the contractual dispute-resolution procedures would give support to the proposition that self-help was the most effective remedy available to the workers. The Court's references to this point as a basis for finding grievance machinery inadequate in *Gardner-Denver* provide further respectability for this view. Yet the board failed to take this route.

The record in *Tanner* did not reveal whether the parties could have turned to impartial arbitration, as they did in *Emporium Capwell,* if the procedure had been proved unfair before the board. Arbitration has serious deficiencies for the resolution of racial grievances[69]—and not only did the District of Columbia Circuit Court of Appeals take note of them in arriving at its decision in *Emporium Capwell,* but the Supreme Court also stressed this theme in *Gardner-Denver. Yet an important point which seemed to escape the board and the courts in both* Tanner *and* Emporium Capwell *is the fact that it is rather difficult to find rapport between union leadership and activist members and, at the same time, to declare the peace machinery inadequate to cope with the problem.* A union which is pressing hard for the elimination of employment discrimination would not knowingly negotiate inadequate procedures for accomplishing this purpose. It is possible that the failure even to refer to any of these factors in *Tanner* indicates that the board has focused its attention on other matters.

Perhaps the board in *Tanner,* rather than limiting the application of arbitration to cases not involving employment-discrimination complaints and thus to matters with which the machinery could cope, desired only to exclude a category of non-contract cases not covered by the negotiated agreement. In *Tanner,* the dispute concerned discrimination in hiring. The board, while addressing itself to the question whether the objectives of the union and the employees were compatible, stated that it would not presume or conclude that "the union knowingly would have taken the unlawful position that it would refuse to represent Negro drivers fairly if hired."[70] *Tanner,* then, may be considered a case in which the collective-bargaining agreement is irrelevant to the dispute, because the agreement does not deal with the subject of the dispute—hiring—but rather with conditions of employment after the employee is on the job. Inasmuch as the industrial unions are generally unconcerned with the hiring of employees the contract's prohibitions against economic action would have no meaning in relation to hiring: the *quid pro quo* relationship assumed to exist in the *Steelworkers' Trilogy* and its progeny may be appropriately regarded as pertaining only to the no-strike clause and the benefits which are traditionally elements of the collective bargain.

The problems with this approach are manifold. First, the unions ought properly to be involved in bargaining for no-discrimination clauses which relate to hiring policies. As the district court in *Detroit Edison* held,[71] a union should have imposed upon it as a matter of law the obligation to represent fairly applicants as well as incumbent employees—that is, to protest and scrutinize employers' discriminatory hiring practices. Dicta in the Ninth Circuit's second *Tanner* opinion, as well as the holding of *Detroit Edison,* support this position. As *Tanner* itself indicated—as well as the Court's holding in *New Negro Alliance*—hiring practices are properly regarded as conditions of employment, and, therefore, disputes about them are "labor disputes" within the meaning of Taft-Hartley and Norris-La Guardia.[72] According to the analysis implied by the board's approach in *Tanner,* stoppages which protest discriminatory union hiring halls, for instance, would become vulnerable because the union would be involved in the hiring process and the use of independent pressure would undermine exclusivity and the negotiated procedures. The result and the reasoning hardly seem sensible or desirable.

Moreover, the no-strike clause often uses the most absolute language and unconditionally obligates the employees to refrain from economic warfare, no matter what the nature of the dispute which might trigger the strike and no matter whether it is arbitrable or bargainable. The Court stated in the *Steelworkers' Trilogy:*

The collective bargaining agreement states the rights and duties of the parties. It is more than a contract; it is a generalized code to govern a myriad of cases which the draftsmen cannot wholly anticipate. . . .

. . . The mature labor agreement may attempt to regulate all aspects of a complicated relationship, from the most crucial to the most minute over an extended period of time.[73]

In regard to the no-strike question, the Court further added that "in a very real sense everything that management does is subject to the agreement, for either management is prohibited or limited in the action it takes, or, if not, it is protected from interference by strikes."[74]* The Court's statements are inconsistent with the proposition that the legal status of the stoppage is determined by whether or not the issue which triggered it was dealt with by the parties at the bargaining table or is necessarily arbitrable. Insofar as the rationale embodied in the statement would weaken the no-strike clause in the contract, it would come as a rude surprise to most employers who have viewed the clause as a much firmer pledge with a base which is unlimited unless the contract states otherwise.

If, on the other hand, *Tanner,* despite its lack of a rationale and the irrationality of its arguments, stands for the proposition that racial disputes have a unique importance in the scheme of national labor policy, it contains a holding which deserves support. The court of appeals' opinion in *Emporium Capwell* seems to stake out the position that they have such importance, although the reasoning employed is not the best. The Supreme Court took a contrary view—partially based on the belief that special consideration for cases involving racial disputes would exacerbate tensions among various groups of workers. Though this view was inconsistent with the implications of *Gardner-Denver* insofar as that decision treats employment-discrimination disputes as different from most labor-management controversies, the fact is that the argument against fair-employment-practices legislation was itself based on the same view. The Court's opinion in *Emporium Capwell* does not say why self-help is apt to be more divisive than litigation—especially since it can be used only when racial minorities are strategically placed in an economically integrated industry, and since it is likely to be more expeditious and effective than protracted class-action litigation, in which the wounds on both sides often fester.

The view that racial disputes stand on a separate plateau is sound for a number of reasons. First, Congress, by passing Title VII as well as the Civil Rights Act of 1866, has made clear its hostility to racial discrimination in employment. The Supreme Court's decision in *Steele* represents a commitment which antedates that involved in the desegregation of public education demonstrated in *Brown* v. *Board of Education.*[75] This commitment, coupled with the history of deliberate bondage and racism which has been the lot of black workers in this country, warrants a special solicitude on the part of administrative agencies and the courts. Although the federal labor policy contained in Taft-Hartley is not to be ignored, the paramount concern must be with the public policy against racial discrimination which is reflected in civil rights legislation and in the Court's *New Negro Alliance* decision, which immunized racial-labor disputes from injunctions under Norris-La Guardia long before the advent of civil rights legislation.[76]

Secondly, Title VII itself, especially through Section 704(a)—as the circuit court's opinion in *Emporium Capwell* noted—specifically protects the right to protest against racial discrimination in employment by protecting employee protests from employer retaliation. As Judge MacKinnon stated:

Where, as here, both the subject matter of the concerted activity and the right to engage in such activity are safeguarded by legislation, we feel such concerted activity cannot be treated identically with other concerted activity which is not so safeguarded for the purpose of determining whether it so violated section 9(a) as to lose section 7 protection.

Neither the Trial Examiner nor the Board took cognizance of the statutory basis of the rights involved in their evaluation of the undermining effect of these concerted activities to section 9(a). While these activities are the subject of review by the Board only because they are deemed to be "concerted activities" within section 7 and also involving "conditions employment" within section 9(a), the Board has an obligation in construing the acts which it administers to recognize, and sometimes reconcile, coexisting and perhaps inconsistent policies embodied in other legislation.[77]

Yet, unless one accepts the absolutism of either Justice Marshall's view or Judge Wyzanski's separate opinion in *Emporium Capwell,* the courts and the board are confronted with the problem of striking the appropriate balance between competing policies of Title VII and Taft-Hartley. If the policies of exclusivity and stability contained in Taft-Hartley are to receive any recognition, the question becomes the following: Under what circumstances is it appropriate to make the factory a battleground where economic pressure is used to settle issues? To begin with, an answer to this question involves a determination of what issues are related to employment conditions, such that employee economic action directed at those issues would properly be protected in the absence of problems relating to exclusivity and stability. Only after ascertaining that can one begin to develop a proper rationale to reach the laudable results inarticulately outlined by the board in *Tanner* and the circuit court in *Emporium Capwell.*

The scheme of labor-management relations created by Congress is designed to deal with factors relating to employment and production. The use of authorized weapons such as the strike to achieve objectives unrelated or only distantly related to these factors should not be allowed.[78*] Yet stating the proposition is considerably easier than applying it to a specific set of facts. Suppose, for instance, that demands are presented to General Motors, Chrysler, and Ford that they pay reparations to black workers because of what is alleged to be the involvement of those companies in this nation's subjugation of Negro workers. Such a protest may seem too generalized and unrelated to plant employment conditions, at least in terms of the particular issues with which the labor board normally deals, to be the kind of dispute which falls within the congressional scheme and consequently is entitled to the protection of *Tanner, Emporium Capwell* or *New Negro Alliance.* Furthermore, whether or not such pressure is properly regarded as unlawful, the reparations example may also smack too much of a political issue best suited to another forum to come within the scope of Section 9.

The problem becomes considerably more difficult, however, when one considers, for example, a stoppage by black workers aimed at making the anniversary of Martin Luther King's death a holiday.[79] This has become a subject of negotiation—the United Auto Workers included the holiday as part of their 1973 collective-bargaining demands. This dispute, like the demand for reparations, has its genesis in a situation not directly related to the employer-employee relationship at a particular establishment. At the same time, the objective is a new holiday—a subject, unlike reparations, quite commonly on the collective bargaining table and therefore perhaps, on that basis alone, a proper subject of protest. (In this connection, it is interesting to note that the Supreme Court has relied upon the prominence of a bargaining item in determining whether a subject must be negotiated under Taft-Hartley.[80]) Furthermore, this particular demand, involving the commemoration of a revered civil rights leader, is, at least symbolically enmeshed in the protest against discriminatory practices, an argument for classifying it with those disputes involving demands to revise seniority systems so as to upgrade black workers, which are clearly within the rubric of "labor disputes."

Even where racial disputes are clearly related to the employer-employee relationship, not all walkouts should be protected in the face of the collective agreement—even if the grievance machinery is inadequate. In regard to the holiday, for example, it might be said that the negotiation of holidays involves considerations which, because of their cost, are extremely important to the employer. Holiday benefits, unlike such costs as retraining hard-core unemployed, recur year after year. Before entering into an agreement providing for more of such benefits, the average employer carefully weights the cost of the concession and may successfully attempt to recapture some of these losses by gaining union concessions in other areas or by making use of technological innovations which save labor costs. Whether or not arbitration is valuable in employment-discrimination cases, once an agreement is entered into, and a benefit is intended to remain unaltered for the term of the contract, arbitration procedures have no relevance. If the employer cannot rely upon that intention, the incentive to enter into long-term binding agreements will decline. Putting aside the question (considered below in connection with union economic pressure) of whether a stoppage over an issue such as the holiday is an unlawful attempt to pressure an employer for a modification of the agreement in violation of Section 8(d)(4),[81]* the governing considerations in determining whether to protect walkouts of this type are ones of contractual obligation. Whether the stoppage can be properly characterized as a labor dispute is not the ruling issue. To give legal protection to economic pressure which upsets basic contractual expectations would interfere too severely with the foundations on which collective bargaining is predicated. Moreover, any number of groups might persuasively argue that special holiday adjustments should be made in their cases also. Here the balance must be resolved in favor of the employer who has bargained in good faith with the workers' representatives—who presumably have resolved differences among employees through internal union debate.

The importance of other areas of dispute may vary from industry to industry. Retraining unemployed blacks, for example, may be a small expense in an industry where job skills are relatively interchangeable and uncomplicated. Consequently, a demand for such retraining would not greatly endanger the contract which has been negotiated between management and the union. However, in industries where technological innovation has severely altered job content and placed a greater premium upon skills, a retraining program might require massive expenditures and probably some loss of production; consequently, where the union and management have made a good-faith effort to integrate black workers into the better paying jobs, a dispute arising from this demand might be treated similarly to one arising from the demand for a new holiday. Disputes arising because of a discriminatory hiring system will not interfere with the economic assumptions upon which collective agreements are based. The overriding theme in all these cases is the same: a consideration of the walkout's compatibility with the industrial relations system's fundamental assumptions as well as a requirement of a conscious, good-faith exploration of the issue and dispute by the parties at the bargaining table.

The expectations of management and labor in regard to the contract which they have negotiated must be balanced against the discriminatory effect which the contract has on black workers. For instance, the Martin Luther King holiday issue does not involve discrimination as such. Where the discrimination involved is illegal under Title VII or another public law, there is no question that a stoppage resulting from that discrimination should be protected despite the reliance of unions and management upon the promise of industrial peace for the term of the contract—just as there is no question that either party to the collective arrangement itself may insist upon modification of the agreement under similar circumstances.

The more difficult problem is posed by the reference in *Tanner* to "unconscionable" discrimination of the kind necessarily alleged in the holiday dispute example as well as in the matter of the seniority system which may not be unlawful but adversely affects the job security of black workers. Such problems are likely to arise in programs involving the hiring of hard-core unemployed, since the job tenure of junior blacks employed in them is threatened by layoffs. Another example is a stoppage aimed at obtaining the company's consent to an "inverse" seniority system, such as that which the United Auto Workers have supported in past negotiations.[82] Such a system would allow whites with greater seniority to opt for layoffs and the receipt of supplemental unemployment compensation. However, where it is not proved that the blacks in a company's work force were individually, harmed by past discrimination, then a "last-hired, first-fired" layoff will probably be sustained by the courts, even if it has the effect of making the work force all white once again.[83] And arbitration is also unlikely to protect the black incumbents in such circumstaces. It seems unfair to permit the company's work force to revert to a lily-white status, even if the only complainants are black incumbents who themselves were not the victims of the company's past refusal to hire blacks. Thus, in the absence of a good-faith effort by the parties to the bargaining relationship to mitigate the undesirable effects of the system, a stoppage aimed at correcting this problem should be viewed as protected.

An even more formidable problem arises in the case of disputes protesting disciplinary action taken because of abesnteeism and poor work habits. "Some unions have been willing to negotiate special probationary arrangements to apply to their companies' hard-core employment programs. But this has been far from universal."[84] While such factors as inferior housing, education, and family environment make reasonable a dual standard in these cases, it is extremely difficult to sanction a walkout over such an issue where it seems to alter the uniform application of regulations which have a bona fide economic justification. One factor which must be considered here is the board's ability to make the distinctions necessary to decide cases of unconscionability. It is ill suited in terms of tradition and expertise to second-guess the judgment of the parties in this critical area.[85] The solution is for the board to stay out of this quagmire of bitter conflict and resentment, although in some cases the unsympathetic nature of union and employer reactions may require it to act.

A Formula for the *Tanner–Emporium Capwell* Issue

In terms of the relationship between black dissidents and their allies and exclusive bargaining agents, the board and court approaches in *Draper, Tanner,* and *Emporium Capwell* have it all backwards. In all these cases the board and the courts have strained to discover a rapport between the union and the workers. In *Tanner,* the record simply did not reflect any such rapport. To some extent, one could be found in *Emporium Capwell.* Yet the board should not strain to discover a rapport inasmuch as no rapport exists normally and inasmuch as the policy enunciated in *Draper* makes absolutely no sense in the context of disputes involving racial discrimination in employment.

Initially, a walkout resulting from such a dispute should be presumed to be protected under Section 7 of the National Labor Relations Act *if and when it is disruptive of the role played by a collective-bargaining representative which is not attempting to eliminate discrimination in the most efficient and expeditious manner possible.* Because Congress passed Title VII out of a profound distrust of events taking place across the bargaining table—a concern which has been buttressed by the record of many unions in the federal courts since 1965—the presumption in these cases should be that the bargaining agent is not doing its best to eradicate discrimination, and the burden should rest upon such a labor organization to show otherwise. The union is the agent through which conflict should properly emerge in such cases. In this respect, the Ninth Circuit's reliance upon *Allis-Chalmers* in the second *Tanner* opinion is quite appropriate. The difficulty is that *Allis-Chalmers,* a decision which permits the board to take into account public policy considerations, presumably beyond the NLRA itself, made no reference whatsoever to racial discrimination and Title VII. As the District of Columbia Circuit Court of Appeals in *Emporium Capwell* stated, the standard for trade unions should be the very highest one; "on the issue of whether to tolerate racial discrimination in employment . . . the law does not give the union an option to tolerate *some* racial discrimination, but declares that *all* racial discrimination in employment is illegal."[86] It is important to note in this context also that the court did not impose the duty-of-fair-representation standard of bad faith upon the union in *Emporium Capwell*. The union's standard is considerably higher—a standard which appears to be in accord with Title VII. That is why the union, although the court did not find it guilty of bad faith, nevertheless had not done enough.

Where the unions are so unresponsive as to require blacks to act on their own, the necessity of ending discrimination requires that self-help be protected. If, on the other hand, a union is pressing to do its utmost on the racial issue and would support the protest, the unauthorized conduct of a black worker should be unprotected. In such circumstances, the rationale of *Allis-Chalmers* should prevail, and there is no justification for bypassing the exclusive representative. The question, of course, is how to determine the nature of the union's policy and how to fashion standards that are sensible and that impose a high level of effort upon the union.

As noted above, the burden should be upon the union to demonstrate that it has "clean hands." In addition to an examination of the union's response to the issue in the particular case before the board, evidence of affirmative action would require a showing of some kind of substantial effort on the part of the union at both international and local levels to resolve race issues among its membership. The establishment of a civil rights department devoted exclusively to the problems of black workers and other racial minorities is not enough. Where blacks are locked into jobs that preclude promotion or are unable to take seniority credits with them to higher paying or skilled trades jobs and where they do not carry the rates of pay that they previously obtained into formerly all-white sectors, the union should be pressing management to eliminate such contractual provisions or practices.

Another relevant factor in considering whether a union is making a bona fide effort to eliminate racial discrimination is the existence of proof that it is integrating, or making substantial efforts toward integrating, its own leadership positions at both the international and local levels. Where blacks constitute a particularly significant percentage of a union's membership, this aspect of the union's record ought to be scrutinized with the grestest of care if there are few or no blacks at leadership level. The leadership's activities are critical here since, despite the protestations about the democratic nature of unions and the fact that the rank and file ultimately determine the vote, it is normally the "slate" sponsored by the leadership, on either a formal or an informal basis, which emerges successful from the electoral process.

To render the black protest unprotected where the evidence reflects an effort at racial justice seems more sensible than the approach adopted by the board, which rewards the strikers only when the union is reported to have acted properly or when the strikers are not militant and adopt a posture in accord with that of the union. The former method would give the board a means of judging those cases which involve unconscionable as opposed to illegal conduct. Such cases, posed as discharge and discipline issues, often arise from black workers' refusal to tolerate what they regard as poor or unsafe working conditions. Rather than judging the nature of the conditions, the board could judge the motives and actual results achieved by the union and allow the union to decide the substantive issues with management at the bargaining table. Again, the union's failure to show that it had exerted all reasonable efforts to integrate leadership positions would be fatal to any effort to undermine the employee's protected status.

For practical reasons, however, the board will become involved in making assessments about what is lawful under Title VII. Although EEOC and the federal courts have primary responsibility in such matters, the board is no stranger to these problems. Not only is it charged with responsibility in the duty-of-fair-representation area, but it must also make determinations—apparently with due consideration of Title VII law[87]—about whether the union may be certified in a Section 9 proceeding. While there is room for disagreement about both the standard for finding a violation and the appropriate remedy, the board cannot and should not avoid its responsibility to make a judgment as to whether the workers had a "reasonable basis" for believing that the law was not bing followed. Making such judgments is the board's normal practice with regard to protests against working conditions—and it is one which permits the workers to make the wrong guess about the law and still protect their jobs under some circumstances. The employer and union are protected from a wide variety of wildcats by disgruntled employees in that the protests must be over something which is arguably unlawful—or over a practice which the workers can be said to have a reasonable basis to believe is unconscionable.

As I noted above, the congressional scheme for maintaining peace between labor and management, as interpreted by the Court in *Lincoln Mills, Steelworkers' Trilogy* and *Boys Markets,* has revolved around the idea of a *quid pro quo* relationship between the right to arbitration and the no-strike pledge.[88] Changes should be made in arbitration procedure to make this tool more applicable to racial disputes; the minimum to be imposed in this connection upon both parties in the handling of such grievances should be the standards articulated in footnote 21 of *Gardner-Denver.*[89]

The pressure that the union mounts to reform arbitration procedures is a central factor to be taken into account in determining whether it is doing all that it can to eliminate discrimination. This, of course, bears upon whether the union is doing the kind of work that makes self-help unnecessary and therefore unprotected under the act. In this respect, the court of appeals opinion in *Emporium Capwell* is entirely inconsistent. For, on the one hand, the court noted that the union was in accord with the workers' objectives, that the union and employees "were not working at cross-purposes, but were both attempting to eradicate racially discriminatory employment practices."[90] Accordingly, the court used this as a peg to make the activity protected under the traditional *Draper* approach. On the other hand, however, the court noted that the union had refused to process the grievance on a group basis and that even in the absence of bad faith, since the union did not choose the most efficacious or expeditious procedure, the workers were justified in walking out. But this difference over timing or procedure is like the auto walkout which takes place in July rather than in September.[91] Such matters involve a fundamental dispute between union and employee. It can be argued that the union is not breaching its duty of fair representation by taking such a posture; yet in *Emporium Capwell* and in *Tanner* the unions were not doing anything resembling all that could have been done under the circumstances. The alleged rapport between the union and the workers was in large part fiction in both cases. The difficulty in *Emporium Capwell* is that the court's approach makes its decision internally inconsistent. The union and the workers must be regarded as in accord for the purpose of the *Draper* rule in determining the protected status of the employees; yet the peace procedures are inadequate, in part, because of the union's lact of zeal—which throws it out of step with the dissident employees. But the court cannot take note of this, because to do so would underscore the inconsistency of the approaches employed: the court's finding of accord between union and worker for the purpose of protected status under *Draper* but its willingness to acknowledge lack of accord in connection with the inadequacy of the arbitration machinery—an inadequacy which is necessary for establishing the protected status of the workers who walk out in the teeth of such procedures.

The justification for imposing a *Gardner-Denver* kind of requirement in connection with finding protected activity in these cases—a requirement totally ignored by the Supreme Court in *Emporium Capwell*—may be extracted from the Court's decision in *Lincoln Mills* and its clarion call for "judicial inventiveness."[92*] It is to be recalled that the decision there held that judicially created arbitral remedies might be devised in the light of guidelines from federal labor law.

For the purpose of determining protected and unprotected activity and employee immunity from discharge and discipline, enforcement of a no-strike pledge should be dependent upon the parties' arbitration procedures as described above. Even where the procedures have been adopted *in toto,* however, the union is behaving properly, the fact of unlawful discrimination should protect a walkout whether engaged in by the union or by dissident individuals or groups of workers. *Mastro Plastics* v. *NLRB,*[93] where the employer's unfair labor practices in effect justified the violation of a broad no-strike ban, provides the analogue for such a policy. While the board has limited the *Mastro Plastics* doctrine to "major" unfair labor practices, public policy considerations argue against a similar limitation of the rule in regard to racial disputes. If, as was the case in *Mastro Plastics,* the goal of industrial peace can be so substantially qualified when the union's very existence is at stake, surely the federal policy against discrimination should protect this kind of walkout. As the Court indicated in *New Negro Alliance,* the latter policy is even more fundamental to our country and to the protection of collective bargaining.

If the board can determine that union's actions violate the law, the no-strike pledge should clearly be deemed of no consequence. Such a conclusion need not await the decision of the Equal Employment Opportunity Commission or the courts, for the board is—or should be—experienced in making determinations in this area. Under these circumstances, however, where changes have been made in the arbitration procedure to comply with *Gardner-Denver,* far more should be required than the *Tanner* standard that the workers have a "reasonable basis" for believing that discrimination or unconscionable conditions exist. In short, where the arbitration procedure has been revised, the requirement of the *Mastro Plastics* rationale should be that the practices must offend the law itself. In light of the havoc caused by labor stoppages, the requirement does not seem unreasonable.

Just as in the *Mastro Plastics* situation, not every violation of law should sustain application of the doctrine. While the unlawful employment-discrimination practice which justifies a walkout need not be massive in the sense apparently contemplated by the Court in *Mastro Plastics,* it would seem sensible and compatible with the goals of industrial peace contained in Taft-Hartley to require that more than a relatively minor or isolated violation take place. At the same time, the relatively strict standards of *Mastro Plastics,* that is, a major unfair labor practice which goes to the foundations of the relationship between the parties, ought not to be required inasmuch as the policies inherent in Title VII are fundamental to the country.

How to achieve this balance is a troublesome problem which lurks in the background of all considerations of the Court's position here—that is, its recognition of the fact that few union-employer relationships are likely to contain arbitration procedures that comport with footnote 21 in *Gardner-Denver.* This fact may provide an argument against examination of the arbitration procedures in connection with determining the protected status of wildcat strikers, on the grounds that the result—the decision that the strikes are lawful because there is no *quid pro quo*—would lead to industrial anarchy, and perhaps to widespread industrial warfare. It may be that a more relaxed standard than that employed in *Gardner-Denver* should be utilized in connection with walkouts resulting from discrimination. The Court's reference to the majoritarian collective-bargaining process in *Gardner-Denver* and the immense difficulties involved in reshaping the system to comport with Title VII bolster one's confidence in such an approach. Yet, *Gardner-Denver* contemplates the promotion of arbitration in discrimination disputes. Justice Powell noted that voluntarism is the preferred method of resolution. Those parties willing to make the investment and effort involved in change should benefit from the standards advocated above in connection with *Mastro Plastics*— that where such procedures are adopted, the board must find the practices engaged in not simply "unconscionable" but also unlawful.

One major objection to the formulas put forth here is that the victims of discrimination have a remedy in the courts; but the difficulties they face in availing themselves of the remedy, as well as the substantial delays involved, make self-help all the more essential. As noted elsewhere, EEOC has a backlog of approximately 120,000 complaints.[94] It has not brought many cases to a conclusion at the trial level on their merits. The collective-bargaining process has been tardy at best and resolves few complaints without the intervention of law. The lesson of *Gardner-Denver* is that this system is a failure thus far. The right to strike and to engage in self-help is not an aberration in national labor policy.[95] Economic pressure and picketing aimed at both labor and management may be the best method under the circumstances.

But what can the employer do when faced with such action? The employer's plight was a matter of great concern to Justice Marshall in *Emporium Capwell*. In the first place, the employer can unilaterally institute a change in the working conditions that are under attack. Second, it can sue to enjoin a walkout called in protest against its attempt to comply with the law.[96] In some circumstances, in the construction industry, for instance, a union's attempt to dissuade another employer's workers from crossing picket lines established at the gate of an employer who complies with the law constitutes an unlawful secondary boycott.[97] Management can also protect itself by pressing the union to change the arbitration procedures. Moreover, if approached by the dissident group, the employer will be in a position to know whether the union has been doing its work in attempting to correct conditions that are perceived to be unconscionable or arguably unlawful.

Should management be required to know whether the employees have attempted to resolve the matter through the union, a procedure specifically favored by both the Ninth and the District of Columbia Circuit Courts of Appeals? In the first place, in my judgment, this should be irrelevant as a matter of law since, if the union is not meeting all standards noted above, the requirement that employees make their initial complaints to the union should be regarded as a requirement that one engage in a futile act[98] where the union is involved in the discriminatory conduct. Second, if it is important to know whether the employees have contacted the union, the employer can inquire without violating the statute—and when the contact between employees and the union has produced no increase in the union's enthusiasm for the matter, the employer is free to act promptly. And for reasons explained below,[99] its dealings with minority group organizations over discrimination issues are not inconsistent with the exclusivity principle or unlawful under Taft-Hartley.

Union Efforts

What of the union's right to strike? Surely striking may be the best and most expeditious way to resolve a dispute involving discrimination for many unions that have a measure of strength—and, in so doing, can meet the standard applied by the District of Columbia Circuit Court of Appeals in *Emporium Capwell*. There appear to be two principal differences between the right of the union to strike and the right of groups of employees to do so—both of which, at least during the term of a contract, make striking more difficult for the unions: (1) Section 8(d)(4)[100] makes it an unfair labor practice to press for a modification of the agreement; (2) the possibility of negotiating arbitration procedures is open to the union. With regard to the second, it would seem that a strike would be legitimate if in fact the union had pressed for arbitration machinery which could deal effectively with the employment-discrimination matters in question but had been unable to obtain it through the collective-bargaining process with the employer. With regard to the first, just as the employer might unilaterally modify an agreement where an effort was being made to comply with law, so also it would seem that union strikes over employment-discrimination issues could be protected in the teeth of both the no-strike clause and the prohibitions of Section 8(d)(4), if in fact the disputed employment practice is unlawful.

The two distinctions noted above also provide protection for the nondiscriminatory employer faced with an unfair union. For the employer confronted with pressure from such a union the stakes are very high. As the Fourth Circuit said in *Robinson* v. *Lorillard:*[101]

> The rights assured by Title VII are not rights which can be bargained away—either by a union, by an employer, or by both acting in concert. Title VII requires that both union and employer represent and protect the best interest of minority employees. Despite the fact that a strike over a contract provision may impose economic costs, if a discriminatory contract provision is acceded to the bargainee as well as the bargainor will be held liable.

In such cases the employer can claim with some justice that it is unfair to make the protected status of a dispute hinge on the union's lack of good faith, and particularly on its failure to establish an integrated leadership. Where the union itself is violating the law a strike by the union is obviously unlawful. Moreover, even with regard to strikes by groups of workers, it is unfair to plunge the employer, as happens under the board's *Draper* rule, into internal union machinations in a futile quest to discover whether or not the striking workers are in derogation of the exclusive bargaining agent. When faced with a recalcitrant union, and conditions which could lead to a protected stoppage by dissident workers as well as Title VII liability should it accede to the union's request, the employer can, as noted above, unilaterally institute appropriate changes.

Suppose nevertheless that the union or a group of workers strikes. The injunction is available as a remedy when the union is thwarting the law despite the strictures of Norris-La Guardia. Another remedy for the employer would be to discharge workers engaged in such a strike on the grounds that the stoppage is aimed at the perpetuation of unconscionable or unlawful discrimination which management is attempting to avoid.

Where the strike occurs during the term of a contract, the Supreme Court's decision in *Boys Markets*[102] is applicable. Should a court operating under the *Boys Markets* doctrine, which permits employers to sue for an injunction in federal and state courts when a union—or, arguably, a group of dissidents[103]—violates a no-strike clause, utilize the same public law considerations which have been proposed in connection with Sections 7 and 8 of the act?

This question would become important if the union or dissidents, engaged in a contract violation, attempted to rely upon Title VII and other employment-discrimination legislation to establish that their walkout would be protected under Section 7 and that it, therefore, would be anomalous to enjoin such a stoppage under Section 301. Although the board, in determining whether a particular stoppage is protected or unprotected activity within the meaning of the act, is not resolving the question of whether an injunction should be issued but is merely deciding whether an employer has the ability to discharge or discipline a worker, it *would be* anomalous as a matter of federal labor policy to permit the court to enjoin stoppages where workers have a protected status for striking under Section 7. While there is considerable disagreement among arbitrators as to the wisdom of their reliance upon law—a factor which we have noted already[104]—the responsibility for the interpretation of the law, of course, lies with the courts. Yet the matter is not so simple. For the Supreme Court has stated that, at least insofar as unfair labor practice is concerned, the NLRB has primary jurisdiction.[105] In the *Boys Markets* context of an employer's request for injunctive relief, the board will not have passed upon the issue in contention. Therefore, review of the matter by a federal district court under Section 301 provides for examination of the issues without the board's involvement.

But on the other hand, the Court has held that, though an issue may be within the exclusive jurisdiction of the board, a breach of contract brings it under the jurisdiction of the federal courts under Section 301.[106] Where employers request *Boys Markets* injunctions, it would seem as though the federal courts could not avoid their duty. Moreover, it seems particularly appropriate that such cases be heard by the federal district courts because they have primary responsibility in any event for resolving employment-discrimination litigation. We have already rejected the view that Title VII and its procedures are the exclusive method for resolving employment discrimination disputes in taking a view in favor of the board's involvement in *Tanner–Emporium Capwell*–type disputes. It seems much easier to do the same when the federal district courts—the same courts which have jurisdiction over employment cases—are involved.

Moreover, the Supreme Court seems to have accepted this point of view in the context of safety disputes in *Gateway Coal Co.* v. *United Mine Workers.*[107] Here the Court, while refusing to renounce its adherence to the view that arbitration and consequent no-strike obligations are presumed in a collective-bargaining agreement,[108]* stated in dicta that it would be inappropriate to enjoin a safety walkout which is protected under Section 502 of the act, so that workers would be shielded against discharge and discipline should the issue come before the board. The Court said in *Gateway:*

The Court of Appeals held that "a refusal to work because of good faith apprehension of physical danger is protected activity and not enjoinable, even where the employees have subscribed to a comprehensive no-strike clause in their labor contract." . . . We agree with the main thrust of this statement—that a work stoppage called solely to protect employees from immediate danger is authorized by §502 and cannot be the basis for either a damages award or a *Boys Markets* injunction.[109]

However, the Court noted that "objective evidence" supporting the view that "such conditions actually obtain" is the prerequisite to the establishment of a defense in a Section 301 proceeding.[110] Similarly, where the union or dissident group attempts to assert such a defense under Title VII in a Section 301 proceeding, the same kind of evidence would be required. Such evidence would support the view that the workers had a "reasonable basis" for believing that unconscionable or unlawful conditions involving racial discrimination "actually obtained." Accordingly, the existence of a no-strike clause or an obligation not to strike which might be inferred from a broad arbitration clause would not support a Section 301 injunction—just as an employer under the same circumstances could not resort to self-help, that is, discharge and discipline the workers who had engaged in a walkout protesting that discrimination.

"Disloyalty" Cases

More than twenty years ago the Supreme Court, in *NLRB* v. *Local 1229, International Brotherhood of Electrical Workers (Jefferson Standard)*,[111] held that disloyal acts performed by workers, albeit in the form of speech associated with a picket line or distribution of handbills, could be regarded as unprotected activity and therefore cause for discharge. The Court said: "The legal principle that insubordination, disobedience or disloyalty is adequate cause for discharge is plain enough. The difficulty arises in determining whether, in fact, the discharges are made because of such a separable cause or because of some other concerted activities engaged in for the purpose of collective bargaining or other mutual aid or protection which may not be adequate cause for discharge."[112]

The *Jefferson Standard* issue promises to become most important in the civil rights area—particularly inasmuch as employers may be prone to retaliate for rough-and-tumble language of the kind used in *Emporium Capwell*. The first question that arises is whether the language relates to the labor dispute itself. Under the *Jefferson Standard* doctrine it appears relatively certain that where the language is unrelated to the dispute it can be characterized as unprotected and therefore a basis for dismissal. But also the trial examiner in *Emporium Capwell*, without deciding the issue of whether the use of terms such as "racist pig" and "colonial plantation" sufficed as cause for discharge, assumed that the mere fact that the language was related to a labor dispute would not in and of itself serve to immunize it.

Yet, given the lexicon of the contemporary civil rights struggle and the breakdown of a personal employer-employee relationship, as well as the rough and tumble of industrial relations generally, it seems that the refusal to countenance attacks such as those employed in *Emporium Capwell* would make civil rights speech which attacks allegedly improper practices in the labor management area a nullity.

The notion that employee disloyalty is a basis for a discharge where minority group workers or their allies protest employment practices or exhort the public to engage in boycotts seems terribly difficult to square with Section 704 and the cases decided under that provision. For instance, the Fifth Circuit in *Pettway* v. *American Cast Iron Pipe Company* held that Title VII provides "exceptionally broad protection" for the "protesters of discriminatory employment practices."[113] The court compared Title VII to the Supreme Court's First Amendment decision in *New York Times* v. *Sullivan*[114]* and noted that the balance involving competing interests was between the protection that must be afforded an employer, on the one hand, for damage caused by maliciously libelous statements, and protection of an employee, on the other, from racial and other kinds of discrimination. The court stated that the balance was to be struck in favor of the employee. Without considering the question whether an employer could sue in civil court for damages incurred as a result of libelous statements made by protesting minority group workers, the Fifth Circuit stated the following:

An employer, consistent with the language and the intent of Title VII, simply cannot avail himself of the retributive discharge as a means of stifling minority group complaints to the EEOC. It may safely be assumed, though we do not so decide in the context of this case, that the malice test established in *Linn*[115]* would govern any libel action stemming from an EEOC proceeding in order to guard against possible abuse of such actions.[116]

Accordingly, though such a decision would hark back to the theme of a uniform federal labor policy enunciated in *Southern Steamship, Lincoln Mills* and *Graziano,*[117] it would appear anomalous and inappropriate for the board to uphold the discharge of minority group workers by virtue of the disloyalty insubordination rubric under Section 7 when under Section 704 of Title VII an employee may engage in speech which is libelous without dismissal. The *New York Times* v. *Sullivan* rule should be applied to the "disloyalty" cases.

Violence and Other Forms of Misconduct: *McDonnell Douglas Corp.* v. *Green*

In *McDonnell Douglas Corp.* v. *Green,*[118] it is to be recalled, the Court concluded that a "stall-in" at an employer's plant by civil rights proponents which interfered with production inasmuch as it limited egress from and ingress to plant premises, was a legitimate nondiscriminatory ground for refusing to hire a qualified black worker. The Court, however, after declaring that the refusal to hire because of involvement in a stall-in was just as valid as the right of employers under the National Labor Relations Act to discharge employees involved in an illegal sitdown strike,[119] indicated that there could be circumstances where despite the employee's involvement in such activity the refusal to hire would be unlawful. It would seem that by implication the Court was protecting peaceful activity of the kind engaged in in both *Tanner* and *Emporium Capwell.*

The Court in articulating the applicable standards in *McDonnell Douglas* indicated that the refusal to hire would not be sustained where it was actually predicated upon "a pretext."[120] In this connection, the burden would shift back to the plaintiff to attack the lawfulness of the defendant's action. With regard to what kind of evidence might be required, the Court stated the following:

Especially relevant to such a showing would be evidence that white employees involved in acts against petitioner of comparable seriousness to the "stall-in" were nevertheless retained or hired. Petitioner may justifiably refuse to rehire one who was engaged in unlawful, disruptive acts against it, but only if this criterion is applied alike to members of all races.

Other evidence that may be relevant to any showing of pretext includes facts as to the petitioner's treatment of respondent during his prior term of employment; petitioner's reaction, if any, to respondent's legitimate civil rights activities; and petitioner's general policy and practice with respect to minority employment. On the latter point, statistics as to petitioner's employment policy and practice may be helpful to a determination of whether petitioner's refusal to rehire respondent in this case conformed to a general pattern of discrimination against Blacks.[121]

However, the *McDonnell Douglas* opinion appears to contain within it some of the elements involved in the balancing approach which the National Labor Relations Board normally utilizes in cases involving employee misconduct and unlawful behavior by employers. As the Court stated in a footnote in the *Green* opinion: "We caution that such general determinations, while helpful, may not be in and of themselves controlling as to an individualized hiring decision, particularly in the presence of an otherwise justifiable reason for refusing to hire."[122] In other words, even where the plaintiff presents evidence of the kind which the Court described as properly leading a court to infer that discrimination is the real reason for the plaintiff's discharge, and that the reason put forward by the employer is simply a "cover up," some grounds for discharge may be so substantial that they constitute "an otherwise justifiable reason" even in the presence of such evidence.

Although *McDonnell Douglas* establishes rules of evidence which are beneficial to Title VII plaintiffs,[123] the rules regarding what constitutes misconduct for the purpose of dismissal or discipline are at least superficially more timid than those articulated under the National Labor Relations Act. For under the NLRA, in the leading case of *Republic Steel* v. *NLRB*[124]—a decision handed down shortly after the Court had held that involvement in an illegal sitdown strike constitutes unprotected misconduct[125]—the Third Circuit held that a certain amount of minor violence was necessarily associated with a strike and did not constitute a basis for dismissal. In *McDonnell Douglas* the petitioner had been involved in a series of protests, all of which presumably were protected by Section 704 of Title VII except, arguably, the stall-in and one other incident. None of the protests involved violence.

Should this kind of misconduct provide a basis for sustaining a discharge that would otherwise appear to be predicated upon protected activity? Under the NLRA ralatively minor kinds of employee misconduct, although unprotected, will not enable the employer to discharge the employee when a general course of conduct which is protected precedes the incident in question. Beyond this, however, the board and the courts have adopted the so-called *Thayer-Kohler* formula[126] according to which a decision as to whether a worker engaged in protected activity may be discharged for misconduct is reached by weighing the kind of employee misconduct involved against the unlawful activity of the employer. *McDonnell Douglas* appears to take this kind of approach since it presupposes that unlawful employer activity may be involved (articulated in the form of a basis for a pretext finding) and that nevertheless a valid reason for dismissal may exist. The pretext approach contemplates that employee misconduct may not be sufficient as a basis for discharge where racial statistics, disparate enforcement of the rules in question, and other kinds of evidence indicate that the unlawful behavior engaged in by the employer is serious. (In terms of a balancing approach, balancing would probably take place where unfair employment practices by the employer or the labor organization directly led to the protected employee activity which included misconduct—just as in the *Thayer-Kohler* context it is the unfair labor practice which leads to a strike that includes employee misconduct.)

What bodes ill for plantiffs is that the board and the courts, in weighing the *Thayer-Kohler* formula, often do not balance at all—particularly where employee violence, as opposed to mere stall-ins, is involved. Here, quite often, the board and courts do not even consider the seriousness of unfair labor practices by the employer, regarding such employee misconduct as sufficient in and of itself for discharge. Even in those cases where balancing explicitly takes place, the board seems to insist upon unfair labor practices which are "massive" or "went to the heart of the Act." Accordingly, there are two reasons for concern in the area covered by *McDonnell Douglas:* (1) the Court's conclusion that the unprotected stall-in is a basis for dismissal, even though it may, like relatively minor misconduct involved in a strike, often be closely tied to perfectly legitimate and protected civil rights protests; (2) the fact that the board and the courts have weighed the balance against employee interests in most instances and have appeared to reinstate employees only where the employer's unfair labor practices were extremely serious.

Sections 8(b)(4) and 8(b)(7) and the "Labor Organization" Issue: Picketing as an Unfair Labor Practice

In 1947 and 1959 Congress amended the National Labor Relations Act to immunize employers dealing with an exclusive bargaining representative from pressure by another "labor organization" to deal with it. Specifically, Congress stated in Section 8(b)(4(C) that it was an unfair labor practice to exert such pressure where "an object" is "forcing or requiring any employer to recognize or bargain with a particular labor organization as the representative of his employees if another labor organization has been certified as the representative of such employees under the provisions of Section 9."[127] In response to the same problem in cases where the employer dealt with a lawfully recognized union which had not been certified under the Section 9 provisions of the act, Congress, in 1959, enacted Section 8(b)(7)(A). The latter provides that it is unlawful to picket or threaten to picket where "an object" of the action is recognition or commencement of bargaining with a "labor organization" or the acceptance of a labor organization as the collective-bargaining representative where "the employer has lawfully recognized in accordance with this Act any other labor organization and the question concerning representation may not appropriately be raised under Section 9(c) of this Act."[128]

One can readily appreciate that these provisions are at odds with some disruptive tactics employed by parties outside of the employer/exclusive representative relationship. Thus, under some circumstances, picketing that is part and parcel of a walkout over discrimination issues may be an unfair labor practice under the act. In this connection, it should be noted that the Supreme Court has equated the right to picket with the right to strike, at least in some contexts, in *NLRB* v. *Teamsters Local 639*.[129]

Apart from their relation to picketing, a weapon of intrinsic importance in the self-help arsenal, the principles which have evolved under Sections 8(b)(4)(c) and 8(b)(7)(A) are worthy of consideration for their relevance in other contexts. For, as we shall see, the courts have been strict in holding that picketing does not violate the act unless done with the object of forcing recognition or bargaining. Picketing without that objective is not prohibited, even though it subjects the employer to pressure outside the collective-bargaining relationship.

This limitation in the reach of Sections 8(b)(4)(C) and 8(b)(7)(A) would seem to have significant implications for the question of the extent to which an employer can deal with a group of minority workers, or a civil rights organization, without running afoul of the exclusivity principle embodied in Section 9. The Court held in *NLRB* v. *Cabot Carbon Co.*[130] that the term "labor organization" as defined in Section 2(5) of the act[131]* applies to groups which merely "deal" with an employer as well as the more traditional types of trade union structure. It might seem to follow that an employer could not "deal" with such a group without violating the polices of Section 9. But the fact that in the context of picketing the courts have refused to find a violation if there is no object of forcing recognition or bargaining may imply that as a general proposition the principles of Section 9 do not impose a bar on conduct which involves the employer in dealings with an employee group outside of the exclusive bargaining relationship unless the group intends to supplant the incumbent union. That is, if the employer has "dealings" with a group which has no intention of supplanting the incumbent, there would seem to be no real threat to the principle of exclusivity. Such a group should probably not be deemed a "labor organization" within the meaning of Section 2(5), and in any event, Section 9 should not preclude the employer from "dealing" with such a group, *Cabot Carbon* notwithstanding.[132]

Prior to the adoption of the 1959 amendments, the board held the view that picketing by an outside labor organization was automatically to be equated with picketing for an unlawful object, that is, recognition or bargaining.[133] This approach was attacked by Archibald Cox,[134] and in *Ford Fanelli Sales*[135] the board specifically overruled its prior holding that a "strike or picketing by a union to obtain reinstatement of a discharged employee 'necessarily' is to compel recognition or bargaining on such matters."[136]

Adopting a fact-oriented test, the board stated: "It may not be gainsaid, of course, that picketing for an employee's reinstatement may in some circumstances be used as the pretext for attaining recognition as collective-bargaining representative of all the employees in a certain unit. But before we are willing to infer such broader objectives, some more affirmative showing of such object must be made than exists here."[137]

The *Ford Fanelli* doctrine brings into play the same considerations which prompted the Fourth Circuit to declare wildcat strikes unprotected in *Draper*—that is, the extent to which dissident groups are pressing for a kind of representation status—and which are bound up with the question whether black workers' groups like the Dodge Revolutionary Union Movement (DRUM), the Association for the

Betterment of Black Edison Employees in Detroit, or the United Construction Workers in Seattle,[138] can truly be regarded as labor organizations within the meaning of the act. For to sanction this use of economic pressure is to permit some kind of contact, perhaps negotiation as well as discussion, between the pickets or protesters and the employer—at least when both are ready for accommodation. In the much publicized arbitration award in San Francisco, *Hotel Employers' Association*,[139] the arbitrator concluded that negotiations and an agreement between a civil rights organization and a unionized employer were unlawful under Section 9. The civil rights agreement was inconsistent with a labor contract and was entered into outside the presence of the exclusive bargaining representative; thus, that aspect of the award would appear to be correct.

It is by no means clear, however, that it would be unlawful for an employer to deal with a civil rights organization or black workers' committee so long as the union was involved in any negotiatons and settlements entered into by management. Moreover, in the *Tanner* context of hiring disputes and industrial unions, if the union had taken no interest in the subject matter, the bargaining agent's presence might be held unnecessary so long as nothing agreed upon was inconsistent with the collective agreement itself. This would certainly hold true in the *Detroit Edison* case where the exclusive agent advised the Association for the Betterment of Black Edison Employees to discuss their problems with management directly and to do the best they could for themselves. Certainly a civil rights group is a less intrinsically disruptive element in the exclusive bargaining framework than a rival union which, by definition, seeks to oust the incumbent union.[140] An organization concerned with the special problems of black workers may be without broader ambitions—although depending upon the situation, the two objectives can merge, especially where blacks constitute a substantial majority of all employees in the bargaining unit.

One circuit court has also applied a strict test in determining what constitutes bargaining for the purposes of the Section 8(b) amendments to the act. In *National Packing Co., Inc.*,[141] the NLRB had to decide whether employees who struck over dangerous working conditions subsequent to a union's defeat in board-conducted elections, and whose strike was enjoined, were entitled to reinstatement and back pay. The board initially held for the dismissed workers because the employer had engaged in unfair labor practices.[142] The Tenth Circuit remanded the case to the board, questioning whether the picketing by the workers violated Section 8(b)(7)(B) in addition to subsection (A)[143] If, the opinion reasoned, the employees had in fact violated the former provision through unlawful picketing, "they should not be able to use the Act to compel reinstatement after the discharge which followed the picketing."[144]

Despite the fact that the strikers had indicated a desire for "someting in writing," the board found on remand that the picketing had not been for an unlawful object, that is, the establishment of a "bargaining" relationship:

We do not view this as an attempt to establish a continuing relationship, but only as an attempt to bind the Respondent to its promises. To accomplish this might have required discussions to the extent necessary to resolve the issues in dispute. This is not to be equated, however, with an attempt to negotiate an overall formal collective-bargaining agreement covering wages, hours, and working conditions. . . .

We have held that Section 8(b)(7)(B) does not preclude picketing to protest an employer's unfair labor practices. We find that Section 8(b)(7)(B) does not preclude employees from protesting, by a peaceful walkout and picketing, their employer's broken promises. To read Section 8(b)(7)(B) as precluding such actions would place employees under due [*sic*] pressure to vote for a union in an election or lose the right for a year thereafter to engage in a concerted protest against any action taken by their employer, however unfair or disadvantageous to the employees.[145]

When the case returned to the Tenth Circuit, the court decided that a finding of an unlawful object could not be avoided by the board's holding that there was no attempt to establish a continuing relationship. "The statute refers to bargaining—not to bargaining for any period of time," said the Tenth Circuit.[146]

This holding, however, is simply wrong. There is a fundamental difference between a full-fledged collective-bargaining relationship and the adjustment of particular grievances, even when the adjustment is formalized in writing as a "contract." Section 9(a) itself recognizes this difference by permitting a degree of individual or group adjustment of grievances in the teeth of the exclusive representative concept. For this same reason, it is not unlawful for an employer to engage in discussions with a minority group workers' organization despite the statute's adherence to the exclusive bargaining representative concept.

The board's decision in *Moss-American, Inc.*[147] was the first application of the 8(b)(4) and 8(b)(7) provisions to a racial dispute. There, the company rejected a request by the NAACP—acting as a representative of some members of a local—that it cease forwarding dues and assessments to the international union (the exclusive bargaining representative) under the checkoff provision until written permission had been obtained from each member of the local. The production and maintenance employees then struck, shutting down the plant. The leaders of the employees' group, which included the officers of the local, stated that they did not consider the contract signed by the international union to be binding and in effect. The trial examiner stated that since the employees in the plant were "predominantly Negro, it seems natural and fitting that the Local's officers sought the counsel and assistance of the local head of the NAACP."[148] The board agreed with the trial examiner that the local could constitute a "labor organization" within the meaning of Section 2(5) of the act, but that since the local was "not seeking to be recognized or bargained with apart from the certified representative," its conduct did not violate Sections 8(b)(4)(C) or 8(b)(7)(A).[149]

One of the demands made by the local, however, was "for a contract." This, coupled with the NAACP's letter concerning dues authorization, brings the case perilously close to the kind of activity prohibited by the statute and a situation where the employer, if it accepted the demands, might be violating the exclusivity doctrine contained in Sections 7 and 8. The statute does not tolerate economic pressure which attempts to circumvent the NLRA election procedures pursuant to which the majority representatives are chosen. *Moss-American* aside, it is clearly inconsistent with *Ford Fanelli* to say that, in the absence of a finding that the exclusive representative has engaged in unlawful racial discrimination,[150]* a local black workers' committee which seeks to oust the international or local union will not violate Sections 8(b)(4)(C) and 8(b)(7)(A).

The trial examiner in *Moss-American* commented in his decision: "The record shows that the great majority of the Company's production and maintenance employees are black; the regional director of the International and his assistants are white men."[151]

Just as it is in my judgment relevant in the *Tanner–Emporium Capwell* context for the purpose of deciding what is protected self-help activity despite the existence of the exclusive bargaining representative under Section 7, this sort of information is useful for the purpose of resolving doubts about the real intentions of the black workers' group, and thus determining whether Sections 8(b)(4) and 8(b)(7) have been violated. All too often the heart of contentions between the unions and the black rank and file may be found in the white leadership's insensitivity to poor or unsafe working conditions which affect black workers. The solution for 8(b) as well as 8(a) problems demands, as a first step, the development of black leadership at the local and international levels. This requirement suggests that the proper policy for the board is to apply Sections 8(b)(4)(C), 8(b)(7)(C), and 8(b)(7)(A) only in instances where there is an outright conflict concerning the continuing exclusive status of the majority representative. Economic pressure may be one of the few viable means through which the unions can be impelled to let Negro workers share elected leadership positions and to involve themselves in the problems of the newly hired "disadvantaged" worker. Although I am somewhat skeptical about the long-range usefulness of the black union trend, one must recognize that if walkouts and picketing do not succeed in their legitimate objectives, black workers may well seek representatives outside the traditional trade union structure or perhaps reject trade unionism in some situations altogether.

Where a trade union itself exerts pressure concerning racial discrimination, both Sections 8(b)(4) and 8(b)(7) may be at issue. Here, of course, there is no question that a labor organization within the meaning of the act is involved. The critical question is whether or not there is an unlawful objective—or whether the objective is, as the union may contend, to remedy unlawful or unconscionable racially discriminatory practices. The only case which appears to deal with this issue is *Vincent* v. *Local 445, International Brotherhood of Teamsters*,[152] where Judge Morris Lasker rejected a union's contention that its picketing was for the purpose of eliminating racial discrimination where the regional director was seeking a temporary injunction to restrain the union from picketing for recognition in violation of Section 8(b)(7)(C). In *Local 445* the court found that the company "actually employs a significant number of Blacks, some in positions of considerable responsibility, who have advanced from lower ranking jobs to the position of foremen"[153] and moreover noted that the evidence supporting the union's contention that discrimination existed was implausible. Accordingly, the court found that the regional director had reason to believe that the union, by its picketing, was engaging in violations of Section 8(b)(7). Here again, however, it would appear that Judge Lasker has adopted the Section 7 approach to these cases enunciated in *Tanner:* that the prerequisite for finding the activity to be protected (or, as in *Local 445,* for finding that the conduct is not prohibited by Section 8(b)), is that employees or the union had reasonable grounds to believe that discrimination was taking place. Statistics, as Judge Lasker's opinion appears to indicate, will undoubtedly play a role in this connection.

An Addendum on Public Employee Strikes

In most jurisdictions, either by common law, by statute, or by judicial decision, the right of public employees to strike is prohibited or substantially limited. In *Bennett* v. *Gravelle*[154] the question of whether a public employees' strike to protest discriminatory conditions could escape the generally applicable prohibition was posed to the Fourth Circuit.

The defendant in *Bennett* was the Washington Suburban Sanitary Commission, a governmental body established by the state of Maryland to maintain public water and sewage facilities in Prince Georges and Montgomery Counties. The plaintiffs were discharged subsequent to the time that they struck in 1970—the reason for the strike being a subject of some conflict. The defendant alleged that it followed the inauguration of a requirement that the plaintiffs and others do "non-emergency outdoor work during inclement weather." The plaintiffs, on the other hand, contended that the strike was the result of a continuous policy of racial discrimination on the part of the defendant. In *Bennett* the Fourth Circuit explicitly stated that the right of public employees to strike could not be determined in light of the considerations which prompted the strike. The court said:

A public employee's right to strike is not, however, resolvable in terms of whether there was good cause or no cause for the strike. Any other conclusion would rob the rule against strikes by public employees of its vitality. To sustain such contention would mean that in every strike by public employees, an attempt would be made to cloud the strike with some appealing purpose, such as to correct racial discrimination or to secure a right of collective bargaining.[155]

The difficulty with this analysis is that the kinds of problems the court mentioned inevitably arise on a fairly regular basis in the public as well as the private sector. Unless employees are to be forced to work under conditions which are deeply at odds with both public policy and conditions required by statute, there is no alternative to judicial scrutiny. Of course, unions and employees may attempt to disguise the reason for striking. It is the duty of administrative agencies and the courts to sort out these problems. The difficulties may be substantial in both the public and the private sector—particulrly where there is a good deal of racial discrimination and/or racial animosity, for here it is likely that the escape valve may be used often.

PART III

THE IMPORTANCE OF
REMEDY AND ENFORCEMENT

10 | The Construction Industry[1]*

> MR. TOBIN: Total membership in the Union [Plumbers' Union No. 12, in Boston], working membership is approximately 1,200 working on building construction.
> REV. DRINAN: And the minority membership is what?
> MR. TOBIN: Eleven apprentices and two journeymen.
> REV. DRINAN: How does that compare with ten or fifteen years ago?
> MR. TOBIN: Excellent. In other words, it is a hundred percent improvement.[2]*

No other industry has been the object of more protest and litigation concerning employment discrimination than has construction. Although the basic ingredients for confrontation have not fundamentally altered during the past decade—and the same can be said in large measure for employment patterns—the attitudes of the participants have hardened. The unions, reluctant to do more than negatively fend off charges of discrimination until 1967–1968, have since contended that their affirmative undertakings negate allegations of racism. Blacks and other minorities, who note both institutional barriers which have the effect of excluding blacks and the slow and numerically small trickle of minorities into the building trades, are hardly convinced that either moral or legal obligations are being met.

In 1964, A. H. Raskin, in writing about a dispute involving the refusal of George Meany's old union, New York City Local 2 of the Association of Plumbers and Pipefitters, to work with black nonunionists remarked, "The general disposition among civil rights spokesmen is to give Mr. Meany high marks for sincerity and for effective action in seeking to implement labor's pledges to wipe out Jim Crow practices."[3] A decade later, however, despite an avalanche of much heralded programs and supposed panaceas for breaking down racial obstacles to access to the trades, even black trade union leaders were denouncing Meany for his recalcitrance as well as for his neutrality during the 1972 election in the face of the Nixon administration's bestowal of generous favors upon the very unions which discriminate most overtly. The irony is that blacks were more trusting at a time when formal color bars had not yet disappeared—not even in Meany's own New York City. The phenomenon is explained by both a rise in black expectations and AFL-CIO smugness about the labor movement's limited efforts toward undoing the past, which Meany himself now admits is a discriminatory one.

The truth is that, despite the multitude of plans and programs, not a great deal has been done to alter the institutional rigidity which limits black access to construction jobs. To be sure, there has been progress in some trades. But EEOC data[4] demonstrate that the pace of change in the high paying mechanical trades is exceedingly slow. In 1967, the statistics on black membership in some of these unions were as follows: Electricians (IBEW), 1.6 percent; Ironworkers, 1.7 percent; Plumbers, 0.2 percent; and Sheetmetal Workers, 0.2 percent. In 1969, for the same unions the figures were, respectively, 1.9 percent, 1.7 percent, 0.8 percent, and 0.69 percent. During the same period the percentage of Spanish-surnamed workers in these unions was as follows: 3.9, 3.8, 1.4, and 4.5. Accordingly, their participation—while not proportionate to their percentage in the population—was more substantial than that of blacks. Moreover, in 1969, 58 percent of the local unions reporting to the commission had no black members.

In 1971 blacks composed 1.8 percent of the Electricians—a substantial move forward from 1967 but a drop from 1969. The black membership in the Ironworkers, which had remained static in the 1960's, had risen to 2.2 percent. For the Plumbers and Pipefitters the percentage was 1.2. The Sheetmetal Workers, with one percent demonstrated the least progress.

The following year the percentage of black Electricians had risen to 2.6, Ironworkers to 2.4, Plumbers and Pipefitters to 1.5, and Sheetmetal Workers to 1.1. There was progress, particularly in the Electricians, but for the most part it was essentially "tokenism." And, of course, the recession of 1974–1975 had a devastating impact upon the construction industry as well as the employment of blacks and other minorities who, as the last to have been hired, were the first to be fired.

Further, it must be noted that black access to construction unions has been limited largely to the apprenticeship level—but many white workers have been able to obtain journeyman cards through other routes. Department of Labor data indicate that a substantial number of journeymen gained admission to these trades without proceeding through apprenticeship programs,[5]* although there appear to be no separate statistics for the racially exclusionary mechanical trades, where it can be assumed that more journeymen have been apprentices because of the relatively formal nature of training required.

Before one examines the roadblocks to black construction jobs and the cause of this sorry record, and attempts to ascertain what efforts have been made and in what respects they are lacking, it is important to determine why so much attention has been given to the construction industry. For, as Meany has pointed out more than once, the skilled trades in manufacturing—in the automotive industry, for instance—hardly have a demonstrably superior record. Even with all the overt racism that exists in the construction industry, the fact is that a good number of manufacturing employers with contracts with progressive industrial unions have only slightly more integrated work forces than their construction trades brethren.

In my judgment, one must look beyond statistics to determine why the black community has focused to such an extent on construction. In the first place, the drift of blacks pushed off the farm by mechanization to the center of northern cities has brought large numbers of them face to face with construction and repair work performed by all-white or predominately white work crews. The visibility of these projects has made them solid targets for black workers excluded from the best jobs in all sectors of the economy. Moreover, blacks have more leverage when the struggle takes place in the ghetto, where whites are surrounded by hostility. Both Detroit and San Francisco have witnessed fine examples of such confrontations. (One factor that works to erode black power in this connection is the shift of a substantial amount of construction work to the suburbs. Discriminatory housing patterns contribute to the exclusion of blacks from the jobs that result.)

Another reason for the amount of attention given to construction is an obvious commonsense one: the extraordinarily high wage rates of the building trades —rates which increased in some of the trades by more than 20 percent immediately prior to Phase I of the Nixon administration's wage restraint policy, and which are soaring upwards again as of this writing. Of course, the wages quoted are on a per-hour basis in an industry noted for its seasonality. Moreover, a rise in the amount of nonunion work indicates that some of the crafts may be pricing themselves out of the market. This more than anything else contributed to the ability of the Construction Industry Stabilization Board to cut down on wage increases during Phases I and II.

Yet, for a community emmeshed in poverty, welfare, and deadend jobs, the construction worker is inevitably the object of a considerable amount of envy now and will remain so for the foreseeable future. Further, the federal government is heavily involved in financial assistance to the construction industry. Of 150 billion dollars expended on construction each year, approximately 30 billion is federally assisted. Of this amount, approximately 7 billion goes to projects which are completely federal, for example, the construction of federal buildings. The remaining 23 billion is spent on projects financed by matching federal and state grants— highway programs, for example—where normally the federal government assumes the lion's share of the cost.[6]* The injustice of racial exclusion is perceived more clearly when such outlays are involved. Moreover, Department of Labor estimates indicate that there will be a substantial increase in the demand for construction manpower during the late 1970's. In what could be an era of rough job competition, construction will be a significant blue-collar beachhead on which black workers must position themselves. One becomes increasingly uneasy about the future plight of black construction workers when one recognizes that the "trowel trade" jobs into which blacks have been congregated (bricklayers, lathers) are declining in number while the nearly all-white trades are the areas of growing employment opportunity.

Racial exclusion is not simply the exclusion of workers. Minority contractors, most of whom employ nonunion workers, are the victims of racial discrimination as well. The significance of this is that the construction industry possesses an identifiable group of minority entrepreneurs who have both expertise in some aspects of the industry and also a financial stake in it. To some extent—how far this position can be pressed is not clear—their personal interest may work at cross purposes with a central goal of national labor policy, the inclusion of minority workers. One reason for such a conflict is that a contractor's concern with joint ventures, bonding problems, and so on, may eclipse consideration of employee integration on a bargaining docket that is already crowded. Second, union membership is an essential element in minority demands, and yet most minority contractors are anxious to continue employing nonunion workers so that they are not deprived of one of their few competitive cost advantages. Moreover, black contractors now appear to employ a disproportionate number of black tradesmen, and, because the unionized white sector of the industry pays higher wages, the effect of increased equal employment opportunity will be to tempt these workers away from their employers—at a time when the latter are seeking to improve their business positions vis-à-vis white employers.

The construction industry's employment problem cannot be discussed without reference to the craft unions involved. In varying degrees and in sharp contrast to their industrial counterparts, these unions control access to the labor market through a variety of measures. Thus, while Meany and writers such as Bok and Dunlop[7]* take great delight in drawing unfavorable comparisons between the construction trades and the auto industry, implying that industrial unions—especially the egalitarian UAW—are hypocritical, they always fail to point out that the UAW has relatively little involvement in the hiring process. Of course, union influence varies considerably depending upon what kind of construction work is involved and what area of the country is considered. For instance, San Francisco and Los Angeles are in sharp contrast, the former city being strongly unionized and the latter containing a substantial nonunion sector that is particularly active in residential work. Indeed, residential building, which accounts for more than a third of construction employment, is an industry in which 80 percent of the workers in the country are unorganized.[8] Sometimes craft unions which represent residential as well as commercial and highway construction workers negotiate special residential rates. Commercial work is the sphere in which the hourly rates are likely to be highest and the overtime most plentiful, and in which the mechanical trades are strongest. It is also in the commercial section that employment of blacks in the mechanical trades is at its lowest level.

The first step in gaining entrance to a craft union—perhaps not a crucial one since it is estimated that between 70 and 80 percent of building tradesmen have never participated—is the apprenticeship program.[9] Although there are no precise statistics for the so-called ''critical'' crafts (so designated because these are the mechanical trades in which earnings are greatest and the work performed is most essential to the industry), most skilled tradesmen seem to have been recruited through the back door: that is, they have become members through job referrals obtained by virtue of recommendations and ''word of mouth'' information provided by friends and relatives, and have received on-the-job training in lieu of following the formal apprenticeship curriculum. However, the percentage of craftsmen who do not proceed through apprenticeship is probably smaller among the mechanical or ''critical'' crafts than in other trades. For instance, a study of construction tradesmen in upstate New York, which indicated that a majority of journeymen had not taken the apprenticeship route, showed that approximately 70 percent of the electricians had completed an apprenticeship program.[10] Workers who are not apprentice graduates gain the experience requisite to a journeyman card by working with friends and relatives as well as by being referred to jobs through "permits." A permit worker is one who is neither journeyman not apprentice—he may be a member of a sister local—and who obtains work when the local's members cannot handle all of it. In time of layoffs, permit workers are required to be pushed off the employment rolls first.

Apprenticeship continues to be the principal route into the craft unions minority group workers, if not for the majority of craftsmen. When one considers the normal selection criteria for spprenticeship in the mechanical trades in particular, the inevitability of confrontation between blacks and unions becomes obvious. The legal backdrop for disputes arising from the selection process is *Griggs*[11] and its condemnation of societal factors which can be mirrored by so-called neutral employment practices (that is, those which are not discriminatory on their face), and also the seniority cases which forbid the carrying forward of past discrimination.[12]

While the selection process is normally handled by a joint union-employer apprenticeship committee, it is not unusual for the crafts to dominate both the committee and the selection process. In some cases, the courts have noted that employer members of such committees were not even aware of hiring decisions made by the committee.[13] To be indentured as an apprentice, normally one must have a high school diploma and a transcript of grades, a birth certificate, and a driver's license. The purpose of the birth certificate is to ensure that age requirements are satisfied, the generally specified age being 17 through 23 or 25. The driver's license is considered necessary by most joint apprenticeship committees on the grounds that work sites are spread out over substantial distances, and the best assurance of an employee's ability to get to work is his possession of a license. While recommendations from incumbent union members are still required in some crafts, they are an obvious target of litigation as a discriminatory device used by an all- or predominantly white membership to exclude blacks.[14] As we have already noted, reliance on subjective criteria by all-white reviewing boards is particularly suspect;[15]* the same is true of decisions arrived at and recommendations made by all-white membership.

Once it is determined that an applicant meets these basic standards, he is notified to that effect and usually takes a written examination and then (sometimes only he succeeds on the exam), is given an interview. Normally, selection is based on the grades in the transcript, the examination, and the attitude demonstrated in the interview. For blacks and other racial minorities, there are a number of immediate problems. Since the interview tends to show in the best light the applicant who demonstrates an interest in and knowledge of the trade, it favors the white who is more likely to know somebody in the trade and therefore something about the craft involved. Further, there is the potential for political and cultural bias to enter in; in one city a joint apprenticeship committee is purported to ask applicants what their view of "law and order" is.

The written examination often assumes knowledge which is to be imparted at a later point through the apprenticeship curriculum—and here the tendency is to favor the white suburbanite who may have taken some algebra and trigonometry rather than the black vocational school graduate. Because of this situation, the Workers Defense League and the A. Philip Randolph Foundation, albeit composed of dedicated civil rights activists, have gained much popularity with the crafts by tutoring blacks—the objective being to overcome educational deficiencies which whites generally do not have. These organizations play by the rules of the game. The assumption is that examinations which require some knowledge of algebra, for instance, and which are suppposedly able to predict an employee's potential ability to read a blueprint, are in some way related to the job content of a journeyman. But in the case of electricians, for example, to whom such tests are often given, it is unlikely, even in major commercial construction, that journeymen will be required to read blueprints. Such a qualification makes sense for professsional personnel, and the work often falls in the jurisdiction of an engineer.

The apprenticeship program is partly aimed at producing an elite for the construction industry—a group that will advance at least to the status of foreman or supervisor. As George Strauss has pointed out, because most employees obtain access to the industry through other routes, contractors rely upon a work force dominated by workers who are semiskilled in the sense of possessing only practice or on-the-job training,[16] and training which in some instances is limited to a portion of the full breadth of a journeyman's work. Much of apprenticeship curriculum, however, is irrelevant even to the work performed by foremen. This interesting exchange appeared in a deposition taken in *United States* v. *Local 638, Pipefitters.*[17]

Q. Mr. Catapano, in your duties as foreman on this job at Tracey Towers, have you had occasion to refer to the specific weight of magnesium?
A. I don't.
Q. Do you know how to figure out the density of a substance if you know its specific weight?
A. No, I don't.
Q. Do you use the principles of Boyle's law?
A. I don't.
Q. Archimedes' principle?
A. I haven't.
Q. Do you use trigonometry tables?
A. Possibly, but not very often. Basic math is necessary, but other than that I don't have to use—I always have references I could refer to if I get stuck on something.
Q. A reference being some kind of table, you mean?
A. Well, I have the same book that you are looking at also. I have other, you know, books I can go back to.
MR. HARRIS: Just to make the record clear we are talking about Plaintiff's Exhibit No. 2 marked for indentification, labeled "Instruction Manual for Steamfitter-Pipefitter Apprentices."
Q. Is that correct?
A. That's correct.
Q. Mr. Catapano, do you know how long a calcium chloride drier should be left in the system?
A. I don't.

Q. Have you had occasion to make use of the chemical properties of gases or liquids in your job as foreman at Tracey Towers?

A. I don't understand the question.

Q. Do you know anything about the chemical properties of refrigerants, various kinds of refrigerants?

A. Well, there is Freon gases and things like that, but I don't get involved with the charging of the units and things. Refrigeration men handle that.

Q. You mean you know what refrigerants are but—

Q. Any further than that you don't have to worry about, is that right?

A. No.

Q. Is that true of the metallic substances used in the pipes, too?

A. That's correct.

Q. You don't get into the expansion, mathematical calculations as to that sort of thing?

A. No, that is all taken care of by the engineers, what size, weight and pipes and so on, what you order and what they call for on that job.

Q. Do you have to make determinations as to what kind of safety boiler water feeders should be selected for the job?

A. No, I don't. That's already in the contract.

Q. Do you have to make determinations as to what kinds of valves should be used?

A. That's also in the contract.

Q. Do you have to calculate on the job the amount of outside air in cubic feet per minute needed to meet ventilation requirements, depending on the size of a room or the number of people in it?

A. No, I don't.

MR. HARRIS: I have no further questions.

While more blacks get into apprenticeship programs through the tutoring efforts of organizations such as the A. Philip Randolph Foundation and the Urban League Outreach—such programs had resulted in the indenturing of approximately 13,000 applicants as of 1972, although not all of them were minorities—progress is slow because the scales are so heavily weighted against blacks. Because whites are more likely to have the requisite educational qualifications and to score well on the exams, the selection process forces blacks to compete where they are weakest, and the subject matter is often not even job-related. Moreover, the fact that standards so far exceed most craft requirements appears to explain, at least in part, both the high dropout rate for both white and black apprentices who go on to greener and more academically demanding pastures, and the oft-repeated statement of craft union apologists that blacks who have the academic requirements are interested only in going to college. Quite obviously, blacks who have such a background are interested in going to college—particularly when there are preferential admission procedures for minorities in the universities. There is absolutely no reason why a minority applicant should seek out the trades in such circumstances; he is "over-qualified" before he begins.

Even if the minority applicant successfully clears all the obstacles already described, there are more to come. The first is that a passing score on the examination may be meaningless, if, as is likely, the apprenticeship committee decides to take in a limited number of workers. The evil here is not so much the fixing of a number, but quite often the artificial manner in which the number is chosen. The Fifth Circuit has held that where this decision does not reflect labor market and industry realities and where past discrimination is present, the court can change the standards created by the parties.[18] The political pressures imposed upon union leadership by journeymen who fear unemployment—some of them choosy about the work that they will accept because of the amount of overtime involved, and some of them insecure because of their lack of ability—can drive the number of members below the needs of the industry. Unions appear to yield to such pressures not so much because they are concerned to keep the supply of workers low as because limited numbers enable them to drive wages up when agreements are negotiated. Whether the motivation is political or economic, however, the effect is the same: to fence out perfectly capable workers. Unfortunately, because of societal conditions which the Court noted in *Griggs,* blacks are generally below the cutoff scores in disproportionate numbers—and yet qualified or qualifiable.

Moreover, even if the applicant is indentured, there may be a period of time before he or she is slotted into a job. This delay compounds the problems alluded to above. In both Cleveland and Newark, New Jersey, I have found substantial ''waiting periods'' during which the lack of interim employment discourages blacks and other minorities from maintaining an interest in the trade.

In most of the cases involving employment discrimination in the construction industry, past discrimination has been evidenced. Nevertheless, the second branch of *Griggs,* which is concerned with neutral practices which reflect societal inequities, has woven its way into these cases as well as into those of the industrial arena.

Nepotism

The craft unions have traditionally rationalized nepotism as being the trade union equivalent of a son's inheriting a father's property, being brought along in the business by the father, or entering a law partnership with his father after graduating from law school. Striking down these neutral practices based upon consanguinity, the courts have not been troubled by the analogy. Judge Murray Gurfein said in *United States* v. *Local 638, Pipefitters:*

There may be some hereditary factors, as there certainly are environmental factors, including motivation, which make the blood relative more likely to do well on the tests. But nepotism as a trade union policy is unhealthy, for while the rich may leave an inheritance for their children, the worker may not bequeath job seniority, for that will take a job from another who has no union ''father.'' Nepotism tends to freeze out blacks because blacks do not have white relatives in the union.[19]

This reasoning, has led the Fifth Circuit Court of Appeals to conclude that policies of nepotism may be struck down under the remedial provisions of Title VII. As the Fifth Circuit noted, such policies are more pernicious than a seniority system which reflects past discrimination since the latter merely slows down the pace of progress, but the former makes the status of exclusion permanent.[20] Where the work force is all or predominantly white, nepotism must be struck down if blacks are to have job access. The same is true even if a token number of blacks are admitted. As the Seventh Circuit pointed out in *United States* v. *Carpenters Local 169,*[21] "Sons of some of local 169's early black transfer members were admitted in later years, which shows, as the district Court found, that 'the nepotism is not racially oriented.' However, when the union opens its doors to a token number of blacks, nepotism applied evenly tends to solidify the miniscule percentage of blacks."[22] Accordingly, what is at issue is not one of those neutral practices referred to in *Griggs* which is societal and therefore stands independent of improper behavior by the employer at the work place. Past discrimination may be a prerequisite to nepotism. Yet, at the same time, since the effect of the consanguinity policy is to exclude blacks just as effectively in the absence of a showing of discrimination—assuming that statistics cannot demonstrate it because in the past there was no substantial number of minority candidates with legitimate backgrounds to fill the job—it is more than arguable that a policy predicated upon either nepotism or word-of-mouth hiring through friends and relatives by an all-white work force would by itself violate the statute because of its permanent exclusionary effect.

Diplomas, Grade Transcripts, and Written Examinations

In questions involving academic records and achievements, that second branch of *Griggs* which is not bound up with consideration of past discrimination is most clearly applicable. The unions have contended that examinations for entrance into apprenticeship programs are not quite within the sweep of *Griggs* because that decision involved a test for a job and the question whether the test was job-related, whereas the apprenticeship examination attempts to predict how the applicant will perform educationally in the curriculum. (Indeed, the AFL-CIO lobbyists were able to insert a provision in the House Labor and Education Committee version of the amendments to Title VII which would have made *Griggs* inapplicable to apprenticeship programs.)[23] This distinction is superficial since what is ultimately being tested in the apprenticeship entrance examination relates to whether the applicant will become a competent electrician, plumber, or whatever.

In one case, *Rios* v. *Steamfitters Local 638,*[24] Judge Frankel mused aloud as to whether *Griggs'* societal branch is applicable only to the portions of the country that have *Brown* v. *Board of Education de jure* segregated schools. As he noted in partial response to his own question, however, the environment of segregated schooling has been found to exist in such northern states as New York.[25] Moreover, the substantial migration to the North during the past quarter century would make such a limited application of *Griggs* difficult to sustain as a logical proposition.

Sometimes the judicial response has been to require the parties to devise a so-called "objective" test without reference to *Griggs* or the rationale of that decision. This is what the Eighth Circuit has done—it being quite clear that the court's purpose is to permit the results of the examinations to be reviewed by an impartial third party.[26] Similarly, Judge Gurfein, in *United States* v. *Local 638, Pipefit-*

ters,[27] specifically required that examinations be composed and reviewed by out-side third parties who can be assumed to have some expertise in the field. It is not at all clear that this response is satisfactory in light of the ability of craft unions to dominate municipal governments, which license the crafts, and some states such as California have taken this function over for themselves.

Age Requirements

Another problem in connection with admission to craft unions relates to age requirements. Normally, the apprenticeship committee will state that applicants must be between the ages of 17 and 25. This has the effect of excluding blacks and members of other racial minorities who could not qualify when they met the age requirements because of the existence of a color bar. Age, like seniority, does not contain within it the "built-in head winds"[28] or societal inequities that exist in connection with the requirement of high school diplomas and written examina-tions, as noted in *Griggs.* Unlike educational qualifications, it is not necessarily synonomous with racial discrimination. Generally, the excluded group can be broken down into two categories: (1) those workers who were excluded when a union had a formal and rigid color bar, prior to the passage of the Civil Rights Act of 1964; (2) those who have been discouraged by the existence of past and explicit discrimination and who regard appliying as a futile act, even though the formal bars have now been dropped, because of the discriminatory reputation of the union and the employer.

The judicial response—the best example being Judge Lindberg's decree in *United States* v. *Local 86, Ironworkers*[29]—has been to take care of both groups by simply revising age requirements of the unions at least for the duration of the decree. In *Local 86, Ironworkers,* in which the decree is to last for a period of five years, the court simply changed the requirement so that anyone under the age of 45 could gain entrance to the apprenticeship program. Age requirements have been revised in other court orders and consent decrees.[30]

Membership Size

The size of the membership class raises questions considered in the third branch of *Griggs*—that concerned with practices which do not necessarily have a dispro-portionate exclusionary effect but which nevertheless preserve the status quo of racial exclusion. Unions attempt to keep their membership low by artificially re-stricting the number of apprenticeship positions, in part because the union leader-ship fears political attack in an election if a large number of employees are coming into the industry while members are short of work. Accordingly, the aim is usually to keep the membership low enough so that members are working for most of the year. The effect here is twofold: (1) to encourage entry into the trade through the back door when the economy is booming and when employees are scarce because of the artificial restrictions placed on apprenticeship entry—a situa-tion which encourages the recruitment of friends and relatives of the existing membership who are predominantly white; (2) to increase reliance upon "permit" employees who are members of other locals of the international or in some instances nonunion and who work on a temporary basis after securing a permit card and often paying a "weekly fee." The qualifications of "permit" workers may often meet journeyman standards. Yet they are the victims of the job scarcity psychosis of American craft unions. For instance, in *United States* v. *Local 638, Plumbers*[31] Judge Dudley Bonsal noted that members of that local's B branch, which included a more substantial percentage of minority employees, worked as "permit" men in the A branch during much of the year because job security, the opportunity for overtime pay, the possibility for advancement, and per-hour wages were all superior in the A branch. The "B" members of Local 638 performed maintenance work which is less desirable, economically and otherwise.

In the *Vogler* decision,[32] the Fifth Circuit Court of Appeals specifically required the union to alter the size of its apprenticeship membership to comport with labor market realities, since the failure to do so would arbitrarily decrease the number of black applicants for whom work opportunities would be available. As Judge Gurfein stated about the New York City Ironworkers, "Local 40's policy of keeping its membership small in order to guarantee work opportunity for its present members has the effect of perpetuating past discrimination and is, therefore, unlawful."[33]

Of course, limitations of membership size are often expressed in terms of journeymen-apprenticeship ratios which assure the layoff of apprentices when a certain number of journeymen are not working—the apprentices being laid off in disproportionate numbers. This practice exists because (1) the journeymen have more political wallop in most unions; (2) they usually have more experience in the trade and are therefore more valuable employees—although employers do not always see it this way. Here also, the courts have not hesitated to revise the ratio where the effect is to perpetuate past exclusionary policies. In a supplemental order in *Local 86, Ironworkers* Judge Lindberg made journeyman-apprenticeship ratios, which were previously optional, mandatory so as to insure the employment of the maximum number of apprentices.[34]

Subjective Criteria

The reliance of Apprenticeship Committees upon subjective criteria and interviews—especially when engaged in by those who are shown to have discriminated in the past—can have the most pernicious kind of influence on future opportunities for minority workers. The courts, particularly the Fifth and Sixth Circuits, have been hostile to the use of subjective criteria when past discrimination is evidenced. As the Fifth Circuit has stated in *Rowe* v. *General Motors Corp.,*[35] an industrial case which has vast implications for the craft unions:

All we do today is recognize that promotion/transfer procedures which depend almost entirely upon the subjective evaluation and favorable recommendation of the immediate foremen are a ready mechanism for discrimination against Blacks much of which can be covertly concealed and, for that matter, not really known to management. We and others have expressed a skepticism that Black persons dependent directly on decisive recommendations from Whites can expect non-discriminatory action.[36]

In some instances an interview results in excluding an applicant even before he has taken the written examination, on the grounds that he has not demonstrated appropriate motivation or enthusiasm for the trade, and that his acceptance will increase the dropout rate. Sometimes the interview is given after the written examination. Regardless of the timing, however, it is quite clear that a black who has had no contact with the trade is more likely to be disqualified when he is judged by the degree of enthusiasm or motivation which he displays at the interview. Accordingly, here also the effect is discriminatory—especially when the decision makers are exclusively white as they are in the five mechanical trades which are racially exclusionary, whether one looks to the unions' or the employers' side of the table.

Publicity

In some states, such as New York, the unions and joint apprenticeship committees are specifically required by statute to publicize apprenticeship opportunities.[37] The court decrees under Title VII have carefully scrutinized the publicity where there is a record of past discrimination. Accordingly, in *United States* v. *Sheetmetal Workers Local 36*[38] the Eighth Circuit Court of Appeals has required that a program involving publicity which was privately initiated be regularized and made mandatory. The court said, on a record which provided no evidence of individual acts of discrimination subsequent to the effective date of the statute, July 2, 1965:

The effectiveness, thoroughness and frequency of the efforts of the Locals to inform Negroes that the apprenticeship programs were at long last being operated in a nondiscriminatory manner must be viewed in the light of (1) the fact that Negroes were excluded from membership in the Locals until 1966, (2) the fact that both Locals historically gave preference to those related to members, and (3) the fact that individual union members will inevitably continue to talk with their sons about opportunities open to them in the trades.

When so viewed, the efforts of the Locals fall short of what is necessary. While it is not the intention of this Court to minimize what has been accomplished by the Joint Committees and the Locals in making the public aware of the now nondiscriminatory character of the program, we cannot believe that what has been done is all that can be reasonably expected. The school appearances do not appear to have been conducted on a regular basis. Only two meetings were held with high school counselors. The A.I.C. bulletins did not indicate that the programs were open to persons of every race and color.

We recognize that the best of publicity programs will not fully convince Negroes that they now have the opportunity to attempt to qualify for apprenticeship training. We also recognize that no such program can hope to be as effective as parental guidance, but a good public information program can help to persuade the doubtful and the skeptical that the discriminatory bars have been removed. Such a program is mandatory.[39]

Promotion within the Industry

But there are many other problems beyond publicity in obtaining access to the mechanical or "critical" crafts. For instance, a disproportionate number of blacks are members of the Laborers Union—employed in the construction industry but represented by a union other than those that have jurisdiction over the high paying crafts. A substantial number of such employees perform work which falls under the Plumbers' and Sheetmetal Workers' jurisdictions. This means that when employment opportunities lag in construction, these unions invariably attempt to push the Laborers out of work which both groups can perform.[40]* The Laborers Union has fought vigorously against such incursions before the construction industry Joint Board (which is authorized to hear jurisdictional disputes in the industry) and in other forums as well, although they have generally come off second best. Moreover, while the Laborers Union vigorously fights jurisdictional battles, it has not generally indicated a strong interest in seeing its members move up into better paying jobs—obviously because that would mean that many of its skilled members, black or white, would be lost to other unions. This attitude, coupled with the racially exclusionary practices of the crafts, has had the effect of overlooking a natural pool from which labor can be recruited.

In fairness to the Laborers Union, however, it faces substantial difficulties with achieving upward mobility for its members—difficulties that are largely attributable to the multiunion character of the industry. In the first place, normally such workers, even though they possess a substantial portion of the skills for a job, would have to begin as apprentices or at an intermediate level (a stage which does not exist for entry purposes in many unions), and in some unions which have referral priority or seniority, they would have to go to the bottom of the ladder. Thus, workers who transferred would have less income and job security than they had previously had as laborers, a substantial deterrent to their taking advantage of any transfer procedure. To some extent, despite their weakness, the so-called "hometown plans" (discussed in Chapter 11) ease these problems, by creating special trainee categories where employees with skills may move without such wage penalties. The hometown plans do not, however, provide seniority or priority credits in connection with a referral at either the trainee or journeyman stage of employment, unlike the procedure established under Title VII in the landmark *Sheetmetal Workers* decision. Further, trainees in the hometown plans do not receive union books and do not have a status equal to apprentices. They are "permit" workers who operate on the fringe of the industry.

Moreover, in addition to the fact that job security problems remain, laborers have nontransferable or portable fringe benefit packages negotiated for them. That the unions have not seen fit to cooperate with one another in negotiating a scheme which would transfer an employee's benefits in the event the employee moves across union lines also acts as a deterrent to transfers by members of the Laborers Union. Finally, the mechanical trades keep a very tight lid on the number of such workers who may obtain "permits." Unions and employers have not remedied this permit problem for black workers who possess some experience. Indeed, as of this writing, the courts have not addressed themselves to "red circling"[41]* and other guarantees for black workers who are in the construction industry, seek upward mobility, and are deterred by the prospect of wage reduction and loss of fringe benefits.

Referral Systems

The means by which construction workers obtain employment is critical to an understanding of the problems of racial discrimination in the industry. Construction unions maintain hiring halls through which applicants are dispatched. (Such institutions also exist in the longshore industry, in shipping, and in the West Coast trucking industry.) The unions control these halls, and usually employers appear to prefer it that way.

The nature of the industry dictates the need for such a system of referral. Work is casual, intermittent, seasonal, and necessarily of limited duration. Work opportunities are scattered at numerous job sites over a large geographical area. Union referral systems eliminate some of the job insecurity inherent in an industry which is filled with so many uncertainties.

The National Labor Relations Act contains two provisions which apply to the hiring hall. The first prohibits the closed shop—the requirement that a worker be a union member prior to employment.[42] The second establishes special rules for the construction industry.[43] This provision, Section 8(f), provides, first, that the construction union can negotiate a collective-bargaining agreement with an employer prior to the time that a majority of the workers in the bargaining unit have demonstrated support for the union as exclusive bargaining representative. The theory here is that since the work may be of extremely short duration, time may not permit workers to demonstrate their free choice. Accordingly, their preference is presumed to be for the union.

Second, although the industrial unions cannot compel membership on the part of workers in the bargaining unit until they have been at work thirty days or thirty days subsequent to the negotiation of an agreement, in the construction industry— once again because of the abbreviated nature of the work—Section 8(f) states that membership can be compelled seven days after employment or the agreement. Third, labor organizations are specifically provided with an "opportunity to refer qualified applicants for such employment," and the agreement between the two parties may "minimum training or experience qualifications for employment or provide [s] for priority in opportunities for employment based upon length of service with such employer, in the industry or in the particular geographical area."

The net effect of these provisions is to permit unions in the construction industry to maintain a tight grip upon access to employment. In effect, the unions are able to maintain a *de facto* version of the closed shop—especially where the hiring hall provides the union with the exclusive right to refer workers to available job opportunities. In the 1964 work stoppage by the Plumbers and Pipefitters in New York City, when white members of George Meany's local refused to work with blacks who were not members of the union, the union, and Meany as well, openly stated that the official union policy was to refuse to work with nonunion workers. The use of hiring halls, exclusive or otherwise, as a means to compel union membership prior to employment in defiance of the Taft-Hartley anti-closed-shop prohibitions, is notorious. Indeed, in many of the Title VII cases involving the construction unions, the courts have made specific reference to the abuses this practice entails.[44] The building trades have openly acknowledged their defiance of Taft-Hartley and in some instances have engaged in walkouts to implement the closed-shop objective.[45] When this tactic was used in St. Louis, the National Labor Relations Board was able to obtain expeditious injunctive relief under the secondary boycott provisions of the NLRA.[46]

Despite these facts of life, the Supreme Court in *Local 357 Teamsters* v. *NLRB*[47] held that the hiring hall is not necessarily a disguised form of the closed shop and does not violate the National Labor Relations Act. The Court held that many union practices and provisions of collective-bargaining agreements might have the effect of encouraging union membership but in the absence of a specific finding of discrimination a violation under the statute could not be made out. The Court's ruling defies reality. The hiring hall is a *de facto* closed shop and does play a significant role in the exclusion of black workers.

Union-dominated referral or hiring systems take a number of forms. A Department of Labor survey[48] found that of 291 collective-bargaining agreements in the construction industry, 131 provided for exclusive work referral, 98 contained provisions which could be characterized as nonexclusive work referral, and 61 had no referral provisions at all.

Of 82 agreements providing for exclusive referral systems which were selected for detailed analysis, all gave responsibility for registering and referring applicants to the union and none gave any to the employer. Seventy-two of the 82 agreements provided that an applicant had to meet certain qualifications in order to register; the other ten contained no provisions on this point. Of the 72 which provided for qualifications, 70 empowered the union alone to review both qualifications and eligibility to register, and two agreements provided that the union and employer would share this responsibility. In those 72 agreements, the qualifications generally related to experience or training prior to referral. Moreover, one agreement specified that an applicant was required to be a resident of the geographical area covered by the collective agreement.

The agreements broke down into two groups: those providing for objective minimum qualifications, and those providing for subjective qualifications. An agreement was classified as subjective if it indicated that experience or training was a requirement but did not specify the amount involved. In 32 of the 33 agreements with objective qualifications, and 38 of the 39 in the subjective category, the union had authority to determine whether the applicant possessed such qualifications.

Agreements providing for subjective criteria generally stated that the applicant had to be a "competent" worker, a "qualified" employee, or a "journeyman."[49] Most of the agreements (29 out of 33) that had objective standards specified that the worker had to have a certain number of years of experience. However, in ten of the 33, an applicant was required to pass an examination in addition. The experience required ranged from "more than one year" to five years, and often it had to have been accumulated under collective-bargaining agreements negotiated by the union in question. The NLRB has held that such contractual provisions do not violate the anti-closed-shop provisions of Taft-Hartley.[50] Here again, as with the Supreme Court's decision in *Local 357,* the reality of industrial relations is substantially different from the assumptions of the law's approach.

Once it has been determined which workers are to have access to the hiring hall, the question of which workers are to have preference in dispatches to job opportunities arises. Of the 82 agreements analyzed in detail, 51 provided that the union was to follow a certain procedure in selecting applicants for referral to employers. Forty-one stated that applicants were to be selected on the basis of the date of registration—"first in/first out." Six provided that applicants be selected on the basis of seniority and experience or competency, and one stated that some applicants should be selected on the basis of registration and others on the basis of experience. Priority groups, which get preference based on time worked in the industry, in a geographical area, and under the collective-bargaining agreement between the parties, raise the same problems of seniority which are discussed elsewhere.[51] To the extent that an agreement permits a union to exercise discretion in selection either by determining the necessary amount of experience or by empowering business agents to dispatch workers to jobs deemed suited to their competence, the subjective criteria cases[52] have relevance. Given the substantial amount of union control involved, it is no wonder that the minority community has focused a good deal of its attention on demands for either (1) a share in the responsibilities connected with selection and referrals; or (2) provision for independent review of the decisions now made exclusively by trade unions.

11 | Private Initiative in the Construction Industry: The How and Why of Imposed and Voluntary Plans

The story of trade union and government programs aimed at eliminating discrimination in the construction industry is a complicated and at times confusing one. Yet its persistent theme is the inadequacy of both private and government efforts. The unions, with the sanction and indeed financial support of the executive branch of the federal government during both Democratic and Republican administrations, have granted union entry to a limited number of minority workers who have had to move up the job ladder—as many have courageously done—without any of the protection or benefits afforded by the law of Title VII. All the programs proposed or supported by the unions have required blacks and other racial minorities to surmount the motivational barriers resulting from unlawful apprenticeship standards and craft referral practices. These practices have emerged unscathed whenever the unions and employers rather than the judiciary have had primary responsibility.

In late January 1967, the Department of Labor provided a grant of $277,688 to the Workers Defense League and the A. Philip Randolph Education Trust to prepare "young men, particularly Negroes and the Puerto Ricans" to take apprenticeship examinations in New York City, Buffalo, Cleveland, and Westchester County, New York. The program, which was predicated upon the belief that unfamiliarity with the examination structure and lack of awareness of and interest in the trades were the greatest obstacles to blacks obtaining access to construction jobs, was geared to provide medical examinations, tests, counseling, and job referrals to minority applicants.

The next action of significance was a February 13, 1968, accord between the Department of Labor and the building trades unions. On February 1, 1968, C. J. Haggerty, president of the Building & Construction Trades Department of the AFL-CIO stated in a letter to Secretary of Labor W. Willard Wirtz[1] that the unions in the department would attempt to foster organized programs which would provide for the recruitment of "qualified applicants for apprenticeship from Negro population and other minority groups" and also programs which would identify "deficiencies affecting the full qualification of Negro and other minority group applicants" with a view toward remedying them "if practical." The assumptions and tone of Haggerty's letter indicated that, in his view, the primary reason for the absence of minority group workers from the building trades was to be found in their own shortcomings. Nevertheless, Secretary Wirtz responded by praising the AFL-CIO's new approach and indicating that the Johnson administration would not change the policies stated in either Executive Order 11,375 or the Bureau of Apprenticeship & Training Regulations. He said "When these proposals are carried out, they will, in my opinion, represent a strong and progressive step toward answering, once and for all, complaints that building trades unions may not be exerting their best efforts in full support of private and public action to eliminate discrimination on the basis of race, creed, color, or national origin."[2]

This, of course, did not put the matter to rest by any means. George Meany himself in a June 1968 report to civil rights organizations in the AFL-CIO magazine, *The Federationist,* stated that "racial discrimination remains a major barrier to Negroes hunting jobs, and labor unions have not done all they can do to eliminate prejudice within their ranks.[3] He continued, "This is not a time to give up, it is a time to fight harder."[4]

To the AFL-CIO, fighting harder meant reliance upon the Urban League's Project Outreach, which was funded by the Department of Labor. The difficulties involved in such an approach, however, were manifold, the most obvious being that the Department of Labor was willing to place its financial *imprimatur* upon apprenticeship programs that in many, if not most, of their practices were in violation of the evolving law of Title VII. In his monograph *Labor Union Control of Job Training,* NAACP Labor Secretary Herbert Hill has detailed the substantial financial subsidization which was provided to AFL-CIO unions and their "front" organizations, such as the A. Philip Randolph Education Trust.[5] Furthermore, according to AFL-CIO Civil Rights Department estimates, minority apprentices covered by the Outreach constituted only approximately 5 percent of the national apprenticeship population.

Dissatisfaction with union attitudes and lack of progress resulted in three demands: (1) that blacks as well as whites be permitted to enter the crafts through routes other than apprenticeship; (2) that more attention be given to results rather than mere revision of procedures; (3) that the revisions dictated by Title VII become part of voluntary programs.

Through promulgation of Executive Order 10925, the Kennedy administration had specifically obligated contractors on federally aided construction projects to undertake affirmative action efforts to recruit minorities. Efforts to improve upon the trade union initiatives began to come forth from the Department of Labor's Office of Federal Contract Compliance which had been created by the Johnson administration in 1965. Area coordinators were appointed to work in fifteen different metropolitan areas or labor markets. However, the executive order under which OFCC operates does not directly cover labor unions which have contracts with employers on federally assisted construction projects. Affirmative action obligations apply only to contractors and subcontractors, even though construction unions play a significant role in the hiring process. This deficiency has always bedeviled contract compliance efforts in construction—and similar programs elsewhere where unions are strong.

The first major step beyond the mere proclamation that the results of recruitment were critical (an assertion irritating to contractors because of its lack of specificity) was the special area program for Cleveland announced in March 1967.[6] The significance of the Cleveland Plan was that it mandated "manning tables" for the employment of minorities. The contractor was required to make a specific proposal on the number of minority workers who would be employed on the project in each trade. The proposal was to be made in advance of the time that the contract was awarded.

This requirement posed a dilemma for the contractors. Would they put pressure on the unions to refer black workers to them? In the first place, there might be too few black union members to enable contractors on federally assisted projects to make a commitment. Also, of course, in most northern cities the contractors were hardly in a position to tell the crafts what to do—especially in this critical area. The only alternative was to hire nonunion blacks. Some federal court decisions made this option a more possible one by holding that the racial inadequacy of the exclusive hiring hall was not a defense to a contractor's failure to hire minorities under the executive order and that if the employer could not find blacks in the exclusive hiring hall, it must find them elsewhere.[7] However, two immediate problems posed themselves: the scarcity of nonunion blacks of journeyman or near journeyman caliber, and the obvious hostility of the unions to the employment of nonunion workers whether black or white.

Union officials were soon heard to criticize the Cleveland Plan as "piles of nonsense and illegal."[8] This viewpoint was appeased by Secretary Wirtz, in a speech to the Building & Construction Trades Department of the AFL-CIO on November 29, 1967, in which he said:

In at least two cases—in Cleveland and in Philadelphia—the Government contract situations had gotten so bad, with antagonism and recrimination piled on top of each other, to the point where symbolism was more important than substance, evidence more important than equity, that there was probably no effective alternative to that kind of ruling. But it isn't right as a general policy, and it won't work. Even if it drags someone who worships his prejudices into line, it demeans someone else who has done the right thing for the right reason.[9]

The second of the two cities mentioned, Philadelphia, assumed a central role in subsequent contract compliance efforts. The first Philadelphia Plan (1967) adopted the manning tables approach.[10] The plan was held invalid by the Comptroller General (who, as the chief controller of the General Accounting Office, authorizes all government expenditures); his rationale for so concluding was that the plan lacked provision for "definite minimum requirements to be met by the bidder's programn and any other standards or criteria by which the acceptability of such program will be judged.[11] At this point OFCC began to devise an approach which has been at the center of the storm ever since—that of goals and timetables for minority representation where there has been a underutilization of such minorities.

This became the revised Philadelphia Plan which, although it met the Comptroller General's specificity objection, he nevertheless regarded as unlawful.[12] The plan was approved in final form by the Attorney General on September 23, 1969.[13*]

The Philadelphia Plan of 1969 was an attempt to prescribe more effective affirmative action requirements under Executive Order 11246 in connection with construction projects for which federal assistance exceeded $500,000. A range of minimum manpower utilization was established for the work forces on all federally assisted projects. This measure was aimed at curing the defect which the Comptroller General had seen in the first Philadelphia Plan, the lack of specificity. Contractors were to be on notice concerning their obligations. At least four factors were to be taken into account in establishing the ranges for the six trades in Philadelphia which were deemed to have "underutilized" mimorities: (1) the extent of minority group participation in the trades; (2) the availability of construction work for minority group persons; (3) the need for training programs in the area and/or the need to assure a demand for those in existing training programs and those who had completed such programs; and (4) the impact of minority group participation upon the existing work force.

While a contractor's bid which failed to promise minority employment in accordance with the ranges and goals formulated in light of these factors was not to be considered, it was to be possible for a contractor to make the promise and yet fall short of the goal if he had made a good faith effort to meet it. "Good faith" was to be measured by the contractor's efforts to (1) notify community organizations which had agreed to refer minority workers; (2) keep lists with names of members of minorities referred and the action taken; (3) properly notify the OFCC area coordinator of union interference; and (4) participate in available training programs.

The United States Senate, in December 1969, tacked an amendment onto a relatively innocuous appropriations bill to block the plan. The provision barred the use of federal funds on any project which the Comptroller General found to be in violation of federal law. The Comptroller General, having found the first Philadelphia Plan unlawful because of its unspecificity, had now declared the revised Philadelphia Plan illegal because of its precisionlthat is, its provision for "unlawful quotas." President Nixon, rarely known to be sympathetic to civil rights issues, nonetheless threatened to veto the Senate act and to keep Congress in session if necessary during the 1969 Christmas holidays. On December 22, the House voted to strike the Senate amendment and to uphold the Nixon administration on this issue. Despite the opposition, therefore, of the Comptroller General, George Meany of the AFL-CIO, and several senators and congressmen, the plan has been implemented during the past seven years. But thus far Tom Wicker's comment appears to have been prophetic: "The primary value of the Philadelphia Plan victory may well be symbolic. The proposal makes only the smallest beginnings on a major problem; yet, as President Kennedy used to say, a journey of a thousand miles begins with but a single step."[14]

The Philadelphia Plan was indeed a small step and a primarily symbolic victory.

It was a beginning, nevertheless, because its impact was felt throughout the nation during the summer and fall of 1969. In Chicago, Pittsburgh, and Seattle, black demonstrators and white hard-hats took to the streets as violence erupted. Civil rights demands were made on the building trades in most northern cities. In the fall of 1969, the AFL-CIO felt compelled both to castigate black militants and simultaneously to claim fidelity to the principles of equal employment opportunity. On September 22, in a statement of policy, its Building & Construction Trades Department, stated the following:

We make the flat and unqualified recommendation to local unions throughout the United States that for a stated period of time they should invite the application of qualified minority journeymen for membership in their respective local unions and should accept all such qualified minority journeymen . . . provided they meet the ordinary and equally administered requirements for membership.

We also recommend that the local unions and the local councils explore and vigorously pursue training programs for the upgrading of minority workers who are not of apprenticeable age. Such programs should be developed in such manner as to prevent undercutting the established apprenticeship programs.[15]

On September 24, one day after the Philadelphia Plan had been declared lawful by the Attorney General, Meany, in a speech to the Building & Construction Trades Department, praised their statement of policy and, quoting portions of the above, asked, "What more do these people want?" He went on:

Still we find the Building Trades being singled out as being "lily-white," as they say, and some fellow the other day said it was "the last bastion of discrimination."

Now, this is an amazing statement, when you figure how small participation of Negroes and other minorities is in, for instance, the banks in this country, the press, on the payroll for newspapers and the communications media, and I think there is one Negro in the United States Senate. That is just 1%, 1 out of 100.

I don't think that when President Nixon looks around his cabinet, I don't think he sees any black faces in there either. But we in the Building Trades are singled out as "the last bastion of discrimination."

I want to tell you I resent it just as much as anyone in this room, or anyone here on the platform. I resent the action of government officials—no matter what department they come from—who are trying to make a whipping boy out of the Building Trades.[16]

Subsequently, however, events were to take a course more satisfying to Meany. In the later part of 1969 and early 1970, it became clear that a version of the Philadelphia Plan was not to be imposed in every situation. Indeed, an entirely different pattern emerged. The dramatic foil for Philadelphia became Chicago, where blacks and whites had already clashed in the streets during September 1969. Community pressure on the construction industry led to demands for minority group involvement in the selection of apprentices and journeymen. Said C. J. Haggerty, at that time still president of the Building & Construction Trades Department:

The teaching of skills must be done by persons in the industry and can never be turned over to unqualified outsiders. . . . I believe we should make it clear again that the conduct, curriculum, and control of our apprentice training programs are going to remain in the hands of our crafts and our contractors. They are not going to be turned over to any coalition.[17]

And indeed they were not. But negotiations nevertheless began to take place in a number of cities between minority coalitions, unions, and contractors. This factor, coupled with the OFCC's failure to hire sufficient staff to supervise imposed plans and a political collapse of will on the part of the Nixon administration, led to the "hometown plan" approach.

The hometown plan approach—regarded as the "best solution" by the Department of Labor—was and still is presumed to have a number of attractions. The first is that plans were voluntarily negotiated—although failure to negotiate one might well mean an imposed plan of the Philadelphia type. Because the hometown plan was voluntary, the expertise of cooperative parties could be tapped and, equally important, the hated numbers or quotas which the unions had railed against in Philadelphia and Cleveland could be accepted more easily because the patients administered their own medicine.

A second attractive point was that the plans dealt directly with unions as well as contractors. Unions were obligated through the negotiations to accept minority apprentices as "trainees," presumably thus placing them on the track leading to a journeyman's card and relative economic security in the geographic area within the union's jurisdiction. Such trainees, while lacking full union status as permanent workers, could be slotted into the union structure at an intermediate stage above the entry level apprentice, depending upon experience—but the unions and employers were to determine when and where such workers were placed and what their experience was worth. Accordingly, where a hometown plan was in effect, "motorcycling" or "checkerboarding"—moving minority employees from one construction project to another—was substantially eliminated. What mattered was not the number of minority workers on a particular project, which was often of short duration, but rather the number of employees moving into a training program which might culminate in the possession of substantial credentials. Under the Philadelphia Plan and other imposed plans like it, employees might gain no union status and no learning experience or exposure to the trade. Such a worker would have a very bleak economic future after a particular project was completed. Third, the hometown approach made sense in that initially the agreements were intended to be tripartite. Labor, management, and the minority community were all to be signatories. Here the theory was that plans which involved those who would benefit from them would tend to be implemented, inasmuch as enforcement was in the self-interest of one of the parties involved.

The hometown approach highlighted some of the imposed plans' deficiencies. When first promulgated, the Philadelphia Plan applied only to minority employee participation on construction projects federally assisted above a certain dollar amount—although this was to change in early 1971. Moreover, the hometown plans were predicated upon the receipt of Department of Labor manpower funding for training projects. Although the Philadelphia Plan contemplated the establishment of training programs, none were not required at the outset. Indeed Assistant Secretary of Labor Fletcher was to announce a year after that plan's adoption that Department of Labor regulations provided the crafts with a veto over training funds in their locality when the program was not to their liking.[18] This helped undermine the Philadelphia Plan inasmuch as the unions were extremely anxious to see it fail and willing to do all in their power to achieve that objective.

Chicago

It was in Chicago that the hometown plan approach began. Although the negotiation of the agreement and its aftermath involved much that was unique to the "Windy City," the Chicago Plan is the model for such plans—not only because it came first, but also because of the high praise it received from AFL-CIO leadership as the answer to Philadelphia.

On July 22, 1969, blacks invaded the offices of the Chicago and Cook County Building Trades Council and demanded that Chicago locals admit more blacks to membership and establish training programs. Formalizing their demands in August, the black groups formed the Coalition for United Community Action. On September 22, the day before the Philadelphia Plan was finally approved, 4,000 blacks and whites held a "black Monday" demonstration in the Civil Center Plaza, protesting the exclusion of blacks from the building trades. Although the crowd was generally peaceful, the Blackstone Nation, one of Chicago's youth gangs which had busied itself during the summer months chasing white workers from construction projects and had thus created an atmosphere in which unions and contractors were more willing to negotiate, clashed with the police when they attempted to block traffic at Clark and Randolph Streets. Later that same week, when the Department of Labor held hearings on the building trades in Chicago, 2,000 white hard-hats blocked the U.S. Customs House where the hearings were being held. The *Chicago Tribune,* on September 26, wrote the preceding day's events: "The construction workers massed around the Customs House and blocked all entrances to the building for four hours and hundreds of them slugged it out with 400 policemen at 1:00 p.m. at or near the intersection of Harrison and Canal Streets."[19]

Despite these incidents, negotiations continued throughout the fall, and on January 12, 1970, an agreement was reached.[20] Torrents of praise poured forth, particularly from those who had condemned the Philadelphia Plan. George Meany, who two days before had attacked the latter, characterized the Chicago Plan as a "significant forward step" and one which was "substantially in line with the policy determination of the recent Building and Construction Trades Department convention and with the continuing policy of the AFL-CIO." He added: "It is an achievable program, that rests four-square on mutual trust. As such, it is vastly superior to any government-imposed quota system—which is, of course, artificial and discriminatory.[21]

Similarly, C. J. Haggerty, the president of the Building & Construction Trades Department of the AFL-CIO, sent his congratulations to those who had devised this "sound approach." Said Haggerty:

Your Agreement provides for skilled training toward a career, rather than a so-called plan which would involve minorities in a reckless numbers game with the ultimate result of only temporary part time employment and further disillusionment. Your Agreement goes much further than the so-called plan developed by bureaucratic staff which by its very implementation would have seriously disrupted the normal procedures and practices of the construction industry in any area where it might have been involved.

And finally, Secretary of Labor George Shultz chimed in, stating that he was "delighted" with the Chicago Plan. He noted that it covered all construction contracts in the Chicago area, and he praised those who had devised the plan for its "realization by contractors and unions that the programs derived from such negotiations will be more successful when non-whites share responsibility and are involved throughout the entire operation."

From the very beginning, however, the Chicago Plan was plagued with certain weaknesses. In the first place, it was signed by the contractors' association and the Building Trades Council and not by the individual unions and employers. Accordingly, the unions always claimed that they had not agreed to do anything inasmuch as they were not parties to the agreement. Second, the agreement was predicated upon the willingness of Mayor Richard Daley, a member of the plan's administrative committee, to enforce it. A third problem, which plagued all the hometown plans, related to the conditional nature of the agreement. These plans were carefully qualified so as to obligate the employment of minorities in specific numbers if "economic conditions" permitted. In Chicago, and inevitably elsewhere, the committees of unions and employers which have had to make such economic determinations have been extremely cautious.

Finally, the Chicago Plan, while it spoke in terms of numbers for an overall commitment by the Chicago Building Trades Council and the employers, did not give goals and timetables for each individual craft. The Philadelphia Plan had done this, and indeed most of the subsequent hometown plans have done it. Quite obviously, commitments obligating the trowel trades and the Laborers Union to improve their minority participation have relatively little significance. The focus of any plan in the construction industry must be upon the mechanical trades from which blacks and other racial minorities are traditionally excluded. The Chicago Plan provided no commitment whatsoever to move forward in these areas. Accordingly, the statements of Meany, Haggerty and Shultz must be regarded as public relations efforts.

Even C. T. Vivian, at that time the leader of the black Coalition for United Community Action, said, "It [The Chicago Plan] will open the seventies to a myriad of possibilities for the black community."[22]

While the Nixon administration was quick to lavish substantial amounts of financial assistance upon the plan—more than $500,000 was bestowed in May 1970, and more than $850,000 during the first eighteen months of its existence—union footdragging soon began to make the accord of January 1970 look hollow and false.

In May 1971, the *New York Times* reported that the plan was "on the brink of failure,"[23] and during the next month its "collapse" was referred to in newspaper reports.[24] Assistant Secretary of Labor Arthur Fletcher stated that the Department of Labor had "no other option" but to impose quotas and that the question was not whether they would be imposed but under what circumstances.[25]

In the summer of 1971 a Department of Labor task force met with representatives of labor, management, and the minority community in Chicago and noted that there were few "hard data available regarding placement of minority group persons in the several trades or identification of their present status." Of seventy-two reported placements, the task force was able to contact only forty-four persons and of these only five were employed at the time of contact. When the task force asked the president of the Chicago Building Trades Council, Tom Nayder, to supply the names and addresses of reported placements, he replied that a "written request" from the Office of Federal Contract Compliance was necessary. A 1971 report compiled by the task force noted: "He [Nayder] further stated that it would probably require a court order to secure this information from the individual crafts because the crafts did not like membership information 'floating around' and other vague reasons."[26] Some of the unions, including the Structural Ironworkers and Sprinkler Fitters, refused even to meet with the operations committee of the Chicago Plan itself. Only the programs of the Pipefitters and Operating Engineers showed any measure of affirmative action. The report came to the following conclusions:

1. The Chicago Plan has not developed a working relationship between the three parties of the Plan. A grave distrust prevails among them. Moreover, all three parties agreed that the Plan has not worked.
2. The Chicago Plan has failed to produce any meaningful jobs at all levels in the construction industry.
3. The Chicago Plan has failed to establish goals for new minority employment from the individual crafts.
4. The Chicago Plan has failed to maintain suitable records of alleged minority placement.
5. The Chicago Plan has failed to provide proper follow-up on minority placements.
6. The nearly $1 million in federal and state funds being expended to support the Chicago Plan have done little to improve the entry of minority workers into the construction industry.[27]

Yet, despite the report and Assistant Secretary of Labor Fletcher's statements, nothing was done by the government. The difficulties were immense, and three groups were responsible: (1) an administration that was lethargic in implementing its programs and indeed hostile to civil rights efforts—now increasingly involved in its new "hard-hat" alliance with Peter Brennan of New York City, soon to become secretary of labor in the second Nixon administration; (2) the building trades in Chicago, whose recalcitrance eventually prompted the Justice Department to file pattern and practice suits against them in the summer of 1972; (3) the Black Coalition which, unlike Seattle's United Construction Workers Association, was composed in large part of some rather disreputable characters who had little interest in civil rights but much enthusiasm for lining their own pockets. The gangs who had seized the Building Trades Council's office in 1969 were hardly interested in or expert at implementing the plan.

Finally, on October 18, 1972, a new Chicago Plan was executed.[28] It was signed by the Building Trades Council, the Building Construction Employers Association of Chicago, and, a new party, the Chicago Urban League. But this plan, contrary to Secretary Fletcher's previous assertions, did not contain imposed quotas and it, too, failed. As Secretary of Labor Brennan was later to admit: "From its inception, the New Chicago Plan was plagued by the inability of the New Chicago Plan participants to voluntarily devise by negotiation and implement an effective affirmative action program. Although all of the parties demonstrated a good faith effort to create a workable and effective affirmative action program, there were too many issues which could not be resolved through good faith negotiation."[29]

Accordingly, without assessing blame or fault on any party, the Department of Labor and the Office of Federal Contract Compliance eventually—on December 19, 1973—imposed a plan in Chicago, the birthplace of the voluntary hometown plan approach.[30] The significance of this step is even more dramatic when one recognizes that (1) former Secretary of Labor Brennan, who was a former president of the Building Trades Council of New York City, had to initiate the action; (2) the statistics for minority participation in Chicago were lower than the national average for the period.[31] The Sprinkler Fitters Union, for instance, had absolutely no minority members, and minority participation in the Sheetmetal Workers was 0.1 percent. Of the Plumbers and Pipefitters Union the minority share was 1.7 percent, and that of the Ironworkers 1.8 percent. Only in the IBEW did the percentage (4.0) compare favorably with nationwide statistics. Accordingly, after more than four years of press announcements and maneuvering by officials in the Nixon administration, the building trades, and the AFL-CIO civil rights department, Chicago is now under an imposed plan.

Boston

Three organizations have played principal roles in the development of equal employment opportunity plans in Boston: the Urban League, the United Community Construction Workers (UCCW), an all-black organization of construction workers representing twenty-six trades, and the Workers Defense League, later renamed the Recruitment and Training Institute, which is part of the A. Philip Randolph Institute. Boston was one of the first cities to develop a voluntary hometown plan, during the summer of 1970, but it has been beset with tension and conflict for the past few years.

Unlike the UCWA in Seattle, the UCCW in Boston has in effect asserted jurisdiction over a number of trades as a "black union." The difficulties, predictably, are that the trades are those to which blacks traditionally have access and the geographical location is exclusively the ghetto areas of Boston, such as Roxbury. The Boston Plan is an attempt to bring minorities into the trades—the skilled mechanical trades foremost among them. But it has suffered from many of the same deficiencies as Chicago, although on balance, it represents one of the best efforts of its kind in the United States.

The plan, a tripartite agreement with the minority community involved, was approved in July 1970,[32] but did not really get off the ground until late the following fall, at which time the Construction Jobs Program of Boston (CJPS), a non-profit corporation, subcontracted recruitment, counseling and orientation of black journeymen and trainees to the Workers Defense League.

In July 1971, a fairly comprehensive audit of the Boston Plan[33] was done to determine whether it had met its goal of 350 placements for all the trades. Only 263 of these placements could be verified by governmental officials. Moreover, the audit gave no indication as to (1) the time of year at which a minority worker listed as a placement had been admitted; (2) the number of hours he had worked during that year; or (3) the number of whites who had been admitted in any capacity to the unions during that period of time. As the result of the problems exposed by the audit, as well as the built-in tensions between UCCW and a program which did not take into account the felt needs of a "black union," a substantial amount of controversy erupted during the late summer and fall of 1971. The Nixon administration determined that the answer was to make the plan a bilateral one, excluding the minority community.[34] In part the theory was that the latter was itself divided and thus its inclusion in the plan simply exaggerated conflict.

In response to the deficiencies of both Boston Plans, the Commonwealth of Massachusetts, acting through its Department of Transportation, proposed a plan of its own in light of the fact that the minority committee did not in any way participate in the Boston Plan II.[35*] It did so because of some of the problems cited above and also because the Massachusetts Commission Against Discrimination had not been provided with any of the information required for an evaluation of the plan. (The commission is an independent agency and less political than the Department of Transportation, which possesses contract compliance responsibility.) Finally the Department of Transportation was critical of the fact that in both Washington and Boston the Office of Federal Contract Compliance has continuously gone through organizational changes and has never been adequately staffed.

The Commonwealth plan did not aim to affect the unions directly but rather to establish quotas for minority workers at job sites located in predominantly minority communities such as Roxbury, Dorchester, and some areas of South Boston.[36*] The objective was to implement the numerical objectives of both Boston Plans more effectively, and no "good faith" escape route was to be permitted contractors who did not adhere to the quotas established. Thus Massachusetts, like the cities of San Francisco and New York, has attempted to move forward with a plan which is more ambitious than the voluntary hometown plans. The Department of Labor, under Brennan, attempted to withhold federal funds and invalidate the plan in court on the grounds that (1) the federal government preempts this field of regulation; and (2) the Massachusetts Plan provided for unlawful quotas. Both contentions were rejected by the First Circuit Court of Appeals[37]—in a case in which the Supreme Court denied certiorari.[38]

Detroit

In Detroit, as in Boston, a black union, Local 124 Allied Workers of America, became embroiled in jurisdictional disputes with the AFL-CIO building trades in 1968 and 1969. Some of its leaders were tied to members of the Ad Hoc Construction Coalition, which presented demands to the Detroit AFL-CIO in the late summer and fall of 1969. But negotiations between the black community, the building trades and the federal government—represented principally by the Department of Housing and Urban Development (HUD)—were plagued by the fact that the Ad Hoc Construction Coalition was dominated by black entrepreneurs. A leadership split soon developed between them and the black trade unionists, who were more interested in employment and also more willing to compromise with the unions.

Threatening work stoppages in the fall of 1969 and engaging in confrontations with the building trades leadership, the Ad Hoc Construction Coalition made the following demands: (1) that the Association of General Contractors (AGC) insure that 50 percent of all building tradesmen on government-funded projects be black; (2) that 50 percent of all subcontractors on government-funded projects be black; (3) that funds be earmarked for a special training program by the Association of General Contractors; (4) that the AGC insure that a percentage of profits from construction projects utilizing public funds be "invested in a black bonding company for the purpose of bonding black contractors"; (5) that 50 percent of union pension funds, union dues and insurance, and other financial investments be deposited in black financial institutions; (6) that 50 percent of all U.S. Department of Labor funds allocated for Detroit be deposited in black financial institutions.[39] Thus the unions were able to say that much of the Detroit leadership was interested in gain for itself in the negotiations. This problem, coupled with the resistance of the building trades and the equivocation of HUD, stalled the implementation of any plan until 1971.[40*]

Essentially, the deficiencies in the plan that emerged, which was vigorously supported by black trade unionists including UAW staffers, related both to the conditional nature of the promises ("when economic conditions permit") and to the fact that control of the selection process was held by the very same unions that had engaged in discrimination previously.

But a new problem arose—one which resembles current problems reflected in the steel and trucking industry consent decrees. The unions sought a *quid pro quo*. The Detroit building trades attempted to coerce the Michigan Civil Rights Commission into relinquishing, in exchange for the plan, its jurisdiction over contract compliance performance by contractors. This attempt was vigorously and properly resisted by Chairman Julian Cook of the Michigan Civil Rights Commission.[41]

Although the plan eventually came into existence, it would appear as though the skeptics, foremost among whom was Chairman Cook, were correct in their assessment. A Department of Labor OFCC audit in October 1972[42*] indicated that none of the trades were meeting their goals and that none of the mechanical trades were even meeting the 50 percent level which OFCC equates with a "good faith" effort. For instance, while the Electricians had a goal of thirty-three placements, they had placed only fourteen workers, or 37 percent. The Operating Engineers reached 32 percent of their goal in placements. The Plumbers placed only 24 percent of their goal and the Pipefitters 6 percent. The Sheetmetal Workers had a 29 percent achievement record, and the Ironworkers and Reinforced Ironworkers placed absolutely no blacks or minorities at all. At this point, the Detroit Plan must be regarded as a failure.

Pittsburgh

In the summer of 1969, Pittsburgh was the center of the disturbances that rivaled those in Chicago. Black civil rights groups and white sympathizers demonstrated in the downtown streets, disrupted traffic, and scuffled with police on a bridge. On August 26, 180 persons were arrested and 45 were injured. The next day the United States Steel Corporation and its $100-million, sixty-four-story building in the downtown area were the target of demonstrators. On September 15, 4,000 blacks and whites marched through downtown Pittsburgh to dramatize their demands for jobs in the skilled trades. While there was no violence, "the well-publicized action, with the possibility of renewed violence, led many shoppers to stay home."[43]

In early 1970, a plan was negotiated among some leaders of the black community, the building trades, and the contractors.[44*] But difficulties soon developed, and in April 1971, after criticisms had been leveled at the plan by black trainees, the Department of Labor requested a report. The story, as reflected in the Department of Labor audit for the fall of 1972, was a familiar one.[45] For the mechanical trades signatory to the plan the percentages in terms of the goals were as follows: Plumbers, 50; Sprinkler Fitters, 50; Sheetmetal Workers, 0; Steamfitters, 46; IBEW, 16.

Indianapolis

Without street demonstrations, the Indianapolis Black Coalition (which included moderate traditional civil rights organizations as well as the Black Panthers) negotiated a voluntary hometown plan in the spring of 1970.[46*] The Black Coalition was less diffuse than its counterpart in Boston and exhibited more strength in connection with follow-up and administration than did the Chicago coalition. Indianapolis is particularly interesting because, on the one hand, its statistical record is much better than those of most other cities, and on the other, the experience under the plan's first two years demonstrated some of the serious deficiencies with the entire hometown approach.

The Indianapolis Plan was fortunate to have an experienced and dedicated black trade unionist, Herman Walker, as its chief mover. Walker did not hesitate to call upon federal agencies including the Department of Justice for assistance in instituting litigation against the building trades when they proved to be recalcitrant—as they fairly often did. One of the problems was trade union resistance to the slotting in of black trainees who had experience. The unions seriously questioned the value of such experience and resisted the trainee concept (which is supposed to be one of the main benefits of the hometown plan) as a back-door evasion of the apprenticeship program.

A second area of conflict was exposed when some black workers dropped out of the trainee program, and Walker took the position that replacements should be recruited immediately so that when jobs became available in the spring such workers would be prepared to accept employment. The proposal was that some kind of stipend should be provided for them during the winter months, prior to the opening of job opportunities. The IBEW's position was that this could not be done, because there were no employment opportunities at the time that admission was being sought. This points up one of the principal problems of the hometown plan. Unless trainees are accepted, and accepted at a time when the economy is down, black workers do not get into the training pipeline. When the boom comes, there is inevitably a shortage of workers, and some gain admittance to the unions through the back door. Invariably, those who do so are white inasmuch as recruitment is done on a friends-and-relatives word-of-mouth basis. And this is most likely to happen when an artificial shortage has been deliberately created in advance of the upswing. One answer is financial assistance for workers who come in during the winter months, to tide them over until the spring. It is quite clear that there will continue to be substantial union resistance to such proposals.

Unlike most other hometown plan leaders from the minority community, who are extremely anxious to please the craft unions to gain their cooperation and also financial support from the Department of Labor, Walker vigorously sought legal assistance when the unions balked. This fact is undoubtedly partially responsible for the relatively good percentage records of the mechanical trades in meeting their placement goals, according to the 1972 Department of Labor audit: Electrical Workers, 68 percent, Ironworkers, 77.5, Operating Engineers, 74, Sheetmetal Workers, 56, and Steamfitters, 60.[47]

New York City

New York City has been one of the focal centers in the disputes about the hometown plans. In 1964, three Puerto Ricans and one Negro tried without success to join Plumbers Union Local 2 on the 25-million-dollar New York City Terminal Market project at Hunts Point in the Bronx. The *New York Times* on May 4, 1964, quoted one of them:

"When I went to the union to apply for membership," Mr. Borges related, "they said: 'Well, first you have to go and get a job in a union shop and then come back.' So I went to a union shop and was told: 'First you have to be a member of the union; so you get your membership.' So . . . what can you do? They work together to keep you out."[48]

President Johnson eventually became involved in this matter, instructing Secretary of Labor Wirtz to intervene so as to "see what could be done" to resolve the controversy. Because Local 2 is AFL-CIO President Meany's home local, he also became involved. As A. H. Raskin wrote in the *New York Times:*

The red flag to the civil rights organizations in the Bronx dispute was Mr. Meany's declaration that he stood unreservedly behind the refusal of the local's members to work with non-union men. He said he would tear up his own card in the local if they ever departed from that stand.

What the Negro groups found most puzzling about the Meany statement was the contrast between it and one he had made in 1960 when Local #26 of the International Brotherhood of Electrical Workers in Washington was refusing to let in Negroes.

At that time, the AFL-CIO President said he would personally recruit non-union electricians to work on Federal office buildings if the local did not end its defiance of anti-discrimination recommendations by the Eisenhower Administration. The electrical local finally opened its ranks under combined government and labor pressure.

The difference between the 1960 situation and the New York Plumbers' conflict as Mr. Meany saw it was that the first genuinely involved bias against Negroes and the second did not. He felt that the three Puerto Ricans and a Negro whose employment caused the trouble in the Bronx were pawns in an attempt by some elements in the civil rights movement to subject him and his home local to unwarranted embarrassment.[49]

In 1968, the administration of Mayor John Lindsay began to hold up city contracts through its Contract Compliance Division because Local 28 Sheetmetal Workers International Association had not reported any Negroes qualified as journeyman mechanics among its more than 3,000 members.[50] Like Local 2, Local 28 had earlier become embroiled in controversy surrounding equal employment opportunity: it had refused to admit black applicants to apprenticeship positions after they performed so well on an examination that the union leadership surmised that they had been provided with the test in advance of taking it.[51] This dispute was eventually litigated in the New York State courts, and the blacks were admitted. But another mechanical trades union had made known its fierce resistance to any change in this area.

In 1969, negotiations began with a view toward establishing a plan for "construction jobs for minority-group workers as the result of four months of union negotiations."[52] The negotiations were announced in April, a few months in advance of the discussions relating to the Philadelphia Plan and others like it. Although the statistics that were accumulated in 1970[53] with regard to minority membership in mechanical trades were better overall than many of the comparable figures in other cities (8.2 percent were black), in unions such as the Plumbers (in which 0.3 percent of the members were black), the figures were as bad or worse. Moreover, the 10.2 percent figure reported for the IBEW was deceptive because most of the black members did not hold cards which entitled them to work on lucrative high rise commercial construction. Finally, figures for some unions, for example, the Sheetmetal Workers, were not reported at all.

On March 22, 1970, the New York City Plan was announced.[54] While the Workers Defense League agreed to be involved in assisting committees in screening applicants, the plan was developed by the New York Building and Construction Industry Board or Urban Affairs, a joint labor and management trustee organization composed of the Building and Construction Trades Council of Greater New York, the Building Trades Employers Association of New York, and the General Contractors Association of New York. The plan's announced goal was the introduction of 800 minority trainees during its first year.[55] The length of the training program was to be determined by the amount of experience the individual possessed upon entrance. Here, again, the concept was that minorities would enter the trades through a route other than apprenticeship. On March 23, the *Wall Street Journal* noted the following:

The New York Plan was immediately dubbed this city's answer to the Philadelphia Plan, a Labor Department effort aimed at getting more minority group members into the construction field. That Plan stipulated that on contracts involving more than $500,000, and involving federal funds, the bidders must take "affirmative action" to train and hire a minority member. The Plan was opposed by both unions and contractors but the Labor Department threatened to extend it to other cities unless other cities came up with proposals of their own.

Advocates of the New York Plan claimed it is a better approach. One main difference is that in the Philadelphia Plan, once a project is completed, the minority group member is right back where he started from. The New York Plan would avoid that shortcoming, they said, because it involves continuing training programs instead of a single project, on-the-job training that the other plan suggested.[56]

But the NAACP in New York labeled the plan a "hoax."[57] Subsequent events were to make their characterization appear more accurate than that of the plan's advocates.

It was not until December 1970 that Governor Nelson Rockefeller and Mayor Lindsay agreed to finance the program, a *sine qua non* for the building trades, which have always insisted that others pay for the recruitment of minorities into previously exclusionary trades. Moreover, unions such as Local 3 IBEW, Local 2 Plumbers, and Steamfitters Local 638 refused to sign up with the plan at all, contending that their apprenticeship programs were in accord with the law and that nothing more was required—even though the last mentioned two unions have been the object of litigation brought by both the federal and the state government. As a result, the *New York Post* noted on March 10, 1971, that "no new traffic lights have been installed in the city since February 1 because of a refusal by electrical contractors to meet the terms" of the New York City Plan and that the "city has withheld more than twenty contracts for refusals to meet the Plan's requirements."[58] On April 10, the *New York Times* noted that city officials reported that more than $55 million in construction contracts "were being held up because of a failure of four building trades unions and contractors dealing with them, to comply with on-the-job training programs for members of minority groups.[59] On July 15, the Lindsay administration announced that more than two hundred million dollars in construction projects for schools, libraries, and firehouses had been held up to pressure the unions. On September 18, construction funds were unfrozen but one of the unions, Local 28 Sheetmetal Workers, was still refusing to bow to city pressure. According to Eleanor Holmes Norton, New York City Human Rights Commission chairman, the union's minority membership was "incredibly poor,"; she noted that the local's 3,386 members included only 44 black and Spanish-surnamed journeymen.[60] But by the following summer the New York City Plan was being denounced as a "failure" and "sham"—a "public relations gimmick dreamed up by Lindsay to con unemployed blacks and Puerto Ricans.''[61] At that point, although the plan had been in existence for eighteen months, not even half the 800 minority training positions projected for the first year had been filled. On July 26, the regional director of the United States Commission on Civil Rights said, ''As far as we are concerned the New York City Plan is dead.''[62] He made this remark on the basis of information given at a City Council hearing, to the effect that only 297 training positions had been produced and only 22 of the persons so trained had been permitted to join the construction unions involved. On July 29, a *New York Times* editorial stated:

Failure has marked the end of the road for another over-touted effort by construction labor and management in this city to prove that the walls excluding blacks and Puerto Ricans from skilled building trades can be leveled without governmental compulsion. The New York Plan, launched with effusive and even then clearly excessive praise by Governor Rockefeller and Mayor Lindsay a year and a half ago, seems to have produced fewer than 300 training opportunities in an industry that normally employs upward of 150,000 craftsmen and laborers. Worse still, according to testimony by assorted experts at a City Council hearing this week, only 22 blacks and Puerto Ricans actually got into construction unions through the plan's operation.

This slack accomplishment came despite a four-month freeze on $200 million in city construction for such needed projects as schools, libraries, and fire houses, which the Mayor ordered in the hope that it would spur laggard locals to join the plan and ensure fulfillment of the decidedly modest goals originally set.

Most of the breakthroughs being made in opening access to construction unions here are still coming under the coercion of Federal court orders. So far as the New York Plan was concerned, its most conspicuous product was bickering over why the city and state were not making government funds available faster to create overhead jobs for union-selected functionaries. But the Plan cannot be rated a total flop. Its original chief administrator has gone off to the White House to serve as special labor advisor to President Nixon.[63]

In the fall of 1972, increased pressure was mounted against Mayor Lindsay to abandon the New York City Plan. Characterizing it as ''short-sighted'' and ''piece-meal,'' Manhattan Borough President Percy E. Sutton stated that Mayor Lindsay had ''taken a big step backward in the struggle of black and Latin workers to secure employment in the construction industry'' and that the plan would ''do little to turn back the tide of racism in the construction trades.''[64] The Lindsay administration admitted that New York had not met its goal of 800 trainees but asserted that it had done a better job than other cities. On January 12, 1973, however, Lindsay announced that the city was immediately withdrawing from the New York City Plan because it was ''very disappointed'' with the plan's results. He requested that the Department of Labor mandate goals and timetables, as is their practice where there is no hometown plan.

Three months later the Lindsay administration itself issued new regulations providing for goals and timetables in connection with construction sites in the city, both private and public.[65] The new regulations provided (1) that minority workers be given jobs and work hours to comport with their percentage of the population; (2) that contractors place one apprentice for every journeyman in each building trades craft; (3) that contractors seek union pledges to advance graduate apprentices to journeyman status; (4) that contractors insure that unions accept new minority apprentices at the rate of one minority apprentice for every three non-minority. But in the summer of 1973, Secretary of Labor Peter Brennan circulated a memorandum among the heads of all federal agencies responsible for the allocation of federal construction money, asserting that state and local attempts to police discriminatory construction contractors were in "conflict" with federally approved hometown plans.[66]* Legal action was commenced against this attempt to coerce more ambitious state and local plans in New York City, Detroit, Seattle, Oakland, and Boston. The resulting court decisions have been contrary to the position taken by the Secretary of Labor.

In the first case dealing with the issue, *Associated General Contractors* v. *Altshuler,*[67] Judge Coffin, speaking for the First Circuit, rejected the view that the Department of Labor through promulgation of the Boston Plan preempted the field so as to void a plan put forward by the Commonwealth of Massachusetts. Said Judge Coffin:

Nothing in the President's Executive Order requires that affirmative action taken under the Order be uniform throughout the country, nor does it necessitate that the federal government be the source for every program. An important aspect of federal implementation is the development of "hometown" plans, conceived and developed by local contractors, unions, and minority representatives. And in at least one instance the federal government has relied upon a plan originally conceived by state officials for their own state funded contracts.[68]

Accordingly, the court rejected the view that the Massachusetts Plan presented a challenge to the supremacy clause. Judge Coffin said:

The only place where the two plans might be found slightly incompatible is in the area of trade union referrals. Recognizing that union reluctance to admit minorities to apprenticeship programs has been one primary reason for the small percentage of minorities in the construction trades, The Boston Plan focusses upon encouraging area-wide minority recruitment in two of the unions, and therefore does not alter the patterns of contractor reliance upon the unions for referrals. The Commonwealth's §1B, however, facilitates referrals from sources other than unions by providing alternative mechanisms for recruiting minority workers.

We think, however, that there is little likelihood that §1B would discourage union initiative in training and recruiting minorities. The Commonwealth's program will operate on a small scale, only within neighborhoods with a high minority population; the contractors for the Boston College project are required to employ thirty minority workers. The federal Boston Plan is designed to train and place sixty minority workers each year drawn from all over the state. Therefore, despite the Commonwealth's program, building trades unions will be obligated to continue their efforts at recruiting minority workers and referring them to contractors. Furthermore, the Commonwealth's program does not prohibit union referrals. It merely provides other sources for referrals. Thus, §1B might actually induce a stepped-up program of union recruitment if the unions are desirous of maintaining contractor reliance upon union referrals.[69]

Judge Lasker reached a similar conclusion in dealing with the New York City Plan and the attempts by Secretary of Labor Brennan to argue the same position. Said Judge Lasker: "We believe it to be settled beyond dispute that the federal government has not preempted the entire field of equal employment regulation."[70]

The court rejected the view that simply because Mayor Lindsay's plan was more demanding than the New York City Plan, the two were inconsistent for the purpose of the supremacy clause. In concluding that the Brennan memorandum was invalid on its face, Judge Lasker noted:

The New York Plan obliges the participating industries to place up to 1,000 minority persons in a training program annually, whereas the Mayor's Plan requires individual contractors to provide on-the-job training to one minority trainee for every four journeymen hired (a ratio which without question will cause the placement of at least 1,000 persons). In addition, the Mayor's Plan promotes a number of objectives not covered by the New York Plan including, for example, achieving specified minority man hour goals, advancement of minority members to journeyman pay scale and status and employment of minority-owned subcontractors. Furthermore, the Mayor's Plan provides for sanctions against the contractors who do not make good faith efforts to comply with its requirements, whereas, under the New York Plan mere agreement to abide by its provisions is deemed to constitute compliance.[71]

The decisions of Judge Coffin and Judge Lasker proved important in blocking the Nixon administration's attempt to assist the building trades and contractors in using the hometown plan as a shield against living up to federal and state equal employment obligations. New York, more than any other city, triggered the resistance to former Secretary of Labor Brennan's sponsorship of the hometown plans.

12 | The Impact of Judicial Decrees: An Empirical Analysis

In employment discrimination litigation, nothing is more significant than the actual impact of judicial decrees. True, the mere institution of litigation and the formulation of a decree radiate consequences which affect others besides the parties directly involved in the case. But in the final analysis, the respect for the law and its potential as an instrument of reform of unlawful employment practices are dependent upon the actual impact of decrees subsequent to their promulgation. This, it seems to me, is the lesson of the Seattle decree discussed in Chapter 13. For only through an understanding of the institutions and their response to court orders can the law be properly analyzed.

Since there is relatively little experience with public employee unions and Title VII as it applies to state and local government, inasmuch as the statute was amended to cover such parties only in 1972, this chapter will concentrate on decrees dealing with the problem of access to the labor market through apprenticeship and referral in the building trades. This area has seen many important and extensively monitored decrees, which provide the kind of data needed for a study of the actual impact of these judicial promulgations. We will examine a variety of decrees, beginning with the least complicated early Title VII litigation through court orders which are more comprehensive and detailed than that of Judge Lindberg in *United States* v. *Local 86, Ironworkers.*

United States v. *Sheetmetal Workers Local 36* (St. Louis)

In this Justice Department suit against Local 36, Sheetmetal Workers and Local 1, IBEW, the trial court found that both locals had excluded blacks prior to 1964. At the time of oral argument, Local 1 had approximately sixteen black members. It did not accept its first Negro apprentice until February 1966, and there was no record of its referring a black for employment before March of that year. Local 36, Sheetmetal Workers had no Negro members at the time of the trial. It had 1,275 white members and accepted its second and third Negro apprentices in 1967. There was no record of any Negro having used the union's hiring hall prior to the date of the trial.

The relief formulated by the Eighth Circuit on September 16, 1969, in *Sheetmetal Workers* seemed reasonably broad at the time.[1]* The court required the modification of the referral system so that blacks reasonably qualified to perform the ordinary work of a journeyman craftsman could be placed in the local's highest priority group for referral, Group 1. Those blacks who gained the requisite experience within the next five years were to be given the same opportunity to move ahead into Group 1 as they qualified. Negroes without construction experience who were beyond the apprenticeship age and who were residents in the area could be placed in Group 1 if they passed an objective journeyman's examination even though they had "other than journeyman construction experience." Also, blacks "without construction experience who are beyond the apprenticeship age shall, upon request to the Local, if they are shown to have other reasonably comparable experience" move into lower priority groups on the basis of such experience. Said the court:

Reasonable steps shall be taken to make it known to the Negro community that all persons are now permitted to use the referral system without respect to race, color or creed.

In requiring the modifications, we impose no quotas, we grant no preferences.

Nor do we deprive any non-Negro craftsmen of bona fide seniority rights. Each such craftsman will remain in the group to which he is now assigned and will move to a higher group when he has satisfied the ability requirements. We do make it possible, however, for qualified Negroes—those who have been deprived of the opportunity to gain experience in the construction industry or to gain experience under the collective bargaining agreement— to be placed in the group where they will have an equal opportunity to be referred for work.[2]

The court also reformed the eligibility-for-membership requirements of both locals. It required that examinations must be objective, although it refused to strike down the membership vote requirement inasmuch as discrimination had not been evidenced in connection with that procedure.

Finally, noting that Negroes had been excluded from membership in both locals until 1966, that both locals had historically given preference to relatives of members, and "that individual union members will inevitably continue to talk with their sons about opportunities available to them in the trades," the court held that current publicity efforts by the local aimed at informing blacks of apprenticeship opportunities fell short of what was necessary to meet the standards of effectiveness, thoroughness, and frequency. Said the Eighth Circuit, perhaps prophetically:

We recognize that the best of publicity programs will not fully convince Negroes that they now have the opportunity to qualify for apprenticeship training. We also recognize that no such program can hope to be as effective as parental guidance, but a good public information program can help to persuade the doubtful and the skeptical that the discriminatory bars have been removed. Such a program is mandatory.[3]

The decree was eventually signed in consent form on December 22, 1969. (A consent decree is agreed upon by the parties and approved by the court.) Over three years later, very little had been accomplished as a result of it. As of January 11, 1972, Local 36, Sheetmetal Workers had only two black journeymen, and had enrolled five black apprentices in a program which included between 110 and 130 apprentices. According to a Justice Department report, insofar as publicity was concerned, "a number of semi-annual advertisements were printed in local papers with little effect." Moreover, said the report, "several letters were addressed to local high school counselors in predominantly black schools."[4*]

Up to 1972, of the total number of persons who applied for referral, 2.02 percent were black (35 out of 1,760). Out of 1,463 referrals, 23 of them, or 1.5 percent, were made for black workers. Of 139 individuals applying for the Sheetmetal Workers' apprenticeship program, only 15, or 10.79 percent, were black.

Regarding Local 1, IBEW, the Justice Department reported: "News releases, Newspaper ads and speaker program requirements were followed with little result." While a substantial number of blacks, 93, were assigned to group 1 between April 1970 and April 1972, they received an infinitesimally small percentage of the number of referrals, 112 out of 6,114 or 1.83 percent. (Similarly, in Seattle, the admission of blacks to apprenticeship under a quota system, as required by the decree discussed in the next chapter, was rendered substantially less significant by referral discrimination which discouraged them from remaining in the apprenticeship program.) Ten out of 19 black applicants had been accepted for membership in the construction classifications in Local 1, but only 7 (or 9.58 percent) of the 73 apprentices completing the program were black. And while membership seemed to be on the upswing, quite obviously the number of dropouts would also rise in all categories because of the discouragingly small percentage of black referrals. As the Justice Department stated in its memorandum: "The decree has proven totally impotent."[5]

The Local 36 decree was one of the earliest. It did not provide for quotas, institutional reform of referral practices (beyond seniority credits for those who had been excluded), or journeyman-apprentice ratios as did *Local 86*. There was no mention of back pay or punitive damages. This decree was therefore doomed to inadequacy from the outset.

United States v. *Local 38, International Brotherhood of Electrical Workers* (Cleveland)

Ray Marshall notes that "Local 38 defied concerted efforts by Negro electricians to get into the union over a period of forty years."[6] Agitation to break down Local 38's barriers began in 1917, and eventually blacks turned to the law, first to the Cleveland Community Relations Board, then in the 1950's to the President's Committee on Government Contracts, and eventually to the Justice Department. Before the Justice Department's involvement, the AFL-CIO and its Civil Rights Committee attempted to intervene. "Finally, Local 38 admitted three Negroes to membership on the last day of June, 1957, after President Meany told the Local to admit the Negroes by July 1 or lose its charter. The Local showed its continued defiance, however, by refusing to admit the man who filed the complaint with the Community Relations Board. Significantly, by July 1964 Local 38 had taken in no more journeymen, Negro or white, and the three Negroes admitted in 1957 were the first journeymen admitted in twelve years."[7]

When the Justice Department became involved, it reported that out of the total of 1,260 members, only two were black. The district court in *Local 38,* however, was confronted with a new political administration in the union, under which "all discriminatory practices had stopped as a result of good faith efforts"[8] following the Civil Rights Act of 1964. Accordingly, the court had refused to order affirmative relief to root out the present effects of past discrimination and, moreover, refused the Justice Department's request that it retain jurisdiction. The evidence before the court at the time of trial was that as of July 1, 1967, Local 38 had 1,316 white members and 2 black members; as of October 1 of the same year there were 1,329 white members and 3 black members and as of September 25, 1968, there were 1,331 white members and 4 black members.

The Sixth Circuit reversed the district court's refusal to order affirmative relief *in United States* v. *Local 238, IBEW.*[9] The court specifically noted that the anti-preferential treatment provisions of Section 703(j) of Title VII could not be construed as a prohibition of affirmative action relief against present practices which had the effect of continuing past discrimination. Judge George Edwards, speaking for the court, said:

Any other interpretation would allow complete nullification of the stated purposes of the Civil Rights Act of 1964. This could result from the adoption of devices such as a limitation of new apprentices to relatives of the all-white membership of a union[10] . . . or limitation of membership to persons who had previous work experience under union contract, while such experience was racially limited to whites[11] . . . or administration of qualification examinations which had no objective standards and which produced unexplained discriminatory results.[12]

Further on in its opinion, the court noted that discrimination had continued for two years after the effective date of the statute. It cited the statistics given above, and noted that during those two years the local had referred 3,487 persons for work in the electrical trades through its hiring hall, of whom only two were Negroes. The opinion also made mention of the fact that these practices "controlled absolutely who got jobs in the organized electrical trades in the Cleveland area" inasmuch as 75 percent of all electrical construction was done under Local 38's contract. With regard to the district court's finding that the new officers of the local favored voluntary compliance, the court stated:

These facts, however, do not in our opinion warrant the District Court's refusal to retain jurisdiction of this case or its refusal of affirmative relief. The record of compliance is very brief—particularly as compared to the long record of discrimination—and even that record has been written under the impact of this litigation. . . . Assuming, as the District Judge plainly did, and as we do, that the new leadership is in utter good faith, it has no mean task ahead in eliminating ingrained discriminatory practices of past decades. In many respects a more specific court order, plus retention of jurisdiction, might serve to support the stated objectives of the new administration of Local 38. And, in any event, such relief is authorized by the Act and called for in this record.[13]

Accordingly, the case was remanded to the district court for further proceedings. On remand,[14] the district court rejected the government's request to eliminate the right of the Local 38 membership to vote upon the acceptance of a journeyman's application. The court stated that no discrimination in this regard had been evidenced in the record and, therefore, there was no basis for eliminating the practice. The decree provided that Local 38 was obliged to give all applicants for referral an application blank and could not require any evidence of past experience and training at that time. Black applicants were to be placed in the various priority groups of Local 38 in a manner similar to that provided for in the *Sheetmetal Workers* order. That is to say, all Negroes who had "a minimum of four years experience in the electrical trade and are residents within the geographical area constituting the normal construction market and have passed an inside journeyman's wireman's examination" given by an IBEW local could be in Group 1. Experience in the trades for the purposes of all groups was to include experience in residential, construction, or maintenance electrical work of either the union or the nonunion variety, or self-employment, or "other employment reasonably related or similar to electrical construction work including such experience in the armed forces, and schooling which is related to the skills required of a jouneyman electrical construction worker."[15] The examination was to be based solely on material contained in the most recent edition of the *National Electrical Code*. The journeyman's examination was to be given semiannually whenever there were applicants. Furthermore,

once a month for the first three months after the entry of this Decree and every six months thereafter, [Local 38] shall place a ¼ page advertisement in the *Call* and *Post* or other newspapers identified with serving the Negro community, describing the work opportunities available through the local, the procedures for obtaining such opportunities and stating that such opportunities are on a non-discriminatory basis. . . . To the extent feasible, Local 38 shall have similar information broadcast by one or more radio stations in the Cleveland area which serve the Negro community.[16]

The joint apprenticeship program was ordered to recruit, receive applications, and evaluate and select applicants so as to give blacks opportunities equal to those of whites. Moreover, the joint apprenticeship committee was ordered to place commercial advertisements in the *Call, Post,* or other appropriate papers, outlining the requirements for the program, the beginning apprenticeship rate of pay, the journeyman scale, the location and business hours of the apprenticeship office, and the equal employment opportunity policy at least once a month for each of the three months preceding the opening date for receipt of applications. The committee was also "obliged to take reasonable steps" to have similar information broadcast by radio stations serving the black community and was to offer to participate in "Career Day" exercises at high schools.

Paragraph 17 stated that "Defendant EJAC [Electrical Joint Apprenticeship Committee] shall select from the Negro applicants for the apprenticeship classes of 1969 and 1970 four additional Negro apprentices who shall be initiated and indentured in the apprenticeship class of September 1970."[17] Finally, perhaps an indication of the way the wind was to blow in the future, Local 38 was ordered to "cooperate in the formulation, execution and implementation of a Cleveland Area Construction Equal Employment Opportunity Agreement designed to facilitate the entry of Negroes into the Cleveland construction industry."[18]

As of April 11, 1973, Local 38 had a membership of 1,501, with 1,064 of those members working.[19] Of this 1,064, 59 were minority workmen. There were 36 black journeymen, one of them Spanish-speaking. (Twelve black apprentices have become journeymen.) As of 1973, there were 11 minority apprentices and 11 "trainees" who were being referred by Local 38 under the Cleveland Plan.[20] Including apprentices and trainees, the union's minority membership was something on the order of 5 percent. As we have previously noted, trainees have no formal union membership status and simply work on permit. Moreover, no apprenticeship classes were indentured between 1970 and 1973 and even the indenturing of the 1970 class had not been completed. Accordingly, considering the economic conditions that Local 38 was confronted with in Cleveland and the fact that the most recent apprenticeship class was only 25 percent minority, five out of twenty, the picture was not particularly bright. (And according to a Local 38 spokesman, only 10 percent of the apprenticeship classes had been minorities since the new leadership came into office.) In late 1972 and 1973, both the Justice Department and the Cleveland Plan were having considerable difficulties with Local 38 because of its refusal to place trainees on jobs while white journeymen were out of work.

Between September and December of 1972, contractors who had affirmative action obligations to fulfill made eight requests for trainees which were not filled by Local 38. In March 1973, the Herbst Construction Company requested a trainee and was rejected by the Local. On several occasions since then, the Electrical Contractors Association has requested trainees in writing and has been rejected. The response is always the same: no work for black trainees and no future apprentices until more white journeymen get back to work. The Justice Department has rigorously protested this position. And two factors make Local 38's case less persuasive than it might initially appear. The first is that it has been able to dispatch a substantial portion of its journeyman membership to other areas of the country, where they have obtained work. Accordingly, quite a few of the so-called "unemployed" are in fact employed elsewhere. In the second place, at the time that the Sixth Circuit ruling came down in 1970, boom conditions existed and 3,000 workers were employed under the jurisdiction of Local 38 in the Cleveland area. Most of them, of course, came from other parts of the country and worked on permit. But that time would have been excellent—politically and economically—for Local 38 to swell its ranks with black members. It did not take advantage of the opportunity—undoubtedly because it assumed that it was not going to be required to operate under a court order imposing the dictates of Title VII.

That the number of black journeymen in Local 38 did increase from three to thirty-six indicates that Title VII can have a substantial impact upon the conduct of defendants. Yet, like the performance of both Local 1, IBEW, and Local 36,

Sheetmetal Workers, in St. Louis, Local 38's performance, albeit in part attributable to economic conditions, indicates that the early Title VII decrees leave something to be desired.

In *Local 38,* there was no request for judicial scrutiny of the union's decision to refuse to indenture new apprentices—a position which contrasts sharply with the Justice Department's refusal to allow Local 38's exclusion of black trainees in 1973, even though white journeymen were unemployed. The government ought to have taken the same position with regard to apprentices who, after all, enjoy more employment security inside the union, and whose employment opportunities can be influenced through revision of the journeyman-apprentice ratio. Moreover, although the Justice Department was fortunate to have an extremely energetic and competent attorney, Louis Ferrand, in charge of the monitoring, here, as in Seattle and St. Louis, the government did not have a staff of its own in the city. Finally, the government was not successful in obtaining quota relief in *Local 38*—although at least it tried to do so, reversing the position it took before the court in *Local 36* and other Title VII cases in the late 1960's.

It is interesting to compare the progress reports relating to the early decrees with those of some of the more recent ones providing for quotas and timetables which the Justice Department has sought. The most illustrative example is *United States* v. *Steamfitters Local Union No. 250* in Los Angeles, where the department sued on February 7, 1968, and entered into a consent decree in September 1969.[21] The decree provided for no goals or timetables even though the local's membership at the time of the Justice Department inquiry showed no blacks or Chicanos in a membership of 3,000, and the minority percentage of the population in the relevant geographical area is 29 percent (10.8 percent blacks and 18.3 percent Chicano). As of the spring of 1972, after a three-year period, the local had one black journeyman. The advertising and so-called affirmative recruiting—all that was required by the first decree—had accomplished nothing. As the result of this failure, the Justice Department insisted upon the negotiation of another consent decree, which was entered into on May 25, 1972.[22]

This decree, in addition to providing for a "reasonable level of employment" (meaning "a parity in hours worked between blacks and whites working within the union's jurisdiction"), record keeping, and the handling of publicity through civil rights organizations and the California State Employment Service, established two eligibility lists for the joint apprenticeship committee program. The JAC obligated itself to select and indenture two apprenticeship classes a year. Paragraph 10 of the consent decree states the following:

In doing so, the defendant JAC shall select and indenture, and the defendant Local union shall accept and refer to work a sufficient number of qualified black applicants to be sure of a reasonable level of black participation in the apprenticeship program. A reasonable level shall be deemed to mean at least 8 blacks per entering class. . . . The obligation of the JAC . . . shall continue until such time as ten classes have been selected or until at least 80 blacks have been selected and indentured as apprentices.[23]

Up to 1973, in addition to four black journeymen taken in by the local, sixteen blacks and twenty-five whites came in under the program. (Moreover, there are five other blacks who were recruited as apprentices prior to the time of the second consent decree.) Although 20 percent of the apprentices have been on the work list, according to Justice Department sources, since the decree not one black employee has been out of work more than one day. Although the numbers are small considering Local 250's entire jurisdiction (the attrition rate is 2 percent) the progress in a one-year period after the May 1972 decree was in startling contrast to what took place before and more encouraging than the records compiled in either Cleveland or St. Louis.

United States v. Lathers Union, Local No. 46

"This case has been very long in process," said Judge Frankel in discussing the New York *Lathers* litigation.[24]

Local 46, Lathers Union, has exclusive jurisdiction over two types of construction work in New York City and Nassau, Suffolk and Westchester Counties. Metallic lathing and furring, "inside" work, is performed by employees who have completed their apprenticeships. "Outside" work, embracing concrete reinforcing, includes no skills requiring an apprenticeship and constitutes a growing proportion of the union's work. Local 46 members perform both inside and outside work. Members of other locals working under Local 46's jurisdiction are restricted to inside work. Permit holders are not union members and perform only outside work. Although the trade is a declining one, it is nevertheless lucrative. As of 1973, New York City Lathers were paid $401.45 for a 35-hour week and $100 in fringe benefits. Job competition is severe in such circumstances.[25]

Local 46 engaged in certain procedures in connection with its job referral and hiring hall which prompted a Justice Department investigation. Employees obtaining outside work under the union's jurisdiction were supposed to appear personally at the hiring hall and place their name on "sign-in" lists. Members of Local 46, who were nearly all white, did not have to follow this procedure, however; they were permitted to telephone to ask to be referred to jobs in New York City and elsewhere, and the union generally made such referrals. Moreover, Local 46 members could call foremen or employers directly and go to a job site and arrange for a job. Nonmembers could not do this. Local 46 members were preferred in referrals over all other categories of workers, and among permit men, the sons and brothers of members were given preference. Telephone requests for specific permit men, sometimes inexperienced, were made by foremen and deputy foremen and generally granted by business agents.

On May 22, 1968, the United States Attorney in New York City filed suit against Local 46 and its Joint Apprenticeship Committee alleging a pattern of practice of racial discrimination in violation of Title VII. A consent decree was entered into on February 7, 1970,[26] which invalidated the union's 1966 apprentice waiting list and required the Joint Apprenticeship Committee to indenture immediately twenty-five nonwhite apprentices to be referred by minority referral sources which were to include New York City's Fight Back and the Workers Defense League (now known as Recruitment and Training). At the time that the suit was brought, Local 46 had three minority members out of a total of 1,597 and there was 1 minority apprentice among 31. In New York City at that time, 16.6 percent of the population was black and 7.75 percent was Spanish-speaking.

The twenty-five minority apprentices were to be between the ages of 18 and 30 and if any of the twenty-five were terminated before completing the program, the Lathers Union joint apprenticeship committee was obligated to "forthwith indenture another such non-white apprentice, it being the commitment of the JAC and the Union to insure that a total of 25 non-white apprentices shall acquire membership and journeyman status in the Union as a result of this affirmative action apprenticeship program."[27] The apprenticeship program was to be exactly the same for nonwhites as for whites in all respects. Under the consent agreement apprentice applicants were to be selected by a random method and ranked in order of selection.

The consent decree also provided for work permits for apprentice applicants who were on the waiting list. Under the terms of the agreement, employees were to obtain registration on the open employment list which the union established in its hiring hall, and with respect to "job referral from the open employment list, job layoff, job transfer, job assignment, work conditions and overtime, the rules and procedures of the Union shall apply equally to all workmen, and shall afford to Negro workmen employment opportunities equal to those afforded to other workmen."[28] Further, the union obligated itself to develop, within six months of the date of the agreement, objective rules and procedures to implement these equal opportunity provisions. Because of the large number of employees who work within the union's jurisdiction on permit and are not members (applicant apprentices who are on the waiting list constitute only a portion of these work permit holders) the agreement provided for an administrator to be appointed by the court (George Moskowitz, a labor arbitrator and attorney, received the appointment). Part of his duties were set forth as follows:

The Administrator shall as soon as practicable make an objective study of the issues relating to the issue of work permits based upon the needs of the industry and taking into account the purpose of achieving equal employment opportunity, which study may include such factors as the total number of work permits to be issued, the number of permits to be issued from time to time, and the manner of issuance, and based upon such study shall recommend such changes, if any, as he deems advisable in the system for the issuance of permits.[29]

Moreover, the administrator was empowered to establish record-keeping requirements, to remedy any breaches of the agreement, and to decide complaints and questions of interpretation arising under it. The union and the JAC were obligated to pay the administrator compensation and expenses.

On February 24, Judge Frankel of the Southern District of New York approved the consent between the parties and ordered that "failure to comply with this order, including breach of this Agreement shall be punishable as a contempt of court."[30]

Soon after the entering of the decree by the court, approximately 165 blacks obtained work permits, and the twenty-five nonwhite apprentices were indentured by the union. Soon after the 165 blacks had acquired the permits, however, the U.S. Attorney's office began to receive complaints about racial discrimination in the hiring hall. While the union did not have an exclusive hiring hall (indeed, one of the problems that emerged in this litigation was the fact that many whites obtained their jobs outside the hiring hall procedures through their contacts with white foremen), blacks alleged that the union acquiesced in unlawful treatment by employers and did not refer minorities out of the hall fairly. Moreover, in June 1970 the union stopped issuing permits, and no more were issued until 1972. Accordingly, the number of blacks working within the union's jurisdiction began to decline substantially in 1970. Finally, the union came forward with a plan to implement the referral and hiring provisions of the agreement which the U.S. Attorney and the court were later to characterize as "trivial" and insubstantial.

Faced with this sequence of events, the U.S. Attorney's office brought an action in federal court before Judge Frankel for contempt on the ground that the agreement had been violated. The judge noted that:

Defendant Local has displayed only measured enthusiasm for the basic objective of non-discriminatory employment, and its key officers have both permitted and participated in the violations outlined below. The "objective rules and procedures" for which the Local had the duty of initiation remain to be formulated. And, above all, the pattern and practice of discrimination has continued.[31]

Judge Frankel sustained the government's application for contempt relating to referrals of permit holders for outside work but found insufficient evidence for other allegations of contempt. With regard to permit holders, the court noted that on "hundreds of occasions" between May 1 and July 30, 1970, white members of Local 46 and white permit holders obtained outside work in the union's jurisdiction without signing the open employment list. White workers often made their own arrangements for work, bypassing the hiring hall altogether with the "acquiescence and tacit blessing of the Local officers."[32] Said the court:

In some cases of this kind, the foremen were told to have the men come through the hall for the ritual of signing the list; in other cases not even the ritual was observed. In some cases, a white applicant would have a job arranged for him even though he was neither a member of the Local nor a permit holder, and would only thereafter acquire a permit.[33]

Moreover, the court noted what has been perceived in many Title VII cases: even though business agents often rely upon an individual's experience in referring him, the agents did not bother to find out the actual experience of black applicants. As Judge Frankel noted: "In fact, some of the blacks waiting in the hall for referrals were experienced in the work for which experience was relevant. Many white permit holders were sent to jobs although they had no experience whatever while experienced (or equally inexperienced) blacks received no referrals or were referred to inferior jobs.''[34]

In short, the court found a method of referral predicated upon ''pull''—a combination of union membership, nepotism, and friendship. Said Judge Frankel in a memorable passage:

The ''hardest'' evidence in the record may be the combination of statistics and accumulated reports by witnesses showing specific cases of favoritism for whites and discrimination against blacks. But there are matters less quantifiable and less objective in appearance that give point and substance to the whole dreary picture. The attitude of witnesses, the bland show of innocence, the forgetfulness about things that ought to be remembered, the occasional revelations of explicitly racist sentiment, the refusal of one agent to sign the settlement agreement to enforce a regime of nondiscrimination because he thought it was ''rammed down the union's throat by the government,'' the evidence of special and focused nastiness to black men in the hiring hall—such things betray a broad undercurrent of hostility to the decree and the commands of the law giving rise to it.[35]

Accordingly, the court found contempt with regard to referral, and established a deadline for the parties to file with the administrator a proposed set of procedures for fair and neutral referrals from the hiring hall. The court specifically admonished the parties to exclude subjective criteria and assessments of ability and work experience by union business agents to the extent that it was possible to do so. The objective established by Judge Frankel was to have the administrator seek agreement about such procedures. On or before June 28, 1971, he was required to submit to the court agreed-upon rules and procedures or his own recommendations in the absence of agreement. Objections to Moskowitz's proposals were to be filed before the court. In establishing this procedure, the court rejected a proposal urged by the U.S. Attorney's office. Judge Frankel stated the following:

The conclusions of the court concerning the development of rules and procedures will resolve the dispute over the Government's proposal that a decree should be entered now requiring a system of ''first in–first out'' as the mode of handling referrals from the hiring hall. The difficulties with this seemingly simple solution—not least the prospect of early-morning riots at Union headquarters—are indicated in persuasive detail by defendant Local. It is obvious, moreover, that if this could be thought to be a genuinely workable arrangement, the Government would have been remarkably derelict in the period of well over a year since the consent decree. At any rate, the court cannot deem it an acceptable remedy to resolve the complexities and the legitimate differences among the job-seekers by merely decreeing their nonexistence.[36]

On June 2, 1971, the administrator submitted his recommendations for rules and procedures, having been unable to achieve agreement between the parties. On July 16, the court adopted those he submitted, with minor modifications.[37] To deal with the problem of referral, a priority list was established by Article IV(C) which provided for a register for referrals to be kept by the business agents. This was to be a cumulative list of those who had been registered during the previous two weeks and the dates on which workmen did not obtain employment. The workmen whose names appeared on the list more than five times in the two-week period were entitled to priority for referral. The priority sequence among such workers was to be established by the number of days that workmen had not been referred to employment. Employees who were entitled to priority, however, had to take responsibility for recording the fact on the daily hiring hall "sign-in." Moreover, the refusal to accept referral would deprive one of priority entitlement during that day, and when two referrals were refused in any one week the employee would be deemed to have waived priority rights for the following week. If more than one man was entitled to the same priority, the worker who registered earlier in the day was to be referred first.

Furthermore, the procedures attempted to regulate the whites' bypass of the hiring hall by requiring the recording of requests for referrals on forms supplied by the administrator. The union was obliged "not [to] grant an employer's request for referral of a specific individual, other than a foreman or deputy foreman. Nothing contained herein shall limit the Union's obligation to grant employers' requests [pursuant to contract compliance obligations under federal, state or local executive orders] that non-white workmen be referred."[38]

Difficulty with these procedures, however, has proved great and leads this observer to question their adequacy. Under the existing system there are always a substantial number of blacks who have priority. Whites generally are not put on the list because they do not have trouble getting work. They benefit from informal contacts in the industry outside the formal hiring hall. The primary problem relates to those blacks who are relatively far down on the list, say, seventh, eighth, or ninth; it takes them a considerable period of time to get to the top, and some never get there.

In an important provision, Article VIII, of the approved procedures the administrator was made responsible for periodically making computer studies of the union's record and reporting violations thus uncovered. He was to rely on the analysis of the data produced by the studies to revise the procedures. As of the late spring of 1973, however, almost two full years after the procedures were approved by the court, no statistical study of racial participation in the industry had taken place.[39] Accordingly, no basis existed, aside from individual complaints by black members who stated that they were not referred, to determine what pattern, if any, had emerged from the referrals—although the evidence that the U.S. Attorney's office continued to receive during this period indicated that blacks were having an exceedingly difficult time being referred under the "priority entitlement" system.

Meanwhile, the matter of work permits remained unaddressed. Although the initial consent decree had provided for the administrator to study the issuance of permits, taking into account considerations involving equal employment opportunity, no such study had been made at the time of Judge Frankel's holding regarding contempt in May, 1971. And, of course, the work permit issue was very much related to referral, since without a permit, blacks, at least, could not obtain referral on any basis. The administrator ordered that past discrimination be remedied by the issuance of enough permits to minority workers to make the minority percentage of the union eventually the same as that of the population. Blacks were to be given the 165 permits that they had received immediately subsequent to the decree in the first instance, and an additional 125 permits were to be given to blacks as well as whites—that is to say, one minority permit for each white permit was ordered. The government accepted the administrator's recommendation in this regard, but the union objected. Judge Frankel, on March 28, 1972, approved the administrator's findings and denied an application for a stay.[40] The work permit remedy was, however, inadequate in two respects: (1) blacks had no permanent security in the industry inasmuch as the permits did not make them union members—although it must be admitted that the wages and overtime earned from permit work probably add up to a substantial increase for many minority workers compared with what they could earn before; (2) the problem of referral itself was still not dealt with adequately.

United States v. Local 638, Steamfitters

The territorial jurisdiction of Local 638 is the five boroughs of New York City and Nassau and Suffolk Counties on Long Island. Local 638 is part of the United Association of Journeymen and Apprentices of the Plumbing and Pipefitting Industry. Like some other unions in that industry, this local has two branches: an A branch whose members do primarily construction work and a B branch whose members work in shops and do repair jobs. Around 1969 or 1970, when the Justice Department began to look at Local 638, of nearly 4,000 journeyman members in its A branch, only 28 were black or minority. Of 351 apprentices, 14 were minority. At the time of the first round of litigation involving Local 638, January 1972, the number of nonwhite journeymen was estimated to be 31. Of approximately 2,800–3,000 members of the B branch, about 500 were nonwhite.[41]

The A branch has a higher hourly rate of pay (in 1971–1972, A branch steamfitters earned $11 an hour). Although Local 638 does not have an exclusive hiring hall with the Mechanical Contractors Association of New York (the trade association of heating, ventilating and air conditioning contractors in the New York area), membership in the A branch is a substantial aid in obtaining a job as construction steamfitter. It is also significant in connection with job security and opportunities for advancement and overtime pay. Members of the B branch are also able to obtain a good measure of work in construction because the A branch is kept so small that employers must obtain employees who work on permit. These permit workers in this case are members of the B branch as well as members of other locals. While working on construction, they receive the same rate of pay as A branch members but do not have the first crack at lucrative overtime assignments and are laid off first.

In August 1971 the Workers Defense League began to recruit approximately a hundred black qualified welders, many of whom were members of the B branch. All of them had at least five years experience in the pipefitting industry, and twenty-five were immediately certified on the basis of a welding test while another twenty-five also scored high. These fifty workers were given welding jobs, and the other men were employed as construction steamfitters by various members of the Mechanical Contractors Association. Meanwhile, approximately seventy other minority workers, some of them members of the B branch and some of them nonunion, were performing the same kind of work as members of the A branch and receiving the same pay but with less job security. In November 1971 a contractor, Sand Courter, decided to lay off workers at the World Trade Center. The only fitters on the job who were not A branch members were black employees. Traditionally, because of the fact that the non-A men were working on permit in construction, they would have been laid off first. In this situation however,—for reasons not exclusively founded on a concern for civil rights—the employer decided to lay off two blacks and forty-nine whites. In other words, it ignored the A-B seniority system.

White workers immediately walked out at the World Trade Center and others throughout New York City soon followed to protest what they regarded as a violation of the layoff procedure. The government, which had previously filed suit against Local 638, sought to enjoin the walkout as an attempt to coerce employers into laying off minority workers instead of whites. The union contended that the stoppage was a wildcat walkout over which it had no control. Although the *New York Times* reported that Judge Bonsal, who was assigned to the case, had ordered the workers to return to work and that the strike continued in defiance of the order, it appears that no order was ever signed.[42]* Whatever the facts are on this score, it is clear that white workers demonstrated vociferously, in a manner reminiscent of the May 1970 Peter Brennan-Cambodia demonstrations in which white students were roughed up. According to the *Times:* "About 1,500 of the workers, some carrying American flags, marched in the morning [December 13, 1971] from Fulton and Church Streets to the Federal Building in Foley Square. John Tracy, business agent of Local 638, said the union had complied with the court order by telling the men to go back to work, even though they had not done so."[43] On December 15, Judge Bonsal told "more than 100 union steamfitters who were seated and standing in his Federal courtroom . . . that he saw no reason for their work stoppage, and that they should go back to work."[44] He reserved decision on the order for a preliminary injunction, however. According to the *Times,* the following took place:

At the end of yesterday's hearing, Judge Bonsal looked beyond the area near the bench and into the spectators' seats. He said he was addressing "the gentlemen who have been in the courtroom all day listening to all of this."
    Practically all of them—some 130—were union members listening to the proceedings.
    The judge said: "This is really a very poor issue to have a work stoppage about. . . . It doesn't seem to me, gentlemen, (reason) [sic] for having any basis for a work stoppage." He added that he hoped that they would go back to work this morning.
    "I'm saying that from the heart and I hope you will appreciate that I'm saying that from the heart," the judge said."[45]

On December 16, the workers returned to their jobs. They did so, however, although it was not reported in the newspapers and not publicized generally, because the employer at the World Trade Center agreed to rehire the fifty-one workers who had been laid off.[46]

On January 3, 1972, Judge Bonsal responded to the government's request for preliminary relief regarding the approximately 170 minority group workers referred to above, who were denied membership in the A branch despite the fact that they were doing the same work as A branch men. The court noted that "the only operative requirements for membership in the A Branch are that each applicant must have at least five years of practical working experience in the plumbing and pipefitting industry and must be of good moral character."[47] Many of the minority workers, the court said, had not only passed welding tests and been given welding jobs but also had "far more" than five years experience in the pipefitting industry. Accordingly, employers had found 169 minority workmen "on the whole to be as competent as A men . . . and wish to keep them on."[48] Since the minority workers desired to become members of the A branch and they all met the requirements, Local 638 was ordered to admit immediately all 169 to full journeyman status in the A branch. Moreover, the court—with reference to the five-year experience requirement—found that the admission policies of Local 638 had the effect of perpetuating past discrimination and was therefore unlawful under Title VII.

Moreover, it appeared that the duration of the apprenticeship program, which was also five years, constituted another artificial barrier to obtaining journeyman status. Testimony in the Local 638 trial subsequent to the issuance of Judge Bonsal's preliminary injunction showed that welding, which the testimony indicated is the most (and perhaps only) skilled portion of steamfitter work, can be taught to a relatively advanced stage in thirteen weeks. Testimony from the Director of Training Programs for the Office of the Assistant Secretary of Defense for Manpower Affairs indicated that military training programs for pipefitting and steamfitting were in the range of eighteen to nineteen weeks. The Navy Seabees train their pipefitters in a fourteen-week course. According to the testimony a utility man in the Seabees could be qualified to work as a journeyman's partner on a construction site, installing pipe, and cutting, hanging, and screwing pipe—in a fourteen-week period. After six months of practical experience he could work as an experienced journeyman. A senior petty officer of the Seabees testified that to become certified it would take a welder at least one year of practical experience following his fourteen-week course. In any event, testimony in the *Local 638* case and in other construction industry litigation indicates that the period of time necessary for training, is substantially shorter than five years—and indeed many whites, outside the formal apprenticeship program, have achieved journeyman status with substantially less training time than the apprenticeship program requires.

When Judge Bonsal fashioned a decree for racial discrimination by Local 638 during the summer of 1973, however, he refused to revise the duration of the apprenticeship program, because, even though there was "some evidence that non-whites drop out of the program with greater frequency than whites,"[49]* the underlying reasons were not disclosed with "specificity" in the evidence at the trial. In other words, while job relatedness of the program's duration was evidenced, the necessary disproportionate impact upon minorities within the meaning of *Griggs*[50] was not evidenced in Judge Bonsal's view. In any event, the decree provided that there should be a minimum of 400 apprenticeships in 1973, of which 175 should be minority. The defendants were obligated to "use their best efforts to provide apprentices with not less than 1,750 hours per year of reasonably continuous employment."[51] Temporary procedures for upgrading from the B to the A branch were provided, and an overall goal of 30 percent nonwhite membership for July 1, 1977, was established. As in *Local 46,* an administrator was appointed.

United States v. *Local 3, Operating Engineers* (Northern California)

Judge Peckham's decree in *Local 3, Operating Engineers* ranks with the *Local 86* order in its comprehensiveness. If it has not been equally effective, the reasons are fundamentally two: (1) the lack of a monitoring device like the court-ordered advisory committee established by Judge Lindberg in *Local 86;* (2) the absence of a minority organization like UCWA to pressure defendants. Private plaintiffs in *Local 3* have played a more prominent and active role than those in Seattle, and Judge Peckham is an activist judge, dedicated to the policies and objectives of civil rights legislation.

When the Justice Department began an investigation of Local 3, approximately 0.6 percent of its 38,000 members who are spread through northern California, Hawaii, Nevada, and Utah, were minority. According to the findings of Judge Peckham, as of July 18, 1972, the following status prevailed:

Of the 35,113 members of Local 3, only .9% are black. This percentage creeps up to 1.2 when Northern California is considered alone, however. Yet in Northern California blacks constitute over 7% of the total population, and even a larger percentage of the workforce. Moreover, of the white union members, almost three-fifths occupy 'A' journeyman status, and therefore are in the first group of referrals. Less than one-fifth of all black union members and less than two-fifths of other minority group union members have attained this coveted status. Finally, of those Union members who are in training but not in the apprenticeship program, only a negligible number (three out of twelve hundred in Northern California) are black.[52]

On January 11, 1972, the Justice Department entered a consent decree with Local 3, Operating Engineers, the Operating Engineers' joint apprenticeship committee, and the Surveyors' apprenticeship committee, as well as the Associated General Contractors of California and the Engineering and Grading Contractors Association, who are parties to collective-bargaining agreements with Local 3 and were named in the complaint as parties defendant for the purpose of relief. Subsequently, private plaintiffs, who had already sued the defendants before the Justice Department entered the fray, sued for a preliminary injunction requesting relief beyond that provided by the consent decree. It is most useful to discuss the contents of that decree within the context of Judge Peckham's response to the request for a preliminary injunction.

Judge Peckham, in his preliminary injunction opinion, referred to the statistics noted above as establishing a prima facie case and specifically found that the union was discriminating against minority group members by varying from its normal procedures when a minority group worker attempted to secure placement as a journeyman or a trainee. The court noted that the union had agreed to make two basic changes in its operations in response to the racial imbalance in its membership which it acknowledged existed. First, it had agreed to a system whereby 30 percent of all employees accepted and dispatched as apprentices were to be black, 30 percent Mexican-American, and 10 percent Oriental or other minorities. In other words, Local 3 agreed to 70 percent minority indenturing. Moreover, tests were not to be used by the union in determining eligibility for the apprenticeship program or continued participation in it. Second, the union had agreed to revise its eligibility requirements for getting onto the ''A,'' ''B,'' or ''C'' journeymen lists. To get their names on the ''A'' list—almost essential for obtaining actual work in the trade on a fairly regular basis—employees had been required to have worked at least 350 hours in each of the last three years under the Master Agreement covering all contractors in Local 3's jurisdiction. The consent decree nullified this rule for minority workers, and they could be placed on the ''A'' list if they had worked as operators 350 hours a year for three consecutive years at any time within the last seven years whether or not this work was obtained under the Master Agreement. Under normal procedures required by Local 3, in order to get on the ''B'' list an individual had to have worked at least 350 hours under the Master Agreement within the last year. Under the consent decree a minority worker could get onto the ''B'' list if he had worked more than 350 hours during any one year within the last seven. In addition, a minority person who had five years experience anywhere and held ''A'' status might be requested by name by an employer regardless of his place on the ''A'' list. And furthermore, as Judge Peckham stated, ''Contractors may call for minorities generically or by name in order to fulfill their affirmative action obligations on publicly funded projects.''[53]

Private plaintiffs, as the judge noted, objected to the changes described on the grounds that they did not ''operate swiftly enough to erase the present effects of past discrimination''—the basic issue in most Title VII litigation ever since the early seniority days. The private plaintiffs were opposed to the apprenticeship program's being the sole means of bringing new minority operating engineers into the industry. They contended that the 4,000-hour apprenticeship program left unchanged by the consent order was ''too long, too abstract, too preoccupied with imparting broad expertise, and too concerned wth classroom as opposed to on-the-job training.''[54] Moreover, the plaintiffs expressed concern that because of the high unemployment rate among operating engineers and the apprentice-journeyman ratio apprentices would not be assured enough work during their training period. Further, they stressed testimony in the form of affidavits from contractors and others to the effect that operating engineers could be trained in a considerably shorter period of time. As Judge Peckham noted, ''Plaintiffs also point out that prior to 1960, when the Operating Engineers first instituted their apprenticeship program, people became journeymen by obtaining employment as 'oilers' in assistance to regular journeymen; these 'oilers' learned their trade by operating machinery during breaks and slow periods, not by undergoing 4,000 hours of structured training.''[55] As the plaintiffs pointed out, the business necessity demonstrated by the defendants for the duration of the apprenticeship program related to the work that an operating engineer might do as a surveyor, because surveying requires substantial amounts of mathematical knowledge. The court specifically considered the traditional argument made by craft unions in connection with apprenticeship programs, that is, testimony "that the apprenticeship program is necessary because it trains people in use of a wide variety of machinery, and without such broad training operating engineers will be unable to obtain steady employment in the working season."[56]* Said Judge Peckham in response to this argument, "Since it is not a matter of business necessity whether operating engineers are steadily employed, however, this argument is wholly unpersuasive."[57]

The plaintiffs also contended that the hours-worked requirements perpetuated the effects of past discrimination in that minority workers who had been excluded from the industry could not have acquired the 350 hours of experience prerequisite to "A" list status. Judge Peckham decided that further evidence was needed to determine whether the hours-worked criterion could meet the business necessity test, or whether an alternative criterion should be formulated if the first criterion did not meet the test. Accordingly, the court ordered further argument and the preparation of detailed proposals for a training program for minorities and stated the following:

Except with respect to the Surveyors' program, then, the Court finds that the contents and administration of the current apprenticeship program prevent minority persons from acquiring journeymen's qualifications as quickly as they are capable of doing so. The Court also finds that insofar as the current courses (except the one for surveyors) last longer than the six months and do not stress on-the-job training, they are not justified by business necessity. And, finally, it is the Court's finding that minority persons should be represented on the directing board of any new program designed to train minority persons more expeditiously, to insure that such a program will be administered in a manner sympathetic to the particular needs of those trainees. . . .

The Court must consider whether the prerequisites for "A" listing under the consent preliminary injunction—350 hours work per year for any three consecutive years within the last seven—are unnecessarily onerous. Are there less burdensome prerequisites which could still provide contractors with competent and safe minority group operating engineers? . . .

Defendants . . . have admitted that an important reason for retaining hours-worked requirements is to protect the seniority of currently working "A" list operating engineers, at a time when unemployment is high [not a business necessity defense].[58]

In the end, the court specifically preserved a portion of the hours-worked provision. Moreover, it let stand a provision of the collective-bargaining agreement, retained by the consent decree, which permitted a contractor to continue to call for those employees who had performed well for him; but it found no justification for a provision allowing a contractor to call by name any man who had worked for ten years in the trade.

The plaintiffs also objected that even if minority workers were admitted to the "A" list in a nondiscriminatory manner (that is, without onerous hours-worked requirements and other unfair criteria), there would remain a likelihood that given "the current high level of unemployment among operating engineers . . . new minority journeymen will sit on the benches unless some kind of proportional hours requirement is established,"[59] that is, a requirement that if minorities constitute X percent of the journeyman pool, they will work X percent of the total hours worked by journeymen. On this issue, the court, while expressing concern about the *possibility* of hostile administrators subverting the decree, took the view that it would be beneficial to determine whether the defendants could be justifiably entrusted with its administration. If such trust turned out to be unjustifiable, it stated, further relief could be provided in the future.

The next step subsequent to the court's order was the negotiation of a new consent decree between the Justice Department and the operating engineers. This decree also met with objections from the plaintiffs but was approved by Judge Peckham, who simply stayed the actions of private plaintiffs until it could be determined how effective the new consent decree would be.[60]

Local 3, Operating Engineers graphically demonstrates the nexus between hours-worked or seniority formulas and the ability of the court to obtain compliance with a decree which provides for the fulfillment of a goal within a specified period of time. In the new consent decree, entitled Permanent Injunction in Partial Resolution of Law Suit, the parties once again acknowledged racial imbalance and obliged themselves to "rectify this imbalance in Northern California within five years." Moreover, minorities once again were permitted to use work experience accumulated outside the collective-bargaining agreement. The basic time-worked provisions which were prerequisites to obtaining "A" journeyman status were not changed, although it became easier to obtain "C" journeyman status (a provision that was largely unimportant because "C" journeymen can work so little considering present employment conditions). Under the new consent decree, the Master Agreement was to be modified so as to permit an employer to call for minority journeymen who hold "A" status by name so that he could fulfill affirmative-action statutory or executive-order requirements at least up to 10 percent of his work force. Further, the defendants obligated themselves to provide minority journeymen who held "A" or "B" referral status with the opportunity for training and skill upgrading at Rancho Murietta. In accordance with Judge Peckham's June 18 decision, four of the fourteen members of the joint apprenticeship committee were to be minority.

The consent agreement required the individual employer to maximize on-the-job training in terms of the actual operation of equipment and to give apprentices maximum opportunity to operate each of the major types. This requirement, coupled with "related off site instruction" at Rancho Murietta, was intended to permit apprentices to be accelerated through the program as they demonstrated ability or skill.

Finally, rather than appointing an administrator of the kind established by Judge Frankel's order in *Local 46,* the court ordered that the government appoint a compliance monitor with the following responsibilities:

[He] shall gather information pertaining to implementation of the provisions of this injunction and . . . shall investigate any complaints arising under it. The Monitor shall be solely responsible to the plaintiff United States and shall have complete access, upon reasonable terms and conditions, to all records of the defendants kept pursuant to this order or any subsequent orders. . . . The reasonable expenses, including salaries, incurred by the Compliance Monitor shall be borne by the defendant in an Affirmative Action Trust Fund.[61]

Private plaintiffs have complained bitterly to the court about this decree. They contend that it makes the apprenticeship program the main, if not the exclusive, conduit through which racial imbalance is to be remedied. As the plaintiffs noted, no attempt was made to reach minority tradesmen who either might have qualified for "A" status on the basis of the decree or might have been in a position to make use of the training provided at Rancho Murietta. Indeed, between January 1972 and January 1973 only seven minority workers came in as apprentices. The plaintiffs have contended that 1,000 hours of work during the last seven years is more than adequate under the business necessity test—especially inasmuch as those who need brush up their skills could go to Rancho Murietta.

The pace subsequently quickened. Between March and December 1973, 89 black and 79 Spanish-surnamed apprentices were indentured. The significance of these figures is lessened by two factors, however. In the first place, 58 or 18.1 percent of the new indentures were "other minorities," and the suspicion was that a substantial number of whites were masquerading as American Indians. To deal with this point, EEOC, which has inherited the monitoring responsibilities for the Justice Department, has proposed that no individual with less than one-fourth Indian blood be classified as Indian.

In connection with a second factor, the duration of the apprenticeship program, the plaintiffs point out that the burden to accelerate is upon the apprentices rather than the Joint Apprenticeship Committee. If the burden were on the committee to explain why apprentices were not being accelerated, a substantial number of minority apprentices might get through the program in considerably less time than the presently required three years. The acceleration question is important because even with a 70 percent minority indenture it can be assumed that no more than between 170 and 180 minority workers will enter the program each year, and thus over a five-year period the total of new minority journeymen would be approximately 900, not quite the population parity—that is, assuming that population parity were measured against the number of journeymen and not, as the consent decree assumes, measured against both journeymen *and* apprentices. However parity is measured, it seems clear that acceleration is the extreme exception—roughly 3 percent of the apprentices have accelerated.

Population parity for journeymen in northern California would require approximately 3,880 minority journeymen, or 22.9 percent of 16,916. Under the present plan, it would take twelve years of 70 percent minority indentures to achieve population parity at the journeyman level. There are a number of problem areas in the Local 3 decree which make parity difficult to achieve. The first is that direct entry to the journeyman level continues to be the principal access route. Between July and December 1973, 82.1 percent of new journeymen came from outside the apprenticeship programs—and during the same period 70.2 percent of the entrants were white, 3.3 black, 8.1 Spanish-surnamed, and 18.4 "other minorities." While blacks and Spanish-surnamed workers must go through the apprenticeship program, many whites do not.

Further, in no month between May and October 1973, the peak construction months, did minority apprenticeships work even half the average number of hours worked by whites. A disproportionately large number of minorities have been "on the bench" or unemployed and thus not obtaining the experience and training prerequisite to journeyman status. As in Seattle, this situation means that the attrition rate is bound to be higher for minorities than for whites. The drop-out rate for minority apprentices was more than twice as high as that for whites. As in Seattle, this phenomenon substantially erodes the quota admission provisions.

Private plaintiffs in hearings before Judge Peckham in the summer of 1974 pointed out that the defendants, in arguing the desirability of an apprenticeship program for minorities, concluded that the journeyman-apprentice ratio would benefit black and Spanish surnamed workers—but precisely the opposite is true. During May–October 1973, minority journeymen worked almost twice as much as minority apprentices. Accordingly, the protection that was envisaged simply did not materialize.

Insofar as on-the-job training is concerned, Rancho Murietta is not being operated at anything close to capacity. One defect of the order is that no stipends are provided trainees. And to compound the problem, nearly 60 percent of the trainee hours have gone to whites—even though the facilities are paid for out of an Affirmative Action Trust Fund which is supposed to be used for the improvement of minority skills.

Another factor contributing to lack of work is the retention of the call-in system which permits employers to call by name for workers who have worked for them previously, as well as to call for minorities generically to fulfill affirmative action commitments required in connection with federal and state projects. From March through August 1973, blacks obtained 0.4 percent of this call-in work, whites 91.3 percent, Mexican-Americans 4.4 percent, and other minorities 3.9 percent.

The picture is hardly a bright one. With a parity goal of 7 percent and 17,932 journeyman members in the local, black journeymen should number 1,255. As of the summer of 1974, there were 133 black journeymen and 191 black apprentices.

As private plaintiffs have noted:

Since it would take between three and four years to graduate these black apprentices, it would be mere fantasy to expect more than roughly 200 new black journeymen to enter the trade during the next four years through the apprenticeship program as it is presently constituted. (Given the increasing minority cancellation rate, this figure is probably inflated.) During the past year, the total number of black journeymen has increased by a mere 24 and 8 of these are accounted for by black graduates from the apprenticeship program. Therefore, unless changes are made, it is unjustifiable to expect more than 64 (16 × 4) new black journeymen to enter the trade within the four years other than through the apprentice program. Adding the present 133 journeymen, the 200 or so expected black graduates from the apprenticeship program, and the 64 or so blacks who enter other than through the apprenticeship program, we get a grand total of roughly 400 black journeymen after the completion of the five year period.

Accordingly, less than one-third of the parity goal will have been attained five years after the decree. It is quite clear that changes will have to be made. As well as the need for further judicial scrutiny of both the training that is given to minorities and the hours necessary to possess an ''A'' card, it would seem as though the following areas are ripe for reform. (1) More staff and authority should be provided the compliance monitor to resolve grievances and disputes. (2) A government presence should be provided. The Justice Department has had no lawyer with substantial authority on the west coast, although to some extent EEOC involvement is increasing the amount of government activity inasmuch as the monitoring is being handled out of the San Francisco Litigation Center. (3) A proportional hours quota requirement should be imposed—something which Judge Peckham initially rejected in 1972. It is quite clear from both the *Local 3* and *Local 86* decrees that unless minorities obtain a substantial amount of work, the cancellation rate will undermine the best of quota admission decrees. (4) There should be a halt to indenturing journeymen and apprentices other than blacks and Spanish surnamed workers until more substantial hours are available.

Further, it may be that the small number of minorities coming in as ''A'' journeymen under the journeyman portion of the decree is attributable to the fact that the Justice Department, even though it has the resources of the F.B.I., has apparently made no efforts to contact minority applicants who might qualify or who might need training at Rancho Murietta. Unfortunately, EEOC does not have the resources of the F.B.I. at its disposal. Yet, it is clear that more of a search, and more publicity, must be undertaken.

13 | The Seattle Building Trades Decree

The Seattle building trades decree,[1] the earliest and, at the time of its issuance, the most comprehensive Title VII decree rendered by any court, illustrates the potential effectiveness of Title VII litigation compared to efforts by the executive branch in attacking discrimination. Predictably, the AFL-CIO lost no time in maligning it. The decree's potential, even more than its accomplishment, poses a substantial threat to the AFL-CIO's position that the law is not a viable way to overcome labor discrimination, that the best method of bringing minorities into the construction trades is through the unions' own apprenticeship plans such as Project Outreach. The Seattle decree not only eliminated existing institutional rigidities in the unions' apprenticeship plans; it also required that the rate of integration be accelerated beyond the "deliberate speed" prescribed for school desegregation by the Warren Court in *Brown* v. *Board of Education* [*II*].[2] Like all novel and ambitious ventures, the decree has had more than its share of difficulties. Nevertheless, experience under the decree indicates that the law can have a substantial impact in providing equal employment opportunities.

Prelude to Litigation: The Seattle Demonstrations[3]*

When Tyree Scott got his discharge papers from the Marine Corps in 1966, he returned to Seattle and went to work with his father, a nonunion electrician, in what he describes as "just about a one-man shop."[4] That year the Scotts, who are black, grossed $9,000. Within three years the construction boom of the late 1960's had given the Scotts substantial new opportunities, and they began to obtain some large contracts. In 1969, they were earning more than ten times as much as they had in 1966. They had hired some skilled journeymen, and Scott had decided that in order to compete for the big contracts he had to come to terms with the International Brotherhood of Electrical Workers (IBEW), Local 46. In Seattle and other cities, the larger and more lucrative commercial contracts cannot be obtained without having a collective-bargaining agreement with a union: the unions which bargain with the general contractor and other subcontractors pressure their own employers to, in turn, force the nonunion contractor to bargain collectively—often as the result of a threatened or actual picket line.[5] The sanction in this situation, of course, is a refusal to cross the picket line.

In August 1969, two black youngsters came into the Scotts' shop and asked for jobs. Says Scott about this encounter: "These guys . . . asked me about a job and I explained that you had to belong to the union, and we had exclusive hiring hall procedures with the unions, and we couldn't hire people just right off the street. And these guys spent another 15 minutes talking to me and then they walked out of the shop."[6] But when they left, says Scott, "the office secretary, who had sons about their age, started talking about their problem: 'You know darned well the white contractors can't hire them.' And I went out in the street and caught up with these guys and told them I wasn't going to turn nobody else down—that I would hire them regardless of the damn union."[7]

This event triggered a series of incidents which has exposed the strengths and frailties of the judicial process. Scott became involved in the Central Contractors Association, an all-black construction employers group in the Seattle area. When he related his story about the black applicants at a meeting of the Contractors Association, he struck a responsive chord in some of the other members. They were concerned about the exclusion of black employees as well as about the fact that black employers found it difficult to get work on construction projects. The association decided to publicize their grievances.

The next day, Scott, along with 13 other black contractors, successfully closed down a swimming pool project which was being built for Seattle's black high school by an all-white work force. The high school, located one block from the spot where Seattle's 1967 riots had been sparked, was hardly the place at which white workers wanted to deliberate fully on a request by blacks to leave. The white construction workers departed quickly.[8] The following day, between 150 and 200 blacks and whites went downtown to a site at which a courthouse was being constructed. Here Scott informed the contractors that employers and unions had an obligation under the President's Executive Order 11,375[9] to employ blacks where federal funds were involved in construction. Construction stopped and momentum increased. From the courthouse the crowd went on to the King County Hospital, the objects being to stop traffic and to ask workers to leave. Again, they succeeded.[10]* Traffic was snarled and white workers left the construction site. Direct action was having an impact. When black trainees were brought onto the job sites subsequent to these demonstrations, however, the building trades members walked out despite a no-strike clause. The Central Contractors Association and Scott sued in federal district court to enjoin these walkouts, and Judge William Lindberg held that an injunction was an appropriate remedy. According to Judge Lindberg, because the walkout was designed to thwart the hiring of black trainees in the respective trades, it was not a labor dispute within the meaning of the Norris-La Guardia Act.[11]

The Nixon administration—not yet locked into its alliance with the white hard-hat unions[12]* had promulgated the Philadelphia Plan during the summer months.[13] One of its leading black officeholders, Assistant Secretary of Labor Arthur Fletcher, threatened its extension to other cities where employers and unions did not take affirmative action.[14] The winds of Philadelphia were being felt throughout the land. The belief that the unions and contractors had obligations to recruit minorities, obligations which could be effected only if "goals" and "timetables" for minority hiring were established, was reflected both in the acceleration of black demands and in a new-found inclination by the white building trades and contractors to negotiate plans. For the first time, a climate which favored meaningful efforts to alleviate employment discrimination was beginning to develop.

The combined impact of Judge Lindberg's injunction and the reverberations of the Philadelphia Plan led the mayor, the county commissioner, and representatives of labor and management to sit down with the black demonstrators in Seattle. The result was an agreement immediately to hire 60 blacks into the mechanical trades at a number of construction sites throughout the city. But the agreement became meaningless once blacks realized that individual black employees—whose place would not be filled by others if they quit or were dismissed—were the only beneficiaries. Accordingly, two weeks later, black demonstrators were back in the streets.

Two of the same projects were closed down again. At this point, the protest began to spread to construction at the University of Washington, where national television recorded the overturning of bulldozers. Scott was well aware of the lesson learned by the unions themselves in the 1930's: if work ceased, negotiations took place. Says Scott: "If [the projects] were closed, they would meet every day. If they were open, they would want to meet on a weekly basis, or whatever."[15]

Almost simultaneously with the university shutdowns, Scott's group started to protest the exclusion of blacks at airport construction projects.[16] Their tactic was to line up in single file and march onto the runways so that the planes could not land. Further negotiations and another agreement resulted.[17] After it became clear that this new agreement would not be implemented, Scott called for more direct action at the airport. In December, an assembly of 300 blacks and some white supporters tied up ticket counters with phony ticket purchases. The police moved in and arrested Scott along with approximately 50 others.[18] The next day the Department of Justice—which had begun to look at Seattle's building trades when the demonstrations began and whose investigatory pace had quickened as blacks escalated the conflict—brought suit against five unions: Local 86, Ironworkers; Local 99, Sheetmetal Workers; Local 46, IBEW; Local 32, Plumbers and Pipefitters; and Local 502, Operating Engineers.[19]* Two months later, Judge Lindberg, the same federal judge who had previously issued an injunction against the building trades walkout, found that the unions and their joint apprenticeship committees (except that of Local 46, IBEW) had violated Title VII of the Civil Rights Act of 1964. Relief was fashioned on June 16, 1970.[20]

Judge Lindberg's Order

The order provides relief which, at the time of its issuance, was more comprehensive and detailed than that set forth by any other judge in any employment discrimination case in the United States.[21]* The court, having carefully documented its findings of fact in a forty-two-page opinion, obligated the defendant craft unions to open up membership to blacks who had been unlawfully excluded from journeyman status.[22] More importantly, Judge Lindberg ordered the unions and their apprenticeship committees to recruit blacks into their apprenticeship programs so that a specific number of graduates could be reasonably anticipated on an annual basis.[23] The court also altered the grounds for admission at the journeyman level and ordered the immediate admission of 45 black journeymen.[24] These requirements were designed to remedy the disadvantages imposed upon blacks by the existing union structure.

Findings of Fact

Judge Lindberg found numerous occasions of union discrimination. The Ironworkers Union, for example, had "on a continuous basis" denied blacks its hiring hall and provided black applicants and workers with false information about employment conditions.[25] The union also referred white workers with little or no experience, enabling them to avoid an apprenticeship and learn valuable skills on the job.[26] Moreover, Judge Lindberg concluded that union estimates of training requirements were considerably exaggerated, noting that the white workers who received preferential treatment had often been referred successfully without going through any apprenticeship program.[27]* In the apprenticeship program itself, the sons and relatives of union members—all of whom were white—had an automatic preference for acceptance. The court also found that aptitude tests imposing higher standards than those in effect prior to 1967 were "at least in part racially motivated" and noted the disproportionate impact that such tests had upon blacks as opposed to whites.[28]

The Sheetmetal Workers Union, like the Ironworkers, gave preference to friends and relatives of union members and union contractors, often by violating its own regulations. One particularly ingenious exclusionary device employed by the union's apprenticeship committee was allowing some white workers to apply while the application books were officially closed. The court noted that blacks were consistently discouraged from applying for entry into the apprenticeship program.[29]

At the time of the trial the number of black construction members in each union was as follows: Ironworkers, 1 out of 920 members; Sheetmetal Workers, 1 out of 900; Electricians, 1 out of 1,715; and Plumbers and Pipefitters, 1 out of 1,900.[30] The Plumbers Union had 93 black members, significantly more than the other unions, but virtually all worked in the nonconstruction trades[31]* where hourly wages were significantly lower than in construction.[32]*

The International Brotherhood of Electrical Workers employed similar kinds of discrimination. For example, the local applied more stringent standards to black marine electricians than to whites seeking construction referral. Moreover, qualified blacks had been refused referral to higher paying construction work. Black applicants were often required to have letters of recommendation from electrical contractors before they could be referred, whereas white marine electricians were regularly referred to construction jobs merely on the basis of their union work records or dues receipts.[33]

Conclusions of Law

Judge Lindberg made numerous conclusions of law from the evidence of widespread racial discrimination on the part of the skilled construction unions.[34] He held unlawful any attempts by a union or its apprenticeship committee.[35]* to give false, misleading, or incomplete information with regard to membership, work referral opportunities, and apprenticeship training. Recruitment programs aimed only at whites and other preferential treatment restricting black employment opportunities were also declared illegal. In addition, application of higher standards or more stringent procedures to blacks than to whites was outlawed by the decree.

Judge Lindberg imposed further limitations on union activities. He prohibited unions which had engaged in racially discriminatory practices from requiring blacks to have experience in the industry as a condition of referral or membership. Such a condition, he reasoned, would perpetuate past discrimination. Moreover, all prerequisites to membership, referral, or apprenticeship training "must bear a reasonable relationship to skills required on the jobn" and the necessary qualifications need only be comparable to those "generally demonstrated by white applicants or members.[36] Judge Lindberg also concluded that a union's reputation and statistical evidence regarding its racial composition are relevant and admissible in proving a policy of discrimination. Finally, he held that a union which has engaged in racial discrimination "must not only refrain from future discrimination but must also undertake whatever affirmative action may be necessary to assure those discriminated against the full enjoyment of their right to equal employment opportunities."[37]

Remedy by Decree

Judge Lindberg issued two decrees based on his findings of fact and conclusions of law. The first dealt with standards and procedures relating to journeyman referral and membership; the second, with apprenticeship and training.

Decree No. 1: Journeyman Referral and Membership Records

The court required all the defendant unions to maintain thorough records. It held that all workers seeking employment had to complete an application for referral with the union which would automatically become a permanent part of the applicant's file.[38]* Only those persons with applications on file were eligible for placement on the out-of-work lists and referral; the locals also had to maintain a register of all requests by contractors for each trade classification of employees.

In addition, the court ordered the unions to transmit copies of items such as referral applications and hiring hall dispatch slips to the Department of Justice. The names of all black applicants not placed on the out-of-work lists or referred for work had to be reported to the government and the decisions justified by the union. Finally, the Department of Justice was instructed to review the data every six months and submit a statistical summary and analysis to the court and the relevant local.

Dissemination of information. Judge Lindberg tried to insure the effectiveness of his decree by ordering dissemination of information to prospective black employees. He required each local union to prepare a brief written statement describing its referral system and its membership requirements for blacks, also indicating that membership is not a prerequisite of initial referral. In addition, the unions had to set forth various employment opportunities and the current rate of pay. The judge obligated the unions to furnish a copy of this statement to each black applicant for employment as well as to the government. The unions also had to place advertisements in newspapers "identified with serving the black community."[39]

Provisions for local unions. In addition to these general requirements imposed on all the defendant unions, the court announced specific standards and procedures for journeyman membership and referral in each local. The Ironworkers local, for example, was ordered to offer journeyman status to blacks who had obtained 700 hours of construction welding, rod work, or structural ironwork experience. The initiation fee charged qualified blacks had to be the most favorable terms offered by the local in the previous five years. Moreover, black applicants for membership were no longer required to provide names of union sponsors or to pass an examination.

With respect to journeyman referral procedures, the court gave the local the option of preserving priority groupings[40]* in the operation of its hiring hall. If the union retained the priority system, the court held, it would have to place black applicants in groups according to experience "reasonably related to the ironwork trade" irrespective of membership status. If the priority system were abandoned, all referrals would have to be made chronologically according to the date the applicant signed the out-of-work list. The court instructed the union not to require any examination or previous experience under the collective bargaining agreement as prerequisites to referral; a black applicant could be referred on the basis of his own statement of experience.[41]* Finally, Judge Lindberg allowed contractors, apart from any established rights to call a worker out of order, to employ blacks without regard to their place on the out-of-work list or prior experience with a particular contractor. He felt such an extraordinary provision was justified by the fact that black journeymen generally had been denied the opportunity to work with contractors. Similar considerations were spelled out for the other local unions.[42]

Decree No. 2: Apprenticeship and Training

Judge Lindberg also ordered the local apprenticeship committees to develop two apprentice programs to meet their affirmative action responsibilities. He imposed separate requirements and procedures on each program.

The regular program. The court compelled the union apprenticeship committees to broaden access to their regular apprentice programs, which train unskilled workers for journeyman status. The unions had to "consider qualified" all applicants for apprenticeship who met the age, education, health, residency, and examination standards set forth by Judge Lindberg.[43]* No other standards could be used by the unions.

In addition, Judge Lindberg required the apprenticeship committees to bring enough black applicants into apprentice programs "to insure a reasonable level of participation sufficient to overcome the present effects of past discrimination."[44] He ordered at least 30 percent of each apprenticeship class to be black, and applied this "minimum participation" figure to the "class of persons remaining in the program for more than three months" as well as to the entering class. Judge Lindberg also obligated the committees to replace blacks whose apprenticeships terminated before three months with newly indentured black apprentices to insure the required quotas would be met.

The special program. Judge Lindberg also forced the union apprenticeship committees to develop and implement special apprenticeship programs. These programs were designed to emphasize on-the-job training for two groups of black applicants whose needs could not be met by the regular programs: "overage black applicants with no previous experience or special skills in the trade" and "any black applicant of apprenticeable age or older who has some previous experience or special skills in the trade but does not meet journeyman standards."[45]

Each apprenticeship committee was permitted to impose "reasonable limitations" upon the size of special apprenticeship classes. The court held, however, that ceilings on class size could not fall below specified minimums.[46]* In addition, the unions had to shorten the training period for the special apprentices in order to speed their access to journeyman status.[47]* The court also specified that the assignment of special apprentices to a construction project had to be "in addition to, and not in lieu of" regular apprentices or other employees already on the payroll.[48]

The Court Order Advisory Committee (COAC)

An important innovation in the court's decrees was the creation of an advisory committee. The committee was to be composed of nine members—two each from labor, the contractors association, the black community, and the interested owners. The court required the ninth person to be from "some minority group other than black." It required the unions and the contractors associations to defray the expenses of the committee until government or pivate funding became available. The advisory committee was delegated the following responsibilities: (1) to communicate within the minority communities both the contents of the court order and the general progress being accomplished in its implementation; (2) to cooperate and consult with the appropriate apprenticeship committees, unions and contractors associations in attempting to formulate "new or altered apprenticeship training programs"; (3) to submit reports to the court expressing its views on the special apprenticeship programs once they were drawn up by the apprenticeship committees; and (4) to issue letters of recommendation for applicants who in its judgment were "likely" successfully to complete the special apprenticeship training programs.[49]*

Retention of Jurisdiction

Finally, the court retained jurisdiction "for such further relief as may be necessary or appropriate to further effectuate equal employment opportunities." At any time subsequent to June 30, 1973, however, any defendant affected by the order could move the court for its termination or modification depending upon the circumstances. Thus, while the court did not anticipate that equal employment opportunity obligations under Title VII would be completely met by 1973, it acknowledged that enough progress might have been made to enable a defendant local to relieve itself from requirements imposed by the 1970 decree. In fact, none of the defendants made enough progress to take advantage of this provision.[50]* Nevertheless, by the summer of 1973 more than 200 black workers were employed in the crafts covered by the decree. This figure represents a considerable accomplishment, especially in a city with such substantial unemployment during the preceding three years that it was described as an economic disaster area. Much of the improvement in the racial composition of the Seattle building trades has come despite inherent weaknesses in Judge Lindberg's order itself and the unions' failure to meet the quotas the order established.[51] The scope and detail of the decrees are in large part responsible for the successes, but Judge Lindberg's order would not have been implemented at all were it not for the militancy of Seattle's relatively small black community[52] and the emergence of a black workers' organization, the United Construction Workers Association. Without street demonstrations and sit-ins by an aroused black community when the order was not complied with, the judge's decrees would have been disobeyed even more than they have been.[53]*

Making the Law a Reality: The Role of the United Construction Workers Association

The lawsuit had been instituted, violations had been found, a remedy had been devised. Yet the remedy still had to be implemented. Only then could the law become a reality for potential black apprentices and journeymen in Seattle—and the city's black community knew that reality required much more than a judge's order.

Shortly after Judge Lindberg's order was entered, Tyree Scott split with the Central Contractors Association, which had been so actively involved in the 1969 demonstrations against the building trades. The association had become preoccupied with its own entrepreneurial problems. Referring derisively to "black capitalism," the promotion of small and often marginal businesses for blacks, Scott noted that Seattle's black contractors were "not totally sold on the job thing."[54]

After leaving the Central Contractors Association, Scott organized, with the help of the American Friends Service Committee, a black workers' organization called the United Construction Workers Association (UCWA). Its avowed purpose was to monitor the court decrees and to supply the apprenticeship committees with able applicants.[55] The UCWA was busy for the next three years meeting its self-appointed responsibilities.

Publicizing Noncompliance

By August 15, 1970, it was already clear that the aspect of the court's order dealing with the hiring of preapprentices was not being implemented.[56*] One of the principal reasons for this lack of progress was that the unions and contractors, through their representatives on the COAC, had begun to negotiate a plan which would cover crafts in addition to those named in Judge Lindberg's decrees. The new approach—completely unauthorized by Judge Lindberg's opinion— broadened the enormous problems and complexities already involved. The attempt to devise a Seattle plan under the court's auspices was something of a disingenuous frolic for the unions and employers. It was a little like former Attorney General John Mitchell's efforts to make voting rights legislation applicable to the North as well as to the South. By stretching one's resources too far, one undermines, sometimes knowingly, the ability to accomplish anything at all.

At the same time that the unions and contractors were evading the court's order, Scott was arrested on charges arising out of the earlier airport demonstrations that provoked the Department of Justice to litigate against the unions in the first place.[57*] Demonstrations and picketing organized by the UCWA underlined a dramatic and important point: the law was being enforced against the civil rights groups but not against the unions and contractors. The Seattle media brought this theme to public consciousness during Scott's imprisonment in September, and the Department of Justice was once again propelled into action. On a motion of the department, Judge Lindberg threatened the Association of General Contractors with contempt of court if a substantial effort to hire 90 blacks were not made by October 1.[58] The threat worked; 90 positions were filled by blacks by the court's deadline.

Recruitment Efforts

The UCWA also worked actively to recruit black applicants, thereby anticipating the frequently used excuse in construction and other industries that blacks have not been hired because no candidates are available for existing opportunities. The recruitment effort made the black community more conscious of the employment opportunities provided by the court order,[59*] but the UCWA leadership was convinced that successful implementation could not be achieved without its own formal participation. The UCWA therefore proposed that it be hired to perform the recruiting and screening functions of the COAC. It pointed out that most potential applicants for the special apprenticeship program were already members of the UCWA. It also argued that these applicants should have a "direct say" in the operation of the program designed for their benefit and that UCWA involvement would be the most effective way to insure such input. Finally, the UCWA reasoned that the reluctance of the unions and contractors to develop the preapprentice program without outside pressure underlined the fact that UCWA participation was a necessary ingredient for any progress in implementing other aspects of the order.

On October 7, 1970, the COAC requested that Scott and the UCWA be engaged to "assist in the day-to-day counseling and troubleshooting of problems related to the Special Apprentices until such time as a program is approved and funded by the Labor Department."[60] Donald Close, of the Electrical Contractors Association and chairman of the COAC, opposed this request.[61] He believed that UCWA involvement would be divisive and would undermine the cooperation contemplated in Judge Lindberg's order. He also made the technical argument that approval by the Department of Labor should be obtained before the COAC subcontracted any work to the UCWA. Austin St. Laurent, the president of the Seattle building trades and a COAC member, opposed this proposal on the ground that the COAC would be fostering dual unionism if it delegated these functions to the UCWA.[62] Yet dealing with the UCWA could not be regarded as dual unionism in the traditional sense of the term—although its existence both in 1970 and today quite clearly embarrasses and challenges the established trade union order. The UCWA, however, never planned to bargain over wages, hours, and conditions of employment for workers or to organize workers with the promise to do so. While it charges dues and has had meetings, the actual dispatch or referral of workers is through the union hiring hall, which generally controls employment opportunities in construction. By December 1970, the Close-St. Laurent views prevailed, and the COAC voted down the UCWA proposal. At this point minorities walked off the committee, creating a crisis situation before the COAC had really begun to operate.

Reorganization of the COAC

Donald Close then resigned because of what he correctly perceived to be a lack of confidence in him by the minorities. Judge Lindberg assigned Judge Sidney Volin, a bankruptcy judge in Seattle, to chair committee meetings on a temporary basis and in February 1971, after consultations with the parties, amended the order insofar as it related to the COAC. The most important modification was the designation of a "nonvoting, impartial chairman, appointed by the Court, who shall be in addition to the nine voting members,"[63] and who would have the authority to make recommendations to the court. Judge Lindberg appointed Professor Luvern Rieke of the University of Washington Law School to this post. He also specifically instructed the COAC to "monitor the progress of each of the special apprentices under this Order, including all phases of recruitment, training and entry into journeyman status."[64] The court hoped to eliminate the acrimony which had arisen toward the end of 1970 through the creation of the new impartial chairman and more specific responsibilities for the COAC. In fact, the amended order did have some effect: the minority members and Close rejoined the committee, and the meetings became less strident in tone. Moreover, the court of appeals for the Ninth Circuit, in a very broad and approving opinion, affirmed Judge Lindberg's order[65]* Yet the UCWA proposal for a formal role in recruitment was rejected,[66] and other practical difficulties were immense. It soon became clear that the order simply was not working well enough to provide the numbers of minority workers which it had envisioned.

Further Problems in Implementing the Decrees

One of the principal reasons why the order proved ineffective was that the numbers established for the special and regular apprentices had been selected without designating a population parity goal or any other ultimate reference point. They had been arrived at on the basis of conferences held between the court, the Department of Justice, and the other parties to the litigation and were the result of nothing more substantial than guesses about future manpower requirements in the construction trades.

A further difficulty was that the case went to trial and was decided when construction jobs were plentiful in Seattle. In fact, the boom in the construction economy provided the court with the decisive proof of discrimination. For example, blacks were being rejected for "lack of experience" when unions and contractors were searching desperately for tradesmen and referring whites with little or no experience—sometimes even as journeymen. In 1971, however, Seattle construction work began to decline, increasing competition between whites and blacks, and making it more difficult to enforce a decree which attempted to promote equal employment opportunities for black tradesmen.

Moreover, throughout 1971 and early 1972, the reports which the court had ordered to be provided by the Department of Justice were simply not forthcoming.[67]* In the Seattle building trades case, as in every litigation in which the Department of Justice has been the plaintiff under section 707, it was extremely difficult to keep on top of the developments from Washington, D.C. Because the Department of Justice had no one in Seattle with fulltime responsibility for the implementation of the decree, it remained ineffective.

Understandably, the UCWA became increasingly disenchanted. After the trial, Judge Lindberg had denied it standing to intervene. The organization remained active in monitoring enforcement of the decrees, even though it had been excluded from a formal role in 1970 with the rejection of its contracting proposal. Arguments and disputes broke out with the union and contractor representatives concerning the number of construction jobs that were actually available in the Seattle community. The UCWA and the minority community continuously took the position that there were many more jobs available than labor and management contended.[68] As there were few data regarding this matter, these debates could not be resolved.

Around the beginning of 1972, however, the UCWA began to sound a theme which would not go away: it maintained that the decree was being violated by the unions which had flouted the law in the past. The best evidence, said the UCWA, was the fact that white apprentices were being indentured while contractors were claiming that they did not have enough work for the number of black apprentices established in the order."[69]

The UCWA also argued that the metering system was being abused by the unions. This system was designed to limit the number of apprentices coming into the trade at a given time by keeping out new applicants unless an adequate number of hours were "metered" for incumbent apprentices. Though the system itself made good sense—it prevented situations in which too many apprentices were working with too few hours to split among them—the UCWA felt that the unions were using it to cover up their failure to incorporate as many new black apprentices as possible into their employment rolls.

By April 1972 none of the trades were indenturing a sufficient number of black special apprentices and all were indicating that they would refuse to take in any more. The Plumbers and Pipefitters apprenticeship committee was supposed to have taken in 50 black apprentices by April 1972. The actual number according to COAC reports was 21—and of those, only 18 were working while attending school. The Ironworkers were to have 40 and had only 12; the Sheetmetal Workers had brought in 18 toward their goal of 40.[70] The Electricians' goal was 50, and although they had 50 special apprentices on their roles, the COAC estimated that only 34 were both employed and attending school. Thus, the number of special apprentices established by the court order in the summer of 1970 was not complied with in the spring of 1972. While union representatives at the COAC continued to claim that they had done everything to comply with the law, contractor representatives, particularly Close, began to sense the deterioration that had set in and came forward with new proposals. The most important of these proposals related to the journeyman-apprentice ratio. It was accepted by the COAC during the spring of 1972.[71]

Close and other contractors recognized that the best method through which employment for apprentices could be obtained—albeit at the price of some unemployment for the less efficient journeymen—was to require that the ratio of apprentices to journeymen be increased. The contractors' idea—later to be adopted by Judge Lindberg—was that the journeyman-apprentice ratio be altered from 10 to 1 to 5-to-1 and that it be made compulsory. Previously, the contractor was obligated not to employ more than one apprentice for every ten journeymen, but the contractor did not have to employ that one apprentice. The proposed change meant that the contractor would be obligated to employ at least one apprentice for every five journeymen. Pressure to employ more was important because small contractors could resist recruiting any apprentice by simply hiring qualified journeymen from the street. Before the court could rule on this proposal, however, the UCWA had once again taken to the streets in an effort to insure compliance with the order. At this time the principal difference betwen the UCWA position and that of some of the contractors was due to UCWA uncertainty about the impact of an alteration of the journeyman-apprentice ratio by itself.

The 1972 Summer Demonstrations and the Judicial Responses

On June 1, 1972, the UCWA brought to the public the message that the decree was not being enforced by closing down a number of projects on Seattle's Interstate 90 and cutting off traffic across a major traffic artery to Seattle. Traffic was stopped for at least two hours. More protests aimed at stopping work were promised. On June 2, demonstrators were succcessful in closing projects at Safeco Tower in the university district and once again on seven building projects at the University of Washington campus. Two days later vandalism erupted in connection with a demonstration at Edison Hall on the Seattle Central Community College campus, causing $15,000 damage[72]

Meanwhile, the court had begun to respond to minority pressure in a manner reminiscent of the fall of 1970. On June 7, Judge Lindberg ordered the journeyman-apprentice ratio altered in accordance with the COAC proposals.[73] Moreover, the court now gave the COAC the responsibility for making recommendations directly to the court to expedite changes in the order. It also instructed the COAC to conduct hearings to determine whether individual employers were employing special apprentices. In those cases where the COAC found compliance was not adequate, a second hearing would be held before the court, which could employ the following penalties for failure to employ: (1) fines not to exceed $1,000 per day, (2) an order to comply under sanction of contempt proceedings, and (3) such other and further remedies as the court might deem just and proper. Significantly, the court reaffirmed its intent to obtain compliance with the numbers set forth in the 1970 decree.[74]*

Of almost equal importance was the fact that the court enjoined the UCWA from interfering with the order by organizing demonstrations involving physical interference with the performance of construction work and ordered a show cause hearing relating to "why they [the UCWA and its leaders] should not be added as parties defendant for purposes of relief."[75] Yet the court opened the possibility for UCWA involvement in implementing the order by allowing the COAC to act through agents or associations "as it deems appropriate" so as to require the employment of apprentices as mandated by the court order.[76]

Nevertheless, the UCWA kept up its protest, for the June 7 order did not specifically resolve the question of whether that organization would be involved in referral dispatch of black apprentices. COAC's Chairman Rieke predicted that 10 to 15 black trainees would be at work by June 10, but Scott replied: "We don't just want the jobs . . . we want some control over them."[77] On June 12, however, Judge Lindberg refused to sign an order proposed by the Department of Justice which would have provided the UCWA with some authority.[78]

UCWA supporters began an around-the-clock vigil on the lawn of the federal courthouse that day. In meetings with Judge Lindberg three days later, the unions sought complete abolition of the COAC.[79] The contractors accepted the UCWA monitoring "in principle," but they believed that this was "a matter requiring careful definition of authority and avoiding unnecessary conflicts.[80]

When Judge Lindberg delayed his decision again on June 15, Scott told supporters in front of the federal courthouse: "We have waited and we have talked to them and the unions refuse to talk to us. The [judge] said, 'Wait some more.' We're not going to wait. We're not waiting any more.[81] On June 16, the UCWA organized demonstrations at a variety of construction sites and shut down jobs at Twenty-seventh and East Alder, the Federal Office Building project, and a low-income project at Sixth and Washington.[82]

On June 21, new demonstrations took place. Forty-nine demonstrators affiliated with or supporting the UCWA were arrested for trespassing at the Seattle Central Community College construction site. Three more were arrested at the Bank of California building construction site the following day.[83] In response to these arrests, the court issued a new order on June 27 in the form of a temporary injunction against UCWA demonstrations, noting that there was a "high probability that property damage, physical injury and construction interruption [would] result."[84]

On July 7, 125 UCWA supporters paraded to the courthouse steps, demanding the right for the UCWA to dispatch black apprentices. At this time Scott took the position that, despite the June 27 order enjoining further demonstrations, such activities would resume unless the court moved forward and met UCWA demands. Said Scott: "We know that these courts can function (quickly) when they want to function. . . . We're here to tell the court it better start to act—and give us what we need and what we got coming."[85]

On July 13, the court finally heard testimony citing racial prejudice on work sites and the problems which plagued black apprentices under the present training system. These difficulties included obtaining books and tuition fees as well as paying the costs of transportation to and from the Seattle Community College's Northgate campus. The court responded by giving the UCWA an opportunity to demonstrate its "ability to recruit and counsel special apprentices and to observe or monitor the dispatch procedures used in referring such apprentices to jobs."[86] On July 17, the court clarified its order and stated that all special apprenticeship applicants were to be initially referred to the UCWA for screening and counseling purposes. The UCWA was then to forward lists of applicants for each of the four trades to the COAC staff office for review and recording. The COAC staff was to transmit the lists "promptly" to the appropriate apprenticeship committee or its subcommittee for final evaluation and acceptance into the programm When any special apprentice was unemployed for five days, the court's order instructed him to first report to the UCWA for counseling. The UCWA would then refer him to the appropriate union or apprenticeship committee for redispatch. Finally, the court required the United States attorney in Seattle to provide reports every ninety days on the progress made under his orders. From this point on—with the court looking to Seattle rather than to Washington, D.C., for its assistance and guidance from the government—the Department of Justice began to play a much more active role in the administration of the decree.

An Evaluation of the Order's Effectiveness

The basic purpose of Judge Lindberg's initial order and its numerous supplements, particularly the creation of the special apprenticeship program, was to insure that sufficient numbers of black workers would achieve the economic security and geographical mobility afforded by journeyman status. The June 7, 1972, order, reflecting impatience with the rate of compliance, required that each union's special apprenticeship program include a fixed number of actively participating blacks by July 1972.[87] The September 1972 report issued by the United States attorney[88] indicated that substantial progress had been made during the summer of 1972; by September the unions appeared close to meeting the July 1972 standards. Yet the number of apprentices decreased by March 1973. The March 1973 United States attorney's report concluded that "only the Electricians have continued to meet the standards for minimum enrollment set last June, and that none of the programs is close to graduating the number specified in the original decree."[89] Moreover, it seems highly unlikely that the goals formulated by the initial 1970 court order will be complied with in the foreseeable future.[90]*

Barriers to Effectiveness

The failure of the original Seattle building trades order to have more impact is attributable to a number of factors. A recession in the construction industry, inherent weaknesses with the admittedly innovative special apprenticeship concept, and continued discrimination both in referral and in the indenture of white apprentices accounted for much of the order's ineffectiveness.

The Recession in Construction

The dramatic decline of work in the construction industry which began in 1971 continued through the spring of 1973. Lack of steady employment had a substantial impact on the high rate of attrition among apprentices; in fact, the rate of attrition was to some degree inversely proportional to the rate of employment. For instance, from November through December 1972, Ironworker apprentices worked an average of 12.8 days. Fifteen apprentices were dropped and the rate of attrition was 44.1 percent. Electricians worked 29.9 days and the number of apprentices dropped was 12. The rate of attrition was 17.6 percent. For Plumbers the average days worked was 23.1, the number of apprentices dropped was 5, and the rate of attrition 15.6 percent.[91]

Practical Problems in the Special Apprenticeship Programs

The special apprenticeship concept, perhaps the most innovative aspect of Judge Lindberg's initial order, was also responsible for many of the practical difficulties in achieving his goals. Judge Lindberg had perfectly understandable reasons for creating a dual system of apprenticeship—the regular and special programs. Substantial evidence was presented at the trial which indicated that there were large numbers of blacks who were too old to qualify for the existing programs or who had some experience in the trade but did not meet journeyman standards.[92] The age limitations of the regular apprenticeship programs were unreasonable for those workers who had been unfairly excluded when they did meet the age qualifications. Moreover, the duration of the existing programs was unnecessary for those workers who had already developed some expertise.

Qualifications of special apprentices. Generally, black workers who entered the special apprenticeship programs with some experience performed satisfactorily.[93] Yet the court's assumptions concerning the skill of the average special apprentice did not work out in practice. A substantial number of black skilled tradesmen in Seattle did not come forward to enter the special apprenticeship program. The most probable explanation of their reluctance is that such workers, often protected from layoffs by pressure from the federal government contract compliance agencies, did not wish to risk their current jobs in a declining construction industry where blacks were traditionally less likely to obtain steady employment than whites. In addition, many black workers in related industries considered themselves close to the journeyman's level already. They did not want to lose what status they had in their current jobs to enter an experimental apprenticeship program. Ironically, those for whom the special program was created were generally deterred from applying.

The result was that the black special apprentice, far from having more skills and experience than the average white apprentice, was often at a considerable disadvantage. Special apprentices often tended to be younger than the white regulars, not older as had been contemplated. Moreover, since black apprentices were less likely to have a white relative or friend who had taught them the trade in the past or who could do so in the future, they did not have the same kind of knowledge and motivation which gives one a competitive edge in the employment arena. Such workers, who probably needed a more substantial training program, were saddled with a program which was inferior to that being given to white regular apprentices.

Curriculum. Moreover, the crafts refused to make a serious effort to revise their apprenticeship programs in order to shorten them in a meaningful fashion for black specials, and the Department of Justice, the COAC, and Judge Lindberg did not require them to do so. As a result, the trades simply lopped off the end of their existing training period. The special apprenticeship program became nothing more than an incomplete regular one. No attempt was made to readapt the curriculum or to determine whether the curriculum was properly job-related. In the Electricians' special program, for example, the lab portion of the regular apprenticeship, which gives the worker a chance to practice what he will be doing on the job, was entirely cut off. Only the two academic years of the regular program were retained.[94] Since many black specials did not have a strong formal education and were therefore less likely to perform well academically, the program devised for them could not have been worse.[95]*

Union referral. The union referral systems, particularly the one employed by the Ironworkers, illustrate further disadvantages with the special apprenticeship concept. Until they were obliged to change their procedures in 1974, the Iron-workers dispatched special apprentices from a hiring list. The dispatcher main-tained one list for regulars and another for special apprentices. When an employer simply requested an apprentice without specifying an individual by name, a regu-lar apprentice was always dispatched. Special apprentices were referred with every fifth journeyman, whether or not they were requested by the employer.[96]

Since union dispatchers did not inquire whether the black special apprentices they sent out were needed, they often knowingly referred specials when there was obviously no work for them. The United States attorney's September 1972 report noted that "at least one first class special apprentice had been sent back to the hall without employment sixty or seventy times."[97] Many employers felt the fifth-man dispatch rule saddled them with employees whose services were worthless or su-perfluous. They had the special do relatively unskilled routine work for a day or two and then sent him back to the hall.[98]* Thus, while special apprentices were dispatched 35 times as often as regulars, they only worked 55 percent as much.[99] The figures cited in the summer 1973 United States attorney's report indicated that the hours worked by black special apprentice Ironworkers continued to be substan-tially below those of regular apprentices.[100]

The fact that special apprentices in unions which have not used the fifth-man dispatch rule also work less than regulars indicates that dispatchers may be using their discretion to send specials to inappropriate jobs or to good jobs at bad times. Moreover, black regulars in all the unions work less than their white counterparts, which suggests that subtle forms of racial discrimination are involved even within the regular program.

Indenture of white apprentices. The fact that the unions continued to indenture a substantial number of white apprentices at the very time that blacks were dropping out as a result of discouragement over inadequate training and referral opportu-nities illustrates another weakness of the special apprenticeship program. The Sheetmetal Union, for example, indentured a class of 31 regulars in 1973, of which only 4 members were black. Only three apprentices were indentured into the special class.[101] The figures for the regular program obviously did not meet the 30 percent "reasonable level of participation" required by Judge Lindberg's initial order. More importantly, however, the admission of a large class of regular apprentices in an industry with limited job opportunities precluded the indenture of a reasonably sized class of special apprentices. As the United States attorney's report pointed out, "if only 30 new apprentice opportunities per year are avail-able, their allocation to a largely white regular class to the exclusion of a fair sized special class is at variance with the affirmative obligations of the degree."[102] The more new whites indentured, the longer it takes to train properly the required quota of black apprentices. If the dual apprenticeship system had not existed, union evasion of the order's numerical goals could not have been accomplished in so effective a manner. Even with the elimination of the dual program, however, problems will abound until and unless ratios are established under which the number of whites indentured and retained is limited in relationship to the number of their black counterparts.

Theoretical Weaknesses of a Dual System

Many of the problems encountered in implementing the court order can be traced to the very notion of a dual system of apprenticeship. The same issue raised by the school desegregation cases also arises in the union discrimination area: can separate but equal ever be equal? In *Sweatt* v. *Painter*, [103] even more clearly than in *Brown* v. *Board of Education*, [104] Supreme Court seriously questioned the proposition that separate facilities for the races could ever be equal for blacks. Because *Sweatt* involved segregated law schools, the Court easily understood that the black graduate would not be able to avoid the stigma of separation in a world dominated by whites. [105*] Yet the *Sweatt* reasoning should apply to craftsmen as well as to professionals. Black special apprentices, like the graduates of the black law school in *Sweatt,* are stigmatized as inferior. Moreover, there are objective and subjective components in both contexts. Blacks in the labor market are harmed by the belief of employers that their skills are inadequate—whether this assumption is accurate or not[106*] as well as by their own history of isolation and deficient training.

Without a unitary apprenticeship system, therefore, black workers are destined to suffer the consequences which the Court perceived so clearly and correctly in *Sweatt.* On the other hand, a conflict exists between the importance of a unitary system and the special need of black workers for an abbreviated training program. It thus appears that abbreviation of unitary apprenticeship programs through the revision of union training procedures which are not justified by a business necessity provides the key to increased black employment. (Of course, in light of the difficulties of revising union training programs and the judicial trepidation in imposing new apprenticeship programs on the unions,[107] quotas and timetables are also essential.)

The question therefore becomes whether the courts would be justified in requiring abbreviated, unitary training programs. In *Griggs* v. *Duke Power Co.*, [108*] the Supreme Court concluded that neutral employment requirements must be job-related when they have a discriminatory impact. The Court found that passing a standardized intelligence test as a condition of employment did not "bear a demonstrable relationship to successful performance of the jobs for which it was used"[109] and therefore outlawed the test. In *Griggs,* the Court referred approvingly to EEOC guidelines which require validation for each race. According to the guidelines, tests are valid only if the results are correlated with job performance. [110] Although dual standards which are predictive for job performance have been adhered to in the written examination context itself,[111] some of the progeny of *Griggs* outside the examination area have not followed the same route. In the arrest record cases the courts have ordered employers to disregard the arrest records of all employees and not simply blacks—even though the discriminatory impact is to be found only with regard to blacks.[112] Similar treatment has been accorded the dismissal of employees because of wage garnishments.[113]

If training programs of substantial duration adversely affect blacks because they are already experienced, as Judge Lindberg thought in *Local 86, Ironworkers,* or because they are more likely to drop out earlier because of the culturally felt need for instant economic gratification,[114] only blacks are harmed. The creation of a remedy for blacks alone, however, may present substantial difficulties because of (1) the practical problems involved in administering two procedures and (2) the discord that is likely to arise between the races in this event. The testing situation can be distinguished from the problems involved here inasmuch as in the testing situation the employer or union is giving all applicants the same examination. It is simply using different cutoff scores in connection with a single application to correlate performance on the job and performance on the test; this may be the only appropriate way in which the test can be validated. On the other hand, very different problems arise in conducting two training programs, problems which the courts have recognized would occur if the employer had separate application forms, only one of which called for information about arrest and conviction records or separate procedures with regard to wage garnishments. Moreover, the lesson of *Local 86, Ironworkers* is that racist trade unions are enabled to engage in evasive action when there are two programs. By refusing to reform the special program for blacks they made it virtually impossible for black graduates to perform as journeymen and moreover made it more likely that blacks will not compete on the same level as white apprentices. It would therefore seem that, under the authority of the *Griggs* progeny, a unitary and abbreviated program could appropriately be established for both races. (This point is developed more fully in Chapter 5.)[115]

Other Judicial Errors

Apart from the recession in the construction industry and problems arising out of the special apprenticeship concept, other factors contributed to the ineffectiveness of the decrees. Judge Lindberg made a serious error in failing to create a specific apprenticeship ratio between blacks and whites. Establishing goals for blacks alone simply invites evasion. The defendant locals, for example, equated the goal for black apprentice recruitment with the goal for the graduation of black apprentices to journeyman status. This interpretation practically insured an insufficient number of black journeymen. Union training programs throughout the country suffer a substantial amount of attrition[116] even without the unique problems encountered in Seattle. Accordingly, a COAC report noted that it was necessary for the recruitment goal to be twice as high as the graduation goal in order for the latter to be successfully implemented within a reasonable period of time. This proposal has never been implemented nor adopted as part of the court's order.[117]

In addition, Judge Lindberg did not use his contempt powers. Theoretically, one of the comparative advantages of Title VII over Taft-Hartley is that the judge who tries the case is subsequently called upon to fashion contempt sanctions if that proves necessary. The judge has a stake in his own decree and is familiar with the facts which gave rise to the litigation. Yet Judge Lindberg, proud of his landmark decree but tired of continuous disharmony, has avoided contempt proceedings whenever possible. He has now begun to use the United States attorney's office in Seattle as a kind of special master or mediator to act as a buffer against excessive judicial involvement in disputes. Whether this should be the Department of Justice's role is somewhat questionable inasmuch as it is supposed to be an advocate. In the Seattle case, the Department of Justice has been extremely timid about instituting contempt proceedings. Either Judge Lindberg or the department could have made the decree work more effectively if they had not allowed their legitimate concern with integrating blacks into the unions to paralyze their will to act. Both understandably feared antagonizing the unions, from whom some measure of cooperation seemed necessary. Yet the unions did not cooperate voluntarily. Use of the contempt power, while creating unfortunate animosity, would at least have increased the chances that the order would be enforced.[118]*

The Positive Impact of the Seattle Order

The failure of Judge Lindberg's order to have all of the practical impact he had intended can be traced to external forces such as pervasive racism and serious unemployment as well as to his own errors in judgment. The deficiencies of the order and the results it produced, however, must be evaluated against a long history of unsuccessful attempts to combat employment discrimination. In fact, Judge Lindberg's opinion is, on balance, the most ambitious and effective approach yet devised.

The principal significance of the Seattle order is that it provided the first decrees which were not content with existing institutions. It went beyond a quota system by devising a comprehensive remedy. Unlike AFL-CIO supported programs, which moved blacks over a number of hurdles previously struck down as discriminatory by the courts, Judge Lindberg's Seattle order assaulted the entire union program. His effort was not an unqualified success, but some progress has been made. Moreover, the Seattle experience has uncovered a good number of the problems which future courts are bound to encounter. Even in his misjudgments, therefore, Judge Lindberg made a substantial contribution. A weaker order would have taught far less. It is also important to recognize that Judge Lindberg's order was the first indication that the courts operating under Title VII had learned the lesson of *Brown* v. *Board of Education* [II].[119] It took fourteen years for the Supreme Court to realize that racist defendants cannot be trusted to act "with all deliberate speed." Not until *Green* v. *County School Board*[120]* did the Court issue a detailed, sophisticated desegregation order to a southern board of education. Yet Judge Lindberg delivered his comprehensive order only five years after the effective date of Title VII. He understood that quotas, though a necessary first step, must be supplemented by specific programs in order to insure implementation. It is to be hoped that other courts will follow his lead and act more quickly against discrimination than they did against school segregation.

Judge Lindberg also recognized that it is important for the black community to be involved in implementing the decree. The establishment of the COAC was the first effort to create an institution which could assist a court in enforcing a Title VII decree.[121]* Blacks, as well as unions and contractors, participated on the board. Their involvement kept pressure on the other groups to insure enforcement[122]* and allowed some cooperation among the previously adversary parties. Moreover, despite initial reluctance, Judge Lindberg gave a black workers' organization, the UCWA, an official role in assuring the decree's effectiveness.[123]*

The March 12, 1974 Order

On March 12, 1974, Judge Lindberg signed four supplemental consent orders[124] which attempt to respond to a number of the problems enumerated above. The 1970 decree had promulgated its quotas for all the trades in terms of the number of blacks indentured in a given year. While it was anticipated that quota indenturing would lead to a substantial change in the racial composition of journeymen, no specific quotas and timetables were set for the number of black journeymen. Because attrition in the trades was substantial, the lack of a numerical goal for graduating journeymen proved to be a troublesome omission—although by no means the cause of the attrition problem. Quite obviously, it was to take more than simply setting quotas for journeymen to cure the underlying problems which frustrated the intent of the 1970 decree.

The number of black journeymen required by the 1974 consent orders were as follows: Electrical Workers, 75; Ironworkers, 78; Sheetmetal Workers, 81; and Plumbers and Pipefitters, 96. These numbers were to be graduated by the following dates: Ironworkers, 1978; Sheetmetal Workers, 1980; Plumbers and Pipefitters, 1981. Because the Electricians had the requisite number of 75 blacks participating in or graduating from their program as of the time of the consent orders, no specific schedule was included for that union.

In effect, the March 1974 consent orders provided some "breathing space" for the unions to comply with the numerical goals while reforms were being instituted elsewhere. In order to deal with the underlying problem of attrition which would defeat the purpose of any quota for journeymen, each joint apprenticeship committee was obligated to develop an indenture policy which would take into account both current participation and past attrition rate so as to reasonably assure that the current rate of indenture and enrollment would implement the timetable.

The separate programs for regular and special apprentices were eliminated. In this regard, the parties and the court gave ground to the craft unions. In effect, the abbreviation of the program to what was thought to be job-related was not accomplished—the reforms thought to be necessary were not imposed upon the unions. Nevertheless, despite these concessions, the 1974 orders seem to be sensible in this respect for the reasons outlined above.[125] As the United States attorney's quarterly report to the court on apprenticeship programs, March 1974, noted:

The theory of the shortened special apprentice program was based on several assumptions: (1) that there was a large pool of partially trained blacks in the community that didn't need full apprenticeship training; and (2) that it was possible to train well-qualified journeymen in a shorter time if sufficient effort was made to condense the apprentice programs.

The single program has worked well for the people that it was originally designed to help. There have been approximately 37 black graduates of the special programs since the inception of the Court order. Most of these graduates were partially trained and experienced prior to their entry into the apprentice programs. These graduates have proven themselves to be competitive in the job market and have worked fairly steadily since their graduation.

Certain problems have emerged, however, with the original theory of the special apprentice program. The pool of partially trained blacks existing in the community is not as large as was originally expected. Most blacks in this category are either in the apprenticeship program or have already graduated from it. Many of the other black apprentices have no significant prior experience in construction, yet are put in a shortened special program where they get less training than is given to regular apprentices. There are continuing questions as to the completeness of the training given to the special apprentices. Apprentice training consists only partially of school work; the majority of apprentice learning consists of on the job training. While it is possible to condense a school program, it is difficult if not impossible to condense work experience. In addition, it is the custom in construction that a first year apprentice, as the low man on the totem pole, spends time doing tasks that are not directly related to learning the craft. An apprentice can better afford to lose all or part of one year's work experience if he is in a four year program. However, it is costly to lose one year's work in a two year program. There has been some continuing resentment over the Court-imposed program that gives blacks quicker access to jobs and to wage increases. There has been concern over whether a graduate of the special apprentice program will be the subject of lasting stima and continuing doubts as to his acquired skills because of his involvement with the program.[126]

Next, because of the charge of craft unions that poor screening was responsible for the attrition rate, the joint apprenticeship committees have been permitted to rank black apprentice applicants. On the one hand, this permits the reappearance of some of the objective and subjective criteria which had been condemned by the court in 1970. On the other hand, the unions must still meet their quotas—they are simply filled with those who have surmounted the ranking hurdles. This procedure may result in a more highly motivated group of apprentices—assuming that some portion of the attrition rate is attributable to a poor screening process.

It is still difficult to assess the full impact of the March 1974 orders. The government has begun to evaluate progress by considering not only the participation rate but also the number of both advanced apprentices and graduates. By this means, future losses can be anticipated and progress can be more realistically estimated. In July 1974, the quarterly report noted that the number of advanced apprentices and graduates, totalled and expressed in terms of the percentage of the court's goal which had been achieved, grew in the following manner between March and June 1974: while the Ironworkers remained at 35 percent, Plumbers and Pipefitters increased from 41 percent to 46 percent, Sheetmetal Workers, from 37 percent to 41 percent, and Electricians, from 45 percent to 61 percent. As the quarterly report noted:

Progress is clearest in the Plumbers' program, where increases in all areas indicate that indenture, training, and graduation are continuing in a slow but orderly fashion toward fulfillment of the required goal. The Sheet Metal and Electrical programs show a decrease in enrollment and total participation, but training progress is evident; there are more senior apprentices and more graduates now than there were in March. Figures for the Iron Worker program indicate a certain loss of momentum. There are more graduates but no increases in the total of seniors and graduates.[127]

In the fall of 1974, the government once again began to speak in its quarterly report of legal action against the Ironworkers:

The Iron Workers have more graduates than any other trade, but a lower level of participation. More important, there are very few seniors—only about a third the number shown in the other three programs. Some new Iron Workers have been indentured but only one first year apprentice has moved up to replace the two seniors who graduated this summer. In short, training has been and continues to be very slow, with few apprentices managing to complete that difficult first year.

The Plumbers program has more graduates than the Electricians and Sheet Metal Workers, a substantial number of seniors, and many new indentures; the participation level is somewhat above that required for this year. If the Plumbers can keep and train the number they have, they should be able to meet the next required increments. . . . New [Sheet-metal] indentures are needed to replace the apprentices who have advanced beyond the first year and to raise the level of participation closer to the required goals.[128]

Finally, elimination of the fifth-man dispatch seems to have steadied employment opportunities for apprentices. The consent orders provide for a "first in–first out" hiring dispatch rule, which has eliminated one of the major problems afflicting black Ironworker apprentices.

Conclusion: The Promise of Private Action

As a result of the 1972 amendments to Title VII, the Department of Justice participation in litigating employment discrimination cases in the private sector has been almost completely phased out. The Equal Employment Opportunity Commission has been given authority to sue, but it has a substantial backlog and is simply unable to take the overwhelming percentage of its meritorious cases to court. Furthermore, the EEOC has been able to try only a handful of cases on their merits in the five years that it has had authority to sue because of procedural objections raised by defendants.[129]

What is even more pernicious and ominous is the willingness of both the Justice Department and the EEOC to align themselves with defendants in consent decrees negotiated in the steel and trucking industries.[130]* The steel decree provides for affirmative action in the form of hiring goals and timetables, seniority carry-over rights for employees locked previously into low-opportunity departments, and back pay. The trucking decree is more modest, primarily because it does not provide any seniority or promotion rights for minority workers inasmuch as the International Brotherhood of Teamsters is not party to the decree. While such decrees, which provide back pay for black workers, have been hailed as multimillion dollar settlements which demonstrate the good faith of companies and unions, the fact is that they are severely deficient in a number of respects. (1) Per capita recoveries are extremely small because the money is spread over a substantial number of workers. (2) The decrees require that workers who accept moneys execute waivers even when they are not advised of the basis for calculating back pay, let alone the availability of front pay and punitive damages (the Court implied in *Bowman* and *Johnson* v. *Railway Express* that both are available).[131] (3) The implementation of the decree either is in essence not provided for at all, as in trucking, where initially the Postal Service and, more recently, the General Services Administration (neither of which can discharge its contract compliance responsibilities which exist independent of the decree)[132] were given monitoring authority, or is handed over to defendants themselves, as in the steel industry, where minorities are excluded from any involvement in monitoring.

All these factors present considerable difficulties for minority plaintiffs. The small amount of relief puts most minority workers, who live on low incomes, to a cruel choice: to submit to a settlement which is demonstratively inadequate in terms of both the past and the future, or to participate in litigation in which the government is not merely passive, as in *Local 86* and *Detroit Edison,* but opposed to the plaintiffs and other members of the groups discriminated against.

The execution of waivers compounds the problem. For as the Court noted in *Albermarle,* monetary relief is an essential ingredient to the deterrence of wrongdoing. Accordingly, it is no coincidence that the pressure for waivers has increased as the judiciary has fashioned more liberal rules relating to back-pay recovery. In trucking, the waivers are provided for even though the minority driver does not know what seniority relief will be obtained through future litigation and decrees.[133] In steel, the waivers are vaguely prospective in nature, thus serving to preclude suits initiated regarding discrimination in the future as well as the past. It seems difficult to contend seriously that such waivers are "voluntary and knowing" within the meaning of *Alexander* v. *Gardner-Denver.*[134] This is especially true in trucking when one considers that counsel for minority plaintiffs, operating under so-called "gag orders," are denied access to the names and addresses of class members, while minorities are subjected to pressure and harassment by defendants. In steel, implementation is equally troublesome, and experience at the Bethlehem Lackawanna plant demonstrates that defendants may use control of the monitoring as both a shield against charges of discrimination and a vehicle for retaliation against the plaintiffs.[135] If the trucking decree is upheld, matters may become worse because the Postal Service will not have the resources to cope with most disputes, and will perform poorly in those that are adjudicated. The involvement of blacks and other affected minorities would do much to alter this picture. The record in *Local 86* testifies to that proposition. Otherwise, every defendant will be standing in line to obtain decrees like those negotiated in the steel and trucking industries. The primary burden for enforcement of Title VII, therefore, must rest on the shoulders of private parties and, perhaps increasingly, minority workers' organizations like the UCWA.

How can private actions be encouraged? Although the courts have begun to attract some attorneys through the award of attorney's fees, large back-pay judgments, and punitive damages for victorious plaintiffs, these inducements may not be sufficient. An attorney may not know what kind of case he has and therefore whether there is a reasonable prospect of financial recovery until after the expenditure of a large amount of money and the hard and detailed investigatory work that goes into getting the facts. It is here, as well as in the critical area of enforcement, that organizations like Seattle's UCWA can play an important role. The association literally brought the Department of Justice to Seattle and made their task considerably easier. It stirred Judge Lindberg to action during the summer of 1972. Similar organizations would be of aid to private attorneys in gathering evidence, bringing actions, and monitoring decrees in other situations.

All these activities cost money, of course. In Seattle, the American Friends Service Committee assisted the UCWA project. One would hope that federal agencies such as the Equal Employment Opportunity Commission and private foundations would find minority organization activity worthwhile enough to finance on a substantial basis in the future. But the EEOC role in Title VII is now a tarnished one and it cannot be counted upon to support plaintiffs when powerful defendants are arrayed against them. One would also hope that actions will be instituted in which organizations like the UCWA can play a role. Financial backing must be made available to both attorneys and private organizations so that private attorneys general can be in a position to have the staying power necessary for protracted litigation and to see that decrees are enforced. For it is that creative interplay between tough court orders and black workers' organizations which holds the greatest promise. The Seattle building trades decree without the UCWA would have been nothing more than an intellectual exercise; without the decree, the UCWA would have floundered like the minority organizations which operate under (and are so often frustrated by) hometown plans fathered by the Nixon administration.

Whether financial resources will be made available to private parties who have the kind of dedication displayed by the UCWA is problematical. But one thing is clear: until an administration demonstrates a great deal more support for minority group aspirations than have the recent Republican ones, the hard work will have to be done by individuals outside of government, if the law is to be enforced. That is perhaps the principal lesson to be derived from the Seattle construction litigation and the few "agitators" who would not let the expectations produced by the June 1970 order flicker out of existence.

14 | Industrial and Public-Employee Unions

Outside of the craft unions, minority employment patterns and systemic discrimination vary. This chapter will examine employment relationships in which a number of noncraft unions are exclusive bargaining representatives, most particularly, the International Brotherhood of Teamsters, the United Automobile Workers, the United Rubber Workers, and the Amalgamated Meat Cutters.

Introduction

For the industrial unions, and for many of their public-employee counterparts, the political dynamics involved in union policy-making on the race issue are considerably different from those discussed previously. For the most part, blacks have been in the industries covered by the industrial unions' jurisdiction in considerable numbers since World War II, a fact largely attributable to manpower requirements of the employers and the drift of blacks from the land to urban centers in the North. This has made black demands inside the industrial unions quite different from those made in the construction trades, where the concern is access to jobs.

In the industrial unions, black demands have had two areas of emphasis. The first relates to type of employment and promotion. For even in unions like the UAW, which has a good reputation in matters of race, based upon the egalitarian stance it took in the 1940's when white auto production workers refused to work with Negroes, the skilled trades have been traditionally a lily-white bastion. The same holds true of supervisory positions, and sometimes the direct contacts between black workers and white supervisors have been incendiary. Resulting protests have involved the industrial unions in issues which are normally beyond their bargaining scope, such as who are to be selected by management as supervisors and, more specifically, what steps management can take to alter the supervisory racial composition.

The second area of protest has involved the question of leadership. As the percentage of blacks in some of the unions has moved continuously upward, dissatisfaction with the all-white or predominantly white leadership at both the international and the local level (but especially the former) has increased. One of the unions in which this issue is most important is the United Steelworkers, whose convention was picketed by members demonstrating their displeasure with the complete absence of minority representation at the international level. At the UAW, in 1968 and 1969, after blacks had cracked the color barrier among elected officials on the international executive board, the question of minority staff appointments was raised.

Black workers, union officials, and delegates are now unafraid to protest in many large unions—sometimes in the most strident and vitriolic language. And the upheaval does not translate itself into words alone. Black caucuses have been formed where none existed before. And even where, as in the case of the UAW, black caucuses were part of the formal union structure, younger workers have formed groups of their own—sometimes working within the union and sometimes attempting to deal with management independent of the collective-bargaining system. Where the bargaining units are composed of a relatively small percentage of the company's employees, as in some portions of the electric power industry, for instance, organizations like the Association for the Betterment of Black Edison Employees at the Detroit Edison Company have been created to speak for both unit and nonunit employees. Local 223, Utility Workers Union in Detroit has acquiesced in this procedure because of its unwillingness or inability to speak for black as well as white members. In short, such groups and organizations take a variety of forms.

On the national level, for some time now black trade unionists have been attempting to address themselves to the problems of minorities within the labor movement. In the 1950's, the Negro American Labor Council was formed, primarily to pressure the AFL-CIO and its constituent organizations to alter practices which were later condemned by Title VII. Initially, the AFL-CIO and even some of the more progressive unions such as the UAW were hostile to NALC. (The UAW was confronted with a particularly active chapter, the Trade Union Leadership Council.) A. Philip Randolph, the president of NALC, incurred the wrath of the AFL-CIO president, George Meany, when Randolph questioned him about segregated locals. Said Meany: "Who in the hell appointed you as guardian of the Negro people?"[1] This same kind of hostile reaction was reported of some UAW leaders, particularly Emil Mazey, secretary-treasurer of the union.

Eventually, however, Randolph made his peace with Meany, the principal basis being AFL-CIO support for Project Outreach programs in the construction trades. What was particularly damaging to the vitality of NALC was the fact that its essential strength came from Negro staffers who were dependent upon white union officials for their appointments. Without an independent political base within the labor movement, black trade unionists could not speak out freely with authority, and the organization declined.

A new and stronger organization, the Coalition of Black Trade Unionists, representing thirty-seven labor unions, appeared on the scene in 1972. A number of factors are responsible for its emergence. A superficial one, which nonetheless served as the immediate catalyst, was Meany's decision to stay neutral during the Nixon-McGovern presidential contest in 1972. Said William Lucy, the black secretary-treasurer of the American Federation of State, County and Municipal

Employees Union: "The AFL-CIO decision did not take into consideration the negative impact Nixon has on the poor, especially the black poor. There is no way black unionists are going to remain neutral in this election."[2] But the coalition was formed for reasons that went far beyond the issue of the 1972 presidential election. Lucy said in the same interview: "It's obvious that the AFL-CIO was not doing its job for black workers. The Federation may consider the problems of poor blacks, but it doesn't understand those problems." Lucy characterized the coalition as neither a "separatist" nor a "civil rights" organization and stated that it would work within the trade union movement for black workers and the black community: "Before now there has been no forum for black militancy within the trade union movement."

Another important factor behind the coalition's existence is the fact that a few black trade unionists have now been able to develop a political base of their own. Foremost amongst these leaders is Lucy himself, in a union which is more than 30 percent black. Not only is he in the vanguard of the coalition's founders, but because he holds an important and independent position inside his own union, he has been able to enlist the help of that union for his movement. Most important, Lucy is able to speak out without a substantial fear of political retaliation.

Because the coalition is a threat to the A. Philip Randolph Institute, financially assisted by the AFL-CIO and headed by Bayard Rustin, and to the notion that Meany, the AFL-CIO civil rights department, and union officialdom generally are doing all that they can to achieve racial equality in jobs, Rustin and the AFL-CIO have attacked the coalition and the media, both of which, in Rustin's words have "ignored the significant progress of the past decade in strengthening the ties between labor and the black community."[3] Meanwhile, the coalition has moved ahead with its plans to mobilize pressure on the labor movement—industrial as well as construction—to integrate more effectively blacks into organized labor.

International Brotherhood of Teamsters

In the South, truck driving was traditionally regarded as a "Negro" job, in large part a legacy of the South's dependence upon Negroes as "draymen" in the post–Civil War period. But this view has altered considerably. As unions have pushed up wages, driving positions have become more attractive to whites, and the number of blacks employed in trucking has declined even in the South. In recent years, blacks and other racial minorities have been excluded from just about all aspects of the industry. But it is the lucrative over-the-road driving jobs to which they have had the most difficulty obtaining access. As Richard Leone has noted:

Although road drivers do not receive their training through formal apprenticeship programs, they have a tendency to view their occupation as a craft. They reserve these jobs for their friends and relatives, just as craft unions practiced nepotism in accepting apprentices into their training programs. We should, therefore, expect to find that Negroes, in their effort to be employed as road drivers, must face some of the problems associated with being accepted in construction crafts.[4]

Furthermore, as Leone notes:

In the key industry—public interstate trucking—the union [International Brotherhood of Teamsters] has few Negro members and has demonstrated little zeal in altering the situation. Moreover, it is the over-the-road truckers on which the Teamsters' union relies to assist in organizing other industries. With the union, therefore, this group is the most powerful, politically and economically. Union officials have been reluctant to advocate positive programs for equal employment because they could effect this internal balance of power.[5]

While approximately 10 percent of the Teamster membership is black, other minorities such as Chicanos and Puerto Ricans are also excluded from lucrative heavy freight. Moreover, there is only one black member of the union's executive board. Only one president of a Joint Council (the sub-regional organizations of the Teamsters) is black. The only blacks working at IBT headquarters in Washington are one secretary and a number of janitors. In short, there is no room at the top for black Teamsters.

Statistics tell a good deal of the story. For instance, with regard to parties operating under the National Master Freight Agreement, according to Justice Department statistics for 1974,[6] of approximately 1,747 road drivers employed by the Pacific Intermountain Express Company, 1.9 percent were black, and 1.1 were Spanish-surnamed American. Apparently, PIE employed their first black over-the-road driver around 1968. In Oakland, California, there are only three black road drivers out of approximately 115—and they are not on the permanent seniority list because their seniority permits them only to obtain irregular employment on the "extra board." Of approximately 2,767 drivers for Consolidated Freightways, 72 or 2.6 percent are black, and 20 or 0.7 percent are Spanish-surnamed.

Although it is clear that both employers and the International Brotherhood of Teamsters play a role in this pattern of exclusion, the union must bear a substantial portion of the blame. As Judge Wright noted in *Macklin* v. *Spector Freight Systems, Inc.,* "Where blacks are in the minority, as they so often are in large industrial unions like the Teamsters, tacit union acquiescence in an employer's discriminatory practices effectively produces the same end result that was condemned in *Steele.*"[7] The union and its members have ample opportunity to engage in word-of-mouth communication and friends-relatives hiring. Because educational qualifications for jobs in the industry are not high, substantial numbers of both blacks and whites are competing. On the west coast, unions play a role in referral—especially in northern California. Local 85 in San Francisco operates a hiring hall, as do Local 70 (which has jurisdiction over the East Bay, including Oakland) and Local 287 (San Jose). In Local 85, of approximately 5500 members in 1973, only 60 were black. The number is much smaller for Local 287—less than 10 blacks in a membership of 3,000. Moreover, in Local 287, as of 1973, there were only one or two black over-the-road black drivers.

Locals 85 and 287 both have "A" and "B" cards, and practically no blacks or Chicanos hold "A" cards, which ensure fairly regular work out of the hiring hall. ("A" cards are given out on the basis of experience, and the holder receives preference in referrals to work opportunities.) Moreover, while an employer may call for a particular employee by name out of the hiring hall, as a practical matter, because of lack of work experience and union pressure, "B" card holders have been unable to benefit from this procedure. Inasmuch as Local 85 has been an exclusionary union, having a father-son preference rule until the 1960's, the work experience requirements for obtaining an "A" card have had the effect of perpetuating past discrimination and excluding blacks from access to the industry. Because there are few jobs for "B" card members, and those jobs are less desirable and of shorter duration, it is extremely difficult for black "B" card holders to obtain the experience that would qualify them for "A" cards. The irony is that a substantial number of employers would like to call for blacks or other racial minorities so as to fulfill their contract compliance requirements, but cannot do so because such drivers are not "A" card holders.

While over-the-road jobs are "coveted" positions, as Judge Wisdom has characterized them in *Rodriguez* v. *East Texas Motor Freight*[8] (for those on the permanent seniority list who are guaranteed work regularly the income is considerable, in some cases, upwards of $30,000 per year), and while blacks and Chicanos are underrepresented in this category, this writer has met many black and Chicano drivers who were previously qualified to work in an over-the-road capacity but who, having acquired family and other responsibilities, no longer desire such work. Of course, as Judge Luther Eubanks noted in *United States* v. *Lee Way Motor Freight:*

From the standpoint of income alone, there is no doubt that the position of road driver is better than any other position mentioned . . . but this position has its drawbacks in that those employed in this category are away from home on many occasions during which they must sleep in an extremely small bunk with the roar of the diesel engine pulling a heavy load in close proximity thereto. Although opinions are divided, most drivers prefer to be in the "over-the-road" category.[9]

Judge Eubanks' opinion points up one of the difficulties blacks and other minorities have encountered when they have attempted to move into over-the-road work. Although the sleeper cab is on the decline with most of the major freight companies, the fact is that many white Teamster members have refused and still refuse to sleep in the same bunk used by a black driver. According to a *Wall Street Journal* article in 1966, the president of Teamsters' Local 100 in Cincinnati said, "Would you like to climb into a bunk bed that a nigger just got out of?" Another Teamster leader, the president of Local 24 in Akron, Ohio, said, "To my knowledge, no law has been written yet that says a white has to bed down with Negroes."[10]

This basic resistance is supplemented by a number of other factors. In the first place, many employers have a prerequisite of two or three years of work experience for hiring an over-the-road driver. A number of major trucking companies on the west coast also require their drivers to have snow and ice experience. The difficulty with these requirements is basically threefold: (1) their disparate enforcement, in that whites have been hired quite often with less such experience; (2) the fact that the duration of the work experience is usually not job-validated and is therefore unlawful under *Griggs* and its progeny; (3) the fact that minorities are least likely to have snow and ice experience, because the only way to obtain it is to work for a major company or to own one's own rig. The effect is to keep out the minorities. Those who have obtained the experience and own their own rigs are deterred from applying by both the union's and the companies' discriminatory reputations and the hope of building business ventures of their own. For younger minority applicants, the answer is a minimal training program providing snow and ice driving experience. The difficulty is that the employers do not respect the product of the training programs that have begun to flourish—and which in all too many instances prey upon the hopes of innocent workers that they can obtain a large per annum salary with a minimum of training. The solution would appear to be a legal requirement that the companies devise their own training programs.

The problem of acquiring skills is made even more difficult by the combination of employer no-transfer practices and separate seniority systems negotiated by the International Brotherhood of Teamsters, sometimes with different locals. Although minorities are underrepresented at all levels of the trucking industry, there are larger proportions of minority workers who are hostlers and dockmen and who work in the terminals—and sometimes there are substantial numbers of minority local drivers, although quite often minorities are excluded from this classification to the same extent they are excluded from over-the-road positions. The International Brotherhood of Teamsters has negotiated guidelines with regard to seniority that are part of the National Master Freight Agreement and the various supplements to it that exist around the country. Although dockmen and local drivers may often be on the same seniority list, generally over-the-road drivers are a separate group. The significance of this, as should be recalled from our discussion of seniority above, is that a dockman or local driver who seeks promotion or transfer rights to the over-the-road classification must relinquish seniority accumulated in his or her classification and go to the bottom of the over-the-road list, a considerable sacrifice inasmuch as those who are on the bottom have no guarantee of working on a regular basis and are especially likely to be laid off during the winter months. Both the loss of seniority and the element of risk are powerful deterrents to minority applications for transfer. Moreover, in many instances a no-transfer policy makes it impossible for the worker to move across to the over-the-road driver classification in any event.

Time and time again, the courts have held that this form of seniority is unlawful insofar as it adversely affects minority drivers.[11] The same basic pattern exists across the country, and neither the Teamsters nor the employers have altered it unless ordered by court decree to do so. As Leone has pointed out, the "consistent phenomenon was that no company appeared ready to alter its hiring and operating procedures . . . the IBT immediately opposed all Post Office Department [the contract compliance agency] recommendations to overcome some of the human problems that might arise should companies hire Negro road drivers."[12]

According to Leone, James Hoffa (and it appears as though Frank Fitzsimmons has maintained this position in recent years) refused to alter the seniority provisions in the National Master Freight Agreement in any way which would make it more likely that blacks would be upgraded:

Hoffa made two points: (1) he defended the industry and maintained that no employer ever denied Negroes employment and (2) he stated categorically that he would never allow any firm to hire drivers under any arrangement other than what was stipulated in the National Master Freight Agreement. Hoffa warned Nagle [the contract compliance officer] that if any single company hired a Negro driver because of government pressure, he would call a strike. "Not a wheel would turn," said Hoffa, and "the Government could give its business to a wheelbarrow."[13]

In part, the Justice Department was prompted to sue the Teamsters and truckers on a nationwide basis because the same issues cropped up in every situation; no matter how many courts declared the seniority provisions of the National Master Freight Agreement and its supplemental agreements to be unlawful, the parties not directly ordered to make changes continued to adhere to the same practices and procedures. The difficulty is that the government, not having the resources to carry its confrontation with the trucking industry to a showdown, entered into a consent decree which covered its beneficiaries inadequately and excluded a substantial number of minority workers who had been harmed by the Teamster and trucker discriminatory practices.[14]*

The Teamsters give little promise of reforming themselves. Neither their tradition nor contemporary events provide much comfort.

The Teamster tradition developed under the presidency of Daniel Tobin, before the election of Dave Beck and Hoffa in the 1950's. Leone states the following:

One of the current union officials stated in a confidential interview: "Tobin did not like Italians, Jews, or Negroes; as a matter of fact, the only people he did like were Irish Catholics." Tobin's attitude, and those of many of the officers of local unions exemplified the craft conscious, work scarcity feelings found in the building trades unions. The milk, bread, and other salesman-driver locals were traditionally white and their customer contact jobs increased their white collar, as well as craft, orientation. Over-the-road drivers added their club-like feelings to the group, all of whom felt that Negroes had little or no place in their midst.

Given these feelings, it is likely that Tobin clearly reflected the feelings of his membership toward Negroes. Even if he did not, however, local autonomy in the union was so pronounced that it is doubtful if Tobin could have done much to insure Negro employment if he had so desired.[15]

In addition, the IBT is traditionally a decentralized organization, which makes it unlikely that an effective response could come from the international even if there was a desire for action at this level. While the international's influence increased considerably under Hoffa, the over-the-road drivers have votes and, more important, the muscle. Thus far, the international has no affirmative-action plan to deal with the transfer-seniority problem. In this respect, the industry on both sides of the bargaining table lags considerably behind the construction trades which, albeit in a stumbling fashion, have made efforts to bring in some blacks through Project Outreach.

A number of specific examples best serve to illustrate the union's attitude. In

1959 the Teamster Rank and File Committee for Equal Job Opportunity, an all-Negro Teamster group in Los Angeles, demonstrated at the Greyhound bus terminal because there were no black drivers. Yet black Teamster members claimed that the Los Angeles Joint Council "frowned" on this activity. The group attempted to meet with Hoffa but were successful only in meeting with the Joint Council and the Western Conference, and these sessions resulted in very little.

In 1962, black Teamsters in Los Angeles picketed the Joint Council because of the absence of black business agents in the organization there. The union agreed to sit down and talk with the black trade unionists, and as of 1973 there were ten Negro business agents in the Joint Council. As one black trade unionist said regarding the international's involvement in the two incidents in Los Angeles, "Hoffa had no awareness of social problems."

In Local 639 (against which Title VII litigation was instituted[16]), a 6,000-member local in Washington, D.C., which is approximately 90 percent black and which had an all-white (and now has a predominantly white) leadership, the efforts of a group of black workers led by Daniel George to alter the leadership composition have met with both resistance and retaliation against George himself in the form of dismissal. The upshot has been protracted litigation involving the National Labor Relations Board, the Department of Labor, and now the federal courts under the Landrum-Griffin Act,[17] even though George's group has not been primarily concerned with the race issue. Rather, here, the old and stratified leadership simply resist the challenge of younger workers who insist upon their democratic rights as trade unionists—the latter group happening to be predominantly black.

The lack of black progress in the Teamsters is not solely attributable to the attitude of union leaders, however. The fact is that black caucuses are not nearly as well developed as in other unions such as the UAW and the United Steelworkers. One reason is that the drivers have less contact with one another than do production workers. There is, in any case, some sense of futility. Indeed, in Washington, George claimed that many blacks have said that his group couldn't do the job of collective bargaining and negotiation, and rejected his campaign with comments such as the following: "It is ridiculous for blacks to aspire for the presidency of a local since you can't go to the country club and go golfing with management."[18]

Yet there have been some stirrings among the black membership. At the 1971 convention, it was reported by the *Miami Herald* that black delegates had received assurances from the union's top command that minorities would be promoted to key leadership positions in the near future. Robert Simpson of Local 743 in Chicago, spokesman for approximately 100 black delegates, met with Frank Fitzsimmons and several other union vice presidents. The *Miami Herald* reported the following:

Behind-the-scenes discussion between the blacks and the Union hierarchy took place before the opening of the Thursday convention session.

Simpson said that blacks have been omitted from high paying leadership positions at the Union's international level, although he declined to use the word discrimination.

He said that the discussion with Fitzsimmons was "frank and open" and that members of his group "didn't hold anything back." . . . The Teamsters' 15-man General Executive Board contains no blacks and Simpson said that to his knowledge there were no blacks who held the title of International Special Organizer—positions paying up to $30,000 a year. . . . Simpson said that Fitzsimmons agreed to form a special committee to give further study to the problem and in the meantime promised that blacks would be considered for vacancies occurring in the General Executive Board before the next Convention.

Five years have passed since that convention, however, and nothing has been done to implement the promises made by Fitzsimmons, although he has since become president. The dilemma for the Teamster leadership is a substantial one. On the one hand, it is obviously loathe to incur the wrath of the powerful white over-the-road drivers. On the other hand, the Teamsters are organizing in many industries where there are substantial numbers of black employees and where black organizers are brought on board in organizational drives. For instance, the minority membership among Teamster warehousemen is far greater than among the employees in the trucking industry. Accordingly, the political picture is more complicated than it might appear at first blush. As blacks begin to develop more of a political toehold in an industry where a sizable number of minority workers are employed at some levels, it may be that the pressure for reform in trucking will grow.

United Automobile Workers

Negroes came into the automobile industry in large numbers in the 1930's and during World War II—and the UAW chose to include them in its organizational efforts rather than to emulate the AFL's exclusionary tactics. This was as much a response to political reality as the result of an egalitarian ethic. The UAW performed the extraordinary task of bringing under one umbrella both blacks and the Poles and Southern whites who were also flocking to the Detroit area and the auto industry. The union took a firm stance against the refusal of white production employees to work alongside Negroes.[19] Moreover, both before and after Walter Reuther's ascension to the presidency of the union, its fair employment practices department waged campaigns to educate auto workers about race relations. Other unions have not generally engaged in efforts of this sort—and when they have done, it has only been during the past few years.

The politics and attitudes of the union toward black workers' aspirations outside the unskilled and semiskilled production jobs which make up approximately 75 percent of the positions in the bargaining unit are another matter entirely. These attitudes are significant because of auto workers' limited mobility in the industry—the only possible upward movement being to skilled-trades jobs in the bargaining unit and the supervisory and salaried jobs outside it. To be sure, the ideological tradition of its leadership as well as the sophistication and size of the union's black membership has made the UAW unique. But at the very time of the

1964 March on Washington, of which Reuther was a leader and in which UAW members were encouraged to participate, and at the very time when the construction unions were being pilloried for their exclusionary tactics, hardly any black UAW members were to be found in the high-paying and prestigious skilled-trade jobs.

At the Ford Motor Company in 1963 only 3.3 percent of the journeymen and 7.1 percent of the apprentices were black. In almost half of the UAW's regions, there were no black skilled tradesmen at all. According to the union's own estimates, only 0.7 percent of the journeymen in the Detroit-based Chrysler Corporation and 2.2 percent of the apprentices were black. In the General Motors Corporation the figures were 0.4 percent of the journeymen and 2 percent of the apprentices. Here also a number of regions reported no black skilled tradesmen at all. What was even more devastating about these statistics was the fact that they covered a wide range of trades. The range is significant; after all, the construction industry would look better than it does if figures for the trowel trades, in which blacks have been able to participate, especially in the South, were included in minority statistics. It is the mechanical trades which have accounted for the bad publicity construction unions have properly received.

One important distinction between the UAW and the construction unions should be noted, however. The construction unions are involved in the decision concerning which worker is to be hired, through their dominance of apprenticeship programs and their control over hiring halls through which, as a practical matter, nonunionists cannot gain entry except under boom conditions which cause a scarcity of labor. The UAW is not directly or formally involved in hiring—although in many plants it may help to know a union official when applying for a job. The union's only security lies in the requirement, where there is no right-to-work legislation prohibiting such agreements, that a worker join the union thirty days after being hired. (Indeed the grace period is merely seven days in construction because of the temporary nature of the work).[20]

Yet this simplifies the matter too much. For the Auto Workers have negotiated the establishment of joint skilled-trades and apprenticeship committees on both the national and local levels. Accordingly, the union participates in the apprentice selection process and in determining whether a worker can be properly classified as a journeyman. While the UAW does not play as activist a role in these decisions as that played by the construction unions, it is, nevertheless, substantially involved.

General Motors Corporation

As of 1974, approximately 2 percent of the General Motors journeymen were minority, and of the minority journeymen approximately 85 percent were black. There are three routes through which one can become a journeyman at General Motors: (1) the apprenticeship program, which covers 22 job classifications. Apprenticeship programs are in existence in 80 of General Motors' 135 plants; (2) the Employees in Training program (between 115 and 120 of General Motors' plants have EIT programs) which takes eight years to complete, as opposed to four years for the apprenticeship programs; (3) application by employees and nonemployees with qualifications for journeymen positions. Until 1958 or 1959 there were no black skilled tradesmen at General Motors at all. Blacks were not selected under the apprenticeship or EIT programs. The international union did nothing about the situation because it regarded racial exclusion as a local union problem. Eleven percent of General Motors' apprentices and 10 percent of EIT workers were minority members as of the spring of 1972. In 1969 and 1970 approximately 16½ percent of the employees selected as apprentices were minority group workers. One preliminary problem with entry into the skilled trades is that the need for skilled tradesmen has declined during the past few years. In 1970 General Motors had 6,000 apprentices and in 1972, it employed 4,745. This was the lowest number to be employed since 1965, when 600 employees were laid off from Fisher Body. The decline in the number of jobs is particularly large among tool and die workers and it is attributable to the state of the economy and, probably even more important, the fact that now model changes are less frequent.

Apprentices are selected from two lists—one being that of employees with seniority and the other being "all other applicants." Two employee applicants must be selected for every applicant from the other list unless there are not sufficient qualified employee applicants. According to management representatives, the mere posting of apprenticeship opportunities has not produced a substantial number of applications from minority group workers. In some circumstances letters have been sent to minority group employees alone and attempts have been made to discuss the possibility of filing an application individually with such workers. Of course, it must be recognized that, apart from plants that are in the Detroit area or other urban areas with large black populations, the mere preference for employee applicants at General Motors does not give minority workers an advantage, because at many of its decentralized plants the minority population is relatively small or even nonexistent.

The duration of the apprenticeship program is four years. As in the construction trades, the selection process involves a point system predicated upon a number of factors: (1) academic background including possession of a high school diploma, grade point average, number of mathematics, science, drawing, and shop courses taken and grades earned (23-point maximum); (2) personal background including marital status, dependent children, and extra schooling including preapprenticeship training (9-point maximum—7 of the points coming under extra schooling); (3) job experience including both General Motors plants and "related work experience" (7-point maximum); (4) aptitude tests including a General Motors arithmetic test, SRA pictorial, General Motors apprentice math test, Minnesota paper form board test, and the Bennett mechanical comprehension (25-point maximum); (5) an interview which takes into account factors such as knowledge of work involved in the trade, strength or desire to enter the trade, and the stability and maturity of the applicant (5-point maximum); and (6) evaluation of applicant's overall qualifications (6-point maximum). The maximum possible score is 75 but a score of 35 will suffice to qualify for either of the two lists. An employee may apply if he has not reached his forty-fifth birthday. On the other hand, a nonemployee applicant must be between the ages of eighteen and 26. Competition is severe inasmuch as there are seven times more applications than there are jobs. The applicants are ranked by the local joint apprenticeship committee.

Both General Motors and the UAW have made some changes in recent years. The academic record counts less than it used to, and the minimum passing score has been reduced. However, company officials do not believe that the alterations have helped minority applicants. According to these officials, there is no disproportionate exclusion of blacks or whites who achieve the minimum score of 35. There is, however, a difference in the way in which blacks and whites perform on the test.

On the basis of cases like *Bethlehem Steel, Lorillard,* and *Local 189, Papermakers*[21] it is easy to see that the basis for transfer from production jobs to apprenticeship classifications is critical to the question of whether a fair employment policy exists for minorities, in industries where blacks have been excluded from skilled-trades jobs in the past.

The 1970 contract between General Motors and the UAW provided for the first time for a red-circling formula in paragraph 151. This provision of the agreement states that "a seniority employee transferred to the apprentice training shall be transferred at his current rate or the rate of \$4.25 per hour, whichever is lower, provided however that in no event shall his 1st Period Rate be lower than a rate of \$4.13 per hour." After completion of his first 916 hours, he shall be paid a minimum of \$4.25 per hour if he is retained.

An apprentice does not obtain seniority as a skilled tradesman until he has completed the four-year program. Once the apprentice obtains journeyman status, he does not retain seniority credits from the production job for the purpose of promotion or layoff. Seniority is predicated upon time spent in the skilled job. The critical question here is whether the skills gap between a production and a skilled-trades job in the auto industry is so substantial that no seniority credit may be given. Here one may note the Eighth Circuit's award of 50 percent seniority credits for black train porters who were seeking promotion to brakemen.[22]

Under paragraph 138 of the agreement, if there is a reduction in the work force, the apprentice who was promoted from a production job will return to a non-interchangeable occupational group—from which lateral transfer is precluded—in which he had seniority at the outset. The apprentices who were hired directly into the apprentice classification may apply prior to layoff in writing and request to be placed on other available work which they are capable of doing and which is comparable to the work they are performing, at the rate paid for the job from which they must transfer.

As I have already noted, there is another route to obtain skilled-trades journeyman status at General Motors. This is the classification of Employees in Training and Employees in Training Seniority (EIT or EITS).

Although some plants appear to rely exclusively upon written examinations to determine entry into the EIT program, generally speaking the factors taken into account are performance upon the Bennett Mechanical Comprehension examination, experience in the trade, and education. No interview is given. Within the past few years classroom training as well as on-the-job training has been established for EIT employees. EITs, unlike apprentices, do not receive grades, although they can be removed from the program for not going to class.

The EIT program originated during World War II when there was a manpower shortage and skilled tradesmen could not be supplied through the normal route. Management utilizes trainees where a new plant is opened and it proves impossible to get the operation off the ground without trainees as well as apprentices. It has been thought that the EIT program would be a route more open to minority workers because the apprenticeship programs have traditionally placed more emphasis on education. Ironically, however, the overall figures for General Motors apprenticeship programs show a higher percentage of minority workers than do those for the EIT program. The UAW pressed for the elimination of the EIT program during negotiations with General Motors in 1961 and 1964. While the number of apprentices gained on the number of EITs for some time, that trend ceased in the early 1970's.

The EIT does not acquire seniority in a skilled-trades classification until four years have passed—the same period of time that must elapse for apprentices. After the four-year period, however, the EIT is in an inferior position vis-à-vis the apprentice in terms of seniority. The EIT receives two years' seniority for four years of work after the four-year period. Moreover, as previously stated, it takes the EIT twice as long as the apprentice to achieve journeyman status (eight years as opposed to four). Like apprentices, both EIT and EITS workers retain and accumulate seniority in the seniority group to which they belonged before transferring to EIT status. The basis for layoff for both EIT and EITS employees is similar to that provided for apprentices.

Even before the 1970 agreement extended red circling to apprentices, EITs were red circled upon transfer from production to skilled-trades jobs. That is to say, if the minimum hourly rate of the skilled-trades classification was not more than 10 cents above the rate he was earning, the employee would immediately be advanced to that minimum rate upon transfer. The 1970 contract also provided: "Where there is more than a 10 cents differential, the employee will be advanced 10 cents over the rate he has been earning, or to a rate of $4.26 per hour . . . whichever rate is higher at the time."

In addition to the problems it raises concerning seniority credits, the eight-year work-experience requirement to qualify as a journeyman under in the plan would appear to be questionable under Title VII. The issue has been raised in at least two plants. In the Chevrolet-Muncie General Motors plant a black worker was hired into the pipefitter classification, and the local union bargaining committee requested proof of journeyman status. As it happens, the black worker in question had been admitted to Plumbers and Steamfitters AFL Local 661 in Muncie, but could not prove to the satisfaction of the UAW bargaining committee that he had eight years' experience. But the central question is whether eight years' experience is a valid prerequisite to obtaining journeyman status. To put it in the language of Title VII cases, once there has been a showing of past-discrimination, decisions in cases such as *Local 3, Operating Engineers*,[23] and *Local 638, Steamfitters*[24] hold that defendants must prove a business necessity. This principle derived from the seniority cases is that the enjoyment of employment opportunities may not be postponed through artificial barriers for the group which possesses skills and is qualified (or would have been qualified in the absence of the defendants' discriminatory conduct). It is probable that past discrimination can be evidenced at Muncie inasmuch as the black pipefitter involved appears to have been the first black pipefitter ever employed.

A second and related issue is raised by a case at the General Motors Fremont, California, assembly plant. At Fremont, as of 1972, there were 27 minority skilled tradesmen, approximately 12 percent of the total skilled-trades work force. (Of these 12 were black, 14 Spanish-speaking and 1 Oriental.) This contrasted with the minority representation in the work force which was approximately 50 percent black and 25 percent Chicano. Of 9 EITs, 3 were minority—1 black and 2 Chicano. No apprenticeship program was established until 1973. Workers were transferred to EIT classification only when it was anticipated that journeymen could not be hired from the street. Apparently all journeymen hired from the street—the principal source of recruitment for the skilled trades—have been white.

A black worker at the Fremont plant has contended that he has been denied the status of journeyman electrician even though he possesses the necessary requirements. This grievance, which has been processed by the union through its machinery may bring into issue paragraph 179 of the agreement, which states the following:

During model change or major plant rearrangement employees may be temporarily transferred to classifications to assist in such work and paid in accordance with the local wage agreement. Seniority of such employees shall remain and accumulate in the seniority group in which it is established at the time of the temporary transfer. *It is understood, therefore, that no employee will be credited with any seniority in such classifications for the purposes of being retained in the classification.* [Emphasis supplied]

A substantial number of production employees—many of them minority-group workers—are temporarily assigned to skilled-trades classification during the model changeover. Paragraph 179 precludes the utilization of such experience for the purpose of obtaining journeyman status at a later date. The theory is that the worker who is only temporarily transferred does not learn a wide variety of skills that are involved in the trade. It is generally contended that the work performed is the more unskilled aspects of the work in the classification. This resembles the construction unions' position that welders, for instance, cannot be admitted as journeyman ironworkers because they do not have all the skills—even though it is unlikely they will be transferred to other work. As Judge Peckham noted in *Local 3, Operating Engineers,* the fact that an employee may be more vulnerable to unemployment as the result of knowing only a portion of the skills involved in the trade does not constitute a business necessity defense in connection with the denial of journeyman or an intermediate status to such a worker.[25] Accordingly, it may be that both paragraph 179 and those provisions of the agreement which established the eight-year previous-experience requirement run afoul of Title VII in the context of past discrimination.

At the General Motors Los Angeles Southgate assembly plant the only routes to becoming a skilled tradesman are the EIT program and being hired from the street. Accordingly, it is not surprising that, in 1972, of 205 skilled tradesmen, nine were Chicano and eight were black. The complete breakdown was as follows:

Job classification	Total work force	Chicanos	Blacks
Air compressor operator	4	0	0
Carpenter	5	0	1
Conveyor-truck maintenance	2	0	0
Electrician	22	1	0
Heater operator	3	0	1
Inspector, jig and fixture	2	0	0
Maintenance machinist	7	0	0
Maintenance painter and glazier	13	2	1
Millwright welder	56	3	2
Plumber and pipefitter	27	2	0
Tool gauge and fixture repair	32	1	0
Tool repair portable	4	0	2
Truck repair, gas and electric	9	0	0
Welding equipment maintenance and repair	19	0	1

At General Motors' Van Nuys plant, in the jurisdiction of UAW Local 645, the number of minority skilled tradesmen is also small. Of 172 skilled tradesmen in 1972, one was black and nine were Chicano. Of the 17 EIT workers, one was black and six were Chicano. Here also, General Motors prefers to hire journeymen from the outside. The 1972 statistics were as follows:

Job classification	Total work force	Chicanos	Blacks
Boiler operator	5	0	0
Building repair	6	2	0
Carpenter	1	0	0
Electrician	23	0	1
Machine repair machinist	1	0	0
Millwright	35	1	0
EIT millwright	5	1	0
Painter and glazier	10	2	0
Pipefitter	15	1	0
EIT pipefitter	1	0	0
Diemaker, jig and fixture	30	1	0
EIT diemaker	7	3	1
Tool repair	7	0	0
EIT Tool repair	2	0	0
Truck repair	4	1	0
Welding equipment maintenance and repair	22	1	0
EIT	2	2	0
Welder	13	0	0

One of the leading cases dealing with Title VII was brought against General Motors, and although it did not involve the skilled trades, it does have some bearing on the issues discussed above. In *Rowe* v. *General Motors Corporation*[26] the issue related to discriminatory practices involving transfer from production to salaried jobs at a General Motors plant in Atlanta. There are two methods by which an employee can secure transfer or promotion from an hourly to a salaried job: (1) unilateral action by the employer, beginning with a recommendation by the immediate foreman to the salaried personnel administrator; (2) an application by the employee on his own. The Fifth Circuit found the General Motors Corporation record "commendable" insofar as it related to the recruiting and hiring of blacks and other minority employees. The court emphasized, however, that the case here did not deal with hiring but rather with promotion and transfer. Noting that a prima facie case of discrimination was made out on the basis of statistics concerning the absence of minorities in salaried jobs at the Atlanta plant, the court rejected General Motors' reliance upon a policy of layoffs on the basis of seniority as an explanation for statistics when those layoffs simply carried forward the consequences of past segregation. The court also stated the following:

Akin to this is the contention that "experience" was essential and only the long-employed Whites—and conversely, not the recently hired Blacks—had the "experience." Without gainsaying, as *Griggs* . . . makes so plain, that *qualifications* are an employer's prerogative, the standards cannot be automatically applied to freeze out newly freed Blacks because for the years of its segregated policy GM hired no Blacks to afford them an opportunity to acquire experience. And on this GM—apart from its incantation of "experience" needs—made no effort to show that in these ebb and flow layoffs and rehirings, that none of the affected Blacks was job-disqualified.[27]

In these circumstances, the court held that the utilization of subjective criteria by the force of foremen, who were all white, was in violation of Title VII inasmuch as there was no "familial or social association between these two groups." Said the court:

All we do today is recognize that promotion and transfer procedures which depend almost entirely upon the subjective evaluation and the favorable recommendation of the immediate foremen are a ready mechanism for discrimination against Blacks much of which can be covertly concealed, and, for that matter, not really known to management. We and others have expressed a skepticism that Black persons dependent directly on the decisive recommendations from Whites can expect non-discriminatory action.[28]

Ford Motor Company

Ford Motor Company has no EIT program. To recruit skilled tradesmen, it relies *exclusively* upon hiring journeymen from the street and recruiting through apprenticeship programs. Like General Motors, Ford also suffered a substantial decline in the number of skilled tradesmen in the early 1970's. In the latter 1960's Ford employed between 3,200 and 3,300 apprentices, and by 1972 this number was down to approximately 1,600. In 1970 the intake of apprentices was approximately half what it was in 1969. In two-thirds of the Ford assembly plants there are apprenticeship programs. According to company sources, only about half a dozen plants have no apprenticeship programs. Approximately half of the employees who became journeymen at Ford "during the past few years" were hired from the street, however, with the other half coming from apprenticeship. The amount of past exclusion at Ford may appear smaller than that at General Motors, primarily because of Henry Ford's relationship to the black community in Detroit. Unlike most employers, Ford in the 1930's established a policy of giving blacks a substantial number of jobs at the River Rouge plant in Dearborn. As a result, some blacks were able to get into the Rouge, but not many were able to obtain employment as skilled tradesmen. This policy existed on a limited basis, however, and was discontinued toward the end of World War II.[29]

Because of a concern about the number of minority employees, the Ford-UAW joint apprenticeship committee (the same basic apparatus described in connection with the GM-UAW agreement exists at Ford and Chrysler as well) adopted a new apprenticeship selection procedure in October 1969. It established three sets of aptitude tests which were to be used to determine whether or not an applicant had a reasonable chance to succeed in the apprenticeship program and on the job. The company attempts to use the tests to determine the candidates' aptitudes, trade preferences, and interests so as to advise and counsel applicants "into a specific trade in one of the three major trade groups." These three groups are: (1) maintenance trades, which include plumbing and pipefitting, millwright work, industrial hydraulics, welding, and sheetmetal work; (2) electrical trades; (3) metal trades, which include toolmaking and diemaking, diesinking, machine repair, and so on. Unlike General Motors, which calls for a high school diploma, Ford sets no educational requirement (previously it had required the completion of tenth grade) and there is no consideration of the high school grade point average, prior Ford experience, or related work experience.

Another significant feature of the 1969 changes is that position of a qualified applicant on the waiting lists for the apprenticeship selection test is now determined by the date of application. Before 1969 an applicant who had a higher score would be placed ahead of the applicant with a lower score even though the latter had met the minimum standard. The rationale for this change is that a substantial number of minority-group applicants met the minimum standards but were placed disproportionately far down on the waiting list because white applicants obtained higher scores. (Under the new procedures, in the event that two applications are made on the same date, the individual with the highest total aptitude points will still be selected. In the event of a tie in total test points, the individual with the highest last four social security numbers will be selected.)

Whether this new procedure is having an impact is difficult to say. Three years after its introduction the parties were still in the process of attempting to obtain validation that would meet EEOC standards, and the subsequent deceleration of apprentice recruitment complicates matters further. The parties have introduced a preapprenticeship program at the Rouge plant and also in some of the parts plants. Unlike General Motors, Ford gives no preference to employees in the selection process. Although there is no age limit for employee applicants (nonemployees must be between 18 and 26) employees above the age of 26 under the contract "shall in no event exceed one to two [of those below the age of 27] in the particular trade involved.'' Two-thirds of all the applications for the program come from within the plant.

The basic provisions relating to seniority credits and red circling of production rates are the same as those of General Motors. At Ford also, the red-circling changes were made in the 1970 agreement. In November 1971 and April 1972 applicants for apprenticeship were tested for the first time since 1970 at the Rouge plant, which was then 50 percent black. While the percentage of black apprentices does not appear to have changed substantially yet, approximately 20 percent of the employees on the waiting list at Rouge in 1972 were minorities.

Although two-thirds of the Ford plants have apprenticeship programs, those that do not will have great difficulty in meeting their Title VII obligations. And it is interesting to note in this connection that at some of these plants the UAW locals have played a pernicious role in thwarting employment opportunities for black workers.

At Ford's Atlanta assembly plant, approximately 25 percent of the work force (the total work force being between 3,100 and 3,200 employees) is black. Until 1961 practically all blacks were employed as janitors and only after 1971 was their seniority revised so that they could move without sacrifice into production jobs. Only a small percentage of minority workers in fact made the transfer. The majority of blacks employed as production workers have been hired since 1965. As of 1972, there were three blacks among approximately 170 skilled tradesmen. One of the three was a painter, however, and one an oiler—hardly two of the more prestigious and high-paying skilled-trades auto jobs. The company has always recruited skilled tradesmen from the street even though it recognizes that this practice has the effect of perpetuating the all-white work force. It is thought that an apprenticeship program may be instituted within the foreseeable future.

At the Pico Rivera, California, assembly plant, minority workers constitute 39 percent of all production employees. Twelve percent are black, and 26 percent are Chicano. Here, as in the Atlanta assembly plant, journeymen are recruited strictly from the outside. Such recruitment does not produce a substantial number of minority employees since there are very few in the labor market who have the requisite skills.

As of December 26, 1971, of 200 skilled tradesmen, 2 were black and 23 were Chicano. By job classification, the minority figures were as follows:

Job classification	Total employees	Spanish-speaking	Black
Electrician	58	11	1
Fork-lift repairman	6	1	0
Millwright	50	1	1
Plumber	39	4	0
Tool maker	14	2	0
Welder	18	4	0
Tin smith	6	0	0
Powerhouse engineer	9	0	0

Management proposed that an apprenticeship program be established at the Pico Rivera plant. One obvious by-product of this proposal would have been that the minority production employees within the plant would have had an opportunity to be trained and upgraded to skilled-trades positions. Despite a fervent plea by international officials, however, the Skilled Trades Committee of Local 923, UAW, the bargaining agent at the Pico Rivera plant, voted the program down. The obvious result is a perpetuation of the racial composition of the skilled trades work force. In the absence of some kind of training program, it is not likely that blacks will obtain more than their present share of the skilled-trades jobs, that is, 1 percent.

At the Milpitas, California, assembly plant the situation is slightly better, but not substantially. Here again most hiring of journeymen is done from the street although the Milpitas plant has established an apprenticeship program for electricians. Curiously enough, although all 11 electrician apprentices are incumbent seniority employees, 6 are Chicano although none are black. The total statistics are therefore only slightly better: in 1972, of 161 skilled tradesmen, 7 were black and 9 were Chicano. The racial composition by skilled trades was as follows:

Job classification	Total employees	Spanish-speaking	Black
Blacksmith	2	0	0
Carpenter	3	0	1
Electrician	49	1	4
Industrial truck repair	10	1	0
Garage serviceman	2	1	0
Millwright	40	2	1
Painter	7	1	1
Plumber, pipefitter	33	0	2
Tin smith	3	1	0
Powerhouse engineer	6	0	0
Powerhouse leader	3	0	0
Oventender	3	0	0

One reason that blacks may have made such a small breakthrough in skilled trades as the result of the apprenticeship program is that in the 1972 solicitation for skilled-trades apprentices, of 156 applicants only 13 were black. It is noteworthy and distressing that at this plant there were only 2 black plumbers and pipefitters and only four black electricians.

Chrysler Corporation

The UAW-Chrysler relationship has given rise to the best record on black employment in the skilled trades of the auto industry and, more important, appears to hold the most promise for the future—although Chrysler's national minority statistics are about the same as General Motors' insofar as apprentices are concerned. (In 1971 25 percent of the new apprentices at Chrysler were minority, as opposed to 16½ percent of those at General Motors. As of 1972, 5 percent of Chrylser's journeymen were black whereas the General Motors figure was 2 percent.)

Three factors support the view that prospects for blacks are best at the smallest of the Big Three auto competitors. Chrysler is Detroit-based to a greater extent than either GM or Ford. Having a substantial number of plants in the Detroit area means that the large black population in Detroit (over 50 percent) is a significant part of its labor market. Indeed, as of 1972, 39.2 percent of all production employees at Chrysler were black, and the statistics were even more dramatic for some of the Detroit-area plants: 68.6 percent at Mack Avenue Stamping; 57.5 percent at Outer Drive and Eight Mile Stamping; 74.1 percent at the Eldon Axle plant. Second, as we shall see, it is Chrysler which has been confronted with the most militant demands from black caucuses and black worker organizations. During the past seven years the Chrysler locals have begun to elect Negro union presidents as white workers have left the industry and Detroit.

Third, the top official in the UAW's Chrysler department is the most liberal and progressive member of the union's executive board, Vice President Douglas Fraser. Fraser, who is also director of the skilled trades department and in charge of the UAW's political efforts in Michigan, lost the UAW presidency to Leonard Woodcock by one vote after Reuther's death (the executive-board vote was 13 to 12). More committed to affirmative action for blacks than any other white UAW executive board member, Fraser has continually urged local union leadership to move quickly to remedy persistent racial imbalance in the auto plants, particularly in the skilled trades. The results have been most dramatic at Chrysler. An example of his efforts is the following message to local union presidents on July 12, 1972:

Obviously, much remains to be done to guarantee fairness and equity to our minority members. It is still accurate to say that random selection among seniority production workers would have produced higher percentages of minorities among skilled occupations. . . .

In regard to hiring temporary employees (upgraders) in skilled classifications, it is important that you insist that your local plant management place a fair share of minorities in skilled jobs.

I strongly urge you to determine what you can do within your local union and in your relationships with your plant management to achieve this result.[30]

To understand the Chrysler situation, it is important to assess the results and impact of the 1967 negotiations between the union and the company. Before 1967, a production worker could take as much as a 35 percent wage cut upon transfer to the apprenticeship program. In 1967, the parties established a red-circle rate for production employees who had transferred or would do so. Contractual preference was established for employees with seniority. Neither General Motors nor Ford moved to red circle such rates for production workers until 1970, and neither company has the preference for incumbent employees with seniority established by Chrysler—although both provide some assurance that production workers will get a portion of the opportunities available.

The upper age limit was also raised to forty-five for all applicants entering the apprenticeship program. The number of tests given as part of the apprenticeship selection process was dropped from eight to four, and the passing score was lowered from 16 to 12 for the screening test. According to UAW sources, results prior to 1967 showed that many blacks had scored between 12 to 16. Moreover, a remedial training course was developed for applicants who failed the apprenticeship test battery, to equip, them to pass on their next try. This is generally a fifteen-week course dealing with mathematics and spacial relationships.

Two apprenticeship selection lists have been established in each plant—one composed of employees with seniority and the other of outside applicants. The outside applicants are placed on the list in the order of their point-system ranking. The seniority list is in order of seniority. (Of course, both lists are composed of individuals whose test scores are above the minimum point score, 12.) As a matter of operating practice, when the seniority list is nearly depleted, the parties reopen it for employee applicants. According to UAW sources, this procedure results in virtually all black apprentices being transferred from production jobs. (This can be shown most clearly by the following statistics for apprentice recruitment between September 1967 and October 1968. Of 526 apprentices, 257 were recruited from the street and of these, 16 were black. On the other hand, of the 269 who had been production employees, 55 or 20.4 percent were black.)

Two other points relating to the period following the 1967 negotiations require discussion. Blacks did not immediately apply for skilled trades jobs in substantial numbers at Chrysler. Accordingly, Fraser, Anthony Connole, and other members of the Chrysler department met with UAW black leaders in the Detroit-area Chrysler plants and organized a recruitment campaign to encourage more blacks to apply. In 1970 the joint apprenticeship committee revised the point system so as to eliminate points for a personal interview. There was a corresponding reduction in the minimum passing score.

As the result of these changes, the racial composition of the apprenticeship work force began to change quite rapidly. This can be seen in comparisons of the number of minority graduates from apprenticeship programs with those who entered at the same time. For example, during September 1971, 37 apprentices graduated from the Chrysler apprenticeship program and only one was a minority group employee. However, 39 apprentices were placed on course during that month, and 15 or 38 percent were minority. In October 1971, 28 apprentices graduated, one of whom was a minority worker. But of the 39 who entered that same month, 10 were minority.

Statistics revealed by the union's Chrysler department in 1973 indicate that progress was spread across all trades. Of 147 minority apprentices which made up 15.7 percent of the total, 23 are diemakers, 25 were electricians, 11 were tool makers, jig and fixture—all sophisticated and prestigious classifications among the skilled trades.

Also, Chrysler, unlike Ford, has an EIT program, which until about 1972 was the main conduit for minority employees into the skilled trades. As of late 1971 in the apprenticeable trades, the number of minority members among EIT workers who were on the eight-year journeyman program at Chrysler continued to run ahead of the number in the apprenticeship program. Twenty-four percent of the EITs in the program and 6.9 percent of the EIT journeymen who had completed it were minority workers.

New Developments in the UAW–Big Three Relationship

UAW Project Outreach

All the Big Three as well as the UAW refer applicants to the UAW Project Outreach, which operates in twenty-two cities and seven states. (Included among these are San Jose, New York City, Detroit, Kansas City, Cleveland, Indianapolis, Atlanta, Gary, Chicago, Minneapolis, and the state of New Jersey.) The UAW Outreach claims to have placed 8,886 "disadvantaged" applicants during a three-year period. The breakdown is as follows: black, 65 percent (5,776); white, 15 percent (1,335); Chicano, 15 percent (1,332); Puerto Rican, 3 percent (265); Indian, 1 percent (90); Portuguese, 1 percent (88). The actual impact Outreach has is difficult to determine, however. Part of the problem is that the Big Three all have their own preapprenticeship programs which are specifically geared toward improving the examination performance of unsuccessful applicants. To what extent Outreach has played a significant part in this process is a difficult question to answer.

Inverse Seniority

About 1968 the Big Three began to accelerate minority hiring through the "hiring-of-the-disadvantaged" programs established at the urging of President Johnson under the auspices of the National Association of Businessmen. The principal motivation was to avoid, if possible, future altercations, civil disorders, and riots similar to those experienced in Los Angeles, Newark, and Detroit between 1965 and 1967.

All the companies suffered cutbacks in early 1969, however, as the so-called Nixon recession began to settle in. This meant that many of the minority employees hired within the past year would have to be laid off because of the seniority system established under the collective-bargaining agreement. The prospect was particularly tragic because the aspirations and ambitions of black employees who had been previously excluded from the labor market were once again to be dashed—this time just as they had begun to accumulate some seniority and experience relatively stable employment.

Accordingly, the UAW proposed in February 1969 a so-called "inverse seniority" system which provided for the layoff of senior and more experienced employees (a higher percentage of whom would be white), who would then draw Supplemental Unemployment Compensation (SUB) benefits that would entitle an auto worker to up to 95 percent of his regular salary for a year. The plan was to give the senior employee a kind of sabbatical which might well provide him with a taste of early retirement. At the same time, the junior black employee who had been recently hired would be retained, would continue to bring earnings into the neediest segment of the community, and would be accumulating the requisite seniority credits to enjoy SUB benefits if and when he was laid off in the future. The Big Three resisted this proposal for a variety of reasons in early 1969 and again during the negotiation of the 1970 contract. The inverse seniority proposal seems to have been quietly dropped as negotiations came down to the "crunch" at some point in September 1970 and as of 1976, it had not been implemented. Accordingly, although the UAW continues to talk about it, it appears not to be a high priority item. Junior black workers with a tenuous foothold in the auto industry do not have the political wallop or sophistication to make their views heard, and there does not appear to be a great demand by senior employees for it. Certainly nothing on the order of the demands regarding the discontinuance of mandatory overtime has been heard from the rank-and-file auto worker.

A number of arguments have been raised by the companies in opposition to the proposal. In the first place, the companies claim that they will lose their highly skilled employees and that employees with lower seniority do not possess the requisite skills to take over their jobs. While ordinary layoffs require the movement of employees from job to job, this is done by "bumping down" from more highly skilled positions, and thus generally does not involve any degree of retraining. The concept of "bumping up," it is contended, presents an altogether different situation. The union's response to this is that where the jobs are more skilled ones—such as the skilled-trades jobs themselves—most of the needed skilled employees would not be able to take advantage of the inverse seniority clause. Only workers with the highest seniority would be able to take the optional layoff. The Big Three have exhibited a good deal of skepticism as to whether the UAW can actually "sell" this position to its membership. Job classification seniority might create dissension if workers with a certain amount of seniority in one classification or department were unable to take advantage of the inverse seniority layoff while workers with less in another department could do so—either because workers in the first classification had less seniority in the appropriate seniority grouping or because the senior employees were unwilling to take advantage of the opportunity.

Another problem is the uncertainty of the parties regarding the number of employees who would take advantage of the opportunity to be laid off. The inverse seniority plan was established at the 1967 negotiations between Deere and Company and the UAW, and as of March 1970 it appeared to be immensely popular with the senior workers. Of the workers laid off, 69.9 percent were senior employees taking advantage of the plan. Some UAW officials nevertheless contend that many senior workers would not want to "sit at home" for a year and that, by doing so, they would be deprived of the substantial overtime pay opportunities that would otherwise be theirs. GM and Ford have pointed out, however, that when there are a large number of layoffs, overtime opportunities are also likely to be declining.

There are also problems relating to recall. Presumably, when there is a need for recall in a particular classification, the employee with the least amount of seniority would be required to return to work first. The UAW takes the position that the employee should be able to return to the job which he left subsequent to the exhaustion of SUB and unemployment. On the other hand, the company officials contend that management should determine the position for which an individual is to be recalled. They have stressed that requiring the employee to take an opening in a comparable job is equitable to him and would avoid the displacement of another employee which, in turn, would start an extremely disruptive chain of bumping. But at Ford, for instance, no returning senior employee under present practices can cause more than three bumps. The company has established distinct seniority groups, each covering a broad type of job, and within each category the employees are divided into three gradations based on the amount of skills involved in the job. The first of these categories, the "designated classification," is the most skilled one. The intermediate category is that of the semiskilled workers, "an undesignated classification." The third of these groups is the unskilled group, that is, the "labor pool." An employee in the top classification can bump an individual who can, in turn, bump the lowest man in the second classification who then can bump the lowest man in the third category. Some kind of limitation along these lines could be placed upon an inverse seniority system as well.

Another problem related to the recall issue is the impact of inverse seniority on area hiring programs. Under the area hiring arrangements negotiated between the Big Three and the UAW, employees laid off in one plant are given preference over nonemployees when applying for new jobs at other plants in the same area. Under inverse seniority, because laid-off senior employees might not want to work, the company might be required to hire new job applicants to a much greater extent. This exaggerates a problem which goes to the heart of management's objections. This is that the costs are extreme when junior employees, either those already in the plant where inverse seniority is in effect, or those who must be newly hired, are being paid at the same time that the senior employees are on layoff and receiving SUB. The intention of SUB was to protect the senior employee in the industry. In effect, through retaining the junior employee and, moreover, providing him with an opportunity to build up the requisite seniority credits to enjoy SUB himself at a later date, the fund is broadened to protect a broader category.

One further problem with inverse seniority relates to state unemployment compensation laws, which generally require that the worker must have been laid off through no fault of his own and be available for work or actively seeking work. Any attempt to circumvent the literal language of such statutes would have to be predicated upon the same goal, that is, the general welfare of society, and the rationale would necessarily be that Title VII and equal employment opportunities in this country are part of society's general welfare, and that since some employee must be laid off, someone will suffer economic hardship through no fault of his own. The UAW has attempted to deal with this problem where it has had inverse seniority systems by instructing senior employees to be laid off and exhaust their regular benefits before applying for SUB rather than requiring them to file an application at the outset—on the theory that in the former situation it cannot be as easily said that the layoff is voluntary. But inverse seniority plans may well require amendment of state unemployment compensation legislation affecting those states where such systems are negotiated.

The Growing Strength of Black Demands

Black Representation in UAW Policy-making

In sharp contrast to the lack of progress within the Teamsters, black political activity and turmoil inside the UAW has produced a climate that may be conducive to expeditious change. The absence of blacks from leadership positions on both the national and the local level, as well as the union's failure to appoint blacks to staff positions in anything resembling numbers proportionate to their share of the membership, has caused considerable controversy in recent years. As noted above, the black percentage of the total union membership is approximately 25–30. Until 1962, there was no black member of the UAW international executive board. As of 1973 the minority percentage of UAW staff on the international payroll was only 14.3—and the digures have not changed much since then.

The issue of black representation at the policy-making level was first raised in the 1940's. It was debated at the 1943 convention in Buffalo (150 of 2000 delegates were Negroes) in the form of a proposal by the left wing (sometimes referred to as the Addes–C.P. caucus) for a special executive-board position for a black member. Reuther, who was later responsible for the UAW's excellent reputation on racial equality, opposed this proposal. Although his opposition was framed in terms of "discrimination in reverse" and "special privileges" allegedly proposed at the meeting, which, it was stated, would lead to Jim Crowism, the fact is that power politics and the weakness of black union members in this context were the essential considerations.

Everyone inside the UAW has known for years that there were black trade unionists qualified for the board in many regions where black members were a minority, and that generally whites would not vote for them. Accordingly, despite the fact that Negroes have constituted a goodly proportion of UAW membership ever since 1940, it was impossible for blacks to be elected. One of the foremost examples of those thus bypassed was the late Willoughby Abner (subsequently director of the American Arbitration Association Center For Dispute Settlement) who, during his membership and activity in the UAW in Chicago, was not recognized by some of the top leaders and was opposed by others.

At the 1962 convention, however, pressure from the Trade Union Leadership Council, the Detroit-based branch of the Negro American Labor Council, made the UAW leadership think again about this question. The executive board was enlarged by the completely dominant Reuther bloc (which did not then have to contend with serious political opposition, as it had in the 1940's) with the specific understanding that one of the new vice presidencies created would be allotted to a black. The Reuther bloc later chose the late Nelson Jack Edwards as the appropriate black candidate.

At the time there was some consternation about the fact that TULC President

388   Black Workers in White Unions

Horace Sheffield (who later became Edwards' administrative assistant) and Abner
had been bypassed. But they had paid the price that militants often do—they had
created the appropriate atmosphere for black representation through their agitation,
but in the process had made themselves *persona non grata* to key elements of the
UAW leadership.

For the six years subsequent to Edwards' election, then, the UAW had one
black executive-board member out of twenty-six (the vacancy created by Edwards'
death was filled by another black, Mark Stepp). In 1968 Reuther took advantage
of an opportunity to increase black representation by one. In Region 1-A, which
covers West Detroit and its suburbs and includes 74,000 UAW members, Joseph
McCusker had been regional director since 1947. On June 24, 1968, McCusker
died at the age of 64. Immediately thereafter, Carl Stellatto (a few years earlier a
staunch left-wing foe of Reuther who had since made his peace with Solidarity
House, the UAW headquarters and establishment), a past president of Local 600,
the bargaining agent at the River Rouge where almost 30,000 of the 74,000
Region 1-A members are located, began to muster support to succeed McCusker.
At the same time, Jack Pellagrine, McCusker's top assistant since 1947, was
promising Negro trade unionists that if he was supported he would step aside in
1970 at the UAW convention for a black candidate. Region 1-A, it should be
noted, is as black in population as any of the UAW regions, but has a black membership of only 28 percent. With a deadlock between Stellatto and Pellagrine on
the horizon, Reuther and his aides responded to the idea of a black candidate as a
preferable alternative. This did not end the competition since, although Reuther
favored Marcellius Ivory, who was, in fact, elected and served until ill health
recently forced his retirement, in both 1968 and 1970 Ivory had to campaign
vigorously to overcome the challenge of Local 600 Vice President Robert Battle
III, who was also black. (Battle has since succeeded him.)

Said Ivory in an interview with the *Detroit Free Press* shortly after his election:
"I subscribe wholeheartedly to the rhetoric of the Black Nationalists. I disagree
with their conclusions. I don't believe in separatism. I don't believe in not voting.
I don't believe in burning down the country. One of the things I give the Black
Nationalists credit for is that they have awakened the Black consciousness and
created pride in Blackness."[31] This statement was even more significant in the
summer of 1968 than it is today. For during that fateful summer black workers
began to stir in the auto factories, to show an independence of the UAW, and to
assert themselves through wildcat stoppages and picket lines—methods that can
raise havoc in an industry which is as interdependent and technologically integrated as the auto industry is.

Black Power and the Local Unions

It was in the Dodge Main plant in Hamtramck, in the jurisdiction of UAW
Local 3 that the first of a number of militant and sometimes violence-prone black
worker organizations was formed, the Dodge Revolutionary Union Movement
(DRUM). At this assembly plant located immediately adjacent to Detroit's East

Side, DRUM found fertile territory. Today approximately 58 percent of the employees represented by Local 3 are black; the percentage was slightly less in 1968. The Chrysler Corporation was experiencing a good year, and speedups on the production line—a phenomenon which has been encountered in automobile factories before—were alleged by a number of UAW local officials. Meanwhile the racial composition of Dodge Main was shifting as blacks entered and whites departed from the Detroit area. Also the work force became younger—according to *Solidarity,* the UAW monthly newspaper, 36 percent of UAW members working for Chrysler at that time were under 30, and more than 51 percent of Chrysler employees represented by the UAW had less than five years' seniority.

A wildcat stoppage took place in May and although DRUM disavowed calling it, seven of the organization's leaders were dismissed. DRUM then began to agitate about their reinstatement, and this triggered another wildcat in July which was enjoined by a Michigan Circuit Court judge (the state trial court) who stated that an injunction should be issued because, among other reasons, the strike and picketing had unlawful objectives, that is, "discrimination in reverse."[32] This finding stemmed from such DRUM demands as a call for the hiring of fifty Negro foremen and ten Negro general foremen.[33] The injunction, however, was not the end of the matter.

Although the UAW had intervened and, according to DRUM, talked Chrysler into reinstating five out of the seven workers who had been discharged, Chrysler refused to take back two of the black leaders. Although further wildcat threats were made, the company continued to refuse to back down. Meanwhile, the activities of DRUM and Local 3 seemed to set in motion a number of events.

The immediate result of the founding of DRUM and its activities during the summer of 1968 was the formation of similar organizations in other UAW units where blacks were strong numerically—particularly in the Detroit area. At the River Rouge complex, black UAW members formed FRUM (Ford Revolutionary Union Movement) and at the Chrysler Gear and Axle Eldon Avenue plant near Six Mile Road, ELRUM emerged. The movement also spread to the farm equipment industry in Chicago where Negroes inside UAW Local 6 at International Harvester called themselves HRUM (Harvester Revolutionary Union Movement). Generally speaking, these organizations had no compunctions about using the most violent, provocative language and excusing violence, including knifings and shootings, when committed by their members. Sometimes they were paper organizations, idolized by the New and Old Left newspapers, but simply mouthing radical slogans and platitudes. Usually they chose not to operate inside the UAW but, where it was possible to do so, to deal directly with management. (A number of management officials in labor relations for Big Three companies admitted to me in off-the-record discussions that meetings with such organizations had been held at a number of plants.)

In about three years the steam had gone out of the movement in most of the auto plants. As early as the fall of 1968, DRUM's candidate Ron Marsh was badly beaten by his white opponent, Joe Elliot, 2,091 to 1,386 in a runoff election for a position on the Local 3 board of trustees. As the *Detroit Free Press* noted, "The balloting was a significant defeat for DRUM, a movement of workers and young activists who use the rhetoric of violence and who seek black control of industry and labor."[34]

Today at Local 3 and the Dodge assembly plant in Hamtramck DRUM is defunct. Most of the other organizations noted above and discussed below either no longer exist or are dormant. In addition, many of their members have been dismissed from the plants and have left the industry. Yet the effects of their impact remain.

Their significance can be gauged in part by the varying reactions of UAW leaders. On March 12, 1969, the executive board castigated DRUM as an organization which was attempting to "spread terror" through the plants. Stating that there were no "black or white answers" to the problems confronting the UAW membership, the board stated that it would not "protect workers who resort to violence and intimidation with the conscious purpose of dividing our Union along racial lines."[35]

For some inside the UAW, the statement was not strong enough, while others found it too strong. On one end of the spectrum was Secretary-Treasurer Emil Mazey, who has a reputation of being on the left because of his views on international affairs, but who has consistently opposed Negro organizations inside the UAW, including the moderate TULC. Mazey, who cast the deciding vote in favor of Woodcock and against Fraser in the executive-board election after Reuther's death in 1970, described the militants in the plant, three days after the board's statement, as a "handful of fanatics who are nothing but black fascists, using the same tactics of coercion and intimidation that Hitler and Mussolini used in Germany and Italy." Conveniently forgetting some of the violence and intimidation engaged in by labor unions in the 1930's and in the Kohler strike, in which Mazey's staff played a prominent role,[36] Mazey, according to the *Detroit News,* stated that the appearance of black workers' organizations was "particularly distressing" because, he argued, the UAW "has done more to further the black man's cause than any other in the nation."[37] On the other hand, Douglas Fraser, while condemning DRUM as a movement to divide the UAW along racial lines, expressed the "hope" that Local 3 leadership would be able to "work on unity with DRUM." Said Fraser: "I don't think that's been tried yet. We owe it to the locals to let them try first."[38] Similar expressions of moderation came from Paul Schrade, the former west coast director of the UAW, when this form of militance began to move to some of the plants in his region. The rationale for the moderate position taken by Fraser and Schrade is obvious—although it went completely unmentioned and unrecognized in Mazey's emotional reaction to DRUM. As lower-level Chrysler management has admitted to me in interviews, the conditions at the Dodge Main were difficult and onerous—particularly for black workers supervised by an all-white work force. It has been generally conceded that the management attitude at Dodge contributed to the problem—the attitude being to "holler and shout" to black workers to "move the line," and to refuse to give line foremen enough authority to make simple decisions such as whether an employee should go to first aid or should be excused to go home when ill. Moreover, quite often the abrasiveness between supervisors and production employees took the form of racial animosity, given the racial composition of each group. What proves these points most clearly is the fact that both management and the union began to change their postures in the wake of the DRUM activities during the summer of 1968. At the Dodge plant itself, in the three-year period immediately after DRUM's initial activities, most of the new people hired as foremen were black. Management appointed its first black general foreman and three black superintendents. Furthermore, the UAW, which like most industrial unions has generally kept itself out of the hiring of supervisory personnel, nevertheless became deeply involved in this matter because of the concern of the work group. Black workers in plants in California and Indiana have had similar problems, and the UAW has inevitably moved into an area which it has always piously contended was none of its concern, the hiring of non–bargaining unit personnel.

Furthermore, the impact can be seen in three other areas. The first is the hiring of minority skilled tradesmen, referred to above. It is no coincidence that the most substantial improvements in the auto industry—and indeed in the country for black blue-collar workers—have been made in the Detroit area Chrysler plants, where one-fourth of the apprentice work force hired in 1971 was minority. Black worker agitation, together with the geographical location of the Chrysler plants and Fraser's progressive attitude, has made these results possible, just as the rough and tumble of union tactics, sometimes including violence, mass picketing, and sit-downs, made the recognition of industrial unions during the 1930's possible. The essential difference, of course, is that the unions became ongoing stable institutions. The black worker organizations do not seem to be able to retain this kind of viability—but, as we have seen, their influence on unions can be substantial. As the *New York Times* recently stated: "Some company and union observers believe that the extremist movement has prompted the company and the union to intensify their efforts to promote Negroes."

Another effect of the organizations has been to increase pressure for changes in staff composition. In the fall of 1968, black UAW officials and blacks in other unions began to point to the fact that not only are blacks disproportionately underrepresented among elected officials, but they also have a small percentage of appointed staff positions. These positions, of course, are political rewards and sometimes a way of eliminating potential political opposition. Solidarity House in Detroit is heavily populated with former office holders defeated at the local level. Blacks pointed out in 1968 that of the about 1,000 UAW staffers, only 75 were black—approximately 7.5 percent—when the black membership was between 25 and 30 percent. A final consequence of this type of agitation was to increase the involvement of Negro UAW members in political activities. More blacks began to run for office, sometimes with the tacit approval and encouragement of Solidarity House. And some of them were successful—although by no means all.

What follows is an attempt to examine a number of important UAW local unions in which either black worker organizations or black caucuses have been particularly active. This discussion begins with those locals where the activity took a more militant form, sometimes involving wildcat stoppages and picketing.

Approximately 80 percent of the UAW Local 961 membership at the Chrysler Eldon Avenue gear and axle plant is black. On January 27, 1969, twenty-five black workers were fired at the Eldon plant after allegedly instigating a production slowdown that day. According to the *Detroit Free Press,* 1,000 Negro employees "refused to enter the Eldon Avenue plant when ELRUM pickets appeared at plant gates to protest what they called management's racist attitude."[39] Here, as at the Dodge Main plant, the allegation was that unsafe and hazardous working conditions had triggered the employee action, and here again the picketing was enjoined. Pickets appeared at Solidarity House on February 11 protesting the lack of satisfactory action by the union. Said Shelton Tappes of the UAW fair employment practices department: "The Union has been processing the grievances, and if there is a greater need to intensify our efforts, that will be done. . . . The first steps have been taken, but sometimes the auto companies are ponderous in fashioning answers."[40]

Until 1967, the executive board of Local 961 had been all white. Elroy Richardson, a black trade unionist, was elected that year as the first black president of the local. According to Richardson, in the past blacks at the Eldon Avenue plant had been consigned to jobs as janitors and matrons, and all supervisory positions had been held by whites. The pattern was the same as that at Dodge Main, as blacks were also excluded from skilled trades jobs. The problems here were complicated by the fact that during the turmoil when blacks were becoming aware of what Douglas Fraser calls the "thirty years of neglect" of black employees at Chrysler, a black had finally become president—but by 1969 he was regarded as too moderate by a substantial number of the black workers.

Accordingly, Jordan Sims, another black candidate, who, while not a member of ELRUM, nevertheless had its support, entered the field in the 1971 Local 961 elections. Richardson was defeated in the primary with the result that there was a runoff between Sims, who had been dismissed as a result of the 1969 walkout, and a white, Frank McKinney. On May 28, 1971, McKinney won the runoff, despite the large black membership, by a vote of 1,178 to 1,142. (Local 961 has a membership of approximately 4,000.) Irregularities were found to exist, however, and Solidarity House ordered a new election which took place in January 1972. Sims was once again defeated, this time by a vote of 1,310 to 1,288, a slightly closer margin with a larger vote. Richardson supported the white candidate, as did many blacks, on the theory that Sims was controlled by ELRUM, as that organization was among his principal supporters. The second election was organized and run by Region 1 director, George Morelli, another UAW official whom, like Mazey, many blacks had come to distrust on the race issue. Sims finally won in the 1974 election, where race was not a divisive issue.

Blacks became a majority in Local 7 (Chrysler) in Detroit around 1964–1965. At that time there were no black full-time officers, and a group called Project 7 was formed to seek greater black representation. After being unable to persuade the incumbent local administration to boost blacks for a full-time position, Project 7 members packed a membership meeting and succeeded in changing the bylaws to make the post of financial secretary, which was held by a black, a full-time position.

In 1969, the incumbent white president did not seek re-election, as he was moving to the international staff. The candidates for the presidency, all running on integrated slates, included several blacks, and the winner was Bill Gilbert, one of the founders of Project 7. Gilbert's margin of victory was substantial—3,000 to 1,100. He was re-elected in 1971 by a margin of 2,700 to 700, and has served on the international negotiating committee.

Although there has been no formal black caucus in Local 7, in early 1971 there were work stoppages and a walkout after a black worker was suspended for striking a white foreman because of harassment. And the DRUM periodical *Voice* was distributed inside Local 7, it being Gilbert's contention that pressure of the sort represented by DRUM results in more leverage for elected black leadership.

At Local 51 (Plymouth), likewise in Michigan, a black majority also existed by 1964, and within a few years a black, Joe Ratcliffe, was elected president in a runoff. In 1971 he was re-elected, again in a runoff which he won by only 85 votes, in a local of over 5,000 members. Ratcliffe's opponent was a white chief steward in the skilled trades who had been at the plant for only four years. As in Local 7, both candidates ran on integrated slates.

Ratcliffe notes that the black majority in Local 51 includes a considerable number of younger new workers, who are politically aware and show an interest in union affairs, often asking for copies of the collective agreement. And while there has been no separate black caucus, black militants have engaged in leafletting and other action, criticizing the local officers, including Ratcliffe, for inaction in seeking to eliminate health and safety hazards, among other issues.

A black majority was achieved at Local 212 (Chrysler) around 1963. Local 212 elected its first black president in 1969 when the incumbent white president moved to the regional staff. Henry Ghant, now the president of this large amalgamated local which has approximately 11,000 members and covers three Chrysler plants as well as nine suppliers, was elected vice president in 1969. In 1971, he was elected president in his own right for the first time by a three-to-one margin with approximately 3,800 voters participating.

In Mahwah, New Jersey, blacks have not achieved representation in the leadership of Local 906 (Ford), although a wildcat stoppage in 1969, engaged in by a black organization called the United Black Brotherhood and some members of the

Students for a Democratic Society (SDS), interfered with production. Allegedly, a white foreman was guilty of a racial slur in dealing with a Negro production worker. On April 28, 500 black workers stayed away from the afternoon shift, interfering with the production of 425 cars. Production resumed at the next shift, however, as the workers refused to accede to the picket line established by the UBB and students. The local filed a grievance against the management representatives and, according to UAW Region 9 spokesmen, this resulted in a suspension and transfer of one of them. In the interim, however, apparently some black workers sought to obtain separate collective-bragaining rights for blacks, and this action produced a backlash among many white trade unionists who defeated the liberal white local president at the next election.

Local 6 is the bargaining agent at International Harvester's Melrose Park plant in Chicago. With approximately 40 percent of the 3,000 members black, at the June 1971 election, four blacks were elected to the thirteen-man executive board. Black candidates for president and vice president lost in runoff elections for those positions. Here blacks are fairly well organized in a large caucus in which whites are included. The 1971 election produced the most substantial black representation ever, although Local 6 had a black president in the early 1960's.

At International Harvester's plant in West Pullman, approximately 25 percent of the 2,000 members of Local 1307 is black. There are no blacks on the twelve-man executive board, the view of many UAW people being that the black vote has been split as a result of poor politics.

The events described above point to a number of conclusions. The first is that black representation does not, in and of itself, remove the problems of employment discrimination and related grievances. Indeed, in both Local 7 and Local 212 shortly after the elections of Gilbert and Ghant, there were wildcat stoppages which had their origin in complaints about harassment by foremen, plant safety conditions, and the treatment given black workers at first aid stations which seemed to them to have racial overtones. Black workers perceive the severe discipline of the auto production line and the authority wielded by white supervisors as impositions, conditions which would not be present were white workers in their place. In any event, regardless of the relationship between safety complaints and race, it seems clear that some of the grievances are legitimate and the election of black representatives has by no means eliminated the turmoil.

The second point that must be made is that the increase in black representation has taken place primarily in locals where blacks have achieved a majority or a near-majority. The one exception to this rule is Local 1248 (Chrysler Motors) where 80 percent of the plant's 989 workers are white.[41] Generally, however, blacks made up a minimum of 45–50 percent of the membership and sometimes considerably more. Two points can be derived from this observation. The first is that where whites are in the majority they still seem to resist voting for black workers. The second is that no one will move the labor movement on the race issue and blacks will not achieve any kind of proportional representation unless they are willing to involve themselves and use political muscle. In all the plants where blacks have been elected they themselves have campaigned on the local level. To be sure, the international has, albeit cautiously, supported blacks, as it did in the case of Marcellius Ivory's election in Region 1-A. But on the local level the international generally avoids involvement.

The third main point shown by these recent events is that, while the immediate impact of black leadership upon the skilled-trades problem is somewhat questionable in light of the fact that none of the black activists in the UAW were skilled tradesmen and therefore were not directly involved in such matters, nevertheless, their election assists in achieving a better climate for upward mobility for blacks. The fact that the greatest strides in both leadership representation and entry into the skilled trades have been made in the UAW locals in Chrysler is not a coincidence. The two, while not directly related, have gone very much hand in hand.

United Steelworkers of America

Probably no industrial union has faced more Title VII trouble than the United Steelworkers of America. Thousands of complaints have been filed against the union and employers with whom they bargain in basic steel, charging racial discrimination at plants in both the North and the South. These complaints relate primarily to problems of upgrading rather than hiring. Negroes have had a good deal of access to employment in steel (they compose upwards of 25 percent of the work force) but have been confined all too often to the dirtiest and hottest jobs and labor pools—all of which offer lower wages and poorer working conditions than those jobs held in the overwhelming number of instances by whites.[42] The pattern is different from the automobile industry where minorities in some companies— particularly GM—are more recent arrivals, and where a partial refusal of both the companies and the union to train nonemployee applicants and to promote from within are all mixed together. Charges relating to discrimination in steel seem to have more of one constant theme.

In the steel industry there is generally a job progression within each department. That is to say, an employee performs one job in order to learn how to handle the next job on the ladder when a vacancy occurs. At certain pay grades, the employee moves into a unit within a department which contains his line of progression. Accordingly, the general rule is that a worker possesses three kinds of seniority, plant, department, and unit seniority—as well as, in some instances, company seniority.

Beginning in 1962, the companies and the union negotiated transfer provisions in collective-bargaining agreements which made it possible for employees in agreed-upon area pools to transfer on a plant-wide basis and, in preference to hiring new workers, also provided such transfer rights to employees with necessary qualifications who were continuously on layoff for sixty days.

Under the 1965 Master Agreement, limited plant-wide transfers became available for the first time to qualified workers who were not on layoff, enabling them to bid on vacancies occurring in any other departments in the plant. Employees in a particular unit, however, continued to retain preference for jobs opening within their unit, and employees in a department where departmental transfer agreements existed continued to retain preference for jobs within that department. Also, workers who were in an area pool continued to retain preference for jobs within those areas. Accordingly, the bulk of vacancies were filled through transfers on an entry-level basis.

But although they broadened transfer rights, neither the 1962 nor the 1965 agreement dealt with the thorny seniority issue. Both before and after the passage of Title VII black workers had been extremely dissatisfied with the operation of seniority arrangements because in the previously all-white departments and units they were penalized by being denied seniority credits which would have been theirs had a fair hiring and transfer policy existed in the first place. As we have noted a complaint on this subject was rejected in *Whitfield* v. *United Steelworkers;*[43] and the Fifth Circuit, dealing with the challenge to seniority rights under the duty-of-fair-representation doctrine imposed upon unions under the National Labor Relations Act, stated that it could not undo what was in effect a "product of the past."[44] The Fifth Circuit has since specifically disavowed *Whitfield* in both *United States* v. *Hayes International Corporation*[45] and *Taylor* v. *Armco Steel Corp.*[46]—the latter involving the very same plant and issue as *Whitfield*. Moreover, the Second Circuit in *Williamston* v. *Bethlehem Steel* (Lackawanna)[47] and more recently the secretary of labor in *Bethlehem Steel* (Sparrow's Point)[48] held that black workers in the steel plants are entitled to seniority credits that they have accumulated in undesirable departments to which they were discriminatorily assigned and may carry with them to the new department both their wage rate and their seniority credits. The impact of these decrees for black employees has been substantial, at least in the Lackawanna plant. Almost a decade after the enactment of the Civil Rights Act, the Steelworkers and their employer counterparts agreed to seniority modification—but only in the context of a consent decree in which black, Chicano, and women steelworkers were required to waive their right to sue under employment-discrimination legislation, and simultaneously accept implementation from which minority workers who were not union members were excluded.[49]

On the one hand, the Steelworkers are to be commended for bowing to the dictates of the law, albeit a decade after Title VII became the law. In accepting the validity of the consent decree, the Fifth Circuit had laudatory comments about the efforts of the government and defendants to negotiate reforms which allowed promotion for employees previously locked into lower-paying lines of progression. The decree is a step forward in the sense that future opportunities are created—but its flimsy enforcement system, which, in sharp contrast to the *Local 86* decree in Seattle, makes the defendants solely responsible for implementation, undermines its promise.[50]

One of the major issues in the Steelworkers union, as in many of the other industrial unions described here, particularly the UAW, has been the question of black representation in both elected policy-making positions and appointed staff jobs. In terms of employment discrimination as well as minority representation in union positions, it is quite clear that the Steelworkers come off a poor second to the UAW. Like many other organizations in America, the Steelworkers, despite the obvious barriers against the upgrading of blacks which they had helped erect in the form of seniority systems which locked minority employees in, continued piously to proclaim their support for civil rights. One must recall former President McDonald's statement, during the debate over Title VII prior to its enactment, to the effect that the Steelworkers were not familiar with discriminatory practices.[51] It also must be recalled that this union played a leading role in the 1966 meeting with representatives of EEOC and in the AFL-CIO's rigid stance against any modification of seniority systems which would improve the lot of black employees. In the 1960's the Steelworkers had no black, Chicano, or Puerto Rican worker in any elected policy-making position; Alex Fuller, the director of the civil rights program, was the only black union member appointed to a policy-making job.

Accordingly, in 1964, around the time of the passage of Title VII, a group of black Steelworkers formed an organization called the Ad Hoc Steelworkers Committee. This organization, chaired by Thomas Johnson of Fairfield, Alabama, attempted to draw attention to the manner in which whites had been appointed to leadership positions at the union's inception so as to justify a similar process for blacks. The Ad Hoc Committee pointed out that between 1936 and 1942 the Steelworkers organizing committee under Philip Murray was in the process of moving to international union status, and prior to 1942 all district directors were appointed. No black was appointed a director or sub-district director at that time although five or six blacks were appointed as international organizers. When the organizing committee became an international union, those who had received leadership positions by virtue of appointment from Murray were in a favorable position to run for election because of the exposure and prestige they had derived from their interim appointment. In effect, the Ad Hoc Committee argued in 1964—and on a number of occasions later—that it was necessary for blacks to gain a district directorship or vice presidency by appointment and then, at a later date, to stand for re-election, just as whites had done at the time that the union was formed—and just as any black would have done had blacks been appointed by Murray sometime between 1936 and 1942.

Within a year after the Ad Hoc Committee had appeared on the scene, the Steelworkers union's first serious political campaign was fought bitterly. A few weeks after the Democratic Convention in 1964, at the Steelworkers' convention in Atlantic City the Ad Hoc Committee met with President McDonald, who promised to call a meeting "before long" of the union's civil rights committee. The meeting was never called. When the Ad Hoc Committee met later that fall in Detroit, the organization, once again committing itself both to the integration of the executive board and district positions and to a reorganization and strengthening of the civil rights committee, endorsed I. W. Abel for the presidency. Abel, despite charges of racial discrimination by the McDonald forces, was able to garner most of the black votes inside the union. After all, in 1960 it was Abel who, with Reuther, had been willing to address the convention of the Negro American Labor Council. McDonald had turned down an invitation to do so.[52] Moreover, Abel had been willing to meet with black Steelworker representatives and to promise the reorganization of the civil rights committee as well as more staff appointments. Only on the question of an integrated executive board did he stop short, noting that a guarantee of minority-group executive-board positions would require a constitutional change.

When Abel was elected in 1965, the civil rights department was reorganized with Alex Fuller as its director, and Fuller hired two black staff men. Additional appointments of Negroes were made to the auditing department, and the research, legal, educational and pension departments as well. There are now two black sub-district directors (in Philadelphia and Detroit), and members of racial minorities are presidents of the three largest locals in District 3 (the Chicago-Gary area).

Yet, as the 1968 convention neared, it was clear that Abel intended to do nothing about the question of black representation on the executive board. Thus in a union which is approximately 30 percent minority, there was and remains a complete absence of minority representation at that level. On the opening day of the convention in Chicago the Ad Hoc Committee stated: "We demand Negroes on the Executive Board and full integration on all levels within the various districts and national offices." The Ad Hoc Committee pointed out that while the Steelworkers have a substantial black voting membership, that membership, as in the UAW and most other industrial unions, is not in a majority in any district. The contention was that a black needed a period of incumbency and the exposure that goes with it in order to be elected. This meant that the president would have to appoint a Negro to the board for an interim period of time.

The Ad Hoc Committee supported constitutional amendments which would have added the office of second vice president to the executive board, with the initially appointed incumbent being required to run for ofice the following February when all members of the international executive board and its officers would have to stand for re-election. Said Johnny Fair of Local 2610, one of the two big locals of Bethlehem Steel in Baltimore: 'I am asking you now, we need a symbol. We need to look up there and know that our people are there, they are in the policy-making framework which we worked so hard for in the mills—I feel it is time now that we change the system and we start changing it right here and put a black man up there so my daughters and daughters of all these Steelworkers of all this country can say, yes, now we're a part, we're a real part, we are in the policy-making part of this Union."

Nevertheless, the union leadership, through the constitution committee, rejected this proposal. Vice President Joseph Molony recommended against adoption of the amendment, stating that "the election of an officer to this union because of race or color, would be a contradiction in the basic theme of the civil rights movement that people should be judged, hired, or elected on the basis of their ability.''[53] Of course, Molony knew and most politicians and trade unionists know that the election of a black is not a mere matter of ability but rather a product of compromise, personalities, and the willingness of the dominant caucus or slate to push for a black to be included as part of the team. This sort of effort the Steelworkers had been unwilling to make, and therefore the Ad Hoc Committee had applied pressure. Said Rayfield Mooty, secretary-treasurer of the Ad Hoc Committee, at the 1968 Convention, ''We believe that there will be an explosive situation in the United Steelworkers of America so long as Abel is unable to appoint and we are unable to elect a member to the Board.''

Later during the week Mayor Andrew Hatcher of Gary, Indiana, in speaking to the convention urged the union to provide for representation of all groups at all levels of the organization.[54]

Meanwhile, at the convention an approach was being made by some Steelworker leaders, including Abel, to Leander Simms, who had recently been made assistant director of District 8 in Baltimore, to run for the directorship. One initial hurdle was never crossed, however. An attempt was made to ask the incumbent white director to step down so that Simms could have the benefit of incumbency. The incumbent, Albert Atallah, stubbornly refused to resign because he had a white staff successor in mind for his position. Apparently, at least before knowing that Atallah would not step down, Abel and some of his associates believed that District 8, which had a black membership of approximately 40 percent, would provide the base for black representation at the international level. This was not to happen.

The political facts of life in Baltimore's District 8 are that, although black membership is 40 percent, blacks among local union presidents constitute a far smaller percentage. Moreover, the black votes are congregated in Locals 2609 and 2610, the two large Bethlehem Steel locals. Simms, who had come from one of the white-collar Steelworkers' units in Crown Cork and Seal Company, was not the ideal politician for black Steelworkers in the rough and tumble milieu of Bethlehem Steel. An even more important factor was that, as might be expected, a racist campaign was waged against him. Finally, some blacks in District 8 spread the word that Simms was a ''safe Negro'' in light of his cordial relationship with Abel. This, of course, points up one of the weaknesses of the Ad Hoc Committee's interim appointment idea: any black who is endorsed by the white leadership is likely to be suspect as—or in fact to be—an ''Uncle Tom.'' (Simms decidedly did not fall in the latter category.)

In February 1969, with a low black turnout, particularly in Local 2610, Simms was beaten. One obvious—and the most publicized—factor in his defeat was the failure of a large number of blacks to vote. This theme was taken up by both Abel and the press at subsequent conventions when the black representation issue was raised again. Indeed, the *Baltimore Afro-American* berated black Steelworkers for ''a remarkable example of lack of interest in their own welfare.''[55] Many blacks, however, while conceding that Negro workers did not vote in substantial enough numbers, still characterize the international's position as one of ''benign neglect.''

Simms himself has stated that the much publicized intervention of Abel was too little assistance too late. Simms and one of his associates point out that nothing was said by the international concerning the campaign until February 6, approximately a week before the election. At that point, Abel said, "If I were in District 8, I would vote for Simms." But the international had great difficulty in making up its mind about even that cautious statement. Moreover, financial assistance was virtually nonexistent. Finally, there was another factor for which neither Simms nor Abel could be held accountable: Abel had a very difficult time during the 1969 election with a spirited challenge from staff lawyer Emil Narick. The incumbents were quite unpopular in certain quarters and the endorsement, albeit a limited and late one, may have harmed Simms' candidacy as well as assisting it.

That election was the last serious and close contest in which a black has attempted to obtain an executive-board position. The Ad Hoc Committee once again raised the issue of black representation at the 1970 convention in Atlantic City. By a decisive voice vote, the 3,500 delegates upheld what was characterized as their officers' "persistent position that minority members must be elected to the top official echelon of that union." This rejection of the possibility of appointment was made in spite of the persuasive argument by delegate Curtis Strong, a staff representative from the union's Chicago District 31 who stated the following during the debate: "Without making the appointment process decisive, the resolution would enhance the possibility of a black getting on the Executive Board. It would enhance the possibility of a woman getting on the Board." Nevertheless, the Steelworkers continue to do what the UAW did before 1962—refuse both to recognize the peculiar difficulties involved in the election of racial minorities, particularly blacks, and to promote the candidacy of a black within the context of a new vice presidency. While the appointment of blacks to lower staff positions may dilute some of the strength of the Ad Hoc Committee's argument, by the same token it may arouse an interest in and awareness of such matters on the part of younger black members who were not involved in the formation of the Ad Hoc Committee.

Amalgamated Meat Cutters and Butcher Workmen of North America

Both the Knights of Labor and the Amalgamated Meat Cutters had serious difficulties in organizing workers in the meat-packing plants around the turn of the century. The strikes of 1894 and 1904 were particularly difficult ones, and even though the Amalgamated survived the 1904 strike in which it was involved, it nearly disappeared in the wake of it. The employers in both 1894 and 1904 were able effectively to combat strikes by importing strikebreakers, some of whom were Negro workers who were discharged soon after the strikes ended. At that time, meat-packing work, which was a continuing upswing because of the advent of both railroads and refrigeration, was performed by white immigrants who were able and willing to do this hard and disagreeable labor. Blacks were not yet in the industry in large numbers and, to the extent that they were involved, it was strictly as strikebreakers.

Of course, the resentment expressed against strikebreakers was visited upon blacks to a greater extent than upon whites because they were visible. This hostility made the job of organizing them—when they finally did begin to come into the industry on a permanent footing at the time of labor shortages during World War I—a very difficult job. Moreover, the interest expressed by the Amalgamated in organizing black workers around 1917 was hardly of the kind to allay previously aroused suspicions. Walter Fogel has described the situation as follows:

Approximately 20 unions, including the Amalgamated, which was by far the largest organization, were affiliated with the [Stock Yards Labor] Council; most of these were skilled craft groups. Only a few of the unions, including the Amalgamated, admitted Negroes to membership. Since there was now a very large number of Negroes in the Chicago yards, "the number increasing in direct ratio to the success of the unions in organizing the white laborers," it was evident that "the Negro problem" had to be dealt with if unionism was to achieve any success. In short, the problem was that black workers had to be organized, but many white workers with strong racial prejudices did not want union "brotherhood" with their colored coworkers. The dilemma was presented to Samuel Gompers, President of the American Federation of Labor, for his recommendation. He suggested the formation of a separate Amalgamated local for Negroes, which would take in all Negroes in the yards, whatever their job. Two colored organizers were hired and local 651 of the Amalgamated was formed. It signed up most of the black workers who did join unions in the Chicago yards, thus enabling the unions of skilled workers to remain all white. Some early successes were obtained in organizing Negroes, but these gains were often temporary and, on the whole, the success of the meat packing unions with Negroes was limited—in the Chicago yards, never more than 15 percent were organized.

Although the effort to organize Negroes appears to have been sincere, it probably appeared more calculating than altruistic to black workers. Many were aware of the fact that, generally, unions did not admit Negroes to membership. Even more realized that Negroes rarely were advanced above semi-skilled positions in meat packing and that unions had done nothing to change the practice. Certainly, all were aware of the antagonistic feelings harbored by many white workers toward members of their race.[56]

Racism is the primary reason why blacks were so difficult to organize. All other factors noted by Fogel flow from this: (1) economic necessity; (2) gratitude for employer paternaism; (3) employer preference for white workers; (4) trade union hostility; (5) union failure to protest lack of job advancement for blacks; (6) the fact that blacks encountered "racially restrictive practices after the beginning of the rapid migration to the North"; (7) mistrust based upon segregated housing, Negroes in the Chicago area being forced to live more than a mile east of the meat-packing yards, unlike the European immigrants who resided in the immediate area.

Not until the 1930's and the advent of the United Packinghouse Workers Union did the labor movement begin to make substantial progress in gaining the organizational allegiance of black workers in the yards. The UPWA's attitude toward black workers was substantially different from that previously displayed by the Amalgamated. Whereas the Amlgamated regarded itself as a craft union of skilled workers and had pride and craft-consciousness which went with that self-image, the UPWA was an industrial union, part of the CIO, and necessarily was concerned with the problems of the black workers. Very few of the Amalgamated's members were black, but a substantial portion of the UPWA's membership was.

In part, this numerical strength dictated a political position which made progress for blacks within the union's structure more possible. In Chicago, for instance, in the 1940's 70 percent of the membership was black. Nationally during that period the black membership was between 40 and 45 percent. By the time of the merger between the UPWA and the Amalgamated in 1968, UPWA black membership had shrunk to aproximately 25–30 percent—for reasons which are explored below.

The UPWA policy with regard to blacks was clearly superior to that of any other major industrial union including the UAW. For at the very time in the 1940's that the UAW and Walter Reuther refused to accede to demands for black representation on the executive board because of the inability of blacks to be elected by a white majority in any region, the UPWA specifically provided for black representation. This resulted in four of the thirteen executive-board seats being held by blacks. The UPWA leadership explicitly stated that blacks had to have some form of proportional representation on the executive board. It was not left to mere chance in the electoral process. This history and tradition are remarkably different from those of all other portions of the labor movement.

Moreover, as John Hope noted in his study of the UPWA conducted in 1955,[57] at that time Negroes held one of three vice presidencies and three of nine district directorships. Three of the eleven heads of administrative departments were black. Of seven international representatives, one was black and one was Mexican-American. Of sixty-five field representatives, eighteen were black and four were Mexican-American. According to Hope, at the end of 1948 83 percent of the locals had Negroes in key positions. More specifically, blacks were on the executive boards in 67 percent of the local unions and Mexican-Americans in 19 percent. Accordingly, unlike all of the other industrial unions, the UPWA did not simply accept blacks into membership. The union moved, more than twenty years before it became fashionable, to include racial minorities in leadership positions. The UPWA national leadership specifically encouraged and, where necessary, insisted upon this.

In addition, the UPWA took its no-discrimination policy much more seriously than did other industrial unions. Walkouts were called to obtain employer adherence to the policy. This action has been rare in American labor history, although the UAW and other unions have taken stances in favor of no-discrimination in the teeth of walkouts by white workers in opposition to a no-discrimination policy. Moreover, the UPWA, once again unlike other industrial unions, concerned itself with fair hiring by employers. Its collective-bargaining agreements addressed themselves to the question of discrimination in hiring as well as in promotion, and in one instance the issue was taken to arbitration, the result being an award which included back pay. Such conduct is extremely rare in the annals of organized labor in this country. As Fogel has noted:

The UPWA continued [to the present] militantly to pursue equal rights for all members after collective bargaining in the industry was well established. . . . Nondiscrimination clauses concerning hiring [in the North as well as in the South] as well as conditions of employment were negotiated in all UPWA agreements. Elimination of segregated plant facilities was pressed. Based partly on a unique self-survey of members' attitudes, educational programs emphasizing the union's antidiscrimination position were conducted. A financial contribution was made by the UPWA to the Southern Christian Leadership Conference in 1957, even before its director, Martin Luther King, Jr., had achieved national prominence. Community fair employment practice and equal rights programs in the North were consistently supported by local and district UPWA leaders. All of these things were done during the 1940's and 1950's, when it had not yet become so fashionable for social and business institutions to be actively concerned with minority rights.[58]

One particularly important insight into the reasons for the UPWA's stance is provided by John Hope's study, which indicates that in the 1940's and 1950's UPWA members on the local level generally thought that their international's no-discrimination policy did not go far enough. According to Hope, the indications of dissatisfaction with the positive aspects of the fair-employment policy were minimal or nonexistent. Of course, the UPWA has had to impose trusteeships upon recalcitrant locals, and it has had, as Hope notes, some serious disagreements on the local level. Nevertheless, on balance, the decline of UPWA membership which ultimately sent membership rolls to a low of 80–90,000 and dictated the merger with the Amalgamated does not seem to have been attributable to the union's position on race. The decline was primarily the result of the relocation of meat-packing plants from large urban areas where the UPWA was strong to relatively rural portions of the Midwest such as Iowa and Minnesota where its perennial rival, the Amalgamated Meat Cutters, had greater strength.

The merger in 1968 between the two unions brought varying traditions and backgrounds together. Primarily because of the UPWA tradition, the merged union, the Amalgamated Meat Cutters, has one of the few integrated executive boards—and indeed probably the most integrated of any industrial union in the private sector. Of 24 executive board members, 3 are black. Of 117 international organizers, 14 are black and 7 are Chicanos. Like the UAW and the Steelworkers—and unlike the Teamsters—the union has a civil rights department which attempts to educate the members about employment-discrimination problems, the law of Title VII, and minority-group rights inside the union. It is chaired by a black official, Harry Alston. It is estimated that approximately 20 percent of the Meat Cutters' merged membership is black or Chicano.

One of the principle difficulties that minority group members in the Amalgamated are faced with today is that the relocation of meat-packing plants in rural areas has meant a decline in Negro employment in that industry and therefore in black membership in that portion of the union. Between 1964 and 1968 the percentage of Negro workers employed in the four largest firms in the meat industry declined from 13.1 to 12.1.[59] Companies such as Swift have hired all employees from the area in which they have relocated. In East St. Louis, which is predominantly black, Swift and Armour operations have shut down. The entire trend of the industry in this regard has had a deleterious impact upon black employment opportunities.

Another problem confronted by black workers in the industry is that seniority is often negotiated on a departmental basis and that blacks, until recently, have been kept out of the mechanical skilled trades. The problem of transfer with seniority credits and wage rates imposes itself again—and neither the union nor the employers seem to have taken any steps voluntarily to cope with it. Blacks have traditionally been limited to the so-called "kill" departments, the slaughtering, which involves the dirtiest and most undesirable jobs. Moreover, once again, as in the automobile industry, all the major companies appear to hire skilled tradesmen, and in some instances apprentices or trainees for skilled-trades classifications, from the street. In most instances workers thus hired appear to be white.

In retail establishments the union's jurisdiction is derived from the old pre-merger Amalgamated—and minorities have had difficulties being employed in retail stores and butchers' jobs. Because work in retail stores involved contact with customers and because the hiring policies tended to follow customer preferences, very few blacks came under the Amalgamated's jurisdiction. This, coupled with the tradition and craft-conscious orientation of most Amalgamated members, limited black entry. Ever since the late 1960's, however, with the advent of violence and riots in ghetto areas, retail employers have begun to change their hiring policies to suit black customers. But some new problems have arisen in this connection. Membership has begun to decline in the black areas as retail stores move more to the white-dominated suburbs. Local 547 of the Amalgamated, based in Detroit, had a membership of 600 in 1967, but by 1972 it was reduced to 400. Ninety percent of that membership is black. Locals 546 and 638 which represent employees in the white areas have continued to grow. The problem of the black workers is that they have generally had no contractual right to follow the work and no right to take their seniority with them, although under the contracts negotiated in 1967 and 1970 they received the right to follow the work if it was supervised by the same individual under whom they had worked before. The Amalgamated's answer to this problem has been that all locals should be merged together. Under this system all workers would have the maximum amount of work opportunities and would be able to follow work without any kind of restriction. The difficulty here is—and this has held up the merger—that whites would outnumber blacks and that blacks fear a loss of black leadership. This problem, of course, is similar to that confronted in connection with *de jure* segregated locals which are merging, although the Chicago Amalgamated locals have been *de facto* racially segregated rather than *de jure*.

Some locals of the Amalgamated have apparently agreed to train minorities to be butchers in New York City and Detroit. Moreover, the Amalgamated, recognizing that, while it is ahead of all other industrial unions insofar as minority representation in union leadership positions is concerned, much remains to be done, has established a new advisory committee which has as an objective the promoting of minority leadership. Of fourteen individuals selected by the international executive board to serve on it, two are black and one is a Chicano. Whether this new procedure will result in more substantial minority representation remains to be seen. Nevertheless, this step, coupled with the minority representation that already exists, clearly indicates that the Amalgamated is one of the most forward-looking unions on the civil rights issue.

International Union of Electrical, Radio and Machine Workers

The number of blacks who are skilled tradesmen in the electrical manufacturing industry is relatively small. As of 1969, 3.7 percent of all males in the industry were blacks; the figure for females was 10.2.[60] The dominant union in the industry is the IUE, although the IBEW and the United Electrical Workers (UE), the left-wing union from which the IUE broke off because of the former's alleged Communist Party leanings, represent employees in electrical manufacturing as well.

The IUE appears to have played a very small role in the promotion of black employees to skilled-trades positions. It has, however, entered into hiring-of-the-disadvantaged "MA-4 contracts" with the Department of Labor. Moreover, within the past four years, the IUE has undertaken an ambitious effort to gather information regarding the racial and sexual composition of the work force and employer affirmative-action programs adopted pursuant to the executive order. Of all the industrial unions, the IUE appears to be the first to concern itself with discriminatory hiring patterns. One can note that the union is obviously responding to threatened litigation by EEOC as well as to a substantial female constituency in its ranks, and still recognize that it has adopted a forward-looking and unique stance on problems of hiring discrimination.

It has done little, however, to protest the absence of minorities in the skilled trades. Apparently most companies hire for these jobs off the street rather than transferring incumbent employees. But a study of black workers in the electrical manufacturing industry indicates that while nonemployee blacks are not in as good a position to compete as their white counterparts, the same may not be true of black incumbent employees vis-à-vis whites:

A better source of Negro applicants is found among employees. They have a knowledge of the job and its opportunities and know the rewards that await the trained mechanic. Companies have instituted special training programs to encourage black employees to register for apprentice training. Although the proportion of Negroes applying for such training, even with special company encouragement, often remains below that of whites in relation to their relative numbers in the workforce, there has been a noticeable rise in Negro apprentices and craftsmen since 1964. The total percentage is still, of course, relatively small.[61]

The IUE role in this regard appears to be a minimal one. Although James Carey, Paul Jennings' predecessor as president of the IUE, was chairman of the AFL-CIO civil rights committee after the AFL-CIO merger, this does not appear to have translated itself into vigorous action insofar as employees or members of the bargaining unit are concerned.

Despite the IUE proclamations, the policies of local unions reflect the realities of their politics. As it has been noted, "if there is a strong black minority among the membership, the local officials are more likely to be concerned with racial problems than if the minority membership is small." Neither the IUE—until its recent demands for information—nor the left-wing UE seem to have been particularly vigorous in their concern. Recent IUE efforts, however, provide a solid basis for believing that the union will push hard for minorities and women.

While some disturbances along the lines of those previously outlined for the auto industry have taken place, the most notable of the more recent incidents in the electrical manufacturing industry occurred at a plant where neither the IUE nor the UE was the collective-bargaining representative. In this situation involving a Hotpoint provision facility of the General Electric Company, where, subsequent to a hiring-of-the-disadvantaged MA-4 contract with the Department of Labor, black workers engaged in sitdowns, picketing and other pressure tactics, the Sheetmetal Workers International Association was the collective-bargaining representative. Given its background, this incident does not seem terribly surprising:

That distrust should develop between the SMWIA local and its black constituents was nearly inevitable. In the summer of 1968 a Negro, Willie Plunkett, ran for local president, lost, and organized a group called The Afro-American Employees of Hotpoint. In October a black and a Puerto Rican employee engaged in a fight while at work, with the former being discharged as the instigator, and the latter suspended. The Afro-American group, by then known as the Black Federation of Labor, launched sitdowns, picketing, and other harassment which actually shut Hotpoint for one day. Plunkett and others were suspended, and it was explained to them that since SMWIA was the certified bargaining agent, the Company could not deal with another union. Finally, the Company sought a directive from the National Labor Relations Board proscribing further interference from the Black Federation.

In October 1969, a coalition of unions including SMWIA struck General Electric plants. A substantial number of employees including many blacks crossed the picket lines and went to work before the four-months strike ended. Now, however, the Sheet Metal Workers local there has a black president and many black stewards, so that union integration is proceeding on a local basis in a quite different manner than appears to be typical in this union's construction locals.[62]

As in the UAW and the Amalgamated Meat Cutters, blacks have some representation in the IUE leadership. On the 29-member executive board, there are two blacks, William White, who is chairman of the board of trustees, and Don Austin, who is secretary-treasurer of IUE District 12 on the west coast. The same kind of demand put forward unsuccessfully at UAW conventions and successfully at UPWA conventions for black representation on the international executive board was put forward in IUE conventions in the 1960's. Informally on a *de facto* basis, the elections of both White and Austin are a response to those demands. White votes are even more at a premium for potential black office holders in the IUE than in the other unions. For instance, in White's district in Indiana, less than 15 percent of the members are black. The international, while disavowing quotas and at the same time praising the 1972 reforms of the Democratic National Committee, has pressed for greater participation by black workers at the local level as well. On balance, it might be said that the international's role is a positive one, demonstrating concern about what other unions have fobbed off as management prerogatives, that is, hiring and composition of the workforce. The IUE occupies an intermediate position on the skilled-trades issue generally, between the best and the worst of the old CIO unions—but is rapidly moving toward the best.

United Furniture Workers of America

This relatively small union (its membership is less than 100,000, and 30 percent are minority) has probably been more ambitious than any other in striving for and achieving minority representation at the national level. In 1968 the convention adopted a resolution calling for such representation. But although only three minority representatives were on the executive board, the resolution did not bring any change. A substantial number of national union officials—both black and white—regarded this figure as inappropriate because the minority membership was so large. Accordingly, at the 1970 convention the constitution was amended, enlarging the executive board from 27 to 31, and providing for 4 vice presidents, as the past constitution had had, representing 4 major geographical areas, and also for "one representative at large from each of the 4 major geographical areas, East, Midwest, the South, and West." Furthermore, the amendment stated that it was adopted "with the expectation that the General Executive Board will reflect the racial make-up of the membership of the United Furniture Workers of America."

The rationale behind this proposal was that the four additional members at large would be minority trade unionists and that their presence on the board would thus represent a start in the direction of racial balance at the leadership level. As Vice President LeRoy Clark put it to me: "We can't permit racism to parade under the banner of Democracy."[63] It was thought desirable, therefore, to take a first step which would attempt both to change the attitudes of white workers who might not otherwise vote for blacks on their own and, equally important, to create a model for black trade unionists which would encourage them to involve themselves in union activities. The hope is that the move will lead to the election of minority members to some of the other 27 positions which are not specifically reserved for them.

The interesting point here is that this step was taken by a union which could have relied upon the kind of color-blind argument put forward by the Steelworkers with even more moral assurance inasmuch as minorities already had some representation. Nevertheless, it took a relatively bold stance and successfully adopted the resolution at its 1970 constitutional convention. Moreover, and much to the consternation of some dissenting delegates, it was clear that the United Furniture Workers had one of the best records in relation to employment discrimination in the labor movement. But as Vice President Clark stated at the convention:

I question sincerely the person who says, "We don't discriminate in our Union and we have never discriminated," when I can look at the staff of that Union and find that it is lily white in a black majority Local Union. I question that. (applause)

The question has also been raised that if you increase the number on the Board to 31 and if you do get 4 minority members more on there, they will have a harder job to bring about change because it is then a bigger Board. But who says it is going to be limited to the four additional? Who says there will not be additional blacks on there or other minority group members? (applause)[64]

United Rubber Workers

Employment patterns in the rubber industry resemble those in basic manufacturing already discussed in connection with the auto and electrical equipment industries. Except in Southern plants, blacks have been hired in smaller numbers than was the case in auto. According to Herbert Northrup, approximately 2.8 percent of the craftsmen employed by the rubber tire companies in 1968 were black.[65] Significantly, in the same year, only approximately 8 percent of the overall work force was black—a relatively small figure for a mass production industry.

Theoretically, all the major industrial unions generally support the concept of plant-wide seniority. Plant-wide seniority is a relatively egalitarian philosophical approach to job bidding, and the industrial unions have accepted the view that a procedure which maximizes opportunities for the greatest number of people is the best policy to follow. Nevertheless, as we have already seen, even though the United Steelworkers, for instance, claim to hold this view, many local agreements instead reflect a department-wide pattern which the international has refused to upset. It appears that the URW and its local constituents have adhered to plant-wide seniority in a greater number of instances than have the industrial unions generally. Although as Northrup notes, the approach of plant-wide seniority was not adopted with a view of benefiting blacks,[66] it seems to have had that impact in a number of instances.

In the Gaston, Alabama, Local 12 collective-bargaining relationship, however, the situation was otherwise. In this case, three separate seniority lists were maintained—for white males, Negro males, and females. Black employees protested the failure of the company to permit their hire when they were on layoff status on the basis of plant seniority rules. Local 12, despite the contrary views of the union's international president, George Burdon, refused to process a grievance concerning the failure to hire on the basis of plant-wide seniority. That refusal to process became the basis of a duty-of-fair-representation allegation before the National Labor Relations Board in which a violation was eventually found, the board's view being subsequently confirmed by the Fifth Circuit Court of Appeals.[67] Unfortunately, for reasons developed more fully below, the relief was not adequate inasmuch as an arbitrator appointed by the union and the employer subsequently denied the black workers' back-pay claims under the collective agreement negotiated by the parties. In this case, and in others as well,[68] local practice departed from what was purportedly the policy at the national level.

Firestone Tire & Rubber Company, which is now attempting to recruit black skilled tradesmen, had as of 1972 an extremely small number of them—23 of 1,746.[69]* One problem has always been that the tire companies, like many of their counterparts in automobile and electrical equipment manufacture, hire skilled employees from the street. These workers are practically always white, because whites are the only group with prior experience in skilled-trades classifications. Moreover, at Uniroyal, Firestone, and other rubber companies, quite often there is no functioning apprenticeship program to provide for upgrading. Sometimes there is no contract provision permitting transfers into the skilled trades. And where such a provision exists, in many instances red circling is not part of the agreement and therefore there is a disincentive to transfer.

One feature of the rubber industry is not present in other manufacturing industries. The classification of tire builder, although not regarded as a skilled-trades job, is more attractive to many production workers than the skilled trades because in many plants the tire builders' incentive wages exceed those of skilled tradesmen. The tire builders' job, on the other hand, is extremely strenuous and physically demanding. Production workers have been upgraded to this job classification, and here blacks appear to have made greater inroads than they have in the skilled trades.

What is the role of the United Rubber Workers in the employment relationship? Like all the other industrial unions, it has prided itself on being open to all employees. Its 200,000 membership is estimated to be approximately 15 percent black and a much smaller percentage Chicano. The percentage of black members in the rubber industry itself appears to be smaller, many blacks being employed in plastics and linoleum plants where the union has bargaining rights. None of the executive-board members is black, and none belongs to any other minority group.

A black caucus is in existence inside the union, but an attempt to secure executive-board representation failed at the 1968 convention when Lyle Skinner of Illinois was defeated at the meeting of the general caucus. (This meeting, as is the case in most unions, is tantamount to endorsement or rejection by the membership.) At the 1970 convention a black caucus of 100 met, but it was unable to alter the racial composition of the executive board.

On the international staff, blacks are also extremely underrepresented. The breakdown as of 1972 was as follows (there is no District 3):

	Total	Black
District 1 (Ohio, Michigan, Indiana, West Virginia, and parts of Virginia, Pennsylvania, and Kentucky)	18	2
District 2 (Massachusetts, Rhode Island, Connecticut, and Vermont)	7	1
District 4 (South)	13	1
District 5 (California, Oregon, Washington)	9	1
District 6 (Canada)	9	0
District 7 (New York, Maryland, Delaware, and parts of Virginia and Pennsylvania)	10	2
District 8 (South)	18	1

While the URW has a civil rights department, its function appears to be largely educational; it operates at a relatively low-key level in comparison to the civil rights department of the UAW.

Utility Workers Union of America

The electric power industry is one of the most discriminatory in the United States. The percentage of minorities employed in 1970 was 8 and that of blacks approximately 6. These are the lowest minority and black participation rates for any industry which employs 500,000 or more.[70] (There are twenty-three industries reporting employment in this amount.) In 1970 one-third of all the utility establishments filing EEO-1 reports with the commission had *no black employees*.[71]

The absence of minorities from utilities, especially electric power, is important because these companies pay higher blue-collar wages than other industries pay to employees of comparable skill. For instance, in Detroit a cleaner at the Edison plant receives almost as much per hour as a semiskilled auto assembler. Moreover, the electric power industry is bound to offer a blue-collar worker greater job security than a manufacturing industry. Cushioned from the pressures of the market by their monopolistic position and assured of their return on investment by state regulation and fixing of prices, utility companies are in a relatively easy economic situation, and there is hardly any possibility of layoff. This is particularly important in cities like Detroit where blue-collar opportunities in other industries are extremely vulnerable to recession, and offer virtually no economic security. Employees will often be willing to take blue-collar jobs at lower wage rates in industries where there is economic security.

Another important reason why the electric power industry is particularly attractive to black workers is that the companies, sometimes through formally negotiated apprenticeship programs, train their own workers. Unlike the automobile, trucking, and electrical equipment industries, utilities do not generally hire skilled tradesmen from the outside. Accordingly, requirements of prior experience, which have a disproportionately exclusionary impact upon blacks in some of the other industries described above, should not be a barrier here. As former Chairman William Brown of the Equal Employment Opportunity Commission has noted:

A common excuse employers use for not hiring is that qualified minorities and women cannot be found. Time and again this claim has been proven false. In the case of the gas and electric utility industry, most of the companies are located in central city locations where the minority workforce is readily available. These companies generally do not hire skilled craftsmen away from other employers. Rather, the specialized nature of their operations requires that utilities train most of their upper-level blue collar employees. This suggests that entry-level occupations can be used effectively as a conduit for the hiring and upgrading of minorities and women.[72]

Yet, this has not happened. If the percentage of minority employees is low, the percentage of minority skilled tradesmen is even worse. This poor record is somewhat surprising when one considers the fact that many electric power companies—particularly in cities with large minority populations—play an important role in the community. In Detroit, for example, Walker Cisler, the president of the Detroit Edison Company, was a community leader involved in sponsoring low-income housing with the United Automobile Workers, and an active member of the NAACP and the Urban League. But the Edison Company practiced racial discrimination in connection with both hiring and employment. Moreover, testimony provided to the Equal Employment Opportunity Commission indicates that Detroit Edison is only the tip of the iceberg in the electric power industry.

An obvious and important factor in the exclusion of minorities from the utility industry is customer preference. Since such companies deal with the public, the discriminatory preferences of consumers are likely to be mirrored in business practices. This is one reason why the job of meter reader, requiring little in the way of background or education, has had a very small minority participation rate. Indeed, it is interesting to note that statistics reflect a continuing absence of minorities in this classification in Detroit Edison, for instance, even when the barriers had begun to break down in jobs that required a substantial amount of skill.

Yet customer preference by no means explains the matter entirely. For the electric power industry has often engaged in behind-the-scenes employment practices which have the effect of excluding minority applicants. Paradoxically, relatively little litigation has commenced in the industry. The most important case, of course, is *Griggs* v. *Duke Power,*[73] which is the leading Title VII holding as of this date throughout all industries. Moreover, the Justice Department has been responsible for actions in the South, *United States* v. *Virginia Electric and Power Company*[74] and *United States* v. *Georgia Power Company.*[75] It has also filed an action against the Philadelphia Electric Power Company and joined in the first class action brought against a public utility in the North,[76] in *Stamps* v. *Detroit Edison Company.* The employment practices described below are in large part a matter of public record because of this litigation.

In the first place, because their level of wages and economic security is high, the electric power companies need not advertise or publicize employment opportunities. An abundance of applications makes it clear that they will have no difficulty in recruiting labor. Considered in a vacuum, an absence of advertising may not be inappropriate. Where discrimination has been practiced in the past, however, and where the work force is all or predominantly white, a refusal to solicit applications will generally perpetuate the racial status quo inasmuch as incumbent employees will tend to notify their friends and relatives about work opportunities. As the Eighth Circuit stated in a case involving the telephone industry, *Parham* v. *Southwestern Bell Telephone Company:*

Appellant also contends that the Company's recruitment policy in February 1967, and prior thereto, which depended primarily upon existing employees to refer new prospects for employment, operated to discriminate against blacks. The validity of Parham's contention is borne out by the Company's employment statistics at that time. With an almost completely white work force, it is hardly surprising that such a system of recruitment produced few, if any, black applicants. As might be expected, existing white employees tended to recommend their own relatives, friends and neighbors, who would likely be of the same race.

Where Title VII has been violated, courts may prohibit or change policies which appear racially neutral on their face but build upon pre-Title VII bias that produces present discrimination. . . . Applying the rationale of the cases in the Government regulation, we determine as a matter of law that the Company's system of recruiting new workers in February of 1967 operated to discriminate against blacks.[77]

The Fifth and Sixth Circuits in public utility cases have similarly condemned word-of-mouth hiring where it has the effect of perpetuating past racial exclusion.[78] Indeed, in *Detroit Edison,* the Justice Department showed clearly that preferential treatment was given to friends and relatives: a random sampling of incumbent employees indicated that 50 percent of them had friends or relatives working at Edison and had "discussed job opportunities" with them.[79]

Second, the utilities, like the trucking industry, have seniority systems which generally have the effect of locking blacks into low-level jobs. This is so for two reasons: (1) generally employees in departments which contain skilled-trades classifications have the opportunity to bid on high-opportunity jobs to the exclusion of outsiders; (2) even if an outsider, who is, proportionately, more often likely to be black than white, is able to bid, he is not able to take his seniority credit with him and may suffer a wage cut. As the Second Circuit noted in *United States* v. *Bethlehem Steel,* "Even a discriminatory system that did not completely deter transfers but only discouraged them should be changed."[80]

The seniority systems have been attacked under the *Local 189, Papermakers* and *Bethlehem Steel* doctrines in all the major electric power company cases: *Griggs, VEPCO, Georgia Power,* and *Detroit Edison.* Generally, the pattern seems to be the relegation of black workers to low-level janitorial service jobs in the central office which offer no possibility of promotion to skilled-trades jobs, unlike labor and apprentice positions in other departments where skilled-trades jobs such as those of lineman, cable splicer, pipefitter, and electrician are present. In *Detroit Edison,* these facts made a substantial economic difference for the black employees involved since the spread between the low-opportunity jobs and skilled-trades classifications was at least $2 per hour.

The negotiation of such seniority systems has made the electric power companies skilled trades as lily-white as the construction trades. An interesting and important difference between construction and the electric power industry, however, relatesto the strength of the unions. As we have seen, in construction the unions have an extraordinary amount of muscle, in part derived from control of apprenticeship programs and hiring halls. In electric power and other utilities, because of technological innovations, employers are able to operate with supervisory personnel during strikes. Accordingly, deprived of their most important weapon in the contemporary collective-bargaining process, the right to strike, trade unions have been relatively weak. Nevertheless, the negotiation of such seniority clauses coupled with discriminatory hiring patterns which are the prerogative of management make the two industries indistinguishable when it comes to assessing discriminatory behavior. As Bernard Anderson has noted in his study *The Negro in the Public Utility Industries:*

Unilateral management control of hiring policy can have important consequences for Negro employment, because craft unions in the electrical industries have traditionally excluded, or seriously limited, Negro membership. Indeed, some electric utilities in several large Northeastern cities had Negro linemen and cable splicers at least a decade before black workers were employed in skilled electrical jobs in the union-controlled building trades located in the same cities. Nonetheless, until recent years, employment of Negroes in skilled jobs was rare within the electric power industry, which suggests that management authority was not used widely to expand occupational opportunity for black workers.[81]

This also, of course, suggests that there is little to choose between management and labor in connection with racially discriminatory practices. It may suggest as well that where employers are involved in a public-utility enterprise protected from competition by a state-granted monopoly, they are all the more prone to cater to the public's discriminatory preferences or what they perceive to be the prejudices of their customers.

The labor unions, however, must share the blame. In the first place, it is the unions which have negotiated the discriminatory seniority systems under attack. Second, these unions, unlike the IUE, for instance, have expressed no interest in pressing management to remedy the hiring policies which permit seniority provisions to carry forward discrimination. Third, the unions, although at one time very much concerned with attacking testing requirements for promotion—primarily before blacks began to come into the industries—have shown no interest in joining with private plaintiffs or the government in attacking discriminatory written examinations under the *Griggs* doctrine. Accordingly, while the unions play a secondary role, their conduuct generally seems to be as poor as that of their construction counterparts.

The unions in electric power are primarily the International Brotherhood of Electrical Workers, which represents skilled tradesmen in overhead lines, and the Utility Workers Union of America, which generally represents semiskilled and unskilled workers. The Utility Workers Union is a relatively small old CIO union with a membership of approximately 100,000. The IBEW is the largest public-utility union in the United States and has a substantial membership in the construction industry as well. Although it may upon occasion refer workers on an informal basis to the employer, it does not have a formal hiring-hall system in electric power, either exclusive or nonexclusive. Although the stance of both unions has been negative, it is the Utility Workers Union which has been the object of more black protest inasmuch as a greater percentage of the unskilled and semiskilled workers it represents tend to be black.

The Utility Workers Union in its attitude toward race gives no indication that it is even as forward looking as its CIO colleagues. The national executive board is all white, as are all local union presidents. In Local 223, Utility Workers Union in Detroit, out of twenty-eight union representatives, Willie Stamps was the only black at the time of the litigation, and he was later voted from office. (Stamps was chairman of the predominantly black property and right of way division.) This, of course, reflects the racial composition resulting from employer hiring patterns. And it also makes for lack of sophistication and sensitivity about race relations among union members. (It should be pointed out, however, that blacks in the Local 223 bargaining unit are actually substantially underrepresented inasmuch as Stamps was the chairman of the only division where, because of the large number of low-opportunity jobs, there is a numerical majority of Negro workers.)

In light of the employment patterns in the industry and the all-white union leadership, it is not surprising that black worker organizations have come onto the scene simultaneously with the hiring of black workers—particularly where most of them have gone into lower-opportunity jobs. At the Detroit Edison Company a black workers' organization, the Association for the Betterment of Black Edison Employees, led by Stamps, has come into existence to demand reform of promotion procedures. In 1969 the association requested that special procedures be adopted at Detroit Edison to facilitate the hiring and upgrading of black workers. Before making such demands, however, the association asked if Local 223 had any objections to a dialogue between the association and the company. The union president indicated that he had no objections and that the black workers should do "the best that they could do for themselves." In effect, Local 233 abdicated responsibility for negotiation in the very important employment sphere of no-discrimination policy. The association took it upon itself to meet with company representatives on a number of occasions and eventually to institute litigation against both the company and the union. So great was the black employee distrust of white union representatives in Local 223 that Stamps, in his capacity as both union representative and president of the association, was soon deluged with requests from black employees who were in other divisions, and thus beyond his jurisdiction, to have him represent them in connection with their grievances.

For a number of years the UAW, Steelworkers, Rubber Workers and other industrial unions have had their own civil rights departments to handle employment discrimination problems. The Utility Workers Union had no such institution until 1972. The change came about as a result of demands made by a hastily formed black caucus at the spring 1971 convention in Washington, D.C. At that convention Stamps and other black members demanded that the international both establish a civil rights department and put pressure upon Local 223 to protest employer discrimination against blacks. In early 1972 the union announced that it would establish a human rights committee. It is interesting that the only dissenting voice at the executive-board level to the establishment of the committee was that of Pete Johnson, former president of Local 223 in Detroit. Curiously, in the monthly publication *Light,* put out by the Utility Workers Union in Washington, D.C., the following was stated: "In most cases the cure for discrimination which the Act [Title VII] provided was voluntary. And most employers and unions took steps to become part of that cure."[82] The fact is that the electric power industry is one of the foremost examples of an industry where *no steps* were voluntarily taken to remedy discrimination insofar as upgrading was concerned. Discriminatory seniority systems remained intact. The only outstanding example of the contrary is that of Consolidated Edison in New York City, which is described below.

To this point, with the exception of urgings by Stamps in Detroit, the union's human rights committee has not really pressed the union on either the national or the local level to revise discriminatory practices. All members of the committee are black and, by definition therefore, none has any influential position in the union's political hierarchy, which doomed the effort to limited impact at best.

Nevertheless, the Association for the Betterment of Black Edison Employees has continued to function on a local level, attempting to galvanize black workers into organized protest. In the first place, as noted above, the association has raised the issue of discrimination on a number of occasions with the company ever since 1969. Second, it has acted as an effective substitute for Local 223 even at that union's invitation. Third, the organization has created a greater solidarity among blacks and has thus been a rallying point for those who have had the courage to challenge Detroit Edison's institutional practices which preserve the racial status quo.

The ability of an organization like the association to effect change is somewhat different from that of the kind of organization which flourished in the Detroit auto plants. The character and conduct of the association are fundamentally different from those of groups like DRUM. The association has always been most concerned with avoiding what could be interpreted as a radical stance, and it has continued discussions with the Detroit Edison Company about training programs for blacks even though it is quite clear that no more training is needed for the average black employee in the electric power plants than is required for white employees. Nevertheless, Stamps, in sworn testimony given to Judge Damon Keith in the *Detroit Edison* litigation, stated that the association desired not to appear too "radical," and that it wanted it to be "reasonable" in its stance. This, of course, contrasts vividly with the kind of positions taken by DRUM, especially at the Hamtramck plant. Also, the association has less ability to effect change at the plant because walkouts and other forms of self-help will not hurt an employer like Detroit Edison. Just as the unions have lost an effective strike weapon in electric power and other public utilities, so also have black worker organizations been required to turn to other means to effectuate their goals. The association has worked with outside community groups and has tried to publicize, especially in the black media, the problems relating to seniority and other matters which brought the organization into existence.

There is one "success story" which contrasts vividly with what is otherwise a relatively somber picture in the industry. This is the example of Consolidated Edison in New York City, which has collective-bargaining relationships with both the Utility Workers Union and the IBEW.[83] It contrasts very sharply indeed with the situation developed before Judge Keith in the *Detroit Edison* litigation. From 1966 through 1971 the minority participation rate at Con Edison went from 8 percent to 17.2 percent. But even more important, the upgrading of minority employees was facilitated by the elimination of all testing for entry-level positions and the creation of a validation program through which an attempt is being made to determine whether other tests discriminate. Moreover, the company does not have a broad policy against employing workers with arrest records. The collective-bargaining agreement provides for company-wide seniority, jobs are posted company-wide, and an employee does not suffer a wage reduction if he moves from one department to another. While it is highly improbable that the employment practices at Con Edison are in all respects completely free of problems in the Title

VII area, nevertheless, it is clear that steps have been taken on both the corporate and the labor union side to eliminate the barriers that impede the advance of black employees at companies like Detroit Edison.

American Federation of Musicians

James Petrillo, the former president, has noted that no other union has had more segregated locals than the American Federation of Musicians. Ray Marshall puts it a bit more mildly: ''As late as 1960 the AFM probably had more segregated locals scattered throughout the United States than any union except the Railway Clerks.''[84] Although some black leaders inside the AFM have always opposed segregation on principle, it appears that most blacks wish to preserve the system of segregated locals. In the 1957 convention forty of the all-black locals voted against merger, five were in favor of it, and two did not vote at all. Even since the passage of Title VII has made the segregation of local unions unlawful per se,[85] some black musicians have nevertheless resisted merger, a fact that AFL-CIO civil rights department people and George Meany seem to take great delight in pointing out. One must recall that it was because of this resistance that Meany reprimanded A. Philip Randolph at the AFL-CIO convention and challenged his right to speak for black workers in the United States.[86] The fact is that there were and are very legitimate reasons for the refusal of blacks in the Musicians and in other unions to merge, and that the AFL-CIO had done little, if anything, to overcome them.

In the first place, it is feared that blacks will lose all political representation inasmuch as they constitute a minority and that whites will be reluctant to vote for blacks. Furthermore, very often blacks have union halls of their own which, as in the case of Pittsburgh, dispatch them to places where black jazz musicians prefer to play. The locals had assets of their own, which upon merger were combined with those of the white-dominated locals. Moreover, in the case of the Musicians Union, the patterns of employment discrimination which were part and parcel of the system of segregated locals remain the same.

Reference to individual experiences in a number of cities makes some of the points noted above clear.

Washington, D.C. In 1967, Local 710 (black) and Local 161 merged after discussions and disputes concerning the circumstances of such a merger had gone on for three years. (Actually by 1967 Local 710 had taken in so many white members that approximately one-third of its membership was white. Local 161 had one black member.) At the time of the merger Local 161 had approximately 1,800 members and Local 710 had 328. The agreement, reached at the strong insistence of the international union, designated the merged union as Local 161-710. Assets of the two unions were to be combined. Local 710 was permitted to elect the following officers and delegates of the merged union: 2 members of the executive board; 2 members of the trial board; 1 delegate to the AFM convention. The administrative vice president was to be the individual elected president of Local 710 at its last election. The agreement provided that the ''remaining officers shall be the persons duly elected by the membership of the Local 161'' (the all-white local) at its previous election. This meant that the parties permitted whites to control the presidency and, at the same time, guaranteed blacks some minority representation through control of the vice presidency and a couple of positions on the executive board. The agreement then provided that most of these offices should be filled by election of all members in March 1969 to serve until April 1, 1972. The administrative vice president was still to be elected by the members of Local 710, however, as were some delegates to conventions and members of the trial board, and an assistant to the president and other officials were to be appointed from Local 710.

During the negotiations Otis Ducker, who was vice president of Local 710 and chairman of the merger committee, had insisted upon a ten-year interim agreement during which period blacks could vote for blacks. Ducker had also raised questions about black admission to the Washington Symphony. The terms were finally agreed upon with a threat hanging over Local 710's head to the effect that it must accept the merger or have its charter revoked.

Soon after the merger, a number of problems began to develop. In the first place, black musicians held the view that the wage scale was rising to the point where the smaller black entrepreneurs who were the prime source of employment for black musicians would simply go nonunion. Part of the argument in this connection was that the pension-plan demands were too costly. Local 710 had not had a pension plan prior to merger and wished to have the plan be optional because many of its members worked in the government and held pension benefits in those jobs. Second, Local 710 had had a more flexible requirement for the number of musicians required to be employed in an engagement. With the merger it was required to accept Local 161's standards, which set as a minimum the employment of twelve musicians. Local 710 had taken the position that trios and quartets were permissible—and the new requirement again forced up costs for the employers of black musicians. Third, certain jobs in addition to the symphony work remained exclusively white. Work at the Watergate Hotel and the park concerts were classic examples of this situation. And finally, Local 710 had previously had its own hall.

Two years after the merger Otis Ducker wrote the following to the executive board:

We have lost ground. Non-union competition is more acute now than ever. The merged union has lost more jobs to non-union competition in the last year than in any five-year period in Local 710's history.

The ironic twist of the situation is that a large percentage of this work is being taken by musicians who were members in good standing of Local 710 on the date of the merger but who have since become "union dropouts."[87]

Ducker's letter went on to specify approximately one dozen establishments which had become nonunion, having previously been under the jurisdiction of Local 710. By 1972, according to Ducker, the black membership in the merged local had decreased from 328 to approximately 80.

Pittsburgh. The problem of political representation emerges very clearly in this city. In Pittsburgh two segregated locals have existed ever since 1908 when they negotiated the so-called Afro-American agreement. The jurisdiction of the black local, Local 471, was restricted to lower-paying jobs in the black neighborhoods. In the 1950's, blacks were excluded from playing at concerts in the municipal park until political pressure coerced the all-white local, Local 60, into retreating from a segregationist position. According to a black Pittsburgh musician, James Petrillo, in responding to the demand that this bar be dropped, stated, pointing to the black musicians: "What makes you think you can play that kind of concert when no other black musicians play them?"

Furthermore, although these discriminatory bars were knocked down in the 1950's, certain jobs have always remained beyond the reach of black musicians. The better-paying jobs in such establishments as Pittsburgh's Holiday House, the Holiday Inn, Nixon Theatre, Syria Mosque, and the Civic Arena have been exclusively white. This is attributable to two factors: (1) black musicians who have qualifications are not known to the contractors (who are union members and all white) who are often called upon to provide musicians for shows; (2) when the union itself has been called upon to refer musicians it has invariably referred whites to available opportunities, even when it is known that blacks have the qualifications. In 1965, a merger agreement was effectuated in Pittsburgh. Under this agreement all assets and liabilities of Local 471 which were "approved by Local 60" would become the responsibility of the merged union. The agreement stated that employment of Negro office employees was to be effected "as reasonably soon after the merge [sic] date as warranted. First consideration shall be given the names of those competent applicants with proper skills as submitted by officers of Local 471." The agreement then went on to provide that for a period of five years starting on January 1, 1966, the executive board of the merged union should consist of nine members in addition to president, vice president and secretary-treasurer. Six members were to be elected from Local 60 and three from Local 471. Also, there were to be two assistants to the president, one appointed by each local. The agreement further provided that in December 1970 the election of officers in the merged union would be an open election with no mandated positions "predicted [sic] on a former affiliation with either Local Union, unless changed by the members of the joined union in this 5 year period." Finally, the agreement noted that the merged union was to be represented at the convention by two delegates from each local.

In 1970 blacks lost all representation and positions on the executive board. Blacks membership is approximately 200 whereas the whites number about 2000. Two blacks ran for the executive board, and their combined vote was equal to the highest vote obtained by any successful candidate. Nevertheless, the only black candidate for a delegate's position was also defeated—even though he did not divide the black votes with any other candidate. Accordingly, it appears that black unity makes it more likely that whites will also unite—against the one black candidate.

In December 1972, after another election in which blacks once again achieved no representation, the Equal Employment Opportunity Commission found reasonable cause to believe that the exclusion of blacks from the jobs referred to above as well as the failure to provide them with proportionate representation at least until the employment discrimination in question ceased was, in the context of past discrimination, a violation of Title VII. The black union musicians in Pittsburgh formed an organization of their own which meets on a fairly regular basis and has a dues structure, the Pittsburgh Black Musicians.

Chicago. The situation in Chicago thus far seems to be much more favorable to blacks than those in Washington and Pittsburgh. Here, in 1964, Local 208, an all-black local and Local 10, the white local, merged as a result of international insistence and eventually of the court order of Judge Julius Hoffman. The agreement and order provided for the continued representation of the membership of Local 208 in the new merged local by guaranteeing positions for members of the previously all-black local on the executive board, examining board and as administrative vice president. The order was to run from January 11, 1966, through January 13, 1969, at which point the agreement was to expire and the merged locals' members were to vote for officials on an at-large basis. Beginning in 1969 an effort was made by the members of former black Local 208 to revive and at least to temporarily retain the interim plan. A resolution introduced on September 8, 1970, stated that the agreement should be extended for five years. This proposal was defeated in a vote of the entire membership. Subsequent to the meeting at which that occurred, the executive board produced a second resolution which would have allowed Local 208 to be represented by two members on the board of directors, two members on the trial board and one administrative vice president. While this resolution had the support of the black local, the international objected. The black local threatened litigation in 1971. In subsequent negotiations, however, a compromise was arrived at whereby blacks agreed to run a slate of officers at the general meeting in October 1971. The election polled the combined membership of the black and white locals, and apparently the whites tacitly agreed to press for the election of black members to the board of directors, the trial board, and the examining committee as well as to delegate positions. These choices have apparently to some extent satisfied demands for black representation inside the local. Accordingly, the sort of difficulties experienced by the Pittsburgh and Washington black locals have not recently been encountered in Chicago.

The Transport Workers Union and the Amalgamated Transit Union

Most big-city transit systems are in the public sector. In 1970, Equal Employment Opportunity Commission statistics collected in Atlanta, Chicago, Detroit, Los Angeles, Philadelphia, and Washington, D.C., indicated that 33.6 percent of all employees and 37.6 percent of blue-collar workers in the urban transit industry were black. Because whites increasingly do not seek transit employment in large numbers—principally because of the urban crime problem—blacks have gained substantial employment even without affirmative-action recruiting policies. Yet this situation has not always existed. The transit industry has shared the mores of the transportation sector of the economy, and, more particularly, the practices of some of the discriminatory railroad unions (which have sometimes had jurisdiction over jobs in transit). In Detroit, where blacks have been hired ever since the early 1940's, the majority of the workers are black. Similarly, in New York City, the majority of the workers are black and Puerto Rican, approximately 40 percent black. It is estimated that of approximately 1,500 new employees hired by the New York City Transit Authority during 1971 and 1972, between 1,100 and 1,200 were black. In Houston and Washington, the percentage of Negro employees is in excess of 40. In Chicago, and Los Angeles, it is in excess of 30 and in Philadelphia the percentage is approximately 25.

As of 1970 approximately 22 percent of the transit industry's craftsmen were Negroes—a figure which compares most favorably with other industries. As is the case with minority employees in transit generally, the percentage rose sharply within a few years. Black craftsmen were "scarce" in the transit industry as of 1966. One of the reasons was that company apprenticeship programs were lacking, and craftsmen were being recruited from other industries instead of lower-level transit employees being upgraded. Here, just as in such industries as trucking, electrical equipment, and automobile, the effect of hiring from the street preserves the racial status quo. But a shortage of craftsmen in the transit industry at the end of the 1960's forced the transit companies to train and upgrade Negro workers to a greater extent than they had done in the past.

The TWU, principal rival of the Amalgamated Transit Union, was affiliated with the CIO before the latter's merger with the AFL. The union has had established civil rights machinery for some time, but it has nevertheless been charged with segregation and discrimination. In Houston, Negroes were not upgraded into platform jobs until 1961 and the TWU, its jurisdiction being limited to operators, therefore had no black members until that time.

On the other hand, in San Francisco, Local 258 which has a membership of 2,100, approximately 75 percent of whom are black, Chicano and Chinese, has a black president, vice president, and secretary-treasurer. On an executive board of twelve members, blacks hold ten of the seats. Similarly, in Local 234 in Philadelphia, black membership is 40 percent. Local 234 has two black vice presidents and a 50 percent black executive board. In Philadelphia in 1944 white bus drivers in the local did not want to break in black workers as bus drivers as provided for by seniority rules. The union leadership took a strong position supporting the blacks who were in line for this training and eventually won out, although white bus drivers did strike and National Guard troops were called out shortly thereafter.[88]

It is Local 100 in New York City in which blacks constitute 40 percent of the membership. Local 100 has two black vice presidents who are also international officers. Eighteen of the thirty-three executive-board members are black, and eleven of the twenty-three business agents. At the international level, however, the picture is a little more bleak. There are two elected black vice presidents, Charles Faulding and Roosevelt Watts. Only eight of twenty-seven elected executive-board members are black, however, and the key positions of president and secretary-treasurer are retained by Irish workers. The Irish once dominated the industry but many of them have now escaped the urban environment to more desirable employment opportunities elsewhere.

Local 100, which is closely tied to the international, has faced litigation commenced by the NAACP, which has alleged a failure to upgrade workers to skilled-trades jobs, the practice allegedly harming blacks disproportionately because a greater percentage of them are hired into menial positions.

Although the Amalgamated Transit Union's membership may well be as integrated as that of the TWU, most certainly its leadership is not. This is particularly true at the national level; there is not one black or one member of any other racial minority group on the executive board. Discussions have been undertaken relating to the feasibility of electing a black board member, and while it is fair to say that union officials express some concern about the racial composition of the leadership, there are no clear signs that the status quo will be altered. Black members of the union have not made a great issue of this matter yet, which means that what is normally the necessary ingredient for any shift in leadership composition is absent.

At the same time, there are a small number of local union officials who are black: the president of the Cleveland local, where a minority of the workers are black; the secretary-treasurer in Detroit, where the local is 70 percent black; the president of Local 1528, the airport transport local in Washington, D.C., which is 75 percent black; the secretary-treasurer in Baltimore; and in Chicago, the president of Local 308, rapid transit, and the secretary-treasurer of Local 241, buses.

Black caucuses are forming in Amalgamated locals in Washington, Richmond, and Norfolk. According to ATU officials, as of 1971 representatives of the Washington black caucus refused to run for office even though the leadership allegedly desired a more racially balanced executive board.

One-third of the membership is black in Oakland, St. Louis, Nashville, and Richmond; the figure is slightly lower in Norfolk. Approximately 45 percent of the membership in Baltimore is black.

In Chicago, until 1968, there were only four Negro members on the twenty-eight-man executive board of Local 241, and there was no black among the full-time leadership. Blacks comprise the majority of the members, but the local permits retirees to vote in elections and almost all its retirees are white. (Of 12,000 members, approximately 4,000 were pensioners and a little in excess of 4,000 were black. Although retirees vote in union elections and are a significant force, they do not vote on or ratify contracts negotiated by the leadership). In the early part of 1968, an organization of black workers calling itself the Concerned Transit Workers (CTW), formed primarily to achieve more black leadership in Division 241 of the ATU in Chicago, began to pressure the union at meetings of the membership for a change in the constitutional rules which would exclude the retirees from voting.[89] The CTW's preoccupation with the issue of leadership was triggered by the announcement that the division president, James Hill, was resigning his position to become financial secretary of the international union. Before his resignation, however, Hill appointed two additional blacks to the board, one in March and another in April.

When CTW was ruled out of order with regard to its objections relating to the retirees voting, the organization turned to other tactics. Two wildcat stoppages were engaged in by the organization in July and August of 1968. The July stoppage began at the Orchard Depot, where approximately 70 percent of the membership was black (although union leaders in that area were white). There and in other areas where black membership was numerically strong, the walkouts met with success. The stoppages were aimed primarily at the elimination of the white retirees' vote, although Amalgamated officials stated that since retirees did not vote in significantly high numbers (some of them having left the area) it would have been a relatively easy matter for blacks to organize politically. Subsequent to the second walkout, timed to take advantage of the presence of the Democratic National Convention in Chicago, approximately 100 workers were discharged by the Chicago Transit Authority. This action seems to have put an end to the CTW's organized efforts.

After the August walkout, the international imposed a trusteeship upon the local because of the allged inability of its leaders to function at local meetings. While the trusteeship was in existence, new elections were held in which a black secretary-treasurer, James Pate, was elected. Pate had been groomed by Hill for a leadership position and had his support, and thus was a part of the administrative slate. Two of three individuals on the Hill slate were victorious at this time.

There is a large black membership in Chicago's Local 308, which represents the rapid transit workers. Their membership totals 11,000, of whom approximately 1,100 are pensioners. Of the remaining 9,900 active members, 60 percent are black. In Local 308, the black membership has increased dramatically during the past eight years, apparently because a large number of black women have taken ticket-agent jobs which white women no longer seem to want.

Some of the members of Local 308 took part in the CTW demonstrations at union meetings as well as the walkouts. Four of 32 CTW members named in an injunction obtained by the Chicago Transit Authority against the second walkout, belonged to Local 308. Apparently, considerably more than 100 blacks from Local 308 joined in the July work stoppage, although the number seems to have been smaller in August.

The political situation inside Local 308 stands in stark contrast to that of Local 241. Of the seven-member executive board, four members are black. Leonard Beattie, the Amalgamated president is black, and the financial secretary-treasurer, High Haggerty, is white. These are the only two full-time positions in the local. Prior to the 1969 elections, the only black leader in the local was an assistant board member. Quite clearly blacks in Division 308 have benefited from the wildcat stoppages and demonstrations engaged in by Local 241. As often happens, the blacks in Local 241 did not benefit from their own actions in equal proportions.

The Detroit transit local is substantially different from those in Chicago—probably because of its larger black membership and also because the transit authority was hiring blacks as bus drivers as early as 1941 and 1942. Since 1963 there has been a majority of black drivers and black union leaders in Division 26, which represents transit workers in Detroit.

The first Negro officer in a full-time position in Detroit—and, for that matter, in any ATU local—was Lee Halley, financial secretary-treasurer, who was elected in 1958 when the black membership was approximately a third of the total. He has won reelection ever since that time. As of 1971, four out of five major offices were held by blacks in Detroit, and only the president was white. According to Halley, the union has pressed hard for promotion of blacks into supervisory positions outside the bargaining unit. While there appears to be less tension inside the union than there is in Chicago, Detroit blacks have joined with full-time Negro officers in ATU locals in Chicago, Cleveland, and Washington to put pressure upon the international union to support a black candidate for executive-board member. Thus far their efforts, now spanning a period of approximately six years, have been completely to no avail.

Summary

Black power in the industrial unions is more than the rhetoric of black nationalists. But the results vary from one setting to another. In both the Teamsters and the IUE blacks represent a small minority, but in trucking there is not only acquiescence in discriminatory patterns, but a fierce resistance to the law. In electrical equipment, the union has adopted a different posture. Aside from New York City, the utility workers' union has done little. In electric power as in trucking, the good wages and good conditions of employment are constants, as both industries are shielded from competition by public-utility regulation of rates. In trucking, effective work-group pressure combines with these factors to permit customer preference and hostility toward blacks to dominate employment decisions.

The Steelworkers Union, which has become caught in an avalanche of litigation, is in an intermediate position. The USW has a substantial number of black and Mexican-American members, which helps to account for the extent of the litigation and the union's willingness to enter into the consent decree. The gap between skilled and unskilled jobs is more important than in the automobile industry and creates more conflict. This difference partly explains the UAW's more positive position.

In industries where there are large numbers of semiskilled or unskilled workers and where minorities can enter easily because whites do not want the work in times of boom conditions, access to jobs is obtained, and political pressure is brought to bear upon the unions. Where the institutional barriers affecting the regulation of jobs are not substantial, change can be produced.

Conclusion

It is now more than a decade since President Johnson signed into law the requirement that unions and companies cease discriminatory employment practices. But although Title VII of the Civil Rights Act of 1964 and related legislation prohibited racial discrimination in employment, it was at least three years before the courts were able to resolve issues on their merits. Well-paid union and company lawyers tied minority-group workers up in knots with procedural objections and other dilatory tactics, even though most of the issues were eventually resolved in the plaintiffs' favor.

When the dust settled in the late 1960's, it became clear that the most important victory for black plaintiffs was to be found in court rulings that the victims of discrimination could maintain class actions on behalf of large groups of workers. Racial discrimination is group discrimination, said the judiciary, and Title VII litigation involves issues that are often common to large numbers of workers—that is, the common complaint arises by virtue of skin color. And *Griggs,* the departmental seniority cases, and the judge-made equation of statistics with a prima facie violation made discrimination relatively easy to prove. But the labor movement, although its seniority and referral practices should have been immediately affected, hardly noticed. The union vigorously opposed the view that their own practices—often built upon the expectations of white workers—were to be altered by Title VII. George Meany and other leaders self-righteously and illogically pointed to their lobbying efforts for employment-discrimination law as a qualification for some kind of merit badge.

The unions, walking in lockstep with their employer counterparts, dug in their heels to litigate against any revision of systematic practices which carried forward the effects of past discrimination—some of the most prominent examples being departmental or job seniority systems negotiated by industrial unions which held blacks in low-level positions. Others were found in work-experience referral procedures and discriminatory apprenticeship barriers adopted by the crafts. Most of the resulting cases involved employment relationships where minorities have been either excluded altogether or consigned to relatively undesirable low-paying work because the effect of the contractual seniority provision or apprenticeship program was to retard or block the integration of the work force. And, in practically every case, hard-earned union dues were wasted in a defendant's defeat. Independent judges appointed with life tenure made short shrift of the *status quo* policy of the AFL-CIO civil rights department.

But the box score of wins and losses did not tell the entire story. For labor as well as management, it was also a question of buying time—just as when the Southern school boards has said "never" to the inevitable, a torturously long judicial process evolved in the wake of *Brown* v. *Board of Education*. The picture quickly changed, however, when the courts, rather than merely altering practices, began to assess large damage awards in the form of back pay, front pay, and punitive damages. As the Fifth Circuit Court of Appeals has noted in *Johnson* v. *Goodyear Tire & Rubber Company*,[1] the courts are now moving into the "recovery stage." But the major burden still falls on the private attorney general whose lawyers are without the financial resources to stand up to defendants who have no difficulty paying costs and more than adequate attorneys fees. The big recent change is that both EEOC and the Justice Department are now no longer simply passive neutrals which can occasionally be counted upon for investigative assistance—a function which Justice performed well in the past. The Government is now antagonistic to and sometimes—as in steel and trucking—actually opposes the plaintiffs. While a government reorganization which accorded cabinet status to an official heading the anti-bias effort might be helpful in ridding us of some of the EEOC and OFCC inefficiencies, the fact is that the recent performance of these agencies makes it appear that minorities are better off without government involvement. The consent decrees show that their aim is to hurt rather than help in the struggle for equality.

What is likely to be the union response in the 1970's and 1980's? Union behavior is difficult to predict. In large measure it may take its cue from government, and here there is not much worthwhile to emulate. Nevertheless, the role of union leadership will be of considerable interest. As previously noted, black trade unionists have made some breakthroughs into leadership positions in unions such as the UAW, Amalgamated Meat Cutters, and the American Federation of State, County and Municipal Employees—and also in others such as the International Longshoremen Workers Union (ILWU–West Coast) and some organizations such as the National Education Association, which has specifically encouraged minority leadership by requiring a racially balanced slate in its constitutional provisions. The emergence of the Coalition of Black Trade Unionists under the leadership of AFSCME Secretary-Treasurer William Lucy may hasten the movement of blacks into leadership positions.

Yet major labor organizations with substantial minority memberships like the International Brotherhood of Teamsters, International Ladies Garment Workers Union, United Steelworkers, United Rubberworkers, and the Amalgamated Transit Union have no room at the top for blacks and other racial minorities. The dreariness of this picture is compounded by the fact that when black trade unionists are elected they are often those who are all too acceptable to a conservative white leadership. Under such circumstances, a racially balanced executive board means little if anything for changes in union policy on the issue of race.

Still, it is possible that the rumblings of the black rank and file in many unions, including the UAW—rumblings which have produced more black local union presidents and staff even inside the United Steelworkers, for instance—will help alter the stance of such unions. The current economic crisis makes such a changing of the guard as well as a statesmanlike policy on the part of the unions all the more imperative. What must be explained is that the attack on "last hired–first fired" is no more an attempt to eliminate seniority than were the judicial rulings in *Quarles* and *Local 189, Papermakers,* and their progeny.

In *Bowman,* the Court has recognized the concept of front pay as an appropriate remedy for the loss of seniority credits—a remedy stressed by Chief Justice Burger. It will take some courage on the part of unions like the Steelworkers to rally to this flag because, as both *Patterson* v. *American Tobacco Co.* and *Detroit Edison*[2] demonstrate, front pay is a double-edged sword which can be used against unions involved in the negotiation of discriminatory seniority systems. It is noteworthy that the United Auto Workers—the most vigorous proponent of the front-pay approach—has less of a concern with liability for such practices.

While seniority systems, as well as other union-negotiated or promulgated procedures such as the hiring hall and closed shop, have operated to exclude blacks and other minorities, the answer to the problem of discrimination is not necessarily the abolishment of such institutions. It may be that other considerations argue for such a result, but that is beyond the scope of this book. In any event, surely the answer is not to substitute employer rule. Some kind of protective device—whether it be grievance-arbitration machinery or something else—represents a deeply felt need in the employment relationship. And as difficult and tortuous as the enforcement of decrees like *Local 86, Ironworkers* has been, such decrees appear preferable to a more systematic government involvement in a variety of work-plan problems.

It is, of course, axiomatic that the best answer to all aspects of discrimination problems lies in full employment. Yet even in the boom conditions of the 1960s, when the problem was that of promotion and transfer and not layoff, the trade union posture was one of intransigence. The lesson is that now responsible trade unionism must reach out to represent *all* workers regardless of color—not just the small baronies of senior workers who are most often white. The labor movement ought to stress the proposition that seniority is not being *eliminated,* but rather an accommodation is being undertaken. This accommodation is necessary in light of the competing policies of labor-management legislation which favors voluntarily negotiated agreements and equal employment opportunity law. And, more important, it is an accommodation which, through its attack on unfairness, as in *Griggs,* has made society question a whole host of arbitrary employment decisions. After all, it was the black civil rights protest of the 1960s which focused attention upon other injustices against, for instance, women, the elderly, and handicapped workers.

The distressing reality, however, is that many unions and employers are participating in a vigorous counterattack on Title VII. They began to do so as soon as it became clear that substantial financial liability for the unions was a real prospect.

Their favorite weapon against class actions relates to a decision of the Supreme Court in 1974, *Eisen* v. *Carlisle & Jacquelin*.[3] *Eisen* established the proposition that formal pretrial notification to the class is required, and the plaintiffs must bear the substantial cost, which can have the effect of eliminating most class actions. But *Eisen* was decided under a rule which is not applicable to employment cases, as the Court itself emphasized.[4] The case involved securities litigation, a field in which the courts are concerned that potentially collusive settlements may enrich a small number of class members—and their lawyers—but not the entire group. In civil rights cases, there is no requirement of written notification at the pretrial stage, although some form of notice is generally considered to be desirable before damages are awarded. Under such circumstances, the defendants bear the expense since their liability has already been established at the trial. Also, the problem of legal ethics is less troublesome since plaintiffs' attorneys' fees are awarded by the court out of the defendants' pockets—and generally, the plaintiffs do not have financial ability to maintain such actions. Accordingly, counsel has less incentive to enter into settlements which enrich lawyers at the expense of the class. Nevertheless, despite the logic of this distinction, it is possible that judges who do not like class actions will apply *Eisen* in employment-discrimination cases.

Another tactic recently mobilized against class actions is to charge the lawyers who bring them with "solicitation" of clients, a practice which is frowned upon by the profession—even though newspaper advertisements to attract plaintiffs have been approved in public-interest litigation.[5] (The Liberty League placed such advertisements when attempting to attack New Deal legislation.) The solicitation ploy was tried in the 1950's as a means to break the civil rights movement in the South. The Supreme Court eventually held in *NAACP* v. *Button*[6] that the regulation of "collective activity" undertaken by organizations, their members, and lawyers to obtain access to the courts for the redress of civil rights is to be scrutinized carefully by the judiciary because First-Amendment rights are at stake. The Court recognized in *Button* that vigorous litigation against racial discrimination possesses a unique character inasmuch as it is "neither profitable or popular. . . . The problem is [therefore] one of an apparent dearth of lawyers who are willing to undertake such litigation."[7] Indeed, the principle that lawyers and others involved in a group effort have a First-Amendment right to communicate with one another which cannot be regulated under the guise of forbidding solicitation has been extended to fee-generating cases[8] where there is more of a potential for "ambulance chasing."

Despite *Button* and its progeny, however, defendants' lawyers are dusting off the old "solicitation" device as a means to attack employment class actions. While generous attorneys' fees can be awarded in Title VII cases (although the courts have not been generous for the most part), the judiciary can control conduct which is regarded as demeaning to the profession by an award which is far below the back-pay judgment on the theory that a lawyer who has asked workers to come forward and testify should not gain from any compensation that they receive regardless of the impact on attorneys' fees.

A conscientious civil rights lawyer must seek out leads, investigate tips, and so on so as to develop a case which represents the class fairly—a presumed objective in class actions. Without this activist approach, class actions cannot be effectively maintained, and more important, witnesses whose testimony may convince the judge that back pay and other relief should be awarded to the class will not be found. Already, however, in two cases in California and Pennsylvania federal judges have enjoined First-Amendment activity as "solicitation"[9]*—and significantly, in both cases union and company lawyers are using these "gag orders" as a means to delay trials so as to enter into inexpensive settlements with the government. And it is the government's anxious desire to enter into deals which grant immunity to defendants that poses the most substantial threat of all to class actions.

The public is now being bombarded by press releases relating to multimillion dollar settlements in the trucking and steel industries which are presumed to represent substantial progress on the employment front. But such consent decrees have all too often had little impact because of both the inadequacy of the relief provided and the ineffective monitoring procedures which offer no assurances against labor-management backsliding. As noted above,[10] what is particularly novel and pernicious about these decrees is the requirement that the employee who wants a back-pay settlement must sign a waiver under which he or she relinquishes a right to sue. On the 1974 Memorial Day weekend, representatives of the Pacific Intermountain Express Company called black and Chicano Teamster drivers into their Los Angeles terminal offices and offered them each $500 if they would sign off on all claims against the company. This was too much for even the Justice Department, which advised PIE that its waivers were invalid.

But that event demonstrates the pattern that is emerging. Government, big unions, and companies are trying to buy off the class and break the collective effort of racial minorities to reform employment practices by making offers on an individual basis without even the representation of counsel. Counsel for private plaintiffs are often unable to communicate with those harmed by discrimination because of solicitation gag orders. Minority workers—like most nonlawyers—are not in a position to weigh the benefits and disadvantages of these offers—and the benefits are all too obvious, cash on the barrel.

Aside from this fundamental unfairness, the decrees obtained by the government in steel, for instance, place the fox among the chickens, for the monitoring of future abuses is left to the very unions and employers who have committed violations of Title VII for the past decade. Similarly, the United States Postal Service, which has a comfortable contract compliance relationship with the racially exclusionary trucking industry, was supposed to monitor that decree. (The equally ineffective General Services Administration has now been substituted.) If employees opt to "take the money and run," they sign waivers which purport to give unions and employers immunity from claims unrelated to the relief which the consent decree grants. The largest amount of back pay to be provided black and Chicano Teamsters is $1,500—about 10 to 20 percent of what many minority workers lose in a year by virtue of their exclusion from the lucrative over-the-road driving positions. Most black steelworkers will get less. Front pay and punitive damages are totally out of the question for both steelworkers and truckers.

For a government that has neither the resources nor the will to litigate and develop imaginative remedies which would directly involve a smaller number of unions and companies as defendants but would nevertheless throw the fear of God into the remainder, the path of "benign neglect" in the employment arena is the best choice available. The evolution of Title VII law in *Griggs* and *Bowman* is essential—but without the deterrents of substantial monetary relief and firmly monitored quota relief (even though the latter is necessarily transitional), the objectives of the statute will be scuttled. The experience with judicial decrees makes that clear enough.

The construction unions, which have been sued all over the country, are salivating at the deals which are being presented to the International Brotherhood of Teamsters and the United Steelworkers. The only party not even invited to the bargaining table is the "private attorney general," the minority community—the very group which is the *sine qua non* for effective monitoring of decrees, as the Seattle experience shows.

The courts have long recognized the key role played by private plaintiffs unaffected by the political pressures that are all too often intertwined in government decision-making—particularly where the decisions affect those who lack power. The award of attorneys' fees to plaintiffs' lawyers is intended to encourage such private involvement. The Justice Department, until 1974 the principal federal law enforcement agency in this field (it has since been phased out of the private-sector cases by amendments to Title VII), never asked the courts for back pay until goaded into doing so by minority plaintiffs.

Thus 1977 finds government, unions, and employers working actively to eliminate the substantial liability created by civil rights class actions. The tragedy is that employment is the key to the attack upon the barriers of racial discrimination in other areas such as education and housing. Redistribution of wealth between the races—on which a very small start has been made as a result of the events of the 1960's and Title VII[11]—is the *sine qua non* for a society in which "lower income" and "black" are not to be synonymous. Although employment, education, and housing must to a certain extent be dealt with together, the fact is that employment is the key to the color-blind society that must remain this nation's objective. Resistance in other areas should decline to the extent that blacks progress up the economic ladder.

Eventually, it will be the task of the Supreme Court, first-rate so far in its disposition of racial employment cases, to determine whether the judiciary keeps the courthouse doors open, or whether the law will be undermined through the new world of notification requirements, gag orders, and waivers. The most ominous sign of all is that the government is now switching sides—just as it did in the school desegregation cases when Nixon first took office eight years ago—and thus aiding and abetting the discriminatory practices of labor and management which remain the shame of our country. One fervently hopes that the Carter administration—elected with substantial black support—will reverse this trend promptly.

Notes

Introduction

1. Anthony Lewis, *Portrait of a Decade* (New York, 1964), p. 193.
2. Among the works which gave the AFL-CIO more credit than it deserves in matters of race are F. Ray Marshall, *The Negro and Organized Labor* (New York, 1965); Derek Bok and John Dunlop, *Labor and the American Community* (New York, 1970), pp. 116–137.
3. Rustin, "Blacks and Unions," *American Federationist,* July 1971, p. 24.
4. B. J. Widick, "Minority Power through Unions," *The Nation,* Sept. 8, 1969, p. 206.
5. *N.Y. Times,* Feb. 16, 1972, C 15, col. 1.
6. "The Unions—IX: Union Ratio of Workers Falls as Economy Rises," ninth in a series of ten articles in the *Washington Post,* April 9–April 19, 1972.
7. *Hearings on Proposed Federal Legislation to Prohibit Discrimination in Employment, Before the Sepcial Subcomm. on Labor of the House Comm. on Education and Labor,* 87th Cong., 2d Sess., at 999 (1962).
8. *Id.,* 1000.
9. *Hearings on S.773, 1210, 1211, and 1937 Before the Sub-Comm. on Employment and Manpower of the Sen. Comm. on Labor and Public Welfare,* 88th Cong., 1st Sess., at 299 (1963).
10. *Local 189, United Papermakers* v. *United States,* 416 F.2d 980, 982 (5th Cir. 1969), *cert. denied,* 411 U.S. 939 (1973), discussed in Ch. 4, beginning at n. 29.
11. *Hearings on H.R. 405 and Similar Bills Before the General Subcomm. on Labor of the House Comm. on Education and Labor,* 88th Cong., 1st Sess., at 83 (1903).
12. A transcript of this meeting is in the author's files.
13. U.S. Comm'n on Civil Rights, *1961 Report,* Bk. 3: Employment 151 (1961).
14. Bok and Dunlop, *Labor and the American Community,* p. 125.
15. *Culpepper* v. *Reynolds Metals Co.,* 421 F.2d 888, 891 (5th Cir. 1970).

1 │ Overview of Constitutional Law in Race Relations

1. 347 U.S. 483 (1954) (*Brown I*).
2. 347 U.S. 497 (1954).
3. Charles Black, "The Lawfulness of the Segregation Decisions," 69 *Yale L.J.* 421, 426 (1960).
4. *Brown* v. *Board of Educ.,* 349 U.S. 294, 300–301 (1955) (*Brown II*).
5. 163 U.S. 537 (1896).
6. *Dred Scott* v. *Sandford,* 60 U.S. (19 How.) 393 (1856).
7. Paul Brest, *Processes of Constitutional Decisionmaking* (Boston, 1975), p. 494.
8. *Id.,* pp. 494–495.
9. *Swann* v. *Charlotte-Mecklenburg Bd. of Educ.,* 402 U.S. 1 (1971).
10. *Green* v. *County School Bd.,* 391 U.S. 430, 439 (1968); see also *Alexander* v. *Holmes County Bd. of Educ.,* 396 U.S. 19, 20 (1969): "The obligation of every school district is to terminate dual school systems at once and to operate now and hereafter only unitary schools."
11. See *Keyes* v. *School District No. 1, Denver,* 413 U.S. 189 (1973), especially Justice Powell's separate opinion, at 217. See generally Frank Goodman, "De Facto School Desegregation: A Constitutional and Empirical Analysis, "60 *Calif. L. Rev.* 275 (1972); J. Skelly Wright, "Public School Desegregation: Legal Remedies for De Facto Segregation," 40 *N.Y.U. L. Rev.* 285 (1965); Paul Dimond, "School Desegregation in the North: There Is but One Constitution," 7 *Harv. Civ. Rights–*

Civ. Lib. L. Rev. 1 (1972); Comment: "De Facto Hangs On," 52 *N.C. L. Rev.* 431 (1973); Comment: "Constitutional Duty to Desegregate De Facto Segregation," 23 *Emory L.J.* 293 (1974); Comment: *"Keyes* v. *School District No. 1:* Unlocking the Northern Schoolhouse Doors," 9 *Harv. Civ. Rights–Civ. Lib. L. Rev.* 124 (1974); Comment: "School Desegregation: New Quandaries and Old Dilemmas," 43 *Fordham L. Rev.* 273 (1974).

12. E.g., *Carson* v. *Warlick,* 238 F.2d 724 (4th Cir. 1956), *cert. denied,* 353 U.S. 910 (1957). See also *Shuttlesworth* v. *Birmingham Bd. of Educ.,* 162 F. Supp. 373 (N.D. Ala.), *aff'd per curiam,* 358 U.S. 101 (1958).

13. E.g., *Carson* v. *Warlick; Hood* v. *Board of Trustees,* 232 F.2d 626 (4th Cir.), *cert. denied,* 352 U.S. 870 (1956); *Holt* v. *Raleigh City Bd. of Educ.,* 265 F.2d 95 (4th Cir.), *cert. denied* 361 U.S. 818 (1959).

14. *Kelley* v. *Board of Educ. of City of Nashville,* 270 F.2d 209 (6th Cir.), *cert. denied,* 361 U.S. 924 (1959).

15. 402 U.S. 1, 25 (1971).

16. On remedies, see Chs. 5 and 6. On the applicability of Title VII to *de facto* discrimination, see Ch. 4, sec.: "Unanswered Questions Relating to Seniority."

17. See Chief Justice Burger's decision as Circuit Justice denying a stay in *Winston-Salem/Forsyth County Bd. of Educ.* v. *Scott,* 404 U.S. 1221, 1227 (1971), in which he expressed concern that the district court and court of appeals might have erred by "misreading . . . the opinion of the Court in the *Swann* case [*supra* n. 9] . . . as requiring a fixed racial balance or quota." See also *Northcross* v. *Board of Educ. of Memphis,* 397 U.S. 232, 236 (1970) (concurring opinion), where the Chief Justice objected to the Court's summary disposition of the case (the Court's decision ordered the district court to apply the *Alexander* holding, supra n. 10 and stated that the Court should have heard argument, since "the time has come to clear up what seems to be a confusion, genuine or simulated, concerning this Court's prior mandates."

18. *Keyes* v. *School District No. 1, Denver, Colo.,* 413 U.S. 189, 217 (1973) (Powell, J., concurring in part and dissenting in part).

19. *Moose Lodge* v. *Irvis,* 407 U.S. 163 (1972).

20. See Charles Black, " 'State Action,' Equal Protection, and California's Proposition 14," 81 *Harv. L. Rev.* 69, 100–103 (1967).

21. 392 U.S. 409 (1968).

22. *Tillman* v. *Wheaton-Haven Recreation Ass'n,* 410 U.S. 431 (1973).

23. *Sullivan* v. *Little Hunting Pack,* 396 U.S. 229 (1969).

24. *Whitcomb* v. *Chavis,* 403 U.S. 124 (1971). See also *Beer* v. *United States,* 44 U.S.L.W. 4435, 4439 n.14 (March 30, 1976). But plaintiffs were able to meet the burden of proof required by *Whitcomb* in *White* v. *Regester,* 412 U.S. 755, 765–770 (1973). The Court has also been unwilling to utilize the Fifteenth Amendment in redistricting cases. See *Beer,* at 4439 n.14.

25. See *Georgia* v. *United States,* 411 U.S. 526 (1973); *Perkins* v. *Matthews,* 400 U.S. 379 (1971); *Allen* v. *State Bd. of Elections,* 393 U.S. 544 (1969). Cf. *East Carroll Parish School Bd.* v. *Marshall,* 44 U.S.L.W. 4320 (March 8, 1976). However, the Court in some recent decisions has taken a less expansive view of the Voting Rights Act. See *Beer* v. *United States; City of Richmond* v. *United States,* 422 U.S. 358 (1975).

26. See *White* v. *Regester.* Cf. *Connor* v. *Johnson,* 402 U.S. 690 (1971).

27. 413 U.S. 189 (1973).

28. *Id.* at 203.

29. 418 U.S. 717, 94 S.Ct. 3112 (1974). During the last two terms the Court exhibited more caution in connection with desegregation remedies. See *Pasadena City Board of Eduction* v. *Spangler,—* U.S. —, 96 S. Ct. 2697 (1976); *Austin Independent School District* v. *United States,—* U.S. —, 45 U.S.L.W. 3413 (1976).

30. *Id.* at 3125.

31. *Id.*

32. *Id.* at 3127.

33. *Id.* at 3140 (dissenting opinion).

34. *Id.* at 3145 (dissenting opinion).

35. *Id.* at 3146 (dissenting opinion).

36. *Id.* at 3161 (dissenting opinion). For developments in the area of interdistrict remedies for school segregation, see "Note: Interdistrict Desegregation: The Remaining Options," 28 *Stan. L. Rev.* 521 (1976). But see *Runyon* v. *McCleary,—*U.S.—, 96 S. Ct. 2586 (1976) prohibiting racial discrimination in private schools.

37. See *Albermarle Paper Co.* v. *Moody,* 95 S.Ct. 2362, 2384 (1975) (Rehnquist, J., concurring); *id.* at 2387 (Burger, C.J., concurring and dissenting); *id.* at 2389 (Blackmun, J., concurring); *Franks* v. *Bowman Transportation Co.,* 424 U.S. 747, 11 EPD ¶10,777 (1976) at 7264 (Burger, C.J., concurring and dissenting); *id.* at 7265 (Powell, J., joined by Rehnquist, J., concurring and dissenting). However, two recent Supreme Court decisions indicate a measure of retreat on employment. See *General Electric Company* v. *Gilbert, et al.,*— U.S. —, 13 FEP Cases 1 (1976) (Rehnquist, J.) and *Washington* v. *Davis,* 426 U.S. 229 (1976) (White, J.).

2 | Framework of Employment-Discrimination Law: An Introduction

1. Exec. Order No. 8802, 3 C.F.R. 957 (1938–1943 Comp.). The role of Randolph's march in bringing about the executive order is discussed by Samuel Krislov, *The Negro in Federal Employment* (Minneapolis, 1967), p. 30; Michael Sovern, *Legal Restraints on Racial Discrimination in Employment* (New York, 1966), p. 9.

2. Exec. Order No. 10,925 3 C.F.R. 443 (1959–1963 Comp.), 5 U.S.C. § *3301 (1970).*

3. The first debarment was of Edgely Air Products, Inc., on Sept. 17, 1971, for failure to comply with the Philadelphia Plan for the construction industry. See 81 *BNA Lab. Rel. Rep.* 118 (Oct. 9, 1972).

4. *Roosevelt:* Exec. Order No. 8802; Exec. Order No. 9001, 3 C.F.R. 1054 (1938–1943 Comp); Exec. Order No. 9346, 3 C.F.R. 1280 (1938–1943 Comp.); *Truman:* Exec. Order No. 10,210, 3 C.F.R. 390 (1949–1953 Comp.); Exec. Order No. 10,277, 3 C.F.R. 739 (1949–1953 Comp.); Exec. Order No. 10,231, 3 C.F.R. 741 (1949–1953 Comp.); Exec. Order No. 10,243, 3 C.F.R. 752 (1949–1953 Comp.); Exec. Order No. 10,281, 3 C.F.R. 781 (1949–1953 Comp.); Exec. Order No. 10,298, 3 C.F.R. 828 (1949–1953 Comp.); Exec. Order No. 10,308, 3 C.F.R. 837 (1949–1953 Comp.); *Eisenhower:* Exec. Order No. 10,479, 3 C.F.R. 961 (1949–1953 Comp.); Exec. Order No. 10,557, 3 C.F.R. 218 (1954–1958 Comp.); *Kennedy:* Exec. Order No. 10,925; Exec. Order No. 11,114, 3 C.F.R. 774 (1959–1963 Comp.), 5 U.S.C. § 3301 (1970); *Johnson:* Exec. Order No. 11246, 3 C.F.R. 339 (1964–1965 Comp.), 42 U.S.C. § 2000e (1970); Exec. Order No. 11,375, 3 C.F.R. 320 (1966–1970), 42 U.S.C. § 2000e (1970); *Nixon:* Exec. Order No. 11,478, 3 C.F.R. 207 (1974), 42 U.S.C. § 2000e (1970).

5. *Ethridge* v. *Rhodes,* 268 F. Supp. 83 (S.D. Ohio 1967).

6. See generally Ch. 7.

7. 323 U.S. 192 (1944).

8. *Id.* at 198.

9. *Id.* at 200.

10. 161 Kan. 459, 169 F. 2d 831 (1946).

11. *James* v. *Marinship Corp.,* 25 Cal. 2d 721, 155 P.2d 329 (1944).

12. *Oliphant* v. *Brotherhood of Locomotive Firemen and Engineermen,* 262 F.2d 359, 363 (6th Cir. 1959), *cert. denied,* 359 U.S. 935 (1959).

13. National Labor Relations Act § 8(b), 29 U.S.C. § 158(b)(1970) as amended by Labor-Management Relations Act (Taft-Hartley Act), Title I, 61 Stat. 136 (1947).

14. National Labor Relations Act § 8(a), 29 U.S.C. § 158(a)(1970), as adopted 49 Stat. 449 (1935) (Wagner Act).

15. *Larus & Brothers Co.,* 62 NLRB 1075, 1983 (1945).

16. *Ford Motor Co.* v. *Huffman,* 345 U.S. 330 (1953). See also *Syres* v. *Oil Workers Local 23,* 350 U.S. 892 (1955).

17. *Local 12, United Rubber Workers* v. *NLRB,* 368 F.2d 12 (5th Cir. 1966), *cert. denied,* 389 U.S. 837 (1967).

18. 355 U.S. 41 (1957).

19. See, e.g., *Richardson* v. *Texas & New Orleans RR,* 242 F.2d 230 (5th Cir. 1957); *Central of Georgia Ry.* v. *Jones,* 229 F.2d 648 (5th Cir.), *cert. denied* 352 U.S. 848 (1956).

20. 262 F.2d 546 (5th Cir.), *cert. denied,* 360 U.S. 902 (1959).

21. *Id.* at 551.

22. 147 NLRB 1573 (1964).

23. See 29 C.F.R. §§ 101.1–101.16(1973) (NLRB Statements of Procedure in Unfair Labor Practice Cases).

24. *Larus & Brothers Co.,* But see *Local 106, Glass Bottle Blowers,* 210 NLRB 943 (1974), *enforced,* 520 F.2d 693 (6th Cir. 1975).

25. 416 F.2d 1126 (D.C. Cir.), *cert. denied,* 396 U.S. 903 (1969).

26. *Farmers' Cooperative Compress,* 194 NLRB 85 (1971). For a discussion of the evidence required to prove a Title VII violation see Ch. 3, sec.: "Statistical Evidence and the Burden of Proof" and *"McDonnell Douglas Corp.* v. *Green."*

27. 192 NLRB 173 (1971), *rev'd and rem'd sub nom. Western Addition Community Organization* v. *NLRB,* 485 F.2d 917 (D.C. Cir. 1973), rev'd sub nom. *Emporium Capwell Co.* v. *Western Addition Community Organization,* 420 U.S. 50, 95 S.Ct. 977 (1975).

28. The changes which the full committee made in the EEOC enforcement provisions recommended by the subcommittee are described in the "Additional Views on H.R. 7152", H.R. Rep. No. 914, Pt. 2, 88th Cong., 1st Sess. (1963), reprinted in United States Equal Employment Opportunity Comm'n, *Legislative History of Titles VII and XI of Civil Rights Act of 1964,* at 2122, 2150.

29. H.R. 7152 § 707; passed Feb. 10, 1964, 110 *Cong. Rec.* 2804–2805 (1964).

30. The efforts of Senators Humphrey, Dirksen, Mansfield, and Kuchel in drafting their substitute bill are described by themselves at 110 *Cong. Rec.* 11935–11937 (1964). See also Francis Vaas, "Title VII: Legislative History," 7 *B.C. Ind. & Com. L. Rev.* 431, 445–456 (1966), for a summary of the changes made by the Mansfield-Dirksen substitute.

31. See Sovern, *Legal Restraints,* ch. 3; Alfred Blumrosen, *Black Employment and the Law* 6 n.11, 9–27 (New Brunswick, J.J., 1971); Herbert Hill, "Twenty Years of State Fair Employment Practice Commissions: A Critical Analysis with Recommendations," 14 *Buffalo L. Rev.* 22 (1964).

32. § 706(b), (c), 42 U.S.C. § 2000e-5(b)(c)(1970), *as amended,* 42 U.S.C. § 2000e-5(c), (d) (Supp. II, 1972).

33. 42 U.S.C. § 20003-5(a)(1970), *as amended,* 42 U.S.C. § 2000e-5(a), (b), (f) (Supp. II, 1972).

34. Sovern, *Legal Restraints,* p. 205.

35. Editorial, *Barron's,* July 17, 1967.

36. § 706(e), 42 U.S.C. § 2000e-5(e)(1970), as amended, 42 U.S.C. § 2000e-5(f)(1) (Supp. II, 1972).

37. § 707, 42 U.S.C. § 2000e-6(1970), *as amended,* 42 U.S.C. § 2000e-6 (Supp. II, 1972).

38. For the major EEOC Guidelines currently in force, see 29 C.F.R. Part 1604 (1973) (Guidelines on Discrimination Because of Sex); 29 C.F.R. Part 1606 (Guidelines on Discrimination Because of Natural Origin); 29 C.F.R. Part 1607 (1973) (Guidelines on Employee Selection Procedures).

39. *N.Y. Times,* Dec. 3, 1969, C-93, col. 6.

40. *N.Y. Times,* June 3, 1970, C-28, col. 4; *N.Y. Times,* June 5, 1970, C-14, col. 7; *N.Y. Times,* June 8, 1970, C-22, col. 1.

41. *Wall Street Journal,* Sept. 7, 1971, p. 1, col. 5.

42. *N.Y. Times,* July 14, 1970, L-75, col. 4.

43. *N.Y. Times,* March 28, 1969, p. 1, col. 3.

44. As of spring 1975 the backlog had reached 120,000. 88 *BNA Lab. Rel. Rep.* 238 (March 24, 1975).

45. *N.Y. Times,* Jan. 25, 1972, M-32, col. 2.

46. 118 *Cong. Rec.* 697 (1972) (remarks of Senator Dominick).

47. § 706(f)(1), 42 U.S.C. § 2000e-5(f)(1) (Supp. II, 1972).

48. See nn.58, 59, 60.

49. See 118 *Cong Rec.* 943 (1972) (remarks of Senator Humphrey).

50. See Carlson, "How Best to Toughen the EEOC," *Wall Street Journal,* Sept. 15, 1971, p. 16, col. 4.

51. See generally Florian Bartosic and Ian Lanoff, "Escalating the Struggle against Taft-Hartley Contemnors," 39 *U. Chi. L. Rev.* 255 (1974).

52. See authorities cited in n.31.

53. See for example the Settlement Agreement between EEOC and AT&T, 1 *CCH Employment Practice Guide* ¶1860–1861 (1973), and the subsequent agreement between the same parties reported in the *Wall Street Journal,* May 31, 1974, p. 5, col. 2.

54. Amdt. No. 878 to S.2515, 118 *Cong. Rec.* 3373 (1972).

55. *Wall Street Journal,* April 25, 1972, p. 48, col. 1.

56. *Wall Street Journal,* Sept. 28, p. 1, col. 3.

57. 88 *BNA Lab. Rel. Rep.* 238 (March 24, 1975).

58. It appears that EEOC has accepted the proposition that actual efforts to conciliate are a jurisdictional prerequisite to a suit by the commission. See *EEOC* v. *Raymond Metal Prods. Co.,* 9 EPD ¶9983 at p. 6655 (D. Md. 1974), *aff'd. in part, rev'd. in part on other grds* 11 EPD ¶10,629 (4th Cir. 1976); *EEOC* v. *Bartenders Local 41,* 369 F. Supp. 827, 828 (N.D. Cal. 1973). In any event, the dis-

trict courts appear to be unanimous in holding that conciliation efforts must be made. In addition to *Raymond Metals* and *Bartenders,* see, e.g., *EEOC* v. *Griffin Wheel Co.,* 360 F. Supp. 424 (N.D. Ala. 1973), *rev'd on other grds.,* 511 F.2d 456 (5th Cir. 1975); *EEOC* v. *Container Corp. of America,* 352 F. Supp. 262 (M.D. Fla. 1972); *EEOC* v. *Westvaco Corp.,* 372 F. Supp. 985, 991–993 (D. Md. 1974) and the Eighth Circuit has stated that "it is beyond dispute that a Commission lawsuit brought before any attempt at conciliation is premature." *EEOC* v. *Hickey-Mitchell Co.,* 507 F.2d 944, 948 (8th Cir. 1974) (dictum). Efforts on the part of EEOC to achieve conciliation are *not* a jurisdictional prerequisite to a suit by private plaintiffs. See n.60(a).

But it is not clear what sort of conciliation effort the commission must make. Compare *Raymond Metals,* at p. 6655 (finding that EEOC failed to make "a sincere endeavor at conciliation") with *Westvaco Corp.* at 992: "That is not to say that the statutory language should be read as requiring the EEOC to affirmatively pursue respondent in an attempt to cajole an agreement from him. Rather the language requires only that the EEOC provide the *opportunity* for conciliation." And see especially *EEOC* v. *Rexall Drug Co.,* 9 EPD ¶9936 (E.D. Mo. 1974) at p. 6930, where the court held that it would not "measure the extent of the Commission's conciliation efforts" as long as the commission "engaged in at least some minimal dialogue with the defendant."

The question has reached the courts of appeals whether, as a matter of procedure, the EEOC must "plead conditions precedent" (such as attempts to conciliate, deferral to state agencies, etc.) "with particularity." Although the district courts were evenly split on this issue, the courts of appeals which have ruled to date have held that the commission can simply plead generally that all conditions precedent to filing suit have been fulfilled, and need not specifically aver that it has deferred the case to the appropriate state agency, *EEOC* v. *Wah Chang Albany Corp.,* 499 F.2d 187 (9th Cir. 1974) or that it has engaged in conciliation efforts, *EEOC* v. *Standard Forge & Axle Co.,* 496 F.2d 1392 (5th Cir. 1974), *cert. denied,* 419 U.S. 1106 (1975); *EEOC* v. *Times-Picayune Publishing Corp.,* 500 F.2d 392 (5th Cir. 1974) *cert. denied,* 420 U.S. 962 (1975). In both *Standard Forge* and *Times-Picayune,* the Fifth Circuit expressly declined to decide whether efforts at conciliation are a jurisdictional prerequisite, holding that the question did not have to be reached since in any event the commission's pleadings had been adequate, and the district court had erred in holding that more definite pleadings were required. But see *Hickey-Mitchell,* (dictum), where it was held that if EEOC fails to notify defendants of the commission's decision that conciliation cannot be achieved, as required by an EEOC regulation, a commission suit must be dismissed. But if there has been no prejudice to defendants, the suit will not be dismissed. *Raymond Metals,* 11 EPD at p. 6638; *EEOC* v. *Kimberly-Clark Co.,* 511 F.2d 1352, 1360–1361 (6th Cir.), *cert. denied,* 423 U.S. 994 10 EPD ¶10,511 (1975); *EEOC* v. *Laclede Gas Co.,* 11 EPD ¶10,709 (8th Cir. 1976).

A related question has arisen as to whether § 706(f)(1), which allows a private party to file suit if EEOC has not done so within 180 days from the filing of the complaint, should be read to imply that the commission loses its power to sue after the 180 days. Again the district courts were split and again the appellate decisions held that EEOC's suit is not barred. *EEOC* v. *Kimberly-Clark Corp.; EEOC* v. *Louisville & Nashville RR,* 505 F.2d 610 (5th Cir. 1974) *cert. denied,* 423 U.S. 824, 10 EPD ¶10,409 (1975); *EEOC* v. *Cleveland Mills Co.,* 502 F.2d 153 (4th Cir. 1974), *cert. denied,* 95 S.Ct. 1328 (1975); *EEOC* v. *E. I. du Pont de Nemours & Co.,* 516 F.2d 1297 (3d Cir. 1975); *EEOC* v. *Meyer Bros. Drug Co.,* 10 EPD ¶10,256 (8th Cir. 1975); *EEOC* v. *Duval Corp.,* 11 EPD ¶10,598 (10th Cir. 1976). These cases are relevant to the question whether conciliation efforts are a jurisdictional prerequisite, in that the cases seem to assume that conciliation must be attempted, and reach their result partly on the grounds that a 180-day limit would not give the EEOC enough time to engage in conciliation, given its backlog of cases. See *Louisville & Nashville,* at 617.

59. Since the EEOC represents a broader interest and possesses greater litigation resources than most private plaintiffs, it would be highly unfortunate if the existence of a private suit were held to limit in any way the commission's ability to litigate. Thus, the commission should be entitled to bring suit regardless of whether a related private suit is pending, has been dismissed or settled, or has proceeded to judgment. Devices such as consolidation, and to some extent doctrines of res judicata and collateral estoppel, should prevent prejudice to defendants in most cases, and of course unusual circumstances can be dealt with on a case-to-case basis. In addition, to save time and expense the EEOC should certainly have the option in most instances of intervening in a private action and expanding the scope of that action, rather than filing a separate lawsuit to deal with matters not adequately raised in the private action.

To date, however, many district courts have taken a rather hostile attitude to attempts by the commission to litigate where a private action has been commenced. But the first appellate decisions indicate that here, as in the areas described in notes 58 and 60, the courts of appeals will not accept the procedural roadblocks fashioned by many of the district courts.

(a) Several district courts have held that once a private plaintiff has filed suit, the EEOC cannot initiate its own suit, but can only intervene. See, e.g., *EEOC* v. *United States Pipe & Foundry Co.,* 7 EPD ¶9331 (E.D. Tenn. 1974); *EEOC* v. *Blue Bell, Inc.,* 7 EPD ¶9332 (W.D. Tex. 1974) *rev'd and rem'd.,* 10 EPD ¶10,305 (5th Cir. 1975) (judgment order); *EEOC* v. *Union Oil Co. of Cal.,* 362 F. Supp. 579 (N.D. Ala. 1974). But see *EEOC* v. *International Paper Co.* 8 EPD ¶9610 (W.D. Mich.). The Eighth Circuit agrees, *EEOC* v. *Missouri Pacific RR,* 493 F.2d 71 (8th Cir. 1974). But in a persuasive opinion the Sixth Circuit has taken the opposite position, *EEOC* v. *Kimberly-Clark Corp.,* 511 F.2d 1352, 1361–1363 (6th Cir. 1975), *cert. denied,* 423 U.S. 994, 10 EPD ¶10,511 (1975). And the Fifth Circuit has elaborated on the reasoning of Kimberly-Clark in *EEOC* v. *Hutting Sash & Door Co.,* 511 F.2d 453 (5th Cir. 1975), holding that unless "the EEOC raises no substantially different issues and seeks no relief other than for the private party," it can bring suit rather than being limited to permissive intervention. (As indicated, the Fifth Circuit also has reversed the district court decision in *Blue Bell.* The reversal was without opinion.) See also *EEOC* v. *Duval Corp.,* 11 EPD ¶10,598 (10th Cir. 1976).

(b) In *Kimberly-Clark,* the Sixth Circuit also reversed the district court's holding that a "court-approved private settlement prevented the EEOC from 'assert(ing) a later cause of action either to undo or to obtain greater relief than was accorded to . . . plaintiffs under the (settlement) order.' " At 361. And in *EEOC* v. *McLean Trucking Co.,* 10 EPD ¶10,522 (6th Cir. 1975), the court held that neither the acceptance of an arbitration award nor the settlement of an action by the original charging party precludes EEOC from filing suit. A district court has similarly held that dismissal of the private plaintiff's suit does not bar a subsequent suit by EEOC. *EEOC* v. *Eagle Iron Works,* 367 F. Supp. 817, 822 (S.D. Iowa 1973). Accord, *Hutting Sash & Door,* where the Fifth Circuit noted that EEOC's claim of the right to file an independent suit is particularly strong where the private suit has been terminated, and duplicative proceedings will therefore not be involved.

(c) It is clear that when the commission files suit, it is not restricted to the issues raised by the charging party's EEOC complaint. See *EEOC* v. *General Electric Co.,* 11 EPD ¶10,627 (4th Cir. 1976). But some courts have been hesitant, once a private suit has been filed, to permit EEOC to expand the issues by intervention. See *Hughes* v. *Timex Corp.,* 8 EPD ¶9776 (E.D. Ark. 1974): EEOC cannot raise claims of sex discrimination by intervention where private action alleged only racial discrimination. Cf. *Van Hoomissen* v. *Xerox Corp.,* 497 F.2d 180 (9th Cir. 1974). In *EEOC* v. *Missouri Pacific RR,* the Eighth Circuit held that the EEOC must be permitted to expand the scope of the suit, see 493 F.2d at 75, and concurring opinion at 75, but as indicated above, the court arrived at its policy of expansive intervention only by holding that the EEOC would not be permitted to file its own lawsuit.

60. The volume of litigation dealing with procedural issues in private actions under Title VII has been remarkable. It is possible only to sketch the major developments—so as to convey some idea of defendants' persistence, and of plaintiffs' success on most of the issues raised:

(a) Suit is not barred by the EEOC's failure to make actual attempts to conciliate the dispute. See, e.g., *Johnson* v. *Seaboard Airline & RR,* 405 F.2d 645, 652–653 (4th Cir. 1968), *cert. denied,* 394 U.S. 918 (1969); *Choate* v. *Caterpillar Tractor Co.,* 402 F.2d 357 (7th Cir. 1968); *Jefferson* v. *Peerless Pumps,* 456 F.2d 1359, 1361 (9th Cir. 1972). Contrast the developments regarding conciliation efforts in suits brought by the EEOC, n.58 *supra.*

(b) The requirement of deferral to state agencies is not violated if plaintiff first files with the EEOC, and the commission then gives the charge to the state agency, and subsequently takes jurisdiction after the statutory period for deferral has run; plaintiff need not refile with EEOC at that time. *Love* v. *Pullman Co.,* 404 U.S. 522 (1972). *Love* enunciates the principle that Title VII, as a remedial statute enforced in large part through charges filed by laymen, should not be undermined by procedural technicalities. *Id.* at 527–528.

(c) Relying on *Love* v. *Pullman,* the Fifth Circuit has held that "the time limitations contained in Title VII . . . [are not] inflexible 'jurisdictional absolutes,' [but are to be] modified . . . in the interest of giving effect to the broad remedial purposes of the Act [in cases where there are] circumstances . . . to excuse the plaintiff from compliance." *Reeb* v. *Economic Opportunity Atlanta,* 516 F.2d 924, 929–930 (5th Cir. 1975). Thus, for example, it has been held that the fact that a right-to-sue notice was issued after the suit was filed, rather than before as called for by § 706(f)(1), does not require dismissal of the action. *Henderson* v. *Eastern Freightways, Inc.,* 460 F.2d (4th Cir. 1972), *cert denied,* 410 U.S. 912 (1973); *Berg* v. *Richmond Unified School Dist.,* 10 EPD ¶10,553 (9th Cir. 1975), and at least one court has refused to bar a suit which was commenced prior even to the filing of charges with EEOC, as long as a right-to-sue notice was eventually issued, *Black Musicians of Pittsburgh* v. *Local 60–471, American Federation of Musicians,* 375 F. Supp. 902, 907, (W.D. Pa. 1974). Furthermore, the right-to-sue letter may be issued before the end of the 180-day waiting period for EEOC conciliation efforts, and the private action may also commence, if there is no likelihood that the EEOC will be able to engage in conciliation efforts during this period. *Gary* v. *Industrial Indemnity Co.,* 7 FEP Cases 193 (N.D. Cal. 1973); *Bauman* v. *Union Oil Co.,* 6 FEP Cases 212 (N.D. Cal. 1973); *Westerlund* v. *Fireman's Fund Ins. Co.,* 11 FEP Cases 744 (N.D. Cal. 1975); *Lewis* v. *FMC Corp.,* 11 FEP Cases 31 (N.D. Cal. 1975); *Howard* v. *Mercantile Commerce Trust Co.,* 10 FEP Cases 158 (E.D. Mo. 1974). *Contra, Jones* v. *Pacific Intermountain Express,* 10 FEP Cases 914 (N.D. Cal. 1975).

(d) A very important consideration which militates against a strict application of the 180-day time limit imposed by § 706(c) or the filing of an EEOC charge is the doctrine of "continuing violations," discussed in n.91.

(e) The 180-day limit on filing an EEOC charge is not tolled when the employee seeks redress through contractual grievance machinery, *International Union of Electrical, Radio and Machine Workers AFL-CIO* v. *Robbins & Myers, Inc.,* — U.S. —, 13 FEP Cases 1813 (1976) (Rehnquist, J.); *Culpepper* v. *Reynolds Metals Co.,* 421 F.2d 888 (5th Cir. 1970); *Malone* v. *North American Rockwell Corp.,* 457 F.2d 779 (9th Cir. 1972); *Sanchez* v. *T.W.A.,* 499 F.2d 1107 (10th Cir. 1974); *Guerra* v. *Manchester Terminal Corp.,* 350 F. Supp. 529, 532 (S.D. Tex. 1972), *aff'd in part on other grds., rev'd in part on other grds,* 498 F.2d 641, 647 n.6 (5th Cir. 1974).

Moreover, in class actions it is not necessary for each class member to have filed a charge; rather the filing of a charge by the named plaintiff tolls the 180-day limitation with respect to all other individuals whose claims arise from acts encompassed within the scope of the charge filed. See, e.g., *EEOC* v. *Detroit Edison Co.,* 515 F.2d 301, 315 (6th Cir. 1975); *Pettway* v. *American Cast Iron Pipe Co.,* 494 F.2d 211, 256 (5th Cir. 1974).

(f) The time limits for filing charges, for deferral to state agencies, for conciliation efforts, and for initiating suit after receipt of a right-to-sue letter are not to be viewed as constituting in the aggregate a 180-day period within which suit must be filed; EEOC's delay in issuing the right-to-sue notice thus does not bar a suit. See, e.g., *Cunningham* v. *Litton Industries, Inc.,* 413 F.2d 887 (9th Cir. 1969); *Richard* v. *McDonnell Douglas Corp.,* 469 F.2d 1249 (8th Cir. 1972).

(g) Technical objections to the form of the EEOC charge are disfavored. See, e.g., *Sanchez* v. *Standard Brands, Inc.,* 431 F.2d 455 (5th Cir. 1970): amending charge after time for filing has expired; *Graniteville Co.* v. *EEOC,* 438 F.2d 32 (4th Cir. 1971): rejecting claim that charge lacked specificity. See also *Huston* v. *General Motors Corp.,* 477 F.2d 1003 (8th Cir. 1973): court action was timely commenced where the plaintiff sent informal papers to the court clerk; formal complaint is not required for purposes of timeliness.

(h) Related to the previous point is the doctrine that the scope of a Title VII action is not limited to the acts specifically alleged in the EEOC charge, but can be as broad as "the scope of the EEOC investigation which can reasonably be expected to grow out of the charge of discrimination." *Sanchez,* at 466. It follows that discovery in Title VII class actions can be very broad. And even in an individual action, the relevance of a statistical picture of the employer's workforce, see *McDonnell Douglas Corp.* v. *Green,* 411 U.S. 792, 804–805 (1973), means that information leading to "an overall statistical picture of an employer's practices" is discoverable. *Burns* v. *Thiokol Chemical Corp.,* 483 F.2d 300, 306 (5th Cir. 1973). See generally Ch. 3, sec.: "Classwide Discovery."

(i) Another much litigated procedural issue in private Title VII actions is that of the adequacy of class representation. See generally Ch. 3, sec.: "Class Representation."

(j) As a final tribute to the prominence of technical procedural defenses in Title VII litigation, mention should be made of the litigation concerning EEOC's now-discontinued "2-letter procedure," under which the commission's practice was to notify the charging party when conciliation had failed and to advise him of his right to request a right-to-sue letter, and subsequently to issue the letter upon request. Literally dozens of decisions were written on the question whether the 90-day period for filing suit, contained in § 706(f)(1), begins to run from the date of the notice that conciliation has failed, or from the date of receipt of the right-to-sue letter. The Eighth and Tenth Circuits held that the date of the notice of failure of conciliation was applicable. *Lacy* v. *Chrysler Corp.,* 11 EPD ¶ 10,746 (8th Cir. 1976); *Tuft* v. *McDonnell Douglas Corp.,* 517 F.2d 1301 (8th Cir. 1975), *cert. denied,* 423 U.S. 1052 1D EPD ¶ 10,595 (1976); *Williams* v. *Southern Union Gas Co.,* 11 EPD ¶ 10,621 (10th Cir. 1976). But see *DeMatteis* v. *Eastman Kodak Co.,* 511 F.2d 306, 310 n.6 (2d Cir. 1975) (dictum). Outside the Eighth and Tenth Circuits, most courts took the opposite position. See *Lacy,* at p. 7126 (concurring and dissenting opinion). Since the EEOC has abandoned the 2-letter procedure, this fertile ground for procedural defenses can no longer be tilled, and the correct interpretation of § 706(f)(1) in that context will apparently remain unsettled.

61. § 705(b)(1), 42 U.S.C. § 2000e-4(b)(1) (Supp. II, 1972).

62. For example Dean St. Antoine, in *Proceedings of the ABA National Institute on Equal Employment Opportunity* (1969), (unpaged), and Sovern in *Legal Restraints,* pp. 70–73, greatly underestimated the effect Title VII would have on seniority systems and on testing. The impact of Title VII on testing and seniority was also underestimated by Arthur Bonfield, "The Substance of American Fair Employment Practices Legislation I: Employers," 61 *Nw. U. L. Rev.* 907, 962–964 (1967). Charles T. Schmidt, "Title VII: Coverage and Comments," 7 *B.C. Ind. & Comm. L. Rev.* 459, 471 (1966), underestimated its impact in such areas as sex discrimination, seniority, and apprenticeship programs. And see generally Carl Rachlin, "Title VII: Limitations and Qualifications," 7 *B.C. Ind. & Comm. L. Rev.* 473 (1966).

63. *United States* v. *Sheetmetal Workers Local 36,* 416 F.2d 123 (8th Cir. 1969).

64. Eight decisions of the Court have been favorable to plaintiffs in virtually all respects. *Griggs* v. *Duke Power Co.,* 401 U.S. 424 (1971) (Burger, C.J.): intent to discriminate need not be proved in order to establish a violation, and use of unvalidated test which has disparate impact on minorities violates the Act (discussed in Ch. 4 sec.: "Societal Discrimination"); *Love* v. *Pullman Co.,* 404 U.S. 522 (1972) (Stewart, J.): procedural technicalities should not bar Title VII suits (discussed in n.60); *McDonnell Douglas Corp.* v. *Green,* 411 U.S. 792 (1973) (Powell, J.): when a qualified black applicant is denied employment, burden shifts to the employer to present a nondiscriminatory reason for the rejection (discussed in Ch. 3); *Alexander* v. *Gardner-Denver Co.,* 415 U.S. 36 (1974) (Powell, J.): arbitration award does not bar Title VII suit (discussed in Ch. 8); *Albermarle Paper Co.* v. *Moody,* 95 S.Ct. 2362 (1975) (Stewart, J.): back pay should normally be awarded for Title VII violations and EEOC testing guidelines should be followed by the courts (discussed in Chs. 5 and 6); *Franks* v. *Bowman Transportation Co.,* 424 U.S. 747, 11 EPD ¶10,777 (1976) (Brennan, J.): retroactive seniority should normally be awarded as part of make-whole remedy for refusal to hire; proof of classwide discrimination shifts to the employer the burden of proving that individual claimants were not victims (discussed in Chs. 4, 5 and 6); *Chandler* v. *Roudebush* — U.S. —, 96 S.Ct. 1949 (1976) (Stewart, J.): federal employees have the same right to a trial *de novo* as do private employees; *McDonald* v. *Santa Fe Trail Transportation Company,* — U.S. —, 12 FEP Cases 1577 (1976) (Marshall, J.): white employees have the right to sue for racial discrimination. In the October, 1975, term, the Court indicated that it had reservations about applying some of its expansive approaches to remedy discrimination. *Washington* v. *Davis,* 426 U.S. 229 (1976) (White, J.): *Brown* v. *General Services Administration,* — U.S. —, 44 USLW 4704 (1976) (Stewart, J.). The same was true in the October 1976 term; *General Electric Company* v. *Gilbert, et al.,* 13 FEP Cases 1 (1976) (Rehnquist, J.); *International Union of Electrical, Radio and Machine Workers AFL-CIO* v. *Robbins & Myers, Inc.,* — U.S. —, 13 FEP Cases 1813 (1976) (Rehnquist, J.). But see *Fitzpatrick* v. *Bitzer,* — U.S. —, 96 S.Ct. 2666 (1976) (Rehnquist, J.): back pay and attorney's fees against state government allowable.

A twelfth decision, *Johnson* v. *Railway Express Agency, Inc.,* 421 U.S. 454 (1975) (Blackmun, J.) (discussed in sec.: "Civil Rights Act of 1866" in this chapter) was decided adversely to plaintiffs on one point (filing of a Title VII charge does not toll the state statute of limitations applicable to a claim under 42 U.S.C. § 1981) but favorably to plaintiffs on a much more important question (42 U.S.C. § 1981 provides cause of action for employment discrimination, totally independent of Title VII).

But a less favorable decision involved employment discrimination issues, albeit not a Title VII case. This is *Emporium Capwell Co.* v. *Western Addition Community Organization,* 420 U.S. 50, 95 S.Ct. 977 (1975) (Marshall, J.) (discussed in Ch. 9), in which the Court took a narrow view of the rights of minority workers to go outside their union in seeking to convince their employer to cease discrimination practices.

65. See, e.g., *United States* v. *Wood Lathers Local 46,* 471 F.2d 408 (2d Cir. 1972), *cert. denied,* 412 U.S. 939 (1973); *United States* v. *Ironworkers Local 86,* 443 F.2d 544 (9th Cir.), *cert. denied,* 404 U.S. 984 (1971); *Carter* v. *Gallagher,* 452 F.2d 315 (8th Cir.), *cert. denied,* 406 U.S. 950 (1972); *United States* v. *Carpenters Local 169,* 457 F.2d 210 (7th Cir.), *cert. denied,* 409 U.S. (1972).

66. See text at n.56.

67. *Stamps* v. *Detroit Edison Co.,* 365 F. Supp. 87 (E.D. Mich. 1973), *rev'd on this grd., aff'd in part on other grds. sub nom. EEOC* v. *Detroit Edison Co.,* 515 F.2d 301 (6th Cir. 1975).

68. 315 F. Supp. 1202 (W.D. Wash. 1970), *aff'd* 443 F.2d 544 (9th Cir. 1971), *cert. denied,* 404

U.S. 984 (1971), *supplemental orders,* 4 FED Cases 1150, 4 FEP Cases 1152 (W.D. Wash, 1972). See especially 4 FEP Cases 1152. See generally Ch. 13.

69. An example is *United States* v. *St. Louis–San Francisco Ry.,* 464 F.2d 301, 309–311 (8th Cir. 1972), *cert. denied,* 409 U.S. 1116 (1973).

70. § 707(c) of the 1972 amendments, 42 U.S.C. § 2000-e 6(c) (Supp. III, 1973) seems on its face to include the public sector when it says simply that "the functions of the Attorney General under this section shall be transferred to the Commission." But Congress clearly intended the Justice Department to retain a special role in suits against state and local governments, since under § 706(f)(1), 42 U.S.C. § 2000e-5(f)(1), after conciliation efforts fail in such cases the commission cannot file suit, but must refer the case to the Justice Department, which is authorized to sue. One might therefore conclude that Congress would not mean to deprive Justice of the authority to file pattern and practice suits in the public sector on its own initiative under § 707, and the legislative history gives some support to this conclusion. See especially the statement of Senator Javits, 118 *Cong. Rec.* 4081 (1972), that in transferring pattern and practice authority "we are dealing not with . . . Government entities but with . . . simply another order of magnitude, from the order of magnitude of the individual suit."

71. Paul Delaney, "Rights Groups and Labor Split on Job Agency Bill," *N.Y. Times,* Oct. 10, 1970, p. 23, col. 5.

72. 118 *Cong. Rec.* 1398 (1972): Senate adopts Amdt. No. 822 to S.2515, deleting transfer of OFCC.

73. See Ch. 11; *City of New York* v. *Diamond,* 379 F. Supp. 503 (S.D.N.Y. 1974).

74. *N.Y. Times,* Sept. 30, 1973, p. 28, col. 1.

75. 392 U.S. 409 (1968).

76. 42 U.S.C. § 1982 (1970).

77. § 1981 states: "All persons within the jurisdiction of the United States shall have the same right in every State and Territory to make and enforce contracts, to sue, be parties, give evidence, and to the full and equal benefit of all laws and proceedings for the security of persons and property as is enjoyed by white citizens, and shall be subject to like punishment, pains, penalties, taxes, licenses, and exactions of every kind, and to no other."

78. 392 U.S. at 427.

79. *Young* v. *International Telephone & Telegraph Co.,* 438 F.2d 757 (3d Cir. 1971); *Brown* v. *Gaston County Dyeing Machine Co.* 457 F.2d 1377 (4th Cir.), *cert. denied,* 409 U.S. 982 (1972); *Sanders* v. *Dobbs Houses, Inc.,* 431 F.2d 1097 (5th Cir. 1970), *cert. denied,* 401 U.S. 948 (1971); *Long* v. *Ford Motor Co.,* 7 FEP Cases 1053 (6th Cir. 1974); *Walters* v. *Wisconsin Steel Works,* 427 F.2d 476 (7th Cir.), *cert. denied,* 400 U.S. 911 (1970); *Brady* v. *Bristol-Meyers, Inc.,* 459 F.2d 621 (8th Cir. 1972); *Macklin* v. *Spector Freight Systems, Inc.,* 478 F.2d 979 (D.C. Cir. 1973).

80. 421 U.S. 454, 466 (1975).

81. Case cited n.79.

82. 427 F.2d at 481.

83. 438 F.2d 757 (3d Cir. 1971).

84. *Id.* at 763, 764.

85. 421 U.S. at 461.

86. See, e.g., *Georgia* v. *Rachel,* 384 U.S. 780, 791 (1966); *Agnew* v. *City of Compton,* 239 F.2d 226, 230 (9th Cir. 1957); *Kurylas* v. *United States Dept of Agric.,* 3-3 F. Supp. 1072 (D.D.C. 1974), *aff'd by judgment order,* 9 EPD ¶10,121 (D.C. Cir. 1975).

87. *Guerra* v. *Manchester Terminal Corp.,* 498 F.2d 641 (5th Cir. 1974).

88. *Kurylas* v. *United States Dept. of Agric.,* n.86, and cases cited therein. But see *Davis* v. *County of Los Angeles,* 13 FEP Cases 1217 (9th Cir. 1976).

89. See, e.g., *League of Academic Women* v. *Regents of Univ. of Cal.,* 343 F. Supp. 638 (N.D. Cal. 1972).

90. § 706(e), 42 U.S.C. § 2000e-5(e) (Supp. 1972).

91. (1) All the courts are agreed that if a violation is "continuing" with respect to an individual, the 180-day limit simply does not begin to run, and therefore the charge can be filed more than 180 days after the violation begins. But the decisions as to what constitutes a continuing violation have been unclear and inconsistent. It has been held that an act which terminates the employment relationship cannot be a continuing violation, and thus the charge must be filed within 180 days of termination, *Evans* v. *United Air Lines, Inc.,* 11 EPD ¶10,665 (7th Cir. 1976); *Terry* v. *Bridgeport Brass Co.,* 519 F.2d 806 (7th Cir. 1975); *Olson* v. *Rembrandt Printing Co.,* 511 F.2d 1228 (8th Cir. 1975) (en banc); *Collins* v. *United Air Lines, Inc.,* 514 F.2d 594 (9th Cir. 1975), even if plaintiff subsequently requests reinstatement and is denied, *Collins,* and even if plaintiff is rehired with loss of seniority, *Evans.* But

see *Burwell* v. *Eastern Air Lines, Inc.,* 394 F. Supp. 1361 (E.D. Va. 1975); *Jamerson* v. *TWA,* 11 FEP Cases 1475 (S.D.N.Y. 1975); Cf. *Healen* v. *Eastern Airlines, Inc.,* 9 EPD ¶10,023 (N.D. Ga. 1973). On the other hand, while a discriminatory layoff alone may not constitute a continuing violation, *Griffin* v. *Pacific Maritime Ass'n,* 478 F.2d 1118 (9th Cir. 1973), if plaintiff alleges a discriminatory failure to recall, the violation is continuing, *Cox* v. *U.S. Gypsum Co.,* 409 F.2d 289 (7th Cir. 1969); *Sciaffra* v. *Oxford Paper Co.,* 310 F. Supp. 891 (D. Me. 1970). Compare *Tippett* v. *Liggett & Meyers Tobacco Co.,* 11 FEP Cases 1294, 1303–1304 (M.D.N.C. 1975), with the same case, 316 F. Supp. 292–296 (M.D.N.C. 1970). Likewise, a single discriminatory refusal to promote may not be deemed continuing by itself, but if plaintiff alleges that others have subsequently been promoted, the violation is continuing. *Moore* v. *Sunbeam Corp.,* 459 F.2d 811, 828 (7th Cir. 1972); see also *Pacific Maritime Ass'n.* v. *Quinn,* 491 F.2d 1294 (9th Cir. 1974); *Belt* v. *Johnson Motor Lines, Inc.,* 458 F.2d 443 (5th Cir. 1972); *Rich* v. *Martin Marietta Corp.,* 552 F.2d 333, 348 (10th Cir. 1975); and a refusal to hire, albeit not a completed act until the vacancy is filled, *Gates* v. *Georgia-Pacific Corp.,* 492 F.2d 292, 294 (9th Cir. 1974) is not otherwise deemed continuing, *Molybdenum Corp.* v. *EEOC,* 457 F.2d 935 (10th Cir. 1972), but if plaintiff reapplies, *Molybdenum Corp.; Jurinko* v. *Edwin L. Wiegand Co.,* 477 F.2d 1038, 1042 (3d Cir. 1973), or is deemed to be still waiting to be called, *Macklin* v. *Spector Freight Systems, Inc.,* 478 F.2d 979, 988 (D.C. Cir. 1973), the violation is continuing.

(2) Several courts have indicated that even if a violation is not continuing with respect to the individual plaintiff, the charge is timely if the plaintiff alleges that the defendant is still discriminating against others. See especially *Kohn* v. *Royall, Koegel & Wells,* 5 EPD ¶8504 at p.7415 (S.D.N.Y. 1973). See also, e.g., *Macklin,* 478 F.2d at 987; *Jamerson,* 11 FEP Cases at 1478; *Cates* v. *TWA,* 10 FEP Cases 334, 336 (S.D.N.Y. 1974). Cf. *Bartmess* v. *Drewrys U.S.A., Inc.,* 444 F.2d 1186, 1188 (7th Cir.), *cert. denied,* 404 U.S. 939 (1971). The courts have often failed to recognize that discrimination "continuing" in this sense is not the same thing as discrimination which is "continuing" with respect to the individual plaintiff. Thus it is not clear whether these cases imply only that the plaintiff whose individual claim is untimely can nevertheless represent a class (see *Olson* v. *Rembrandt Printing Co.,* at 1234), inasmuch as an individual with a losing claim can serve as a class representative, see, e.g., *Huff* v. *N.D. Cass Co.,* 485 F.2d 710 (5th Cir. 1973) (discussed in Ch. 3, sec.: "Class Representation"), or whether the allegation of an ongoing pattern of classwide discrimination can serve to enable an individual to recover for a claim which would otherwise be untimely. *Kohn,* seems to adopt the latter position. And the holding in *United States* v. *Georgia Power Co.,* 474 F.2d 906, 922 (5th Cir. 1973), that the 180-day filing period "is in no sense a limitation on the period for which one may receive back pay relief" and that instead the relevant state statute of limitations will be applied with respect to back pay, has been interpreted by at least one court to mean that any class member who was denied employment or transfer within the period provided by the state statute of limitations (rather than within 180 days prior to the filing of a charge by the class representative) can recover back pay, as well as seniority credits. *EEOC* v. *Detroit Edison Co.,* 515 F.2d 301, 315–316 (6th Cir. 1975). See also *Pettway* v. *American Cast Iron Pipe Co.,* 494 F.2d 211, 258 (5th Cir. 1974).

But the Third Circuit has held that if an individual's claim arose more than 180 days before the class representative filed a charge, the claim is barred. *Wetzel* v. *Liberty Mutual Ins. Co.,* 508 F.2d 239, 246 (3d Cir. 1975), *cert. denied,* 95 U.S. 2415, 9 EPD ¶10,176 (1975). *Accord, Doski* v. *Goldseker Co.,* 10 EPD ¶10,582 at p. 6406 (D. Md. 1975); *Hecht* v. *C.A.R.E.,* 351 F. Supp. 305, 308–309 (S.D.N.Y. 1972).

92. § 706(g), 42 U.S.C. § 2000e-5(g) (Supp. II, 1972).

93. See, e.g., *United States* v. *Georgia Power Co.,* 474 F.2d 906, 922–925 (5th Cir. 1973). See generally Ch. 6, beginning at n.39.

94. See *Laffey* v. *Northwest Airlines, Inc.,* 7 FEP Cases 687, 688–689, (D.C.D.C. 1974); *Bing* v. *Roadway Express, Inc.,* 485 F.2d 441, 454 (5th Cir. 1973), *Head* v. *Timken Roller Bearing Co.,* 486 F.2d 870, 878 (6th Cir. 1973).

95. See "Racial Discrimination in Employment under the Civil Rights Act of 1886," 36 *U. Chi. L. Rev.* 615, 621–637 (1969).

3 | The Substantive Law of Title VII: An Introduction

1. *Oatis* v. *Crown Zellerback Corp.,* 398 F.2d 496, 499 (5th Cir. 1968). On the point that individual class members need not file charges but can rely on the charge filed by the class representatives, see also *Pettway* v. *American Cast Iron Pipe Co.,* 494 F.2d 211, 256 (5th Cir. 1974) and cases cited *id.* n.134; *EEOC* v. *Detroit Edison Co.,* 515 F.2d 301, 315 (6th Cir. 1975).

2. *Newman* v. *Piggie Park Enterprises, Inc.*, 390 U.S. 400, 402 (1968) (Title II); *Jenkins* v. *United Gas Co.*, 400 F.2d 28, 32 (5th Cir. 1968) (Title VII).

3. See e.g., *Jenkins* v. *Blue Cross Mutual Hospital Insurance, Inc.*, 13 FEP Cases 52 (5th Cir. 1976); *Blue Bell Boots, Inc.* v. *EEOC*, 418 F.2d 355 (6th Cir. 1969); *Parliament House Motor Hotel* v. *EEOC*, 444 F.2d 1335 (5th Cir. 1971); *Motorola, Inc.* v. *McLain*, 484 F.2d 1339 (7th Cir. 1973); *Parham* v. *Southwestern Bell Telephone Co.*, 433 F.2d 421, 425 (8th Cir. 1970); Cf. *EEOC* v. *General Electric Co.*, 11 EPD ¶10,627 (4th Cir. 1976); *Sanchez* v. *Standard Brands, Inc.*, 431 F.2d 455 (5th Cir. 1970); *Rich* v. *Martin Marietta Corp.*, 522 F.2d 333, 343–345 (10th Cir. 1975) and cases cited therein.

4. 400 F.2d 28, 33 (5th Cir. 1968).

5. See *id.* at 33; Note: "Work Environment Injury under Title VII, 82 *Yale L.J.* 1695, 1697–1698 (1973). Cf. *Senter* v. *General Motors Corp.*, 11 EPD ¶10,741 at p. 7089 (6th Cir. 1976) and cases cited therein.

6. *Cypress* v. *Newport General & Nonsectarian Hosp. Assn.*, 375 F.2d 648, 658 (4th Cir. 1967).

7. *Anderson* v. *City of Albany*, 321 F.2d 649, 657 (5th Cir. 1963).

8. 400 F.2d at 33.

9. See *Sprogis* v. *United Air Lines, Inc.* 444 F.2d 1194 (7th Cir.), *cert. denied*, 404 U.S. 991 (1971).

10. 472 F.2d 631 (9th Cir. 1972).

11. *Id.* at 633, 634.

12. Fed. R. Civ. P. Rule 23(a), 28 U.S.C. (1970).

13. 485 F.2d 710 (5th Cir. 1973).

14. *Id.* at 713, citing 7A Wright & Miller, *Federal Practice and Procedure* § 1785 p. 131 (1972).

15. *Id.* at 714.

16. *Id.*

17. *Roberts* v. *Union Co.*, 487 F.2d 387, 389 (6th Cir. 1973). See also *Gibson* v. *ILWU, Local 40*, 13 FEP Cases 997 (9th Cir. 1976).

18. 485 F.2d at 713.

19. *Id.* at 713, citing *Hutchings* v. *United States Industries, Inc.*, 428 F.2d 303, 310 (5th Cir. 1970).

20. *Wetzel* v. *Liberty Mutual Ins. Co.*, 508 F.2d 239 (3d Cir. 1975), *cert. denied*, 9 EPD ¶10,176 (1975); *Carr* v. *Conoco Plastics, Inc.* 423 F.2d 57 (5th Cir.) *cert. denied*, 400 U.S. 951 (1970); *Johnson* v. *Georgia Highway Express, Inc.*, 417 F.2d 1122 (5th Cir. 1969); *Tipler* v. *du Pont Co.*, 443 F.2d 125, 130 (6th Cir. 1971); *Reed* v. *Arlington Hotel Co.*, 476 F.2d 721 (8th Cir. 1975). And see generally *Rich* v. *Martin Marietta Corp.*, 522 F.2d 333, 340–341 (10th Cir. 1975) and cases cited therein. See also *Barnett* v. *W. T. Grant Co.*, 518 F.2d 543 (4th Cir. 1975), and cases cited therein; *Senter* v. *General Motors Corp.*, 11 EPD ¶10,741 (6th Cir. 1976).

21. *EEOC* v. *Detroit Edison Co.*, 515 F.2d 301, 311 (6th Cir. 1975).

22. See, e.g., *Williams* v. *Sheet Metal Workers Local 19*, 5 FEP Cases 888 (E.D. Pa. 1973).

23. 405 U.S. 727, 739 (1972).

24. 95 S.Ct. 2197, 2211–2212 (1975). The Court expressly stated that an organization has standing if "any one of" its members has been harmed.

25. *United States* v. *Students Challenging Regulatory Agency Procedures* (SCRAP), 412 U.S. 669 (1973).

26. *Id.* at 686; *Sierra Club, supra* n.23, at 738.

27. *Warth* v. *Seldin*, 95 S.Ct. at 2211–2212; *Environmental Defense Fund, Inc.* v. *Corps, of Engineers*, 348 F. Supp. 916 (N.D. Miss. 1972).

28. 409 U.S. 205 (1972).

29. *Air Lines Stewards & Stewardesses Ass'n; Local 550* v. *American Airlines, Inc.*, 455 F.2d 101 (7th Cir. 1972); *Lynch* v. *Sperry Rand Corp.*, 6 FEP Cases 1306 (S.D.N.Y. 1973). Cf. *Air Lines Stewards & Stewardesses Ass'n, Local 550* v. *American Airlines, Inc.*, 490 F.2d 636, 639–642 (7th Cir. 1973).

30. *Chemical Workers* v. *Planters Mfg. Co.*, 259 F. Supp. 365 (N.D. Miss. 1966); *Local 186, Pulp, Sulphite & Paper Mill Workers* v. *Minnesota Mining & Mfg. Co.*, 304 F. Supp. 1284, 1293 (N.D. Ind. 1969); *Oakland Federation of Teachers* v. *Oakland Unified School Dist.*, 9 EPD ¶10,079 (N.D. Cal. 1975). But cf. *Air Lines Stewards & Stewardesses Ass'n* v. *American Airlines, Inc.*, 490 F.2d 636, 639–642 (7th Cir. 1973), *cert. denied*, 94 S.Ct. 2406 (1974): union must satisfy traditional tests as to adequacy of class representation.

31. §§ 706(b), (f), 42 U.S.C. §§ 2000e-5(b), (f) (Supp. II, 1972).

32. *Chemical Workers*, at 368.

33. EEOC Decision No. 70–09, *CCH EEOC Decisions* ¶6026 (July 8, 1969). Accord, *Waters* v. *Heublein, Inc.*, 13 FEP Cases 1409 (9th Cir. 1976). Cf. "Work Environment Injury." But see *Ripp* v. *Dobbs Houses, Inc.*, 366 F. Supp. 205 (N.D. Ala. 1973); *Thomas* v. *Ford Motor Co.*, 396 F. Supp. 52, 61–62 (E.D. Mich. 1973), *aff'd on other grds*, 516 F.2d 902 (6th Cir.), *cert. denied*, 95 S.Ct. 1991 (1975).

34. Race Relations Act 1968 (c.71) § 8(2). But note that § 8(2) is seemingly of benefit only to immigrants, since § 8(4) states that for the purposes of § 8(2), all individuals wholly or mainly educated in Britain shall be deemed to be members of the same racial group. Section 8(2) is one of the most controversial provisions of the Race Relations Act. See Anthony Lester and Geoffrey Bindman, *Race and Law*, (London 1972), pp. 208–213.

35. See e.g., Officers for *Justice* v. *Civil Service Comm'n*, 371 F. Supp. 1328 (N.D. Cal. 1973); *Western Additional Community Organization* v. *Alioto*, 360 F. Supp. 733 (N.D. Cal. 1973); *Vulcan Society* v. *Civil Service Comm'n*, 360 F. Supp. 1265 (S.D.N.Y. 1973), *aff'd* 490 F.2d 387 (2d Cir. 1973).

36. *Arkansas Education Ass'n* v. *Board of Educ. of Portland*, 446 F.2d 763, 766 (8th Cir. 1971); *United Minority Workers* v. *Local 701 Operating Engineers*, 10 EPD § 10,581 (D. Ore. 1975); *Bridgeport Guardians Association* v. *Bridgeport Civil Service Commission*, 354 F. Supp. 778, 783 (D. Conn. 1973), *aff'd* 482 F.2d 1333 (2d Cir. 1973); *NAACP* v. *Allen*, 340 F. Supp. 703, 705 (N.D. Ala. 1972), *aff'd* 493 F.2d 614 (5th Cir. 1974).

37. 357 U.S. 449 (1958).

38. *United States* v. *Local 86, Ironworkers*, 315 F. Supp. 1202 (W.D. Wash. 1970), *aff'd*. 443 F.2d 544 (9th Cir. 1971), *cert. denied*, 404 U.S. 984 (1971), *supplemental orders*, 4 FEP Cases 1147, 4 FEP Cases 1150, 4 FEP Cases 1152 (1972) (discussed in Ch. 13). See especially 4 FEP Cases 1152.

39. § 706(b), 42 U.S.C. § 2000e-5(b) (Supp. II, 1972), amending 42 U.S.C. § 2000e-5(a) (1970).

40. See generally Ch. 9. In *Local 86, Ironworkers*, the United Construction Workers Association clearly did not supplant the union, since UCWA was required to send referrals to the union for final evaluation, 4 FEP Cases 1152.

41. *State of Alabama* v. *United States*, 304 F.2d 583, 586 (5th Cir. 1962), *aff'd per curiam*, 371 U.S. 37 (1962).

42. *Parham* v. *Southwestern Bell Telephone Co.*, 433 F.2d 421, 426 (8th Cir. 1970).

43. *United States* v. *Jacksonville Terminal Co.*, 451 F.2d 418, 442–443 (5th Cir. 1971), *cert. denied*, 406 U.S. 906 (1972). Accord, *Pettway* v. *American Cast Iron Pipe Co.*, 494 F.2d 211, 225–239 (5th Cir. 1974).

44. Where a job requires educational or professional training which the employer and/or union do not generally provide, proper analysis of statistical proof of discrimination becomes more complicated. See, generally, Note: "Title VII and Employment Discrimination in 'Upper Level' Jobs," 73 *Colum. L. Rev.* 1614 (1973).

45. *United States* v. *Local 86 Ironworkers*, 443 F.2d 544, 551 n.19 (9th Cir.), *cert. denied*, 404 U.S. 984 (1971).

46. OFCC Revised Order No. 4, *Affirmative Action Guidelines*, 41 C.F.R. § 60-2.11 (1973). See, e.g., "Timken To Be Denied Federal Contracts in Unusual Dispute over Minority Hiring," *Wall Street Journal*, March 23, 1976, p. 4 (firm must expand affirmative action recruiting to include town located 25 miles from plant).

47. 365 F. Supp. 87, 111 (E.D. Mich. 1973), *rev'd in part on other grounds*, 515 F.2d 301 (6th Cir. 1975).

48. 42 U.S.C. § 2000e-2(j) (Supp. II, 1972).

49. 428 F.2d 144, 149 (6th Cir.), *cert. denied*, 400 U.S. 943 (1970).

50. Thus, the Interpretative Memorandum of Senators Clark and Case stated that although "there is no requirement in Title VII that an employer maintain a racial balance in his workforce. . . . [Nonetheless] the presence or absence of other members of the same minority group in the workforce may be a relevant factor in determining whether in a given case a decision to hire or to refuse to hire was based on race" 110 *Cong. Rec.* 7213 (1964).

51. See *Afro American Patrolmen's League* v. *Duck*, 8 FEP Cases 22, 24–25 (N.D. Ohio 1973), *aff'd in part on other grds., rev'd in part on other grds.*, 503 F.2d 294 (6th Cir. 1974).

52. See, e.g., *Castro* v. *Beecher*, 459 F.2d 725 (1st Cir. 1972); *Chance* v. *Board of Examiners*, 458 F.2d 1167 (2d Cir. 1972).

53. On the proper meaning of § 703(j) with respect to remedies, see generally Ch. 5.

54. *H. K. Porter Co.* v. *NLRB*, 397 U.S. 99 (1970).

55. 431 F.2d 245 (10th Cir. 1970), *cert. denied*, 401 U.S. 954 (1971).

56. 451 F.2d 418, 445 (5th Cir. 1971), *cert. denied* 406, U.S. 906 (1972).

57. *Jones* v. *Lee Way Motor Freight, Inc.*, at 247.

58. 457 F.2d 1377, 1382, 1383 (4th Cir.), *cert. denied*, 409 U.S. 982 (1972).

59. *Marquez* v. *Omaha District Sales Office, Ford Division*, 440 F.2d 1157, 1162 (8th Cir. 1971).

60. An employer must preserve such forms for at least 6 months due to an EEOC rule, 29 C.F.R. § 1602.4 (1973).

61. §§ 706(b), 709(e), 42 U.S.C. § 2000e-5(b) (Supp. II, 1972), § 2000e-8(e) (1970).

62. 472 F.2d 1147, 1152 (5th Cir.) (*en banc*), *cert. denied*, 412 939 (1973).

63. See text at n.41–43.

64. *United States* v. *Sheet Metal Workers Local 36*, 416 F.2d 123, 127, n.7 (8th Cir. 1969).

65. *Rowe* v. *General Motors Corp.*, 457 F.2d 348, 359 (5th Cir. 1972). See also *Senter* v. *General Motors Corp.*, 11 EPD ¶10,741 at pp. 7093–7095 (6th Cir. 1976).

66. *Stamps* v. *Detroit Edison Co.*, 365 F. Supp. 87, 112 (E.D. Mich. 1973), *aff'd in part, rev'd in part on other grds. sub. nom. EEOC* v. *Detroit Edison Co.*, 515 F.2d 301 (6th Cir. 1975).

67. 483 F.2d 300, 306 (5th Cir. 1973).

68. See generally Note: "Work Environment Injury under Title VII," 82 *Yale L.J.* 1695 (1973).

69. See *Jones* v. *Milwaukee Country*, 10 EPD ¶10,448 at p. 5938 (E.D. Wis. 1975) and cases cited; *Samuel* v. *Virgin Islands Telephone Corp.*, 11 EPD ¶10,643 at pp. 6699–6701 (D.V.I. 1975).

70. 411 U.S. 792, 804–805 (1973).

71. *Motorola, Inc.* v. *McLain*, 484 F.2d 1339, 1346 (7th Cir. 1973). See also *Local 104 Sheet Metal Workers* v. *EEOC*, 439 F.2d 237 (9th Cir. 1971).

72. Subdivision of the class is provided for by Fed. R. Civ. P. 23(c) (4). See Judicial Panel on Multidistrict Litigation, *Manual for Complex Litigation* § 1.42.

73. 416 U.S. 979 (1974).

74. For the proposition that a Title VII action may properly be brought under Rule 23(b)(2) even where back pay is sought and awarded see, e.g., *Franks* v. *Bowman Transportation Co.*, 495 F.2d 398,422 (5th Cir. 1974), *rev'd on other grds*, 424 U.S. 747 (1976), 11 EPD ¶10,777 (1976). And the Third Circuit has held that where a Title VII suit brought in good faith for injunctive relief as well as back pay is certified as a Rule 23(b)(2) class action and the district court subsequently determines that injunctive relief will not be appropriate, the action may continue under Rule 23(b)(2) and need not be recertified as a Rule 23(b)(3) action. *Wetzel* v. *Liberty Mutual Ins. Co.*, 508 F.2d 239 (3d Cir.), *cert. denied*, — U.S. —, 9 EPD ¶10,176 (1975). Moreover, the *Wetzel* court rejected defendants' contention that even if the action may continue under Rule 23(b)(2) a notice requirement similar to that under Rule 23(b)(3) should be imposed. However, several district courts have imposed notice requirements in Rule 23(b)(2) Title VII actions. See, e.g., *Meadows* v. *Ford Motor Co.*, 7 EPD ¶9103 (W.D. Ky. 1973), *aff'd in part on other grds., rev'd in part on other grds.*, 510 F.2d 939 (6th Cir. 1975); *Martinez* v. *Bechtel Corp.*, 10 EPD ¶10,570 at pp. 6355–6356 (N.D. Cal. 1975); *Freeman* v. *Motor Convoy, Inc.*, 8 EPD ¶9798 at p. 6339 (N.D. Ga. 1974).

75. 411 U.S. 792 (1973).

76. *Id.* at 802.

77. *Id.*

78. *Id.* at 805.

79. 424 U.S. 747 (1976), 11 EPD ¶10,777 (1976).

80. Id. at p. 7263. Unlike *Green, Bowman* was a class action. The implications of the quoted passage from *Bowman* for classwide seniority remedies are discussed in Ch. 4, Secs.: "*Franks* v. *Bowman Transportation Co.*" and "Seniority Credits." The implications for classwide back pay remedies are discussed in Ch. 6, sec.: "The Circumstances under which Back Pay is Awarded."

81. See, e.g., *Stamps* v. *Detroit Edison*, 365 F. Supp. at 99–100, 113. (The 6th Circuit did not reverse on this point.) And in *Franks* v. *Bowman*, the jobs in question had been filled.

82. See *East* v. *Romine, Inc.*, 518 F.2d 332, 340 (5th Cir. 1975): when qualified minority applicant is passed over, employer must prove "that each of the others [hired] had a better work record."

4 | Discrimination, Seniority, and the *Griggs* Progeny

1. 407 F.2d 1047 (5th Cir. 1969).

2. 407 F.2d at 1054.

3. *Id.* at 1054.

4. See, e.g., 110 *Cong. Rec.* 486–489 (1964) ("The Civil Rights Bills—A Blow to Labor Union Freedom"—a speech of Senator Lester Hill).

5. 42 U.S.C. § 2000c-5(g) (Supp. II, 1972).

6. 42 U.S.C. § 2000-2(a) (2) (Supp. II, 1972) (Employers); § 2000e-2(c) (2) (Supp. II 1972) (labor organizations).

7. See *Kober* v. *Westinghouse Electric Corp.,* 480 F.2d 240, 245–246 (3d Cir. 1973), and cases cited.

8. 110 *Cong. Rec.* 7217 (1964).

9. 110 *Cong. Rec.* 7213 (1964).

10. 110 *Cong. Rec.* 7207 (1964) (my italics).

11. 42 U.S.C. § 2000e-2(h) (1970).

12. *Whitfield* v. *United Steelworkers,* 263 F.2d 546, 551 (5th Cir.) *cert. denied,* 360 U.S. 902 (1959). See Ch. 2, text beginning at n. 20.

13. In 1967 the author published an article based on the report. William B. Gould, "Employment Security, Seniority and Race: The Role of Title VII of the Civil Rights Act of 1964," 13 *How. L.J.* 1 (1967).

14. 349 U.S. 294, 300 (1955).

15. See the Clark-Case memorandum quoted above (employers "would not be obliged—or indeed, permitted—to fire whites in order to hire Negroes"). See also, the speech of Senator Hill, n.4.

16. *United Steelworkers* v. *American Mfg. Co.,* 363 U.S. 564 (1960), *United Steelworkers* v. *Warrior & Gulf Navigation Co.,* 363 U.S. 574 (1960); *United Steelworkers* v. *Enterprise Wheel & Car Corp.,* 363 U.S. 593 (1960). See generally Ch. 8.

17. § 706(f)(5), 42 U.S.C. § 2000e-5(f)(5) (Supp. II 1972).

18. For discussion of the "but for" approach to seniority credits, see Gould, pp. 37–42.

19. The 1966 report stressed that the employer's line of progression "must be carefully scrutinized to see if it is rationally constructed" in the sense that each job along the line provides experience essential to developing skills needed for the next job on the line. See Gould, p. 42. The following discussion assumes that the line of progression in question meets this strict test. If it does not, the 1966 report noted that blacks should be permitted to skip certain jobs on the line of progression. *Id.* at 47. See sec.: "Further Thoughts on 'Freedom Now.'"

20. See text at n.75. See generally Ch. 5.

21. 279 F. Supp. 505 (E.D. Va. 1968).

22. *Id.* at 513.

23. *Id.* at 514.

24. *Id.* at 517.

25. *Id.* at 518.

26. *Id.* at 516.

27. 416 F.2d 123 (8th Cir. 1969).

28. *United States* v. *Chesapeake & Ohio Ry.,* 471 F.2d, 582, 586–587 (4th Cir. 1972), *cert. denied,* 411 U.S. 939 (1973).

29. 416 F.2d 980 (5th Cir. 1969), *cert. denied,* 397 U.S. 919 (1970).

30. *Id.* at 982–983.

31. *Id.* at 986–987.

32. *Id.* at 988.

33. *Id.*

34. *Id.*

35. *Id.* Although the 1966 report contained criticisms of what it termed the "rightful place" approach (see Gould, pp. 41–48), the approach referred to as "rightful place" in the report was essentially the approach identified as "freedom now" in the lexicon of *Local 189,* and the criticisms expressed in the report—essentially that "rightful place" calls for the immediate promotion of blacks without regard for their ability to perform the work in question, and that the bumping of white incumbents would be required—do *not* apply to the "rightful place" doctrine as the term came to be used in *Local 189.* The approach recommended by the 1966 report—careful scrutiny of lines of progression, carryover of seniority and wage rates, use of rational residency rules, etc.—is in fact the "rightful place" approach adopted in *Local 189* and subsequent cases. See, e.g., *Taylor* v. *Armco Steel Corp.,* 429 F.2d 498 n.1 (5th Cir. 1970).

36. 416 F.2d at 989.

37. *Id.* at 992.

38. *Id.*, citing 279 F. Supp at 518.

39. 444 F.2d 791 (4th Cir.) *cert. dismissed,* 404 U.S. 1006 (1971). "Red circling" is now routinely utilized in departmental seniority cases. See, e.g., *Stevenson* v. *International Paper Co.,* 516 F.2d 103, 112–113 (5th Cir. 1975); *Rogers* v. *International Paper Co.,* 510 F.2d 1340, 1355 (8th Cir.), *vacated and rem'd on other grds.,* 423 U.S. 809, 10 EPD ¶10,409 (1975), *new trial ordered on other grds,* 526 F.2d 722 (8th Cir. 1975); *Pettway* v. *American Cast Iron Pipe Co.,* 494 F.2d 211, 249 (5th Cir. 1974).

40. 424 U.S. 747, 11 EPD ¶10,777 (1976). The remedial provisions are in § 706(g), 42 U.S.C. § 2000e-5(g). See 11 EPD at p. 7260.

41. 495 F.2d 398 (5th Cir. 1974).

42. 11 EPD at p. 7260–7361.

43. NLRA § 10(c), 29 U.S.C. § 160(c).

44. 11 EPD at p. 7262, citing *In re Phelps Dodge Corp.,* 19 NLRB 547,600 & n.39, 603–604 (190), *modified on other grds,* 313 U.S. 177 (1941); *In re Consolidated Copper Corp.,* 26 NLRB 1182, 1235 (1940), *enforced,* 316, U.S. 105 (1942).

45. 11 EPD at pp. 7264–7265.

46. *Id.* at 7266–7268.

47. *Id.* at 7268–7269.

48. NLRB § 10(b), 29 U.S.C. § 160(b).

49. 11 EPD at p. 7260.

50. *Id.* at 7265 (concurring and dissenting opinion).

51. *Id.* at 7260 n.21 (opinion of the Court).

52. See Sec.: "The 'Last-Hired, First-Fired' Controversy."

53. 451 F.2d 418 (5th Cir. 1971), *cert. denied,* 406 U.S. 906 (1972).

54. *Id.* at 454. Cf. also *Carey* v. *Greyhound Bus Co.,* 500 F.2d 1372, 1377 (5th Cir. 1974).

55. See *Franks* v. *Bowman Transportation Co.* 495 F.2d 398 (5th Cir.), *cert. denied,* 419 U.S. 1050 (1974); *U.S.* v. *Navaho Freight Lines, Inc.* 525 F.2d 1318 (9th Cir. 1975); *Hairston* v. *McLean Trucking Co.,* 520 F.2d 226 (4th Cir. 1975); *U.S.* v. *T.I.M.E.–D.C., Inc.,* 517 F.2d 299 (5th Cir. 1975); *Sabala* v. *Western Gillette, Inc.,* 516 F.2d 1251 (5th Cir. 1975); *Rodriguez* v. *East Texas Motor Freight, Inc.,* 505 F.2d, 40 (5th Cir. 1974); *Herrara* v. *Yellow Freight Systems, Inc.* 505 F.2d 66 (5th Cir. 1974); *Resendis* v. *Lee Way Motor Freight, Inc.,* 505 F.2d 69 (5th Cir. 1975); *Bing* v. *Roadway Express, Inc.,* 444 F.2d 687 (5th Cir. 1971); *Belt* v. *Johnson Motor Lines, Inc.,* 458 F.2d 443 (5th Cir. 1972); *Witherspoon* v. *Mercury Freight Lines,* 457 F.2d 496 (5th Cir. 1972); *U.S.* v. *Roadway Express, Inc.,* 457 F.2d 854 (6th Cir. 1972); *Jones* v. *Lee Way Motor Freight,* 431 F.2d 235 (10th Cir.) *cert. denied,* 401 U.S. 954 (1971); *U.S.* v. *Central Motor Lines,* 388 F. Supp. 532, 352, F. Supp. 1253 (W.D.N.C. 1971); *U.S.* v. *Pilot Freight Carriers, Inc.,* 54 F.R.D. 519 (M.D.N.C. 1973); *U.S.* v. *Lee Way Motor Freight, Inc.,* 6 FEP Cases 274 (C.D. Cal. 1973).

56. 11 EPD at p. 7263.

57. *Id.,* quoting *United States* v. *Bethlehem Steel Corp.,* 446 F.2d 652, 663 (2d Cir. 1971).

58. 416 F.2d at 970.

59. The Court of Appeals in *Local 189* was not presented with an attack by plaintiffs against the requirement of low-level entry, the residency requirements, etc. Indeed, the court noted that in a decree issued subsequent to the decree which was before the Court of Appeals, the district court had ordered that black employees be allowed to "skip" certain jobs along the lines of progression, and that the residency requirements be reduced. At 986 n.6.

60. *Stevenson* v. *International Paper Co.,* 516 F.2d 103, 111–112 (5th Cir. 1975). See also, e.g., *Robinson* v. *Lorillard Corp.,* 444 F.2d 791 (4th Cir.), *cert. dismissed,* 404 U.S. 1006 (1971), *Long* v. *Georgia Kraft Co.,* 450 F.2d 557 (5th Cir. 1971); *Pettway* v. *American Cast Iron Pipe Co.,* 494 F.2d 211, 245–247 (5th Cir. 1974); *Rogers* v. *International Paper Co.,* 510 F.2d 1340, 1354–1357 (8th Cir. 1975), *vacated and rem'd on other grds.,* 423 U.S. 809, 10 EPD ¶10,409 (1975), *new trial ordered on other grds.,* 526 F.2d 722 (8th Cir. 1975); *Patterson* v. *American Tobacco Co.,* 11 EPD ¶10,728 at p. 7015 (4th Cir. 1976).

61. *Robinson,* 444 F.2d 791 (4th Cir.) *cert. dismissed,* 404 U.S. 1006 (1971); *Bethlehem Steel,* 446 F.2d 652 (2d Cir. 1971); *Watkins* v. *Scott Paper Co.,* 530 F.2d 1159 (5th Cir. 1976).

62. 444 F.2d at 798.

63. 446 F.2d at 662.

64. *Pettway,* at 246. See also *Robinson,* at 799–800.

65. See, e.g., *Patterson,* at p. 7015.

66. See cases cited n.60 especially *Stevenson, Pettway, Rogers.*

67. *Stamps* v. *Detroit Edison Co.,* 365 F. Supp. 87, 121–122 (E.D. Mich. 1973), *aff'd in part, rev'd in part on other grds.,* 515 F.2d 301 (6th Cir. 1975).

68. *Patterson* v. *American Tobacco Co.,* 9 EPD ¶9909 at pp. 6779–6780 (E.D. Va. 1974), *aff'd in part, rev'd on this grd.,* 535 F.2d 257 (4th Cir. 1976).

69. *Patterson* v. *American Tobacco Co.,* 535 F.2d 257 (4th Cir. 1976). But see *Sabala* v. *Western Gillette, Inc.* 516 F.2d 1251, 1265–1266 (5th Cir. 1975): finding no abuse of discretion in denial of front pay. The *Patterson* approach to front pay differs from that of Judge Keith in *Detroit Edison* in that under *Patterson* the discriminatee is awarded in advance a sum of money which is the estimated present value of the pay he will lose while waiting to achieve his rightful place, while under Judge Keith's approach the discriminatee is awarded the actual difference between his "rightful place" wages and the wages he is earning, until the discriminatee is, in fact, promoted to his rightful place. Front pay has also been awarded by the Second Circuit. See *EEOC* v. *Enterprise Association Steamfitters, Local No. 638,* 13 FEP Cases, 705, 714 (2d Cir. 1976).

70. See, e.g., *Sabala* v. *Western Gillette, Inc.,* 516 F.2d 1251, 1256 (5th Cir. 1975); *Rodriquez* v. *East Texas Motor Freight,* 505 F.2d 40, 64 (5th Cir. 1974); *Hairston* v. *McLean Trucking Co.,* 520 F.2d 226, 232 (4th Cir. 1975); *Bing* v. *Roadway Express, Inc.,* 485 F.2d 441, 451 (5th Cir. 1973); *United States* v. *Navaho Freight Lines, Inc.,* 525 F.2d 1318, 1326 (9th Cir. 1975). But see *Thornton* v. *East Texas Motor Freight,* 497 F.2d 416, 420–421 (6th Cir. 1974). Compare *EEOC* v. *Detroit Edison Co.,* 515 F.2d 301, 316 (6th Cir. 1975).

71. *United States* v. *Navaho Freight Lines,* at 1326.

72. N.27 *supra.*

73. 365 F. Supp. at 120–121. The Sixth Circuit, however, excluded the rejected applicants from the suit on the grounds that it had not been sufficiently established that the named plaintiffs could adequately represent this group (or the rejected applicants). 515 F.2d at 311. The court also stated that "there was no allegation that [Edison's discriminatory] reputation actually deterred anyone from applying" (at 312). But the court did approve relief for employees who "indicated a desire to transfer to a vacant job, but did not do so because it would have been futile under existing company practices" (at 316).

74. *United States* v. *Jacksonville Terminal Co.,* 451 F.2d 418, 453–454 (5th Cir. 1971), *cert. denied,* 406 U.S. 906 (1972).

75. See § 703(j), 42 U.S.C. § 2000e-2(j). See generally Ch. 5.

76. 416 F.2d at 995.

77. *Franks* v. *Bowman Transportation Co.,* 495 F.2d 398, 418 (5th Cir. 1974), *reversed,* 424 U.S. 747, 11 EPD ¶10,777 (1976).

78. *Id.* at 417.

79. 11 EPD at p. 7263.

80. See cases cited n.70.

81. *Acha* v. *Beame,* 11 EPD ¶10,740 p. 7084 (2d Cir. 1976).

82. See text at n.15.

83. 369 F. Supp. 1221 (E.D. La. 1974), *judgment entered* 8 FEP Cases 729 (E.D. La. 1974), *rev'd and rem'd,* 516 F.2d 41 (5th Cir. 1975).

84. 457 F.2d 348 (5th Cir. 1972).

85. *Id.* at 358.

86. 369 F. Supp at 1231.

87. See *Jersey Central Power & Light Co.* v. *Local 327, IBEW,* 508 F.2d 687 (3d Cir. 1975); *Waters* v. *Wisconsin Steel Works,* 502 F.2d 1309 (7th Cir. 1974) And compare *Chance* v. *Board of Examiners,* 11 EPD ¶10,633 (2d Cir. 1976), with *Acha* v. *Beame,* 11 EPD ¶10,740 (2d Cir. 1976).

88. 516 F.2d 41 (5th Cir. 1975).

89. *Id.* at 44–45.

90. *Id.* at 45. See generally Clyde Summers and Margaret Love, "Work Sharing as an Alternative to Layoffs by Seniority," 24 *U. of Penna. L. Rev.* 893 (1976).

91. 516 F.2d at 46.

92. *Franks* v. *Bowman Transportation Co.,* 11 EPD at p. 7263 n.38 (Brennan, J., for the Court); *id.* at 7264 (Burger, C.J., concurring and dissenting).

93. Compare Chief Justice Burger's opinion for the Court in *Griggs* v. *Duke Power Co.,* 401 U.S. 424 (1971), with his concurring and dissenting opinion in *Albermarle Paper Co.* v. *Moody,* 422 U.S. 405, 449 (1975).

94. See discussion in sec.: "Societal Discrimination."

95. *Quarles* v. *Philip Morris,* n.21; see also *Patterson* v. *American Tobacco Co.,* 11 EPD ¶10,728 at p. 7016.

96. *Keyes* v. *School District No. 1, Denver, Colo.,* 413 U.S. 189 (1973), discussed in Ch. 1, text at n.28.

97. 401 U.S. 424 (1971).

98. The Chief Justice made the statement in a CBS television interview.

99. 401 U.S. at 429–431.

100. 422 U.S. 405, 416, 418 (1975).

101. 401 U.S. at 430–431.

102. 395 U.S. 285 (1969).

103. 42 U.S.C. § 1973 et seq. (1970).

104. 401 U.S. at 432 (italics in original).

105. 422 U.S. at 423.

106. See Ch. 3, sec.: "Statistical Evidence and the Burden of Proof."

107. See, e.g., *Chance* v. *Board of Examiners,* 458 F.2d 1167 (2d Cir. 1972); *Castro* v. *Beecher,* 459 F.2d 725 (1st Cir. 1972); *Vulcan Society* v. *Civil Service Comm'n,* 490 F.2d 387 (2d Cir. 1973); *Bridgeport Guardians, Inc.* v. *Bridgeport Civil Service Comm'n,* 482 F.2d 1333 (2d Cir. 1973). But see *Washington* v. *Davis,* 426 U.S. 229 (1976) for constitutional standards.

108. See the discussion of the 1866 Act and *Jones* v. *Alfred H. Meyer Co.,* in Ch. 2, Sec.: "Civil Rights Act of 1866."

109. 395 U.S at 289.

110. *San Antonio Independent School District* v. *Rodriquez,* 411 U.S. 1 (1973).

111. § 703(h), 42 U.S.C. § 2000e-2(h).

112. 472 F.2d 631 (9th Cir. 1972). But see *Jimerson* v. *Kisco Co.,* 13 FEP Cases 997 (8th Cir. 1976).

113. *Green* v. *Missouri-Pacific RR.,* 523 F.2d 1290 (8th Cir. 1975). See also *Carter* v. *Gallagher,* 452 F.2d 315, 326 (8th Cir.), *cert. denied,* 406 U.S. 950 (1972).

114. On the impediments to rape convictions, and the factors which discourage an estimated 80 percent of rape victims from reporting the crime, see generally "Comment: Rape and Rape Laws: Sexism in Society and Law," 61 *Calif. L. Rev.* 919 (1973).

115. 494 F.2d 674 (8th Cir. 1974).

116. For example, the Supreme Court's decision in *Fibreboard Paper Prods. Corp.* v. *NLRB,* 379 U.S. 203 (1964), that an employer has a duty to bargain to impasse over certain types of subcontracting decisions, turned in part on the impact such decisions have on employees (at 211–212). And the NLRB has subsequently stressed the "impact" criterion in cases involving decisions to subcontract, e.g., *Westinghouse Elec. Corp.,* 150 NLRB 1574 (1965), even where a major change in business operations is involved, *Adams Dairy,* 137 NLRB 815 (1962), *enforcement denied,* 322 F.2d 553 (8th Cir. 1963), remanded for reconsideration, 379 U.S. 644 (1965), original opinion affirmed on reconsideration, 350 F.2d 108 (8th Cir. 1965), *cert. denied,* 382 U.S. 1011 (1966), as well as in cases involving decisions to close part of a business, *Ozark Trailers, Inc.,* 161 NLRB 561 (1966).

117. *Gregory* v. *Litton Systems, Inc.,* 316 F. Supp. 401, 403 (C.D. Cal. 1970), *aff'd as modified,* 472 F.2d 631 (9th Cir. 1972).

118. Since school segregation in the North is generally *de facto* rather than *de jure,* most northern segregation will continue to go unremedied until the courts recognize segregation to be unconstitutional even in a *de facto* context. There are some promising signs that *de facto* segregation will eventually be declared unconstitutional; see the authorities cited in Ch. 1, n.1. Judge Marvin Frankel noted in *Rios* v. *Steamfitters Local 638,* 326 F. Supp. 198, 203 n.4 (S.D.N.Y. 1971), that cases such as *Taylor* v. *Board of Educ. of New Rochelle,* 1971 F. Supp. 181 (S.D.N.Y.), *aff'd,* 294 F.2d 36 (2d Cir.), *cert. denied,* 368 U.S. 940 (1961), the first major case ordering desegregation in the North, cut against the notion that *Griggs* is a southern, rather than a national, case.

5 | Remedies (I): Quotas, Ratios, Goals, and Timetables

1. § 706(g), 42 U.S.C. § 200e-5(g) (Supp. II, 1972).

2. *Id.*

3. 118 *Cong. Rec.* 1661–1676, 4917–4918 (1972).

4. *United States* v. *IBEW Local 212,* 472 F.2d 634, 636 (6th Cir. 1973). Curiously, Judge Paul Hays of the Second Circuit completely ignored this legislative history while dissenting in *Rios* v. *Enterprise Ass'n. Steamfitters Local 638* 501 F.2d 622, 634 (2d Cir. 1974).

5. Exec. Order No. 11478 § 23 C.F.R. 207 (1974), 42 U.S.C. 200e (1970). See Ch. 2, sec.: "The Presidential Executive Order."

6. 380 U.S. 145, 154 (1965).

7. *Local 53, Heat & Frost Insulation* v. *Vogler,* 407 F.2d 1047 (5th Cir. 1969), discussed in Ch. 4 at n.1.

8. Several courts have held that, even apart from practices of nepotism, Title VII may be violated if a union keeps its membership lower than industry needs justify. See, e.g., *Local 53, Heat & Frost Insulators* v. *Vogler,* 407 F.2d 1047, 1055 (5th Cir. 1969); *United States* v. *Lathers Local 46,* 471 F.2d 408, 414 (2d Cir. 1973), *cert. denied,* 412 U.S. 939 (1974); *United States* v. *Local 638 Steamfitters,* 347 F. Supp. 169, 181 (S.D.N.Y. 1972). Although in each of these cases the discriminatory impact of the exclusionary practices on blacks was shown, Judge Frankel has suggested (albeit with regard to nepotism and other practices of favortism) that "because courts may know what all the world knows, [such] practices . . . could, and probably should, be condemned as inevitably discriminatory *per se.*" *United States* v. *Lathers Local 46,* 328 F. Supp. 429, 436 (S.D.N.Y. 1971).

9. For data on the uneven employment advances made by blacks (e.g. over 25 percent of employers reporting to EEOC have no black employees), see Andrew Brimmer, "Widening Horizons: Prospects for Black Employment," 25 *Labor L.J.* 323, 327 (1974).

10. On the effects of discriminatory reputation, see, e.g., *United States* v. *Sheet Metal Workers Local 36,* 416 F.2d 123 (8th Cir. 1969); *Sabala* v. *Western Gillette, Inc.,* 516 F.2d 1251, 1256 (5th Cir. 1975); *Hairston* v. *McLean Trucking Co.,* 520 F.2d 226, 232 (4th Cir. 1975); *Rodriguez* v. *East Texas Motor Freight,* 505 F.2d 40, 55 (5h Cir. 1974); *Bing* v. *Roadway Express, Inc.,* 485 F.2d 441, 451, (5th Cir. 1973); *Jones* v. *Lee Way Motor Freight,* 431 F.2d 245, 247 (10th Cir. 1970), *cert. denied,* 401 U.S. 954 (1970); *United States* v. *Local 86 Ironworkers,* 315 F. Supp. 1202, 1234 (W.D. Wash. 1970), *aff'd* 443 F.2d 544 (9th Cir. 1971), *cert. denied,* 404 U.S. 984 (1971); *United States* v. *Central Motor Lines, Inc.,* 338 F. Supp. 532 (M.D.N.C. 1971).

11. Ch. 12, at n.6.

12. 347 U.S. 483 (1954) (Brown I); 349 U.S. 294 (1955) (Brown II). On the school desegregation cases see generally Ch. 1.

13. 373 U.S. 526 (1963).

14. *Id.* at 539.

15. 391 U.S. 430, 438, 439 (1968) (emphasis in original).

16. 402 U.S. 1 (1971).

17. *Id.* at 25.

18. Ch. 11, text at n.10–14.

19. 442 F.2d 159 (3d Cir.), *cert. denied,* 404 U.S. 854 (1971).

20. *Id.* at 170.

21. *Id.* at 177.

22. *Id.* at 173.

23. *Id.* at 172.

24. *Id.* at 173.

25. 452 F.2d 315 (8th Cir.) (reporting both panel and en banc opinions), *cert. denied,* 406 U.S. 950 (1972).

26. *Id.* at 325.

27. *Id.* at 325–326.

28. *Id.* at 328.

29. *Id.* at 329, *citing United States* v. *Ironworkers Local 86,* 443 F.2d 544 (9th Cir.), *cert. denied,* 404 U.S. 984 (1971) (discussed in Ch. 13,), *Local 53, Heat & Frost Insulators* v. *Vogler,* 407 F.2d 1047 (5th Cir. 1969) (discussed in Ch. 13, at n.1); *United States* v. *Central Motor Lines, Inc.,* 325 F. Supp. 478 (W.D.N.C. 1970).

30. 452 F.2d at 330–331.

31. *Id.* at 332.

32. 340 F. Supp. 703 (M.D. Ala. 1972); reconsideration directed 7 EPD ¶9089 (5th Cir. 1973); *decree reaff'd after reconsideration sub. nom. NAACP* v. *Dothard,* 373 F. Supp. 504 (M.D. Ala. 1974), *aff'd,* 493 F.2d 614 (5th Cir. 1974).

33. 340 F. Supp. at 705.

34. 493 F.2d 614 (5th Cir. 1974).

35. *Id.* at 618.

36. *Id.* at 619.

37. *Morrow* v. *Crisler,* 479 F.2d 960 (5th Cir. 1973), *aff'd in part and rem'd in part on rehearing,* 491 F.2d 1053 (5th Cir. 1974), *cert. denied,* 419 U.S. 895, (1974).

38. *Id*. at 964.

39. *Id*.

40. *Id*. at 971.

41. *Id*. at 972.

42. *Id*.

43. *Id*.

44. *Morrow* v. *Crisler,* 491 F.2d 1053 (5th Cir. 1974) (en banc).

45. *Id*. at 1055.

46. *Id*. at 1056.

47. *Id*.

48. 493 F.2d at 620–621.

49. 501 F.2d 622, 631 (2d Cir. 1974). *Rios* seems to have ushered in a period of uncertainty in the Second Circuit with regard to quotas—an uncertainty apparently not shared by other circuits. Prior to *Rios* unanimous panels of the Second Circuit had approved quota remedies in both the public sector, Bridgeport Guardians, Inc. v. *Civil Service Commn,* 482 F.2d 1333 (2d Cir. 1973); *Vulcan Society* v. *Civil Service* v. *Civil Service Commn,* 490 F.2d 387 (2d Cir. 1973), and private sector, *United States* v. *Wood, Wire & Metal Lathers Local 46,* 471 F.2d 408 (2d Cir.), *cert. denied,* 412 U.S. 939 (1973); see also *Patterson* v. *Newspaper & Mail Deliveries Union,* 514 F.2d 767 (2d Cir. 1975).

But in *Rios* the unanimity was broken; the panel approved the quota remedy but Judge Paul Hays dissented. Subsequently in *Kirkland* v. *New York State Dep't of Correctional Services,* 520 F.2d 420 (2d Cir. 1975), a panel of the Second Circuit adumbrated a sharply narrowed view of the permissible role of quota remedies. The *Kirkland* approach, as described in *EEOC* v. *Local 638 Sheet Metal Workers,* 11 EPD ¶10,757 at p. 7181 (2d Cir. 1976) is that "the imposition of a racial goal can be justified only when two conditions are met: there must be a long and egregious pattern of past discrimination and the effects of the goal cannot fall upon a relatively small, identifiable group of reverse discriminates." Judge Walter Mansfield, joined by Chief Judge Irving Kaufman and Judge James Oakes, vigorously dissented from the denial of rehearing en banc in *Kirkland,* in an opinion which described the case as a clear departure from precedent in the Second Circuit and eight other Circuits 10 EPD ¶10,547 (2d Cir. 1975).

In addition, a panel of the Second Circuit, Judge Oakes dissenting, has relied on *Kirkland* in rejecting a broad attack on a "last-hired, first-fired" seniority system. *Chance* v. *Board of Examiners,* 11 EPD ¶10,633 (2d Cir. 1976). Compare *Acha* v. *Beame,* 11 EPD ¶10,740 (2d Cir. 1976).

In addition to the dissents in *Rios, Kirkland,* and *Chance,* separate concurring opinions were written in *Patterson, Local 638,* and *Acha.* The court is obviously deeply divided, and it is far from clear whether *Kirkland* will ultimately emerge as the law of the Second Circuit.

Although goals and timetables have been upheld in the absence of a finding of past discrimination, *Contractors Association* v. *Schultz,* 442 F.2d 159 (3d Cir. 1971), *cert. denied* 404 U.S. 854 (1971); *Southern Illinois Builders Association* v. *Ogilvie,* 471 F.2d 680 (7th Cir. 1972), it would seem as though something akin to a judicial proceeding may be required. *Associated General Contractors* v. *Altshuler,* 490 F.2d 9 (1st Cir. 1973), *cert. denied* 416 U.S. 957 (1974). See especially *Weber* v. *Kaiser Aluminum & Chemical Corporation,* 45 U.S.L.W. 2018 (E. La. 1976).

50. 491 F.2d at 1056.

51. See Ch. 4 n.73.

52. 501 F.2d st 632.

53. 369 F. Supp. 1221, 1231 (E.D. La. 1974), *judgment entered* 8 FEP Cases 729 (E.D. La. 1974), *rev'd and rem'd,* 516 F.2d 41 (5th Cir. 1975), discussed in Ch. 4, sec.: "The 'Last Hired/First Fired' Controversy."

54. 485 F.2d 441 (5th Cir. 1973).

55. See also *United States* v. *T.I.M.E.–D.C., Inc.* 517 F.2d 299, 318 (5th Cir. 1975); *Rodriquez* v. *East Texas Motor Freight,* 505 F.2d 40, 63 (5th Cir. 1974); *United States* v. *Navajo Freight Lines, Inc.,* 10 EPD ¶10,503 at p. 6142 (9th Cir. 1975).

56. 369 F. Supp. at 1232.

57. 495 F.2d 398, 417 n.17 (5th Cir.) *cert. denied,* 419 U.S. 1050 (1974).

58. Cases cited n.29.

59. *United States* v. *Jacksonville Terminal Co.,* 451 F.2d 418 (5th Cir. 1971), *cert. denied,* 406 U.S. 906 (1972).

60. *Waters* v. *Wisconsin Steel Works, 502 F.2d 1309 (7th Cir. 1974).*

61. *Id.* at 1318, 1320. See generally Ch. 4, sec.: "The 'Last Hired/First Fired" Controversy."

62. John Kaplan, "Equal Justice in an Unequal World: Equality for the Negro: The Problem of Special Treatment," 61 *Nw. L. Rev.* 363, 375 (1966).

63. 424 U.S. 747, 11 EPD ¶10,777 at p. 7263 (1976).

64. 446 F.2d 652, 663 (2d Cir. 1971).

65. 482 F.2d 1333, 1341 (2d Cir. 1973).

66. 360 F. Supp. 1265, (5.D.N.Y. 1973), *aff'd,* 490 F.2d 387 (2d Cir. 1973).

67. *Id.* at 1278. However, Judge Edward Weinfeld subsequently fashioned a temporary quota remedy in *Vulcan,* see 490 F.2d at 391, which was approved by the Court of Appeals, *id.* at 398–399.

68. 340 F. Supp. at 706.

69. 457 F.2d 348 (5th Cir. 1972).

70. Kaplan, pp. 370–371.

71. See Ch. 13.

72. See cases cited in Ch. 4, n.55.

73. See *United States* v. *Roadway Express, Inc.,* 457 F.2d 854 (6th Cir. 1972).

74. 10 EPD ¶10,503 (9th Cir. 1975).

75. 493 F.2d at 618–619.

76. *Id.* at 621.

77. *See* e.g., *Erie Human Relations Comm'n* v. *Tullio,* 493 F.2d 371, 374–375 (3d Cir. 1974); *United States* v. *Lathers Local 46,* 471 F.2d 408, 414 n.12 (2d Cir. 1973), *cert. denied,* 412 U.S. 939 (1974); *Rios* v. *Steamfitters Local 638,* 501 F.2d 622, 628 n.3 (2d Cir. 1974).

78. 388 U.S. 1 (1967). *Loving* makes it clear that a law based on an "invidious" racial classification cannot stand, even if the law applies equally to whites and blacks. The doctrine that classifications (such as those based on race) which affect "discrete and insular minorities" are constitutionally suspect had its genesis in the famous footnote 4 in *United States* v. *Carolene Products Co.,* 304 U.S. 144 (1938).

79. 411 U.S. 677, 684 (1973).

80. *Id.* at 686.

81. Civil Rights Act of 1886, 14 Stat. 27, *as amended* 42 U.S.C. §§ 1981, 1982 (1970); 1870 Enforcement Act, 16 Stat. 140, as amended 18 U.S.C. § 241 (1970); Civil Rights Act of 1871, 17 Stat. 13, *as amended* 42 U.S.C. § 1938, 28 U.S.C. § 1343(3) (1970), Civil Rights Act of 1875, 18 Stat. 335, 337, Civil Rights Act of 1957, 71 Stat. 634, 5 U.S.C. § 5315(19), 8 U.S.C. §§ 1843, 1861, 42 U.S.C. 1995; 73 Stat. 724, 42 U.S.C. §§ 1971, 1975, 1975a-e, 1995; 73 Stat. 724, 42 U.S.C. § 1975c; 74 Stat. 89, 42 U.S.C. §§ 1971, 1975d; 75 Stat. 559, 42 U.S.C. § 1975c; 77 Stat. 271, 42 U.S.C. § 1975c; 78 Stat. 249, 42 U.S.C. §§ 1975a-d; 81 Stat. 582, 42 U.S.C. §§ 1975c, 1975e; 84 Stat. 1356, 1357, 42 U.S.C. §§ 1975a, b, d, e (1970); Civil Rights Act of 1960, 74 Stat. 86, 18 U.S.C. §§ 837, 1074, 1509, 20 U.S.C. §§ 241, 640, 42 U.S.C. §§ 1971, 1974–1974e, 1975d) (1970); Civil Rights Act of 1964, 78 Stat. 241, 28 U.S.C. § 1447, 42 U.S.C. § 1971, 1975a-1975D, 200a-200h-6) (1970). Voting Rights Act of 1965, 79 Stat. 437, 42 U.S.C. §§ 1971, 1973–1973p; 52 Stat. 75, 42 U.S.C. § 1973; 84 Stat. 315, 42 U.S.C. §§ 1973b, 1973c, 1973aa-bb-4; 84 Stat 314, 315, 42 U.S.C. §§ 1973, 1973b, c, aa-bb-4 (1970).

82. Paul Brest, *Processes of Constitutional Decisionmaking* (Boston, 1975), p. 482.

83. 493 F.2d at 621.

84. Kaplan, p. 381.

85. *Id.* p. 380 (emphasis added).

86. *Id.* p. 374.

87. Bayard Rustin, "The Failure of Black Separatism," *Harper's,* Jan. 1970, pp. 25, 31.

88. Kaplan, p. 374.

89. 334 F. Supp. 930, 943, 945 (D. Mass. 1971), *aff'd in part, rev'd in part,* 459 F.2d 725 (1st Cir. 1972), *consent decree entered,* 365 F. Supp. 655 (D. Mass. 1973).

90. 459 F.2d 725, 731 (1st Cir. 1972).

91. 365 F. Supp. 655 (D. Mass. 1973).

92. Boris Bittker, *The Case for Black Reparations* (New York, 1973), p. 21.

93. *Id.* p. 91.

94. Kaplan, p. 379.

95. 416 F.2d 980, 995 (5th Cir. 1969), *cert. denied,* 397 U.S. 919 (1970) (emphasis added).

96. 451 F.2d 418, 459–460 (5th Cir. 1971), *cert. denied,* 406 U.S. 906 (1972).

97. See *McDonnell Douglas Corp.* v. *Green,* 463 F.2d 337, 352–353 (8th Cir. 1972), remanded on other grounds, 411 U.S. 792 (1973) Cf. *United States* v. *St. Louis-San Francisco Ry.,* 464 F.2d 301, 310 (8th Cir. 1972), *cert. denied.* 409 U.S. 1116 (1973).
98. The text of the decree is reported at *BNA FEP Manual* 431: 73 (1973).
99. 411 U.S. 792, 802 (1973), discussed in Ch. 3, sec.: *"McDonnell Douglas Corp.* v. *Green."*
100. 352 F. Supp. 135, 137, 141 (E.D. Mich. 1972), *reversed,* 496 F.2d (6th Cir. 1974).
101. 496 F.2d 500, 505 (6th Cir. 1974).
102. 440 F.2d 1157 (8th Cir. 1971).
103. 315 F. Supp. 1202, 1247–1249 (W.D. Wash. 1970), *aff'd* 443 F.2d 555 (9th Cir. 1971), *cert. denied,* 404 U.S. 984 (1971).
104. See Ch. 12.
105. The proposed Partial Consent Decree, pending in the case of *United States* v. *Trucking Employers, Inc.,* No. 74–453 (D.C.D.C. 1974), is being challenged by intervenor plaintiffs and is not yet in effect at the time of this writing.
106. 431 F.2d 245, 250 (10th Cir. 1970), *cert. denied,* 401 U.S. 954 (1971).
107. 416 F.2d at 990.
108. *Id.* at 983.
109. *Id.* at 988.
110. 464 F.2d 301 (8th Cir. 1972), *cert. denied,* 409 U.S. 1116 (1973).
111. *Id.* at 310.
112. "Record of Removal of Membership Restrictions Based on Race by AFL-CIO Affiliates, 1942–1963," memorandum prepared by AFL-CIO Department of Civil Rights, in *Hearings on S. 773, S. 1210, S. 1211, and S. 1937 Before the Subcomm. on Employment and Manpower of the Sen. Comm. on Labor and Public Welfare,* 88th Cong., 1st Sess. 160–162 (1963).
113. § 703(c)(2), 42 U.S.C. § 2000e-2(c)(2) (Supp. II, 1972).
114. *EEOC* v. *International Longshoremen's Ass'n,* 511 F.2d 273 (5th Cir. 1975), *cert. denied,* 96 U.S. 421, 10 EPD ¶10,511 (1975). See also *Ethridge* v. *Rhodes,* 268 F. Supp. 83, 88–89 (S.D. Ohio 1967).
115. 347 U.S. 483 (1954), discussed in Ch. 10.
116. 163 U.S. 537, 552 (1896) (dissenting opinion).
117. 343 U.S. 768 (1952).
118. Archibald Cox, "The Duty of Fair Representation," 2 *Vill. L. Rev.* 151, 158 (1957).
119. 460 F.2d 497 (4th Cir. 1972), *cert. denied,* 409 U.S. 1007 (1972). See also *EEOC* v. *ILA, supra* n. 114.
120. 460 F.2d at 500.
121. 262 F.2d 359, *cert. denied,* 359 U.S. 935 (1959).
122. 329 F. Supp. 1226 (E.D. Pa. 1971).
123. *Id.* at 1233, 1238.
124. *United States* v. *Chesapeake & Ohio Ry.,* 4 EPD ¶7637 (E.D. Va. 1971), *vacated in part on other grounds and remanded,* 471 F.2d 582, 585 (4th Cir. 1972), *cert. denied,* 411 U.S. 939 (1973); *Hicks* v. *Crown-Zellerbach Corp.,* 310 F. Supp. 536 (E.D. La. 1970); *Fluker* v. *United Papermakers, Locals 265 and 940,* 6 FEP Cases 92 (S.D. Ala. 1972); *English* v. *Seaboard Coast Line RR,* 4 FEP Cases 904 (S.D. Ga. 1972). But see *Long* v. *Georgia Kraft Co.,* 455 F.2d 331 (5th Cir. 1972): *Pettway* v. *American Cast Iron Pipe Co.,* 332 F. Supp. 811 (N.D. Ala. 1970), *rev'd and rem'd,* 494 F.2d 211, 266 (5th Cir. 1974).
125. *United States* v. *Chesapeake & Ohio Ry.*
126. See text at n.72.
127. 403 U.S. 124 (1971).
128. And subsequent to *Whitcomb* the Court has found a redistricting plan to violate the Fourteenth Amendment where past discrimination was shown. *White* v. *Regester,* 412 U.S. 755, 765–770 (1973).
129. *Georgia* v. *United States,* 411 U.S. 526, 534 (1973); *see also Allen* v. *State B. of Elections,* 393 U.S. 544, 569 (1969); *Perkins* v. *Matthews,* 400 U.S. 379 (1971).
130. But see *City of Richmond* v. *United States,* 422 U.S. 358 (1975). See generally Ch. 1, text at n.24–26.
131. See, e.g., *Vaca* v. *Sipes,* 386 U.S. 171 (1967); *Ford Motor Co.* v. *Huffman,* 345 U.S. 345 U.S. 330, 337–338 (1953).
132. 455 F.2d 331 (5th Cir. 1972).
133. *Id.* at 334.

134. *Id.* at 332.

135. *Id.* at 335–336.

136. EEOC Decision No. 73-0458, *CCH EEOC Decisions* ¶6377 (1972).

137. 494 F.2d 211 (5th Cir. 1974).

138. *Id.* at 266.

139. *Id.* at 266, citing *White* v. *Regester,* 412 U.S. 755, 765–770 (1973); *Connor* v. *Johnson,* 402 U.S. 690 (1971).

140. *Schultz* v. *Local 1291, ILA,* 338 F. Supp. 1204 (E.D. Pa. 1972), *aff'd* 461 F.2d 1262 (3d Cir. 1972) (per curiam); *Tucker* v. *Tobacco Workers Local* 183, 488 F.2d (4th Cir. 1973).

141. *Schultz,* at 1207–1208.

142. 457 F. 2d 348 (5th Cir. 1972).

143. *Smith* v. *YMCA,* 462 F.2d 634, 649–650 (5th Cir. 1972).

6 | Remedies (II): Back Pay, Punitive Damages, Attorneys' Fees, and Test Validation

1. § 706(g), 42 U.S.C. § 2000e-5(g)(1970).

2. 422 U.S. 405, 417 (1975). Before *Albemarle* was decided, the Fourth, Fifth, and Sixth Circuit Courts of Appeals had paved the way in developing the doctrine that backpay is generally to be awarded where discrimination is proved. In *Robinson* v. *Lorillard Corp.,* 444 F.2d 791, 803 (4th Cir.) *cert. dismissed,* 404 U.S. 1006 (1971), the Fourth Circuit concluded that the Title VII grant of remedial authority should be broadly read so as to make the victims of discrimination "whole." In *Head* v. *Timken Roller Bearing Co.,* 486 F.2d 870, 876 (6th Cir. 1973), the Sixth Circuit said that "the clear intent of Congress that the grant of authority under Title VII should be broadly read and applied mandates an award of back pay unless exceptional circumstances are present." And in *Johnson* v. *Goodyear Tire & Rubber Co.,* 491 F.2d 1364 (5th Cir. 1974); *Pettway* v. *American Cast Iron Pipe Co.,* 494 F.2d 211 (5th Cir. 1974); and *Baxter* v. *American Cast Iron Pipe Co.,* 494 F.2d 211 (5th Cir. 1974); and *Baxter* v. *Savannah Sugar Refining Co.,* 495 F.2d 437 (5th Cir.), *cert. denied,* 419 U.S. 1033 (1974), the Fifth Circuit further developed the "exceptional circumstances" approach, as well as the doctrine that once classwide discrimination is established, the burden shifts to the employer to prove that the individual class members were not in fact victims of the discriminating practices. Accord, *Stewart* v. *General Motors Corp.,* 13 FEP Cases 1035 (7th Cir. 1976).

3. *Id.* at 419–420.

4. *Id.* at 421.

5. *Id.* at 417, quoting *Griggs* v. *Duke Power Co.,* 401 U.S. 424, 429–430 (1970), discussed in Ch. 4, sec.: "Societal Discrimination." But this aspect seems to have been deemphasized by the line of cases which requires that public assistance be deducted from back pay because of the statute's compensatory objectives. See *EEOC* v. *Enterprise Association Steamfitters Local 638,* 13 FEP Cases, 705, 714–715 (2d Cir. 1976); *Satty* v. *Nashville Gas Co.,* 522 F.2d 850 (6th Cir. 1975), and compare the approach adopted under the National Labor Relations Act in *NLRB* v. *Gullett Gin Co.,* 340 U.S. 361 (1951).

6. 479 F.2d 354, 379 (8th Cir. 1973), quoted in part in *Albemarle,* 422 U.S. at 417–418.

7. 491 F.2d 1364, 1375 (5th Cir. 1974). Economic harm need not be evidenced. *Swint* v. *Pullman-Standard Company,* 13 FEP Cases, 605, 614 (5th Cir. 1976.)

8. *Id.*

9. *Id.* at n.30. See *Albemarle,* 422 U.S. at 414 n.8.

10. 494 F.2d 211, 259 (5th Cir. 1974).

11. *Id.*

12. *Id.* at 259–260.

13. 495 F.2d 437 (5th Cir. 1974), *cert denied, 419 U.S. 1033 (1974).*

14. *Franks* v. *Bowman Transportation Co.,* 424 U.S. 747, 11 EPD ¶10,777 at p. 7263 (1976).

15. 495 F.2d at 445. The Fifth circuit has recently reaffirmed the *Johnson, Pettway,* and *Baxter* approach to what the court termed "stage II" back pay proceedings, in which the entitlement of individual class members to back pay is determined following the "stage I" proof of classwide discrimination. In *United States* v. *United States Steel Corp.,* 520 F.2d 1043 (5th Cir. 1975), the court stated that "[t]o the extent that actual, historical vacancies in the employer's workforce can be flow-charted with reasonable accuracy, the court should award the back pay to the minority employees who, in its

sound judgment, would have occupied those vacancies but for discrimination. . . ." *Id.* at 1055. But the court stressed that where such a determination is impossible, the district court should not deny back pay but should use any of a number of "classwide approaches" which the court described. *Id.* at 1055–1056. Clearly, the inability of a class member to show that in the absence of discrimination he would have been hired into, or promoted into, a particular vacancy does not bar his recovery of back pay under the Fifth Circuit approach. Rather than being a matter for strict proof by the class members, entitlement to back pay is a matter for the "sound judgment" of the court (or special master); and where individual entitlement is impossible to ascertain, the court must be guided by the goal of "making the affected *class* whole." *Id.* at 1055 (emphasis added).

That the Fifth Circuit approach is proper seems clear from the Supreme Court's favorable citation of *Baxter* and the court's statement that where "a discriminatory hiring pattern and practice" is proved with respect to a class, "the burden will be upon [the defendant] to prove that individuals who reapply were not in fact victims of previous hiring discrimination. In *Franks* v. *Bowman Transportation Co.*, 424 U.S. 747, 11 EPD ¶10,777 at p. 7263 (1976). These matters are discussed further in sec.: "The Method of Computation."

16. *Pettway*, 494 F.2d at 252–253.

17. 347 U.S. 483 (1953), discussed in Ch. 1.

18. 339 U.S. 629 (1950).

19. 339 U.S. 637 (1950).

20. Bittker, *The Case for Black Reparations*, pp. 42–43.

21. 422 U.S. at 422.

22. *LeBlanc* v. *Southern Bell T&T Co.* 460 F.2d 1228 (5th Cir. 1972); *Manning* v. *General Motors Corp.*, 466 F.2d 812 (6th Cir. 1973). See also *Kober* v. *Westinghouse Electric Corp.*, 466 F.2d 240 (3d Cir. 1973).

23. 462 F.2d 1002, 1007 (9th Cir. 1972).

24. 293 F. Supp. 1219 (C.D. Cal. 1968), *aff'd* 444 F.2d 1219 (9th Cir. 1971).

25. 462 F.2d at 1007.

26. See Ch. 2, sec.: "Civil Rights Act of 1866."

27. *Steele* v. *Louisville & Nashville RR*, 323 U.S. 192 (1944), discussed in Ch. 2.

28. *Local 189, United Papermakers* v. *United States*, 416 F.2d 980, 991. (5th Cir. 1969), *cert. denied*, 397 U.S. 919 (1970), discussed in Ch. 4, text beginning at n.29.

29. 263 F.2d 546 (5th Cir. 1959), *cert. denied*, 360 U.S. 902 (1959).

30. *Griggs* v. *Duke Power Co.*, 401 U.S. 424 (1971), discussed in Ch. 4, sec.: "Societal Discrimination."

31. 457 F.2d 1377, 1379 (4th Cir. 1973), *cert. denied*, 409 U.S. 982 (1972).

32. *Jones* v. *Alfred H. Mayer Co.*, 392 U.S. 409 (1968), discussed in Ch. 2, beginning at n.76.

33. 457 F.2d at 1387 (dissenting opinion).

34. *United States* v. *National Lead Industries*, 479 F.2d at 379.

35. *Id.* at 380.

36. *Johnson*, 491 F.2d at 1377. See also *U.S. Steel*, at 1058–1059. Unlike *Brown*, where the defendant's argument was based on the unsettled state of employment discrimination law prior to the enactment of Title VII, in these cases the argument was that even the defendants' Post-Act testing and seniority practices were not foreseeably illegal until decisions such as *Griggs* and *Local 189* were handed down. That such arguments must be rejected is clear from *Albemarle*, where the District Court had accepted as a defense to back-pay liability the fact that "judicial decisions had only recently focused directly on the discriminatory impact of seniority systems." 422 U.S. at 422 n.15. The Supreme Court rejected the defense, noting that Title VII specifically immunizes employer conduct undertaken in reliance on "any written interpretation or opinion" of the EEOC, 42 U.S.C. § 2000e-12(b), and that "it is not for the courts to upset this legislative choice to recognize only a narrowly defined 'good faith' defense." *Id.* at 423 n.17.

37. *Pettway*, 494 F.2d at 253; *Johnson*, 491 F.2d at 1377.

38. *Johnson*, 491 F.2d at 1376.

39. See *House Rpt.* No. 92–238 at 65–66 (1971); 117 *Cong. Rec.* 31973, 31974 (1971) (remarks of Congressman Erlenborn); 117 *Cong. Rec.* 31979 (1971) (remarks of Congressman Dent); 117 *Cong. Rec.* 31981 (1971) (remarks of Congressman Erlenborn); 117 *Cong. Rec.* 40290 (1971) (reprint of article by Senator Dominick).

40. § 706(g), 42 U.S.C. § 2000e-5(g) (Supp. II, 1972).

41. 474 F.2d 906, 922–925 (5th Cir. 1973).

42. *Id.* at 922.

43. See, e.g. *Jones* v. *United Gas Improvement Co.,* 8 FEP Cases 821, 829 (E.D. Pa. 1974); *Waters* v. *Wisconsin Steel Works,* 427 F.2d 476, 488 (7th Cir.) *cert. denied,* 400 U.S. 911 (1970); cf. *Lazard* v. *Boeing Co.,* 322 F. Supp. 343, 345–345 (E.D. La. 1971); E. Richard Larson, ''The Development of Section 1981 as a Remedy for Racial Discrimination in Private Employment,'' 7 *Harv. Civ. Rights*–Civil Lib. L. Rev. 56, 81–82 (1972).

44. See, e.g., *Green* v. *McDonnell Douglas Corp.,* 318 F. Supp. 846, 849 (E.D. Mo. 1970), *aff'd* 463 F.2d 337, 340 (8th Cir. 1972), *rev'd on other grds.,* 411 U.S. 792 n.5 (1973); *Broadnax* v. *Burlington Industries, Inc.,* 7 FEP Cases 252, 255–256 (M.D.N.C. 1972); *Page* v. *Curtiss-Wright Corp.,* 322 F. Supp. 1060, 1065, (D.N.J. 1971). However, these cases dealt with the issue of which statute of limitations governed the timeliness of the filing of the complaint in a§ 1981 suit, not the question of the period over which back pay would accrue under Title VII, and there does not appear to be a case applying a contracts statute of limitations to the back pay question.

45. See, e.g. *EEOC* v. *Detroit Edison Co.,* 515 F.2d 301, 315 (6th Cir. 1975); *Marlowe* v. *Fisher Body,* 489 F.2d 1057, 1063 (6th Cir. 1973); *Johnson* v. *Goodyear Tire & Rubber Co.,* 491 F.2d 1364, 1378 (5th Cir. 1974). Persuasive arguments that Title VII cases, with their wide range of equitable remedies, cannot be analogized to common law tort actions for damages, appear in the *Jones* and *Lazard* cases and the Larson article, all cited in n.43.

46. See, e.g., *United States* v. *Georgia Power Co.,* 474 F.2d 906, 924 (5th Cir. 1973); *Franks* v. *Bowman Transportation Co.,* 495 F.2d 398, 405–406 (5th Cir. 1974); *Pettway* v. *American Cast Iron Pipe Co.,* 494 F.2d 211, 258 (5th Cir. 1974); *Boudreaux* v. *Baton Rouge Marine Contracting Co.,* 437 F.2d 1011, 1017 n.16 (5th Cir. 1971).

47. 474 F.2d at 924.

48. *Hamm* v. *City of Rock Hill,* 379 U.S. 306 (1964).

49. 494 F.2d at 255–256.

50. 491 F.2d at 1378.

51. *Id.* at 1379.

52. 494 F.2d at 261.

53. *Id.* at 262.

54. 371 F. Supp. 385, 392–393 (S.D. Tex. 1974), *aff'd. on this grd., rev'd in part on other grds.,* 516 F.2d 1251 (5th Cir. 1975).

55. 328 F. Supp. 429, 433 (S.D.N.Y. 1971).

56. *Id.* at 444–445.

57. See, e.g. *NLRB* v. *Izzi Trucking Co.,* 395 F.2d 241 (1st Cir. 1968); *NLRB* v. *Rice Lake Creamery Co.,* 365 F.2d 8888 (D.C. Cir. 1966); *Mastro Plastics Corp.,* 136 NLRB 1342 (1962).

58. Government's Memorandum in Support of Back Pay Claims, *United States* v. *Lathers Local 46,* No. 68 Civ. 2116 (S.D.N.Y. Jan. 8, 1973), at 13–15, 22, 24–27, 37; Government's Reply Memorandum in Support of Back Pay Claims (Feb. 16, 1973), at 8–17. See generally Ch. 12, sec.: *United States* v. *Lathers Union, Local No. 46.''*

59. For example, in cases involving discrimination in transfer and promotion, some courts, faced with the impossibility of determining which class members would have been promoted into which vacancies in the absence of discrimination, have simply estimated the employer's total liability and divided it among the class members in some equitable fashion. See *Head* v. *Timken Roller Bearing Co.,* 7 FEP Cases 987 (S.D. Ohio 1974); cf. *United States* v. *U.S. Steel Corp.,* 520 F.2d 1043, 1055–1056 (5th Cir. 1975): use of ''pro rata shares''.

60. 494 F.2d at 260–261.

61. See generally Ch. 4, sec.: ''Further Thoughts on 'Freedom Now.' ''

62. 365 F. Supp. 87, 121–22 (E.D. Mich. 1973), *rev'd in part on other grds.,* 10 FEP Cases 239 (6th Cir. 1975).

63. *Patterson* v. *American Tobacco Co.,* 535 F.2d 257 (4th Cir. 1976). But see *Sabala* v. *Western Gillette, Inc.,* 516 F.2d 1251, 1265 (5th Cir. 1975). Subsequently front pay was accepted by the Sixth and Seventh Circuits. See *Detroit Edison, supra,* and *EEOC* v. *Enterprise Association Steamfitters Local 638,* n.5.

64. 8 FEP Cases 729 (E.D. La. 1974), *entering judgment following* 369 F. Supp. 1221 (E. D. La. 1974), *rev'd and rem'd,* 516 F.2d 41 (5th Cir. 1975). See generally Ch. 4, sec.: ''The 'Last-Hired, First-Fired.' ''

65. *Id.* at 731.

66. 100 *Cong. Rec.* 7213 (1964).

67. *Franks* v. *Bowman Transportation Co.,* 424 U.S. 747, 11 EPD ¶10,777 at p. 7263 n.38.

68. *United States* v. *Navaho Freight Lines, Inc.*, 525 F.2d 1318, 1327–1328 (9th Cir. 1975).

69. Holding punitive damages awardable under Title VII: *Mills* v. *Memorex, Inc.*, 12 FEP Cases 593 (N.D. Cal. 1974); *Claiborne* v. *Illinois Central RR*, 11 FEP Cases 811 (E.D. La. 1974); *Gary* v. *Industrial Indemnity Co.*, 7 FEP Cases 193 (N.D. Cal. 1973); *Dessenberg* v. *American Metal Forming Co.*, 6 FEP Cases 159 (N.D. Ohio 1973); *Tooles* v. *Kellogg Co.*, 336 F. Supp. 14 (D. Neb. 1972; *Tidwell* v. *American Oil Co.*, 2 FEP Cases 1121 (D. Utah 1970); *Wells* v. *Bank of America*, 7 FEP Cases 885 (S.D. Cal. 1973). Cf. *Evans* v. *Sheraton Park Hotel*, 503 F.2d 177 (D.C. Cir. 1974). *Contra, EEOC* v. *Detroit Edison Co.*, 515 F.2d 301 (6th Cir. 1975); *Waters* v. *Heublein, Inc.*, 12 FEP Cases 617, 622 (N.D. Cal. 1975); *Opara* v. *Modern Mfg. Co.*, 12 FEP Cases 378, 380–381 (D.Md. 1975); *Tietz* v. *Iron Workers Local 10*, 12 FEP Cases 381 (W.D. Mo. 1975); *Carrenthers* v. *Alexander*, 11 FEP Cases 475, 481 (D. Colo. 1974); *Smith* v. *Liberty Mutual Ins. Co.*, 11 FEP Cases 732 (N.D. Ga. 1973); *Bradshaw* v. *Zoological Society*, 10 FEP Cases 1268, 1271 (S.D. Cal. 1975) *Grohal* v. *Stauffer Chemical Co.*, 10 FEP Cases 785 (N.D. Cal. 1974); *Hunter* v. *United Air Lines*, 10 FEP Cases 787 (N.D. Cal. 1974); *Howard* v. *Mercantile Commerce Trust Co.*, 10 FEP Cases 158–160 (E.D. Mo. 1974); *Jiron* v. *Sperry Rand Corp.*, 10 FEP Cases 731 (D. Utah 1975); *Loo* v. *Gerarge*, 374 F. Supp. 854 (D. Hi. 1974); *Howard* v. *Lockheed-Georgia Co.*, 372 F. Supp. 854 (N.D. Ga. 1974); *Van Hoomissen* v. *Xerox.*, 368 F. Supp. 829 (N.D. Cal. 1973); *Mills* v. *Cox*, 13 FEP Case 1009 (E.D.N.Y. 1976); *Whitney* v. *Greater N.Y. Corp.*, 13 FEP Cases 1194 (S.D.N.Y. 1976).

70. *Johnson* v. *Railway Express Agency*, 421 U.S. 454, 460 (1975).

71. H.R. Rep. No. 88–914 (1963) at p. 60.

72. *Culpepper* v. *Reynolds Metals Co.*, 421 F.2d 888, 891 (5th Cir. 1970).

73. Comment, "Developments in the Law: Employment Discrimination and Title VII of the Civil Rights Act of 1964," 84 *Harv. L. Rev.*, 1109, 1261 (1971). See also "Comment, Implying Punitive Damages in Employment Discrimination Cases," 9 *Harv. Civ. Rights Civ. Lib. L. Rev.* 269 (1974).

74. *Murry* v. *American Standard, Inc.*, 488 F.2d 529 (5th Cir. 1973); *Culpepper* v. *Reynolds Metals Co.*, 421 F.2d 888 (5th Cir. 1970); *United States* v. *Hayes International Corp.*, 415 F.2d 1038 (5th Cir. 1969).

75. *Hayes International.*

76. *Murry; Culpepper.*

77. *Culpepper*, at 895.

78. 480 F.2d 69 (5th Cir. 1973).

79. *Id.* at 72. Accord, *Berg* v. *Richmond Unified School Dist.*, 10 EPD ¶10,533 (9th Cir. 1975). Even where preliminary injunctive relief is not sought, it may be possible to bring a private action without waiting 180 days, if the EEOC backlog will prevent the commission from engaging in conciliation efforts during that period. See Ch. 2, n.60.

80. See cases cited in Ch. 8, n.68.

81. 390 U.S. 400–402 (1968).

82. 422 U.S. at 415. Distinction of actions arising under 42 U.S.C. § 1981, arguably compelled by the Court's decision in *Alyeska Pipeline Service Company* v. *Wilderness Society*, 421 U.S. 240 (1975), has been set aside by the more recent Kennedy-Tunney Act, Public Law 74–559 (Oct. 19, 1976), granting courts the power to grant attorneys' fees in effecting relief under the Civil Rights Act of 1866.

83. 390 U.S. at 401–402.

84. *Clark* v. *American Marine Corp.*, 320 F. Supp. 709, 711 (E.D. La. 1970), *aff'd per curiam*, 437 F.2d 959 (5th Cir. 1971).

85. 6 *CCH EPD Cases* ¶8946 (N.D. Cal. 1973).

86. 488 F.2d 714 (5th Cir. 1974).

87. 6 *CCH EPD Cases* at p. 6033.

88. *Schaeffer* v. *San Diego Yellow Cabs, Inc.* 462 F.2d 1002, 1008 (9th Cir. 1972).

89. 488 F.2d at 218.

90. *Id.*

91. *Id.*

92. *Id.* at 719.

93. *Id.* at 719–720.

94. 401 U.S. 424 (1971). See Ch. 4, sec.: "Societal Discrimination."

95. 401 U.S. at 433–434. The "Guidelines on Employee Selection Procedures" appear at 29 C.F.R. pt. 1607 (1974).

96. 422 U.S. at 425.

97. 29 C.F.R. § 1607.3 (1974).

98. 29 C.F.R. § 1607.4 (1974).

99. See *Bridgeport Guardians, Inc.* v. *Civil Service Comm'n,* 482 F.2d 1333, 1337 and n.6 (2d Cir. 1973), and cases cited. In *Washington* v. *Davis,* 426 U.S. 229 (1976), the Court, albeit in the context of constitutional standards relating to public employment, seemed to relax some of the *Griggs* standards.

100. *Robinson* v. *Lorillard Corp.,* 444 F.2d 791, 798 n.7 (4th Cir.) *cert. dismissed,* 404 U.S. 1006 (1971).

101. 474 F.2d 906, 913 (5th Cir. 1973).

102. A showing of disproportionate exclusion may not be required under what I have described as the third branch of the *Griggs* decision, relating to practices which "freeze the status quo." See Ch. 4, text at n.67.

103. *Johnson* v. *Goodyear Tire & Rubber Co.,* 491 F.2d 1364, 1373 (5th Cir. 1974).

104. 29 C.F.R. § 1607.5(a)(1974) permits content or construct validation "where criterion-related validity is not feasible."

105. "Whatever Criteria are used they must represent major or critical work behaviors as revealed by careful job analyses." 29 C.F.R. § 1607.5(b)(3)(1974).

106. 29 C.F.R. § 1607.3(1974).

107. 29 C.F.R. § 1607.5(c)(2)(1974).

108. 29 C.F.R. § 1607.5(c)(1)(1974).

109. 474 F.2d at 915.

110. *United States* v. *Jacksonville Terminal Co.,* 451 F.2d 418, 456 (5th Cir. 1971), *cert. denied,* 406 U.S. 906 (1972).

111. 474 F.2d at 914.

112. See text at n.96.

113. 459 F.2d 725 (1st Cir. 1972).

114. 458 F.2d 1167 (2d Cir. 1972).

115. 459 F.2d at 733.

116. 458 F.2d at 1170.

117. *Id.* at 1176.

118. *Id.* at 1177.

7 | Some Aspects of Taft-Hartley and Racial Discrimination

1. 147 NLRB 1573 (1964).

2. *Pioneer Bus Co.,* 140 NLRB (1962).

3. 473 F.2d 471 (8th Cir. 1973).

4. *Id.* at 474.

5. *Id.* at 477.

6. See *General Motors Corp.,* 120 NLRB 1215 (1958). The Board's current craft severance criteria are presented in *Mallinckrodt Chemical Works,* 162 NLRB 387, 397 (1966). For a post-*Mallinckrodt* case in which the board gave weight to the fact that the industrial union had fairly represented the special interests of the craft workers, see *Holmberg, Inc.,* 162 NLRB 407, 410 (1966). See also *Dow Chemical Co.,* 202 NLRB 17, 19 (1973).

7. On the legitimacy of "benign classifications," see generally Ch. 6.

8. Bernard Meltzer, "The National Labor Relations Act and Racial Discrimination: The More Remedies, the Better?," 42 *U. Chi. L. Rev.* 1, 10 (1974). Compare Herbert Hill, "The National Labor Relations Act and the Emergence of Civil Rights Law: A New Priority in Federal Labor Policy," 11 *Harv. Civ. Rights Civ. Lib. L. Rev.* 299 (1976).

9. *Local 357 Teamsters* v. *NLRB,* 365 U.S. 667 (1961).

10. See Ch. 10, text at nn.42–49.

11. *Vaca* v. *Sipes,* 386 U.S. 171, 183 (1967).

12. See William B. Gould, "The Negro Revolution and the Law of Collective Bargaining," 34 *Fordham L.Rev.* 207, 231 (1965).

13. 140 NLRB 181 (1962), *enforcement denied,* 326 F.2d 172 (2d Cir. 1963).   .

14. NLRA § 7, 29 U.S.C. § 157(1970).

15. Michael Sovern, "The National Labor Relations Act and Racial Discrimination," 62 *Colum. L. Rev.* 563, 591–593 (1962).

16. NLRA § 7, 29 U.S.C. § 157(1970).

17. NLRA § 7, 29 U.S.C. § 157(1970).

18. 370 U.S. 9 (1962).

19. Concerted activities are protected even if they are "unnecessary and unwise." *NLRB* v. *Washington Aluminum Co.*, 370 U.S. 9, 16 (1962). *Accord, NLRB* v. *Mackay Radio & Telegraph Co.*, 304 U.S. 333, 344 (1938). Where such activities are in protest of racial discrimination, it is enough that the employees have a "reasonable basis" for believing there has been discrimination. *Tanner Motor Livery, Ltd.*, 166 NLRB 551, n.6 (1967).

20. 148 NLRB 1402 (1964), *remanded,* 349 F.2d 1 (9th Cir. 1965), *aff'd* 166 NLRB 551 (1967), *vacated and remanded,* 419 F.2d 216 (9th Cir. 1969).

21. On the "economic striker's right to reinstatement in the absence of permanent replacement, see *NLRB* v. *Mackay Radio & Telegraph Co.*, 304 U.S. 333 (1938); *NLRB* v. *Fleetwood Trailer Co.*, 389 U.S. 375 (1967); *Laidlaw Corp.*, 171 NLRB 1366 (1968) *aff'd,* 414 F.2d 99 (7th Cir. 1969), cert. denied, 397 U.S. 920 (1970); cf. *NLRB* v. *Great Dane Trailers, Inc.*, 388 U.S. 26 (1967); *NLRB* v. *Erie Register Corp.*, 373 U.S. 221 (1963). "Unfair labor practice strikers" are entitled to reinstatement even if permanent replacements have been hired, and even if the strike also had economic causes, e.g., *NLRB* v. *My Stones, Inc.*, 345 F.2d 494, 498 (7th Cir. 1963), *cert. denied,* 382 U.S. 824 (1965). Employer conduct can convert an economic strike into an unfair labor practice strike. *NLRB* v. *Pecheur Lozenge Co.*, 209 F.2d 393 (2d Cir. 1953), *cert. denied,* 347 U.S. 953 (1954).

22. Consider, for example, the range of union disciplinary measures which have been held not to constitute violations of § 8(b)(1)(A), especially the power to fine a member for exercising his § 7 "right to refrain" from crossing a picket line, *NLRB* v. *Allis-Chalmers Mfg. infra* n.153, and the power to expel a member for filing a decertification petition; see n.159.

23. See the discussion of the legislative history in *NLRB* v. *Teamsters Local 639, infra* n.24.

24. 362 U.S. 274, 290 (1960).

25. 366 U.S. 731 (1961).

26. See *General Motors Corp.*, 147 NLRB 509 (1964), *enforcement denied,* 345 F.2d 516 (6th Cir. 1965), where a board majority held that the union violated § 8(b)(1)(A) by contracting away a minority union's right to solicit and distribute literature on company property. See *NLRB* v. *Magnavox Co.*, 415 U.S. 322 (1974).

27. NLRA § 8(b)(2), 29 U.S.C. § 158(b)(3)(1970).

28. 150 NLRB 312 (1964), *enforced,* 368 F.2d 12 (5th Cir. 1966) *cert. denied,* 389 U.S. 837 (1967).

29. NLRA § 8(b)(3), 29 U.S.C. § 158(b)(3)(1970).

30. NLRA § 8(d), 29 U.S.C. § 158(d)(1970).

31. 147 NLRB at 1591–1592 (concurring and dissenting opinion).

32. *Id.* at 1593 (concurring and dissenting opinion), where Chairman Frank McCulloch and Member John Fanning, dissenting, adverted to an "isolated statement" by Congressman Hartley which indicated that the unions were to have a duty of good faith toward the individual worker as well as toward the employer. The dissenters, however, treated this as "certainly not sufficient to offset the language of the statute and the overwhelming burden of the legislative history." *Id.*

33. Sovern, p. 588.

34. Archibald Cox, "The Duty of Fair Representation," 2 *Vill. L. Rev.* 151, 173 (1957).

35. 368 F.2d 12 (5th Cir. 1966), *cert. denied,* 389 U.S. 387 (1967).

36. *Id.* at 20.

37. *Local 100, United Ass'n of Journeymen* v. *Borden,* 373 U.S. 690 (1963). *Accord, Local 207 Bridge Workers* v. *Perko,* 373 U.S. 701 (1963).

38. 368 F.2d at 23.

39. *Id.* at 24.

40. Author's interview with John Truesdale, executive secretary of NLRB.

41. 473 F.2d at 472.

42. *Id.* at 473.

43. See 93 *Cong. Rec.* 4400–4401 (1947), in which Sen. Claude Pepper sought and received assurance from Senators Joseph Ball and Robert Taft "that there is no provision of the bill which denies a labor union the right to prescribe the qualifications of its members, and that if the union wishes to discriminate in respect to membership, there is no provision in the bill which denies it the privilege of doing so."

44. "Mr. Taft . . . Let us take the case of unions which prohibit the admission of Negroes to membership. If they prohibit the admission of Negroes to membership, they may continue to do so." 93 *Cong. Rec.* 4193 (1947).

45. 473 F.2d at 474–475.

46. Sovern, pp. 607–608.

47. A transcript of this meeting is in the author's files.

48. Copies of a preliminary draft of the regulations were distributed to the NLRB's regional directors and a subcommittee of the ABA Labor Law Section for comment. See *BNA Labor Relations Yearbook* 1973, p. 77. But the proposed regulations were never published.

49. *Bekins Moving & Storage Co. of Florida, Inc.* 211 NLRB No. 7, 86 LRRM 1323, 1327 (1974).

50. *Id.*, 86 LRRM at 1325.

51. *Id.*, 86 LRRM at 1325.

52. *Id.*, 86 LRRM at 1326.

53. *Grants Furniture Plaza,* 213 NLRB No. 80 (1974). A second major gap in the *Bekins* doctrine was created by *Bell & Howell Co.,* 213 NLRB No. 79 (1974), in which the board, Chairman Edward Miller and Member Howard Jenkins dissenting, held that *Bekins* would not be applied to claims that a union engaged in sex discrimination. Members John Fanning and John Penello, who had dissented in *Bekins,* were joined by Member Ralph Kennedy, who stated that unlike race, sex is not clearly a "suspect classification." A third troubling development in the *Bekins* progeny is a reluctance to consider the effects of discrimination at the international union level. In *NLRB* v. *Bancroft Mfg. Co.*, 516 F.2d 436 (5th Cir. 1975), the court enforced the board's decision that the employer's subpoena for statistical data concerning the union's racial composition should be revoked because the employer had failed to make out a prima facie case of discrimination for purposes of a *Mansion House* defense. The court noted that the only evidence of discrimination presented by the employer concerned the international and regional organizations, and that the employer "failed to establish or even to allege any nexus between policies at the international and regional level and policies at the local level." *Id.* at 447. This requirement of a "nexus" is not unreasoable; what is more troubling is the court's apparent belief that a sufficient nexus will seldom exist. Said the court: "Both *Mansion House* and *Bekins* dealt with union discrimination at the local level only, and it is clear that it is the local unit with which the rule of those cases is ordinarily concerned, for it is the local—and not the regional or international union organization—which usually bargains with employers and is charged with fair representation of all its members" (*id.* at 446). For this proposition the court cited *Grants Furniture Plaza,* where the board seemingly gave no weight to the discriminatory features of the National Master Freight Agreement negotiated by the International Brotherhood of Teamsters—despite the fact that the NMFA clearly has at least as much impact on the employment conditions of black drivers as any actions taken at the local level. See also *Master Slack Corp.,* 221 NLRB No. 149 (1975).

54. For example, in *Williams Enterprises, Inc.,* 212 NLRB No. 132, 87 LRRM 1044 (1974), *enforced,* 89 LRRM 2190 (4th Cir. 1975) (per curiam), the Administrative Law Judge, whose findings and conclusions were adopted by the board, rejected a *Mansion House* defense in a case in which the respondent contractor complained that the union's refusal to refer black sheet metal workers for employment was frustrating his effort to comply with the Washington Plan for affirmative action in the construction industry. The Administrative Law Judge stated that the fact "that no minority employees were referred to the Respondent by the Union . . . does not establish a discriminatory membership or referral policy by the Union." 87 LRRM at 1047. And while noting that the percentage of minority union members was "substantially smaller than the minority population in the District of Columbia," the Administrative Law Judge was satisfied with the mere conjecture that "the gap may be narrower in the Union's total jurisdictional area." *Id.* at 1048. The judge also indicated that any inference of discrimination would be rebutted by the union's participation in affirmative action programs.

55. *NLRB* v. *Radio & Television Broadcast Engineers Local 1212* (CBS), 364 U.S. 573 (1951).

56. 197 NLRB 1250 (1972).

57. 198 NLRB No. 116, 80 LRRM 1775 (1972).

58. Id., 80 LRRM at 1777.

59. *Id.*, 80 LRRM at 1777 n.3, citing *Local 1367 ILA,* 148 NLRB 897 (1964), *aff'd,* 368 F.2d 1010 (5th Cir. 1966), *cert. denied.* 389 U.S. 837 (1967).

60. See *Vaca* v. *Sipes,* 386 U.S. 171, 197–198 (1967).

61. See, e.g., *Chemical Workers* v. *Planters Mfg. Co.* 259 F. Supp. 365 (N.D. Miss. 1966); *Local 186 Pulp, Sulphite & Paper Mill Workers* v. *Minnesota Mining & Mfg. Co.,* 304 F. Supp. 1284, 1293 (N.D. Ind. 1969). But unions may encounter difficulties when they attempt to maintain class actions. See *Airline Stewards & Stewardesses Ass'n Local 550* v. *American Airlines, Inc.,* 455 F.2d 101 (7th Cir. 1972); *Lynch* v. *Sperry Rand Corp.,* 62 FRD 78, 6 FEP Cases 1306 (S.D.N.Y. 1973); *Airline Stewards & Stewardesses Ass'n Local 550* v. *American Airlines, Inc.,* 490 F.2d 636 (7th Cir. 1973), *cert. denied,* 416 U.S. 993 (1974).

62. *Farmers Cooperative Compress,* 169 NLRB (1968), *remanded sub nom. United Packinghouse Workers* v. *NLRB,* 416 F.2d 1126 (D.C. Cir.) *cert. denied,* 396 U.S. 903 (1969), *aff'd on remand* 194 NLRB 85 (1971).

63. *Id.* at 1132.

64. *Id.* at 1132.

65. *Id.* at 1134, n.12.

66. *Id.* at 1135.

67. See nn.43, 44.

68. See, e.g., *Tanner Motor Livery, Ltd., supra* n.20. See generally Ch. 9.

69. See the legislative history discussed in *Curtis Bros., supra* n.24.

70. 416 F.2d at 1135 (empahsis in original).

71. 347 U.S. 483, 494, n.11 (1954), discussed in Ch. 1.

72. See *EEOC* v. *International Longshoremen's Ass'n,* 511 F.2d 273, 277–278 (5th Cir. 1975); *Ethridge* v. *Rhodes,* 268 F. Supp. 83, 88–89 (S.D. Ohio 1967).

73. Dodge Revolutionary Union Movement (DRUM). See Ch. 14, sec.: "Black Power and the Local Unions."

74. See Julius Getman and Stephen Goldberg, "The Myth of Labor Board Expertise," 39 *U. Chi. L. Rev.* 681 (1972).

75. 194 NLRB 85 (1971).

76. 202 NLRB 272 (1973).

77. *Id.* at 272.

78. *Id.* at 272. On the meaning of "mandatory subjects of bargaining," see sec.: "Racial Discrimination and the Duty to Bargain."

79. *Id.* at 272. Does this requirement of a "nexus" apply to union conduct? In *Local 106, Glass Bottle Blowers,* 210 NLRB 943 (1974), *enforced,* 520 F.2d 693 (6th Cir. 1975), the board held that sex-segregated locals violate § 8(b)(1)(A), but not necessarily § 8(b)(2), of the act. The decision of the board did not discuss *Jubilee.* The decision reasoned that sex segregation can "generate a feeling of inferiority among the females as to their work status" (*id.* at 944), and can also adversely affect the working conditions of both sexes. As an example of the latter point, the board noted that in the case before it, the grievance mechanisms were sex-segregated, and yet under the collective bargaining agreement the outcome of any grievance was binding on both sexes. "These employees have therefore, solely because of sex, been denied a voice in the resolution of matters affecting their working conditions." *Id.* In a footnote to the decision of the board, Chairman Edward Miller stated that he viewed the locals as having violated the duty of fair representation in that separate but allegedly equal representation is not fair representation." *Id.* n.5. The chairman stated that this factor distinguished *Jubilee,* which had not involved union conduct.

Member John Penello, concurring, stressed the nature of the grievance mechanisms involved in the case as making out "an actual nexus between the discriminatory conduct and interference with, and restraint of employees in the exercise of rights protected under the Act," thus distinguishing *Jubilee.* Member Ralph Kennedy concurred in the finding of an § 8(b)(1)(A) violation only because of the separate processing of grievances which denied a voice to employees affected by the outcome of a grievance. But he viewed the majority as holding that separate locals constitute a *per se* violation of the act, and thought this to be inconsistent with *Jubilee's* requirement of "actual evidence, as opposed to speculation, of a nexus." *Id.* at 946. Member Howard Jenkins concurred with respect to the § 8(a)(1)(B) violation but dissented from the failure to find a § 8(b)(2) violation.

80. 202 NLRB at 272.

81. *Id.* at 272–273.

82. *Id.* at 273.

83. Section 8(a)(5), 29 U.S.C. § 158(a)(5)(1970), makes it an unfair labor practice for an employer "to refuse to bargain collectively with the representatives of his employees, subject to the provisions of section 9(a)" [which defines the "exclusive bargaining representative" concept].

84. Section 8(b)(3), 29 U.S.C. § 158(b)(3)(1970), makes it an unfair labor practice for a labor organization "to refuse to bargain collectively with an employer, provided it is the representative of his employees subject to the provisions of section 9(a)."

85. The requirements of good-faith bargaining are spelled out in section 8(d), 29 U.S.C. § 158(d)(1970), which states in pertinent part: "For the purposes of this section, to bargain collectively is the performance of the mutual obligation of the employer and the representative of the employees to meet at reasonable times and confer in good faith with respect to wages, hours, and other terms and

conditions of employment, or the negotiations of an agreement, or any question arising thereunder, and the execution of a written contract incorporating any agreement reached if requested by either party, but such obligation does not compel either party to agree to a proposal or require the making of a concession.''

86. On the scope of the duty to bargain in good faith, see generally Charles Morris, ed., *The Developing Labor Law*, Ch. 11 (1971). On the board's lack of power to require concessions, see *H.K. Porter Co.* v. *NLRB*, 397 U.S. 99 (1970). On abstinance as one of the indicia of a lack of good faith, see *United Steelworkers* v. *NLRB*, 390 F.2d 846 (D.C. Cir. 1967), *cert. denied*, 391 U.S. 904 (1968); *H.K. Porter Co.*, 153 NLRB 1370, 1372 (1965), *enforced*, 363 F.2d 272 (D.C. Cir. 1966), *cert. denied*, 385 U.S. 851 (the earlier stages of the H.K. Porter litigation which culminated in 397 U.S. 99, cited above); *General Electric Co.*, 150 NLRB 192 (1964), *enforced*, 418 F.2d 736 (2d Cir. 1969), *cert. denied*, 397 U.S. 965 (1970); *Herman Sausage Co.*, 122 NLRB 168 (1958), *enforced*, 275 F.2d 229 (5th Cir. 1960).

87. *NLRB* v. *Wooster Division of Borg-Warner Corp.*, 356 U.S. 342 (1958).

88. *Tanner Motor Livery, Ltd.*, *supra* n.20, 347 F.2d 1, 4; *Mason-Rust*, 179 NLRB 434 (1965); *Washington State Service Employees State Council No. 18*, 188 NLRB 957 (1970).

89. 444 F.2d 340 (5th Cir. 1971).

90. *Id.* at 344.

91. *Id.* at 346.

92. *Local 189 Papermakers* v. *United States*, 416 F.2d 980 (5th Cir. 1969), *cert. denied*, 397 U.S. 919 (197), discussed in Ch. 4 beginning at n.28.

93. *Local 53 Heat & Frost Insulators* v. *Vogler*, 407 F.2d 1047 (5th Cir. 1969), discussed in Ch. 4 at n.1.

94. See e.g., *Pettway* v. *American Cast Iron Pipe Co.*, 494 F.2d 211, 218 n.10 (5th Cir. 1974); *United States* v. *Jacksonville Terminal Co.*, 451 F.2d 418, 441 (5th Cir. 1971), *cert. denied*, 406 U.S. 906 (1972), and cases cited. See generally Ch. 4.

95. See n.21.

96. *United States* v. *Jacksonville Terminal Co.*, 451 F.2d 418, 454 (5th Cir. 1971), *cert. denied*, 406 U.S. 906 (1972).

97. 316 U.S. 31 (1942).

98. 353 U.S. 448 (1957).

99. *Id.* at 457.

100. 316 U.S. at 47.

101. 195 NLRB 1,2 (1972).

102. *Western Addition Community Organization* v. *NLRB*, 485 F.2d 917, 927 (D.C. Cir. 1973), reversed *sub nom. Emporium Capwell Co.* v. *WACO*, 420 U.S. 50 (1975).

103. 420 U.S. at 66, 73 n.26.

104. NLRA § 9(a), 29 U.S.C. § 159(a)(1970).

105. *Emporium Capwell* v. *WACO*, 420 U.S. at 61 n.12. See genearally, Kurt Hanslowe, ''Individual Rights in Collective Labor Relations,'' 45 *Cornell L.Q.* 25 (1959): Sanford Rosen, ''The Individual Worker in Grievance Arbitration: Still Another Look at the Problem,'' 24 *Maryland L. Rev.* 362 (1962); Clyde Summers, ''Individual Rights in Collective Agreements and Arbitration,'' 37 *N.Y.U.L. Rev.* 362 (1962); Bernard Dunau, ''Employee Participation in the Grievance Aspect of Collective Bargaining,'' 50 *Colum. L. Rev.*

106. *Douds* v. *Local 1250, Retail-Wholesale Union*, 173 F.2d 764 (2d Cir. 1949).

107. See *Black-Clawson Co.* v. *IAM Lodge 355*, 313 F.2d 179 (2d Cir. 1962); *Broniman* v. *Great A&P Ten Co.*, 353 F.2d 559 (6th Cir. 1965); *Hughes Tool Co.*, 56 NLRB 981 (1944), *enforced*, 147 F.2d 69 (5th Cir. 1945); *U.S. Automatic Corp.*, 57 NLRB 124 (1944); *Federal Telephone & Radio Co.*, 107 NLRB 649 (1953).

108. NLRA § 2(5), 29 U.S.C. § 152(5)(1970).

109. 360 U.S. 203 (1959).

110. See generally Ch. 13. See also Ch. 9, n.142.

111. See Ch. 13.

112. *United States* v. *Local 86, Ironworkers*, 4 FEP Cases 1152 (W.D. Wash. 1972).

113. 457 F.2d 348 (5th Cir. 1972).

114. See also Ch. 3, sec.: *''McDonnell Douglas Corp.* v. *Green.''*

115. *Government Employees Relations Report* No. 487, Janaury 22, 1973, at BB-12.

116. The union security provisions of the NLRA, § 8(a)(3), 29 U.S.C. § 158(a)(3), do not permit

an employer and union to enter into an agreement whereby union membership will be a prerequisite to hiring. In effect, the most stringent form of union security permissible is the "agency shop," whereby an employee is required to join the union within thirty days after hire—but no obligation can be put on the employee other than the obligation to pay an initiation fee and periodic dues. See *NLRB* v. *General Motors Corp.*, 373 U.S. 734 (1963).

117. See n.9.

118. 379 U.S. 203 (1964).

119. Indeed, many antidiscrimination clauses specifically include hiring. See *BNA Collective Bargaining Negotiations and Contracts* 55:12 (1975). And hiring is generally included in joint employer-union equal employment opportunity pledges, which are becoming increasingly prevalent. See *id.* at 95:511–514.

120. Civil Rights Act of 1964, Title VII, § 703(c)(2), 42 U.S.C. § 2000e-2(c)(2)(1970).

121. In several recent cases the International Union of Electrical, Radio and Machine Workers (IUE) has successfully argued before Administrative Law Judges of the NLRB that a union has a right under § 8(a)(5) of the NLRA to information concerning all aspects of the employer's practices relating to race and sex, including hiring. See *Automation & Measurement Div., Bendix Corp.*, Case No. 9-CA-8762 (May 20, 1975); *East Dayton Tool and Die Co.*, Case No. 9-CA-8887 (May 30, 1975); *Westinghouse Electric Corp.*, Case No. 6-CA-7680 (Feb. 17, 1976). But see *White Farm Equipment Co.*, Case No. 9-CA-8835 (May 30, 1975) (union not entitled to information if it will not be used for purposes of collective bargaining).

122. 313 U.S. 177 (1941).

123. *Id.* at 186.

124. 343 U.S. 768 (1952).

125. The Supreme Court has held that the duty of fair representation, first developed under the Railway Labor Act, *Steele* v. *Louisville & Nashville R.R.*, 323 U.S. 192 (1944); *Tunstall* v. *Locomotive Firemen*, 323 U.S. 210 (1944); *Bd. of R.R. Trainment* v. *Howard supra* n.125, fully applies to the NLRA, *Ford Motor Co.* v. *Huffman*, 345 U.S. 330 (1953); *Syres* v. *Oil Workers Local 23*, 350 U.S. 892 (1955), and has used the same approach under both statutes.

126. See Cox, pp. 157–159.

127. 404 U.S. 157 (1971).

128. *Id.* at 181 n.20.

129. See generally Ch. 13.

130. 303 U.S. 552 (1938).

131. § 4 of the Norris-La Guardia Act, 29 U.S.C. § 104 (197C), provides: "No court of the United States shall have jurisdiction to issue any restraining order or temporary or permanent injunction in any case involving or growing out of any labor dispute to prohibit any person or persons particpating or interested in such dispute . . . from doing, whether singly or in concert, any of the following acts . . . [at which point there follows an expansive list] (Section 13, 29 U.S.C. § 113 (1970), further defines the terms of § 4).

132. 303 U.S. at 561.

133. N.20.

134. 148 NLRB at 1404.

135. 166 NLRB 551 (1967).

136. 454 F.2d 234, 238 (5th Cir.), *cert. denied,* 406 U.S. 957 (1972).

137. 143 NLRB 409 (1963) *enforced,* 349 F.2d 449 (5th Cir. 1965), *cert. denied,* 382 U.S. 1026 (1966).

138. *Mobil Oil Co.,* 147 NLRB 337 (1964).

139. NLRA § 8(b)(1)(B), 29 U.S.C. § 158(b)(1)(B)(1970).

140. 417 U.S. 790, 804–805 (1974).

141. 204 NLRB No. 32, 83 LRRM 1443 (1973), *enforced,* 503 F.2d 192 (D.C. Cir. 1974).

142. 204 NLRB No. 32 at p. 2 (slip op.)

143. *Id.*

144. 503 F.2d at 194.

145. 194 NLRB 386 (1972).

146. *Id.* at 386 (dissenting opinion).

147. EEOC Decision No. 71–359 (Oct. 22, 1970), 2 FEP Cases 1104.

148. See Ch. 12, text beginning at n.89.

149. 388 U.S. 175 (1966).

150. *Id.* at 179, 180, 181.

151. 394 U.S. 423, 429, 430 (1969).

152. 391 U.S. 418 (1968).

153. *National Grinding Wheel Co.,* 176 NLRB 628 (1969); *Tusco Glass, Inc.,* 177 NLRB No. 37 (1969). Similarly, a union violates § 8(b)(1)(A) if it disciplines a member for refusing to take part in unlawful activity such as a secondary boycott, *B.D. Morgan & Co., Inc.,* 205 NLRB No. 75, 84 LRRM 1319 (1973), or a strike which is unlawful by virtue of the union's failure to comply with the notice provisions of § 8(d), *N.Y. Telephone Co.,* 208 NLRB No. 31, 1974 CCH NLRB ¶ 26, 129 (1974), or an action which constitutes an attempt by the union to unilaterally alter the existing collective-bargaining agreement, in violation of § 8(b)(3), *Rochester Telephone Corp.,* 194 NLRB No. 144 (1972).

154. 181 NLRB 992 (1970).

155. *Smith Lee Co.,* 182 NLRB 849 (1970); *Blackhawk Tanning Co.,* 178 NLRB 208 (1969); *Tawas Tube Products,* 151 NLRB 46 (1965).

156. See *Radio Officers Union* v. *NLRB,* 374 U.S. 17 (1961); cf. *United Nuclear Corp.* v. *NLRB,* 340 F.2d 133 (1st Cir. 1965). See also *Union Starch & Refining Co.* v. *NLRB,* 186 F.2d 1008 (7th Cir. 1951), *cert. denied,* 342 U.S. 815 (1951); Vincent Macaluso, "The NLRB 'Opens the Union,' Taft-Hartley Style," 36 *Cornell L.Q.* 443 (1951).

157. NLRA § 8(a)(3)(B), 29 U.S.C. § 158(a)(3)(B)(1970).

158. 181 NLRB at 994 (Trial Examiner's Decision).

159. *Id.* at 995 (Trial Examiner's Decision).

160. *Id.* at 995 (Trial Examiner's Decision).

161. *Id.* at 992 n.6.

162. 133 NLRB 451, 456–457, n.12 (1961), *enforcement denied on other grounds,* 303 F.2d 428 (6th Cir. 1962), *rev'd,* 373 U.S. 734 (1963).

163. 367 U.S. 740 (1961).

164. See text at n.7.

8 | Grievance Arbitration Machinery and Title VII

1. On the history of labor arbitration in the United States, see generally Robben Fleming, *The Labor Arbitration Process* (Urbana, Ill., 1965), Ch. 1; Maurice Trotta, *Labor Arbitration* (1961), ch. 1; Clarence Updegraff, *Arbitration and Labor Relations* (Washington, 1970), pp. 2–3. On the role of the War Labor Board, see also Jesse Freidin and Francis Ulman, "Arbitration and the National War Labor Board." 58 *Harv. L. Rev.* 309 (1945).

2. The veto message appears at 20 LRRM 22 (1947). See generally R. Alton Lee, *Truman and Taft-Hartley* (1966), ch. 4. Interestingly, one of Truman's objections was that the bill ignored the "wide agreement that the interpretation of the provisions of bargaining agreements should be submitted to the processes of negotiation ending in voluntary arbitration . . . In introducing damage suits [under § 301] as a possible substitute for grievance machinery, the bill rejects entirely the informed wisdom of those experienced in labor relations." 20 LRRM at 25.

3. Section 301(a), 29 U.S.C. § 185 (a)(1970) provides: "Suits for violation of contracts between an employer and a labor organization representing employees in an industry affecting commerce as defined in this chapter, or between any such labor organizations, may be brought in any district court of the United States having jurisdiction of the parties, without respect to the amount in controversy or without regard to the citizenship of the parties." And see n.2.

4. 29 U.S.C. § 173(d) (1970).

5. 353 U.S. 448 (1957)

6. *Id.* at 455.

7. *International Ass'n of Machinists* v. *Cutler-Hammer, Inc.,* 271 App. Div. 917, 67 N.Y.S. 2d 317, *affirmed,* 297 N.Y. 519, 74 N.E. 2d 464 (1947).

8. Classic examples of the common law attitude toward arbitration include *Insurance Co.* v. *Morse,* 87 U.S. (20 Wall) 445 (1874); *Kill* v. *Hollister,* 1 Wilson 129 (K.B., 1746) (considered to be the first statement of the "ouster of jurisdiction" objection); *Vynior's Case,* 4 Co. Rep. 302, 305 (K.B. 1609). A more sympathetic attitude began to emerge with *Scott* v. *Avery,* 25 L.J. Ex. 308 (1856). See generally *Kulukundis Shipping Co.* v. *Amtorg Trading Corp.,* 126 F.2d 978, 982–985 (2d Cir. 1942), (Frank, J.); Charles Gregory and Richard Orlikoff, "The Enforcement of Labor Arbitration Agreements," 17 *U. Chi. L. Rev.* 233, 235–238 (1950); Paul Sayre, "Development of Commercial Arbitration Law," 37 *Yale L.J.* 595 (1928).

9. *United Steelworkers of America* v. *American Mfg. Co.*, 363 U.S. 564 (1960); *United Steelworkers of America* v. *Warrior & Gulf Navigation Co.*, 363 U.S. 574 (1960); *United Steelworkers of America* v. *Enterprise Wheel & Car Corp.*, 363 U.S. 593 (1960).

10. N.9.

11. *Warrior & Gulf Navigation Co.*, at 582.

12. *Id.* at 578 and n. 4.

13. *Id.* at 581–582.

14. N.9.

15. 363 U.S. at 597.

16. *Id.* at 597 (emphasis supplied).

17. *Republic Steel Corp.* v. *Maddox*, 379 U.S. 650 (1965).

18. *Vaca* v. *Sipes*, 386 U.S. 171 (1967).

19. 398 U.S. 235 (1970). See William B. Gould, "On Labor Injunctions, Unions, and the Judges: The Boys Markets Case," 1970 *Sup. Ct. Rev.* 215.

20. *Collyer Insulated Wire*, 192 NLRB 837, 843 n.18 (1971).

21. BNA Collective Bargaining: Negotiations and Contracts 95:5 (1975). This is up from 46 percent in 1970 and 28 percent in 1965. Ten percent of these antidiscrimination clauses include a statement that the company will comply with laws prohibiting discrimination.

22. 393 U.S. 324 (1969).

23. *Id.* at 330–331. The Glover principle that resort to arbitration will not be required in duty of fair representation cases alleging racial discrimination, is also applied to Title VII where the courts have held that exhaustion of contractual remedies is not required. *Evans* v. *Local 2127 IBEW*, 313 F. Supp. 1354, 1358 (N.D. Ga. 1969); *King* v. *Georgia Power*, 295 F. Supp. 943 (N.D. Ga. 1968); *United States* v. *Georgia Power*, 301 F. Supp., 538 (N.D. Ga. 1969); *Reese* v. *Atlantic Steel Co.*, 282 F. Supp. 905 (N.D. Ga. 1967); *Dent* v. *St. Louis-San Francisco Ry.*, 265 F. Supp. 56 (N.D. Ala. 1967), *rev'd on other grds.*, 406 F.2d 399 57 (5th Cir. 1972). The same holds true of suits under 42 U.S.C. § 1981. *Waters* v. *Wisconsin Steel Works*, 502 F.2d 1309, 1316 (7th Cir. 1974).

24. For cases recognizing the importance of the "plenary powers" of the federal courts in Title VII cases, see, e.g., *Alexander* v. *Gardner-Denver Co.*, 415 U.S. 36, 47 (1974); *Sprogis* v. *United Air Lines, Inc.*, 444 F.2d 1194, 1201–1202 (7th Cir.), *cert. denied*, 404 U.S. 991 (1971); *Hutchings* v. *United States Industries, Inc.*, 428 F.2d 303, 311–312 (5th Cir. 1970); *Bowe* v. *Colgate-Palmolive Co.*, 416 F.2d 711, 715, 719–721 (7th Cir. 1969); *Parham* v. *Southwestern Bell Telephone Co.*, 433 F.2d 421, 428–429 (8th Cir. 1970); *Jenkins* v. *United Gas Corp.*, 400 F.2d 28 (5th Cir. 1968).

25. This legislative history is discussed in *Alexander* v. *Gardner-Denver Co.*, 415 U.S. 36, 48, n.9 (1974).

26. *Tipler* v. *E. I. Dupont Co.*, 443 F.2d 125 (6th Cir. 1971). And see generally *Guerra* v. *Manchester Terminal Corp.*, 498 F.2d 641 (5th Cir. 1974).

27. *McDonnell Douglas Corp.* v. *Green*, 411 U.S. 792, 798 (1973); *Robinson* v. *Lorillard Corp.*, 444 F.2d 791, 800 (4th Cir. 1971), *cert. dismissed*, 404 U.S. 1006 (1971); *Fekete* v. *U.S. Steel Corp.*, 424 F.2d 331 (3d Cir. 1970).

28. *Alexander* v. *Gardner-Denver Co.*, at 48 n.8 (dictum); *Cooper* v. *Philip Morris, Inc.*, 464 F.2d 9 (6th Cir. 1972); *Ferrell* v. *American Express Co.*, 8 EPD ¶9567 (E.D.N.Y. 1974); cf. 42 U.S.C. § 2000e-5(b) (Supp. II, 1972).

29. 452 F.2d 889 (2d Cir. 1971), *cert. denied*, 406 U.S. 918 (1972).

30. *Id.* at 893.

31. See *Alexander* v. *Gardner-Denver Co.*, at 52 and n.15: "(P)resumably an employee may waive his cause of action under Title VII as part of a voluntary settlement. In determining the effectiveness of any such waiver, a court would have to determine at the outset that the employee's consent to the settlement was voluntary and knowing."

32. *United States* v. *Local 3, Operating Engineers*, 4 FEP Cases 1088 (N.D. Cal. 1972).

33. *Williamson* v. *Bethlehem Steel Corp.*, 468 F.2d 1201 (2d Cir. 1972), *cert. denied*, 411 U.S. 931 (1973).

34. See *Collyer Insulated Wire*, 192 NLRB 837 (1971); *Spielberg Mfg. Co.*, 112 NLRB 1080 (1955).

35. *Vaca* v. *Sipes*. And see generally sect.: "Third-Party Intervention" in this chapter.

36. 150 NLRB 312 (1964), *enforced* 368 F.2d 12 (5th Cir. 1966), *cert. denied*, 389 U.S. 837 (1967).

37. *Id.* at 316–317.

38. *Goodyear Tire & Rubber* (Gadsden, Ala.), 45 LA 240 (Paul N. Lehoczky, 1965).

39. See, e.g., *Robinson* v. *Lorillard Corp.,* 444 F.2d 791 (4th Cir.) *cert. dismissed,* 404 U.S. 1006 (1971); *Glus* v. *G.C. Murphy Co.,* 329 F. Supp. 563 (W.D. Pa. 1971).

40. 47 LA 873 (Robert E. Burns, 1966). This award is discussed in William B. Gould, "Labor Arbitration of Grievances Involving Racial Discrimination," 118 *U. Pa. L. Rev.* 40 (1969).

41. Study of arbitration awards involving discrimination grievances for the period 1969–1973, prepared by Oscar Rosenbloom, Stanford Law School, class of 1975, for William B. Gould (unpublished).

42. See, e.g., *Pacific Gas & Electric Co.,* 73-2 CCH ARB § 8604 (William Eaton, 1974), *Chippewa Valley Bd. of Education,* 62 LA 409 (James R. McCormick, 1974); *CLIO Education Association,* 61 LA 37 (Board of Arbitrators, James R. McCormick, Chairman, 1973); Milwaukee Area Technical College, 60 LA 302 (Reynolds C. Seitz, 1973); *Simoniz Co.,* 70-1 CCH ARB § 8024 (Robert G. Howlett, 1969).

43. Rosenbloom study.

44. The Rosenbloom study found only one award which made an explicit finding of racial discrimination in sustaining a grievance; the award is *Lianco Container Corp.,* 60 LA 938 (Paul C. Dugan, 1973). In the other awards sustaining a grievance where racial discrimination was alleged, the arbitrators found violations of the "just cause" clause, the seniority provisions, or other contract terms, but refused to find that race was the causative factor.

45. In the Rosenbloom study, of the 15 grievances involving promotion or transfer, 12 were rejected and only 3 were sustained. This contrasts with the 30 discharge-demotion-discipline grievances, of which 17 were rejected and 13 were sustained.

46. For example, at the Workshop on Seniority and Ability held during the Ninth Annual Meeting of the National Academy of Arbitrators: "A fairly basic proposition was made, which seemed to command general support. This was that the determination of ability must be made by the management, and the issue should not be one of the arbitrator's judgment versus that of the management but whether the company's discrimination was arbitrary, capricious (the proponent's adjective was "whimsical"), or discriminatory. If not, this should end the matter. While each side must seek to persuade the arbitrator of his position, it was recognized that it is a managerial responsibility to make the determination and initiate the action, that there is an area of latitude for judgment and discretion and that within this area, bound as it were by the adjectives suggested, the employer's decision should not be overruled on grounds that the arbitrator might have reached a different conclusion." Management Rights and the Arbitration Process, Proceedings of the Ninth Annual Meeting of the National Academy of Arbitrators 45–46 (1956). The view that promotion disputes and other grievances which involve questions of employee ability call for a substantial deference to management prerogatives still commands a consensus among arbitrators; see Clarence Updegraff, *Arbitration and Labor Relations* (1970), 304–305.

47. *U.S. Postal Service,* 60 LA 206, 215–216 (G. Allan Dash, Jr., 1973).

48. 61 LA 421, 427 (Alex J. Simm, 1973).

49. *Griggs* v. *Duke Power Co.,* 401 U.S. 424 (1971), discussed in Ch. 4, sec.: "Societal Discrimination"; *McDonnell Douglas Corp.* v. *Green,* 411 U.S. 792 (1973), discussed in Ch. 4, sec.: "Franks v. Bowman Transportation Co."

50. 53 LA 101, 110 (Edgar Jones, Jr., 1969).

51. 54 LA 1210, 1213 (Howard S. Block, 1970).

52. *Signal Delivery Service, Inc.,* 60 LA 339 (Charles Morgan, Jr., 1973).

53. 54 LA 330 (Robert G. Howlett, 1970).

54. See, *International Harvester Co.,* 9 LA 894 (1947); cf. *Consolidated Paper Co.,* 33 LA 840 (1959); *United States Indus. Chem. Co.,* 33 LA 335 (1959); *Elberton Crate & Box Co.,* 32 LA 228 (1959); *International Paper Co.,* 31 LA 494 (1958); *United States Rubber Co.,* 13 LA 839 (1949). One of the more extraordinary arbitral remedies issued to date is *Jack Meilman,* 34 LA 771 (1960), where the arbitrator ordered a company to cease operations at its new location, to reestablish its operation at its former location, and to pay damages to the union for wages and other contract benefits lost by the company's breach of contract. See, generally, Robben Fleming, "Arbitrators and the Remedy Power," 48 *Va. L. Rev.* 1199 (1962).

55. See text at n.36.

56. 60 LA 760 (John F. Caraway, 1973).

57. *Albemarle Paper Co.* v. *Moody,* 422 U.S. 405 (1975); *Johnson* v. *Goodyear Tire & Rubber Co.,* 491 F.2d 1364 (5th Cir. 1974); *Pettway* v. *American Cast Iron Pipe Co.,* 494 F.2d 211 (5th Cir. 1974); *Baxter* v. *Savannah Sugar Refining Corp.,* 495 F.2d 436 (5th Cir. 1974); *cert. denied,* 419 U.S. 1033 (1974). These cases are discussed in Ch. 6, sec.: "The Circumstances under Which Back Pay Is Awarded."

58. Although "refusal [of arbitrators] to award punitive damages is so universal that the number of such cases is few and far between," nevertheless "punitive damages are awarded on rare occasions when the circumstances are such that there is strong justification for so doing." *ACF Industries, Inc.*, 62 LA 364, 365 (J. Earl Williams, 1974). Plaintiffs have also frequently sought punitive damages in suits under § 301 of the NLRA for breach of the collective-bargaining agreement, and here, while the courts are split, the trend appears to be in favor of allowing punitive damages in appropriate cases. See *Butler* v. *Yellow Freight System, Inc.*, 514 F.2d 442, 454, (8th Cir.), *cert. denied.*, 423 U.S. 924 (1975), and cases cited.

59. 61 LA 942 (Edgar A. Jones, Jr., 1973).

60. *Id.* at 943.

61. 350 F. Supp. 632, 636 (S.D. Ga. 1972).

62. 61 LA at 946–947.

63. CCH ARB 72-1 ¶8360 (Adolph Koven, 1972).

64. *Id.* at 4259.

65. 415 U.S. 36 (1974).

66. *Id.* at 44.

67. *Id.* at 45, 49–50.

68. One question which has been litigated in the wake of *Gardner-Denver* is whether the filing of a grievance tolls the 180-day time limit for the filing of an EEOC charge. If not, there is the possibility that the charge will have to be filed before the grievance has been decided, an event which could certainly affect the disposition of the grievance. In *Sanchez* v. *TWA*, 499 F.2d 1107 (10th Cir. 1974), the court held that nothing in Alexander changed the previously settled view that the filing of a grievance tolls the 180-day period. But in *Guy* v. *Robbins & Myers, Inc.*, 525 F.2d 124 (6th Cir. 1975), the court relied on *Johnson* v. *Railway Express Agency*, 421 U.S. 454 (1975), decided subsequent to *Sanchez*, which held that the filing of an EEOC charge does not toll the state statute of limitations applicable to a claim under 42 U.S.C. § 1981, and the *Guy* court concluded that the filing of a grievance does not toll the 180-day period. This decision was recently affirmed by the Supreme Court in *International Union of Electrical, Radio and Machine Workers AFL-CIO* v. *Robbins & Myers, Inc.*, — U.S. —, 13 FEP Cases 1813 (1976).

69. *Id.* at 58–60.

70. *Id.* at 60, n.21.

71. 416 F.2d 711 (7th Cir. 1969).

72. *Id.* at 714.

73. See Ch. 3, sec.: "Class Representation."

74. 416 F.2d at 715.

75. See *Newman* v. *Avco Corp.*, 451 F.2d 743, 746 n.1 (6th Cir. 1971).

76. See text at n.67.

77. 428 F.2d 303 (5th Cir. 1970).

78. 467 F.2d 54 (5th Cir. 1972).

79. 482 F.2d 569 (9th Cir. 1973).

80. 428 F.2d at 310, 311.

81. See text at n.66.

82. See text at n.29.

83. 482 F.2d at 572.

84. *Id.* at 572.

85. See nn.86, 87, 89.

86. 482 F.2d at 573. See *Gardner-Denver*, 415 U.S. at 54.

87. 482 F.2d at 573. See *Gardner-Denver*, 415 U.S. at 54.

88. 415 U.S. at 54.

89. 482 F.2d at 574. See *Gardner-Denver*, 415 U.S. at 54–55.

90. 482 F.2d at 574.

91. *Id.* at 574.

92. 467 F.2d at 57.

93. *Id.* at 58.

94. 415 U.S. at 59.

95. *Id.* at 59.

96. See e.g., William B. Gould, "Substitutes for the Strike Weapon: The Arbitration Process in the United States," 28 *Arb. J.* 111 (1973); Harold Davey, "What's Right and What's Wrong with Grievance Arbitration: The Practitioners Air their Views," 28 *Arb. J.* 209 (1973).

97. 429 F.2d 324 (6th Cir. 1970), *aff'd per curiam,* 402 U.S. 690 (1971).

98. See text at n.15.

99. 429 F.2d at 332.

100. Before reaching the question of the effect of the arbitration award, the Sixth Circuit held that the district court's finding of a Title VII violation was "clearly erroneous." *Id.* at 331. Thus even apart from the question of the finality of the award, the Sixth Circuit would have reversed the district court's judgment for the employee. Since the Supreme Court affirmed without opinion, it is impossible to know which of the Sixth Circuit's two grounds for reversal was approved by the Court, or whether it approved both grounds.

101. 446 F.2d 120 (6th Cir. 1971).

102. *Id.* at 123.

103. 451 F.2d 743 (6th Cir. 1971).

104. *Id.* at 745.

105. *Id.* at 746–47 (emphasis in original).

106. *Id.* at 747.

107. *NLRB* v. *Union of Marine & Shipbuilding Workers,* 391 U.S. 418 (1968).

108. See *Glover* v. *St. Louis-San Francisco Ry.,* n.22.

109. 451 F.2d at 747–748 (footnote omitted).

110. *Id.* at 749.

111. *Id.* at 748.

112. 291 F. Supp. at 789.

113. N.101.

114. 415 U.S. at 58 n.19.

115. *In re Soto,* 7 N.Y. 2d 397, 165 N.E. 2d 855, 198 N.Y. 2d 282 (1960). However, see the strong dissent of Judge John VanVoorhis in *Chupka* v. *Lorenz-Schneider Co.,* 12 N.Y. 2d 1, 7, 186 N.E. 2d 191, 193, 233 N.Y.S. 2d 929, 932 (1962).

116. *McElroy* v. *Terminal R.R. Ass'n,* 392 F.2d 966 (7th Cir. 1968); *Estes* v. *Union Terminal Co.,* 89 F.2d 768 (5th Cir. 1937).

117. *International Harvester Co.,* 138 NLRB 923 (1962), *enforced sub nom. Ramsey* v. *NLRB,* 327 F.2d 784 (7th Cir. 1964).

118. *Id.* at 928.

119. 99 N.W. 2d 132, 137 (Sup. Ct. Wis. 1960).

120. *Id.* at 138.

121. 375 U.S. 335 (1964).

122. *Id.* at 349–351.

123. "Were the Dealers employees, if the union was going to oppose them, deprived of a fair hearing by having inadequate representation at the hearing? Dealers employees had notice of the hearing . . . and three stewards representing them went to the hearing at union expense and were given every opportunity to state their position. . . . The Dealers employees made no request to continue the hearing until they could secure further representation and have not yet suggested what they could have added to the hearing by way of facts or theory if they had been differently represented." *Id.* at 350–351.

124. 404 U.S. 528 (1972).

125. 386 U.S. 171 (1967).

126. See n.129.

127. 415 U.S. at 58 n.19.

128. 404 F.2d 169 (5th Cir. 1968), *cert. denied,* 394 U.S. 987 (1969).

129. *Id.* at 171. It will be recalled that the Court's holding in *Vaca* is predicated in part upon the exclusive bargaining representative status accorded unions under the NLRA. See *J.I. Case Co.* v. *NLRB,* 321 U.S. 332 (1944). However, section 9a) contains a proviso which indicates that "any individual employee or a group of employees shall have the right at any time to present grievances to their employer and to have such grievances adjusted, without the intervention of the bargaining representative, as long as the adjustment is not inconsistent with the terms of a collective-bargaining contract or agreement then in effect: Provided further, that the bargaining representative has been given opportunity to be present at such adjustment." NLRA § 9(a), 29 U.S.C. § 159(a). On the meaning of this proviso, and the extent to which it applies to the presentation of grievances by employee organizations or civil rights groups as well as by individual grievants, see Ch. 7, text beginning at n.106, and authorities cited in nn.107, 108, 109 therein.

130. 404 F.2d at 171 n.3.

131. See, e.g., *Tenneco Chemicals, Inc.* v. *Teamsters Local 401,* 520 F.2d 945 (3d Cir. 1975). And the Third Circuit has recently held that even where a strike is unauthorized, the no-strike clause gives rise to an implied obligation on the part of the union to use "every reasonable means" to end the strike, and the failure to do so makes the union liable for damages. *Eazor Express, Inc.* v. *Teamsters,* 520 F.2d 951 (3d Cir. 1975).

132. *Textile Workers Union* v. *Lincoln Mills,* 353 U.S. 448, 457 (1957) (emphasis added).

133. 195 NLRB 1,2 (1972); 316 U.S. 31 (1942).

134. *Graziano Construction Co., supra* n.133.

135. *Southern S.S. Co.* v. *NLRB, supra* n.133.

136. See generally Ch. 14, and Ch. 5, sec.: "The Segregation and Merger of Local Unions." See also William B. Gould, "Black Workers in White Unions," *The Nation,* Sept. 8, 1969, at 203; Gould, "The Negro Revolution and Trade Unionism," 114 *Cong. Rec.* 24872 (1968).

137. 379 U.S. 650 (1965) (employee must exhaust contractual grievance procedures before suing employer for breach of contract).

138. Note, "Federal Protection of Individual Rights under Labor Contracts," 73 *Yale L.J.* 1215, 1228 (1964).

139. See text at n.40.

140. See, William B. Gould, "Non-Governmental Remedies for Employment Discrimination," 20 *Syracuse L. Rev.* 865 (1969).

141. See *Glover* v. *St. Louis-San Francisco Ry.,* text at n.22, and the cases cited at n.23.

142. James Atleson, "Disciplinary Discharge, Arbitration, and NLRB Deference," 20 *Buffalo L. Rev.* 355 (1971); Bernard Meltzer "Labor Arbitration and Overlapping and Conflicting Remedies for Employment Discrimination," 39 *U. Chi. L. Rev.* 30, 45 (1971).

143. 415 U.S. at 58 n.19.

144. On the record of the local unions, see generally Ch. 14.

145. It is settled that a federal district court cannot refuse to entertain a class action merely because the named plaintiff does not have a meritorious claim, e.g., *Huff* v. *N.D. Cass Co.,* 485 F.2d 710 (5th Cir. 1970) (en banc). See generally Ch. 3, sec.: "Class Representation."

146. 88 *BNA Labor Relations Reporter* 238 (March 24, 1975).

147. § 706(f)(5), 42 U.S.C. § 2000e-5(f)(5) (Supp. II 1972).

148. N.125.

149. N.138.

150. *Id.* at 653.

151. 386 U.S. at 192.

152. *Id.* at 186–187 (emphasis added; footnote omitted).

153. Exhaustion of contractual grievance machinery is not a prerequisite to § 301 suits involving racial discrimination, *Glover* v. *St. Louis-San Francisco Ry.,* n.22, nor to Title VII suits, see cases cited in n.23.

154. 415 U.S. at 54–55.

155. 398 U.S. 235 (1970).

156. *Sinclair Refining Co.* v. *Atkinson,* 370 U.S. 195 (1962), interpreting § 4 of the Norris-LaGuardia Act, 29 U.S.C. § 104 (1970).

157. Bureau of Labor Statistics, U.S. Dept. of Labor, *Major Collective Bargaining Agreements-Arbitration Procedures,* Bull. No. 1425-6 (1966).

158. Since *Atkinson* applied only to federal courts, it was possible to obtain injunctions in state courts where a state did not have a "Baby Norris-La Guardia Act" which was subject to the Atkinson construction. But see *Avco Corp.* v. *Aero Lodge No. 735,* 390 U.S. 557 (1968), which complicated the picture by allowing removal of such state court injunctive proceedings to federal court.

159. See text at nn.86–88.

160. 415 U.S. at 54.

161. *Id.* at 55.

162. *Stamps* v. *Detroit Edison Co.,* 365 F. Supp. 87, 124 (E.D. Mich. 1973), *aff'd in part, rev'd on this grd.,* 515 F.2d 301 (6th Cir. 1975). See generally Ch. 6, sec.: "Punitive Damages."

163. *NLRB* v. *Wooster Division, Borg-Warner Corp.,* 356 U.S. 342 (1958). On the implications of *Borg-Warner* with respect to bargaining over contract terms relating to racial discrimination, see generally Ch. 7, sec.: "Racial Discrimination."

164. 415 U.S. at 51–52.

165. *Id.* at 52 n.15.

166. *Id.* at 51.

167. Cf. *Stamps* v. *Detroit Edison Co.,* 365 F. Supp. 87, 108–109 (E.D. Mich. 1973), *rev'd in part on other grounds,* 515 F.2d 301 (6th Cir. 1975).

168. See n.54, and text.

169. N.101.

170. See text at n.171.

171. *United Steelworkers* v. *Warrior & Gulf Navigation Co.,* 363 U.S. 574, 582 (1960).

172. 347 U.S. 483 (1954), discussed in Ch. 1.

173. *Rios* v. *Reynolds Metals Company,* 467 F.2d 54, 58 (5th Cir. 1972).

174. Cf. *NLRB* v. *Acme Industrial Co.,* 385 U.S. 432 (1967).

175. Here the ''just cause'' criterion provides the arbitrator with ample room to look to other sources; *United Steelworkers* v. *Enterprise Wheel & Car Corp.,* 363 U.S. 593, 597 (1960).

176. See n.21.

177. Mark Kahn provided the author with this proposal during a telephone conversation in 1969. Moreover, the EEOC General Counsel now possesses statutory authority to render advisory opinions.

178. The settlement agreement is unreported; a copy is in the author's files.

179. See *Basic Vegetable Products, Inc.,* 64 LA 620 (1975) (William B. Gould).

9 | Self-Help under the National Labor Relations Act and Federal Labor Law

1. Chief Justice Stone in *Steele* v. *Louisville & Nashville Ry.,* 323 U.S. 192, 200 (1944) (emphasis added).

2. *Textile Workers Union* v. *Lincoln Mills,* 353 U.S. 448 (1957); *United Steelworkers of America* v. *American Mfg. Co.,* 363 U.S. 564 (1960); *United Steelworkers of America* v. *Warrior & Gulf Navigation Co.,* 363 U.S. 574 (1960); *United Steelworkers of America* v. *Enterprise Wheel & Car Corp.,* 363 U.S. 593 (1960). See also *Boys Markets, Inc.* v. *Retail Clerks,* 398 U.S. 235 (1970). See generally Ch. 8, sec.: ''The Institutional Framework.''

3. 414 U.S. 368 (1974).

4. *Id.* at 385.

5. See *NLRB* v. *Washington Aluminum Co.,* 370 U.S. 9 (1962). The statutory basis is provided in 29 U.S.C. §§ 157, 158(a)(1) (1973): [§ 157]: Employees shall have the right to self-organization, to form, join, or assist labor organizations, to bargain collectively through representatives or their own choosing, and to engage in other concerted activities for the purpose of collective bargaining or other mutual aid or protection . . . . [§ 158(a)]: It shall be an unfair labor practice for an employer—(1) to interfere with, restrain, or coerce employees in the exercise of rights guaranteed in section 157. . . .

6. *NLRB* v. *Sands Mfg. Co.,* 306 U.S. 332 (1938). Cf. *Teamsters Local 174* v. *Lucas Flour Co.,* 369 U.S. 95 (1962). However, a more limited no-strike obligation will project the walkout. See *Ford Motor Co.,* 131 NLRB 1462 (1961); *Young Spring & Wire Corp.,* 138 NLRB 643 (1962); *Mid-West Metallic Prods., Inc.,* 121 NLRB 1317 (1958).

7. 350 U.S. 270 (1956).

8. The no-strike clause could not, however, be read to specifically preclude its application to the situation involved in *Mastro Plastics.*

9. 350 U.S. at 281.

10. *Arlan's Department Store,* 133 NLRB 802, 807 (1961) (emphasis added).

11. 29 U.S.C. § 143.

12. *Gateway Coal Co., supra* n. 3, at 385–387.

13. *NLRB* v. *Draper Corp.,* 145 F.2d 199 (4th Cir. 1944). See also *NLRB* v. *Serv-Air, Inc.* 69 LRRM 2476 (10th Cir. 1968); *Rubber Rolls, Inc.* v. *NLRB,* 388 F.2d 71 (3d Cir. 1967); *Packers Hide Ass'n* v. *NLRB,* 360 F.2d 59 (8th Cir. 1966); *NLRB* v. *Cactus Petroleum, Inc.,* 355 F.2d 755 (5th Cir. 1966); *NLRB* v. *R.C. Can Co.,* 328 F.2d 974 (5th Cir. 1964); *Western Contracting Corp.* v. *NLRB,* 322 F.2d 893 (10th Cir. 1963); *NLRB* v. *Kearney & Trecker Corp.,* 237 F.2d 416 (7th Cir. 1956); *NLRB* v. *Sunbeam Lighting Co.,* 318 F.2d 661 (7th Cir. 1963); *NLRB* v. *Lundy Mfg. Corp.,* 316 F.2d 921 (2d Cir.), *cert. denied,* 375 U.S. 895 (1963); *NLRB* v. *Kaiser Aluminum & Chemical Corp.,* 217 F.2d 366 (9th Cir. 1954); *Simmons, Inc.* v. *NLRB,* 315 F.2d 143 (1st Cir. 1963); *Confectionery & Tobacco Drivers Union* v. *NLRB,* 312 F.2d 108 (2d Cir. 1963); *Plasti-Line, Inc.* v. *NLRB* 278 F.2d 482 (6th Cir. 1960); *NLRB* v. *Sunset Minerals, Inc.,* 211 F.2d 224 (9th Cir. 1954); *Harnischfeger*

Corp. v. *NLRB*, 207 F.2d 575 (7th Cir. 1953); *NLRB* v. *American Mfg. Co.*, 203 F.2d 212 (5th Cir. 1953); *NLRB* v. *J.I. Case Co.*, 198 F.2d 919 (8th Cir. 1952); *NLRB* v. *Deena Artwear, Inc.*, 198 F.2d 645 (6th Cir. 1952); *NLRB* v. *Warner Bros. Pictures, Inc.*, 191 F.2d 217 (9th Cir. 1951). See generally Archibald Cox, "The Right to Engage in Concerted Activities," 26 *Ind. L.J.* 319, 332 (1951); Gould, "The Status of Unauthorized and 'Wildcat' Strikes under the National Labor Relations Act," 52 *Cornell L.Q.* 672 (1967).

14. *NLRB* v. *Draper Corp.*, 145 F.2d 199, 202–203 (4th Cir. 1944).

15. See *Consul Lee A. Co.*, 175 NLRB No. 93 (1969); Gould, "The Status of Unauthorized and 'Wildcat' Strikes under the National Labor Relations Act," 52 *Cornell L.Q.* 672 (1967).

16. I have taken the position that union involvement and notification from union officials are prerequisites for the exercise of protected rights under Section 7 where an exclusive bargaining representative has been selected by the employees. *Id.* at 696–697. However, as indicated here, I would not apply such standards to disputes which have their origin in protest concerning racially discriminatory practices. Public policy and statutory consideration concerning racial equality argue for a different approach to this problem.

17. *R. C. Can Co.*, 140 NLRB 588, 596 (1963), *enforced*, 328 F.2d 974 (5th Cir. 1964).

18. 380 U.S. 300, 302–304 (1965).

19. The board refuses to regard a walkout as unprotected where the international representative's "reservation concerning the walkout appears to relate to its tactical wisdom." *R. C. Can Co.*, at 596.

20. See *American Ship Building, supra* n.18, 380 U.S. at 309–313; *NLRB* v. *Brown*, 380 U.S. 278, 283–290 (1965). The Court has also carefully inquired into the actual impact of the contested practice in determining the legality of various management actions affecting strikers. See *NLRB* v. *Erie Resister Corp.*, 373 U.S. 221, 227–231 (1963). See also *NLRB* v. *Great Dane Trailers, Inc.*, 388 U.S. 26 (1967); *NLRB* v. *Fleetwood Trailer Co.*, 389 U.S. 375 (1967); *NLRB* v. *Mackay Radio & Telegraph Co.*, 304 U.S. 333 (1938).

21. 148 NLRB 1402 (1964), *remanded*, 349 F.2d 1 (9th Cir. 1965), *original order aff'd* 166 NLRB 551 (1967), *vacated and remanded*, 419 F.2d 216 (9th Cir. 1969).

22. *New Negro Alliance* v. *Sanitary Grocery Co.*, 303 U.S. 552 (1938), holding that picketing to force the employment of blacks is a "labor dispute" within the meaning of the Norris-La Guardia Act, and hence is not subject to an injunction.

23. 349 F.2d 1, 3, 5 (9th Cir. 1965).

24. 166 NLRB 551–552 (1967).

25. See, e.g., *NLRB* v. *Marshall Car Wheel & Foundry Co.*, 218 F. 2d 409 (5th Cir. 1955); *NLRB* v. *Cowles Publishing Co.*, 214 F.2d 708 (9th Cir. 1954); *NLRB* v. *Southern Silk Mills, Inc.*, 209 F.2d 155 (6th Cir. 1953); *Modern Motors Inc.* v. *NLRB*, 198 F.2d 925 (8th Cir. 1952); *Carter Carburetor Corp.* v. *NLRB*, 140 F.2d 714 (8th Cir. 1944); *NLRB* v. *Peter Cailler Kohler Swiss Chocolates Co.*, 130 F.2d 503 (2d Cir. 1942).

26. 166 NLRB at 551 n.6.

27. 419 F.2d 216, 220 (9th Cir. 1969).

28. 388 U.S. 175 (1967).

29. Case cited n.1; discussed in Ch.2, sec.: "The National Labor Relations Act."

30. 394 U.S. 423 (1969).

31. The Court stressed the fact that the strike vote had been taken in a "fair and democratic" manner, 388 U.S. at 195, that the fines were "reasonable" in amount, *id.* at 193, and that all of the fined employees "enjoyed . . . full union membership," *id.* at 196. That "full union membership" cannot be required of an employee follows from *NLRB* v. *General Motors Corp.*, 373 U.S. 734 (1963), which interpreted the NLRA as authorizing only the "agency shop," whereby an employee can be required only to pay dues and an initiation fee. It is now clear that if an employee chooses to resign his "full union membership," he is not subject to union fines. *NLRB* v. *Granite State Board, Textile Workers*, 409 U.S. 213 (1972); *Booster Lodge 405, IAM* v. *NLRB*, 412 U.S. 84 (1973). However, *Allis-Chalmers'* qualification with respect to "unreasonable" fines has recently been removed by *NLRB* v. *Boeing Co.*, 412 U.S. 67 (1973), which held that the reasonableness or unreasonableness of a fine is not relevant to the determination of whether the fine constitutes an unfair labor practice.

32. 419 F.2d at 221.

33. *Id.*

34. 188 NLRB 957 (1971).

35. *Id.* at 958–959.

36. *Id.* at 959.

37. 415 U.S. 36 (1974). The Court held that a Title VII claim is not precluded by the submission of

the dispute to arbitration. The Court also rejected any strict rule of deferral to the arbitration award, relying on what it perceived as inadequacies of the arbitral forum in disputes involving Title VII claims. See *id*. at 56–58. In commenting on "the weight to be accorded an arbitral decision," the Court again stressed the importance of careful examination of the adequacy of the arbitral forum. See *id*. at 60 n.21. See generally Ch. 8, sec.: "The *Gardner-Denver* Decision."

38. *The Emporium*, 192 NLRB 173 (1971), *rev'd sub nom. NLRB* v. *Western Addition Community Organization*, 485 F.2d 917 (D.C. Cir. 1973), *rev'd sub nom. Emporium Capwell* v. *Western Addition Community Organization*, 95 S.Ct. 977 (1975).

39. 192 NLRB at 185.

40. *Id*.

41. *Id*. at 173 n.2.

42. 485 F.2d 917.

43. *Id*. at 926.

44. 415 U.S. at 47.

45. Section 704(a), 42 U.S.C. § 2000e-3(a), provides: "It shall be an unlawful employment practice for an employer to discriminate against any of his employees or applicants for employment, for an employment agency to discriminate against any individual, or for a labor organization to discriminate against any member thereof or applicant for membership, because he has opposed any practice made an unlawful employment practice by this subchapter, or because he has made a charge, testified, assisted, or participated in any manner in an investigation, proceeding, or hearing under this subchapter."

46. 485 F.2d at 929.

47. *Id*. at 928–929 (emphasis in original).

48. *Id*. at 929 (emphasis in original).

49. 398 U.S. 235 (1970). See text at n.113.

50. 485 F.2d at 929–930.

51. *Id*. at 930.

52. *Id*.

53. *Id*. at 931 (emphasis in original).

54. *Id*. at 931–932.

55. *Id*. at 937 (dissenting opinion).

56. *Id*.

57. *Southern Steamship Co*. v. *NLRB*, 316 U.S. 31 (1942). See also *Lincoln Mills*, at 457; *Graziano Construction Co*., 195 NLRB 1,2 (1972). See generally Ch. 7, text at nn.87–92.

58. 485 F.2d at 938–939 (dissenting opinion).

59. *Id*. at 940 (dissenting opinion).

60. 95 S.Ct. 977.

61. *Id*. at 938–984.

62. *Id*. at 987–988, 990 n.26.

63. 166 NLRB at 552.

'64. See text at nn.15–19.

65. See generally Ch. 3, sec.: "Class Representation."

66. See text at n.24.

67. See text at nn.51–53, 62.

68. See *Denver-Chicago Trucking Co*., 132 NLRB 1416, 1421 (1961).

69. See generally Ch. 8.

70. 166 NLRB at 551–552.

71. See Ch. 7, sec.: "Duty-of-Fair-Representation Doctrine." *Stamps* v. *Detroit Edison*, 365 F. Supp. 87, 115 (E.D. Mich. 1973), *aff'd in part, rev'd in part on other grds. sub nom. EEOC* v. *Detroit Edison*, 515 F.2d 301 (6th Cir. 1975).

72. Cf. *Phelps Dodge Corp*. v. *NLRB*, 313 U.S. 177 (1941).

73. *United Steelworkers of America* v. *Warrior & Gulf Navigation Co*., 363 U.S. 574, 578, 580 (1960).

74. *Id*. at 583. That a broad no-strike clause should in many cases be applied even to non-arbitrable disputes may seem inconsistent with a "quid pro quo" relationship between the no-strike and arbitration clauses. But the quid pro quo approach has not been literally applied by the courts. For example, where a no-strike clause is not unqualified, the courts have nonetheless applied the same approach to arbitrability as was fashioned in *United Steelworkers of America* v. *American Mfg. Co*., 363 U.S. 564 (1960), where the no-strike clause was unqualified. See William B. Gould, "Labor Injunctions, Unions, and the Judges," 1970 *Sup. Ct. Rev*. 215, 250, and cases cited in n. 129 thereat.

75. 347 U.S. 483 (1954).

76. See n. 22.

77. 485 F.2d at 927.

78. Thus, if a union insists to the point of impasse on a subject that is not a term or condition of employment, and hence is not a "mandatory subject of bargaining" (see *NLRB* v. *Wooster Div. of Borg-Warner Co.*, 356 U.S. 342 (1958)), the union is in violation of § 8(b)(3). See, e.g., *NLRB, Local 1082, Hod Carriers,* 384 F.2d 55 (9th Cir. 1967), *cert. denied,* 390 U.S. 920 (1968); Local 3, Bricklayers, 162 NLRB 476 (1966); *District Council 16, Southern California Pipe Trades* 167 NLRB No. 143 (1967).

79. See *Bechtel Corp.,* 194 NLRB 386 (1972), discussed in Ch. 7, text at nn. 149–152. See also *N.Y. Times,* Jan. 20, 1969, at 26, col. 2. Cf. *Sligo, Inc.,* 50 LA 1203 (1968); *American Standard, Inc.,* 52 LA 736 (1969).

80. See *Fiberboard Paper Products, Inc.* v. *NLRB,* 379 U.S. 203, 212 (1964). Cf. *NLRB* v. *Wooster Div. of Borg-Warner Corp.*

81. Section 8(d)(4), 29 U.S.C. § 158(d)(4), provides in pertinent part: "That where there is in effect a collective-bargaining contract covering employees in an industry affecting commerce, the duty to bargain collectively shall also mean that no party to such contract shall terminate or modify such contract, unless the party desiring such termination or modification—(1) serves a written notice upon the other party to the contract of the proposed termination or modification sixty days prior to the expiration date thereof, or in the event such contract contains no expiration date, sixty days prior to the time it is proposed to make such termination or modification; (2) offers to meet and confer with the other party for the purpose of negotiating a new contract or a contract containing the proposed modifications; (3) notifies the Federal Mediation and Conciliation Service within thirty days after such notice of the existence of a dispute, and simultaneously therewith notifies any State or Territorial agency established to mediate and conciliate disputes within the State or Territory where the dispute occurred, provided no agreement has been reached by that time; and (4) continues in full force and effect, without resorting to strike or lock-out, all the terms and conditions of the existing contract for a period of sixty days after such notice is given or until the expiration date of such contract, whichever occurs later."
See text at n. 100.

82. See "Auto Workers Proposal for Inverted Seniority," 70 LRRM 313 (1969); Dietsch, "Hardcore Blacks and the Shiny Auto," *New Republic,* Mar. 10, 1969.

83. See *Watkins* v. *Steelworkers Local 2369,* 516 F.2d 41 (5th Cir. 1975), discussed in Ch. 4, sec.: "The 'Last Hired, First Fired' Controversy."

84. Wallen, "Industrial Relations Problems of Employing the Disadvantaged," in *Arbitration and Social Change: Proceedings of the 22d Annual Meeting, Nat'l Academy of Arbitrators* 65, 68 (1970).

85. See, e.g., *NLRB* v. *Insurance Agents' Int. Union,* 361 U.S. 477 (1960); *NLRB* v. *Gamble Enterprises, Inc.,* 345 U.S. 117 (1953); *American Newspaper Publishers Ass'n* v. *NLRB,* 345 U.S. 100 (1953); *NLRB* v. *American National Insurance Co.,* 343 U.S. 395 (1952).

86. 485 F.2d at 928.

87. See *NLRB* v. *Mansion House Center Management Corp.,* 473 F.2d 471, 477 (8th Cir. 1973), discussed in Ch. 7, secs.: "Racial Discrimination by a Union" and "Duty-of-Fair-Representation Doctrine."

88. See cases cited n.2

89. See n.37.

90. 485 F.2d at 930.

91. See text at n.18–19.

92. In discussing what law the courts are to apply in Section 301 suits to enforce collective bargaining agreements, the Court said: "The Labor Management Relations Act expressly furnishes some substantive law. It points out what the parties may or may not do in certain situations. Other problems will lie in the penumbra of expressed statutory mandates. Some will lack express statutory sanction but will be solved by looking at the policy of the legislation and fashioning a remedy that will effectuate that policy. The range of judicial inventiveness will be determined by the nature of the problem." *Textile Workers Union* v. *Lincoln Mills,* 353 U.S. 448, 457 (1957).

93. 350 U.S. 270 (1956). See text at n.7.

94. 88 *BNA Labor Relations Reporter* 238 (March 24, 1975).

95. See, e.g., *NLRB* v. *Insurance Agents Intl. Union,* 361 U.S. 477 (1960).

96. See, e.g., *Central Contractors Ass'n,* v. *Local 46, IBEW,* 312 F. Supp. 1388 (W.D. Wash. 1969); *United States* v. *Local 189 United Papermakers,* 282 F. Supp. 39 (E.D. La. 1968).

97. *Building & Construction Trades Council,* 164 NLRB 313 (1967); cf. *NLRB* v. *Denver Bldg. & Constr. Trades Council,* 341 U.S. 675 (1951).

98. See *Glover* v. *St. Louis-San Francisco Ry.,* 393 U.S. 324 (1969).

99. See sec.: "Picketing as an Unfair Labor Practice."

100. See n. 81.

101. 444 F.2d 791, 799 (4th Cir. 1971).

102. 398 U.S. 235 (1970).

103. See *Sinclair Oil Corp.* v. *Oil Workers Union,* 452 F.2d 49, 54, n.10 (7th Cir. 1971), noted 86 *Harv. L. Rev.* 447, 454 (1972).

104. See Ch. 8, text at nn.42–58.

105. *Garmon* v. *San Diego Bldg. Trades Council,* 359 U.S. 236, 244–245 (1959).

106. *Smith* v. *Evening News Ass'n,* 371 U.S. 195 (1962). See also *Carey* v. *Westinghouse Electric Corp.,* 375 U.S. 261 (1964).

107. 414 U.S. 368 (1974).

108. The Court, while noting that the obligation to arbitrate a labor dispute arises from contract rather than by operation of law, *id.* at 374, reaffirmed the "well-known presumption of arbitrability," *id.* at 377, which was fashioned in *United Steelworkers of America* v. *Warrior & Gulf Navigation Co.,* 363 U.S. 574, 582–83 (1960). The Court also reaffirmed that "a contractual commitment to submit disagreements to final and binding arbitration gives rise to an implied obligation not to strike over such disputes," *id.* at 381, as held in Local 174, *Teamsters* v. *Lucas Flour Co.,* 369 U.S. 95 (1962). The Court stated that "(a)bsent an explicit expression [to the contrary] . . . , the agreement to arbitrate and the duty not to strike should be construed as having coterminous application." 414 U.S. at 382.

109. *Id.* at 385.

110. *Id.* at 386.

111. 346 U.S. 464 (1953).

112. *Id.* at 475.

113. 411 F.2d 998, 1006 n.18 (5th Cir. 1969). See generally *Houchstadt* v. *Worcester Foundation for Experimental Biology,* 13 FEP Cases, 805 (1st Cir. 1976).

114. 376 U.S. 254 (1964) (public official cannot recover damages for defamatory falsehood relating to his official conduct unless he proves that the statement was made with "actual malice"—i.e., with knowledge that it was false or with reckless disregard of whether it was false or not).

115. *Linn* v. *United Plant Guard Workers,* 383 U.S. 53 (1966) (where union publishes defamatory falsehoods regarding employer during organizing campaign, employer can recover damages under state law of defamation, if he proves that the statement was made with "malice," as the term was defined in *New York Times, supra* n.114).

116. 411 F.2d at 1007 n.22.

117. See n.64.

118. 411 U.S. 792 (1973), discussed in Ch. 3, sec.: *"McDonnell Douglas Corp.* v. *Green.*

119. *Id.* at 803–804, citing *NLRB* v. *Fansteel Corp.,* 306 U.S. 240 (1939).

120. 411 U.S. at 804.

121. *Id.* at 804–805.

122. *Id.* at 805 n.19.

123. See Ch. 3, sec.: *"McDonnell Douglas Corp.* v. *Green."*

124. 107 F.2d 472, 479 (3d Cir. 1939), *modified on other grds.,* 311 U.S. 7 (1940).

125. *NLRB* v. *Fansteel Corp., supra* n.119.

126. See *NLRB* v. *Thayer Co.,* 213 F.2d 748 (1st Cir.), *cert. denied,* 348 U.S. 883 (1954); Local 833, *UAW* v. *NLRB (Kohler Co.),* 300 F.2d 699 (D.C. Cir.), *cert. denied,* 370 U.S. 911 (1962).

127. 29 U.S.C. § 158(b)(4)(C).

128. 29 U.S.C. § 158(b)(7)(A).

129. 362 U.S. 274 (1960).

130. 360 U.S. 203 (1959).

131. Section 2(5), 29 U.S.C. § 152(5) (1973), provides: "The term 'labor organization' means any organization of any kind, or any agency or employee representation committee or plan, in which employees participate and which exists for the purpose, in whole or in part, of dealing with employers concerning grievances, labor disputes, wages, rates of pay, hours of employment, or conditions of work."

132. See Ch. 7, text at nn.113–117.

133. *Meat & Provision Drivers Union,* 115 NLRB 890 (1956).

134. Archibald Cox, "The Landrum-Griffin Amendments to the National Labor Relations Act," 44 *Minn. L. Rev.* 257, 266–270 (1959).

135. 133 NLRB 1468 (1961).

136. *Id.*

137. *Id.* at 1468–1469. See also *Bldg. & Constr. Trades Council* v. *NLRB,* 396 F.2d 677, 683 (D.C. Cir. 1968); *Restaurant Management, Inc.,* 147 NLRB 1060 (1961); *Eastern Camera & Photo Corp.,* 141 NLRB 991, 997 (1963); *Mission Valley Inn,* 140 NLRB 433 (1963); *Woodward Motors, Inc.,* 135 NLRB 851 (1962). Cf. Leo Weiss, "The Unlawful Objective in 8(b)(7) Picketing," 13 *Lab. L.J.* 787 (1962).

138. For a discussion of these and similar organizations, see Ch. 14.

139. 47 LA 873 (1966).

140. See generally *Bronian* v. *Great A&P Tea Co.,* 353 F.2d 559 (6th Cir. 1965); *Black-Clawson Co.* v. *Lodge 355, IAM,* 313 F.2d 179 (2d Cir. 1962); *Federal Tel. & Radio Co.,* 107 NLRB 649 (1953); Dunan, "Employee Participation in the Grievance Aspect of Collective Bargaining," 50 *Colum. L. Rev.* 731, 751–760 (1950). But cf. *Douds* v. *Local 1250, Retail, Wholesale & Department Store Union,* 170 F.2d 695 (2d Cir. 1948).

141. 147 NLRB 446 (1964), *enforcement denied,* 352 F.2d 482 (10th Cir. 1965), *original order aff'd,* 158 NLRB 1680 (1966), *enforcement denied, and order set aside,* 377 F.2d 800 (10th Cir. 1967). See generally, George Schatzki, "Some Observations and Suggestions Concerning a Misnomer—'Protected' Concerted Activities," 47 *Tex. L. Rev.* 378, 398–403 (1969); Comment, "Employee Picketing and Section 8(b)(7)(B)," 47 *Tex. L. Rev.* 294 (1969).

142. 147 NLRB 446 (1964).

143. 352 F.2d 482, 485 (10th Cir. 1965).

144. *Id.* at 485.

145. 158 NLRB at 1688.

146. 377 F.2d 800, 804 (10th Cir. 1967).

147. 178 NLRB 189 (1969).

148. *Id.* at 192.

149. *Id.* at 189 n.1.

150. Presumably, §§ 8(b)(4) and (7) cannot be used as a shield by parties that discriminate, any more than § 9. See *Hughes Tool Co.,* 147 NLRB 1573 (1964); *Pioneer Bus Co.,* 140 NLRB 54 (1962). Cf. *Hughes Tool Co.,* 104 NLRB 318 (1953). In the absence of racial discrimination, the collective bargaining relationship is preserved by the board through 39. See *Leonard Wholesale Meats, Inc.,* 136 NLRB 1000 (1962).

151. 178 NLRB at 192 n.11.

152. 76 LRRM 2409 (S.D.N.Y. 1970).

153. *Id.* at 2412.

154. 451 F.2d 1011 (4th Cir. 1971), *cert. denied,* 407 U.S. 917 (1972).

155. *Id.* at 1012.

10 | The Construction Industry

1. Specific examples of many of the practices discussed in this chapter are to be found in Chs. 12 and 13.

2. U.S. Comm'n on Civil Rights, *Contract Compliance and Equal Employment Opportunity in the Construction Industry* 266–267 1969) (transcript of open meeting in Boston, Mass., June 25–26, 1969, before the Massachusetts State Advisory Committee to the United States Commission on Civil Rights).

3. A. H. Raskin, "Labor and Civil Rights," *N.Y. Times,* May 20, 1964.

4. Data provided to the author by EEOC Office of Research.

5. U.S. Dept. of Labor, Formal Occupational Training of Adult Workers, Manpower/Automation Research Monograph No. 2 (1964). Howard Foster and George Strauss conclude that although there are "no adequate statistics" on apprenticeship in construction, it is nevertheless "clear that apprenticeship provides a 'port of entry' for only a fraction of the industry's workers." Foster and Strauss, "Labor Problems in Construction: A Review," 11 *Ind. Rel.* 289, 295–296 (1972). See also Strauss, "Apprenticeship: An Evaluation of the Need," in Arthur Ross, ed., *Employment Policy and the Labor Market* 299–332 (1965). The "fraction" appears to be in the neighborhood of 20–307. See Foster, "Nonapprentice Source of Training in Construction," 93 *Monthly L.L. Rev.,* Feb. 1970 at p. 21.

6. These statistics were provided in a lecture by Nathaniel Pierson, Director of Contract Compli-

ance, Veterans' Administration and former Director of the Special Construction Unit, OFCC, in the Employment Discrimination Seminar at Stanford Law School, Oct. 1972.

7. Derek Bok and John Dunlop, *Labor and the American Community* 127 (1970). For an excellent review of this book, see Clyde Summers, "Straw Men of Union Leadership," 80 *Yale L.J.* 687 (1971).

8. See Foster and Strauss, p. 305, and authorities cited therein; *Wall Street Journal,* Aug. 29, 1972, p. 1, col. 5.

9. See n. 5.

10. Foster, p. 23, n.5.

11. *Griggs* v. *Duke Power Co.,* 401 U.S. 424 (1971), discussed in Ch. 4, sec.: "Societal Discrimination."

12. See generally Ch. 4.

13. See, e.g., *United States* v. *Iron Workers, Local 10,* 6 FEP Cases 59, 67 (W.D. Mo. 1973); cf. *United States* v. *Local 86, Ironworkers,* 315 F. Supp. 1202, 1234 (W.D. Wash. 1970), *aff'd* 443 F.2d 544 (9th Cir. 1971), *cert. denied,* 404 U.S. 984 (1971).

14. Cf. *Local 53 Heat & Frost Insulators* v. *Vogler,* 407 F.2d 1047 (5th Cir. 1969); *Rios* v. *Steamfitters Local 638,* 360 F. Supp. 979 (S.D.N.Y. 1972), *aff'd with modifications,* 501 F.2d 622 (2d Cir. 1974); *United States* v. *Sheet Metal Workers Local 36,* 416 F.2d 123 (8th Cir. 1969); *United States* v. *Pipefitters Local 638,* 347 F. Supp. 169 (S.D.N.Y. 1972). Cf. also the cases cited in n.15.

15. *Rowe* v. *General Motors Corp.,* 457 F.2d 348 (5th Cir. 1972), discussed in Ch. 5 at n.65 and Ch. 3 at n.63. The theme appears in several of the apprenticeship cases; see, e.g., *United States* v. *Sheet Metal Workers, Local 10,* 6 FEP Cases 1036 (D.N.J. 1973); *United States* v. *Plumbers, Local 24,* 364 F. Supp. 808, 829 (D.N.J. 1973); *United States* v. *IBEW Local 357,* 356 F. Supp. 104 (D. Nev. 1972); *United States* v. *Bricklayers Local 1,* 5 EPD ¶8480 at p. 7317 (W.D. Tenn. 1973), *aff'd with modifications subnom United States* v. *Masonry Contractors,* 497 F.2d 871 (6th Cir. 1974), see also *United States* v. *IBEW, Local 38,* 428 F.2d 144 (6th Cir.), *cert. denied,* 400 U.S. 943 (1970).

16. Strauss, pp. 311–313.

17. Deposition of Frank Catapano, taken by plaintiff in *United States* v. *Local 638, Pipefitters,* No. 71 Civ. 2877, (S.D.N.Y. May 26, 1972), pp. 16–19.

18. *Local 53 Heat & Frost Insulators* v. *Vogler,* 407 F.2d 1047 95th Cir. 1969). See also *United States* v. *Local 638 Pipefitters,* 347 F. Supp. 169, 181 (S.D.N.Y. 1972); *United States* v. *Lathers Local 46,* 471 F.2d 408, 414 (2d Cir. 1973), *cert. denied,* 412 U.S. 939 (1974).

19. 347 F. Supp. 169, 176 (S.D.N.Y. 1972).

20. *Vogler* at 1054.

21. 457 F.2d 210 (7th Cir. 1972), *cert. denied,* 409 U.S. 851 (1972).

22. *Id.* at 215 n.8.

23. See *H.R. Rgt.* No. 92–238 (1971) at 22.

24. 326 F. Supp. 198 (S.D.N.Y. 1971).

25. *Id.* at 203 n.4.

26. *United States* v. *Sheetmetal Workers, Local 36,* 416 F.2d 123, 136 (8th Cir. 1969).

27. 347 F. Supp. 169, 184 (S.D.N.Y. 1972).

28. *Griggs* v. *Duke Power Co.,* 401 U.S. 424, 432 (1971).

29. 315 F. Supp. 1202, 1246–47 (W.D. Wash. 1970), *aff'd* 443 F.2d 544 (9th Cir. 1971), *cert denied,* 404 U.S. 984 (1971), discussed in Ch. 13.

30. See, e.g., *United States* v. *Local 638 Steamfitters,* 360 F. Supp. 979, 993 (S.D.N.Y. 1973), *affirmed with modifications,* 501 F.2d 622 (2d Cir. 1974); *United States* v. *Local 357 IBEW,* 356 F. Supp. 104, 121 (D. Nev. 1973).

31. 337 F. Supp. 217 (S.D.N.Y. 1972).

32. N.18.

33. 347 F. Supp. 169, 183 (S.D.N.Y. 1972).

34. 4 FEP Cases 1147 (W.D. Wash. 1972).

35. See n.15.

36. *Id.* at 359.

37. See Sovern, pp. 189–90 (1966).

38. 416 F.2d 123 (8th Cir. 1969).

39. *Id.* at 139–140.

40. For example, the Laborers have successfully challenged, as an unconstitutional denial of equal protection, municipal ordinances which require certain outside pipelaying work, which laborers are

capable of performing, to be done by licensed plumbers. *White* v. *City of Evansville,* 310 F. Supp. 569 (S.D. Ind. 1970); see also *Utility Contractors Ass'n of New Jersey* v. *Toops,* 507 F.2d 83 (3d Cir. 1974).

41. "Red circling" refers to a remedy which has been employed in the industrial union seniority cases, namely the freezing of an employee's wages at their existing level so that he will not be deterred from making a transfer (typically from a previously all-black line of progression to a previously all-white line) by the fact that a cut in wages would be involved. See Ch. 4 at n.38.

42. NLRA § 8(a)(3), 29 U.S.C. § 158(a)(3)(1970).

43. NLRA § 8(f), 29 U.S.C. § 158(f) (1970).

44. See, e.g., *Rios* v. *Local 638 Steamfitters,* 326 F. Supp. 198 (S.D.N.Y. 1971); *United States* v. *Local 638 Steamfitters,* 347 F. Supp. 169, 180 n.7 (S.D.N.Y. 1972).

45. *NLRB* v. *Local 2, United Association of Plumbing and Pipefitting Industries,* 360 F.2d 428 (2nd Cir. 1966) enforcing 152 NLRB 1093 (1965).

46. *Building & Construction Trades Council,* 164 NLRB 313 (1967).

47. 365 U.S. 667 (1961).

48. U.S. Dept. of Labor, Labor Management Services Administration, *Exclusive Union Work Referral Systems in the Building Trades* (1970).

49. *Exclusive Union Work Referral Systems,* p. 48.

50. *Typographers, Local 6 (N.Y. Times Co.),* 133 NLRB 1052 (1961).

51. See generally Ch. 4. See *Kaplan* v. *I.A.T.S.E.,* 525 F.2d 354 (9th Cir. 1975).

52. See n.15.

11 | Private Initiative in the Construction Industry: The How and Why of Imposed and Voluntary Plans

1. *N.Y. Times,* Feb. 14, 1968, p. 23.

2. *N.Y. Times,* Feb. 14, 1968, p. 23.

3. *N.Y. Times,* June 25, 1968, p. 29.

4. *Id.*

5. Herbert Hill, *Labor Union Control of Job Training: A Critical Analysis of Apprenticeship Outreach Programs and the Hometown Plans* 42–46 (Howard University Institute for Urban Affairs and Research Occasional Paper vol. 2, no. 1, 1974).

6. For a discussion of the Cleveland Plan, see Richard Nathan, *Jobs and Civil Rights* 109–111 (1969) (publication of U.S. Comm'n on Civil Rights).

7. *Ethridge* v. *Rhodes,* 268 F. Supp. 83 (S.D. Ohio 1967). See also *Todd* v. *JAC,* 223 F. Supp. 12 (N.D. Ill. 1963), *vacated as moot,* 332 F.2d 243 (7th Cir. 1964), *cert. denied,* 380 U.D. 912 (1965).

8. Nathan, p. 110.

9. *Id.* at 110.

10. *Id.* at 111.

11. 47 Comp. Gen. 666, 670 (1968). See also 48 Comp. Gen. 326 (1968).

12. 49 Comp. Gen. 59 (1969).

13. The revised Philadelphia Plan appears in *BNA FEP Manual* 401:255, supplementing 401:251, and *CCH Employment Practices Guide* ¶1710, supplementing ¶1708. It was amended, effective March 1, 1971, to include non-federally involved construction activities of covered contractors and subcontractors. The legality of the Plan was upheld in *Contractors Ass'n of Eastern Pennsylvania* v. *Schultz,* 442 F.2d 159 (3d Cir. 1971), *cert. denied,* 404 U.S. 854 (1971).

14. Tom Wicker, "In the Nation: Whispering Hope," *N.Y. Times,* Dec. 30, 1969, p. 326, col. 3.

15. Excerpts from the statement appear in *N.Y. Times,* Sept. 23, 1968, p. 56, col. 3.

16. AFL-CIO Dept. of Public Relations Press Release, Sept. 24, 1969.

17. *Wall Street Journal,* Sept. 26, 1969, p. 14, col. 4.

18. *Wall Street Journal,* July 6, 1970, p. 6, col. 4.

19. *Chicago Tribune,* Sept. 26, 1969, p. 1, col. 8.

20. *Chicago Tribune,* Jan. 13, 1970, at sec. 1, p. 17, col. 2; *N.Y. Times,* Jan. 13, 1970, p. 28C, col. 3.

21. AFL-CIO Department of Public Relations Press Release, Jan. 15, 1970.

22. *N.Y. Times,* Jan. 13, 1970, p. 28C, col. 3.

23. *N.Y. Times,* May 30, 1971, p. 37, col. 3.

24. *N.Y. Times,* June 5, 1971, p. 1, col. 7.

25. *Id.*

26. *OFCC-MA Task Force Report* 9 (1971).

27. *Id.* at 11.

28. *Detroit News,* Oct. 19, 1972, p. 19-A, col. 1. For a description of this plan, see *N.Y. Times,* Dec. 16, 1972, p. 32, col. 2.

29. 41 C.F.R. § 60–11.3 (1974).

30. The Chicago Plan, in its current form, appears in 41 C.F.R. § 60-11 (1974).

31. The statistics appear at 41 C.F.R. § 60–11.11 (1974).

32. *N.Y. Times,* June 21, 1970, p. 28, col. 1.

33. Memorandum from Reginald Brown, Contract Compliance Advisor, OFCC Region I, to John Wilks, Director, OFCC, re Boston Plan Review.

34. See *Wall Street Journal,* Sept. 7, 1971, p. 5; *Boston Globe,* Nov. 3, 1971, p. 3; *Boston Globe,* Nov. 12, 1971, p. 10.

35. See *Associated General Contractors* v. *Altshuler,* 490 F.2d 9, 13–14 (1st Cir. 1973), *cert. denied,* 416 U.S. 957 (1974). The announcement of the Mass. Dept. of Transportation's plan, and the Department's criticism of Boston Plan II, were contained in the Department's press release of May 30, 1972.

36. On the differences between the Boston Plan and the Commonwealth's provisions, see *Associated General Contractors,* at 14–15.

37. *Associated General Contractors.*

38. *Id.* 416 U.S. 957 (1974).

39. *Detroit Free Press,* Oct. 7, 1969, p. 3, col. 4–8.

40. On the resistance of the building trades to implementing the plan, see *Detroit Free Press,* May 9, 1970, p. 3–A; *Detroit News,* May 9, 1970, p. 7-A; *Detroit News,* Sept. 22, 1970, p. 3-A. On the conditional nature of the obligations imposed by the plan, and its general weakness, see William B. Gould, "Letter to the Editor," *Detroit News,* March 10, 1971, p. 6-B; *Detroit News,* March 23, 1971, p. 1-A (reporting comments of Michigan Civil Rights Commission); *Detroit Free Press,* July 7, 1972, p. 3-A (reporting comments of Herbert Hill).

41. *Detroit Free Press,* Feb. 23, 1971, p. 1, cols. 2–5.

42. The results of the audit appear in Report of Findings Regarding Audits Conducted by Sepcial OFCC Audit Detail (report from Robert G. Owens, Acting Associate Director, OCCO, to Philip J. Davis, Acting Director, OFCCO at p. 1 (1972).

43. *N.Y. Times,* Sept. 16, 1969, p. 61, col. 2.

44. *N.Y. Times,* Jan. 31, 1970, p. 20-C. The "memorandum of understanding" signed on Jan. 30 developed into a plan which was approved by the Federal government on Oct. 24, 1970. *N.Y. Times,* Oct. 25, 1970, p. 46, col. 2.

45. The results of the audit appear in Report of Findings, p. 8.

46. Much of the information which follows regarding the Indianapolis Plan derives from the author's interview with Herman Walker, director of the Indianapolis Plan, on April 21, 1971 (transcript on file with the author).

47. The results of the audit appear in Report of Findings, p. 2.

48. *N.Y. Times,* May 4, 1964.

49. A. H. Raskin, "Labor and Civil Rights," *N.Y. Times,* May 20, 1964.

50. *N.Y. Times,* Oct. 3, 1968.

51. *Id.;* see also *N.Y. Times,* Dec. 30, 1967, p. 20, col. 1.

52. *N.Y. Times,* April 28, 1969, p. 37M, col. 1.

53. *N.Y. Times,* Feb. 15, 1970, p. 79, col. 5.

54. Damon Stetson, "Builders and Unions Here Offer Minorities Training," *N.Y. Times,* March 22, 1970, p. 1, col. 6.

55. *Id.*

56. *Wall Street Journal,* March 23, 1970, p. 7, col. 2.

57. *N.Y. Times,* April 2, 1970, p. 33C, col. 2.

58. *N.Y. Post,* March 10, 1971, p. 28.

59. *N.Y. Times,* April 10, 1971, p. 1, col. 2.

60. *N.Y. Times,* Sept. 19, 1971, p. 1, 30.

61. *N.Y. Post,* June 26, 1972, p. 2, col. 1.

62. *N.Y. Times,* July 27, 1972, p. 35-C, col. 7.

63. *N.Y. Times*, July 29, 1972, p. 24, col. 1.

64. *N.Y. Times*, Oct. 12, 1972, p. 51.

65. *N.Y. Times*, April 18, 1973, p. 1, col. 5.

66. For the text of the original Brennan memorandum, see *City of New York* v. *Diamond*, 379 F. Supp. 503 509–510 (S.D.N.Y. 1974). This memorandum was not published in the Federal Register, but subsequently the Department of Labor has promulgated a regulation based on the memorandum. 41 C.F.R. section 60-1.4, 39 Fed. Reg. 2365 (Jan. 21, 1974). The regulation as well as the initial memorandum were held in *Diamond* to be invalid on the ground that they were improperly promulgated, as well as for the substantive grounds discussed in text at nn.70–71.

67. N.35.

68. *Id.*, 490 F.2d at 14–15.

69. *Id.* at 15–16.

70. *City of New York* v. *Diamond*, 379 F. Supp. 503, 519 (S.D.N.Y. 1974).

71. *Id.* at 520.

12 | The Impact of Judicial Decrees: An Empirical Analysis

1. *United States* v. *Sheetmetal Workers Local 36*, 416 F.2d 123 (8th Cir. 1969). The decree broke new ground by reaching not only blacks who had applied for membership or referral, but also those who had been deterred from applying by the union's discriminatory reputation.

2. *Id.* at 133–134.

3. *Id.* at 139–140.

4. Department of Justice Memorandum to David L. Rose, Chief, Employment Section, from Grover G. Hankins, Attorney, Employment Section, re: Review of Compliance Reports: Sheetmetal Workers Local 36 and IBEW Local 1, St. Louis, at p. 2 (1972).

5. *Id.* at p. 3.

6. F. Ray Marshall, *The Negro and Organized Labor* (New York, 1965), p. 113.

7. *Id.* at 113–114.

8. *United States* v. *IBEW Local 38*, 428 F.2d, 144, 146 (6th Cir.), *cert. denied*, 400 U.S. 943 (1970), reversing 1 FEP Cases 673 (N.D. Ohio 1969).

9. *Id.*

10. *Local 53 Heat & Frost Insulators* v. *Vogler*, 407 F.2d 1047 (5th Cir. 1969), discussed in Ch. 4, at n.1., and Ch. 10 at nn.18, 20, 32.

11. *Local 189, Papermakers* v. *United States*, 416 F.2d 980 (5th Cir. 1969), discussed in Ch. 4.

12. 428 F.2d at 149–150.

13. *Id.* at 151.

14. *United States* v. *IBEW Local 38*, 3 FEP Cases 362 (N.D. Ohio 1971).

15. *Id.* at 365–365.

16. *Id.* at 366.

17. *Id.* at 367.

18. *Id.*

19. *Id.*

20. The Cleveland Plan is discussed in Ch. 11, text at nn.6–9.

21. Consent Decree, *United States* v. *Steamfitters Local 250* No. 68–190-DWW (C.D. Cal. Sept 10, 1969) (unreported).

22. Consent Decree, *United States* v. *Steamfitters Local 250*, No. 68–190-DWW (C.D. Cal. May 25, 1972) (unreported).

23. *Id.* at p. 4.

24. *United States* v. *Lathers Local 46*, 341 F. Supp 694, 698 (S.D.N.Y. 1972), *aff'd* 471 F.2d 408 (2d Cir. 1973), *cert. denied*, 416 U.S. 939 (1973).

25. *Id.*

26. 2 EPD ¶10, 266 (1970).

27. 2 EPD ¶10,226 at p. 878.

28. *Id.*

29. *Id.* at 879.

30. *Id.* at 876.

31. *United States* v. *Lathers Local 46*, 328 F. Supp. 429, 434 (S.D.N.Y. 1971).

32. *Id.* 435.

33. *Id.*

34. *Id.*

35. *Id.* at 437.

36. *Id.* at 441 n.13.

37. Memorandum Confirming Rules and Procedures, *United States* v. *Lathers Local 46,* No. 68 Civ. 2116 (S.D.N.Y., July 16, 1971).

38. *Id.,* part III.B, p. 3.

39. Letter to William B. Gould from Joel B. Harris, Assistant U.S. Attorney for the Southern District of New York, March 6, 1973.

40. *United States* v. *Lathers Local 46,* 341 F. Supp. 694 (S.D.N.Y. 1972), *aff'd,* 471 F.2d 408 (2d Cir.), *cert. denied,* 412 U.S. 939 (1973).

41. *United States* v. *Local 636 Steamfitters,* 337 F. Supp. 217, 218 (S.D.N.Y. 1972).

42. The *N.Y. Times* reported that Judge Dudley Bonsol signed a temporary restraining order. *N.Y. Times,* Dec. 11, 1971, p. 1, col. 3; *N.Y. Times,* Dec. 14, 1971, p. 34, col. 4. However, Assistant U.S. Attorney Joel B. Harris advised the author in an interview of July 7, 1972, that in fact Judge Bonsol did not formally sign the TRO.

43. *N.Y. Times,* Dec. 14, 1971, p. 34, col. 4.

44. *N.Y. Times,* Dec. 16, 1971, p. 33, col. 1.

45. *Id.*

46. Interview with Assistant U.S. Attorney Joel B. Harris, July 7, 1972.

47. *United States* v. *Local 638 Steamfitters,* 337 F. Supp. 217, 218 (S.D.N.Y. 1972).

48. *Id.* at 219.

49. *United States* v. *Local 638, Steamfitters,* 360 F. Supp. 979, 994 (S.D.N.Y. 1973), *aff'd and remanded for modification,* 501 F.2d 622 (2d Cir. 1974). The *U.S.* v. *Local 638* suit was consolidated for trial with *Rios* v. *Local 638, Steamfitters,* an action in which Judge Frankel had issued a preliminary injunction compelling Local 638 to admit three named black plaintiffs to full journeymen status, 326 F. Supp. 198 (S.D.N.Y. 1971).

50. *Griggs* v. *Duke Power Co.,* 401 U.S. 424 (1971), discussed in Ch. 4, sec.: "Unanswered Questions Relating to Seniority."

51. 6 FEP Cases at 337.

52. *United States* v. *Local 3, Operating Engineers,* 4 FEP Cases 1088, 1090 (N.D. Cal. 1972).

53. *Id.* at 1091.

54. *Id.* at 1091.

55. *Id.* at 1091.

56. The AFL-CIO continually defends apprenticeship programs designed to provide graduates with far more skills than are needed for most jobs in the trades. See, e.g., 1970 *BNA Labor Relations Yearbook* 271, 278–279 (interview with Gregory Meany).

57. *Id.* at 1096.

58. *Id.* at 1097.

59. *Id.* at 1091.

60. The consent decree is unreported; Permanent Injunction in Partial Resolution of Lawsuit, *United States* v. *Operating Engineers Local 3,* Civil No. C-71-1277 RFP (N.D. Cal. Feb. 8, 1973). The private plaintiffs' suits were stayed in Corrected Order, Civil No. C-71-1277 RFP (Feb. 1, 1973).

61. Permanent Injunction, para. 19, p. 15.

13 | The Seattle Building Trades Decree

1. *United States* v. *Local 86, Ironworkers,* 315 F. Supp. 1202 (W.D. Wash. 1970), *aff'd,* 443 F.2d 554 (9th Cir.), *cert. denied,* 404 U.S. 984 (1971).

2. 349 U.S. 294 (1955). See Ch. 7.

3. During the period Jan. 1971 through Feb. 1974, numerous interviews were conducted with Tyree Scott and Harley Bird, both of the United Construction Workers Association, Alice Paine of the American Friends Service Committee, Salley Kenyon, Stuart Pierson, and Frank Petramale, all of the Department of Justice, Kenneth McDonald, former counsel to the Court Order Advisory Committee, Donald Close, of the Electrical Contractors Association, Austin St. Laurent, president of the Seattle Building Trades Council, and Professor Luvern Rieke, chairman of the Court Order Advisory Committee.

4. Interview with Tyree Scott, in Seattle, Wash., Feb. 1, 1971, p. 3 [hereinafter cited as Scott Interview] (on file with author).

5. See D. Mills, *Industrial Relations and Manpower in Construction* (1972), p. 33; *NLRB* v. *Denver Bldg. & Construction Trades Council,* 341 U.S. 675 (1951); Bldg. & Construction Trades Council, 164 NLRB 313 (1967).

6. Scott Interview, p. 4.

7. *Id.*

8. *Id.,* p. 5.

9. See Ch. 8, sec.: "Institutional Framework."

10. Scott Interview, p. 6. Seattle was not the only city where such events occurred during the late summer and fall of 1969. Street gangs roamed Chicago's South Side chasing white workers from construction sites in the ghetto. *N.Y. Times,* Sept. 23, 1969, at 56, col. 3. "Black Monday" marches took place in Pittsburgh. *Id.,* Sept. 16, 1969, at 36, col. 2. Black "hard-hat" demonstrators protested job discrimination in Detroit. *Detroit Free Press,* Oct. 11, 1969, at A3, col. 2. In urban areas throughout the country, the same demands were heard.

11. *Central Contractors Ass'n.* v. *Local 4 IBEW,* 312 F. Supp. 1388, 1391 (W.D. Wash. 1969), construing 29 U.S.C. § 107 (1970). For a criticism of this approach, see William B. Gould, *Black Power in the Unions: The Impact upon Collective Bargaining Relationships,* 79 Yale L.J. 46 (1969). See generally Gould, *On Labor Injunctions, Unions, and the Judges: The Boys Market Case,* 1970 Sup. Ct. Rev. 215.

12. This alliance originated with Peter Brennan's "hard-hat" demonstrations in the spring of 1970. See Gould, *Labor & Nixon: Moving the Hard-Hats In, The Nation,* Jan. 8, 1973, at 41.

13. See Ch. 11, text beginning at n.11.

14. *N.Y. Times,* Sept. 30, 1969, p. 1, col. 2.

15. Scott Interview, p. 8.

16. *Id.,* p. 9.

17. *Id.,* p. 11–A.

18. *Id.,* p. 13–15.

19. *United States* v. *Local 86, Ironworkers,* 315 F. Supp. 1202 (W.D. Wash. 1970), *aff'd,* 443 F.2d 554 (9th Cir.), *cert. denied,* 404 U.S. 984 (1971). The Operating Engineers entered into a consent decree without trial. For an examination of the progress made under the consent decree, see Report to the Court on Progress under Judgment and Decree, Oct. 24, 1973.

20. 315 F. Supp. at 1202.

21. State agencies have also attempted to combat employment discrimination, but they have generally been even less successful than the courts. The experience of Howard Lewis, a black welder with thirty years of experience, illustrates both the nature of union discrimination and the inadequacies of administrative remedies.

Lewis was employed as a permit workman; he was obliged to pay dues to the local Ironworkers Union, but he had no status as a union member. In order to gain job security, he applied for membership. The union sent him a letter which stated an examination date but did not contain any instructions concerning the nature of the examination or other prerequisites to membership. At the examination Lewis was informed that he would have to return with a withdrawal card from a union to which he previously belonged, certification papers, and a letter of recommendation from a supervisor. Nothing more was required.

The following month Lewis again appeared before the examination board. One of the board members specifically stated to him: "There is no question about your welding. We know that you are a damn good welder." Yet he was asked whether he could tie knots and was advised that he could not become a member of the union unless he knew how to do so. At the conclusion of this second examination, the examining board offered to assist Lewis in learning to tie the required knots. He could not take advantage of this offer, however, because he worked too far away. Although none of the union workers who worked on the same job could tie the knots he was forced to learn, a nonunion machinist finally taught him. After practicing for more than a month, Lewis received a third examination.

At this examination Lewis proceeded to demonstrate his knot-tying ability by tying seven different knots. He was then asked to tie a knot which he never knew existed. At this point his patience and good-faith efforts collapsed. When asked if he wished to return to the examining board after further practice, he stated: "No, I do not, because I think regardless of what I do I am not going to pass this board."

The Washington Board Against Discrimination regarded the knot-tying requirement as an arbitrary hurdle which had been placed in Lewis' way: "Mr. Lewis' successful work at the Wells Dam project, as well as construction work performed both before and after that time, establish that the work of a welder ironworker does not involve knot-tying to any significant extent, and that it can be performed without the extensive knowledge and skill required to pass the examination which the Union purportedly gave all applicants. The Union has suggested that knot-tying abilities are required not only for performance of a welder's work but also for the protection of the individual workman as well as other workmen who might be injured if a welder undertook to move material with a line improperly tied. Such an argument might be entitled to weight if it were not evident that the Union has during the past years referred hundreds of 'permit' welders to work on construction sites without attempting to determine their abilities at knot-tying." *Lewis* v. *Local 86, Ironworkers,* BNA Daily Lab. Rep. No. 55, at D-6 (Wash. State Bd. Against Discrimination 1969). The board also found a pattern of racial discrimination by the union: "The almost total absence of outside Negro Ironworkers sharply contrasts with the 300 to 400 Negroes working as welders in Seattle manufacturing plants, shipyards, and even in construction work as sheetmetal workers." *Id.* at D-9.

It concluded that the knot-tying requirement had been applied in a discriminatory manner in the Lewis case and that "some limitation" needed to be imposed upon the use of such tests in connection with future application. The examiners' substantial discretion in choosing difficult or easy knots for the applicant to tie permitted them to discriminate on the basis of race. The Washington Board Against Discrimination left the type and number of knots to be determined by the examination board but insisted that requirements be applied uniformly to all applicants. Further, the union was required to prepare a written statement of its standards and procedures in connection with the examination of applicants. The purpose of this requirement was to insure that the subjects and degree of knowledge would be publicized and that applicants would be in a position to prepare—something that Lewis had been unable to do.

The board also noted that because of the union's discrimination, future referrals based upon either union membership or length of service would be the equivalent of a referral on the basis of race and therefore would constitute an unlawful practice. It concluded that the referral system could be reinstated only when the proportion of blacks employed in the trade reached the 10 percent proportion which blacks constitute in the area where the union's members live. Finally, the board stated that no further changes were to be made with regard to referral policies without its approval.

The board's decision, often referred to as the "knot-tying decision," was an important one. It suspended referral procedures until a quota was implemented, and it attempted to clarify membership application procedures. The fact remained, however, that it was binding upon only one of Seattle's building trades. The board also established very little in the way of substitute referral criteria or guidelines for such criteria. Moreover, the thrust of the board's order related only to two black workers who had been adversely affected and did not deal with broader problems of employment discrimination.

22. 315 F. Supp. at 1239–1243.

23. *Id.* at 1247.

24. *Id.* at 1239–1245.

25. *Id.* at 1207.

26. *Id.* at 1208.

27. "The bulk of the work which a rodman does consists in the placing and tying of rods on reinforcing jobs. The evidence establishes that the skills ordinarily required of a rodman can be learned and developed on the job in considerably less time that [sic] the two year minimum contended for by the union." *Id.*

28. *Id.* at 1211.

29. *Id.* at 1217–1218.

30. *Id.* at 1204, 1212, 1219, 1228.

31. The union often told experienced black laborers that no work was available in the construction trades when there was in fact a shortage of skilled workers. See *id.,* at 1221. Moreover, white workers with significantly less experience were referred. *Id.*

32. Virtually all of the blacks were employed as marine pipefitters, where the hourly wage for journeymen was $4.18. The hourly rate for journeymen in the construction trades, where only one black worker was employed, was $6.25. *Id.* at 1219.

33. *Id.* at 1231–1233.

34. *Id.* at 1235–1238.

35. Apprenticeship committees are legally distinct from their respective unions. See generally Mills, p. 187. Judge Lindberg found, however, that the unions were at least partially responsible for the discriminatory racial policies of the apprenticeship committees: "In practical effect the unions' policies and practices have established the framework within which the apprenticeship committees have worked. Union influence has been further supplemented by equal representation on each committee, by physical proximity to apprenticeship offices, and by varying degrees of control over the day to day operation of committee functions." 315 F. Supp. at 1234.

36. *Id*. at 1236.

37. *Id*. at 1236–1237.

38. The applications were to be serially numbered and had to contain at least the following information: "name, address, telephone number, age, race, union affiliation (if any) and summary and explanation of the applicant's experience in the particular union's trade or any related trade." *Id*. at 1237.

39. *Id*. at 1238.

40. A priority grouping is a work referral system based upon criteria such as length of previous employment in the particular field. U.S. Department of Labor, Exclusive Union Work Referral Systems in the Building Trades 58 (1970).

41. The union, however, retained the right to verify applicant's relevant statements. 315 F. Supp. at 1240.

42. *Id*. at 1240–44.

43. The Plumbers and Pipefitters apprenticeship committee and the Sheetmetal apprenticeship committee were ordered to "consider qualified" all applicants who were between the ages of 18 and 25, had a high school diploma or its equivalent, passed the aptitude test administered by the Washington State Division of Employment Security, and had no disabling physical defects. For the Ironworkers apprenticeship committee, eligible applicants needed to be between 18 and 30 and have 10 years of school, a high school transcript, a passing score on the aptitude test, no physical disabilities, and residency in the jurisdiction of the local for one year. *Id*. at 1246. The court did not find discrimination against blacks by the Electrical Workers apprenticeship committee and therefore did not impose specific admission standards upon it. See *id*. at 1251.

44. *Id*. at 1247.

45. *Id*. The overage applicants, however, had to be below the age of 45.

46. A class size from which one could "reasonably anticipate" an annual graduating class of at least twenty-five workers was imposed on the Plumbers and Pipefitters committee. A goal of twenty graduates was imposed on the Ironworkers and Sheetmetal Workers committees. *Id*. at 1248. The Electrical Workers committee was not required to form special apprenticeship programs because it had not discriminated against blacks, but the court encouraged the contractors' association and the Department of Justice to persuade the committee to establish one in order to achieve uniformity among the unions. *Id*. at 1251. The court instructed the Electrical Workers to set a goal of twenty-five graduates in the event it formed a special program. *Id*. at 1248.

47. The court required a two-year maximum for all the special programs except for that of the Plumbers and pipefitters, on which a three-year maximum was imposed. *Id*. at 1248.

48. *Id*.

49. *Id*. at 1249. The court also allowed the committee to designate other persons or organizations to issue such letters.

50. The aggregate of the quotas established by the 1970 order would be 483 black apprentices. As of June 11, 1972, there were 85 special apprentices and 10 operating engineer trainees, 388 fewer positions than prescribed in the 1970 order. *Seattle Post-Intelligencer,* June 11, 1972, at A18, col. 1.

51. See text accompanying nn.87–118.

52. As of 1970, blacks constituted 8 percent of Seattle's population. *United States Bureau of Census–Characteristics of the Population,* pt. 49, at 59 (1970).

53. The black community's willingness to engage in self-help has generally been devoid of the black nationalist rhetoric which has drained many other new organizations. This absence of rhetoric accounts for much of the effectiveness of black action in Seattle.

54. Scott Interview, p. 12.

55. *Id.,* p. 27–29.

56. Judge Lindberg ordered the union apprenticeship committee and the contractors with whom the unions had collective-bargaining agreements to establish "preapprentice" programs for blacks. These interim programs were designed to provide training for black workers pending the implementation of the more comprehensive special apprenticeship programs, which would eventually supersede them.

The court's order contemplated the placing of employees on contractor payrolls within two months. Yet by August 15, two months had passed and nothing had been done by either the unions or the contractors. For a discussion of the preapprentice program, see 315 F. Supp. at 1248–1249.

57. See text accompanying nn.16–18. Scott was arrested for criminal trespass at the demonstrations. He was tried subsequently and fined $175, but he refused to pay. When a warrant was issued for Scott's arrest in late August 1970, he surrendered and fasted in jail for eight days.

58. 3 FEP Cases 428, 429 (W.D. Wash. 1970).

59. The UCWA built substantial solidarity among black workers and could effectively encourage applications. Word-of-mouth communication, traditionally the means through which good jobs have been preserved for whites, was used for the first time by blacks. Tyree Scott has reported the impact UCWA meetings have had on spreading information about employment opportunities. See Scott Interview, pp. 31–32.

60. Minutes of COAC Meeting, in Seattle, Wash., Oct. 7, 1970, p. 1. The vote was six in favor and one opposed.

61. Interview with Donald Close, in Seattle, Wash., July 19, 1973.

62. Minutes of COAC Meeting, p. 1.

63. Order of Feb. 16, 1971, at 2, *United States* v. *Local 86, Ironworkers,* Civil No. 8618 (W.D. Wash. Feb. 16, 1971).

64. *Id.* at 4.

65. "In his carefully written and excellent opinion, covering some 50 pages, Judge Lindberg made separate findings of fact as to each party, carefully analyzing the supportive evidence found in the record. In these findings of fact Judge Lindberg has pointed out by page reference to the record, the testimony, stipulations, admitted facts, and exhibits upon which his findings were based. . . . Having reviewed the findings and the record before us, we are fully convinced that the findings are amply supported by the evidence." *United States* v. *Local 86, Ironworkers,* 443 F.2d 544, 550 (9th Cir.), *cert. denied,* 404 U.S. 948 (1971).

66. See Order of Feb. 16, 1971, at 4, *United States* v. *Local 86, Ironworkers,* Civil No. 8618 (W.D. Wash. Feb. 16, 1971).

67. Judge Lindberg later recognized this problem himself: "Such a report was not furnished by the plaintiff until approximately one year after the entry of the Decree [July 1971] and then only as a result of solicitation and urging by the Court. The plaintiff, United States, has never assigned a full-time Assistant United States Attorney to monitoring its Decree. As a result, when emergencies have developed, the plaintiff has sent Mr. Petramalo, who is not stationed in Seattle, here to deal with emergency situations, obviously after they have occurred. Mr. Petramalo is an able, dedicated lawyer but he has other obligations of a most substantial nature which prevent his attending to this matter, which itself requires substantial commitment in terms of time and ability." *United States* v. *Local 86, Ironworkers,* 4 FEP Cases 1152, 1153 (W.D. Wash. 1972).

68. *Seattle Post-Intelligencer,* June 11, 1972, p. A18, col. 1.

69. See text accompanying n.102.

70. *Special Plumbers and Pipefitters Subcommittee Report,* Apr. 24, 1972, at 1; *Ironworkers Special Apprentice Program Report,* Apr. 24, 1972, at 1; *Sheetmetal Special Apprentice Program Report,* Apr. 24, 1972, at 1; *Electrical Apprenticeship Subcommittee Report,* Apr. 21, 1972, at 1.

71. Minutes of COAC Meeting, p. 1.

72. *Seattle Post-Intelligencer,* June 8, 1972, p. A3, col. 1.

73. *United States* v. *Local 86, Ironworkers,* 4 FEP Cases 1147, 1148 (W.D. Wash. 1972).

74. "In order to meet the goals of this Court's orders of June 16, 1970, the COAC shall exercise fully its power under this and prior orders in this case to require the acceptance of a sufficient number of special apprentice applicants to bring the total number of actively participating special apprentices up to at least the following levels by July 7, 1972: Electricians 50; Ironworkers, 40; Plumbers, 50; Sheet Metal Workers, 40." *Id.* at 1149.

75. *Id.*

76. *Id.* at 1148.

77. *Seattle Post-Intelligencer,* June 10, 1972, p. A1, col. 3.

78. *Seattle Times,* June 13, 1972, p. A17, col. 1.

79. *Seattle Post-Intelligencer,* June 16, 1972, p. A11, col. 1.

80. *Id.*

81. *Id.*

82. *United States* v. *Local 86, Ironworkers,* 4 FEP Cases 1150–1151 (W.D. Wash. 1972).

83. *Seattle Post-Intelligencer,* June 23, 1973, p. A1, col. 2.
84. 4 FEP Cases at 1151.
85. *Seattle Times,* July 8, 1972, p. A4.
86. *United States* v. *Local 86, Ironworkers,* 4 FEP Cases 1152, 1153 (W.D. Wash. 1972).
87. See n.74.
88. U.S. Attorney's Report to the Court on the Special Apprentice Program, Sept. 11, 1972.
89. U.S. Attorney's Quarterly Report to the Court on Apprentice Programs, Mar. 1973, at 3.
90. U.S. Attorney's Quarterly Report to the Court on Apprentice Programs, Dec. 1973, at 3:

	Ironworkers	Plumbers	Sheetmetal	Electricians
Specials				
Class I	0	3	6	10
Class II	4	7	5	14
Class III	12	10	14	20
Class IV	15	4	13	28
Subtotal	31	24	38	72
Black Regulars	8	15	12	0
Graduates	9	8	5	6
Total	48	47	55	78
No. Required	78	96	81	75
Ratio of Participation to Goal	61.5%	49.0%	67.9%	104%

91. U.S. Attorney's Quarterly Report to the Court on Apprentice Programs, Mar. 1973, at 5.
92. 315 F. Supp. at 1247.
93. Special Report of COAC, Sept. 13, 1973, p. 5.
94. U.S. Attorney's Quarterly Report to the Court on Apprentice Programs, Summer 1973, at 22–23.
95. Luvern Rieke has remarked that lack of work experience was a deficiency of all special apprenticeship programs: "[W]ork experience is a major part (perhaps 3/4) of apprentice training. A special apprentice gets only 1/2 of the work experience of a regular apprentice. Thus, even though it may be possible to condense a school curriculum, it is impossible to condense work experience. This problem is compounded by the fact that the first year of apprentice experience is often spent doing nonsubstantive chores as the low man on the totem pole. The first year is often useless. This is not a great problem in a four year course, but it is in a two year course." Interview with Luvern Rieke, in Seattle, Wash., July 18, 1973.
96. U.S. Attorney's Report to the Court on the Special Apprentice Program, Sept. 11, 1972, at 12.
97. *Id.*
98. U.S. Attorney's Quarterly Report to the Court on Apprentice Programs, Summer 1973, at 13: "There are several aspects to employment under the 5th-man dispatch rule, the main source of jobs for specials, which are disturbing. First, the special sent out under that provision has not been requested by the employer, which indicates that he may not be needed on the job. If this is the case, the dispatch will not provide a good training situation, and the unwanted apprentice will be laid off as soon as possible. Secondly, the opening exists only because the employer has not maintained the proper journeyman/apprentice ratio, a fact suggesting that he is not particularly sensitive to his responsibilities in the area of apprenticeship. It is therefore even less likely that he will try to provide good training, or that he will keep the special any longer than necessary. In contrast, an employer who voluntarily asks for an apprentice has a real need for such an employee, or at least has recognized an obligation to hire one; he can more logically be expected to provide good training and a longer term of employment. Obviously, there will be many exceptions on both sides, but it seems reasonable to assume that jobs obtained under duress, through the 5th-man dispatch rule, may be inferior in quality and shorter in duration than jobs filled at the employer's request."
99. U.S. Attorney's Report to the Court on the Special Apprentice Program, Sept. 11, 1972, at 16.
100. U.S. Attorney's Quarterly Report to the Court on Apprentice Programs, Summer 1973, at 5.
101. *Id.* at 19, 27.
102. U.S. Attorney's Quarterly Report to the Court on Apprentice Programs, Summer 1973, at 27.
103. 339 U.S. 629 (1950).

104. 347 U.S. 483 (1954). See Ch. 2.

105. "Whether the University of Texas Law School is compared with the original or the new law school for Negroes, we cannot find substantial equality in the educational opportunities offered white and Negro law students by the State. In terms of number of the faculty, variety of courses and opportunity for specialization, size of the student body, scope of the library, availability of law review, and similar activities, the University of Texas Law School is superior. What is more important, the University of Texas Law School possesses to a far greater degree those qualities which are incapable of objective measurement, but which make for greatness in a law school. Such qualities, to name but a few, include reputation of the faculty, experience of the administration, position and influence of the alumni, standing in the community, traditions and prestige. It is difficult to believe that one who had a free choice between these law schools would consider the question closed.

"Moreover, although the law is a highly learned profession, we are well aware that it is an intensely practical one. The law school, the proving ground for legal learning and practice, cannot be effective in isolation from the individuals and institutions with which the law interacts. Few students and no one who has practiced law would choose to study in an academic vacuum, removed from the interplay of ideas and the exchange of views with which the law is concerned. The law school to which Texas is willing to admit petitioner excludes from its student body members of the racial groups which number 85% of the population of the State and include most of the lawyers, witnesses, jurors, judges, and other officials with whom the petitioner will inevitably be dealing when he becomes a member of the Texas Bar. With such a substantial and significant segment of society excluded, we cannot conclude that the education offered petitioner is substantially equal to that which he would receive if admitted to the University of Texas Law School." 339 U.S. at 633–634.

106. Many Seattle contractors, for example, expressed satisfaction with the performance of black specials on their own payroll. At the same time, however, they complained that most specials were substandard. U.S. Attorney's Quarterly Report to the Court on Apprentice Programs, Summer 1973, app. F.

107. See, e.g., *United States* v. *Local 3, Operating Engineers,* 4 FEP Cases 1088 (N.D. Cal. 1972). See generally Ch. 12, discussing *Operating Engineers* and other decrees.

108. 401 U.S. 424 (1971). The Court emphasized that the consequences of employment practices rather than the motivation behind their adoption is the test of discrimination. It noted that "good intent or absence of discriminatory intent does not redeem employment procedures or testing mechanisms that operate as 'built-in headwinds' for minority groups and are unrelated to measuring job capability." See generally, Ch. 4, sec.: "Societal Discrimination."

109. *Id.* at 431.

110. *Id.* at 433 n.9, citing EEOC Guidelines on Employee Selection Procedures, 29 C.F.R. § 1607.4(c) (Supp. 1973).

111. See, e.g., *United States* v. *Georgia Power Co.* 474 F.2d 906 (5th Cir. 1973); *United States* v. *Jacksonville Terminal Co.,* 451 F.2d 418 (5th Cir. 1971), *cert. denied,* 406 U.S. 906 (1972). See generally Ch. 6, sec.: "Testing."

112. See, e.g., *Gregory* v. *Litton Systems, Inc.,* 316 F. Supp. 401 (C.D. Cal. 1970), *aff'd. as modified,* 472 F.2d 631 (9th Cir. 1972).

113. See *Johnson* v. *Pike Corp.,* 332 F. Supp. 490 (C.D. Cal. 1971). But cf. *Wallace* v. *Debron Corp.,* 494 F.2d 674, 677 (8th Cir. 1974).

114. See generally Dennis Yeager, "Litigation Under Title VII of the Civil Rights Act of 1964, the Construction Industry, and the Problem of the 'Unqualified' Minority Worker," 59 Geo. L.J. 1265 (1971).

115. Ch. 6, text beginning at n.67.

116. See U.S. Bureau of Apprenticeship and Training, Dropouts from Apprenticeship (1960), cited in Mills, p. 231 n.24.

117. Special Report of COAC, pp. 10–11.

118. Judge Lindberg might have been cautious because he feared that relief could not cover the international unions, which were not parties to the litigation. He might have been concerned that Seattle journeyman credentials would not be recognized in other cities. One possible answer to this problem is to join the international for purposes of relief. See, e.g., *United States* v. *Chesapeake & O. Ry.,* 471 F.2d 582, 592–593 (4th Cir. 1972), *cert. denied,* 411 U.S. 939 (1973).

119. N.2.

120. 391 U.S. 430 (1968). The same vigilance and impatience is demonstrated by the Court's

decisions in *Swann* v. *Charlotte-Mecklenberg Bd. of Educ.*, 402 U.S. 1 (1971), and *Alexander* v. *Holmes County Bd. of Educ.*, 396 U.S. 19 (1969). See generally Ch. 7.

121. The second effort is Judge Damon Keith's order in *Stamps* v. *Detroit Edison Co.*, 365 F. Supp. 87 (E.D. Mich. 1973), *rev'd. in part*, 515 F.2d 301 (6th Cir. 1975).

122. The minority members who walked off the COAC in December 1970, for example, provoked modification of the committee's structure and function.

123. See text accompanying nn. 76–86. Although there have been difficulties involved in the failure of unemployed black apprentices to contact the UCWA, the UCWA role, on balance, has been constructive and effective. Both prior and subsequent to the July 1972 order which gave it an official role, the organization played a critical role in the placement and counseling of black apprentices. The agitation of its founders in 1969 was responsible for the Department of Justice's instituting suit in the first instance. Its demonstrations and agitations in the streets as well as involvement in both the COAC and the special screening subcommittees have been of critical importance in the implementation of the decree. They have filled the vacuum which would otherwise have been left by the Department of Justice's sporadic involvement and the limits that are inherent in legal intervention.

In *Stamps* v. *Detroit Edison Co.*, Judge Keith gave another black workers' organization, the Association for the Betterment of Black Edison Employees, an official role in implementing his decree.

124. *United States* v. *Local 86, Ironworkers*, 8 EPD ¶9586 (W.D. Wash. 1974).

125. See sec.: "Barriers to Effectiveness."

126. U.S. Attorney's Quarterly Report to the Court on Apprentice Programs, March 1974, at 5–6.

127. U.S. Attorney's Quarterly Report to the Court on Apprentice Programs, July 1974, at 14.

128. U.S. Attorney's Quarterly Report to the Court on Apprentice Programs, September 1974.

129. See Ch. 2, nn. 57–59.

130. Both consent decrees have been challenged as inadequate and unlawful by minority intervenors. The steel decree was upheld in *United States* v. *Allegheny-Ludlum Industries, Inc.*, 517 F.2d 826 (5th Cir. 1975). The trucking decree is pending in the case of *United States* v. *Trucking Employers, Inc.*, Civil Action No. 74-453 (D.D.C.), and is not yet in effect.

131. See Ch. 6, secs.: "Front Pay" and "Punitive Damages."

132. See "Policing of Federal Contractors to Find Possible Job Bias is Lax, GAO Aide Says," *Wall Street Journal*, Sept. 12, 1974, at 9, col. 1. Cf. United States Commission on Civil Rights, The Federal Civil Rights Enforcement Effort 133–362 (1970); United States Commission on Civil Rights, The Federal Civil Rights Enforcement Effort: One Year Later 14–25 (1971).

133. The International Brotherhood of Teamsters is not even joined as a party to the decree in *U.S.* v. *T.E.I.*

134. 415 U.S. 36, 52 n. 15 (1974).

135. Petition of George Williamson, filed March 31, 1976 in *United States* v. *Bethlehem Steel Corp.*, C.A. 1967-432 (W.D.N.Y.) seeking modification of decrees and citation for contempt.

14 | Industrial and Public-Employee Unions

1. Philip Foner, *Organized Labor and the Black Worker, 1619–1973*, 329 (New York, 1974).

2. *N.Y. Times*, Oct. 3, 1972, at 33, col. 2.

3. "Letter to the Editor," *N.Y. Times*, Oct. 20, 1972.

4. Richard Leone, *The Negro in the Trucking Industry*, (Philadelphia, 1970) p. 20.

5. *Id.* at 31–32.

6. *United States* v. *Trucking Employers, Inc.*, No. 14–463 (D.C.D.C.).

7. 478 F.2d 979, 989 (D.C. Cir. 1973).

8. 505 F.2d 40, 53 (5th Cir. 1974).

9. 7 EPD par. 9066, at 6466 (W.D. Ok. 1973).

10. *Wall Street Journal*, March 31, 1966, p. 1.

11. See cases cited in Ch. 4, n.55.

12. Leone, p. 96.

13. *Id.* at 96–97.

14. At the time of this writing the Proposed Partial Consent Decree is pending in the case of *United States* v. *Trucking Employers, Inc.*, No. 74–453 (D.C.D.C.), and has not yet taken effect. Plaintiffs in intervention are challenging the legality and adequacy of the decree, primarily because of its failure to reform the seniority system, and the failure of the proposed waiver forms to inform minority drivers

adequately of the rights and claims which they will waive if they accept the back pay provided by the proposed decree.

15. Leone, pp. 29–30.

16. *Macklin* v. *Spector Freight Systems, supra* n.6.

17. See *Jacobs Transfer, Inc.*, 201 NLRB 210 (1973) (ordering reinstatement of George after discharge stemming from his activities as member of Committee for Reform of Local 639); *Brennan* v. *Teamsters Local 639*, 494 F.2d 1092 (D.C. Cir. 1974) (setting aside union election for violation of Landrum-Griffin Act).

18. Interview with the author.

19. See generally Irving Howe and B. J. Widick, *The UAW and Walter Reuther*, Ch. 10 (1949).

20. NLRA 58(f), 29 U.S.C. 5158(f).

21. *United States* v. *Bethlehem Steel Corp.*, 446 F.2d 652 (2d Cir. 1971); *Robinson* v. *Lorillard Corp.*, 444 F.2d 791. (4th Cir.), *cert. dismissed*, 404 U.S. 1006 (1971); *Local 189, Papermakers* v. *United States*, 416 F.2d 980 (5th Cir. 1969), *cert. denied*, 397 U.S. 919 (1970). See Ch. 4, text at n.29–81.

22. *United States* v. *St. Louis-San Francisco Ry.*, 464 F.2d 301 (9th Cir. 1972), *cert. denied*, 409 U.S. 1107, 1116 (1973).

23. *United States* v. *Local 3, Operating Engineers*, 4 FEP Cases 1088 (N.D. Cal. 1972), discussed in Ch. 12, sec.: *"U.S.* v. *Local 3, Operating Engineers."*

24. *United States* v. *Local 638, Steamfitters*, 360 F. Supp. 979 (S.D.N.Y. 1973), *aff'd with modifications*, 501 F.2d 622 (2nd Cir. 1974), discussed in Ch. 12, sec.: *"U.S.* v. *Local 638, Steamfitters."*

25. 4 FEP Cases at 1096.

26. 457 F.2d 348 (5th Cir. 1972).

27. *Id.* at 358.

28. *Id.* at 359. See also *Senter* v. *General Motors Corp.*, 11 EPD par. 10.741 at p. 7095 (6th Cir. 1976).

29. Herbert Northrup, *The Negro in the Automobile Industry* (Philadelphia, 1968) pp. 12–15, 20.

30. Letter from Douglas Fraser to all Chrysler local union presidents, July 12, 1972.

31. *Detroit Free Press*, Aug. 15, 1968, p. 2E, col. 1.

32. *Detroit Free Press*, Aug. 16, 1968, p. 3A, col. 6.

33. *N.Y. Times*, July 13, 1968, p. 28, col. 2.

34. *Detroit Free Press*, Oct. 4, 1968, p. 3.

35. *N.Y. Times*, March 13, 1969, p. 22C, col. 1.

36. See generally Walter Uphoff, *Kohler on Strike* (Boston, 1966).

37. *Detroit News*, March 16, 1969, p. 4B, col. 1.

38. *Michigan Chronicle*, Aug. 24, 1968, p. 4A.

39. *Detroit Free Press*, Jan. 28, 1969, p. 9A.

40. *Detroit Free Press*, Feb. 11, 1969, p. 6A.

41. See Tom Brooks, "Drumbeats in Detroit", *Dissent*, Jan.–Feb. 1970.

42. See generally Richard Rowan, *The Negro in the Steel Industry* (Philadelphia, 1968).

43. 263 F.2d 546 (5th Cir.), *cert. denied*, 360 U.S. 902 (1959), discussed in Ch. 4, text at n.13.

44. *Id.* at 551.

45. *United States* v. *Hayes International Corp.*, 415 F.2d 1038, 1042 n.6 (5th Cir. 1969).

46. *Taylor* v. *Armco Steel Corp.*, 429 F.2d 498 (5th Cir. 1970). See also *Taylor* v. *Armco Steel Corp.*, 8 EDP par. 9550 at 5402–5403 (S.D. Tex. 1973).

47. Case cited n.23.

48. In the Matter of Bethlehem Steel Corp., Decision of the Secretary of Labor, Docket No. 102–68, January 15, 1973, reported in *CCH Employment Practices Guide*, New Developments par. 5128.

49. The consent decree was approved in *United States* v. *Allegheny-Ludlum Industries, Inc.*, 517 F.2d 826 (5th Cir. 1975).

50. See generally Ch. 13, sec.: "Conclusion."

51. See Introduction, text at n.9.

52. Foner, p. 405. On the McDonald-Abel contest, see generally J. Herling, *Right to Challenge: People and Power in the Steelworkers Union* (New York, 1972).

53. Foner, p. 398.

54. *N.Y. Times*, Aug. 24, 1968.

55. *Baltimore Afro-American*, Feb. 22, 1969, p. 6, col. 3.

56. Walker Fogel, *The Negro in the Meat Industry* (Philadelphia, 1970), p. 31.

57. John Hope II, *Equality of Opportunity: A Union Approach to Fair Employment* (1956).

58. Fogel, p. 70.

59. *Id.*, p. 82.

60. Theodore Purcell and Daniel Mulvey, *The Negro in the Electrical Manufacturing Industry* (Philadelphia, 1971), p. 122.

61. *Id.*, p. 60.

62. *Id.*, p. 101.

63. Interview with author, May 2, 1971.

64. Proceedings, 16th Constitutional Convention, United Furniture Workers of America, AFL-CIO, (1970) p. 155.

65. Herbert Northrup, *The Negro in the Rubber Tire Industry* (Philadelphia, 1969), p. 73.

66. *Id.*, p. 48.

67. *Local 12, United States Rubber Workers,* 150 NLRB 312 (1964) *enforced* 368 F.2d 12 (5th Cir. 1966), *cert. denied,* 389 U.S. 837 (1967), discussed in Ch. 7 text beginning at n.28.

68. See Northrup, *The Negro in the Rubber Tire Industry,* p. 111.

69.

Job classification	Total	Black
Machinist	111	1
Pipefitter	183	1
Carpenter	30	0
Electrician	230	3
Millwright	442	5
Welder	95	1
Instrument	137	3
Oiler	96	1
Painter	47	1
Sheetmetal worker	51	1
Tractor mechanic	106	2
Die and mold stamper	6	0
Blacksmith	3	0
Leadman	7	0
Cement finisher	19	1
Engraver	4	0
Crane operator	2	1
Refrigeration and heating	27	1
Mold repair	4	1
Powerhouse operator	99	0
Rubber die maker	16	0
Scale repair	10	0
Fireman, furnace	12	0
Pump operator	3	0
Battery man	5	0
Elevator mechanic	1	0
	1,746	23 (1.3%)

Source: Data in author's possession.

70. U.S. Equal Opportunity Comm'n, *Promise* v. *Performance: A Study of Equal Employment in the Nation's Electric and Gas Utilities,* p. 5.

71. *Id.*

72. *Id.*, p. iv (Foreword by Chairman William H. Brown III).

73. 401 U.S. 424 (1971) discussed in Ch. 4, sec.: "Societal Discrimination."

74. *United States* v. *Virginia Electric and Power Co.,* 327 F. Supp. 1034 (D.Va. 1971), consent decree entered, 4 EPD par. 7502 (D.Va. 1971).

75. *United States* v. *Georgia Power Co.,* 474 F.2d 906 (5th Cir. 1973).

76. *Stamps* v. *Detroit Edison Co.,* 365 F. Supp. 87 (E.D. Mich. 1973), *aff'd in part, rev'd in part sub nom. EEOC* v. *Detroit Edison Co.,* 515 F.2d 301 (6th Cir. 1975).

77. 433 F.2d 421, 426–427 (8th Cir. 1970).

78. *United States* v. *Georgia Power Co.,* at 925–926; *EEOC* v. *Detroit Edison Co.,* at 313.

79. 365 F. Supp. at 103.

80. *United States* v. *Bethlehem Steel Corp.,* 446 F.2d 652, (2d Cir. 1971). See also *Head* v. *Timken Roller Bearing Co.,* 486 F.2d 870, 878 (6th Cir. 1973).

81. Bernard Anderson, *The Negro in the Public Utility Industries* (Philadelphia, 1970), p. 38.

82. "UWUA Human Rights Committee Dedicated to Equal Opportunity," *Light,* April 1972, p. 1, col. 1.

83. *Promise* v. *Performance,* pp. 35–36.

84. Ray Marshall, *The Negro and Organized Labor* (New York, 1965) p. 103.

85. *United States* v. *International Longshoremen's Ass'n.,* 460 F.2d 497 (4th Cir. 1972), *cert. denied,* 409 U.S. 1007 (1972); *EEOC* v. *International Longshoremen's Ass'n,* 511 F.2d 273 (5th Cir. 1975), *cert. denied,* — U.S. — , 10EPD ¶10,511 (1975). See generally Ch. 5, sec.: "The Segregation and Merger of Local Unions."

86. See text at n.1.

87. Letter of Otis Ducker to Executive Board, Local 161–710 AFM, Feb. 18, 1969. Copy in author's possession.

88. Philip Jeffress, *The Negro in the Urban Transit Industry* (Philadelphia, 1970), p. 35.

89. See *Wall Street Journal,* Nov. 29, 1968, p. 1, col. 1.

Conclusion

1. *Johnson* v. *Goodyear Tire & Rubber Co.,* 491 F.2d 1364, 1380 (5th Cir. 1974).

2. See Ch. 6, sec.: "Front Pay."

3. 417 U.S. 156 (1974).

4. See Ch. 3, n.74.

5. See D.C. Bar Ass'n. Comm. on Legal Ethics and Grievances, Report (January 26, 1971). See also A.B.A. Comm. on Professional Ethics, Opinions, No. 148 (1935); A.B.A. Comm. on Professional Ethics, Informal Opinions, Nos. 992 (1967); 888 (1965); 786 (1964).

6. 371 U.S. 415 (1963).

7. *Id*. at 443.

8. *Brotherhood of Railroad Trainmen* v. *Virginia,* 377 U.S. 1 (1964). See also *United Mine Workers* v. *Illinois Bar Ass'n,* 389 U.S. 217 (1967); *United Transportation Union* v. *State Bar of Michigan,* 401 U.S. 576 (1971).

9. In the Pennsylvania case, the court of appeals held that the district court lacked the statutory authority to promulgate its anti-solicitation rule. And the court indicated quite strongly that in addition, the application of the rule was unconstitutional. *Rodgers* v. *U.S. Steel Corp.,* 508 F.2d 152 (3d Cir.), *cert. denied,* 423 U.S. 832, 10 EPD ¶10,409 (1975). The California case is *Jones* v. *Pacific Intermountain Express,* No. C-73-2296 RHS (N.D. Cal.) (order entered March 22, 1974).

10. See Ch. 13, sec.: "Conclusion."

11. See generally Andrew Brimmer, "Economic Situation of Blacks in the United States," Federal Reserve Bulletin, March 1972, p. 257.

Table of Cases

This table lists cases mentioned in the text and notes. Page references are given only for those discussed in the text.

Index

**BLACK WORKERS IN
WHITE UNIONS**

Designed by R. E. Rosenbaum.
Composed by Vail-Ballou Press, Inc.,
in 10 point VIP Times Roman, 2 points leaded,
with display lines in VIP Times Roman Bold.
Printed offset by Vail-Ballou Press
Warren's No. 66 text, 50 pound basis.
Bound by Vail-Ballou Press
in Joanna book cloth
and stamped in All Purpose foil.

Library of Congress Cataloging in Publication Data
(For library cataloging purposes only)

Gould, William B
  Black workers in white unions.

  Includes index.
  1. Discrimination in employment—Law and legislation—United States. 2. Trade-unions—Afro-American membership. I. Title.
KF3464.G6   344'.73'01133   76-50263
ISBN 0-8014-1062-2